Polytheism and Soci
at Athens

Worshipping Athena: sacrificial animals brought to an altar on which stands Athena's owl; beside the altar a column bears a votive relief.

Polytheism and Society at Athens

ROBERT PARKER

OXFORD
UNIVERSITY PRESS

OXFORD
UNIVERSITY PRESS

Great Clarendon Street, Oxford OX2 6DP

Oxford University Press is a department of the University of Oxford.
It furthers the University's objective of excellence in research, scholarship,
and education by publishing worldwide in

Oxford New York

Auckland   Cape Town   Dar es Salaam   Hong Kong   Karachi
Kuala Lumpur   Madrid   Melbourne   Mexico City   Nairobi
New Delhi   Shanghai   Taipei   Toronto
With offices in
Argentina   Austria   Brazil   Chile   Czech Republic   France   Greece
Guatemala   Hungary   Italy   Japan   South Korea   Poland   Portugal
Singapore   Switzerland   Thailand   Turkey   Ukraine   Vietnam

Oxford is a registered trade mark of Oxford University Press
in the UK and in certain other countries

Published in the United States
by Oxford University Press Inc., New York

ISBN 978-0-19-921611-6

Printed in the United Kingdom by
Lightning Source UK Ltd., Milton Keynes

For Lucy
Lux mea, qua viva vivere dulce mihi est

Preface

I began this work while holding the Mark Fitch Research Readership of the British Academy from 1995–6, and after six years spent on other matters I was able to bring it almost to completion during a sabbatical year granted by the University of Oxford in 2002–3. I am very grateful to the institutions (the British Academy, Oxford University and Oriel College) which made possible these prolonged periods of study, as also to New College for the excellent facilities which I here enjoy. All students of antiquity in Oxford are fortunate to be able to use the fine new Sackler library. Enid Barker, Dorothy McCarthy and Lavinia Porter have guided my book helpfully through the press, and I particularly thank Belinda Baker for expert copy-editing. Among the many friends to whom I am grateful for discussion of topics treated in this work I must single out Jan Bremmer, Esther Eidinow, Sally Humphreys, Michael Jameson (whose recent death so many Hellenists mourn), Barbara Kowalzig, Robin Lane Fox, Angelos Matthaiou, Robin Osborne, Olga Palagia, Nikolaos Papazarkadas, Peter Thonemann. I owe particular thanks to Stephen Lambert, who has kept me abreast of his own important work on Athenian religious inscriptions in advance of publication, and has checked readings for me in Athens rapidly and expertly. Simon Hornblower's gift to me of his own copy of Mommsen's *Feste der Stadt Athen*, a rare book, is only one of many kindnesses for which I am indebted to him. I thank above all Christiane Sourvinou-Inwood for the blend of intellectual engagement, instant and complete mastery and warmly encouraging enthusiasm with which she has discussed with me my studies of Athenian religion over many years.

R. P.
New College
May 2005

Contents

III

List of Illustrations

Conventions and Abbreviations

Abbreviations of periodicals and works of reference are those recommended in the *American Journal of Archaeology (AJA)*, 95 (1991), 1–16 (as expanded at http://www.ajaonline.org.), with a few supplements listed below. For ancient authors the abbreviations in S. Hornblower and A. Spawforth (eds.), *The Oxford Classical Dictionary*[3] (1996), supplemented by those in Liddell/Scott/Jones, *A Greek English Lexicon with a revised supplement* (Oxford 1996), have been followed, with a few trivial divergences. I have restored the speech commonly known as [Dem.] 59 to its author, as Apollod. *Neaer*. Abbreviations of epigraphical and papyrological publications are from Liddell/Scott/Jones (with some supplements listed below). Comic fragments are cited from R. Kassel and C. Austin, *Poetae Comici Graeci* (Berlin 1983–), fragments of Aeschylus and Sophocles from the editions of Radt (*TGrF*), of Euripides, failing other indication, from that of Nauck.

On much-debated topics, I sometimes cite only a recent contribution, adding the symbol [+] to stress that this work refers to earlier studies which remain important.

Op. cit. refers back to works cited in the same note or one of its five predecessors.

For a note on the datings adopted here of Athenian inscriptions see *Athenian Religion*, p. xi; for the period 261/0 to 234/3, where archon datings remain very unsettled, I accept those of S. V. Tracy, *Athens and Macedon* (Berkeley 2003), 165–8.

AION	*Annali del' Istituto Orientale di Napoli.*
Agora	*The Athenian Agora: Results of the Excavations Conducted by the American School of Classical Studies in Athens* (Princeton 1951–). Note esp. *Agora* XV (1974): *Inscriptions: The Athenian Councillors*, eds. B. D. Meritt and J. S. Traill; *Agora* XVI, *Inscriptions: the Decrees*, ed. A. G. Woodhead; *Agora* XIX (1991): *Inscriptions: Horoi, Poletai Records, Leases of Public Lands*, eds. G. V. Lalonde, M. K. Langdon, and M. B. Walbank.

Aleshire, *Asklepieion*

S. B. Aleshire, *The Athenian Asklepieion: The People, their Dedications and the Inventories* (Amsterdam 1989).

Aleshire, *Asklepios*

S. B. Aleshire, *Asklepios at Athens: Epigraphic and Prosopographic Essays on the Athenian Healing Cults* (Amsterdam 1991).

Architectural Sculpture

D. Buitron-Oliver (ed.), *The Interpretation of Architectural Sculpture in Greece and Rome. Studies in the History of Art*, 49 (National Gallery of Art, Washington 1997).

Arnott, *Alexis*

W. G. Arnott, *Alexis. The Fragments. A Commentary* (Cambridge 1996).

Arrigoni, 'Donne e sport'

G. Arrigoni, 'Donne e sport nel mondo greco. Religione e società', in ead. (ed.), *Le Donne in Grecia* (Bari 1985), 55–201.

Athena in the Classical World

S. Deacy and A. Villing (eds.), *Athena in the Classical World* (Leiden 2001).

Athenian Religion

R. Parker, *Athenian Religion: A History* (Oxford 1996).

Athens and Attica

W. D. E. Coulson and others (eds.), *The Archaeology of Athens and Attica under the Democracy* (Oxford 1994).

Auffarth, *Drohende Untergang*

C. Auffarth, *Der drohende Untergang. Schöpfung in Mythos und Ritual im Alten Orient und in Griechenland* (Berlin 1991).

Before Sexuality

D. M. Halperin, J. J. Winkler, and F. I. Zeitlin (eds.), *Before Sexuality: The Construction of Erotic Experience in the ancient Greek World* (Princeton 1990).

Bell, *Ritual*

C. Bell, *Ritual: Perspectives and Dimensions* (Oxford and New York 1997).

Bell, *Ritual Theory*

C. Bell, *Ritual Theory, Ritual Practice* (New York and Oxford 1992).

Bérard, *Anodoi*

C. Bérard, *Anodoi. Essai sur l' imagerie des passages chthoniens* (Rome 1974).

Bergemann, *Demos und Thanatos*

J. Bergemann, *Demos und Thanatos. Untersuchungen zum Wertsystem der Polis im Spiegel der attischen Grabreliefs des 4. Jahrhunderts v. Chr. und zur Funk-*

	tion der gleichzeitigen Grabbauten (Munich 1997).
Bierl, *Dionysos*	A. F. H. Bierl, *Dionysos und die griechische Tragödie* (Classica Monacensia 1, Tübingen 1991).
Boegehold, *Lawcourts*	A. L. Boegehold, *The Lawcourts at Athens* (*Agora* XXVIII, Princeton 1995).
Boersma, *Building Policy*	J. Boersma, *Athenian Building Policy from 561/0 to 405/4 B.C.* (Groningen 1970).
Boethius, *Pythaïs*	A. Boethius, *Die Pythaïs* (Uppsala 1918)
Bonnechere, *Sacrifice humain*	P. Bonnechere, *Le Sacrifice humain en Grèce ancienne* (Athens/Liège 1994).
Borgeaud, *Mère des dieux*	P. Borgeaud, *La Mère des dieux* (Paris, 1996).
Borgeaud, *Pan*	P. Borgeaud, *Recherches sur le dieu Pan* (Bibliotheca Helvetica Romana 17, 1979).
Bourriot, *Génos*	F. Bourriot, *Recherches sur la nature du génos: Étude d' histoire sociale athénienne–périodes archaïque et classique* (Lille 1976).
Bowden, 'Oracles for Sale'	H. Bowden, 'Oracles for Sale', in P. Derow and R. Parker (eds.), *Herodotus and his World* (Oxford 2003), 256–74.
Bravo, *Pannychis*	B. Bravo, Pannychis e Simposio (Pisa and Rome 1997).
Brelich, Paides *e* Parthenoi	A. Brelich, Paides *e* Parthenoi (Rome 1969).
Bremmer, *Afterlife*	J. N. Bremmer, *The Rise and Fall of the Afterlife* (London 2002).
Bremmer, *Greek Religion*	J. N. Bremmer, *Greek Religion* (Oxford 1994, repr. with addenda 1999).
Bremmer/Horsfall, *Roman Myth*	J. N. Bremmer and N. M. Horsfall, *Roman Myth and Mythography* (*BICS* supplement 52, 1987).
Bruck, *Totenteil*	E. Bruck, *Totenteil und Seelgerät im griechischen Recht* (Munich 1926).
Brulé, *Fille d'Athènes*	P. Brulé, *La Fille d'Athènes: La Religion des filles à Athènes à l'époque classique. Mythes, cultes et société* (Paris 1987).
Brulé, 'Panathénées'	P. Brulé, 'La Cité en ses composantes: remarques sur les sacrifices et la pro-

cession des Panathénées', *Kernos* 6 (1996), 37–63.

Brumfield, *Agricultural Year*
A. C. Brumfield, *The Attic Festivals of Demeter and their Relation to the Agricultural Year* (Salem, NH 1981).

Burkert, *Greek Religion*
W. Burkert, *Greek Religion: Archaic and Classical*, tr. J. Raffan (Oxford 1985; German orig. 1977).

Burkert, *Homo Necans*
W. Burkert, *Homo Necans: The Anthropology of Ancient Greek Sacrificial Ritual and Myth*, tr. P. Bing (Berkeley 1983; German orig. 1972).

Burkert, *Mystery Cults*
W. Burkert, *Ancient Mystery Cults* (Cambridge, Mass. 1987).

Cahill, *Household and City*
N. Cahill, *Household and City Organization at Olynthus* (New Haven 2002)

Calame, *Choeurs*
C. Calame, *Les Choeurs de jeunes filles en Grèce archaique* (Rome 1977).

Calame, *Thésée*
C. Calame, *Thésée et l'imaginaire athénien* (Lausanne 1990).

Camp, *Agora*
J. M. Camp, *The Athenian Agora* (London 1986).

Camp, *Athens*
J. M. Camp, *The Archaeology of Athens* (New Haven 2001).

Camps-Gaset, *L'Année des Grecs*
M. Camps-Gaset, *L'Année des Grecs. La Fête et le Mythe* (Annales Littéraires de l'Université de Besançon 530, 1994).

Carpenter, *Archaic Dionysian Imagery*
T. H. Carpenter, *Dionysian Imagery in Archaic Greek Art* (Oxford 1986).

Carpenter, *Fifth-Century Dionysian Imagery*
T. H. Carpenter, *Dionysian Imagery in Fifth-Century Athens* (Oxford 1997).

Cavanaugh, *Eleusis and Athens*
M. B. Cavanaugh, *Eleusis and Athens. Documents in Finance, Religion and Politics in the Fifth Century B.C.* (Atlanta 1996).

Ceccarelli, *Pirrica*
P. Ceccarelli, *La pirrica nell' antichità greco romana* (Pisa/Rome 1998).

City of Images
C. Bérard et al., *A City of Images*, tr. D. Lyons (Princeton 1989).

Clairmont, *Tombstones*
C. W. Clairmont, *Classical Attic Tombstones* (Kilchberg, 1993–5).

Clinton, *Myth and Cult*
K. Clinton, *Myth and Cult: The Iconography of the Eleusinian Mysteries* (Stockholm 1992).

Clinton, *Sacred Officials*　　　　K. Clinton, *The Sacred Officials of the Eleusinian Mysteries* (*TAPS* NS 64, Philadelphia 1972).

Clinton, 'Thesmophorion'　　　　K. Clinton, 'The Thesmophorion in central Athens and the celebration of the Thesmophoria in Attica', in R. Hägg (ed.), *The Role of Religion in the Early Greek Polis* (1996), 111–25.

Cohen, *Athenian Nation*　　　　E. E. Cohen, *The Athenian Nation* (Princeton 2000).

Cole, *Ritual Space*　　　　S. G. Cole, *Landscapes, Gender, and Ritual Space* (Berkeley 2004).

Comptes et Inventaires　　　　D. Knoepfler (ed.), *Comptes et inventaires dans les cités grecques* (Geneva 1988).

Cook, *Zeus*　　　　A. B. Cook, *Zeus: A Study in Ancient Religion* (3 vols., Cambridge 1914–1940).

Cox, *Household Interests*　　　　C. A. Cox, *Household Interests* (Princeton 1998).

Crux　　　　P. Cartledge and F. D. Harvey (eds.), *Crux: Essays Presented to G.E.M. de Ste. Croix on his 75th Birthday* (= *History of Political Thought* 6/1–2, 1985).

Csapo, 'Riding the Phallus'　　　　E. Csapo, 'Riding the Phallus for Dionysus: Iconology, Ritual and Gender-Role De/construction', *Phoenix* 51 (1997), 253–95.

Csapo/Slater, *Ancient Drama*　　　　E. Csapo and W. J. Slater, *The Context of Ancient Drama* (Michigan 1995).

DAGM　　　　E. Pöhlmann and M. L. West, *Documents of Ancient Greek Music* (Oxford 2001).

Daraki, *Dionysos*　　　　M. Daraki, *Dionysos* (Paris 1985).

Daux, *Delphes*　　　　G. Daux, *Delphes au IIE et au IER Siècle* (Paris 1936).

Davies, *Propertied Families*　　　　J. K. Davies, *Athenian Propertied Families* (Oxford 1971).

Democracy, Empire and the Arts　　　　D. Boedeker and K. Raaflaub (eds.), *Democracy, Empire and the Arts in Fifth-Century Athens* (Harvard 1998).

Dentzer, *Banquet couché*　　　　J. M. Dentzer, *Le Motif du banquet couché dans le proche-oriente et le monde grec du*

	viie au ive siècle avant J.-C. (*BEFAR* 246, Rome 1982)
Detienne, *Apollon*	M. Detienne, *Apollon le couteau à la main* (Paris 1998).
Detienne, *Jardins*	M. Detienne, *Les Jardins d'Adonis* (Paris 1972; Engl. tr. J. Lloyd, *The Gardens of Adonis*, Harvester Press 1977).
Detienne, 'Violentes "eugénies" '	M. Detienne, 'Violentes "eugénies". En pleines Thesmophories: des femmes couvertes de sang', in M. Detienne and J. P. Vernant, *La Cuisine du sacrifice en pays grec* (Paris 1979), 183–214.
Detienne/Sissa, *Vie quotidienne*	M. Detienne and G. Sissa, *La Vie quotidienne des dieux grecs* (Paris 1989).
Detienne/Vernant, *Mètis*	M. Detienne and J. P. Vernant, *Les Ruses de l' intelligence. La mètis des grecs* (Paris 1974) (Engl. tr. J. Lloyd, *Cunning Intelligence in Greek Culture and Society*, Chicago 1991).
Deubner, *Attische Feste*	L. Deubner, *Attische Feste* (Berlin 1932).
Deubner, 'Weinlesefest'	L. Deubner, 'Das attische Weinlesefest', *AbhBerl* 1943, no. 12 (reprinted in his *Kleine Schriften zur klassischen Altertumskunde*, Meisenheim 1982, 713–25).
DHA	*Dialogues d'histoire ancienne.*
Dickie, *Magicians*	M. W. Dickie, *Magic and Magicians in the Greco-Roman World* (London and New York 2001).
Dillon, *Girls and Women*	M. Dillon, *Girls and Women in Classical Greek Religion* (London 2002).
Dover, *Frogs*	K. J. Dover, *Aristophanes* Frogs, *edited with introduction and commentary* (Oxford 1993).
Dover, *Greek Popular Morality*	K. J. Dover, *Greek Popular Morality in the Time of Plato and Aristotle* (Oxford 1974).
Dowden, *Death and the Maiden*	K. Dowden, *Death and the Maiden: Girls' Initiation Rites in Greek Mythology* (London 1989).
DT	A. Audollent, *Defixionum Tabellae* (Paris 1904). Numbers refer to items, not pages.

DTA — R. Wuensch, *Inscriptiones Atticae* III (*IG* III), Appendix, *Defixionum Tabellae* (Berlin, 1897). Numbers refer to items, not pages.

Durand, *Sacrifice et labour* — J. L. Durand, *Sacrifice et labour en grèce ancienne* (Paris/Rome 1986).

Ellinger, *Légende nationale phocidienne* — P. Ellinger, *La Légende nationale phocidienne* (*BCH* supp. 27, Paris 1993).

Faraone, 'Agonistic Context' — C. A. Faraone, 'The Agonistic Context of Early Greek Binding Spells', in *Magika Hiera*, 3–32.

Faraone, *Love Magic* — C. A. Faraone, *Ancient Greek Love Magic* (Cambridge, Mass. 1999).

Farnell, *Cults* — L. R. Farnell, *The Cults of the Greek States*, 5 vols. (Oxford 1896–1909).

Ferrari, *Figures of Speech* — G. Ferrari, *Figures of Speech: Men and Maidens in Ancient Greece* (Chicago 2002).

Follet, *Athènes* — S. Follet, *Athènes au IIe et au IIIe siècle. Études chronologiques et prosopographiques* (Paris 1976).

Fontenrose, *Delphic Oracle* — J. Fontenrose, *The Delphic Oracle* (Berkeley 1978).

Food in Antiquity — J. Wilkins, D. Harvey and M. Dobson, *Food in Antiquity* (Exeter 1995).

Foucart, *Mystères* — P. Foucart, *Mystères d' Éleusis* (Paris 1914).

Foxhall, 'Women's ritual' — 'Women's ritual and men's work in ancient Athens', in *Women in Antiquity*, 97–110.

Frontisi-Ducroux, *Le Dieu-masque* — F. Frontisi-Ducroux, *Le Dieu-masque. Une figure du Dionysos d' Athènes* (Paris/Rome 1991).

Gager, *Curse Tablets* — J. G. Gager (ed.), *Curse Tablets and Binding Spells from the Ancient World* (New York and Oxford 1992).

Gauthier/Hatzopoulos, *Loi gymnasiarchique* — P. Gauthier and M. B. Hatzopoulos, *La Loi gymnasiarchique de Beroia* (Athens 1993).

Georgoudi, 'Lisimaca' — S. Georgoudi, 'Lisimaca, la sacerdotessa', in N. Loraux (ed.), *Grecia al femminile* (Rome 1993), 157–95.

Gernet, *Droit et société* — L. Gernet, *Droit et société dans la grèce ancienne* (Paris 1955).

Gifts to the Gods	T. Linders and G. Nordquist (eds.), *Gifts to the Gods* (= *Boreas: Acta universitatis Uppsaliensis* 15, Uppsala 1987).
Giuliani, *Oracolo*	A. Giuliani, *La città e l' oracolo* (Milan 2001).
Giuman, *Dea, Vergine, Sangue*	M. Giuman, *La dea, la vergine, il sangue* (Milan 1999).
Goddess and Polis	J. Neils (ed.), *Goddess and Polis. The Panathenaic Festival in Ancient Athens* (Hanover, NH and Princeton 1992).
Goette, *Sounion*	H. R. Goette, Ὁ ἀξιόλογος δῆμος Σούνιον. *Landeskundliche Studien in Südost-Attika* (Rahden/Westf. 2000).
Goette, *Attica*	H. R. Goette, *Athens, Attica and the Megarid. An Archaeological Guide* (London 2001).
Golden, *Children*	M. Golden, *Children and Childhood in Classical Athens* (Baltimore 1990).
Gordon, 'Imagining Magic'	R. Gordon, 'Imagining Greek and Roman Magic', in *The Athlone History of Witchcraft and Magic in Europe,* ii. *Ancient Greece and Rome* (London 1999), 159–275.
Graf, *Nordionische Kulte*	F. Graf, *Nordionische Kulte* (Rome 1985).
Graf, *Orphische Dichtung*	F. Graf, *Eleusis und die orphische Dichtung Athens in vorhellenistischer Zeit* (Berlin 1974).
Habicht, *Athens from Alexander*	C. Habicht, *Athens from Alexander to Antony*, tr. D. L. Schneider (Cambridge, Mass., 1997; German original 1995).
Habicht, 'Fluchtafeln'	C. Habicht, 'Attische Fluchtafeln aus der Zeit Alexanders des Großen', *ICS* 18 (1993), 113–18 (= id., *Athen in hellenistischer Zeit*, Munich 1994, 14–18).
Habicht, *Studien*	C. Habicht, *Studien zur Geschichte Athens in hellenistischer Zeit* (Göttingen 1982).
Hadzisteliou Price, *Kourotrophos*	T. Hadzisteliou Price, *Kourotrophos: Cults and Representations of the Greek Nursing Deities* (Leiden 1978).
Halliwell, 'Le Rire rituel'	S. Halliwell, 'Le Rire rituel et la nature de l'Ancienne Comédie attique', in M.-

	L. Desclos (ed.), *Le Rire des Grecs* (Grenoble 2000), 155–68.
Hamilton, *Choes*	R. Hamilton, *Choes and Anthesteria: Athenian Iconography and Ritual* (Ann Arbor 1992).
Harris, *Treasures*	D. Harris, *The Treasures of the Parthenon and Erechtheion* (Oxford 1995).
Harrison, *Law*	A. W. R. Harrison, *The Law of Athens*, i. *The Family and Property* (Oxford 1968), ii. *Procedure* (Oxford 1971).
Harrison, *Prolegomena*	J. E. Harrison, *Prolegomena to the Study of Greek* Religion, ed. 2 (Cambridge 1908).
Hatzopoulos, *Rites de passage*	M. B. Hatzopoulos, *Cultes et rites de passage en Macédoine* (Athens 1994).
Haussoulier, *Vie municipale*	B. Haussoulier, *La Vie municipale en Attique* (Paris 1884).
Healey, *Eleusinian Sacrifices*	R. F. Healey, *Eleusinian Sacrifices in the Athenian Law Code* (diss. Harvard 1961; published New York and London 1990).
Henrichs, 'Between Country and City'	A. Henrichs, 'Between Country and City: Cultic Dimensions of Dionysus in Athens and Attica', in M. Griffith and D. J. Mastronarde (eds.), *Cabinet of the Muses* (Scholars Press 1990), 257–77.
Hornblower, *Commentary*	S. Hornblower, *A Commentary on Thucydides*, i, bks. I–III (Oxford 1991); ii, bks. IV–V.24 (Oxford 1996).
Humphrey/Laidlaw, *Archetypal Actions*	C. Humphrey and J. Laidlaw, *The Archetypal Actions of Ritual* (Cambridge 1994).
Humphreys, *Strangeness*	S. C. Humphreys, *The Strangeness of Gods; Historical Perspectives on the Interpretation of Athenian Religion* (Oxford 2004).
Humphreys, 'Demes'	S. C. Humphreys, 'A Sense of Agency: religion in the Attic demes', in Humphreys, *Strangeness*, 130–96.
Humphreys, 'Family Tombs'	S. C. Humphreys, 'Family Tombs and Tomb Cult in Ancient Athens: Tradition or Traditionalism?', *JHS* 100 (1980), 96–126, reprinted with minor changes in *The Family, Women and*

	Death (London 1983; ed. 2 Michigan 1993, with addition of a review of I. Morris, *Burial and Ancient Society* (first published in *Helios* 17, 1990, 263–68)).
Hurwit, *Acropolis*	J. M. Hurwit, *The Athenian Acropolis* (Cambridge 1999).
Initiation	D. B. Dodd and C. A. Faraone (eds.), *Initiation in Ancient Greek Narratives and Rituals* (London 2003).
IOropos	B. K. Petrakos, ʾΟι ʾΕπιγραφὲς τοῦ ʾΩρωποῦ (Athens 1997).
IRhamnous	B. K. Petrakos, ʿΟ Δῆμος τοῦ ʿΡαμνοῦντος (Athens 1999), ii, ʿΟι ʾΕπιγραφὲς. Numbers refer to inscriptions, not to pages. Cf. s.v. Petrakos, *Rhamnous*.
Isler-Kerenyi, *Dionysos*	C. Isler-Kerenyi, *Dionysos nella Grecia arcaica. Il contributo delle immagini* (Pisa/Rome 2001).
Jacoby, *Atthis*	F. Jacoby, *Atthis* (Oxford 1949).
Jameson, 'Domestic Space'	M. H. Jameson, 'Domestic Space in the Greek City-State', in S. Kent (ed.), *Domestic Architecture and the Use of Space: An Interdisciplinary, Cross-Cultural Approach* (Cambridge), ch. 7.
Jameson, 'Private Space'	M. H. Jameson, 'Private Space and the Greek City', in O. Murray and S. Price (eds.), *The Greek City from Homer to Alexander* (Oxford 1990), 171–95.
Jameson, 'Sacred Space'	M. H. Jameson, 'Sacred Space and the City: Greece and Bhaktapur', *International Journal of Hindu Studies* 1.3 (December 1997), 485–99.
Jameson, 'Sacrifice and husbandry'	M. H. Jameson, 'Sacrifice and animal husbandry in Classical Greece', in C. R. Whittaker (ed.), *Pastoral Economies in Classical Antiquity* (PCPS supp. 14, Cambridge 1988), 87–119.
Jameson, 'The spectacular and the obscure'	M. H. Jameson, 'The spectacular and the obscure in Athenian Religion', in *Performance Culture*, 321–40.

Jameson *et al.*, *Selinous* M. H. Jameson, D. R. Jordan, R. D. Kotansky, *A Lex Sacra from Selinous* (*GRBM* 11, 1993).

Jeanmaire, *Couroi* H. Jeanmaire, *Couroi et Courètes* (Lille 1939).

Jeanmaire, *Dionysos* H. Jeanmaire, *Dionysos* (Paris 1951).

Jenkins, *Parthenon Frieze* I. Jenkins, *The Parthenon Frieze* (London 1994).

Johnston, *Restless Dead* S. I. Johnston, *Restless Dead. Encounters between the Living and the Dead in Ancient Greece* (Berkeley 1999).

Jones, *Associations* N. F. Jones, *The Associations of Classical Athens* (New York and Oxford 1999).

Jones, *Rural Athens* N. F. Jones, *Rural Athens under the Democracy* (Philadelphia 2004).

Judeich, *Topographie* W. Judeich, *Topographie von Athen*^{2} (Munich 1931).

Kahrstedt, *Magistratur* U. Kahrstedt, *Untersuchungen zur Magistratur in Athen* (Stuttgart 1936).

Kavoulaki, 'Processional Performance' A. Kavoulaki, 'Processional Performance and the Democratic Polis', in *Performance Culture*, 293–320.

Kavoulaki, 'Ritual Performance' A. Kavoulaki, 'The Ritual Performance of a *Pompê*: Aspects and Perspectives', in *Δώρημα. A tribute to the A.G. Leventis Foundation on the Occasion of its 20*th *Anniversary* (Nicosia 2000), 145–58.

Kearns, *Heroes of Attica* E. Kearns, *Heroes of Attica* (*BICS* Suppl. 57, London 1989).

Kephalidou, *Νικητής* E. Kephalidou, *Νικητής* (Thessaloniki 1996).

Kerényi, *Die Mysterien* K. Kerenyi, *Die Mysterien von Eleusis* (Zurich 1962).

Kerényi, *Eleusis* K. Kerenyi, *Eleusis. Archetypal Image of Mother and Daughter*, tr. R. Mannheim (Princeton 1967).

Knigge, *Kerameikos* U. Knigge, *Der Kerameikos von Athen* (Athens 1988).

Korrés, 'Architektur' M. Korrés, 'Ein Beitrag zur Kenntnis der attisch-ionischen Architektur', in E. L. Schwandner (ed.), *Säule und Gebälk. Bauforscherkolloquium Berlin 16–18.8.1994* (Berlin 1996), 90–113.

Kraus, *Hekate* T. Kraus, *Hekate* (Heidelberg 1960).

Pickard-Cambridge, *Dramatic Festivals*[2]   A. W. Pickard-Cambridge, *The Dramatic Festivals of Athens*, rev. J. Gould and D. M. Lewis (Oxford 1968; reissued with suppl. 1988).

Pingiatoglou, *Eileithyia*   S. Pingiatoglou, *Eileithyia* (Königshausen 1981).

Pinney, 'Pallas and Panathenaea'   G. F. Pinney, 'Pallas and Panathenaea', in J. Christiansen and T. Melander (eds.), *Ancient Greek and Related Pottery* (Copenhagen 1988), 465–77.

Pirenne-Delforge, *L'Aphrodite grecque*   V. Pirenne-Delforge, *L'Aphrodite grecque* (*Kernos* Supplément 4, Liège 1994).

Pomeroy, *Families*   S. B. Pomeroy, *Families in Classical and Hellenistic Greece* (Oxford 1997).

Price, *Religions*   S. Price, *Religions of Ancient Greece* (Cambridge 1999).

Pringsheim, *Archäologische Beiträge*   H. G. Pringsheim, *Archäologische Beiträge zur Geschichte des eleusinischen Kults* (Munich 1905).

Pritchett, 'Παννυχίς'   W. K. Pritchett, 'The Παννυχίς of the Panathenaia', in *ΦΙΛΙΑ ΕΠΗ ΕΙΣ ΓΕΩΡΓΙΟΝ Ε.ΜΥΛΩΝΑΝ* ii (Athens 1987), 179–88.

Pritchett, *War*   W. K. Pritchett, *The Greek State at War*, vols. i–v (Berkeley and Los Angeles, 1971–91).

Pugliese Carratelli, *Lamine d'oro*   G. Pugliese Carratelli, *Le Lamine d'oro orfiche* (Milan 2001).

Pulleyn, *Prayer*   S. Pulleyn, *Prayer in Greek Religion* (Oxford 1997).

Rappaport, *Ritual and Religion*   R. A. Rappaport, *Ritual and Religion in the Making of Humanity* (Cambridge 1999).

RE   *Paulys Real-encyclopädie der classichen Altertumswissenschaft, Neue Bearbeitung*, ed. G. Wissowa, W. Kroll, K. Ziegler (Stuttgart/Munich, 1894–1980).

Redfield, *Locrian Maidens*   J. M. Redfield, *The Locrian Maidens: Love and Death in Greek Italy* (Princeton 2003).

Reeder, *Pandora*   E. D. Reed, *Pandora. Women in Classical Greece* (Princeton 1995).

Rhodes, *Boule*   P. J. Rhodes, *The Athenian Boule* (Oxford, 1972).

Rhodes, *Commentary* Ath. Pol.   P. J. Rhodes, *A Commentary on the Ar-istotelian* Athenaion Politeia (Oxford 1981).

Richardson, *Hymn to Demeter*   N. J. Richardson, *The Homeric Hymn to Demeter* (Oxford 1974).

Riedweg, *Mysterienterminologie*   C. Riedweg, *Mysterienterminologie bei Platon, Philon und Klemens von Alexandria* (Berlin 1987).

Ritual, Finance, Politics   S. Hornblower and R. Osborne (eds.), *Ritual, Finance, Politics: Democratic Accounts Rendered to D.M. Lewis* (Oxford 1994).

RO   P. J. Rhodes and R. Osborne, *Greek Historical Inscriptions, 404–323* (Oxford 2003). Reference unless otherwise noted is to inscription number, not page.

Robertson, 'Palladium Shrines'   N. Robertson, 'Athena and Early Greek Society: Palladium Shrines and Promontory Shrines', in M. Dillon (ed.), *Religion in the Ancient World* (Amsterdam 1996), 383–475.

Robertson, 'Proerosia'   N. Robertson, 'New Light on Demeter's Mysteries: The Festival Proerosia', *GRBS* 37 (1996), 319–79.

Rosivach, *Public Sacrifice*   V. J. Rosivach, *The System of Public Sacrifice in Fourth-Century Athens* (*American Classical Studies* 34, Atlanta 1994).

Rubinstein, *Adoption*   L. Rubinstein, *Adoption in IV. Century Athens* (Copenhagen 1993).

Rudhardt, *Pensée religieuse*   J. Rudhardt, *Notions fondamentales de la pensée religieuse et actes constitutifs du culte dans la Grèce classique*, 2nd edn. (Paris 1992).

Sacrifice   *Le Sacrifice dans l'antiquité* (*Entretiens Hardt* 27, Vandoeuvres 1981).

Sanctuaire grec   *Le Sanctuaire grec* (*Entretiens Hardt* 37, Vandoeuvres 1992).

Scarpi   P. Scarpi (ed.), *Le Religioni dei misteri*, I, *Eleusi, Dionisismo, Orfismo* (Fondazione Valla 2002).

Schachter, *Cults*   A. Schachter, *Cults of Boiotia*, 4 vols. (*BICS* supplements 38.1–4, London 1981–94).

Schaps, *Economic Rights* D. Schaps, *The Economic Rights of Women in Ancient Greece* (Edinburgh 1979).

Schlesier, 'Dionysos in der Unterwelt' R. Schlesier, 'Dionysos in der Unterwelt. Zu den Jenseitskonstruktionen der bakchischen Mysterien', in R. von den Hoff and S. Schmidt (eds.), *Konstruktionen von Wirklichkeit* (Stuttgart 2001), 157–72.

Schmitt Pantel, *Cité au banquet* P. Schmitt Pantel, *La Cité au banquet* (Rome 1992).

Schöne, *Thiasos* A. Schöne, *Der Thiasos. Eine ikonographische Untersuchung über das Gefolge des Dionysos in der attischen Vasenmalerei des 6. und 5. Jhs. v. Chr.* (Göteborg 1987).

Seaford, *Reciprocity and Ritual* R. Seaford, *Reciprocity and Ritual* (Oxford 1994).

Sfameni Gasparro, *Misteri e culti mistici* G. Sfameni Gasparro, *Misteri e culti mistici di Demetra* (Rome 1986).

SGD D. R. Jordan, 'A Survey of Greek Defixiones not included in the Special Corpora', *GRBS* 26 (1985), 151–97. Numbers refer to items, not pages.

Shear, *Kallias* T. L. Shear, Jr., *Kallias of Sphettos and the Revolt of Athens in 286 B.C* (*Hesperia* Suppl. 17, Princeton 1978).

Shear, 'Polis and Panathenaia' J. L. Shear, 'Polis and Panathenaia: The History and Development of Athena's Festival' (diss. Pennsylvania 2001).

Simon, *Festivals* E. Simon, *Festivals of Attica: An Archaeological Commentary* (Madison, Ill. 1983).

Sjövall, *Hauskult* H. Sjövall, *Zeus im altgriechischen Hauskult* (Lund 1931).

Smarzyck, *Religionspolitik* B. Smarzyck, *Untersuchungen zur Religionspolitik und politischen Propaganda Athens im Delisch-Attischen Seebund* (Munich 1990).

Sophocles Revisited J. Griffin (ed.), *Sophocles Revisited* (Oxford 1999).

Sourvinou-Inwood, *Death* C. Sourvinou-Inwood, *'Reading' Greek Death* (Oxford 1995).

Sourvinou-Inwood, *Girls'* | C. Sourvinou-Inwood, *Studies in Girls'*
Transitions | *Transitions: Aspects of the Arkteia and Age Representation in Attic Iconography* (Athens 1988).

Sourvinou-Inwood, 'Festival and Mysteries' | C. Sourvinou-Inwood, 'Festival and mysteries: aspects of the Eleusinian cult', in M. B. Cosmopoulos, *Greek Mysteries* (London 2003), 25–49.

Sourvinou-Inwood, 'Reconstructing change' | C. Sourvinou-Inwood, 'Reconstructing change: ideology and the Eleusinian Mysteries', in M. Golden and P. Toohey (eds.), *Inventing Greek Culture* (London 1997), 132–64.

Sourvinou-Inwood, *Tragedy and Religion* | C. Sourvinou-Inwood, *Tragedy and Athenian Religion* (Lanham 2003).

Steinhauer, Ἱερὸς νόμος Αἰξωνέων' | G. Steinhauer, Ἱερὸς νόμος Αἰξωνέων', in A. Matthaiou (ed.), Ἀττικαὶ Ἐπιγραφαί. Συμπόσιον εἰς μνήμην Adolf Wilhelm (1864–1850) (Athens 2004), 157–76.

van Straten, *Hierà kalá* | F. T. van Straten, *Hierà kalá: Images of Animal Sacrifice in Archaic and Classical Greece* (Leiden 1995).

van Straten, 'Votives and Votaries' | F. T. van Straten, 'Votives and Votaries in Greek Sanctuaries', in *Sanctuaire Grec*, 247–84.

Svoronos, *Nationalmuseum* | J. N. Svoronos, *Das Athener Nationalmuseum* (Athens 1908–37).

Tagalidou, *Herakles* | E. Tagalidou, *Weihreliefs an Herakles aus klassischer Zeit* (Jonsered 1993).

Taplin, *Stagecraft* | O. P. Taplin, *The Stagecraft of Aeschylus* (Oxford 1977).

Taylor, *Salamis* | M. C. Taylor, *Salamis and the Salaminioi* (Amsterdam 1997).

The Sacred and the Feminine | S. Blundell and M. Williamson, *The Sacred and the Feminine in Ancient Greece* (London 1998).

Thompson/Wycherley, *Agora* | H. A. Thompson and R. E. Wycherley, *Agora* XIV: *The Agora of Athens: The History, Shape and Uses of an Ancient City Center* (Princeton 1972).

Threatte, *Grammar* | L. Threatte, *The Grammar of Attic Inscriptions*, I. *Morphology*, II. *Phonology* (Berlin 1980–96).

Todd, *Athenian Law* — S. C. Todd, *The Shape of Athenian Law* (Oxford 1993).

Tracy, *Attic Letter-Cutters* — S. V. Tracy, *Attic Letter-Cutters of 229 to 86 B.C.* (Berkeley 1990).

Tracy, 'Panathenaic Festival' — S. V. Tracy, 'The Panathenaic Festival and Games: An Epigraphic Enquiry', *Nikephoros* 4 (1991), 133–53.

Tragedy and the Historian — C. B. R. Pelling (ed.), *Greek Tragedy and the Historian* (Oxford 1997).

Tragedy and the Tragic — M. Silk (ed.), *Tragedy and the Tragic* (Oxford 1996).

Travlos, *Bildlexikon* — J. Travlos, *Bildlexikon zur Topographie des antiken Attika* (Tübingen 1988).

Travlos, *Pictorial Dictionary* — J. Travlos, *Pictorial Dictionary of Ancient Athens* (London 1971).

Tresp, *Kultschriftsteller* — A. Tresp, *Die Fragmente der griechischen Kultschriftsteller* (Giessen 1914).

Trümpy, *Monatsnamen* — C. Trümpy, *Untersuchungen zu den altgriechischen Monatsnamen und Monatsfolgen* (Heidelberg 1997).

Vérilhac/Vial, *Le Mariage grec* — A. M. Vérilhac and C. Vial, *Le Mariage grec* (*BCH* suppl. 32, Athens and Paris 1998).

Vernant, *Figures, idoles, masques* — J.-P. Vernant, *Figures, idoles, masques* (Paris 1990).

Vernant, *Mythe et pensée* — J.-P. Vernant, *Mythe et pensée chez les Grecs*, 2 vols. (Paris 1965; Engl. tr. by J. Lloyd, *Myth and Thought among the Greeks*, London 1983).

Vernant, *Mortals and Immortals* — J.-P. Vernant, *Mortals and Immortals: Collected Essays* (Princeton 1991).

Versnel, 'Beyond Cursing' — H. S. Versnel, 'Beyond Cursing: The Appeal to Justice in Judicial Prayers', in *Magika Hiera*, 60–106.

Versnel, *Transition and Reversal* — H. S. Versnel, *Transition and Reversal in Myth and Ritual* (Leiden 1993).

Veyne, *Mythes* — P. Veyne, *Les Grecs ont-ils cru à leurs mythes?* (Paris 1983).

Vian, *Guerre* — F. Vian, *La Guerre des géants: le mythe avant l'époque hellénistique* (Paris 1951).

Vidal-Naquet, *Chasseur Noir* — P. Vidal-Naquet, *Le Chasseur noir: Formes de pensée et formes de société dans le monde grec* (Paris 1981; Engl.

	tr. by A. Szegedy-Maszak, *The Black Hunter*, Baltimore 1986).
Vikela, *Pankrates-Heiligtum*	E. Vikela, *Die Weihreliefs aus dem Athener Pankrates-Heiligtum am Ilissos* (*AM Beiheft* 16, Berlin 1994).
Vollkommer, *Herakles*	R. Vollkommer, *Herakles in the Art of Classical Greece* (Oxford 1988).
Walter, *Akropolismuseum*	O. Walter, *Beschreibung der Reliefs im kleinen Akropolismuseum in Athen* (Vienna 1923).
Whitehead, *Demes*	D. Whitehead, *The Demes of Attica, 508/7 B.C.–c. 250 B.C.* (Princeton 1986).
Wilamowitz, *Glaube*	U. von Wilamowitz-Moellendorff, *Der Glaube der Hellenen* (2 vols., Berlin 1931–2) (cited from 1959 Darmstadt reprint, which has slightly different page numbers).
Winkler, 'Laughter of the oppressed'	J. J. Winkler, 'The laughter of the oppressed', in id., *The Constraints of Desire* (New York and London 1990), 188–209.
Wilson, *Khoregia*	P. Wilson, *The Athenian Institution of the* Khoregia (Cambridge 2000).
Women in Antiquity	R. Hawley and B. Levick (eds.), *Women in Antiquity: New Assessments* (London 1995).
Woodford, 'Herakles in Attika'	S. Woodford, 'Cults of Herakles in Attica', in *Studies presented to George M.A. Hanfmann* (Mainz 1971), 211–25.
Worshipping Athena	J. Neils (ed.), *Worshipping Athena: Panathenaia and Parthenon* (Wisconsin 1996).
Wycherley, *Stones of Athens*	R. E. Wycherley, *Stones of Athens* (Princeton 1978).
Wycherley, *Testimonia*	R. E. Wycherley, *Agora* III: *Literary and Epigraphical Testimonia* (Princeton 1957).
Ziehen, 'Panathenaia'	L. Ziehen, *RE* article s.v. 'Panathenaia', 457–89 (1949).

Introduction

εἴ τις γῆ θεοὺς ἐπίσταται | τιμαῖς σεβίζειν, ἥδε τῷδ' ὑπερφέρει: 'if any land understands how to pay reverence to the gods with honours, in that this land [Attica] excels' (Sophocles, *OC* 1006–7)

Ἄνδρες Ἀθηναῖοι, κατὰ πάντα ὡς δεισιδαιμονεστέρους ὑμᾶς θεωρῶ: 'Men of Athens, I see that you are very god-fearing in all respects' (Paul on the Areopagus, Acts 17: 22)

In the most down-to-earth Athenian writings, gods, cults and rituals are everywhere. Aristophanes' first play, *Acharnians* (to take an example almost at random), contains extended evocations of two major festivals of Dionysus. Theophrastus constantly brings out the singularity of his various *Characters* through their religious behaviour: when the man proud of trifles has sacrificed an ox, he pins the skull outside his front door to make a show of his expensive offering; caught in a storm at sea, the coward asks anxiously whether any of his fellow-passengers is not initiated; at sacrifices to Heracles the opsimath or aged adolescent throws off his cloak and seeks to pick up the ox . . . [1] Aristophanes and Theophrastus are not religious writers; they merely reflect the way in which acts of cult and piety are taken for granted in Athenian everyday reality.[2] And examples could be multiplied almost ad infinitum, from art as well as from literature, from public as well as from private life. This book is a kind of long commentary on the religious themes in Aristophanes and Theophrastus and the rest. It is about the pervasiveness and the taken-for-grantedness of religion in Attic life.

It treats the religious life of just one Greek city. Yet it aspires to extend the scope of curiosity about Greek religion, not to restrict it. In anthropology, it is the precise, detailed and varied information about a particular community to be found in monographs which allows imaginative engagement with human behaviour in society. Rich and varied (and even in some measure precise and detailed) information is available about the religious life of Athens as of no other Greek city; indeed there may be no other polytheistic city in the ancient world the religious life of which is illuminated from so many different angles.

---

[1] Theophr. *Char.* 21.7; 25.2; 27.5; there are scores of further examples.
[2] Cf. 'An encounter with lived Islam challenges conventional definitions of religion as consisting primarily of beliefs and practices set apart from everyday life': C. Delaney, *The Seed and the Soil. Gender and Cosmology in a Turkish Village Society* (Berkeley 1991), 25.

The allure and potential of the subject lies in its diversity, and the challenge is to do justice to the diversity, to keep the many-faced prism of the evidence in motion, to investigate all the cracks and fissures into which this 'embedded religion' spreads out and down. That challenge has certainly been only very partially met here.[3] But it is incompatible with the no less important challenge of comparativism, whether within the Greek societies or outside them. The monograph is not the enemy of the work of synthesis or comparison. But one must do one thing at a time.

This book is a complement to an earlier work, *Athenian Religion: A History*.[4] In the introduction to that work I argued that the religion lived day by day by any Greek was the religion of a particular society within Greece, not an abstract and synthetic 'Greek' religion. The particularism of the religion of the Greek cities applies not just to festivals but also, if less obviously, to the gods honoured; the names of the main gods may be largely the same from state to state, but the division of functions between gods, the balances and combinations and emphases within the pantheon, differ radically from place to place.[5] Greeks bring out the individuality of a local pantheon, in their own way, by the connection that they often draw between gods and territory. Particular gods 'hold' or 'have as their portion' particular territories; Aeschines and his associates, says Demosthenes, have surrendered to Philip 'territories in which the gods should have been honoured by you and your allies' and feel no shame before 'the sun nor the native land on which they stand nor its shrines and tombs'; but it is precisely the tie to 'shrines and ancestral tombs', responds Aeschines, which has made impossible for him the kind of treachery of which he is accused by Demosthenes.[6] Temples necessarily belong to a particular place; the gods who inhabit them belong to that place too.

There were, on a modern estimate, 30,000 adult male citizens in Attica in the fourth century, and 100,000 male and female Athenians in all; also perhaps 20,000 adult male metics and a total metic population of 80,000. Hyperides speaks of there being 'more than 150,000' working male slaves in the fourth century. The citizen population is generally agreed to have been much larger in the mid-fifth century than in the fourth, perhaps even twice as large. Even if (in Thucydides' vague phrase) 'most' Athenians lived in Attica rather than Athens itself before the Peloponnesian war, they were tied in to

---

[3] I am very conscious that a different author could have made much more extensive use of visual evidence than I have done. This is not, however, the reason for which such evidence plays a smaller role in my discussion of festivals than it has often done. Students of iconography themselves have criticized many received associations between images and particular festivals (cf. p. 305); they are also much less inclined than their predecessors to treat images as if they were photographs of specific situations or events. For interesting recent reflections on the painters' use (which she sees as largely decorative and formal) of religious themes see A. F. Laurens in *Kernos* 11 (1998), 35–62.

[4] Oxford 1996.   [5] On the methodological implications of this point cf. p. 394.

[6] Dem. 19. 257, 267; Aeschin. 2. 23. Gods who hold a land: see p. 396, n. 35.

the life of the city in innumerable ways both formal and informal.[7] Athens was certainly an 'archaic city' in the senses defined by anthropology, an urban centre smaller, more homogeneous and traditional than the cities of the modern world but larger and more complex than the very small-scale communities studied by traditional anthropology (from a coalescence of several of which an archaic city typically emerges).[8] We can only guess the number of inhabitants of Attica who gathered in the city at the *Great Panathenaea* every five years. But there were surely tens of thousands.

Athenian Religion: A History attempted to say what can be said about the changing structures within which the religious life of these many inhabitants of Attica took place in the 500 years from *c.*750 to *c.*250 BC;[9] it also treated other topics that can be pinned down in time, such as the introduction of new cults, the trials of Socrates and other impious intellectuals, the restoration of cults and temples by Lycurgus. But our evidence for many religious practices at Athens does not allow a proper historical treatment; we can merely say 'this was the ritual performed in the fifth and fourth centuries'. The present book is a thematic study of (in the main) that central period, the period for which documentation is at its richest. Much evidence will, however, be quoted from later authors alongside that which is genuinely contemporary, and a word of justification and of distinction may be in place. The Attic authors whom later antiquity judged canonical wrote in the fifth and fourth centuries; much effort was expended from the third century onwards on explaining not just the vocabulary of their texts but also the institutions and practices there mentioned. The preferred method was the search for parallels within the author under consideration or others of the same period. The approach of this tradition of ancient scholarship can best be seen in the very important *Lexicon to the Ten Orators* of Harpocration, but the explanations of Attic customs found in numerous other places (in particular, scholia to ancient texts and lexicographers/encyclopaedists such as Hesychius, fifth to sixth century AD, Photius, ninth century, and the Suda, tenth to eleventh century) stand in the same tradition. Harpocration wrote in the second century AD, but the world he described was that of the orators of the fourth century BC whom he admired, and he had access to much evidence from that period now lost to us. Only at a very literal level can one dismiss a particular practice as 'unattested before the second century AD' if that attestation in the second century comes in Harpocration; and there is usually no reason to reject the testimony of a good historian such as Plutarch to classical Athenian practice when that is what he professes to describe (but often he speaks of his native Boeotia, sometimes of the Athens of his own day).

---

[7] Hyperides: fr. 29 Blass[3]; Thuc. 2.16.1. Modern estimate: see M. H. Hansen, *The Athenian Democracy* (Oxford 1991), 52–4, 90–4.

[8] See the application by Jameson, 'Sacred Space', of the ideas of Levy, *Mesocosm*. Cohen, *Athenian Nation*, is a bracing if extreme critique of the 'village Athens' model.

[9] Mikalson, *Hellenistic Athens*, continues the story to *c.*31 BC.

Other authors sought to recreate the lost world of classical Athens for very different purposes. The fictional Epistles of Alciphron (second century AD) are set in the Athens of the admired Menander, and Alciphron strives to give them the feel of that world. But he is no scholar, and, though he has occasionally dipped in the tradition of learned commentary just mentioned, he is capable of attaching his patches of local colour in quite the wrong places.[10] In his case great suspicion is indeed in order (if, that is, one perversely seeks to extract from his sugared confections hard nuggets of fact). The surviving commentaries on ancient authors (those on Aristophanes are particularly important here) contain a mixture of genuinely well-informed material with ad hoc guessing no more valuable than what an examination candidate faced with the same passage might improvise today. No infallible litmus test is available to distinguish learned tradition from guesswork, though there are certain diagnostic symptoms.[11] Different again are the sparse but interesting allusions to Attic festivals in authors such as Philostratus and Himerius writing in the third and fourth centuries AD. In principle they have in view the festivals as celebrated in their own day, though literary flourishes and gestures to a famous past may always adorn the plain record of experience. Enough of this: the simple point is established that what matters is the character of a source, not its date.

No book has previously been published that treats the same range of topics as this one. The predecessor closest in theme is *Attische Feste* of Ludwig Deubner, which appeared in 1932. Two distinct histories, both true, could be written of the ways in which the world of Athenian Religion has changed since the publication of that distinguished work. Deubner had no fragment of the state sacrificial calendar at his disposal, only one calendar of a deme, no indication that bodies such as *gene* issued documents of that type at all; the great excavations in the city centre of Athens had barely begun, and the sanctuary of Artemis Brauronia still lay beneath the mud of the Erasinos. The data available to us have, therefore, changed not trivially but profoundly. The second history would treat the developments in anthropological thought which have occurred since Deubner wrote or which, in common with most classical scholars of his day, he largely neglected even though they took place in his lifetime. And here the simple conclusion would be that Deubner was affected by none of the anthropological theorists and none of the students of Greek religion whose thought exercises most influence today.

Both new data and new theoretical perspectives extend, sometimes in complementary ways, the range of questions that can usefully be posed. No cult has been more discussed in recent years than the initiatory cult for young

[10] See Appendix 2.
[11] Citation of independent evidence usually indicates the learned tradition. But abbreviation sometimes causes the omission of the evidence which parallel texts prove originally to have underlain a particular interpretation. And scholiasts who guess occasionally guess on the basis of facts or factoids which they adduce.

girls of Artemis Brauronia—dealt with by Deubner in a mere page or so—and it would be hard to say whether a stronger impulse for these studies came from anthropological work on girls' initiations, or from the spectacular results of the excavations in the valley of the Erasinos. Again, if the religious topography of Attica is now an attractive subject to discuss, this is partly a product of theoretical reflection on centres and peripheries, partly of epigraphic and archaeological discoveries which have added so much shading to parts of the map of Attica which had once been blank. Some scholars tend temperamentally to put their trust for the future in new data, some in new theories; but, in the sublunary world, the antithesis is too sharp.

Yet most contemporary scholars differ drastically from Deubner even in areas where new data have not emerged to suggest new perspectives. We interpret the same data differently, which is predictable, and, more insidiously, we are interested in different things. At the festival of *Dipolieia*, a trial was held to establish culpability for the killing of an ox, and, after the human participants had disclaimed responsibility, the sacrificial knife itself (in a variant the axe) was found guilty and thrown into the sea. At the *Thargelia*, two individuals dressed in necklaces of figs (the one dispatched 'for the men' wore black figs, the one 'for the women' white) were driven out of the city as scapegoats. Surprising practices to detect in the city of Socrates!—and of the utmost interest to Deubner's generation. But other festivals served as showcases for drama and for sport and scarcely seem religious at all to modern eyes; for Thucydides' Pericles, festivals as a class are 'relaxations from toil'.[12] The *Thargelia* itself was the occasion not only for the expulsion of scapegoats but also for an elaborate and spectacular competition between cyclic choruses. By choosing which elements to emphasize, one can make Athenian religion as alien or as familiar as one pleases, almost *ad libitum*. Scapegoats and axe-trials are rather unfashionable today; we tend to prefer festivals which can be interpreted as some kind of expression of civic identity. And there are arguments of some force which can be used in justification: mentions of the scapegoat ritual are strangely few, if it was still a major focus of attention in the fifth and fourth centuries; as for the *Dipolieia*, the ritual already seemed quaint to Aristophanes.[13] Contemporary priorities are defensible, therefore. But there can never be a wholly objective standpoint from which to select the themes to emphasize or to pass over lightly.

The book has three parts. The first, Chapters 1–7, presents different contexts in which cult activity took place or reflection on religious topics was to be heard; it also treats religious personnel. 'Contexts' and 'personnel' sometimes bring with them distinctive religious practices with which they are associated, as for instance in Chapter 6 religious professionals introduce magic. Part two, Chapters 8–16, broadly coincides in subject matter with

[12] Thuc. 2.38.1.
[13] Ar. *Nub.* 984–5. On *Dipolieia* and *Thargelia* see Appendix 1.

the standard books on Attic festivals. But it seeks to break away from the festival-by-festival approach adopted in those books, which prevented broader questions about the nature and functions of festivals from even being raised. The short third part consists of two chapters which treat gods and heroes. These chapters are placed at the end not by way of a final revelation, but because the study of individual festivals has laid much groundwork for them.

In one sense, however, these chapters do indeed represent a conclusion to which the whole work has tended. The specific issues raised by the character of polytheism are confronted directly only in this part of the book. But the gods have been omnipresent throughout, and the implications of the fact that each god is one among many have never (I hope) been lost from view. The book bears the title that it does in order to emphasize that any study of Greek religion must in the end confront the logic or illogic of polytheism.

I

1

Ancestral Gods, Ancestral Tombs: The Household and Beyond

'Starting from Hestia' was for Greeks, according to a proverb, the proper way to begin; and in describing an Athenian's religious world it seems natural to do just that—or at least to start from the unit of which Hestia is the symbol, the individual household (*oikos*) with its associated cults. The Athenians themselves did not think in terms of 'the religion of the household' or 'household gods', as we shall see. But houses did have altars within and without their walls, at some of which members of the household joined together to worship.[1] So with due reservations we too can 'start from Hestia'.

What then was an *oikos? Oikos* and *oikia* have physical, social and economic applications. Our concern is with the social sense, but this cannot be neatly isolated from the other two. The members of a social *oikos* typically lived in the same physical house, and the practice known from Athens as from other states of 'razing the house' of a bad citizen was obviously directed against a social unit, not against bricks and mortar.[2] But the metaphysical idea of a family was also closely associated with the idea of heritable property. In none of its senses was the *oikos*, it seems, a legally defined entity in Athens. In some Greek states the word *oikos* or an equivalent appears in legal or quasi-legal contexts where it ought to have a clearly specified meaning: the Locrian settlers in Naupaktos, for instance, are allowed to return home provided that one male is left in each 'hearth'.[3] But any comparable contexts that may have existed in Athens are not revealed by our documents. The *kurios* who was the legal representative of women and minors was apparently the *kurios* of each of these individually, and not in virtue of a role as *kurios* of the whole *oikos* or head of household. And it was as 'son of X', not as 'member of the *oikos* of X', that the future citizen was entered on a deme register. (The contrary is often asserted in both cases, but evidence is never quoted.) For financial purposes, to judge liability to levies and liturgies, there must have been at least a set of

---

[1] The first item of household equipment listed in Xen. *Oec.* 9.6 is οἷς ἀμφὶ θυσίας χρώμεθα.

[2] W. R. Connor, 'The Razing of the House in Greek Society', *TAPA* 115 (1985), 79–102; 'the symbolic aspects of the house were inseparable from the literal edifice', comments L. Kurke, *The Traffic in Praise* (Ithaca, NY 1991), 16.

[3] See D. M. MacDowell, 'The *Oikos* in Athenian Law', *CQ* 39 (1989), 10–21; L. Gernet, intr. to Budé ed. of [Dem.]. 43, p. 91: *oikos* is not 'une notion proprement juridique'; Harrison, *Law*, i, 92. Locrians: ML 20.7, 16, cf. ibid. 5.28.

shared assumptions as to the scope of an *oikos*.[4] But in general *oikos*, like family, was a concept much deployed but little defined. All that can be done with it is to note the different implicit definitions that underly usage. Individuals sometimes pronounced conditional curses upon themselves, their *oikia* and *genos*. Doubtless they knew roughly what they meant, but this does not show that a definition applicable to all usages existed.

The *oikos*, it is often claimed, is fundamental, the frame from within which the individual experienced his world, the building block with which the society of the polis was made.[5] But what alternative conception is such a formulation intended to exclude? Is the point that we might have expected the Greeks to work with units smaller than the *oikos*, or larger? One interpretation of the slogan certainly sets the *oikos* in opposition to modern individualism. The Greek's fundamental sense of himself, it is said, was as a member of a group larger than himself that existed before his birth and would persist after his death: *stat fortuna domus, et avi numerantur avorum*.[6] A society which distinguished between proper uses for 'ancestral' and 'acquired' wealth, in which squandering one's patrimony was actually an actionable offence,[7] evidently did see the financial fortunes of the house as something held in trust. But the Athenians seem in general to have had no great interest in their grandfathers' grandfathers (for what it is worth, the naming convention whereby grandsons were named after grandfathers implies a much flatter conception of family history),[8] and many of the Athenians' understandings of the *oikos* reveal it as a principle of discontinuity and a kind of individualism. A much-quoted passage in the Demosthenic corpus tells how:

There was a man called Bouselos of Oion, jurors, who had five sons.... All these sons of Bouselos grew to be men, and their father Bouselos divided his property between them fairly and justly, as was right. After dividing the property amongst themselves, each married a wife in accordance with your laws, and they all had children and grandchildren, and so five *oikoi* came from the single *oikos* of Bouselos, and each son lived separately and had his own *oikos* and his own descendants. (43.19)

A happy story indeed of a flourishing family! But under inspection the *oikos* turns out to consist on this view of not more than a single adult male

---

[4] Joint *choregiai* of fathers and sons (*IG* II² 3095; 3096) are attested in two demes but not to my knowledge in the city (Nikias and his brothers probably won on separate occasions, Pl. *Gorg.* 472a, Plut. *Nic.* 3.3, Löhr, *Familienweihungen*, no. 62; for collective commemoration of separate victories, in the *anthippasia*, see *IG* II² 3130, Löhr, *Familienweihungen*, no. 108). Fathers and sons could perform separate liturgies more or less contemporaneously: for several instances in Isae. 6 see Davies, *Propertied Families*, 562–6. Note too Lys. 18.21: ἐκ μιᾶς οἰκίας τρεῖς ὄντες (two brothers and a cousin) τριηραρχοῦμεν.

[5] So e.g. Todd, *Athenian Law*, 204; J. Jones as cited and endorsed by Kurke, op. cit., 8–9.

[6] Virg. *Georg.* 4. 209.

[7] Lys. 19.37; Bruck, *Totenteil*, 181–9; Gernet, *Droit et société*, 144.

[8] See L. Foxhall, *CQ* 39 (1989), 28, n. 32; Jameson, 'Domestic Space', 112, n. 26. The inheritance group starts from an ἀρχὴ τοῦ γένους one higher, the great-grandfather: Isae. 8.32; Bourriot, *Génos*, 223–6.

Athenian and his dependents; when the sons of an *oikos* grow to manhood, they split off and form new *oikoi*, which in time replace that into which the sons were born. In place of a single *oikos* surviving through time, we have new *oikoi* created (and vanishing) generation by generation.[9] A broader use of the term was, certainly, also possible, by which the *oikoi* of the five sons of Bouselos could be subsumed into 'the *oikos* of Bouselos'. Inheritance lawyers adopt this broader use from time to time, for clearly visible tactical purposes.[10] But the more restricted use is much the more characteristic. For the writers on household management, the house consists merely of a husband, wife and their dependents, even parents being left somewhere outside the field of vision.[11] We meet the restricted sense above all whenever there is talk of 'an *oikos* being made empty' (ἐρημοῦσθαι) for lack of descendants. In the orators, that poignant phrase normally refers to the death of an individual without issue, not to the extinction of the whole lineage of a remoter ancestor. My *oikos* perishes if I die childless even if my brother leaves ten sons.[12]

The fragmenting *oikos* we have described is a product of the system of partible inheritance. Just as a man's physical property is split between his sons, so too is his metaphysical *oikos*. How to describe the life-cycle of the self-dividing *oikos* is a delicate problem.[13] Five *oikoi* result from the one *oikos* of

[9] Cf. Gernet, *Droit et société*, 149: 'une contradiction se dénonce dans le système ... tout Athénien male, du vivant meme de son père, représente un οἶκος en puissance'; L. Foxhall, *CQ* 39 (1989), 28, n. 32.

[10] The speaker of [Dem.] 43 makes great play with an '*oikos* of Hagnias', with reference to Hagnias the grandfather of the Hagnias whose property is in dispute (11, 12, 14, 17, 28, 29, 49–50, 68, 72, 73 and so on). But this is just rhetorical manipulation: the claimant whom the speaker supports falls just inside, the counter-claimant just outside, this 'house of (descendants of the elder) Hagnias' which he has arbitrarily conjured up as though it gave title to inherit, and the coincidence in name allows the speaker to insinuate that his client somehow belongs also to the house of the younger Hagnias. In e.g. [Dem.] 43. 49–50, 83–4, the '*oikos* of Hagnias' is certainly that of the elder Hagnias. But in e.g. 11–14 jurors would certainly think of the younger. See W. E. Thompson, *De Hagniae Hereditate* (*Mnem.* Suppl. 44, Leiden 1976), 75–6; cf. D. M. MacDowell, *CQ* 39 (1989), 18 (the speaker in effect treats the *anchisteia*, the inheritance group which allowed membership in the female line, as an *oikos*). In Isocr. 19.46 the speaker can claim to belong to the same *oikia* as his father's sister and cousin.

[11] See G. Sissa, 'La famille dans la cité grecque' (an excellent survey), in A. Burguière and others, *Histoire de la famille* (Paris 1986), 163–94, at 179.

[12] Note e.g. Isae. 2.35: it will be a case of ἐρήμωσις οἴκου if the estate of Menekles goes to his brother, who has a son. Cf. D. Asheri, 'L'οἶκος ἔρημος nel diritto successorio attico', *Archivio Giuridico* 159 (1960), 7–24: he discusses, 14–15, the tendentious extension of the term in [Dem.] 43.

[13] Cf. D. M. MacDowell, *CQ* 39 (1989), 16–17. A closely related question is that of residence practices. 'Neolocal' residence for married couples is Plato's ideal, but his text clearly implies that residence with either set of parents often occurred (*Leg.* 776a–b; cf. [Dem.] 25.88 on tensions arising where 'a father and sons and perhaps the son's children' all live together). Plut. *Per.* 16.5 seems to show even the wealthy Pericles sharing a large menage with his married sons. The speaker of Dem. 39 and 40, who married very young, brought his bride home to his father's house, 40.50 (which, however, was only semi-occupied by his father, entangled with another woman, 39.26, 40.9, 40.11); further complications follow after the father's death, but the physical house was so central to the dispute of Dem. 40 (Gernet even suspects it was an ἐνοικίου δίκη: Budé introduction, p. 31) that all statements about the house and its use must be

Bouselos, we are told; but when do they emerge precisely? And was there a
point at which there were not five but six, those of the sons and that of the
father? Would the father have retained a separate *oikos* only if he retained a
physical house of his own?[14] Similarly, would there still have been five *oikoi* if
the sons had lived together and not in separate houses? Or if they had left their
inheritance undivided? Could a single *oikos*, in the sense of physical house,
contain several *oikoi* in the sense of 'a property-owning male and his dependents'? Not only are these questions hard to answer; it is hard even to discern
the extent to which they would for Athenians have been real and significant
questions, whether in practical or symbolic terms. But a central consideration
appears to be the following. An Athenian of the high property classes commonly handed over his property (some or all) to his sons if he lived to see them
reach maturity. It was perhaps this act more than any other, or failing it the
transmission of the father's property by his death, that created new *oikoi*; for
both Philoctemon, who received property from his father but died during the
father's lifetime, and Archiades, who inherited but never married, could none
the less be held to need heirs 'to prevent their *oikos* becoming desolate'.[15] An
individual therefore has his own *oikos* once he has his own property (though
it might not be natural to say so in his lifetime). We also see from these cases
one sense in which these questions are not merely academic ones. If one
brother among several dies without heirs, one might expect his property to be
sucked straight back into the family pool and divided among the surviving
brothers. But at Athens there existed the institution of posthumous adoption,

viewed with suspicion. In Plaut. *Most.* 754–9 (source unknown) a father supposedly plans to add
a *gynaeceum* to his house to accommodate a bride for his son. In *Leg.* 931a Plato implies that many
families had parents and grandparents 'worn out with age' living at their hearths (the situation
familiar from the plot of Ar. *Vesp.*). We know of one family, in the trierarchic class, where two
brothers had divided their property and one, a bachelor, lived apart, another (marital status
unknown) with his father ([Dem.] 47.34–6, 53); we also hear of two brothers, one married and
one unmarried, who lived separately after the death of their father but left their property
undivided ([Dem]. 44.10). The Bouselids lived apart from one another (what their father did is
not clear). If separation of brothers was the norm, among the wealthy at least, and in cases of co-
residence of married son and father the father's *oikos* was subsumed in the son's, the sum comes
out neatly with one social *oikos* for each physical house. Perhaps then, according to the cultural
ideal, an *oikos* should be seen as 'an adult property-owning male living, with dependents, in a
house shared by no other adult property-owning male (except a father in retirement)'. But the
oikos of Pericles (above) is a significant exception. For texts which speak of a πατρῴα οἰκία see
Golden, *Children*, 142. On the residence of the widowed mother see Cox, *Household Interests*, 143.

[14] The language of Pl. *Lys.* 209c, of a father entrusting (ἐπιτρέπειν) to his son καὶ αὐτὸν καὶ τὰ
αὐτοῦ (cf. Ar. *Vesp.*) suggests that a 'retired' father no longer had an *oikos*; cf. the situation of
Philocleon in Ar. *Vesp.* On 'retirement' see Gauthier/ Hatzopoulos, *Loi gymnasiarchique*, 52.

[15] Isae. 6 *passim*, esp. 5 (evidence for a possibility, despite the complication of the actual case:
Harrison, *Law*, i, 139–40; D. M. MacDowell, *CQ* 39, 1989, 14 n. 11); [Dem.] 44.10, 18–19.
Archiades, the bachelor, perhaps adopted an heir in his lifetime (contrast [Dem.] 44.46 and 61
with 19: Rubinstein, *Adoption*, 117; L. Gernet, *REG* 34, 1921, 370, seems wrong to deny that a
bachelor could have an *oikos*). Archiades and his brother left the property undivided. This case
shows, therefore, that it was not division of the estate that created *oikoi*.

which could provide the heirless with heirs after death.[16] And it was the fact of 'having an *oikos*' which made a dead man a candidate for acquiring such a posthumous heir.

Before we turn to the gods situated in and around the house, two further caveats must be made. First, it is unavoidable in such a study to speak of 'ideal homes' and to ignore the differences that must have existed between those of the 'fat' and of the 'many'. Second, not every event that takes place within the walls of the *oikos* is itself an activity of the whole household. Most conspicuously, one principal room of the house, location no doubt of many of its sacrificial banquets, was open to male outsiders but, in the main, closed to the women. The outsiders so admitted might be blood kin, affines or members of that category of intimate non-kin known precisely as *oikeioi*, persons associated with the house.[17] Women too had their neighbourhood networks and celebrated rites in the house together, in honour of Hecate as well as of Adonis. The most basic act of domestic piety, it is tempting to suppose, is the burning of small offerings of food and the pouring of libations at meals.[18] But 'whose meal?', one must ask; for we should probably imagine arrangements in an Athenian household on the analogy of the reliefs that depict 'banqueting heroes'—a male waited on by a woman who has eaten elsewhere—rather than of the modern family meal.[19] Occasions when all the members of the *oikos* and they alone met together for worship are hard to identify.

I turn at last to the gods situated in and around the house. From various allusions in the *Homeric Hymns*—not of course in the main Athenian texts—we learn that Hestia has 'an everlasting seat' in 'the middle' of the house of every mortal, and receives the first and last libation at every banquet; like her friend Hermes she 'lives in the fair houses' of men.[20] Early in the fifth century the East Locrians still spoke of a household or family as a hearth.[21] The hearth remained the symbolic centre of the Athenian household, to which new members of all types were in different ways introduced. Brides (but also grooms) and newly bought slaves were led to it, made to sit, and greeted with a shower of light foodstuffs such as nuts and figs (καταχύσματα) 'as a symbol of prosperity'; children were informally acknowledged a few days after birth at the *Amphidromia*, which took its name from an act (just how or by

---

[16] Cf. p. 34 below.
[17] On the relative importance of kin and friends, esp. neighbours, see Golden, *Children*, 141. For a friend at a domestic sacrifice see Ant. 1.16–18; the host's παλλακή waits on the two men.
[18] So Jameson, 'Domestic Space', 105; id. 'Private Space', 193; cf. Porph. *Abst.* 2.20. Networks: Dem. 55.23. Hecate: Ar. *Lys.* 700–1.
[19] So Golden, *Children*, 36–8; see too Pomeroy, *Families*, 30. But for a sacrifice shared by husband and wife see Xen. *Oec.* 7.8.
[20] *Hymn. Hom.* 5.29–32; 29; cf. 24.
[21] ML 20.7, 16; cf. Hdt. 1.176.3, 5.40.2, 6.86δ; ὁμεστίοι in C 43 of the Labyadai inscription (RO 1); and especially πυρόκαυσις as a near synonym of οἰκία in the new section of the Macedonian military law: M. B. Hatzopoulos, *L'Organisation de l'armée macédonienne sous les Antigonides* (Athens 2001), 91, n. 1.

whom performed is unclear) of 'running around' the hearth. Offerings to
Hestia were in theory shared only among members of the household, if we
may trust the explanation offered of the proverb 'he's sacrificing to Hestia',
which meant 'you'll get nothing from him'.[22] The dying Alcestis in Euripides
entrusts her children to the charge of Hestia in a moving prayer. Alcestis is a
tragic queen, but the speaker of Lysias 1 has to face the charge that he killed
the adulterous Eratosthenes even though the latter had 'fled to the hearth' of
the speaker's far from palatial home. The wife of the exiled general Phocion
prayed to 'dear hearth' and laid beside it the remains of her husband, brought
home at last from Megara.[23]

Hestia, the fixed centre, can be seen as a symbol of the *oikos'* continuity over
time. The child is born of a mother presented to the hearth, and is presented to
the hearth itself; the boy child eventually leads a bride 'from her paternal
hearth' to his own and begets a child to perpetuate the process, the girl child
eventually goes out to another hearth in exchange.[24] Cults and myths flirt,
perhaps, with the fantasy of a child born literally 'from the hearth'.[25] But we
have noted that the *oikos* was not continuous, but old *oikoi* were constantly
being replaced by new. Did new *oikoi* fetch fire from the paternal hearth, after
the fashion of the colonies to which Plato compares them?[26] Or were there
rituals to establish a new hearth? Or did one simply emerge when fire was
lighted in the new house? These questions remain unanswerable.

Whatever the answer might be, however, it is startling to read an authoritative judgement on the archaeological evidence for Greek houses in the
classical period: fixed rectangular hearths are a rarity, fixed circular hearths
are unknown, and we must conclude that most households used movable
braziers or lit temporary fires wherever was convenient. The fixed centre of
the turning world[27] turns out to have been portable. That conclusion is not
universally accepted, some preferring to suppose that if, say, six out of thirty

[22] Symbolic centre: e.g. Pl. *Leg.* 740b, 771c. Introductions: Ar. *Plut.* 768–9, 788–799; Dem.
45.74 (slaves); Theopompus fr. 15 (the newly married); also lexicographers, esp. Hesych. κ 1525
(seated posture) and Suda κ 877 ('prosperity'). First-time ambassadors and *theoroi* were also so
greeted (at the hearth in the prytaneum?): Suda loc. cit. For καταχύσματα and (perhaps) a
welcoming Hestia on wedding vases see Oakley/Sinos, *Wedding,* 34 (cf. *LIMC* s.v. *Hestia,* nos.
26 and 27). The word περιστίαρχος perhaps preserves a trace of ritual purification of the domestic
hearth: Parker, *Miasma,* 21; RE s.v. *Hestia,* 1280–1. *Amphidromia:* see most recently R. Hamilton,
GRBS 25 (1984), 243–51; M. Golden, *EchCl* 5 (1986), 252–6; Brulé, *Fille d' Athènes,* 58–9.
Offerings to Hestia: see Zenobius 4.44, citing Theopompus fr. 29; cf. fr. 71.
[23] Eur. *Alc.* 163–9 (for greetings to the hearth see Eur. *HF* 599); Lys. 1.27 (cf. e.g. Eur. *HF*
715); Plut. *Phoc.* 37.5. Sacrifice of a δέλφαξ to Hestia: Eupolis fr. 301, and cf. Ar. *Vesp.* 844.
[24] So Phot. ζ 28 s.v. ζεῦγος ἡμιονικόν (= Paus. Att. ζ 3 Erbse). Pl. *Leg.* 773a speaks of marriage
as 'a union of hearths' (ταῖς συνιούσαις ἑστίαις).
[25] On all this see L. Gernet, *Anthropologie de la Grèce Antique* (Paris 1968), 387–8; Vernant,
Mythe et pensée, 129–38 (131–8 in the Engl. tr.); Bremmer/Horsfall, *Roman Myth,* 51.
[26] *Leg.* 776a–b; cf. I. Malkin, *Religion and Colonization in Ancient Greece* (Leiden 1987), 114–34
(on *Etym. Magn.* 694. 28–31 s.v. πρυτανεία).
[27] Eur. fr. 944 N.; Pl. *Phaedr.* 247a; cf. Vernant, *Mythe et pensée,* 126, n. 7 (162, n. 7, in the
Engl. tr.).

houses of a given type still display hearths, those of the other twenty-four have been carried off, fine shaped blocks as they are, for use elsewhere. And, since the evidence for domestic architecture almost all comes from northern Greece or beyond the Aegean, one is at liberty to imagine that at Athens itself Hestia remained fixed firm. (Two stone hearths have in fact been tentatively identified from the scanty domestic remains of the Piraeus.)[28] But if the more radical conclusion proved correct, what it would force us to adjust might be an over-literal conception of how the traditional symbol was embodied, in new living conditions, not necessarily our understanding of the symbol's continuing importance.

Hestia sat in the seclusion of the *oikos*, like the women who guarded its property, and may have been seen as ταμίας or stewardess of its riches. (She bears that title, though in a public context, in Hellenistic Cos.[29]) But the power explicitly associated with the wealth of the household was a different god, Zeus Ktesios. 'If the property of a house is destroyed, it may be replaced, by grace of Zeus Ktesios (Κτησίου Διὸς χάριν)', says the Argive king in Aeschylus' *Supplices* (443–4); rage seizes me, says a character in Menander, 'when I see a parasite entering the women's quarters, and Zeus Ktesios not keeping the storeroom (ταμιεῖον) locked, and little whores running in'.[30] Zeus Ktesios was concerned, therefore, both with the acquisition of property and with its preservation, in that storeroom where his own image was set. A typical prayer to him was 'to grant health and prosperous acquisition/ ownership' (ὑγίειαν διδόναι καὶ κτῆσιν ἀγαθήν).[31] According to Isaeus, one head of household who was a particular enthusiast for sacrifices to Zeus Ktesios treated them, like the supposed sacrifices to Hestia of olden days, as confined to household members, and free ones at that; but we hear of another who saw such a sacrifice as a good opportunity to entertain a friend.[32] A turn of expression in this second case—'he chanced to have a sacrifice to Zeus

---

[28] Authoritative judgement: Jameson, 'Domestic Space', 98, 105; id., 'Private Space', 193, with reference e.g. to V. Hadjimichalis, *BCH* 80 (1956), 483 n. 3, ibid. 95 (1971), 218. For fixed hearths at Olynthus (in 6 out of 29 houses) see W. Hoepfner and E.-L.Schwandner, *Haus und Stadt im klassischen Griechenland*, ed. 2 (Munich 1994), 100; the character of the part of the house in which they appear is disputed: Cahill, *Household and City*, 138, 154, 156, 160. Piraeus: see Hoepfner/Schwandner, op. cit., 34 (J. Kraounaki) and 40, the latter a re-interpretation of the remains shown in *ArchDelt* 30 (1975) *Chron.* fig 29a, where the square stone object in question is clearly visible. A hearth was supposedly found in a corner of a room in a 5th-c. house in Paeania (A. D. Keramopoullos, *ArchEph* 1932, 58, without further details); that of 'house D' in the 'Industrial region' west of the Areopagus is thought to have belonged to a foundry (R. S. Young, *Hesperia* 20, 1951, 222–3). Hoepfner/Schwandner locate the Attic hearth in a substantial 'living room', distinct from the *andron*, not in a kitchen or court. The presence of a hearth in an *andron*-type room at Ano Voula is taken to disprove domestic use, Lohmann, *Atene*, 132. See further several essays in N. Fisher, J. Whitley and R. Westgate (eds.), *Building Communities: House, Settlement and Society in the Aegean and Beyond* (British School at Athens, in press).

[29] *LSCG* 169 A 9; cf. Gernet, op. cit., 397–8.

[30] Fr. 410 (452 Koerte).   [31] Isae. 8.16.

[32] Isae. 8.16 (the old man also, supposedly, admitted the speaker, who was, supposedly, his daughter's son); Ant. 1.16 (where the easiest interpretation is that Philoneos, who sometimes lodged in Athens, 14, lived in the Piraeus).

Ktesios (to perform) in Piraeus'—suggests that the occasion even for these private celebrations could be fixed by convention. The head of the household in Isaeus excluded slaves, but the speaker implies that others might have been less strict. At household sacrifices slaves could always at least hope for a share.[33]

One of the rare surviving fragments of exegetical literature concerns his cult: 'This is how to set us symbols (σημεῖα) of Zeus Ktesios'.[34] What follows is corrupt in detail, but the main action certainly concerned a new two-handled jar (καδίσκος) with a lid, which was to be hung with white wool and filled with a mixture, known as 'ambrosia', of pure water, olive oil and 'all fruits' (παγκαρπία). Pots were sometimes used, perhaps as foundation offerings, to 'set up' statues, but it looks as if the jars of Zeus Ktesios were themselves the tokens of the god's presence, the only ones apart perhaps from small altars.[35] If so, Zeus Ktesios was within the means of any household. Votives to him are not found in Attica, not surprisingly, since it was not the practice to make dedications within the house. Had representations of the god existed, they might perhaps have shown him, as does one from Thespiae in Boeotia, as a snake.[36]

Zeus Herkeios is more complicated. Every candidate for an archonship at Athens was asked 'if he had an Apollo Patroos and a Zeus Herkeios, and where these shrines were'.[37] Every citizen—or at least every citizen from the higher property classes—had therefore an association of some kind with Zeus Herkeios. The *herkos* is the wall or fence that surrounded the external courtyard of the Homeric house—and by extension the courtyard itself—and we regularly find an altar located there in the Homeric poems and in myths which reflect that world (above all that of the death of Priam).[38] The typical Athenian house had an internal courtyard, and it is often and reasonably supposed that Zeus Herkeios transferred at Athens to this internal αὐλή, as in

[33] Men. *Dysc.* 563–9 (Getas' grumbling that he will get nothing implies that the thing was at least conceivable); in *Dysc.* 560 Sostratos invites both his new friend Gorgias and Gorgias' servant to share a family sacrifice. Slaves are full participants in Dicaeopolis' private celebration of the *Rural Dionysia* in Ar. *Ach.* 247–50. [Arist.] *Oec.* 1344b 19–21 recommends that 'sacrifices and enjoyments' be held for the sake of slaves more than of freemen, because of their greater capacity for low pleasure.

[34] Autokleides, *FGrH* 353 F 1 ap. Ath. 473b–c (Tresp, *Kultschriftsteller*, 45–7); on the text see Sjövall, *Hauskult*, 56–63 [+]; Nilsson, *Geschichte*, 404, nn. 9–10. The parallels quoted for this striking use of σημεῖον (Aesch. *Supp.* 218; *IG* XII.3.452 = *LSCG* 133.5) are not very close.

[35] Cf. Aesch. *Ag.* 1038, κτησίου βωμοῦ πέλας; *IG* XII.3 *Supp.* 1361 is a probable example of such a small altar from Thera, and cf. Nilsson, *Geschichte*, 404, nn. 7–8. The state could also make offerings: see the Dodona prophecy ap. Dem. 21.53 requiring Διὶ κτησίῳ βοῦν λευκόν, *Agora* XV 171.9 (offering by prytaneis of 190/89).

[36] M. P. Nilsson, *AM* 33 (1908), 279–88 (reprinted in *Op. Sel.* i); on the extra Attic cult see *RE* XA (1972), 326 and (Zeus Pasios) 350. Nilsson suggests that the contents of the jars were symbolic food for the household snake (op. cit., and *Geschichte*, 403–6).

[37] Arist. *Ath. Pol.* 55.3; cf. 7.4, and e.g. Cratinus Junior fr. 9.

[38] Hom. *Il.* 16.231, *Od.* 22.335; Eur. *Tro.* 483; Sjövall, *Hauskult*, 7–10 (who argues that it was a cult confined to the well-off, 11–12).

effect a Zeus Auleios. The ancient scholars who claimed, however mis-
guidedly, that the Athenians called the house ἕρκος and the guardian of the
house Zeus Herkeios evidently took the cult to be a domestic one; and
Herodotus, in recounting a story set in sixth-century Sparta (admittedly in
the king's residence), certainly supposes that the altar of Zeus Herkeios would
be within the house.[39] The difficulty with this view is to see what force it
allows to the archon's question 'have you a Zeus Herkeios?' If it meant 'do
you belong to an *oikos*?', it constitutes the only evidence that the 'house' was,
or had once been, in any formal sense one of the building blocks of Attic
society. Possibly the cult of Zeus Herkeios, like that of Apollo Patroos, was
attached to the larger kinship groups, phratry or *genos* (or even to the
deme)—as the obscure expression '*gennetai* of Apollo Patroos and Zeus Herkeios'[40] might suggest. (This would not preclude individual altars in the
courtyards of prosperous households.) However this may be, we have a
clear item of evidence that for the Athenians Zeus Herkeios was not merely
a form of Zeus located conveniently close to hand (as he may appear to be in
Homer), nor merely a guardian of the physical space of the household, but
specifically associated with the social ties holding together the close family.
'Whether she is my sister's child or closer in blood than the whole (family
linked by) Zeus Herkeios, she and her sister shall not escape a dreadful death',
says Sophocles' Creon, terribly, of his niece Antigone.[41] Demaratus' appeal to

---

[39] Hdt. 6.68. Ancient scholars: Phot. ε 1926; *Σ* Pl. *Euthyd.* 302d; *Anecd. Bekk.* 1.256.21–2.
Sacrifice in the *aule* was possible (Pl. *Resp.* 328c); 7 out of 106 houses on the N. hill at Olynthus
yielded stone courtyard altars (*Olynthos VIII*, 321–2; Cahill, *Household and City*, index s.v. *altars*;
I know no Attic instance). Portable terracotta altars have often been found in houses (*Olynthos
VIII*, 322–5; Cahill, op. cit., index of artefacts s.v. *altars, portable*; Nilsson, *Op. Sel.* iii, 265–70; C. K.
Williams, *Hesperia* 48, 1979, 136–40), but in such cases findspots demonstrate place of storage,
not place of use (Jameson, 'Domestic Space', 111, n. 17). Consecration 'by pots' (Ar. fr. 256; n. 53
below) would certainly fit a domestic context.
[40] [Dem.] 57.67; Solon used the word ὁμοερκής, Poll. *Onom.* 6.156 (F 59 Ruschenbusch); cf. H.
J. Rose, *Euphrosyne* I (1957), 99; A. Andrewes, *JHS* 81 (1961), 7–8. Zeus Herkeios is mentioned
in association with phratry gods in Pl. *Euthyd.* 302d, but the only groups we positively know to
have worshipped the god are a *genos*, of special type (the *Eumolpidai*: Nicomachus calendar, *BSA*
97, 2002, 364, fr. 3. 73), and rather surprisingly a deme: at Thorikos he receives three offerings,
at least once in association with Demeter (*SEG* XXXIII 147. 22; left side by 41; right side by 44);
the offering mentioned in *IRhamnous* 180.87 may also derive from the deme Rhamnus (on this
link with the demes see Jameson, 'Domestic Space', 105). Other Attic evidence is unhelpful: there
was an altar in or near the Pandroseion (Philochorus, *FGrH* 328 F 67: cf. Travlos's speculative
reconstruction, *Pictorial Dictionary*, 218, fig. 281), and an altar by the Dipylon gate apparently
addressed to him as guardian of the ἕρκος of the city (so U. Köhler, *AM* 4, 1879, 288, on *IG* II²
4983). *Syll.*³ 991 is (probably) a *horos* from an Ionian colony in Thrace (perhaps Galepsos, a
colony of Thasos): Διὸς Ἑρκείο Πατρώιο καὶ Διὸς Κτησίο (cf. *IG* XII *suppl.* 407, from Thasos): the
need for a *horos* may imply a cult that was not merely domestic. There is little other non-Attic
evidence: *RE* XA 309.
[41] Soph. *Ant.* 487; cf. his reference to Ζεὺς σύναιμος at 658–9. Demaratus: Hdt. 6.68. But how
precisely the group who might worship Zeus Herkeios together was defined (and was it defined, or
constituted according to individual circumstances?) is unknown. Plato's reference to ὁμογνίων
θεῶν κοινωνία (*Leg.* 729c) seems to imply something similar.

his mother by Zeus Herkeios to tell the truth about his birth implies something similar.

In the porch of many Athenian houses stood some among three further gods.[42] Apollo Aguieus is familiar to readers of drama, but the physical form in which he was manifested is controversial. An 'Aguieus' was, according to lexicographers, a 'pillar ending in a post', a 'conical pillar'.[43] But some ancients believed that these pillars were 'proper to the Dorians' and that the Athenians had altars instead: in Harpocration's words, 'the Aguieus mentioned by Attic authors must be the altars in front of the houses mentioned by Kratinos and Menander and Sophocles in the *Laokoon*, where he says, transferring Athenian customs to Troy,

> The *aguieus* altar gleams with fire, steaming with
> drops of myrrh, perfumes of the barbarians.'[44]

Certainly, it is not strictly demonstrated that the Attic Aguieus was a pointed column, of the kind that can be seen on the coins of (for instance) Megara and Apollonia.[45] But greetings such as 'lord Aguieus, neighbour, guardian of my front door', common in tragedy and comedy, imply the presence of an emblem of the god, not an altar alone.[46] (A subsidiary question then arises whether small altars have also to be postulated, to burn the kind of offerings mentioned by Sophocles.) The references in comedy imply that pillars of Aguieus were common, though they cannot support the no doubt unguarded claim of the lexicographers that every household had one. No example has yet been identified archaeologically.

A comic oracle in Aristophanes declares that one day every one of the litigious Athenians will have a little private law court outside his porch 'like a

[42] On the porch (which is archaeologically detectable) see Jameson, 'Domestic Space', 97–8; Soph. *El.* 1374–5, ἔδη | θεῶν ὅσοιπερ πρόπυλα ναίουσιν τάδε.

[43] Σ vet. Ar. *Vesp.* 875b; Phot. α 277: for further references see Nilsson, *Geschichte*, 203.

[44] Harpocr. α 22, citing Soph. fr. 370; for the association with the Dorians cf. Dieuchidas of Megara, *FGrH* 485 F 2. Harpocration also believes that the common oracular instruction κνισᾶν ἀγυιάς (Dem. 21.51, 43.66; cf. Ar. *Eq.* 1320, *Av.* 1233) should be accented not ἀγυιάς, 'fill the streets with smoke', but Ἀγυιᾶς, 'make the Aguieus altars smoke'. On either view the Aguieus altars may have been used: through them perhaps households could participate in a more collective celebration.

[45] See E. de Filippo Balestrazzi in *LIMC* s.v. *Apollon Agyieus*, nos. 2–7; V. Fehrentz, 'Der antike Agyieus', *JdI* 108 (1993), 123–96, at 138–54; or e.g. J. E. Harrison, *Themis* (Cambridge 1912), 406; M. P. Nilsson, *Greek Popular Religion* (Colombia 1940), 154, fig. 30. The symbol's complicated later history is discussed in *LIMC* and V. Fehrentz, locc. citt.

[46] Ar. *Vesp.* 875; cf. Aesch. *Ag.* 1081; Eur. *Phoen.* 631; Pherecr. fr. 92; also the appeals in similar contexts to an Apollo, not named as Aguieus, in Men. *Sam.* 444, Plaut. *Bacch.* 172–3, and the tragic passages cited by Mastronarde on Eur. *Phoen.* 631; also the oath 'by this Apollo', Men. *Dysc.* 659 with Sandbach's note. Small altars: denied most recently by J. P. Poe, *ClAnt* 20 (1989), 134, who argues that the one source which distinguishes altar from pillar (Helladius ap. Phot. *Bibl.* 279, 535b 33–8) is confused. In fact, *Anecd. Bekk.* 1.268.9 also speaks of βωμίσκοι καὶ στύλοι, but not necessarily with good authority. Fehrentz, op. cit., 133, adduces Hesych. α 856 ὁ πρὸ τῶν θυρῶν ἑστὼς βωμὸς ἐν σχήματι κίονος and supposes for Attica a small pillar-shaped altar.

Hecataeum everywhere in front of the doors'.[47] Small Hecataea have been found in Attica in good numbers, though perhaps few if any antedate the Hellenistic period. Almost all take the form of the 'triple-bodied Hecate' round a pillar, an iconographical type said by Pausanias (whom archaeology has not refuted) to have been invented by Alcamenes in the second half of the fifth century 'for the Hekate Epipurgidia of the Athenian acropolis'. Simpler forms can be postulated for earlier Hecataea—three masks hung on a pillar, for instance—but this is speculation.[48] How frequent Hecataea may have been we do not know. We can apply to them the usefully vague expression applied by Thucydides to the last of the doorstep gods, the 'stone herms of native, four-cornered form': of these, he said, there stood in the city of Athens 'many, both outside private houses and in shrines'.[49]

We do not know what a Hecataeum of, say, the year 500 would have looked like. But, that uncertainty aside, none of the gods commonly found in or near Greek houses is straightforwardly represented in human form. Hestia is the hearth, Zeus Ktesios a pot, Apollo Aguieus a pillar, Hermes a block with head and phallus; Zeus Herkeios had an altar, but was perhaps not further represented. A strange collection they would make, lined up in a row! One elegant explanation is that it was precisely because these gods lived near to men that their otherness needed to be stressed.[50] Even the Hecataea of classic type presented a Hecate humanized indeed, but tripled and so made alien.

Any log can be made into a pillar or a god, said a proverb; and it was probably in regard to household images that the paradox was particularly obvious.[51] Vases show herms being carried, lifted into place, even under attack from an axe.[52] The transformation from brute matter to god was probably managed by a ritual of 'foundation with pots' (suitable, according to a speaker in Aristophanes, for a 'crumby little herm', μέμφομενον Ἑρμίδιον, and doubtless other household images). Women carried the pots, in which

---

[47] Ar. *Vesp.* 804. According to Bentley's minimal adjustment to Ar. *Lys.* 64 the wife of Theagenes 'consulted the Hecataeum' (θοὐκάτειον ἤρετο) before coming out. Recent editors see no humour in this and print van Leeuwen's τἀκάτειον ἤρετο (hoisted the sail/raised the jug). But Suda ε 361 s.v. Ἑκάτειον speaks of a παροιμία. Θεαγένους Ἑκάτειον· οὗ ἐπυνθάνετο πανταχοῦ ἀπιών, and both παροιμία and the reference to Theagenes rather than his wife may suggest that this is not just a guess based on a corrupt text of the Aristophanes passage. The point in Arist. would then be that Theo/agenes' wife was as eccentric as her husband (on this problematic figure see I. Storey, *Eupolis*, Oxford 2003, 148).

[48] Cf. Nilsson, *Geschichte*, 724, n.10; T. Kraus, *Hekate* (Heidelberg 1960), 107–11.

[49] 6.27.1; for more on herms see *Athenian Religion*, 80–3 and now B. Rückert, *Die Herme im öffentlichen und privaten Leben der Griechen* (Regensburg 1998). Jameson, 'Domestic Space', 112, n. 21, suggests that stone doorway herms were 'a fashion among well-to-do and prominent Athenian families', while wooden herms were perhaps more common. He notes that the herms so often seen on vases are seldom in doorways (the loutrophoros Karlsruhe, Bad. Land. Mus. 69/78, *ARV²* 1102 (iii) 2, C. Bérard and others, *Cité des images*, Lausanne 1984, fig. 12, being an exception).

[50] Frontisi-Ducroux, *Le Dieu-masque*, 217–18.

[51] Epicharmus fr. 129 (131 Kaibel); cf. Hor. *Sat.* 1.8.1 and *Priapea* 10.4.

[52] *LIMC* s.v. Hermes, nos. 170–3, 179.

pulses had been cooked, in procession to the site and there offered the pulse to
the new god. No source states what was then done with the pots, but perhaps
they were buried as 'foundation offerings'.[53]

The main household gods have now been reviewed. Hestia is the *oikos* itself,
its permanence; Zeus Ktesios its wealth; Zeus Herkeios (wherever precisely
located) the bond of kinship. The gods of the porch have something to do with
the transition from the private space of the house to the public world. Hermes
promises safe journeys (though he may also have some connection with the
material prosperity of the house); Apollo and Hecate are probably there as
protectors from intrusive evil. Hecate was herself an ambiguous figure, and by
planting her as a protectress at the threshold one perhaps insisted that she did
not enter the house. It was no aimiable trait in Euripides' Medea to have a
Hecate who 'lives in the recesses of my hearth', actually within the house.[54]

Individual households hosted other cults. The dying Alcestis, after her
prayer to Hestia, crowned and prayed to 'all the altars in Admetus' house'.
The house of Theophrastus' *Superstitious Man* contains 'hermaphrodites', and
wherever he sees a sacred snake in the house he 'founds a hero-shrine'; only
the second of these points is presented as a symptom of his excess. A full
catalogue of possible household gods cannot be written, because, as Plato
complains, there could in principle be as many as any individual cared to
establish. There was much crowning of altars and images and bringing of
small offerings at the new moon; and archaeology has revealed further widely
practised but enigmatic domestic rituals apparently unknown to the literary
sources.[55] We leave the list of gods and rites, therefore, necessarily incomplete, and turn instead to the question of what in Greek terms these powers
were.

Greeks occasionally spoke of particular gods as 'inhabiting the fair houses'
of men or 'sitting in hearths' or something similar.[56] But no classical text
presents us with a class of 'household gods'. Rather, the group we are tempted
to identify as such are a subset of a larger class which Greeks do indeed

---

[53] Ar. *Pax* 923–4 with Σ vet. 923c (a shorter form = Σ vet. Ar. *Plut.* 1198), *Plut.* 1197–9 (the
Σ on Ar. *Pax* 923c quotes Ar. fr. 256, a paratragic fr. which speaks of χύτραι used to found an
altar of Zeus Herkeios); Nilsson, *Geschichte*, 404, n. 10 [+]. A more dignified 'founding with an ox'
appears in Ar. fr. 591.85–6.

[54] Eur. *Med.* 396–7; on Hecate cf. pp. 414–15 below, and on Hermes p. 391.

[55] Eur. *Alc.* 170–1; Theophr. *Char.* 16.4, 10; Pl. *Leg.* 909d–910e. For non-Attic evidence see
Nilsson, 'Greek and Roman Domestic Cult', *OpRom* 1 (1954), 77–85 = *Op. Sel.* iii, 271–85, esp.
80/275–7. Crowning etc. esp. at the new moon, Ar. *Vesp.* 96; Theopompus comicus fr. 48; cf.
Porph. *Abst.* 2.16.4 (p. 146.7–8 Nauck); Men. *Dysc.* 50–1 (on the festive character of the new
moon day see too p. 192, n. 2). Enigmatic rituals: *AR* 1996–7, 7; 1997–8, 4; 1999–2000, 6;
2001–2, 5 (all from the agora excavations): shallow pits within houses containing assemblages of
small vases, traces of burning and a few bones (4th–3rd c.).

[56] Eur. *HF* 609 θεοὺς προσειπεῖν πρῶτα τοὺς κατὰ στέγας; Aesch. *Cho.* 800–2 οἵ τ᾽ ἔσωθε
δωμάτων | πλουτογαθῆ μυχὸν ἐνίζετε (Seidler: νομίζετε M)/ κλύετε, σύμφρονες θεοί; *Hymn. Hom.*
29. 1–3, 9.

mention repeatedly, that of the πατρῷοι θεοί, an untranslatable phrase which we will render 'ancestral gods'.[57] Greek women are snatched away at marriage 'from their ancestral gods and their parents'. These must be the gods the virgins grew up with in the houses of their fathers. But they are described as ancestral, not as household gods.[58] In the black days after the defeat at Chaeronea, the ignoble Leocrates fled from Athens and even 'exported his ancestral sacred objects', thereby, according to Lycurgus, 'exporting the good will of the gods in so far as it lay in his power'. Leocrates had presumably carted off to Megara such things as his 'jar of Zeus Ktesios'.[59] Before the great battle in the harbour at Syracuse, Nicias produced all the stock exhortations 'by wives and children and ancestral gods' that desperate men have recourse to, says Thucydides; and the 'ancestral gods' or 'shrines' appear constantly in contexts of strong patriotic emotion or other charged appeals ('the gods nearest and dearest to you').[60]

Ancestral gods are gods whom one has inherited a relation to, gods whom one's father worshipped (much as a ξένος πατρῷος is a family friend). The breadth of that group will vary greatly according to context. In a certain sense, the gods of Athens en masse are πατρῷοι θεοί for every Athenian citizen, and appeals to protect or respect the 'seats of the ancestral gods' normally refer in this broad way to the whole pantheon of the state concerned. There coexisted, however, a narrower sense in which the ancestral gods were the gods of the restricted groups into which one was born, above all it seems those of the household and the phratry, perhaps also those of the deme. The clearest evidence for the relation to a social unit comes from Thasos, where were found a series of inscriptions of such forms as 'of Zeus Patroos of the Neophantideis' or 'of the Nymphs Korades Patroiai of the Amphoterideis'.[61] Here an 'ancestral'

---

[57] Cf. the note of W. Wyse on Isae. 2.1; C. Rolley, 'Le Sanctuaire des dieux patrôoi et le Thesmophorion de Thasos', *BCH* 89 (1965), 441–83; *OCD* ed. 3 s.v. *patrooi theoi*.

[58] Soph. fr. 583.8 (*Tereus*), women at marriage are traded away θεῶν πατρῴων τῶν τε φυσάντων ἄπο; cf. Eur. fr. 318.4 (*Danae*), the male *genos* unlike the female stays at home θεῶν πατρῴων καὶ τάφων τιμάορον; Aesch. *Ag.* 1277 (Cassandra speaks) βωμοῦ πατρῴου δ' ἀντ' ἐπίξηνον μένει; cf. an eloquent passage quoted from Fustel de Coulanges by Pomeroy, *Families*, 70 (I do not understand her denial that a woman left her ancestral gods on marriage). See more generally Soph. *El.* 1374, πατρῷα ἕδη of the gods of the porch; [Lys.] 6. 11–12 for an 'ancestral' Hermes; Lysias fr. 82a Thalheim (Rut. Lup. *De fig.* 1.13): 'constat igitur, iudices, Simonem domo sua, ab suis diis penatibus ... esse exturbatum'.

[59] Lycurg. *Leoc.* 25–6, 56. Lycurgus' claim that he had thereby emptied 'temples' (25, 38) is scarcely credible: surely he could not have removed *sacra* even of his phratry. Elsewhere Lycurgus accuses him of 'betraying' by abandonment his πατρῷα μνήματα (8, 97) and other (public) πατρῷα ἱερά. The ἱερά which Hyperides proposed be removed to the Piraeus after Chaeronea ([Plut.] *XOrat.* 849a) will have been a probably larger class of movable objects, including some belonging to phratries.

[60] Thuc. 7.69.2; cf. e.g. Hdt. 2.30.4, Aesch. *Pers.* 404, Din. 1. 99; charged appeal: e.g. Soph. *Ant.* 839, *Phil.* 933, *OC* 756. For prayers to θεοὶ πατρῷοι see Soph. *El.* 411, Ar. *Vesp.* 388.

[61] See Rolley, op. cit., who also quotes examples from other states. Among gods who receive the epithet are some we have already encountered: Zeus Ktesios (Rolley, 443, no. 2; *IG* XII suppl. 407, also from Thasos); Zeus Herkeios (n. 40 above). For the distinctive form of expression whereby the name of a group who 'own' the god is attached in the genitive cf. K. Forbes, *Philologus* 100 (1956), 235–52; F. Graf, 'Apollon Lykeios in Metapont', in Πρακτικά του Η' Διεθνούς Συνεδρίου Ελληνικής και Λατινικής Επιγραφικής II (Athens 1987), 242–5.

god is explicitly associated with a particular group based on real or fictive kinship. The same relation is implicit in the common Attic form of expression whereby certain gods are spoken of not as being worshipped by individuals or groups but as belonging to them: 'do you have a Zeus Patroos?', or 'Artemis Orthosia of the Demokleidai'. τὰ πατρῷα is a man's patrimony, and πατρῷοι θεοί too are a kind of property, like the ancestral altars (πατρῷοι βωμοί) at which they are worshipped. By the law of Solon, bastards were excluded from the rights of inheritance (ἀγχιστεία) 'both of sacred and non-sacred things' enjoyed by the legitimate heir.[62] This relationship between πατρῷα and πατρῷοι is not casual or insignificant. Both inheritances created a sense of rootedness and obligation, and the strong emotional force of each was re-inforced by that of the other. Now that Eurystheus has been defeated, says Alcmene to her grandchildren in Euripides, in strikingly technical language, 'you will take legal possession of your plots of land' (κλήρους ἐμβατεύσετε χθονός) 'and sacrifice to your ancestral gods'. One reason to adopt an heir was to have someone 'to honour the ancestral shrines' or 'go to the ancestral altars' 'on behalf of oneself'.[63]

For Attica, the character of the *patrooi* has been obscured by one prominent but misleading text.[64] Questioned by the sophist Dionysodorus, Socrates explains that he does indeed possess 'domestic and ancestral' altars and shrines and the rest of such things 'just like other Athenians', but not a Zeus Patroos: 'none of the Ionians have this title, neither those who were colonized from this city nor we ourselves, but rather we have Apollo Patroos, because of the birth of Ion. We do not call Zeus Patroos, but Herkeios and Phratrios, and Athena Phratria'. Here then the epithet is taken to indicate the god from whom a people claims origin, and a sharp distinction is drawn between the single authentic *patroos* and other traditional gods who make do with different titles. The word *patroos* was open to various understandings (despite Socrates' denial, for instance, a Zeus Patroos does appear in Attic texts, as a 'protector of Fathers')[65], and doubtless, where a particular 'ancestral god'

---

[62] Isae. 6.47. [Dem.] 43.51 (Solon fr. 50b Ruschenbusch); for inheritance of ἱερὰ καὶ ὅσια see Isae. 9.13, Dem. 39.35 (for the same expression in a context of political entitlement Dem. 23.65, 59.104; Ant. 5.62). The conception is much played up by Plato in *Laws*, with stress on the heir's duty to maintain the cult (878a, 740b–c, 773e). On the word πατρῷος see E. Benveniste, *Le Vocabulaire des institutions indo-européennes* (Paris 1969), i, 272–4. Ancestral altars: Isae. 9.7.

[63] Eur. *Heraclid.* 876–7; Isae. 2.46 (cf. 9.13), 9.7; cf. Lysias fr. 40 Thalheim (XXVI.I Gernet-Bizos). In Isae. 2.46 the heir is said to act ὑπέρ, in 9.13 ἀντί, the dead man. The approach to the ancestral altars is distinct from performance of grave cult, which is normally mentioned in the same context. Here and always in Isaeus (see esp. 2.1) the primary reference seems to be to the phratry altars.

[64] Pl. *Euthyd.* 302c–d. Socrates' generalizations about the Ionians are not quite accurate, as for instance the Thasian Zeus Patroos mentioned in the text shows. On Apollo Patroos see *Athenian Religion*, 64, n. 31, also Dem. 18.141, and cf. Ar. *Av.* 1527.

[65] Ar. *Nub.* 1468 (paratragic); cf. Pl. *Leg.* 881d. The concern of *patrooi theoi* for the kin who share their altars (Isae. 2.1; Plut. *De frat. amor.* 7, 481d) is distinct.

could also be seen as a forefather, an interpretation such as Socrates' was common.[66] But numerous uses cannot be understood in this way. There is the regular practice of speaking of θεοὶ πατρῷοι in the plural; there are occasional references to 'maternal' as well as 'paternal' gods;[67] there is, above all, the application of the term to goddesses, often virgins. Even the Platonic passage gets its point from the way in which ancestral gods are treated as a form of property. Quibbling Dionysodorus deliberately chooses gods of whom it is natural to ask not 'do you honour X?' but 'do you have an X?', in order to put to Socrates the modest proposal that, since a man may after all dispose of his own property as he pleases, he might care to sell or indeed sacrifice his ancestral gods.

Male children of citizen parents were introduced to their father's phratry at age about 3; it may be that from then on for the rest of their lives they met their *phratores* annually at the great festival celebrated phratry by phratry, the *Apatouria*. It is frustrating that we do not know where in the range from about 200 to about 1000 to put the membership of a typical phratry, but it is clear that any individual's *phratores* must have consisted both of actual kin and of others to whom he was only notionally related. Whatever the size of the whole phratry, the very character of the three-day festival will have encouraged strong bonding, renewed year by year, among smaller sub-groups of *phratores*. Some individuals belonged to further hereditary groups such as *genē* (which might meet for sacrifice on numerous occasions each year), societies of *orgeones* of a hero, *thiasoi* of Heracles and the like.[68] Young men were not registered in their father's deme until 18, but they perhaps tagged along to deme sacrifices from a much younger age. Plato in a famous passage speaks of children learning to believe in the gods by watching the solemn acts of worship performed by their parents 'for themselves and their children'.[69] It was at the altars of their ancestral gods that this socialization into the religion of the city took place.

A final category of 'ancestral things' are the ancestral tombs: they are constantly mentioned in association with 'ancestral shrines', as they were for instance in the questions put to candidates for archonship.[70] With them

[66] For worship of Zeus Patroos by his mythological descendants see e.g. Soph. *Trach.* 288, 753; Apollod. 2.8.4, and more generally the prominence of the cult in Dorian cities. A dedication to Heracles Patroos comes from the Macedonian royal palace at Vergina, *ArchDelt* 25 (1970), *Chron.* 394; M. Andronikos, *Vergina* (Athens 1984), 38.

[67] For an appeal πρὸς θεῶν πατρώων καὶ μητρῴων see Xen. *Hell.* 2.4.21; other instances are much later, Lucian, *De mort. Peregr.* 36, the spurious preface to Xen. *Cyneg.* (1.15) and doubtless *IG* II² 5016. Goddesses: e.g. Athena: in Thasos, *BCH* 89 (1965), 447, no. 6; 448, no. 7; in Gonnoi, *SEG* XXXV 567; Artemis: Paus. 2.9.6; Hestia: Xen. *Cyr.* 1.6.1; Meter Phrygia *IEphes.* 1217–18.

[68] For phratries and the *Apatouria* see *Athenian Religion*, 104–8 (on the size of phratries 107, n. 19); Appendix 1 below s.v. *Apatouria*. For *genē orgeones, thiasoi* see *Athenian Religion*, 56–60, 108–11, 333–4.

[69] Pl. *Leg.* 887d; cf. J. N. Bremmer, 'The Family and Other Centres of Religious Learning in Antiquity', in J. W. Drijvers and A. MacDonald (eds.), *Centres of Learning* (Leiden 1995), 29–38.

[70] Arist. *Ath. Pol.* 55.3; cf. e.g. Isae. 9.36, n. 59 above. For pride in ancestral tombs see Aeschin. 2.23; Menander fr. 835 [612 Koerte]. For πατρῷος applied to tombs see e.g. Thuc. 3.59.2, Dem. 57.28, 70, Plut. *Phoc.* 37.5, ? Din. 2.17.

we revert to the *oikos*, in its more compact or more extended form. The funeral itself of an adult was normally a responsibility of the presumptive heir, which is why competitions could occur for the honour of performing the pious duty.[71] No women were allowed to mourn the dead except those over 60 and those 'up to the children of cousins'.[72] Since the right to inherit in absence of a direct heir also extended up to 'children of cousins' on both sides, the group of recognized mourners and of potential heirs was identical. A question faced by the heir who organized the funeral—unless the dead man had made dispositions in advance, as may often have happened—was where to site the tomb. The regular principle was for men and unmarried women to be buried with their paternal kin, married women with their husbands', but exceptions of various kinds to that division are quite frequent; the circumstances of particular families prevailed over any strict patrilineal rule.[73] More drastically, burial in 'ancestral tombs' of whichever branch of a family was an ideal rather than a general reality. A passage concerning the *Bouselidai* is again very instructive:[74]

There is a memorial ($\mu\nu\hat{\eta}\mu\alpha$) shared by all the descendants of Bouselos (it is called 'of the *Bouselidai*', a large enclosed area of the kind that was customary in the old days), and in this memorial all the other descendants of Bouselos—Hagnias and Euboulides and Polemon and all the other kin, numerous as they are—these all share this

---

[71] See above all Isae. 8.21–7, 38–39 ('The parties contended for the body as if it were one of the assets', Wyse ad loc.); also Dem. 44. 32–3, Isae. 6. 39–41, 4.7; Humphreys, 'Family Tombs', at 98–9. For the corresponding argument that X, not having performed burial rites, ought not to inherit see Isae. 4.19 (cf. 26), 9.3–4; [Dem.] 43.64. 'Those who inherit the money' or, failing them, relatives could be forced by law to meet the burial expenses, [Dem.] 43.57–8, Dem. 24.107, cf. Aeschin. 1.13–14 (supposed infractions Lys. 31.21, Dem. 25.54). On burial expenses see G. J. Oliver in id. (ed.) *The Epigraphy of Death* (Liverpool 2000), 77; Pl. *Leg.* 959d allows 100–500 dr. (depending on status), but his aim is explicitly to limit expenditure, and higher figures appear in oratory: at least 1000 dr., Dem. 40.52; 2500, Lys. 32.21; 2 talents, Dem. 45.79.

[72] [Dem.] 43.62. For bilateral mourning note the black figure funerary plaque which identifies three 'aunts' and specifies that one is a $\tau\epsilon\theta\grave{\iota}s$ $\pi\rho\grave{o}s$ $\pi\alpha\tau\rho\acute{o}s$: Louvre MNB 905, cf. J. Boardman, *BSA* 50 (1955), 62, no. 28; H. A. Shapiro, *AJA* 95 (1991), 630 fig. 1, 638. For the role of $\sigma\upsilon\gamma\gamma\epsilon\nu\epsilon\hat{\iota}s$ at the classical funeral see [Dem.] 44.32–3, Isae. 8.26 (and *a contrario* 9.19); Lys. 1.7–8 (a daughter-in-law); for $\phi\acute{\iota}\lambda o\iota$ e.g. Isae. 9.4, Lys. 12.87–8. For the 6th c. see Humphreys, 'Family Tombs', 105.

[73] *IG* II² 6218 apparently attests 'intrusion' by a wife's father (but the further intrusions postulated by Kirchner are unnecessary: Attabos and Euthippos may be brothers), 7528 (cf. 7501) by a son of a woman of the house (Humphreys, 'Family Tombs', 120), [Plut.] *XOrat.* 838b-c (Isocrates: Humphreys, 120) by a maternal aunt and her son. There are several apparent instances (5479, 5712, 5753, 6216: Humphreys, 117) of brother(s) and sister + sister's husband (sometimes + brother's wife, which is more predictable), a pattern which can be explained either as 'intrusion' by a wife's brother or as 'retention' of a married sister and attraction of her husband (for this see 6230 with 6217). *IG* II² 5374 with 5376 seems to show intrusion by a wife's brother and his son (Humphreys, 119; Bergemann, *Demos und Thanatos*, 185). The incorporation of Heragoras of Samos and descendants into his wife's family plot (6417) is a special case, since naturalized Samians lacked ancestral tombs of their own.

[74] The following depends heavily on Humphreys' pioneering 'Family Tombs' and now on Bergemann, *Demos und Thanatos*. The status of multi-figure grave reliefs as evidence is unclear: almost certainly they do not reflect actual joint burial (some of the figures being alive at the time of commissioning), but at most an intention (cf. Clairmont, *Tombstones*, intr. vol., 119–21).

memorial. But the father and grandfather of this Makartatos don't share it, but have made their own memorial apart from the Bouselid memorial.   ([Dem.] 43.79)

Another passage of Demosthenes speaks of 'an ancestral tomb, shared by all members of the *genos*.'[75] Having subtracted the pious outrage, we learn from the first passage that the five sons of Bouselos (known from elsewhere in the speech) decided to found a shared funerary enclosure. This project inevitably meant a rupture with whatever the previous tradition of the family may have been. In the next generation, some branches of the family continued to use the Bouselid monument (and went on doing so into the next generation), but one broke off to found its own. Even the memorial of the Bouselids then, a paradigm case of the solidarity of the broader *oikos*, reveals the limits of that solidarity. The tradition reaches no great distance back in time, and within a generation of its creation one branch of the family has rejected it.

Archaeological and epigraphical evidence is abundant, and increases by the day as the new excavations reveal more of the pompous procession of funeral enclosures that approaches the fort at Rhamnus.[76] (A 'monument of five brothers, who left offspring' is a pleasing parallel to the Bouselids.) Some caution is needed, since it is never possible to insist that every single individual originally deposited in a given *peribolos* has been uncovered. Even an inscribed list of those buried in a plot can be demonstrably incomplete. So no argument can be based on the apparent absence from a family's *peribolos* of an attested member, nor on the implausible narrowness of the line of descent (one male only per generation) sometimes found in lists.[77] We can only be sure that family members were separately buried when, as sometimes occurs, their monuments have actually been uncovered in separate places.[78] But the

---

[75] 57.28, cf. 67.

[76] See now Petrakos, *Rhamnous*, 335–413. The most important Rhamnusian *periboloi* post-dating Humphreys, 'Family Tombs', are those of Pytharchus, of Phanocrates, and of Aristoklea and Antimachus. The most important find elsewhere is the tomb-plot of the Lycurgi, A. P. Matthaiou, *Horos* 5 (1987), 31–44 (*SEG* XXXVII 160–2). Bergemann, *Demos und Thanatos*, 183–210, now replaces the useful 'A first catalogue of Attic peribolos tombs' by R. S. J. Garland, *BSA* 77 (1982), 125–76; the monuments also now appear in Clairmont's fundamental repertoire, *Tombstones*.

[77] Such as *BCH* 99 (1975), 379 or *IG* II² 6008 ('apparet hoc monumentum hereditate ad primogenitos pervenisse', Kirchner ad loc.; but he himself mentions a memorial of a 'second son' apparently deriving from the same plot, *IG* II² 6859). On all this see Bergemann, *Demos und Thanatos*, 14. 'Demonstrably incomplete': see Garland, op. cit., 168, on *CEG* 473. 'Five brothers': *IRhamnous* 273 (*CEG* 597 [+]). The father of the five sons was buried with them, as were members of the two generations subsequent to them, and some wives and servants (Petrakos, *Rhamnous*, 387–98; *IRhamnous* 270–83; Bergemann, *Demos und Thanatos*, 199–200). A later family member, Lykeas son of Kephisios, is commemorated on the outside of a different *peribolos* (*IRhamnous* 248).

[78] See *IG* II² 5479 with 6474–75, 6480 (Humphreys, 'Family Tombs', 117), or 6097 with 6135 (ibid.); 5450 with 5448 (Humphreys, 120), is less clear. *IG* II² 6008 may attest a sold plot (Garland, op. cit., 142, n. 57), and 'the *peribolos* of Diogeiton' hosted non-members of that family, and them only, in the 3rd c. (Petrakos, *Rhamnous*, 368; *IRhamnous* 245–8). Humphreys' inference (120) from the silence of the learned source (A. Scholl, *JDAI* 109, 1994, 240–1) of [Plut.] *XOrat.* 838b–c that Isocrates was buried away from several of his siblings seems justified.

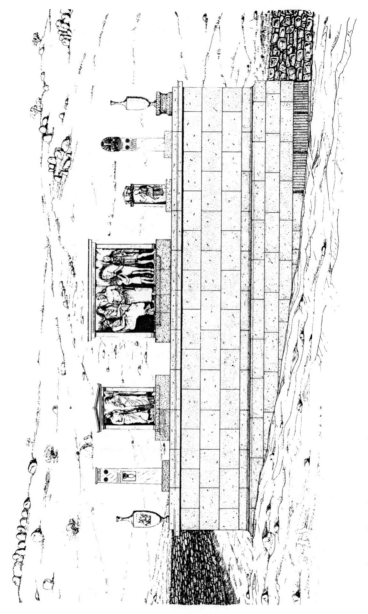

Fig. 1. The tomb enclosure of the family of Hierokles at Rhamnus.

divisions among the *Bouselidai* seem to be just as typical as their partial unity. Exaggeration in the other direction should, doubtless, also be deprecated. An ideal of collective burial existed, and was often realized in some measure. Funerary sculpture emphasized not the individual but the family, with particular stress on the idea of continuity between the generations. Multi-figure commemorative reliefs (always a chronological puzzle) may sometimes have been set up, it has been suggested, when the older members were already long dead.[79] But there were always other pressures working against the collective ideal. *Periboloi* that remained in use for as long as that of the *Bouselidai* are not common, though we should certainly note Meidon of Myrrhinus, buried with his great-great-great grandson and several members of each intervening generation. *Periboloi* that contained as many as twenty graves are all but unknown.[80]

All this evidence concerns the 110 years from *c*.430 onwards, during which monumental enclosures and numerous inscribed stelai provide uniquely convenient subjects for investigation. But grouped burial over long stretches of time does not seem to have been any more common in earlier periods. It was in fact in those 110 or so years that the idea of marking off ancestral tombs architecturally as belonging to a particular family received uniquely clear expression in Athenian history.[81]

The family tombs were the site for commemorative rites, not just those performed in the days immediately following the funeral but also, more interesting, those that in theory were repeated every year until the child or heir's own death. Of a certain commemorative rite among the Issedones of Thrace, Herodotus says that they perform it annually 'son for father, just as the Greeks perform the *Genesia*' (i.e. probably rites relating to parents, *genetai*). The generations of men pass life to one another like a torch in a relay, says Plato in one of the many passages of *Laws* where he seeks to inculcate this long, individual-squashing perspective.[82] The heir's moral obligation to perform these recurrent 'customary rites' (τὰ νομιζόμενα) is a theme on which the

---

[79] Bergemann, *Demos und Thanatos*, 25–32, cf. 91; ibid. 87–8 on the continuity of generations.

[80] For statistics see Bergemann, *Demos und Thanatos*, 14–15. Multi-generational use is now seen to be a little more frequent than allowed by Humphreys, 'Family Tombs', 118–20, but her basic picture remains correct. Meidon: *CEG* 473 [+]; Bergemann, 202–3.

[81] So Bergemann, *Demos und Thanatos*, 24. For earlier centuries, see the review of possible cases of group burial in Bourriot, *Génos*, 831–1042, and Humphreys, 'Family Tombs', 105–12 (who maintains that it was actually less common then); also now U. Knigge in W. Koenigs, U. Knigge, A. Mallwitz, *Kerameikos XII. Rundbauten im Kerameikos* (Berlin 1980), 72 (cf. Knigge, *Kerameikos*, 96–7). As for a different skewing of our evidence, we doubtless know less about how poor citizens grouped their graves than about how the rich did, even if T. H. Nielsen and others, 'Athenian Grave Monuments and Social Class', *GRBS* 30 (1989), 411–20, are right that almost any citizen could afford a cheap monument (similarly Bergemann, 131–41: criticism in G. J. Oliver, 'Athenian Funerary Monuments: Style, Grandeur and Cost', in id. (ed.), *The Epigraphy of Death*, Liverpool 2000, 59–80). But the poor are unlikely to have been more clannish than the rich.

[82] Hdt. 4.26.2; Pl. *Leg.* 776b, cf. 721b–c, 773e (on the duty to marry), 923a (property belonging to the whole past and future *genos*), and, on the permanent family cult, 740b–c, 878a.

orators harp constantly. Unfortunately, a crucial detail is ambiguous. A lexicographer records, very reliably, that *Genesia* was 'a public festival at Athens', celebrated on the fifth of Boedromion and mentioned by Solon in the *Axones*. Sacrifice was certainly offered on this occasion to Earth, abode of the dead, source of fertility and wealth for the living;[83] and sacrifices made on the fifth of Boedromion at Erchia to the ancestral hero Epops, and on the fifth of an unidentified month in Athens to Erechtheus, have also been associated with the festival.[84] Such a calendrically fixed festival of the dead is attested in several Greek states.[85] The question is whether we should postulate, in addition to the public festival, private *Genesia* performed on a date determined by the biography of the individual concerned, more probably the day of his death than the day of his birth. If there was only the single, public ceremony, all *oikoi* remembered their dead collectively on one day, Boedromion 5, and all the branches of an *oikos* which had dead in a particular plot will presumably have assembled at the ancestral tombs on that day. On the other view, a public ritual on Boedromion 5 (content largely unknown) coexisted with private rites dispersed throughout the year: no burial plot will ever have been thronged, but a pious descendant with dead kinsmen buried in several places could have honoured them all in due season. If they existed, these would be the rites to which the orators regularly refer, 'private', but in social terms, for the son or heir at least, compulsory to perform. No decisive argument is available in favour of either conception: private, individually dated rites for the dead are certainly found at various times and places in the Greek world,[86] but to assess the Attic norm we need, and lack, specific evidence.

---

[83] *Anecd. Bekk.* 1.86.20–25 s.v. Γενέσια (= Solon fr. 84 Ruschenbusch, Philochorus *FGrH* 328 F 168); Hesych. γ 337; growth from the dead: Hippoc. *Vict.* 4. 92; Ar. fr. 504. See F. Jacoby, 'Γενέσια. A Forgotten Festival of the Dead', *CQ* 38 (1944), 65–75, at 74–5; S. Georgoudi, 'Commemoration et celebration des morts dans les cités grecques: les rites annuels', in P. Gignoux (ed.), *La Commemoration* (Louvain/Paris 1988), 73–89. Γενέσια is linked with γενέται and dissociated from γενέθλια by W. Schmidt, *Geburtstag im Altertum* (Gießen 1908), 37–8, followed by Jacoby, op. cit., and the etymological dictionaries. Commemorative rites held on the birthday of the dead man are attested from *c.*300 (Diog. Laert. 10.18, the will of Epicurus: for other exx. see Schmidt, op. cit., 41–4, or Humphreys, 'Family Tombs', 101), and probably encouraged the late antique confusion between γενέσια and γενέθλια (Jacoby, op. cit., 74–5). But the practice is unlikely to have earlier roots, since the will of Epicurus in fact provides the first firm evidence (for earlier vagueness see Pl. *Lys.* 207b–c) for interest in an annual birthday in Greece (the birthday within the month—'on the 4th'—appears much earlier: Schmidt, 12–16). Rites on the anniversary of the day of death, by contrast, are implied by the expression τὰ ἐνιαύσια (*LSCG* 97 B 5–6; cf. RO 1, the *Labyadai* inscr., C 48; *Anecd. Bekk.* 1.187.17), since in comparable expressions ('third day rites', 'thirty day rites') the count is from the day of death.

[84] See S. D. Lambert, *ZPE* 139 (2002), 75–81; *BSA* 97 (2002), 367–8.

[85] Georgoudi, op. cit., draws attention to the Νεκύσια of Bithynia (Eust. in *Od.* 9. 60, p. 1615.3), the *Agriania* of Argos (Hesych. α 750 and 788), a newly attested commemoration at Kyme (*Bull. Épigr.* 1983 no. 323, p. 134) and the occurrence of Genesia/Genetios/Genesios as a month name.

[86] For the Hellenistic period see n. 83 above; Bruck, *Totenteil*, 158–89, and the works cited by Humphreys, 'Family Tombs', 122, n. 63; on the implications of the term τὰ ἐνιαύσια see n. 83

Our picture of the rites performed 'by son for father', whenever this occurred, is also vague. Normally they are simply (and in one sense revealingly)
'the customary rites'. Occasionally Isaeus speaks of descendants who 'make
burnt offerings' (whether of animals or merely, for example, of cakes is
unclear) 'and libations' (as so often in tragedy).[87] Analogy makes it very
likely that 'seasonal produce' (τὰ ὡραῖα) was also offered. It was doubtless on
this occasion that the dead were 'called on three times', their existence being
re-evoked by the use of their name, and urged to 'send up good things hither'
or to 'make a fair return to those who bring these offerings'.[88] The ceremony
evoked the perpetual succession of death and growth, the recycling of nature.
It was doubtless the ideal that more distant ancestors too should not be
forgotten. A dying man, says Isaeus in one passage, desires an heir who
will perform the customary rites for himself and his forebears. Even Epicurus
made provision in his will for the continuing commemoration of his parents
after his own death.[89] But the ideal could only readily be realized when father
and forefathers were buried in the same plot. Herodotus speaks merely of
performance by son for father, and this is all that is mentioned elsewhere in
Isaeus.[90]

Mothers had the same right to honour as fathers;[91] they would normally be
buried in the same plot, but we do not know how the children by a first
marriage of a woman who remarried and was buried elsewhere reconciled
their obligations (perhaps these simply passed to offspring of the second
marriage); nor indeed how the pious duty was divided when a couple had
more than one son. The role of women in these rites is particularly intriguing.
From the Electra plays we think of maidens as the 'libation-bearers' par
excellence, and those who prepare for or perform that 'visit to the tomb' so
often depicted on Attic white ground lekythoi are characteristically women.
These scenes may indeed suggest that such visits were much more frequently
paid than we would otherwise guess, at least in the early period after a

---

above. The Delphic injunction that 'relatives should sacrifice to the dead on the appropriate day'
([Dem.] 43.66–67) is no help.

[87] 'Customary rites': Isae. 2.4 with W. Wyse's note ad loc. ἐναγίζουσι καὶ χέονται: Isae. 6.51,
6.65: cf. Wyse's note on 2.46 (where ἐναγίζειν alone is mentioned, as e.g. in the will of Epicurus,
Diog. Laert. 10.18). Pl. *Leg.* 717e, which speaks of sharing wealth with the dead, suggests that
significant expense might be involved. 'Seasonal produce': Thuc. 3.58.4, and texts cited by W.
Wyse in his commentary on Isae. 2. 46, p. 269, cf. 271. Aesch. *Cho.* 483 speaks of δαῖτες ἔννομοι.

[88] Ar. *Ran.* 184 and 1176, with K. J. Dover's notes; Ar. fr. 504.14, with Kassel/Austin's notes;
Aesch. *Cho.* 91–2 (where the dead are urged either ἔσθλ' (Elmsley) or ἴσ' (Bamberger) ἀντιδοῦναι).
On naming as a preservation of memory see Georgoudi, loc. cit., 77 (who cites Artemid. 1.4,
p. 13.6–9 Pack, and Pl. *Leg.* 873d for the refusal to name those who commit suicide).

[89] Isae. 9.7; Diog. Laert. 10.18.

[90] At funerals, lament for older dead might be barred by law (Plut. *Sol.* 21.5, RO 1, the
Labyadai inscr., C 39–42).

[91] Isae. 6.64–5.

Fig. 2. White ground lekythos showing a tomb visit by a woman, 475–450 BC.

death.[92] But it was on the male heir that the real burden of obligation lay, and we must suppose that the women paid their tribute with his authorization and in a sense on his behalf. What happened at marriage to the girl who had hitherto visited the tombs of her paternal *oikos*? The 'marriage libations' that

---

[92] See H. A. Shapiro, *AJA* 95 (1991), 651–5 [+]. The presence of tomb markers on these vases, in a period when at least in marble they were not erected, is a standing puzzle (Shapiro 655, nn. 167–8). For monthly death commemorations see Soph. *El.* 277–81 (a perverted form) and Diog. Laert.10.18. For modern parallels see L. Danforth, *The Death Rituals of Rural Greece* (Princeton 1982), ch. 5.

Aeschylus' Electra promised to bring her dead father would perhaps have been as a farewell; for we hear elsewhere in tragedy that it is the man who 'stays always in the house, defender of the ancestral gods and tombs'.[93] A married woman known from oratory who paid a *mna* for a commemoration of her recently dead father was an heiress (*epikleros*) and so perhaps a special case;[94] the *epikleros* may have been expected to perform the customary rites for her father, for lack of any male heir to do so. In other cases the norm was presumably for married women to deck their in-laws' tombs.

Beyond the individual named forebears lay the anonymous ancestors, the Tritopatores. Almost uniquely, we can compare various 'native exegeses' of these figures,[95] and they turn out to be intriguingly various. For Demon they were winds, for Philochorus primeval beings, offspring of Earth and Sun, third down from the beginning of the world, for others apparently great-grand-fathers, third up from oneself; the 'author of the *Exegetikon*' (an Athenian) offered yet another interpretation of the 'three' in their name by identifying them with Hesiod's three 'Hundred-handers', monstrous offspring of Heaven and Earth. Phanodemus records that 'the Athenians alone pray and sacrifice to them for the birth of children, when they are about to marry'. Unity has been found in this diversity, not unconvincingly, through the hypothesis that they are ancestors (just how remote matters little), who care for the continuation of their line; they enter new bodies to be reborn themselves, or at any rate fructify young wombs, in the form of winds.[96] Further details remain vague. Outside Attica it was certainly not only on the occasion of a forth-coming marriage that they needed to be honoured. One might expect the distinctive context of their cult to be the ancient descent groups, the phratries and *gene*, and indeed one *genos*, the *Pyrrhakidai*, worshipped a Tritopator, and two groups of uncertain type (*Zakyadai, Euergidai*) had Tritopatores;[97] but the earliest surviving monument of their cult is an archaic enclosure in the Ceramicus which presumably belonged to the whole citizenry (no restriction

[93] Aesch. *Cho.* 486–8; Eur. fr. 318. Of course the many women who married close kin (e.g. father's brother) and the few whose parents were buried with their husband's (n. 73) could maintain contact.

[94] Dem. 41.11, money spent εἰς τὰ Νεμέσεια (Γενέσια? - *Athenian Religion*, 246, n. 101) τῷ πατρί. The context seems to require a single ceremony at which the fairly large sum in question (100 dr.) could have been spent. Schaps, *Economic Rights*, 15, speaks of 'funeral expenses': this is good sense, but funerals were not called τὰ Νεμέσεια. The guardians of minors performed 'the customary rights' on their behalf, Isae. 1.10. My concern here is with commemorative rights; women could certainly attend the funerals of their natal kin.

[95] See Harpocration τ 32, where appear Demon *FGrH* 327 F 2, Philochorus *FGrH* 328 F 182, Exegetikon *FGrH* 352 F 1, Phanodemus *FGrH* 325 F 6 (and Orphica fr. 318 K).

[96] See Jameson *et al.*, *Selinous*, 112 [+], and for a full survey of Attic and non-Attic evidence ibid. 107–14; Bourriot, *Génos*, 1135–79 remains valuable, and see too S. Georgoudi in G. Hoffmann (ed.), *Les Pierres de l'offrande. Autour de l'œuvre de Christoph W. Clairmont* (Zurich 2001), 152–63.

[97] *IDél.* 66; *IG* II² 2615; *Agora* XIX H 20 (*Athenian Religion*, 323).

being indicated), and they receive sacrifice in the calendar of two demes.[98] It does not look as if every Athenian *oikos* had a tie with a particular altar of the Tritopatores. Nor do we know how widespread the practice of sacrificing to them before marriage in fact was.

I have talked of the religion of the *oikos*, but not yet of the *oikos* as itself a quasi-religious entity needing to be respected and preserved. But the danger that death may 'empty an *oikos*' is one that is constantly evoked in court cases concerning inheritance.[99] What was this danger, and how greatly was it feared?

We noted earlier that the *oikos* at issue in such formulations is, almost without exception, a very narrow one: an *oikos* is extinguished when a man dies without natural or adopted issue, however many brothers and nephews may survive him. It is for an individual therefore that the prospective voiding of an *oikos* is a disaster. What does he lose by it?[100] Not heirs of his own stock; for there were rules for the transmission of property to collateral relatives, and never a shortage of claimants. Nor yet funeral honours: as we have seen, it was the recognized duty, and, where title was in dispute, the much fought-for privilege, of a man's heirs to see to his burial and to associated rites. Possibly he was deprived of the commemorative rites performed subsequently year by year; for the possibility that these, as distinct from the funerary rites, might be carried out by collateral heirs is raised by Isaeus only once, within a piece of characteristically far-fetched hypothetical reasoning, whereas it is regularly stated or implied that to overthrow the title of an adopted heir in favour of a collateral will deprive the dead man of the recurrent rites.[101] If the *Genesia* were carried out 'by son for father', it was not the strict duty, perhaps not even the proper function, of, say, a nephew to observe them for an uncle from whom he had inherited. Such rites preserved the memory of the deceased, and possibly also—but the point is never raised by orators—improved his condition in the afterlife. Beyond this, we hear that a man desires a successor who will 'approach the ancestral altars on his behalf', perform religious and social functions 'in his place', and preserve his name.[102] What this seems to mean is

[98] Demes: *LSCG* 18 δ 41–46; Marathon calendar (*ZPE* 130, 2000, 45–7), A, col. 2, lines 32, 52. For the enclosure (identified by *IG* I³ 1066–7, the former speaking of it as an ἄβατον) see Travlos, *Pictorial Dictionary*, figs. 394–5; Knigge, *Kerameikos*, 103–4 [+].

[99] Isae. 1.44; 2.15, 35; 6.5; 7.30; Isoc. 19.3, 47; [Dem.] 43. 11–12, 68, 72, 80, 84; [Dem.] 44. 2, 15, 27, 33, 43, 47–8; Pl. *Leg.* 925c; n. 12 above.

[100] All that follows is heavily dependent on Rubinstein, *Adoption*.

[101] So Rubinstein, *Adoption*, 73–6. Far-fetched reasoning: Isae. 1.10; deprivation: ibid. 2.46, 7.30–2. For instances of actual funerals conducted by collaterals see Rubinstein, 71, n. 32.

[102] Isae. 2.46; 9.7, 13 (n. 63 above); for the fear that the dead or his *oikos* may become 'nameless' see too Isae. 2. 36–7; Dem. 43.80; Isoc. 19.35 (and for an attempt to base title to inherit on 'family names' [Dem.] 43.49–50, 76). On 'family names' see Golden, *Children*, 24–5. This is a variant of concern for memory survival via commemorative monuments, on which see Sourvinou-Inwood, *Death*, index s.v. 'memory survival'. On 'memory' as the main function of funerary cult see Pl. *Leg.* 717e.

that 'Demetrius of Acharnae' desires that an individual known as 'X son of Demetrius of Acharnae' should continue to perform what had been his own customary activities, should as it were fill the gap in the social world left by his death, and should ideally in due course name his own son 'Demetrius of Acharnae' (or even change his own name to that[103]). In Plato's *Laws*, the ideal receives a different, less individualistic inflection: the successor is needed to pass on the torch of life and, above all, to perpetuate the family's service of the gods.[104] From the orators alone, one would not guess that the gods suffered from the cessation of cult in a given *oikos*.

But how strong was the impulse to leave a replacement for oneself? The orators regularly present it as a serious motive for action: 'all those who are about to die take thought for themselves, and consider how they can avoid leaving their houses empty, and have someone to make offerings to them and perform all the customary rites. And so, even if they die childless, they adopt children to leave behind them.'[105] And it has been widely held that the main purpose of the epiklerate—the institution whereby the daughter of a man without sons married a kinsman and as it were held her father's property in trust for the grandsons she would bear him—was to perpetuate the *oikos*. It may seem indeed that the main function of adoption in its Greek form was to give the childless the opportunity to secure a replacement; for the adopted child entered the *oikos* of the adopted father, from whom he acquired full title to inherit. He was henceforth known as 'son of' the adopted, not of the natural father. But the case of the epiklerate is unclear, since the grandson would continue the grandfather's *oikos* only if adopted into it (thereby losing the right to inherit from his own father), and it is not known how commonly such adoption in fact took place. (But perhaps we can allow that the ideal was that it should occur.[106]) Nor is the argument from other forms of adoption

---

[103] On name-changes at adoption see C. A. Cox, ZPE 107 (1995), 249–51, who refers to Davies, *Propertied Families*, 44 (Thrasyllos III), 45–7 (Hippolochides II), 86 (Makartatos II).

[104] See nn. 62 and 82 above. Characters in tragedy can urge the gods to save them in order to ensure future cult (Aesch. *Cho.* 255–7).

[105] Isae. 7.30; cf. e.g. 2.10, 6.5. As W. E. Thompson observes, *Prudentia* 13 (1981) 19–20, the opportunism with which the orators exploit the *topos* shows how persuasive they thought it.

[106] For various views see Harrison, *Law*, I, 92 n.1; Schaps, *Economic Rights*, 32–3 (who raised the difficulty); N.R. Fisher, CR 31 (1981), 72–4; Lane Fox, 'Inheritance', 226–7; Rubinstein, *Adoption*, 88–92. Isae. 3.73 shows that the father of an *epikleros* could enjoin that such adoption be performed (it was not obligatory, therefore). The one attested instance ([Dem.] 43.11–13) is double-edged: the dead man's injunction seems to have been ignored until the heirs had their own interested motives for honouring it (Schaps, *Economic Rights*, 32). No other direct evidence is available, but Rubinstein observes that the practice of adopting a daughter is easier to understand if the adopter had good hope that a son of hers would be introduced into his *oikos*. On the other hand, Gernet was right to argue (REG 34, 1921, 337–79), that the most distinctive feature of the epiklerate—the right of collateral kin to the *epikleros*' hand—has nothing to do with preservation of the nuclear *oikos*. See too the acute comments of Sissa (n. 11 above), 192–3. Plato normally associates inheritance with adoption (878a, 923e, 924a, 925c) but says nothing in this case; under his system, however, the husband of an *epikleros* would not normally have an *oikos* in the sense of a *kleros* of his own.

straightforward, since there were reasons why an individual might wish to secure an heir apart from a desire to perpetuate his *oikos*.[107] When, however, the testator adopted the relative who would have inherited from him even if not adopted,[108] no motive can be identified except that of continuing the *oikos*. And we evidently cannot attribute personal motives to an individual who died without a will and into whose house the heir *ab intestato* was adopted posthumously.[109] The relatives who carried such adoptions through may have had reasons of their own quite unconnected with piety. But society had no reason to respect such motives: in permitting, none the less, the practice of posthumous adoption, it paid tribute to the principle of preserving the *oikos*. This was, therefore, a socially recognized value of some importance. This importance was not, in every instance, overriding: cases can be found such as that of a father who allowed an only son to be adopted out of his *oikos* (which was thereby doomed to extinction), presumably to secure a larger inheritance elsewhere. And Isaeus' claim that 'by law the city enjoins the archon to prevent *oikoi* becoming empty' appears to be rhetorical distortion, given that no case of such an intervention by a magistrate is recorded.[110] But values and aspirations do not have to be universally binding, nor protected by law, in order to be real values and aspirations.

The matter has another aspect, however.[111] It was a recurrent ambition of Greek political philosophers and, according to them, of archaic lawgivers to keep the territory of the city divided into a constant total of roughly equal 'plots' or 'portions'. Partible inheritance and childlessness permanently threatened the balance even where total population remained constant: the plot of A, fertile, was divided into fragments, that of B, childless, went to a collateral who was perhaps already waxing fat on a rich paternal plot. Sometimes the two sources of imbalance must have corrected one another: a plot divided between three sons was re-assembled if two died without issue (and in such a case the possibility of perpetuating a childless *oikos* by adoption worked against the ideal of preserving a steady state of plots). But the Athenian

---

[107] See Rubinstein, *Adoption*, 62–86. An adopted heir was obliged to tend his 'parent' in old age; and many think that in order to exercise the right of free bequest created by Solon the will-maker was obliged to adopt his designated heir (so de Ste. Croix, *CR* 20, 1970, 387–90, followed by Lane Fox, 'Inheritance', 225; *aliter* W. E. Thompson, *Prudentia* 13, 1981, 22; Rubinstein, *Adoption*, 81–6).

[108] See Rubinstein, *Adoption*, 76–86. As she shows, the orators treat this as a possible case; its frequency cannot be established.

[109] As in the cases recorded in [Dem.] 43.11 and 44, *passim*; note too Isae. 11.49. On the practice see Rubinstein, *Adoption*, 25–8; 105–12.

[110] Only son adopted out: so apparently Thrasyboulos in Isae. 7.23; [Dem.] 42.21 probably attests an only son of a deceased father who allowed himself to be adopted by a maternal grandfather (Davies, *Propertied Families*, 552). Isaeus' claim: on the distortion see Rubinstein, *Adoption*, 105–9, following W. Wyse's note on Isae. 7.30.8–9; D. Asheri, *Archivio Giuridico* 159 (1960), 11–12; cf. Harrison, *Law*, I, 93, n. 1.

[111] See Lane Fox, 'Inheritance', 224–8. 'Philosophers': Pl. *Leg.* 923c–924a; Arist. *Pol.* 1265b 12–16 (on Pheidon of Corinth), 1274b 2–5 (on Philolaus of Thebes, who passed adoption laws 'to preserve the number of *kleroi*').

system whereby the spare son of a fecund home was transferred into a barren one was doubtless, over a broad number of cases, a much more effective corrective. A crucial feature of Athenian adoption needs to be underlined here: if I was born Kephisios son of Kephisodotos of Phaleron but became by adoption Kephisios son of Dionysios of Marathon, I surrendered all title to the property of Kephisodotos of Phaleron. One could not multiply inheritances by adoption, and in consequence the natural candidates for adoption were those without expectations of a large inheritance under their own natal identity. The prosperous adopted the less prosperous.

So far, so good. But a simple functional account whereby Athenian adoption practices served as a check on unbalanced accumulation of wealth cannot explain the sentiments of those who performed the adoptions. Dying men do not conceive the desire for a successor out of concern for the equitable distribution of property in society at large (though a prejudice was undoubtedly available to be exploited against those who enjoyed the fruits of 'two houses'[112]). Must we then imagine a fortunate congruence between general social utility, as envisaged by a 'wise lawgiver', and the deepest urges of individual Athenians faced by death? Is it not possible rather that the desire for personal perpetuation was itself a product of the institution, adoption, without which it was sure of disappointment in a good number of cases? There were, it seems, many Greek societies where adoption on the Athenian model was not practised.[113] In such a society, the belief that if one died without issue one's house died with one would have been very ill-placed; for infertility is commonplace, and such despair-inducing extinction would inevitably have been the fate of many *oikoi*. The Athenian notion that in order to live on one had to leave behind a kind of replacement for oneself was surely not the only possibility. One could live on in one's uncle's or one's brother's or one's sister's children, and one's memory could be preserved in other ways. There were doubtless other ways too of ensuring a continuation of cult at the tomb. But the Athenians had their own ideal; the survival of the *oikos* was paramount, but for each male Athenian it was in effect a matter of 'l'*oikos*, c'est moi'. This highly individual understanding of the survival of the *oikos* could arise because adoption meant that there was always a viable alternative to obliteration. The individual's desire for a form of self-perpetuation is distinct from the lawgiver's concern for an equitable distribution of property, but the law decisively shaped the contours of the individual's yearnings.

This chapter has presented that curious array of gods whose images, none of them conventionally anthropomorphic, were physically present in Greek houses. Hestia and Zeus Ktesios within the house, Apollo Aguieus, Hecate

---

[112] Dem. 42.21, 43.77–8, 44.23; cf. Isoc. 19.44.
[113] See Gernet, *Droit et société*, 141, on ML 20. It is hard to know what reliance to place on the assertion of Isocrates that, by the early 4th c., the principle of adoption was accepted 'by all the Greeks' (19.50–1, cf. 12–14).

and Hermes just outside it, Zeus Herkeios perhaps in the internal courtyard, perhaps at a more distant site shared with other households, have all been surveyed. We have visited the ancestral tombs. The shrine of a 'neighbouring hero' just round the corner will be mentioned in due course.

The chapter has sought in one sense to restrict the *oikos* and in another to extend it. The restrictive argument was an argument in favour of a 'small' interpretation of the *oikos* which makes it, in effect, just a single male along with his wife, children and servants. The *oikos* which is threatened with becoming 'empty' (a real anxiety to many Athenians, if for complicated reasons) is 'small' too. It is not denied that a 'large' *oikos* can be found, if less readily, in Athenian sources, and that the idea of the large *oikos* doubtless had its own emotional force. Some few Athenians were buried along with their great-great-grandfathers and may, before their own death, have brought them offerings. But smaller tomb groupings with less historical depth were much more common.

The extending argument was that 'household' gods (as we call them) were merely a subset of the gods whom the Greeks themselves called 'ancestral' gods, a group in some contexts identical with the gods of the city but more particularly associated with the phratry (or the *genos*). This argument relocates some of (we may guess) the strongest religious emotions of the individual in a context broader than that of the 'small' *oikos* (though not in fact identical with the large one; for *oikoi* trace kinship bilaterally, phratries only through the father).

The picture created by this pair of arguments remains incomplete. There is more evidence for religious activity within the small *oikos*, and more for the impossibility of isolating the religious practices of the *oikos* from a wider context. But these matters demand a short chapter of their own.

2

'Those with Whom I Sacrifice'

In the previous chapter, I sought to qualify the importance of the family unit in cult: the 'household gods' of the moderns are not a class recognized as such by the ancients, but merely some among what they termed 'ancestral gods'. I turn now, by contrast, to look at aspects of the religious role of the household that are commonly almost entirely overlooked. The theme will be the role of cult in holding social groups together in amity or at least intimacy. But the bonding so created was not confined to members of the same household or to kin; the shared sacrifices of non-kin are a further central aspect of private religion, and the chapter will move on to that theme.

Theophrastus' *Superstitious Man* goes each month to the Orpheotelest to be initiated 'with his wife (or the nurse, if his wife is busy) and his children'.[1] Only a man of exaggerated piety, it may seem, would insist on seeking divine favour *en famille*. But to conclude so is to neglect the evidence of that common type of votive relief which shows a god approached by worshippers.[2] A large and readily studied group is that coming from the sanctuary of Pankrates/ Herakles by the Ilissus. Twenty-six reliefs are well enough preserved to allow a sure or probable judgement of the number of worshippers who were originally depicted. Nine show a man or a group of men, two a woman or women, while the remaining fifteen mix the sexes. Of these mixed sex groups (the number of which would be much increased if we added in fragments) two present a couple, five a couple with a child, one a pair of couples (?) with children, five a couple, usually with child or children, plus a 'spare man' (or woman), and two show more complicated mixtures; servants are also often present. At the Asklepieion we find five reliefs showing a man or men, one a woman and one apparently two women, and another sixteen that mix the sexes in various combinations; almost always it is plausible that a married couple forms the nucleus, and children are often present. Another numerous group is that of the 'banqueting hero' reliefs (though we must certainly remember that despite their shared iconography they derive from cults of

---

[1] *Char.* 16.12.

[2] See van Straten, 'Votives and Votaries', 274–84—a pioneering study. Detailed evidence is collected in the lists at the end of this chapter. Löhr, *Familienweihungen*, is a catalogue raisonné of joint dedications by family members, dedications made by one family member 'for' another, and dedications of statues of other family members; 'family reliefs' dedicated by one individual are excluded.

Fig. 3. Third-century votive relief showing a family in the shrine of Pankrates (cf. p. 419): incribed Πείθων εὐχὴν Πανκράτει.

different heroes, and even gods, whom we can seldom identify). Here the bourgeois ideal prevails yet more: some fifteen reliefs present a couple plus child(ren) (often plus servant), another eleven a couple plus child(ren) plus further adults or near adults, one a woman and child, one five adults of both sexes, and only some four a single man. (On a different type of hero-relief, where a hero and heroine stand together or a hero holds or rides his horse,[3] single male worshippers were perhaps more common; the sample is not large, however.) From the shrine of Artemis at Brauron come five reliefs, of which four show extended families or groups of families (the average number of adults per relief is noticeably higher than at other sites), one a single male worshipper. No other sanctuary or type of cult has yielded material in quantity, but a good number of gods are approached by families on one or two reliefs: almost all the other healing gods of Attica, predictably (Asclepius

---

[3] See van Straten, *Hierà kalá,* 92–4.

in the Piraeus; Amynos; Amphiaraus at Rhamnus and Oropus); Aphrodite at
Daphni; Kalliste in the Ceramicus; Zeus Meilichios and Zeus Philios at several
sites; Athena Polias (though amid the abundant votive material offered to her
this type is rare),[4] Heracles, Demeter and Kore, Nymphs. Several major gods
are absent from the list (Apollo, Dionysus, Poseidon), but votive material of
any kind relating to them is sparse. In a striking instance of cultural assimilation we find the type used by 'Mitradates and his wife' (an Iranian name) for
a dedication to Men (an Anatolian god) found at Thorikos.

About twenty 'family reliefs' (i.e. reliefs depicting what is probably a family
group) still have the dedicatory inscription attached. In most cases they are
identified as the offering of a single individual, who in nine cases is a man and
in eight a woman. (Even where the dedicant is a woman, on the relief her
husband normally precedes her.[5]) Of the three or four such reliefs that
explicitly present themselves as offerings by both a man and a woman, only
one appears to be made by native Athenians.[6] Similarly, among the dedicatory inscriptions that are now detached from their associated offering, only a
handful are made by a man and a woman jointly, whereas joint dedications
by two or more men—very often brothers, or fathers and sons—are common.
But if reliefs, when they are present, regularly reveal a family context which
the dedicatory inscriptions disguise, it seems to follow that those men and
women who made the innumerable 'individual' dedications known only from
inscriptions did not necessarily suppose that they were acting in their own
interests alone. A text such as the following neatly illustrates the point:
'Phaidimides of Probalinthos, son of Protarchos, dedicated this lovely object
to Athena' (individual donor); 'grant prosperity to him himself, his children
and his descendants' (group beneficiaries).[7] In that case the added element

---

[4] See O. Palagia, Hesperia 64 (1995), 493–501, who suggests associating the main family
relief dedicated to Athena, Athens Acr. Mus. 581, with Athena Phratria and the Apatouria. It is
however very unclear whether women had much role at that festival. Van Straten's conclusion,
Hierà kalá, 76–7, from the scarcity of family reliefs that families had little interest in Athena Polias
scarcely squares with the evidence of inscriptions.

[5] For counter cases see van Straten, 'Votives and Votaries', 276–7; note too LIMC s.v. Artemis,
658, no. 459 (Brauron 1171 (77)).

[6] IG II² 4627, dedicated by a man and two women; the other cases are IG II² 4684, 'Mitradates
and his wife'; Hesperia 12 (1943), 51, no. 10 (names too fragmentary to interpret: no children
shown), and Hesperia 17 (1948), 137 (van Straten, Hierà kalá, R 90), Πάνις Αἰγίριος Ἡρ[α]κλεῖ,
where neither name (if two names is what they are) is otherwise attested in Attica. IG II² 4426
(van Straten, R 39) lacks a formal dedication, but the names of a woman and three men (husband
plus two sons?) are inscribed, as identification, over the relief.

[7] IG II² 4319 (CEG 760); cf. IG II² 4321 (CEG 761). Of course, not all individual dedications
can be seen as 'crypto-familial': many reliefs which depict worshippers show only men or only
women—some such appear, for completeness, among the 'family reliefs' listed in the annexe to
the chapter; note too (men only) Athens NM 2505 (IG II² 4423), Hesperia 12 (1943), 49, no. 9
and (two women) IG II² 4565. 'Single parents' with children are also found (whether through the
death of the spouse or for other reasons cannot be known): mother and child(ren) NM 2756 (IG
II² 4548); NM 1779 (Cook, Zeus, ii, 1115, fig. 947); NM 1406 (IG II² 4623); NM 1408 (van
Straten, Hierà kalá, R 45: two women with children); man and child(ren) IG II² 4553, 4556 (?: see
p. 47).

beyond the individual dedicator himself is merely his children and theirs, without explicit mention of women (but Phaidimides' wife may have been dead), and the many joint dedications by brothers and by fathers and sons may also be thought to support the idea of an *oikos* conceived primarily as a succession of males. (One specimen is even dedicated by Autophilos, three sons and three grandsons—the grandsons, however, are all sons of daughters, in a spectacular demonstration of the bilateral strand in Athenian kinship.) But in the reliefs themselves, as we have seen, women have their place. Another offering bears two dedicatory inscriptions: one in prose speaks of 'X, his wife, and children', while its verse companion mentions the paterfamilias alone.[8]

We should also note here the common formula whereby a dedication is made by one person, who is often said to 'have made a vow' 'on behalf of' ($\dot{v}\pi\acute{\epsilon}\rho$) another, most commonly a child or children.[9] 'On behalf of' here does not indicate 'instead of' but 'for the welfare of'. Such vows and dedications were made to various gods, even if the acknowledged healers were much the commonest recipients, and it does not look as if they were exclusively a response to illness, even when addressed to healers. A formula used particularly by women, 'on behalf of herself and her children', suggests that the general well-being of the family was what was sought. Family reliefs may often be the upshot of vows, even though only one presents itself explicitly as being made (by a woman) 'on behalf of her children'.[10] (Several offerings are said to have been vowed by one family member and dedicated by another. The situation here is probably different, the death of the vowmaker before discharge of the vow: 'we owe a cock to Asclepius'.[11] Different again may normally have been the motivation for the practice that emerged in the fourth century of dedicating portraits or statues of one's kin in sanctuaries.[12])

---

[8] *IG* II² 4318 (*CEG* 759). Autophilos: *IG* II² 4327: on the maternal grandfather see J. N. Bremmer, *ZPE* 50 (1983), 173–86.

[9] From the pre-Roman period I have noted about 20 instances of $\dot{v}\pi\acute{\epsilon}\rho$ dedications addressed to healers (of which perhaps three-quarters are dedicated by men), also *IG* I³ 857 (a woman's tithe to Athena 'for herself and her *genea*'—for use of this formula or variants by women see *IG* II² 4446, Asclepius, and 4883, uncertain god); ? *IG* II² 4338 (Athena: sex. incert.); *IG* II² 4593 (? Athena: by a woman); *IG* II² 4588 (Demeter and Kore: a woman); 4637 (Aphrodite: sex. incert.) and *SEG* XXI 784 (?Aphrodite); the instances $\dot{v}\pi\grave{\epsilon}\rho$ $\tau\hat{\omega}\nu$ $\pi\alpha\iota\delta\acute{\iota}\omega\nu$ given in p. 439, n. 83; and *IG* II² 4923 (uncertain deity: by a man). In Xen. *Mem.* 2.2.10 Socrates treats the behaviour of a mother who makes and discharges vows on behalf of ($\dot{v}\pi\acute{\epsilon}\rho$) her son in sickness as typical.

[10] *IG* II² 4613.

[11] *IG* I³ 659, ? 701, 705, 735, 773; *IG* II² 4368 (*CEG* 772), 4649 (*CEG* 781). In *IG* I³ 773 it is on oracular or divinatory advice of some kind that a son fulfils his mother's vow. *IG* II² 4325, if correctly supplemented, implies the possibility of long delay. Aristotle's will stipulates dedications to be made on his behalf post mortem, Diog. Laert. 5.15. But possibly in a case such as *IG* II² 4368 (*CEG* 772) a father was meeting the expenses of a vow made by a still-living daughter. The non-Attic instances listed by Lazzarini, 'Formule', 99, do not help in understanding the usage.

[12] We assume that statues of little children, apparently anonymous, found in the sanctuary of Artemis Brauronia or Eileithyia were at least in part intended to put the real children they represented under the goddess's protection. Statues of named children dedicated by parents such as Löhr, *Familienweihungen*, nos. 106 (Miles, *Eleusinion*, 189, no. 10) and 127 (*IRhamnous*

What emerges from this survey? It might be naive to take the many depictions of families bringing animals to the altar as simple snapshots of actual family parties. Such reliefs have sometimes been dedicated in discharge of a vow, and in such a case the depicted sacrifice is less the record of an event than a translation into visual terms of the idea of 'honouring the god' which the dedication exists to convey. Again, the man who gave a relief to Asclepius in gratitude for being 'rescued from the wars and ransomed and freed' probably added his wife, his daughter and another man as a way of indicating the circle whom the god's saving aid had benefited most.[13] But it would be odd if the visual image 'family sacrificing to god X together' served as a vehicle for the idea 'family honouring god X together' if such sacrifices were not in fact a very familiar practice. Surely the fine reliefs at Brauron showing extended families were there at least in part to be admired by other such extended family groups physically present at the shrine. Menander's *Dyscolus* contains an admirably clear example of a sacrifice held by a rich family in a deme's sanctuary of Pan; it is attended by the whole family but had been initiated by the mother, who according to her son was for ever on the move around the deme planning one sacrifice or another.[14] On any view the reliefs illustrate the extent to which Athenians tended to see themselves, in their relations with the gods, not as individuals but as members of an *oikos*; women did so more than men ('mother of the sons of Dionysius', one calls herself[15]), but men did so too to a significant degree.

All the reliefs which we have been considering were dedicated at shrines to which everybody had access; some of these shrines were also the site of major public festivals. Whether the 'family reliefs' dedicated at Brauron say or Eleusis were made (or vowed) on the occasion of the great public ceremonies or in consequence of independent visits to the shrines can scarcely be determined.[16] However that may be, the crucial conclusion is inescapable that 'the religion of the *oikos*' is not to be looked for within the confines of the *oikos*, or

123) could be seen in the same way. But the dedication e.g. of statues of parents by children also became common, and the only expressed motives were to honour the god by the gift and to preserve the memory of the parent (who might even be dead): for such statues described as gifts to the god see Löhr, *Familienweihungen*, nos. 149 (*IG* II² 4596; *CEG* 775); 136 ([Plut.] *XOrat.* 839b), and for commemoration 89 (*IG* II² 3838; *CEG* 780), 136 again, and esp. 162 (Diog. Laert. 5.15, Aristotle's will). Löhr, *Familienweihungen*, no. 161 (*IG* II² 3829) is a five-member family group.

[13] Vow: so e.g. the relief of Aristonike, Brauron Museum 1151 (van Straten, *Hierà kalá*, R 73). Asclepius: *IG* II² 4357.

[14] Men. *Dysc.* 259–64; 393–455; 557–73; 773–83; the sanctuary is envisaged as being regularly so used, 197–9, 444–7. Literary references to private sacrifices in public shrines are not very frequent (but Plaut. *Poen.* 529; *Rudens* 142–3, 342–3 may come from Greek originals), but both sanctuary architecture and sacred laws show the practice to have been standard.

[15] *IG* II² 4573; cf. van Straten, 'Votives and Votaries', 282. None of this is intended to dispute Sourvinou-Inwood's undeniably correct conclusion that the smallest unit of action in Greek religion is the individual (*Oxford Readings*, 44–7).

[16] But it is certain that offerings to Artemis Brauronia were not made only at the time of the penteteric *Brauronia*: see p. 232.

even at the altars of the phratry, alone. *Oikos* members and their *oikeioi* could also supplicate for their mutual well-being at the public shrines.

Another point of connection needs to be recognized between the religion of the *oikos* and public cults. The festivals of the city had far greater reverberations within individual *oikoi* than is generally acknowledged. The one case that is generally allowed is that of the *Anthesteria*, since the private drinking parties which formed the core of the public festival almost certainly took place in individual houses. It must also have been in private households that the feasting together of masters and slaves attested for the *Kronia* took place.[17] Both cases are in fact ambiguous, since, as we have seen, rites performed within the house are not necessarily rites of the house, and women probably attended festivities that involved drinking, if at all, only to serve. (But let us signal a mysterious fragment of Menander, unfortunately deprived of a context, which reveals the Greek for 'family party', τρίκλινον συγγενείας, and shows senior family members of both genders roistering together.[18]) We also have explicit testimony that groups of 'kinsmen' (συγγενεῖς) dined together— but probably at the site of the festival in this case—at the *Diasia*; the god of the *Diasia*, Zeus Meilichios, is one to whom 'family reliefs' were very often dedicated, and actually functions as a god explicitly tied to kin-groups in many states outside Athens.[19] And the *Apatouria* was by definition a festival at which kinsmen came together. But apart from the quasi-familial aspects, perhaps chiefly involving men, of these four festivals, we must remember the special foodstuffs associated with many others. Not all these foods were prepared and consumed within each individual household, but surely many were. And for the festival of Sacred Marriage, *Hieros Gamos*, we have the unambiguous evidence of a joke in Menander about the outrageous Chairephon, who 'said that he would hold a sacred marriage at home (καθ' αὑτόν) on the 29th, so that he could dine out on the 27th [the proper day for the festival]'. More conventional folk therefore celebrated the festival by dining at home on the 27th, doubtless with their wives.[20]

We have surveyed the shared religious activities of blood relations. But, as was noted at the outset, cult activity was an essential bond between non-kin

---

[17] See pp. 293–4 and 202.   [18] Fr. 186 (209 Koerte).

[19] See the evidence from Thera, Cyrene and Selinous cited by Jameson et al., *Selinous*, 78, 86, 89–91. Kin at *Diasia*: Ar. *Nub.* 408–9. In Xen. *Anab.* 7.8.5, where Xen. speaks of sacrificing to Zeus Meilichios τῷ πατρίῳ νόμῳ, πατρῴῳ is a variant in a ms. group of some standing (c). The variant would underline the familial character of the cult in Athens. But I know no parallel for πατρῷος applied to an abstraction such as νόμος. Sacred laws from outside Attica quite often anticipate and even require private sacrifices at the time of public festivals and as a part of them: see S. Georgoudi, *Ktema* 23 (1998), 325–34.

[20] Men. fr. 225 (265 Koerte); cf. F. Salviat, *BCH* 88 (1964), 647–54; I. Clark in *The Sacred and the Feminine*, 18–19. This festival is now twice mentioned in deme calendars (below, p. 76); and the sacrifice to Zeus Heraios in the month Gamelion in the calendar of uncertain type *IG* I³ 234. 21 (*LSCG* 1) has long been associated with it. Ritual details are not known, but note that the first libation at banquets could honour 'the timely marriage of Zeus and Hera', Aesch. fr. 55. On festival foods see p. 164.

too. The seamlessness of the transition from kin to non-kin is suggested by the word *oikeios*, 'of the *oikos*', which is applied both to relatives and to other intimates. *Philos* too is used of kin as well as of friends, as English 'friend' still was in the language of Jane Austen. One's *oikeioi* were *oikeioi* because they came to one's house, to share in sacrifices above all. A young man in Menander invites the brother of the girl he loves (and, interestingly, his servant) to a sacrifice which his mother is organizing, and explains 'after sharing in the rites they will be more helpful allies for us later for the marriage'; when the intended guest seeks to excuse himself, the young man protests 'Heracles, what man on earth refuses to come to dine when one of his circle has sacrificed?'[21] In inheritance cases, the question of who a testator did and did not invite to his sacrifices becomes an important index of intimacy (whether deriving from supposed kinship or not). 'When he sacrificed to Dionysus, and invited all his *oikeioi* and many other citizens too, he made no effort to summon Pherenikos.' 'He never held a sacrifice without us, but whether he was making large offerings or small, we were always present and sacrificed along with him.'[22] An alternative (or perhaps a mark of lesser intimacy) was to send out portions of sacrificial meat to friends by carrier, like slices of wedding cake;[23] the slaves who distributed these μερίδες traced out on their journeyings the networks of ancient Athens.

The good life as generally conceived, according to Adeimantus in the *Republic*, includes 'making one's own sacrifices to the gods' and then entertaining guests. The ideal was perhaps one of reciprocity, but an element of social ranking inevitably crept into relations based upon sacrifice, whereby men (and women) of wealth and standing distributed meat more often than they received it, and were indeed expected to do so. There is pressure on the rich Kritoboulos to sacrifice with a free hand, says Xenophon's Socrates, from both gods and men.[24] Yet this was still not a mere display of wealth, but a sociable sharing of it. Only Theophrastus' Shameless Man would salt and store meat from a sacrifice, and then dine away from home.[25] It is not a coincidence that Theophrastus' little masterpiece is full of sacrificial details

[21] Men. *Dysc.* 558–62, 612–14; cf. e.g. Antiphon 1.16, Apollod. *Neaer.* 65. The sacrifice in Menander is in a shrine of the deme, not at home, but the main point is unaffected. On sacrifice and bonding see *Athenian Religion*, 1, and such passages as Isocr. 19.10; Dem. 19.128, 190; 58.40; Aeschin. 3.52; Din. 2.9.

[22] Isae. 1.31, 8.15.

[23] Men. *Sam.* 403; Ephippus fr. 15. 11–13; Theophr. *Char.* 17.2 (perhaps too the obscure 15.5); cf. Ar. *Ach.* 1049.

[24] Reciprocity: Xen. *Mem.* 2.3.11. Adeimantus: Pl. *Resp.* 419a. Kritoboulos: Xen. *Oec.* 2. 5, cf. 11.9 and, for a characteristic example, Alcibiades in Plut. *Nic.* 7.7; for the patronal aspect, Xen. *Mem.* 2.9.4 (on sacrificial expenditure as honourable expenditure see Arist. *EN* 1122b 20). But giving (or sending) sacrificial pieces could be spoken of as a way of 'honouring' the recipient, by way perhaps of a kind of courteous euphemism: Xen. *Hiero* 8.3 (and perhaps Theophr. *Char.* 15.5). The provision by the polis of numerous public sacrifices eroded but did not wholly destroy such forms of patronage (cf. *Athenian Religion*, 127–9 [+]).

[25] Theophr. *Char.* 9.2 (cf. 22.4, sale); other sacrificial details 10.11, 12.12, 17.2, 21.7, 30.4, 30.16.

such as this: the work studies the quirks of character as revealed in social interaction, and one prime context for observation is the sacrificial feast. All these private sacrifices, some conducted in the house, some in public shrines, some on the occasion of festivals, some at the pleasure of the host, some inspired by specific religious motives such as a rescue from danger, many held chiefly for the pleasure of the feast, are a largely unobservable but very important face of ancient religion. The guardian who is prosecuted in a speech of Lysias charged his wards 500 drachmai a year for expenditure on sacrifice at the *Dionysia* and for 'the other festivals and sacrifices'. As he normally divided costs between himself and the boys, the claimed total of expenditure on sacrifices and festivals by one household was 1000 drachmai, more than that of any of the demes of which we have record.[26]

More formal than these ad hoc banquets were the sacrifices of private religious associations. But we will do no more than note them,[27] and pass instead to a different context of religious sociability. 'A life without *theoria* is a life not worth living': here is a proposition on which the most philosophical Athenian and the least would have been able to agree. But whereas for a philosopher *theoria* was contemplation, for unreformed man it meant attendance at a festival where there was plenty to see. In Aristophanes' *Peace* Theoria appears on stage in female form as one of the delights of peace from which the Athenians have been shut off for so long. The most familiar application of the nouns *theoria* and *theoros* relates to state delegations sent to the panhellenic festivals, and at this level they represent a privilege open to few citizens. But the journey to Artemis' festival at Brauron too was a *theoria*, and the 'theoric fund' subsidized attendance at festivals even within the city: *theoria* is simply 'going to a (religious) show'.[28] Like sharing in sacrifices, 'going to festivals together', συνθεωρεῖν, is a symptom and a reinforcement of close social bonds.[29]

This short chapter has sought to show that the *oikos* functioned as a religious unit in more ways than are commonly recognized. In the process it has emerged that the walls of the *oikos* did not divide the religion of the *oikos* from that of the city at large. It is altogether a fallacy to suppose that the temples of the acropolis and the festivals of the city hosted a formal and civic religion detached from the more personal and urgent religious concerns of the Athenians. Civic festivals were important events in the life of individuals and

[26] Lys. 32.21–2 (cf. 20). The speaker's point is, however, that the claimed total was fraudulent. On private sacrifices see G. Berthiaume, *Les Rôles du Mágeiros* (*Mnemosyne Suppl.* 70, Leiden 1982), 32–7.

[27] Cf. pp. 373–4 below.

[28] See I. Rutherford, *CQ* 50 (2000), 133–8; Hdt. 6.87 speaks of a πεντετηρίς at Sunium, with a θεωρὶς ναῦς. Female form: Ar. *Pax* 713, 871–6 (with ribald jokes about the Brauron *theoria*); εἰς πανηγύρεις θεωρεῖν is an ideal already, ibid. 342.

[29] [Lys.] 8. 5; Isoc. 19.10, 'we were more than brothers to one another, and there was no sacrifice or *theoria* or other festival which we did not share'; Isae. 8.15–16 (cf. 9. 30); Pl. *Ep.* 7, 333e. For friends arranging to process together at the *Dionysia* see Aeschin. 1.43.

families. But the *oikos* itself was not a sealed unit. Sacrificing together and attending festivals together were the most important contexts for the expression of social intimacy, but one might engage in these activities with one's kin, with one's friends, or with a mixture of both. Midway between private sacrifices and festivals of the city there were the rites of phratries and *thiasoi* and the like. A different point has emerged almost clandestinely, but deserves now to be given a place in the light. Offering one's own sacrifices and entertaining guests were, we saw, an essential ingredient of the good life; 'going to the show' at festivals was a pleasure full-flavoured enough even for an Aristophanic hero. The argument about different types of social bonding reinforced by cult has also been an argument about the comforts of religion, *à la grecque*.

GODS TO WHOM 'FAMILY RELIEFS' ARE DEDICATED, AND THE
COMPOSITION OF THE 'FAMILY' GROUPS

NM in these lists stands for the National Archaeological Museum of Athens.

Pankrates/Herakles: The following reliefs allow sure or probable judgement of the number of figures in the original composition; the numeration is that of Vikelas, *Pankrates-Heiligtum*. Sure: A 1, 3, 4, 5, 8, 9, 11–18, 22; B 5–6, 7 (gender?), 8, 10, 12 (gender sometimes unclear), 14, 16, F 11; probable: F 3, F 8. I exclude A 2, 10, 20; B 15, 19.

Man/men: A 1, 17, 18, 22; B 5, 7, 8, 16; F 11. Woman/women: A 13, B 14. The other scenes are mixed (mixed groups in fragmentary reliefs also A 2, couple with child; B 15, couple?; F 4, woman + two men?; F 6, couple and children). Couple: A 5, 12; couple with child/children: A 3 (the child is unusually mature), 9, 14, 16; B 10; two couples (?) with children: F 3; couple with child(ren) and 'spare' man: A 4, A 8, B 6; and spare woman A 15, B 12 (no children). More complicated mixtures: A 11, a bearded man with a fully grown young man (?), two women, two children; F 8, a couple, a younger man, and a boy: perhaps to be seen as a couple with two children.

Asclepius in the Asclepieum: My list was compiled with the help of U. Hausmann, *Kunst und Heiltum* (Berlin 1948), 185, and van Straten, *Hierà kalá*, 275–81, but I omit reliefs of undemonstrated provenance except where stated.

Man/men: NM 1332, 1338–9, 1347, 1376: the first shows six men, the rest one only. Woman/women: IG II^2 4415; NM 1372. Couples: NM 1355, 1841, 2926 (uncertain provenance); couples + spare man: 1331, 1354, Walter, *Akropolismuseum*, no. 394b (which also includes a child); couple with children NM 1356, 1361, Walter, no. 96 (five girls according to Walter!), NM 1344 (with a nurse); two couples with children NM 1374; more complicated groups: NM 1333, a couple, a girl, a man, a small boy, a servant; NM 1345, four men, one clearly aged, a woman, two children, one servant; NM 1342, a couple, a girl, a man, three women (?); NM 1367, a couple followed by a young woman and a girl; NM 1377, four couples, two having a child, and servants (so van Straten, *Hierà kalá*, 279). NM 1334 may show a man and two young women: unusual if so.

Banqueting hero reliefs: I cite by the numbers of the reference list in Dentzer, *Banquet couché*.

Couple plus children: 103a, 148, 151, 153, 193, 195–6, 200–1, 203, 205 (?), 237, 244; 145 and 146 have a single, rather large male child. Couple plus children plus spare man: 119, 192 (an eldest son?), 226 (no children), 233; plus spare woman 152, 154, 224 (no children), 228; 103b, 225 and 229 have a spare woman clearly marked as younger. Woman and child: 143. Five adults: 235. Single man: 126 (?), 139 (?) 197, 236. I omit 100 and 121 as unclear. These are the figures for reliefs with an assured Attic provenance: for panhellenic figures, based on almost 200 specimens, see van Straten, 'Votives and Votaries', 281–2: *c*.75 per cent of instances show couples, of which *c*.55 per cent have children.

Hero-reliefs of different types: Single male worshipper: E. Mitropoulou, *Corpus I: Attic Votive Reliefs of the 6th and 5th Centuries B.C.* (Athens 1977), nos. 37, 57 (cf. the pieces of uncertain provenance 61, 64, 103, 117, 130); man and child, ibid. 47; Louvre Ma 743 = M. Hamiaux, *Musée du Louvre. Les Sculptures grecques* I (Paris 1992), no. 135 (Theseus: *IG* II^2 4553); families NM 1410 (Svoronos, *Nationalmuseum*, pl. LXV), 1411 (Svoronos pl. XXXIII, 7).

Artemis at Brauron: Brauron museum 1151 (Travlos, *Bildlexikon*, 72, fig. 77): four couples, each with a child; ibid. 1152 (Travlos, 72, fig. 78): a couple, another woman, four children; ibid. 1153 (Travlos 73, fig. 79): child, woman, three bearded men, two children, a youth (all these reliefs—R 73–5 in van Straten, *Hierà Kalá*, with pp. 80–1—also contain servants); ibid. 1171 (77) (*LIMC* s.v. *Artemis*, no. 459): woman, man (children may be missing from beside them), three women (one with a girl), three youths progressively smaller in size; Brauron 1182 (1) (*LIMC* s.v. *Artemis*, no. 463): a single man. There is also a document relief showing five male worshippers, Brauron Museum 1172, Lawton, *Document Reliefs*, 118, no. 73 with fig. 39.

Other gods: Numbers are too few in each case for it to be worth giving details of the worshippers; the point from here on is to list the gods who received this type of dedication.

Asclepius in the Piraeus, Amynos, Amphiaraus: van Straten, *Hierà kalá*, R 27–31, 36–40. **Aphrodite** at Daphni: NM 1598, cf. 1597, 1601. **Kalliste** in the Ceramicus: *BCH* 51 (1927), pl. viii (Travlos, *Pictorial Dictionary*, 322, fig. 423: no children) = *IG* II^2 4666. **Zeus Meilichios and Philios**: van Straten, *Hierà kalá*, R 41–8, also *ArchEph* 1885, 90 = *IG* II^2 4624 (Philios: Cook, *Zeus*, ii, 1174, n. 1); NM 1405 = *IG* II^2 4623 (Philios: Cook, ibid. 1174, fig. 976); NM 1431 = *IG* II^2 4618 (Meilichios: Cook, *Zeus*, ii, 1106, fig. 942); NM 1779 (Cook 1115, fig. 947), 2356 (Svoronos, *Nationalmuseum*, pl. CXLII),

2357 (Svoronos pl. CXLII) and 2809 (Svoronos CCXXI: Attic provenance of the two latter not stated), the last four dedicated to unidentifiable Zeuses; *Hesperia* 12 (1943), pp. 49–51, nos. 9–10 (Meilichios: no children). **Athena Polias**: Akr. Mus. 581 = van Straten, *Hierà kalá*, R 58 (*Hesperia* 64, 1995, pl. 114) (cf. the fragmentary R 59, *Hesperia* 1995, pl. 115b); the worshippers in van Straten, *Hierà kalá*, R 60 (*Hesperia* 1995, pl. 115a), all male, are doubtless officials, and NM 2960 (Svoronos, *Nationalmuseum*, pl. CLXXXXIII = M. Mangold, *Athenatypen auf attischen Weihreliefs des 5. und 4. Jhs. v. Chr*, Bern 1993, no. 54) is quite unclear. **Heracles**: van Straten, *Hierà kalá*, R 89 and 90 (though note that women are not shown among the worshippers in the characteristic 'Heracles in columnar shrine' type of relief, ibid. pp. 88–9). **Demeter and Kore**: van Straten, *Hierà kalá*, R 64, 66–7, ? 68, cf. ? 62–3; G. Schwarz, *Triptolemos* (Graz 1987), 67 R 9 with fig. 32; Eleusis museum 5057 (K. G. Kanta, *Eleusis*, Athens 1979, 71); there are also some all-male processions, van Straten, *Hierà kalá*, R 61 (?), 65, NM 1461 (Svoronos, *Nationalmuseum*, pl. LXXVII). **Nymphs**: NM 2798 (Svoronos, *Nationalmuseum*, pl. CXXXVII). Worshippers are seldom present in the very common 'Nymph reliefs', but note *LIMC* s.v. *Achelous*, no. 174 (van Straten, *Hierà kalá*, R 99; *IG* II² 4886): three men, two women; Athens Ag. Inv. 2905 (van Straten, R 101): a couple. Single men also in NM 1329 (*IG* II² 4545, Archandros relief); NM 4466 (van Straten R 100; Travlos, *Bildlexikon*, 334, fig. 420, Agathemeros relief); NM 2646; two men in NM 2351 (*IG* II² 4592); three in NM 4465 (Travlos, *Bildlexikon*, 334, fig. 419); six in NM 1966; two women in *IG* II² 4565 (NM 3529). **Apollo, Dionysus ??** (identification or Attic origin uncertain): van Straten, *Hierà kalá*, R 87 (Dionysus), ibid. 83 (Apollo). *IG* II² 4556 (*CEG* 751), a 4th-c. ded. to Apollo, bears a relief which as recarved in the 18th (?) c. shows a man and two boys as worshippers; that combination is very unusual. **Men**: NM 1406 (Svoronos, *Nationalmuseum*, pl. LIX, *IG* II² 4684; note too M. B. Comstock and C. C. Vermeule, *Sculpture in Stone*, Boston 1975, no. 78).

Dedicators of family reliefs identified by inscription

Men: Vikelas, *Pankrates Heiligtum*, A 4, ? A 5, B 10; *IG* II² 4357 (NM 1354); 4568; 4589; 4624 (for the relief see I. C. Dragatses, *ArchEph* 1885, 90); 4886 (van Straten, *Hierà kalá*, R 99: no children among the worshippers); 4928 (NM 1513; *SEG* XXII 161; Dentzer, *Banquet couché*, R 392), if Attic (Wilson, *Khoregia*, 385, n. 81).

Women: Vikelas, *Pankrates Heiligtum*, A 2, A 16; *IG* II² 4569 (van Straten, *Hierà kalá*, R 44); van Straten, *Hierà kalá*, R 73–4 (Brauron); *IG* II² 4613 (van Straten R 89, ὑπὲρ τῶν παιδίων); 4618 (see under Zeus Meilichios and Philios above); 4666 (see under Kalliste above).

NM 2351 (*IG* II² 4592) is a relief showing a group of men dedicated by a single man.

Men and women: see p. 39, n. 6.

Dedications with more than one named dedicator

I turn away here from reliefs which depict families to inscribed dedications of whatever type which describe themselves as being offered by more than one individual. The bond uniting the joint dedicators is often demonstrably one of kinship, and may be so more often than can be demonstrated.

Two men: IG I³ 526, 566, 597 (brothers?), 614, 620, 636 (?), 695, 702, 716 (brothers), 731 (brothers), 740, 751 (brothers), 755, 785, 833 (brothers), 834, 843, 848, 873 (brothers), 954 (brothers), 994; IG II² 4332, 4339a, 4442(a), 4459, 4615, 4640, 4658, 4679; IOropos 355 and 356 (separate but related dedications by brothers); cf. IG I³ 701 (unspecified number of brothers), 820 (X and his two brothers). IG I³ 654, 659 (siblings), 671, 705, 727, 859 bis, 909 are joint dedications one partner in which could in theory be female, though doubtless very seldom is. In IG II² 4442(a), 4615, 4640, 4679 the joint dedicators come from different demes and in IG II² 4339a have different fathers; in the other cases they might be brothers even where this is not indicated above.

ὁ δεῖνα **and his son(s)**: IG I³ 610 (?), 655c (?), 696 (five sons!), 701, 706 (?), 722, 783, 830, 855 (?), 868 (?), 950; IG II² 3829 (the objects dedicated are images of many further family members); 4611; SEG XXXIX 235; cf. IG I³ 635, 718, 811 (these three present themselves as 'memorial of X and his children/*genea*'—573 is of the same type but dedicated by a woman); 1014, a new dedication set alongside a father's by his ἔγγονοι (699 is similar); IG II² 4362/3, separate but related dedications by father and son (cf. IG II² 4329 + Hesperia 9, 1940, 58 no. 7 for separate deds. to Athena Ergane by a pair of brothers); IG II² 4603, dedication by παῖδες Φαλέου (I assume παῖδες in such contexts to be male, as demonstrably in IG I³ 696; IG II² 4327).

ὁ δεῖνα **and his sons and the sons of his sons**: IG II² 4327.

Larger male groups: IG I³ 672 (?), 701 (brothers), 723 (non kin), 762, 802; IG II² 4375, 4402 (non-kin[30]), 4651. (I omit collective dedications by large groups of the poor or slaves such as IG II² 2934, 4650, 4832).

Mixed sex: IG I³ 644 (female Εὐαρχίς, as in LGPN, despite the doubts in IG I³);[31] IG II² 4318 (CEG 759, man, wife and children: but the associated epigram credits the man only); 4333 (mother with son and daughter?); 4364, 4403 (a couple ὑπέρ τῶν παιδίων); 4596, two sisters and the son of one of them (dedicating portrait statues of themselves); 4609, 4685 (non-citizens?—cf. 4684), probably Hesperia 12 (1943), 51, no. 10 (3rd c.) and the late IG II² 4696, 4710.

---

[30] I include this relief even though it lacks a formal dedication: the names merely identify figures in the relief (NM 1335, Svoronos pl. XXXVI, van Straten, *Hierà kalá*, R 10).

[31] Similarly the postulate of a unique male Κάλλις in IG I³ 814 (so IG I³ and LGPN, despite eight attestations of Καλλίς) is unnecessary, since women could vow tithes: IG I³ 536.

Two or more women: *IG* I^3 573, 700, 745 (probably sisters: with a prayer for their *genea*), 858 (sisters?), 1030 bis (sisters); *IG* II^2 4565, 'daughters of Kleonothos'.

3

Places of Cult: Athens and the Demes

The 'what?' and the 'why?' and 'to whom?' of cult are traditional questions in the study of ancient religions. 'Where?' has tended to be neglected, except in relation to certain distinctive types of location such as caves. There is little explicit reflection in ancient texts on such matters, though questions put to oracles about the siting of particular shrines show how the issue could become one of practical concern.[1] In the main, ancients seem simply to take it for granted that sanctuaries should be distributed around the townscape and landscape, and scholarship long tended to accept this self-evident truth of the ancients as indeed self-evident. Some phenomena may have seemed too self-explanatory to merit comment, such as the tendency to locate gods of the agora in the agora, or sea-gods on the shore. But the easy cases ought to encourage thought about the harder ones, not to close the dossier. If, as structuralism teaches, individual gods are defined by their *differentia* from other gods, 'where?' is very likely to be an important point of difference, and one that may position gods in relation to differences within the human world. Under the inspiration of structuralism on the page or in the air, the topic has in fact at last begun to attract attention. Different approaches are possible, which in an ideal intellectual world would be made to converge. Distinguished studies have been made of the ways in which communities use sanctuaries to ground and root their sense of having rights over land.[2] Here what is crucial is the link between territory and people created by the sacred place; the identity of the gods involved is of secondary concern. But the question 'what gods where?' is the urgent one for students of the pantheon.[3]

---

[1] See e.g. L. Migeotte, *Les Souscriptions publiques dans les cités grecques* (Geneva 1992), no. 28 (*LSCG* 72: Tanagra); Parke, *Oracles of Zeus*, 261, no. 5 (*SEG* XV 397). Texts sometimes recommend that temples should be sited in secluded (Xen. *Mem.* 3.8.10; Paus. 9.22.2) but conspicuous (Xen. loc. cit., Arist. *Pol.* 1331a 28–30) spots, which would tend to be on heights (Paus. loc. cit., Arist. loc. cit.) also conferring security (Arist. loc cit., Pl. *Leg.* 778c–d). Aristotle and Plato (locc. citt.) assume that magistrates' buildings and courts should share the location of temples; cf. Jameson, 'Sacred Space'.

[2] F. de Polignac in many studies, particularly *Cults, Territory, and the Origins of the Greek City-State* (tr. J. Lloyd, Chicago 1995).

[3] See Bremmer, *Greek Religion*, 29–31 [+]. Various essays in *Le Sanctuaire grec* and S. Alcock and R. Osborne (eds.), *Placing the Gods* (Oxford 1994) are relevant to both these enquiries; and see Cole, *Ritual Space*.

Our knowledge of the religious landscape of Attica is immeasurably more fine-meshed than that of any other Greek territory. In one sense Athens is centre and Attica periphery. But Attica contains more than a hundred rural demes, many if not all of which will have been felt by their inhabitants to have themselves a religious centre and religious periphery. On this point the evidence of the sacred calendar of the deme Erchia is decisive. A cluster of cults, including one of 'Zeus of the City', are sited 'on the acropolis'; as for the sense of a periphery, the instruction to perform a sacrifice 'out towards Paiania' is eloquent.[4] And there are many further complications. The cults of Artemis at Brauron and of Nemesis at Rhamnus look, viewed from a distance, very similar: both are important cults of goddesses located in outlying coastal regions. But from literary sources we know their actual roles in religious life to have been to a surprising degree different, the one but not the other destination of a procession from the city, and site of a major public festival. Religious organizations of many different types—phratries, *gene*, groups of *orgeones*, private cult societies—all had their own altars somewhere. At one level, all these altars collectively simply constitute the sacred places of 'the gods and heroes who hold Attica'. It was good to know that a particular local hero was being honoured, even if one did not belong to the group whose inherited right and duty it was to honour him. But only at that very general level would a simple map which marked all the attested cult sites of Attica without differentiation have a bearing on what the complex and many-layered religious life of the region was actually like.

I lay these complexities aside for the moment, and start in the city itself. The treatment will need to be almost scandalously broad-brushed,[5] and must come with the caveat that even some major sanctuaries remain unlocated; about the Anakeion and the Theseum, for instance, substantial places both, no more can be said than that they were somewhere in the centre of the city. The sanctuaries that have received most attention, in studies of cities other than Athens, are those that can be assigned to the acropolis, to the agora, or to a 'suburban' or 'periurban' band; 'gate-holding' gods too are a familiar category. But one cannot begin to fit all the shrines of Athens into these three or four categories. The acropolis, it is true, works well enough, with its sanctuaries of such central 'city-holding' or civic gods and heroes as Athena, Zeus and Poseidon, and of associated heroes and heroines such as Erechtheus and Pandrosus. Where else could the irretrievably tangled skein of ancient

---

[4] See p. 68 below. For a bracing critique of the notion of 'marginality' as applied to Attica see I. Polinskaya in *Initiation*, 85–106.

[5] Fine-pencilled annotation would therefore be out of place. Milchhoefer, *Schriftquellen*; Travlos, *Pictorial Dictionary*; Wycherley, *Testimonia*; Thompson/Wycherley, *Agora*, are fundamental (Judeich, *Topographie*, is largely outdated); also very useful are Wycherley, *Stones of Athens*; Hurwit, *Acropolis*; Camp, *Agora*; Camp, *Athens*; Goette, *Attica*. Recent bibliography on buildings mentioned can easily be recovered from these last four works.

piety that is the Erechtheum be properly located?[6] Artemis of Brauron is of
different character, but the point of giving her a place on the acropolis was to
establish an anchor within the heart of the city for what was fundamentally
an extra-urban cult; no source records that the procession to Brauron started
from the shrine on the acropolis, but we can guess that it did, just as the
procession to Eleusis was formed at the Eleusinion. (The Eleusinion was
another such anchor, in a different but still central location, at the foot of
the acropolis and on the fringe of the agora.[7]) But alongside the gods of the
acropolis we have to set a further category largely unknown to theoretical
analysis, that of the rather numerous 'periacropolitan' cults, some comfortably resting, some perched a little precariously, on the slopes of the great rock.
Here we find (among others) Aphrodite in two guises, Pan, Aglaurus, Asclepius, 'Bride' (Nymphe), Dionysus and, eventually at least, 'Apollo under the
rocks'. [8] The easiest case to categorize is the cave of Pan; by finding this
location under the acropolis the Athenians were able to square the circle,
both granting their honoured new divine guest a place near the heart of
things, and also respecting that strange wildness which made him unsuitable
to occupy an ordinary temple. Can we extrapolate, and identify the other
periacropolitan gods too as problematic or ambiguous powers?[9] The suggestion is an insult to several estimable figures. The important civic heroine
Aglaurus, we may feel, has merely tumbled over the edge of the acropolis, and
could perfectly well have been honoured with her sister Pandrosus on its
heights. As for the others, Aphrodite, Asclepius and Nymphe to a large extent
met personal needs, and the best formulation may be the negative one that
these cults did not need the civic emphasis that a place on the acropolis or in
the agora would have given them.

West of the Acropolis stood Areopagus and Pnyx. The cave of the Semnai
below the former, a very sacred place, has never been identified, but an
unexpected recent discovery is the outline of foundations on the east peak
of the hill; they are taken to imply a small temple (of Ares?) of the same design
as Athena Nike's.[10] The Pnyx perhaps contained a magnificent monumental
altar which was relocated in the agora in or near the Augustan period and
has been ascribed to Zeus Agoraios. A small hill a little further west could
even—*rus in urbe*—host a cult of the Nymphs.[11] But the hills of Areopagus

---

[6] Detienne/Sissa, *Vie quotidienne*, 211: 'l'*Erechteion* est tout en niches, en autels agglutinés ...
et sur le sol les signes de hautes épiphanies, les cicatrices d'une histoire, celle de l'autoctonie'.

[7] See Miles, *Eleusinion*.

[8] A comprehensive account would need to include the 'propylaean' gods too (on the symbolic
importance of the acropolis entry see n. 21 below); but I am concerned here with major
complications, not subordinate ones. With Wycherley, *Stones of Athens*, 167, n. 29, 177, n. 9,
I do not believe in cults of Apollo Pythios or Zeus Astrapaios under the acropolis.

[9] Roughly so, in the case of Asclepius, F. Graf in *Le Sanctuaire grec*, 159–99.

[10] Korrés, 'Architektur', 113, n. 70.

[11] Wycherley, *Stones of Athens*, 188. A little way north there was also apparently a shrine of
Zeus Meilichios: Jameson, *Selinous*, 81.

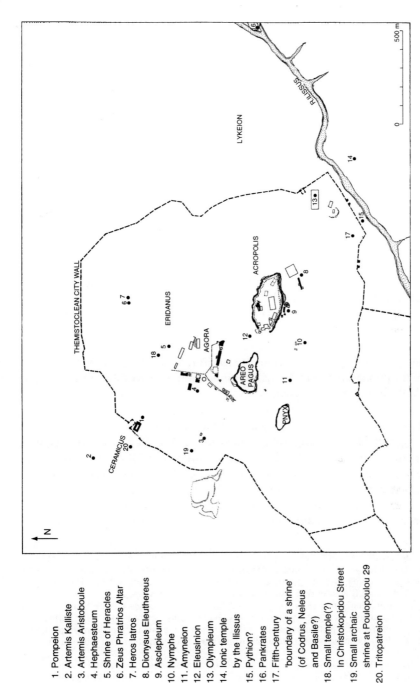

1. Pompeion
2. Artemis Kalliste
3. Artemis Aristoboule
4. Hephaesteum
5. Shrine of Heracles
6. Zeus Phratrios Altar
7. Heros Iatros
8. Dionysus Eleuthereus
9. Asclepieum
10. Nymphe
11. Amyneion
12. Eleusinion
13. Olympieum
14. Ionic temple
    by the Ilissus
15. Pythion?
16. Pankrates
17. Fifth-century
    'boundary of a shrine'
    (of Codrus, Neleus
    and Basile?)
18. Small temple(?)
    In Christokopidou Street
19. Small archaic
    shrine at Poulopoulou 29
20. Tritopatreion

Fig. 4. Archaeologically located temples and sanctuaries in Athens, excluding those of the Acropolis and Agora.

and Pnyx stood up within what scholarship has termed the industrial region west and north-west of the acropolis. In and among houses and workshops are shrines: those of Amynos, Artemis Aristoboule and two more of unidentified ownership (heroes?) have been located on the ground;[12] that of Heracles Alexikakos known from literary sources must have been somewhere hereabouts. We know that in colonial foundations it was normal for minor shrines to be located cheek by jowl with houses, but an additional factor in Athens is that the city was divided into five demes, which may each have wished to have some sanctuaries that they could consider their own; the little temple of Artemis Aristoboule was certainly in the city deme of Melite, and it was a prosperous man of Melite, Neoptolemus, who in the fourth century paid for its repair.[13] Perhaps we need to think even of Melite in terms of a centre and a periphery ... such possibilities defy exploration. We are left with the negative formulation used above that these were cults which could do their work without reinforcement by a prominent central site.

The large sweeps of the city between the agora and the walls to north and east have yielded very little: perhaps a sanctuary of Heracles quite close to the agora, and further to the north-east a fine altar of Zeus Phatrios and nearby, probably, the shrine of 'Hero Doctor'.[14] It is doubtless fair to assume that there were no major sanctuaries in these parts. (None of the sanctuaries in the residential and industrial district just discussed can count as major, either.) But many lesser shrines, hero-shrines above all, may lie hidden. Heroes did not shun prestigious locations such as acropolis and agora, but could be found almost anywhere.[15]

I turn to the agora. As is well known, a number of sizeable classical temples, and one monumental altar, were brought block by block from other locations and re-assembled in the agora in or near the reign of Augustus. This singular phenomenon is often and rightly taken as an index of the dereliction of the Attic countryside, where these masterpieces of fifth-century architecture had now become surplus to requirements. But in a different perspective we can note that the agora was now for the first time well stocked with conspicuous temples. The Hephaesteum, the one temple comparable in splendour to those

---

[12] See Travlos, *Pictorial Dictionary*, fig. 219 (and 28); the localization there accepted for Herakles Alexikakos is controversial. For the anonymous shrines (Poulopoulou 29; Vassilis 18–20) see *Athenian Religion*, 74, n. 25. Also in Melite was the Eurysakeion. On the region near the Pnyx see H. Lauter-Bufe and H. Lauter, *AM* 86 (1971), 101–24.

[13] The Amyneion, however, was certainly administered by orgeones, not the deme. The grisly facts about contemporary Melite (repository for executed corpses and for nooses and garments of those hanged) recorded by Plutarch in this context (*Them.* 22. 2) are puzzling: surely such things would not have happened inside the walls in the 5th c., but why then does Plutarch mention them?

[14] Travlos, *Pictorial Dictionary*, 274, 573 with fig. 219. Note too *ArchDelt* 19 (1964), *Chron.* 50–2 (Boersma, *Building Policy*, 168), for traces of a temple (?) in Odos Christokopidou, a little beyond Odos Ermou if one moves north from the agora.

[15] On the shrines of the ten eponymous heroes see *Athenian Religion*, 119, n. 62; Jones, *Associations*, 156–61.

imported in the Augustan period, overlooked the agora but was not one of the buildings that actually abutted the open central square; it looked also towards the adjacent inner Ceramicus, and the potters and craftsmen whose patron Hephaestus was. Other temples (of Apollo Patroos, and of the Mother of the Gods; some think of Zeus Phratrios too) were small, if important. One sizeable building was consecrated to a god, but it was a stoa, that of Zeus Eleutherios, not a temple. What used to be identified as a lawcourt has now been assigned to a hero, Aeacus.[16] Aeacus enjoyed an unpredictable prominence if the identification is sound, perhaps in consequence of the singular circumstances in which his cult was introduced, but this was still not a temple. Two monumental altars or enclosures containing altars are also found. The altar of the Twelve Gods was an appropriate symbolic centre of the whole of Attica: distances were measured from here. Title to the second is disputed, frustratingly, between Aphrodite Ourania and Hermes Agoraios.[17] These altars were one of the many ways in which gods and heroes were evoked in and around the agora: there was also the region of the Herms, there was the monument of the Eponymous Heroes, and several small but not for that reason insignificant hero-shrines were marked off with care. (How frustrating it is not to be able to give a name to these heroes and heroines honoured in so prominent a place!) In the hellenistic period a precinct of Demos and the Graces was carved out on the north-western fringe. The case is not then that the agora was a place without gods. But at Athens it was not a place for monumental religious display, for emphasizing a god's importance to the state through weight of stone.

When the Pisistratids sought to build the largest temple in the world, they located it not in the agora (old or new) but south of the acropolis where, according to Thucydides, sanctuaries had traditionally been sited in good numbers: he names Zeus Olympios, Apollo Pythios, Earth, Dionysus in the Marshes 'and other ancient shrines'.[18] Thucydides speaks vaguely of 'south' but modern speculation concentrates on a more limited zone south-east of the acropolis; it positions here both Thucydides' shrines and a whole series of others, some of which at least are very likely to belong here.[19] The two most important religious zones in Athens are therefore not acropolis and agora, but rather acropolis and this area around and beyond the Olympieum.

[16] See R. Stroud, *The Athenian Grain-Tax Law of 374/3 B.C.* (*Hesperia* suppl. 29, 1998), 85–108.

[17] See M. Osanna, *ASAtene* n.s. 48–9 (1988–9), 73–95; id., *Ostraka* 1 (1992), 215–22, arguing for Hermes against the excavators.

[18] Thuc. 2.15.3–4; see Judeich, *Topographie*, 55–60 and A. W. Gomme's notes ad loc. I say nothing in this regard of an 'old agora' because I do not now think that the one source who speaks of one (Apollodorus *FGrH* 244 F 113) is at all likely to have had access to information on the subject, or indeed to be doing anything other than engaging in aetiological speculation. The hypothesis that an old agora existed is anything but implausible, but we gain nothing from directing our own speculations on the subject by those of Apollodorus.

[19] For an extreme example see Travlos, *Pictorial Dictionary*, fig. 379. Figure 4 on p. 53 above understates the case, because it omits shrines approximately located in this area by literary sources.

Thucydides' explanation is robust and straightforward: old shrines were located here because this is where the men of old had their homes. In truth we know so little of the history of private habitation in Athens that all arrows here are shot in the dark. Our architectural histories are (perhaps perforce) histories of monuments, not of the growth of a city inhabited by men. One might rather suspect that this was a region kept somewhat reserved for the gods. But whether Thucydides is right or wrong, the sanctuaries extended out beyond the inhabited area. Zeus Olympios was well within the Themistoclean city walls, but the gymnasium of Heracles at Kynosarges and the sanctuary of Aphrodite in the Gardens were outside them, so too apparently the precinct of Apollo Pythios ('Dionysos in the Marshes' is unclear, but we might guess outside). There was a further cluster of shrines at Agra/Agrai across the Ilissus, which here, which will not be a coincidence, is at its closest to the city. At Agrai, Artemis Agrotera and 'Mother' are the main claimants to ownership of the small Ionic temple so charmingly depicted by Stuart and Revett twenty-five years before its final destruction in 1778.[20] In neither case is the reason for an extra-mural location obscure: Artemis Agrotera is (to simplify) a goddess of the wilds, while 'Mother at Agrai' presides over the *Lesser Mysteries*. (But celebration outside the walls was only one way to veil mysteries from profane eyes. How the female mysteries of the *Thesmophoria* were normally kept from view in Attica is unfortunately not clear.) Which-ever of the two asocial deities the temple belonged to, it was only two hundred metres or so distant, across river and walls, from the temple of Olympian Zeus. This was a single, if diversified, sanctuary zone.[21]

Agrai was also host to a major festival, the *Diasia* of Zeus Meilichios, which took the form of a huge penitential picnic.[22] Is it enough to say that a picnic for all the city had necessarily for practical reasons to be celebrated outside it? Or was an external location in some way required by the grimness of the occasion? The sanctuary of Zeus Pankrates, an awe-inspiring figure some-what comparable to Zeus Meilichios, was also outside the walls and beyond the Ilissus, some way to the north east. Eileithyia was yet one more deity honoured at Agrai, in accord with an attested tendency to locate the shrines of birth-goddesses outside the walls; but she seems also to have had a place or places within them.[23] The main gymnasia (Academy,[24] Lyceum, Heracles at Kynosarges) were all located outside the walls, for reasons that some will

---

[20] See p. 344, n. 76.

[21] According to Jameson, 'Sacred Space', 489, it was the walls of the acropolis that had symbolic value in the classical city, not the extended defensive walls.

[22] See p. 466.

[23] Eileithyia at Agrai: Clidemus *FGrH* 323 F 1, *IG* II² 5099; but for further sites see Paus. 1.18.5 and *Agora* XIX L 6.98. The many dedications have very varied provenances. Attested tendency: Bremmer, *Greek Religion*, 36, n. 20.

[24] Most of the classical cults of the Academy (Paus. 1.30.1–2) relate in different ways to the young who exercise there (Eros, Muses, Hermes; altar of Prometheus, starting place of a torch race).

consider merely practical (exercise requires space), others also symbolic (inchoate citizens belong beyond the walls). Not many futher periurban cults can be identified.[25] The precinct of 'Kalliste and Ariste' is just outside the walls on the north-west side of the city. Kalliste and Ariste were, in Pausanias' judgement, forms of Artemis, and the siting of the shrine supports his view, though the dedications attest a concern for women's health rather than the life of the wild. Artemis Soteira too had a home in this area, unfortunately not located precisely.[26] Also nearby was the great Ceramicus graveyard, and one wonders whether it is more than coincidence that two cults of Artemis should be located just here. Inside the graveyard were honoured not only the Tritopatores, the collective ancestors, but also (at least in the Roman period) Hecate, a goddess close in many of her forms to Artemis.[27] Yet gods and goddesses, even Artemis, shunned that pollution of death in which Hecate revelled, and the cautious view must be that the proximity of these cults of Artemis to the Ceramicus is indeed just coincidence.

Not a long way beyond the walls to the north lies Kolonos Hippios, with its cluster of local cults memorialized for ever by Sophocles and W. B. Yeats.[28] The cults of Kolonos are the cults of Kolonos, not mere adjuncts to those of Athens, and the men of other periurban demes doubtless felt the same about their own gods and heroes, even if there was no Sophocles to hymn them. The view from the city walls will not then be the proper perspective on such cults. But Athenians went out to the precinct of Poseidon at Kolonos, and Aristophanes can casually allude to the shrine of Genetyllis on cape Kolias as if it were an Athenian shrine like any other;[29] festivals too often took city-dwellers out into the countryside or to the sea-coast. (Let us note in passing that the very numerous coastal sanctuaries of Attica were typically intended to be approached by land. Many were apparently located in these secluded spots because they hosted girls' or women's cults. Among seaside cults other than those of the Piraeus, those that actually relate to the sea or are directed to the needs of seafarers are the exception.[30]) Of the six quadrennial festivals (*penteterides*) listed in *Athenaion Politeia* probably only one, the *Panathenaea*,

[25] For an Ionic temple probably at the site of the ruined church of Hagioi Pantes, just north east of Lykabettos, see Korrés, 'Architektur', 103–6.

[26] Kalliste and Ariste: Paus. 1.29.2; A. Philadelpheus, *BCH* 51 (1927), 155–63; Travlos, *Pictorial Dictionary*, 322. Soteira: IG II^2 1343, 4695 (both found in the Roman 'precinct of Hecate' in the Ceramicus, but in secondary use); A. G. Woodhead, *Hesperia* 28 (1959), 279.

[27] See Knigge, *Kerameikos*, 127–30 on the 'shrine of Hecate' (but I have not found a detailed justification for the identification).

[28] See, in any edition of his collected poems, 'Colonus' Praise', a free rendering of Soph. *OC* 668–719.

[29] Thuc. 8.67.2; it was apparently 'the Posidonion' beside which decrees honouring cavalry officers were displayed, *SEG* XXI 525.43. Genetyllis: see p. 432, n. 58.

[30] The sanctuaries at Sunium and perhaps those of Apollo at Cape Zoster and Prasiai can count as such. But for women's cults by the sea note, in addition to Genetyllis at Cape Kolias, the Artemis sanctuaries of Brauron, Munichia and Halai Araphenides and the coastal celebrations of

was held in the city; one was outside Attica altogether, on Delos, while three others were near its limits (at Eleusis, Brauron, and the Amphiareum at Oropus); the sixth, the *Herakleia*, was probably held at Marathon, though a location nearer the city cannot be altogether excluded.[31] And there were processions to Skiron, to Phaleron and to the Piraeus at annual festivals. No line can be drawn around the city to mark the point at which we pass from 'Athenian' to 'Attic' religion.

If any cult anywhere in Attica might in principle serve the needs either of Athenians at large or of local residents only, it would certainly be desirable to sort the attested cults between the two groups. And many cases are clear. At the sacrifices listed in deme calendars, non-members of the deme were not entitled to a cut of meat except by special permission. The *penteterides* just mentioned, by contrast, were organized by state magistrates and were open to all. They constituted, among other things, a statement about the unity of Attica. There is a grey area in the middle, so coloured partly because of the unclarity of our evidence, partly because the reality itself was complicated. Several sites of the Attic countryside received in the third quarter of the fifth century temples of a splendour that seems to imply more than local pretensions, and would have placed a strain on local financial resources.[32] Prima facie then we might expect state involvement in the cults of Poseidon at Sunium, Nemesis at Rhamnus, Athena Pallenis at Pallene and perhaps Demeter at Thorikos (if the mysterious Doric building in the plain there, hybrid of temple and stoa, is indeed hers); the cult of Artemis Tauropolos at Halai Araphenides will fall on the borderline of this category, while that of Apollo at Cape Zoster will illustrate by contrast, with its humble late sixth century (?) temple, never replaced, what a deme could achieve from its own resources.[33]

Thesmophoria at Halimus and/or Eleusis. De Polignac has proposed two models for the interpretation of coastal sanctuaries, that they mark out the confines of territory controlled by a community, and that they are places of international encounter and exchange. He himself applies the latter model to Attica (in A. Verbanck-Piérard and D. Viviers, *Culture et cité*, Brussels 1995, 93), but the former seems to me much more appropriate. The exchanges implied by the common narrative motif of 'women snatched by pirates/enemies while celebrating rites' are strictly involuntary!

[31] Arist. *Ath. Pol.* 54.7, with the notes of Rhodes ad loc.

[32] A. Burford, 'The economics of Greek temple building', *PCPS* n.s. 2 (1965), 21–34, reckons a cost of 40–50 talents for a temple such as Poseidon's at Sunium. The total for capital in the mid 5th-c. accounts of Nemesis is a bit less than 10 talents (*IG* I³ 248 (ML 53) 38); the gap seems rather large to be made up in a small community by the kind of subscription which Burford envisages (cf. the attested totals listed by L. Migeotte, *Les Souscriptions publiques dans les cités grecques*, Geneva 1992, 349).

[33] On the first four see e.g. Camp, *Athens*, 108–17 (on Athena Pallenis cf. p. 398, n. 43); on Cape Zoster Travlos, *Bildlexikon*, 468 [+], 477; Goette, *Attica*, 197. On the temple of Artemis at Halai see M. B. Hollinshead, *AJA* 89 (1985), 435–8 [+], who writes, 436, 'not only the size, but also the conception and execution of this temple are decidedly modest'. Important if enigmatic are the finds of fine Ionic capitals, implying small temples, at Acharnai, Jeraka and on Penteli: Korrés, 'Architektur', 112.

This prima facie presumption is strengthened, in the cases of Poseidon at Sunium and Nemesis at Rhamnus, by the dramatic position of their temples at the two tips of east Attica; surely, we feel, these monumental markers of the two limits of Attic territory were not intended merely for local eyes. 'Poseidon prayed to at Sunium', as Aristophanes calls him, was certainly present to the imagination of many Athenians.[34] But, if we then apply the two further most relevant criteria, the picture becomes blurred.[35] Festivals attended by non-locals are attested for Sunium (though rather shakily), for Halai Araphenides, and for Pallene; this last, however, is not a state festival of familiar type, but one based originally on a league of demes in a crescent from north to east of Athens.[36] External participation in the *Nemeseia* at Rhamnus only began, to our knowledge, when Lycurgus established the new model ephebate in the fourth century; about Thorikos nothing relevant is known. As for administration, there are signs of city involvement at Sunium and Pallene, but the Rhamnusians and men of Halai Araphenides seem to have run their own goddesses' affairs and to have seen their festivals as belonging, significantly if not exclusively, to the deme; Thorikos again is a blank.[37]

Were the evidence fuller, it might emerge that Poseidon at Sunium belonged unambiguously with Artemis of Brauron as a god of city rather than of deme. But the ambiguities relating to Nemesis and Artemis Tauropolos appear irreducible. In one sense all this matters little. A young Athenian who travelled out to Halai Araphenides in search of amusement at the *Tauropolia* doubtless did not care very much whether he had deme or city to thank for the entertainment. The cult of Demeter and Kore at Eleusis was certainly primarily one of the city; but local residents were proud of it, and the demarch of Eleusis might sometimes be happy to become involved.[38] Yet, if

---

[34] Ar. *Eq.* 560; cf. Eur. *Cycl.* 293–4.

[35] T. Linders, *The Treasurers of the Other Gods in Athens and their Functions* (Meisenheim 1975), 12–16, argues that all cults brought under control of those Treasurers were already state cults: this argument if correct is decisive for Apollo Zoster, Athena Zosteria, Poseidon of Sunium and Athena Pallenis. But the case of Apollo Zoster is controversial (Whitehead, *Demes*, 183, n. 34). The priesthood was apparently reserved for men of Halai Aixonides, and a deme decree praises a priest as if he were answerable to deme alone; it also shows demesmen involved with upkeep of the shrine (*SEG* XLII 112 = RO 46). But a different text has the priest praised by council and people (*AD* 11, 1927–8, 39, no. 3: for a similar case see *IG* II² 2849). Clearly then at some point in the year the priest 'prayed for Athens'. The story that the young Euripides was *pyrphoros* in the cult (p. 00, n. 00) also implies a measure of non-local involvement. (The late theatre seat, *IG* II² 5081, by contrast proves little.) We appear as often to be faced with a hybrid.

[36] Halai: Men. *Epitrep.* 1119; Pallene: *Athenian Religion*, 331. Sunium: Hdt. 6.87 attests for the 6th c. a πεντετηρίς, with a θεωρὶς ναῦς, 'at Sunium'; *IG* I³ 8.18 as read by Lewis gives a τριετηρίς; Lys. 21.5 mentions a ship-race there (festival unspecified); a bronze hydria bears the inscription *ΑΘ[Ε]ΝΑΙΟΙ ΑΘΛΑ ΕΚ ΠΟΣΕΙΔΟΝΙΟ* (Kefalidou, *ΝΙΚΗΤΗΣ*, 117); and the Thorikos calendar *SEG* XXXIII 147.19 records an offering sent from neighbouring Thorikos. But by the 4th c. no regular *theoria* is attested.

[37] Sunium: *IG* I³ 8; Pallene: *Athenian Religion*, 331; Rhamnus: ibid. 26, n. 56; Halai: *SEG* XXXIV 103; on the issues discussed in what follows see now Cole, *Ritual Space*, 92–104.

[38] *IG* II² 949.7 (*Haloa*); local pride: e.g. *IG* II² 1186 and especially Men. *Sik.* 187, where Eleusis is 'the deme of the goddess'; similarly Ar. *Ran.* 886–7. Diodorus comicus fr. 2. 23–4 is a fine instance of blurring: 'the city' honours Heracles splendidly by sacrifices 'in all the demes'.

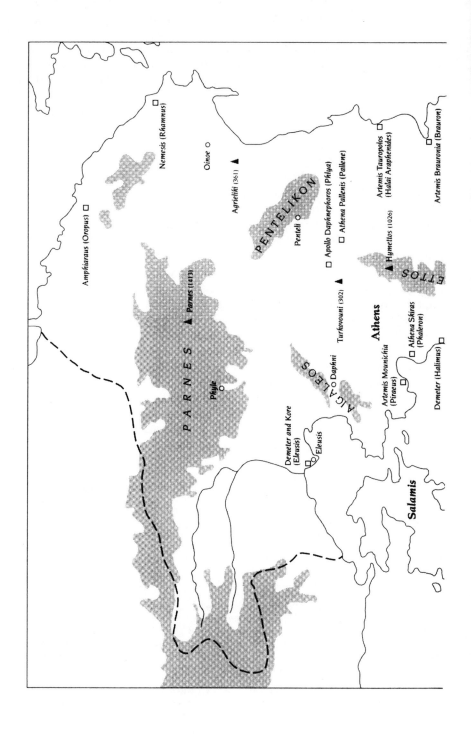

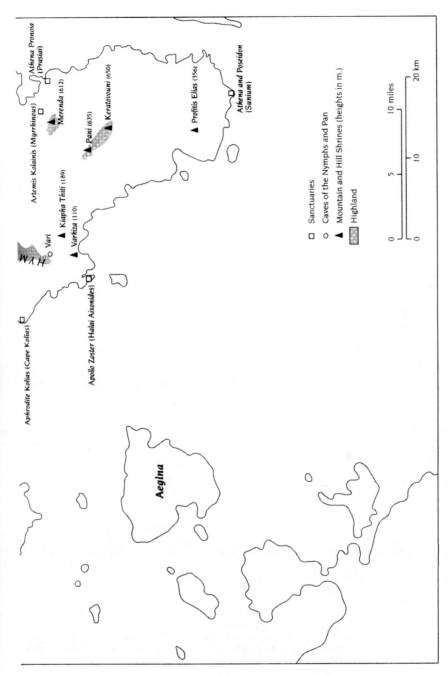

Fig. 5. Caves of Pan, mountain and hill shrines and principal sanctuaries outside Athens and the Piraeus.

the young Athenian at the *Tauropolia* was entitled to a share in sacrificial meat, this had to be paid for by somebody; practical questions always arose which also raised larger issues of inclusion and exclusion. A deme decree from Plotheia of the late fifth century reveals the organizational complexities of religious life with vivid obscurity. The Plotheans belonged to various networks, and had to finance their share in each. What is particularly intriguing here is a special fund established for 'exemption'. Apparently the deme was now going to pay en bloc for its members to participate in certain rites for which hitherto they had been required to contribute individually. The fragments surviving to us of Solon's state calendar of sacrifices reveal three or four instances of local sacrifices paid for by the city; there were doubtless many more.[39] Hybrid forms (festivals organized by one body, but part financed by another) doubtless abounded; *gene* too could be involved. A sharp line of division between city and demes cannot be drawn.

With that warning, we can turn at last to the demes.[40] The best introduction is perhaps a famous passage of Thucydides, in which he deploys all his powerful resources of pathos to describe the feelings of rural Athenians when forced to evacuate the countryside at the start of the Peloponnesian war:

They were distressed and resentful at leaving their houses and the shrines which had been traditionally theirs right from the time of the ancient constitution, and at being forced to change their way of life and to do no less than each abandon his own native city.   (2.16)[41]

'Do no less than each abandon his own native city': such was the emotional significance of leaving his deme to an Attic countryman in 432. Some of the demes were in fact, by most normal criteria except that of political structure, small *poleis*;[42] some had even been called *poleis* before the reforms of Clisthenes changed the nomenclature, Eleusis, for instance, so described in the *Homeric Hymn to Demeter*, Thorikos on the east coast, mentioned as a *polis* by Hecataeus,[43] and the four villages of the Marathon region that made up the so-called Tetrapolis. The identity of some demes was so marked that it

---

[39] Plotheia: *IG* I[3] 258.7, 28–33, with Whitehead, *Demes*, 168–9. Solon: Steph. Byz. s.v. Ἀγνοῦς (fr. 83 Ruschenbusch); *LSS* 19. 20 and 86 (Porthmos, near Sunium); Oinoe, in the calendar of Nicomachus (*BSA* 97, 2002, 365, fr. 12.4 and ? 10); Callim. fr. 103 Pf. with A. S. Hollis, *ZPE* 93 (1992), 7 (the 'hero at the stern' of Phaleron).

[40] What follows is a reworking of my article 'Festivals of the Attic Demes', in T. Linders and G. Nördquist (eds.), *Gifts for the Gods* (Stockholm 1987), 137–44; an appendix, 144–7, containing a translation and discussion of the Thorikos calendar, is not repeated here. For fuller details Whitehead, *Demes*, 176–222, is a basic resource. The possibility that units smaller than demes, *komai*, might also have had cults is considered by S. D. Lambert, *ZPE* 130 (2000), 75–80. I do not exclude it, but the attested cult groupings with names such as Tetrakomoi combined *komai* that under Clisthenes became demes.

[41] I have tried to translated the last phrase in the light of D. Whitehead's argument in *CQ* 51 (2001), 604–6.

[42] So S. Hornblower, *The Greek World, 479–323 B.C.*, ed. 3 (London 2002), 134.

[43] *Hymn. Hom. Dem.* 114, 151; *FGrH* 1 F 126.

gave rise to deme-jokes, about the litigiousness of the Prospaltians or the big talk of the men of Diomeia, for instance.[44]

Not all the demes were of such ancient renown as Eleusis and Thorikos; and 'deme-jokes' remind us that all demes were different. Size, typical mode of livelihood of inhabitants, and distance from Athens all varied drastically, and these variations cannot but have affected religious life[45] even if we cannot confidently track the consequences. It is unfortunate that the demes we know best, from the survival of their calendars, all chance to be located some way from Athens. The pattern of settlement within country demes is another striking variable.[46] (The matter is controversial and the picture changes constantly, but it seems certain that no universal form will be identified.) Unmistakable 'villages' are still there to be seen at two sites in Attica today, Thorikos and Ano Voula (ancient Halai Aixonides). But this simple picture needs to be complicated in several ways. Halai Aixonides was made up (again the evidence is on the ground) not of one village but of two, divided by about 400 metres of clear ground; and in the territory of Thorikos too further outlying settlements may have been identified.[47] It seems to have been common for a deme to have consisted of several distinct clusters of habitation; the lesser villages which formed part of a classical deme sometimes emerged with their own names in the extended class of 'late Roman demes'. We must also doubtless allow (though controversy on this point is at its most intense) that isolated farms were a not unfamiliar feature of the Attic landscape.[48] The extreme case is the deme of Atene in south-west Attica, which, it has been argued, consisted simply of isolated farms with no centre of habitation at all. But the spaces between plots recorded in the Mesogaia can also be so large (120 to 250 metres) that, even if these plots show some clustering, the distinction between 'nucleated' and 'dispersed' settlement loses its clarity.

---

[44] See Haussoullier, *Vie municipale*, 196–200; Whitehead, *Demes*, 333.

[45] For a less static and less synthetic account than mine see Humphreys, 'Demes'.

[46] See above all G. Steinhauer, 'παρατηρήσεις στην οικιστική μορφή των αττικών δήμων', in *Athens and Attica*, 175–90; on Halai, I. Andreou, 'ο δήμος των Αιξωνίδων Αλών', ibid. 191–210; Lauter, *Landgemeinden*, 27–70; Lohmann, *Atene*, 129–34; on the Mesogaia G. Steinhauer in *Mesogaia*, 81–139, esp. 128–9; on S. W. Attika Lohmann, *Atene*, passim (for Atene without a centre esp. 126–9; see too an overview in English in B. Wells (ed.), *Agriculture in Ancient Greece*, Stockholm 1992, 29–58); on Sunium Goette, *Sounion*, 114–16; on komai or subordinate villages Lauter, op. cit., 131–51; Lohmann, *Atene*, 134–6; S. D. Lambert, *Rationes Centesimarum* (Amsterdam 1997), 220–1.

[47] M. Oikonomakou, *ArchDelt* 46 (1991), Chron. 67–9. I accept the common view that the two villages at Ano Voula both belong to Halai, but the point is not beyond the reach of doubt (Lauter, *Landgemeinden*, 150—but he inclines, 146, to follow the received view).

[48] On the archaeological issues see in brief the discussions after the papers of Osborne and Lohmann in Wells, op. cit. in n. 46. On the literary evidence see J. Roy, *Liverpool Classical Monthly* 13 (1988), 57–9 (on Demosthenes 55) and id. in J. Salmon and G. Shipley (eds.), *Human Landscapes in Classical Antiquity* (London 1996), 98–118 (on Eur. *El.* and Men. *Dysc.*). On the whole topic see esp. the *mise au point* by R. Osborne, *Topoi* 6 (1996), 54–7; contrast now Jones, *Rural Athens*, 17–47.

Yet we have no reason to suppose that even Atene failed to work as a community.[49] The political system established by Clisthenes imposed a structure. And as far as we can tell all demes were busily active as religious groupings. Of about forty-five demes from which we have relevant documents of any type, about thirty demonstrably had cults of their own; probably no other aspect of deme life is, in our random evidence, so consistently attested. Radical scepticism is not called for. Two little demes that shared a bouleutic quota of just three have recently turned out also to share two festivals of Heracles, and we might suspect here a trace of the difficulties faced by small communities in running a varied ritual programme from their own resources. But a text which reveals, as we have already noted, multifarious religious activities comes from one of the smallest of all the demes, Plotheia.[50] How to pay for cult was always a problem. That preoccupation dominates the decree from Plotheia, and it underlies too two of our main sacrificial calendars from the demes: that from Erchia is divided rather arbitrarily into five columns of equal cost, apparently so that each could be assigned to a separate local liturgist, while the calendar of the Marathonian Tetrapolis bears on its back a list of contributions to a fund doubtless intended to finance the sacrifices listed on the front.[51] Financing cult was a struggle, but the demes seem to have made shift and managed.

In many respects the religious life of a deme can be seen as that of a mini polis, comparable on a small scale to that of Athens itself. Cult was a recognized public activity of the deme: sacrifices were made 'on behalf of' the deme, the assembly debated questions of cult, and performing the sacrifices was a part, a large part probably, of the official responsibilities of the demarch.[52] The demesmen probably assembled much more often for religious purposes than for political. The demarch shared ritual duties with priests and priestesses, who, whatever their precise manner of appointment, were certainly treated as being answerable to deme officials and the assembly of the deme. A single deme could have several priests and priestesses; an extraordinary fourth-century text apparently from Aixone which has been discovered bit by bit regulated, at the last count, the perquisites due to no less than six priestesses and three priests.[53] As at the national level, these local priests

---

[49] Contrast Cohen, *Athenian Nation*, 112–29, 'Anonymity and Mobility: The Reality of Deme Life'. Cohen argues that so many Athenians lived away from their deme of registration ('hereditary deme' as he calls it) that the effective entity must have been the informal 'territorial deme'; this sounds plausible a priori, but scarcely accounts for the evidence.

[50] *SEG* XXXIX 148, a joint decree of Kydantidai and Ionidai; *IG* I³ 258.

[51] So S. Lambert, *ZPE* 130 (2000), 66, following S. Dow.

[52] 'On behalf of': *IG* I³ 258.26–7; *Hesperia* 8 (1939), p. 178, lines 9–10; *SEG* XLIII 26 A 4; cf. *IG* II² 1215.18. Assembly: *IG* I³ 258; *IG* II² 1183 (RO 63) 32–6. Demarch: e.g. *IG* I³ 244 (*LSCG* 10) A 13, C 2–4: see further Whitehead, *Demes*, 128. In *SEG* XLIII 26 A the demarch is replaced, surprisingly, by the *tamias*.

[53] On the probable infrequency of political deme assemblies see Hausoullier, *Vie municipale*, 6–7; but Whitehead, *Demes*, 90–2, stresses the deficiencies in our evidence. Priests: see R. Garland, *BSA* 79 (1984), 108–9. Whitehead, *Demes*, 180–5, points out that local election of priests is only

might have a set of *hieropoioi* to assist them, and they even retained financial responsibilities of a kind that in the city had mostly been transferred to special commissions.[54] There were of course temples and sacred precincts: a lease issued by the Teithrasians of eastern Attica mentions, just to locate a piece of land, a Herakleion, a precinct of Zeus, a Koreion and a 'property of the hero Datylos', and there were at least a dozen sacred sites at Erchia, even if some of them may have been little more than a rough-hewn altar in a field.[55] Repairs to shrines, and how to pay for them, are naturally a concern that appears in the deme decrees. Two familiar financial practices of state religion, the leasing of temple precincts and the loaning of temple capital, are also found in the demes: the Piraeans in the fourth century had the cultivable areas around their Theseion, Thesmophorion and further unnamed precincts out to lease, while in the 440s 9-10 talents belonging to Nemesis at Rhamnus were on loan to private borrowers.[56] And local cults seem to be financed in the same complex mix of ways as state cults, by a blend of specific endowments, taxes, general public income, locally organized liturgies and the contributions of 'honour-loving' individuals.[57]

The sacrificial calendars of the demes (more cautiously, 'some demes'), like that of the city, listed complex and varied programmes of sacrifices running throughout the year. The earliest surviving specimen is probably that from Thorikos, which appears to date from the 430s.[58] The evidence for such deme calendars is now quite abundant, whereas clear examples do not survive of comparable calendars published by other bodies to which all Athenians

---

demonstrable in one case (Dem. 57. 46–8, 62, Halimus); in theory then they could have been provided by *gene*. But they were subject to orders from the deme. Aixone: A. Matthaiou, *Horos* 10–12 (1992–8), 133–69, adds a new fragment to *IG* II² 1356 (*LSCG* 28) and assigns the text to Aixone; a further large fragment is published by Steinhauer, Ἱερὸς νόμος Αἰξωνέων'. The text remains incomplete at the start; at least one further officiant, probably a priestess, was there mentioned; further priests and priestesses from Aixone appear in *IG* II² 1199 (n. 85 below). For priests/priestesses see too *IG* II² 1175, and three priestesses mentioned in the Erchia deme calendar *LSCG* 18 α 21, cf. ε 7 (Heroines—the same priestess, presumably, serves in two places), α 50, cf. δ 39 (Dionysus and Semele), β 38 (Hera). (S. Dow argues, *BCH* 89, 1965, 207, that priests are not mentioned at Erchia because their title to perquisites is self-evident; but this is not very compelling). On priestesses (and women in general) in deme religion see Jones, *Associations*, 123–32.

[54] *IG* II² 1199; 1183 (RO 63) 27–32.   [55] *SEG* XXIV 151; *LSCG* 18, *passim*.
[56] Repairs: *IG* II² 1215. Leasing: *IG* II² 2498. Loans: *IG* I³ 248 (ML 53).
[57] Endowments: *SEG* XXVIII 103; taxes: *IG* II² 1215 (a levy on office-holders for repairs); general income: *IG* I³ 258; liturgies: n. 51 above, and Whitehead, *Demes*, 152, 171–5; benefactors: *IG* II² 1215. On the whole subject of cult finance see Whitehead, *Demes*, 163–775.
[58] *SEG* XXXIII 147 (*IG* I³ 256 bis, p. 958); important new readings in Jameson, 'The spectacular and the obscure', 329–30. The text itself proves neither that it was issued by Thorikos nor by a deme at all, though both points seem to me probable: cf. S. D. Lambert, *ZPE* 139 (2002), 81, n. 21, citing Jameson and expressing doubts also about the Erchia calendar. On the date see D. M. Lewis, *ZPE* 60 (1985), 108, n. 3; M. Jameson in C. R. Whittaker (ed.), *Pastoral Economies in Classical Antiquity* (PCPS suppl. vol. 14 1988), 115, n. 7; the high dating is supported by the feminine dative plurals in -ησι (cf. H. T. Wade-Gery, *JHS* 51, 1931, 78–83; W. S. Barrett's note on Eur. *Hipp*. 101), as Martin West has pointed out to me.

belonged, phratry, tribe and (a doubtful case aside)[59] trittyes. Phratries and tribes certainly had religious functions, and phratries may have had more before the epigraphic record begins, but it looks as if, at least from about the middle of the fifth century, the two most important levels of religious organization in Attica were deme and city.[60]

Just what took place at the sacrifices so curtly and drily listed in the calendars is often obscure. Some must have been the occasion of an institution attested in a variety of sources, a communal deme banquet or ἑστίασις. The men of Plotheia resolve, for instance, that sweet wine should be provided, from public funds, at all the communal rites (ἱερὰ τὰ κοινά) at which the Plotheans feast together. Sometimes the demes bestow on outsiders who live in the deme the right to receive a portion of meat, a μερίς, at feasts of this kind ('except in shrines which Piraeans but no one else may enter', adds one striking example).[61] Such grants of *communio sacrorum* to favoured aliens are sometimes made by true *poleis*. Individuals too sometimes 'feasted their demesmen' (whether voluntarily, or in fulfilment of a liturgy, is not certain).[62] If every offering listed in a calendar, barring those where a victim was to be burnt whole or even sold, was destined for the demesmen en masse, then we would have to envisage, for an average deme, perhaps twenty such banquets each year. But in a deme of, say, three hundred adult males, a single sheep would not have made for a very sumptuous feast. The lesser offerings may have been reserved for officers of the deme, in company possibly with a specified subdivision of the demesmen.[63] A blend of worship by participation and worship by proxy is characteristic of the practice of the city; in cases of proxy the priests or magistrates who conducted the sacrifice reported to the

---

[59] *IG* I³ 255, on which see Jameson's notes and now S. D. Lambert, *ZPE* 130 (2000), 71–5. On the problem of whether trittyes had cults see *Athenian Religion*, 103, n. 4.

[60] Cf. *Athenian Religion*, 107; on 115 I also postulate, much more speculatively, an important religious role for pre-Clisthenic 'proto-demes'. For an overview of the deme calendars see Whitehead, *Demes*, 185–204.

[61] Plotheia: *IG* I³ 258.34–36. Portion: *IG* II² 1187.20–23 (Eleusis), 1204.12–16 (Lamptrai), 1214.11–17 (Piraeus). In *IG* II² 1183 (RO 63) 32–6 the demarch of Hagnous (?) is required to sacrifice 'the *plerosia*' on a date lost ([πέμπτ]ει editors; I would prefer [ἑβδόμ]ει despite the pointless repetition it creates) and on the 7th to distribute the meat τοῖς π[αροῦσιν κ]/αὶ συναγοράζουσιν καὶ συνενεχυράζουσιν. ... The final word appears, extraordinarily, somehow to involve the demesmen assembled for their feast in loan transactions regulated earlier in the text.

[62] *Communio*: see L. and J. Robert, *Fouilles d'Amyzone en Carie* (Paris 1983), 123; N. F. Jones, *Public Organization in Ancient Greece* (Philadelphia 1987), 400. Feasting demesmen: Men. *Sicyonius* 184–6, with Sandbach's note. Feasting the demesmen's wives at the *Thesmophoria* was a liturgy, Isae. 3.80.

[63] Twenty banquets: so Rosivach, *Public Sacrifice*, 34–5. On attested subdivisions of demes see *IG* II² 1203, 1214.18; Whitehead, *Demes*, 147–8, and, for the newly attested *pentekostyes* of Aixone, Steinhauer, 'Ἱερὸς νόμος Ἀιξωνέων', 159, Lines 36–7. The Erchia law has a few specifications about recipients of meat: *LSCG* 18 A 48–50, B 49–51, C 35–7, D 36–8, E 36–8. Sale of meat: six offerings in the Thorikos calendar are marked πρατόν, which I take to mean 'saleable' as e.g. πλωτός means 'navigable' (on –τος formations see W. S. Barrett's note on Eur. *Hipp.* 677–9): this against the doubts of Rosivach, op. cit., 23, n. 40. Cf. *IG* I³ 244 C 18. Jameson, 'The spectacular and the obscure', 329–31, argues that offerings made outside the deme or on its margins, at places inconvenient for a feast, tended to be sold.

boule on its successful outcome, and the boule resolved to 'accept the good things that had occurred in the sacrifice'. In just the same way we find the demarch of the Icarians being praised for having 'performed all the sacrifices' and 'reported that they all turned out well'.[64] Here too, it seems, a verbal report was used to transfer the divine favour secured by a vicarious sacrifice to the general good.

A decree of Skambonidai appears to grant metics equal rights with demesmen at one sacrifice. As this is almost the only decree of a city-deme to survive, it might indicate a broader tendency within the city. On the other hand, the grants mentioned above of *communio sacrorum* to favoured aliens show that, in the demes concerned, only demesmen had an automatic right to a cut of the sacrificial meat. It need not follow that non-demesmen were excluded from every aspect of deme festivities: at the *Rural Dionysia* all-comers were certainly free to attend local dramatic productions, if perhaps on payment. Whether informal conventions allowed broader participation on other occasions we can only guess. A policy of complete exclusion would have been remarkable, given that at least in demes in or near the city there must have lived not merely many metics but many citizens registered in other demes.[65]

One would like to be able to locate the many cult acts of a deme in a landscape. But sacrifices known from inscriptions can seldom be associated with cult places still visible on the ground; when the calendars give topographical indications, these usually convey little to us, whereas both the divine and the human proprietors of surviving rustic sanctuaries[66] tend to be unknown. Textually, much the most suggestive evidence is that of the Erchian calendar. Every sacrifice is given a location. Apart from a vague and very frequent 'at Erchia', we find as sites for offerings four sanctuaries (Pythion; Delphinion; [shrine] of Hekate; [shrine] of Hera: used once each[67]), the agora (used once, for Hermes), eight places within the deme and one (Hymettus) outside it; there are also five sacrifices on two days in Athens itself. Of the places within the deme, the only two that host more than one sacrifice or sacrificial cluster are 'Hill' (Pagos), which is used four times, and 'Acropolis' (Polis), used twice. In reference to both these places the definite article is omitted because, we assume, there could be no doubt what Polis and Pagos were being referred to; these must have been very familiar

---

[64] *SEG* XXII 117.

[65] Skambonidai: *IG* I³ 244 C 7–9: strangely, the sacrifice is one for which exclusivity might have been predicted, to the tribal hero Leos. *Rural Dionysia*: Pl. *Resp.* 475d. On the problem see Whitehead, *Demes*, 205; for maximalist assumptions about metic participation see Cohen, *Athenian Nation*, 73, 123–4.

[66] No synthetic treatment exists; a promised work by U. Linnemann has not been published. The catalogue in A. Mersch, *Studien zur Siedlungsgeschichte Attikas von 950 bis 400 v. Chr.* (Frankfurt 1996), 91–232, is useful for the period covered, as are, for their regions, Lohmann, *Atene*; Goette, *Sounion*; Lauter, *Landgemeinden*. I cannot begin to survey the archaeological evidence here.

[67] By 'used once' I mean used on one day, though perhaps for more than one sacrifice.

landmarks, like the Polis and (Areo)pagos of Athens, which also omit the article.[68] The acropolis of Erchia hosts a mysterious local festival of Athena, the *Erosouria*, and a nameless festival on Skirophorion 3 at which sacrifices were made to Kourotrophos, Aglaurus, Zeus Polieus, Athena Polias, Poseidon, and one other power. Attempts have been made to identify the anonymous event with one of the known Athenian festivals, but what is really striking about the list of recipients is the fidelity with which it evokes the chief gods of the Athenian acropolis.[69] Other demes had sanctuary-bearing hills or mountains in their vicinity, but we cannot know whether they viewed them as an 'acropolis', comparable to that at Athens, in quite this way.[70] The other places named in the calendar (Schoinos, Petre, Sotidai, Pylon, 'the Peak', 'towards Paiania') mostly sound as if they lie away from any deme-centre that Erchia may have had. This leaves no central religious sites at all other than 'Hill' and 'Acropolis',[71] but we can imagine the four named sanctuaries mentioned above (Pythion and the rest) near the centre if we choose; they give no clues as to their location. However that may be, the fidelity with which the Polis and Pagos of Erchia replicate the two high places of central Attica is very striking.

On the ground, easily the most revealing site to consider is that of Halai Aixonides.[72] We noted earlier that the deme seemed to be built from two (at least) separate villages. That to the south-east is full of little sanctuaries: it contains what seems to be a Hekataion at a crossroads, and four small temples (between about 2.85 and 4 metres in length) sometimes and perhaps always situated in their own *temene*. Two of these small temples are in and

---

[68] This in answer to Lohmann's linguistic puzzlement, *Atene* 134, n. 1029. He has forgotten the exact expression used on the stone when, 134, n. 1031, he refers the sacrifices ἐμ Πόλε to the acropolis at Athens: the stone says ἐμ Πόλε Ἐρχιᾶσι. Humphreys, 'Demes', 182, notes the distinctive character of two of the sacrifices on 'Hill' (an all black lamb for Hera Telkhinia; a holocaust for Zeus Epopetes).

[69] So Kearns, *Heroes of Attica*, 26. M. H. Jameson, *BCH* 89 (1965), 156–8, identified the 'one other power' (*LSCG* 18 ε 65 ff.) as Pandrosus and saw the cluster of sacrifices as an Erchian *Arrephoria*; N. Robertson, *HSCP* 87 (1983), 281–2, thinks rather of *Plynteria*.

[70] Steinhauer, *Παρατηρήσεις* (n. 46 above), 184, mentions the relation of Halai Aixonides to Kastraki (below), Anagyrous to Lathuresa, Lamptrai to Panagia Thiti, Sphettos to Christos Koropiou. These cases need to be reviewed one by one. The acropolis at Athens is a few minutes walk from the agora; a walk of an hour or even thirty minutes would quite change the relation. The Mycenaean graves on the acropolis of Thorikos received cult in the archaic period, but I do not know evidence that the acropolis housed other 'deme-protecting' gods, likely though this is. On the topography of Erchia see E. Vanderpool, *BCH* 89 (1965), 21–4 (traces of a temple in the plain); Steinhauer in *Mesogaia*, 93.

[71] Mersch (n. 66), 57, remarks provocatively 'Vor dem 4 Jh. können in Attika fast nur extraurbane Heiligtümer festgestellt werden', and the calendars certainly imply a tendency to scatter altars widely.

[72] See the works of Andreou, Lohmann and Lauter cited in n. 46 above: the fullest discussion is by Lauter (and the best plans are his pl. 29 and 34); excellent plates also in Lohmann. I mention only in a note, as not directly relevant to deme organization, the 'clubhouses' of religious *koina* detected by both Lohmann, 132, and Lauter, 124–5 (but the building on Odos Kalymnou there discussed is now identified as the Aphrodision: n. 74 below); particularly important and puzzling is the house on odos Athinon within the deme cemetery (Andreou, pl. 17).

among houses, two in more open ground on the edge of the village. At least
one more lay at some distance from both villages. These pocket-sized shrines
have been seen as expressions of private piety,[73] but they could have served
deme needs if we are right that many deme sacrifices were attended by only a
representative handful of worshippers; demes may well in fact sometimes
have made use of altars owned by families or other groups. The north-west
village contains a larger if still modest temple (8.50 × 5.75 metres) built so
close to contemporary housing that the whole has been seen as a single
complex, 'sacred house with temple enclosed'. However that may be, the
temple can fortunately now be identified epigraphically as the Aphrodision of
Halai, an important sanctuary where decrees of the deme were sometimes
displayed.[74] Uniquely,[75] a second sanctuary controlled by the deme and used
as a place of display is also known, that of Apollo Zoster at Cape Zoster three
kilometres or so south of the villages; the quite well-preserved small temple
(10.8 × 6 metres), still visitable within a bathing establishment at Vouliag-
meni, is perhaps the most evocative monument of this local religion that now
survives. So at Halai both 'urban' and 'extra-urban' sanctuaries are unambiguously attested. A kilometre or so south of the south-east village rose a
hill, Kastraki, which was certainly built on in antiquity and might, it has
been suggested, have served the Haleans as an acropolis.[76] That it might
have hosted a cult is far from implausible, but we cannot be sure that there
was, so to speak, an acropolis function that needed to be discharged in
every deme.

Archaeologically, the two most familiar types of cult site in rural Attica are
mountains and caves; and both have a certain connection with the demes.
Once a year some Erchians left their own territory to sacrifice to Zeus of the
Heights on Hymettus; perhaps they went to one of the two small but well-
preserved temples (honorand unknown) on Hymettus' east slopes above
Koropi. No calendar lists an offering to Pan, but Menander's *Dyscolus* takes

---

[73] Lauter, *Landgemeinden*, 124. Only one shrine amid houses has been identified at Thorikos to
my knowledge, and the identification has been contested (*Athenian Religion*, 176, n. 80).

[74] See G. Steinhauer, *AM* 113 (1998), 235–40 (*SEG* XLIX 141–3). Single complex: Lauter,
Landgemeinden, 47–49. IG II² 2820 is a 4th-c. dedication to Aphrodite made by the twenty-four
men of Halai who were elected by their demesmen to 'make the statue for Aphrodite' and were
crowned by them on completion. The findspot was Athens, but all logic seems to suggest that the
original place of dedication was the Halai Aphrodision (particularly if the object dedicated was in
fact the statue).

[75] What is unique is the possibility of identifying two deme sanctuaries on the ground (several
demes may have had more than one place of display: for Aixone see A. Matthaiou, *Horos* 10–12,
1992–8, 167–8). The only other surviving sanctuaries that I can think of which definitely
belonged to demes are the Pythion of the Icarians, so identified by an inscription (*IG* II² 4976),
and the cave of Pan at Phyle (Travlos, *Bildlexikon*, 319, 325–6), associated with the deme by
Menander (*Dysc.* 3). The Icarian Pythion can be allowed to bring the neighbouring Dionysiac
monuments with it (Travlos, *Bildlexikon*, 85–90). Then there are the perhaps hybrid cases,
Artemis Tauropolos and others (above, n. 33).

[76] So I. Andreou in *Athens and Attica*, 195–6.

Fig. 6. The Temple of Apollo Zoster.

place in the vicinity of what is described as the 'Paneion of the Phylasians'.[77] Such sanctuaries have therefore a place in the life of the demes, but not apparently a hugely important one. Explanations for this lack of prominence are available: perhaps the cult of Pan functioned primarily at the level of families, as we see in Menander's play; as for mountain sanctuaries, it is generally believed that their acme had passed even by the fifth century and that cult at many had ceased completely by the fourth.[78] There is doubtless some truth in both hypotheses. But there may be truth also in the proposition that cults of mountain and of cave have a false prominence in the archaeo-logical record because they are easy to detect. The calendars reveal them for what they were, just some among a vast range of possibilities.

From sites I now turn to gods worshipped (or 'gods and heroes' as a decree of Acharnae more properly puts it). As a mini polis, each deme had its own pantheon, what Sophocles calls, in a unique variant on the familiar idea of gods who protect the city, 'deme-holding' (δημοῦχοι) gods.[79] Any deme's gods

[77] *LSCG* 18 E 58–64; Men. *Dysc.* 3. On such cults see *Athenian Religion*, 29, n. 3, 164, n. 38; on the constituencies served by the mountain cults also now A. d'Onofrio, *Annali di Archeologia e Storia Antica*, n.s. 2 (1995), 57–88. The classical material from the shrine on Kiaphi Thiti has now been published by J. Christiansen, *Kiapha Thiti* III.1 (*MarbWPr* 1996, 2000); very unusually, the votive material (female figurines, votive *poloi*, one loomweight) suggests a female recipient, identified by Christiansen as the Nymphs.

[78] On the problem see recently the differing positions of Lohmann, *Atene*, 120–1 and Lauter, intr. to *Kiapha Thiti* III.1 (previous note), 13–15.

[79] Soph. *OC* 458. *Demos* here is poised between 'people' and 'deme'. Acharnae: *SEG* XLIII 26 A 3–4.

and heroes are a blend of some who might be worshipped anywhere and others of merely local appeal. Thus through its pantheon a deme could assert its specific identity and interests without declaring total independence from the larger Attic or Greek world.[80] The proportion of local to pan-Attic gods and heroes varies from deme to deme. Erchia has few distinctively Erchian cults, but even at Erchia a nugget of local myth has recently been shown to underlie a sacrifice to the hero Epops.[81] In other calendars, the largest offerings, the ones that unquestionably brought together the demesmen for a feast, are often made to local figures. The identifiable recipients of bovines in the calendar of Marathon are a hero (name lost), Earth, Aristomachus, Neanias, Athena Hellotis, and Eleusinian Demeter:[82] three heroes, therefore, Athena worshipped under a distinctive local epithet, as Athena Hellotis, and two goddesses, Earth and Demeter, who were often no doubt in the thoughts of the farmers of the region. Not every deme can be shown to have worshipped an 'eponymous' or 'founder' (*archegetes*) hero, but many did,[83] and the founder hero could be the deme's point of contact with the mainstream of Attic and Greek myth. Ikaria was celebrated as the place where Ikarios received Dionysus on the god's arrival in Attica and was taught winemaking by him. The deme's accounts were divided into three funds, Dionysus', Ikarios', and non-sacred;[84] the god and the hero must have dominated the religious life of the deme. One of the most singular local cult complexes was that of Aixone, where Hebe the wife of Heracles occupied the deme's main shrine and had an important festival, and the Herakleidai and Alcmene too were honoured. Tales were told of a 'reception of Heracles' in the deme, even if in the version preserved for us the host is not the deme's founder hero but his grandson.[85]

A strong local emphasis is a particularly striking feature of the calendar from Thorikos.[86] This ancient community had an unusually rich mythology. It was the home of Cephalus, who was carried off as a youth by Dawn and

---

[80] Cf. Osborne, *Demos*, 178–81 (with a different emphasis).

[81] See A. S. Hollis, *ZPE* 93 (1992), 11–13; S. D. Lambert, ibid. 139 (2002), 75–82.

[82] Marathon calendar (*ZPE* 130, 2000, 45–47), A, col. 2, lines 8, 20, 21, 35, 43–4. The recipient in 6 is unknown.

[83] For both points see Whitehead, *Demes* 208–11; see further Kearns, *Heroes of Attica*, 92–102. Since Whitehead wrote, the Heros Archegetes of Sunium has vanished (Goette, *Sounion*, 35), but evidence for the importance of the founder hero at Rhamnus has increased considerably (Petrakos, *Rhamnous*, 117–19; *IRhamnous* 77–82; an unpublished inscr. even attests an *agon* for him, Petrakos, *Rhamnous*, 119) and actual cult of the archegete of Aixone (cf. Whitehead, 210, on Pl. *Lys.* 205d) has been demonstrated (in the new fragment of *IG* II² 1356 published by Steinhauer, Ἱερὸς νόμος Αἰξωνέων'). *IG* II² 1932.11–14 appears to show that the wealthiest cults of Phegaia were those of Menelaus Archegetes and Heracles Archegetes.

[84] *IG* I³ 253. For other deme eponyms who hosted gods (Semachos, Erchios) see Kearns, *Heroes of Attica*, 98 n. 93: as she notes, the absence of Erchios from the Erchian calendar is part of the same problem as the absence from that calendar of Demeter, whom he hosted.

[85] See *IG* II² 1199 (cf. *SEG* XLVI 154); 2492.22; Pl. *Lys.* 205c–d (with 204d); n. 91 below. On the shrine of Hebe, A. Matthaiou, *Horos* 10–12 (1992–1998), 146–69.

[86] See n. 58 above.

later accidentally shot his wife, the king's daughter Procris. According to an obscure variant it was also the home of the nymph Philonis, who was seduced by Hermes and Apollo in the same afternoon, and so became mother both of thieving Autolycus and tuneful Philammon. Off Thorikos lay a long thin island called 'Helen' because there, they said, the union of Paris and Helen was first consummated on the journey from Sparta to Troy. It was at Thorikos that Demeter landed on her arrival in Attica.[87] Cephalus (16, 54), Procris (17, ?56), Philonis (44) and Helen (37) all receive one or more offerings in the calendar, and Demeter is given several (21, 38, 44). (The offerings to Helen and Demeter can, certainly, be explained without reference to local mythology,[88] but any Thorikian who attended the rites is likely to have thought of the myths.) The two largest sacrifices, of oxen, are made to Cephalus and a figure as thoroughly local as the obscure eponymous hero Thorikos (28, 54).[89] Perhaps if we knew more of Thorikian traditions we might be able to interpret two offerings that at the moment are obscure, one to the west-Attic hero Nisus (49), and one to, of all people, Phoenix ('right side', by 13). Sacrifices are also listed to a string of heroes and heroines who apparently guard areas of Thorikian territory, perhaps the heroines of the nearby promontory of Koroneia ('left side', by 58), and certainly 'He above the plain' (Hyperpedios, 48–9) and 'Gatekeeper' (Pylochos, 50–1), both with corresponding heroines; while the Thorikians' maritime interests are in the care of 'Save-ship' (Sosineos, 50).[90] About distinctive rites that may have accompanied such offerings to local figures, at Thorikos or elsewhere, we can usually say nothing. But some rites confined, so far as we know, to a single deme did acquire the distinction of a name. A complete list of Attic festivals should not omit the *Zosteria* of Halai Aixonides, in honour of Apollo Zoster, the *Amarysia* of Athmonon, honouring Artemis Amarysia, the *Areia* of Acharnae, the *Nemesia* of Rhamnus or the mysterious *Erosouria* of Erchia.[91]

---

[87] Cephalus and Thorikos: Pherecydes, *FGrH* 3 F 34, with corrigenda; Apollod. *Bibl.* 2.4.7; Ant. Lib. *Met.* 41. Philonis: Konon, *FGrH* 26 F 1.7. Helen: Eur. *Hel.* 1674 with commentaries ad loc. Demeter: *Hymn Hom. Cer.* 126. For fuller references see J. Labarbe, *Thorikos, Les Testimonia* (Ghent 1977), 15–24.

[88] The sacrifice of a τριττύα to Helen with the Anakes/Dioscuri is attested by Paus. Att. α 111 Erbse, by implication for Attica (cf. Eur. *Or.* 1637); but the Thorikos calendar provides the first epigraphic evidence for Helen cult in Attica, though offerings to τῶ ἄνακε (dual) are common: B. Hemberg, *ΑΝΑΞ ΑΝΑΣΣΑ und ΑΝΑΚΕΣ als Götternamen* (Uppsala 1955), 32–44.

[89] They were surely intended for eating, like so many sacrifices to heroes in Attica: G. Ekroth, *The Sacrificial Rituals of Greek Hero-Cults* (Liège 2002), 150–69. Thorikos the hero was mentioned by Eratosthenes fr. 23 Powell (A. S. Hollis, *ZPE* 93, 1992, 9).

[90] The sense of 'heroines of Koroneans' is obscure. The 'gates' could be a geographical feature (as in Thermopylae), not man-made; but cf. G. Dunst, *ZPE* 25 (1977), 253. On the groups of 'heroines' see Larson, *Heroine Cults*, 31–4.

[91] *SEG* XLII 112.5; *IG* II² 1203.17; *SEG* XXI 519.16; *IRhamnous* 7.9, 17.28; *LSCG* 18 B 28. It is not clear whether the named festivals of *IG* I³ 258.5–9 are local or national. Note too the *Herakleia Spondeia* and *Therina* jointly celebrated by Kydantidai and Ionidai (*SEG* XXXIX 148); for ἑορτή used of a deme festival e.g. *SEG* XXVIII 103.32; *SEG* XLVI 154. At the Aixonian sacrifice to Hebe there was a παννυχίς, *IG* II² 1199. 22.

In spite of all these eagerly cultivated local traditions, the demes were not in fact independent republics. It is to the relation in religious matters between the demes and the true polis of Athens that we must now turn. In the good old days, Isocrates tells us,[92] many demesmen did not even go up to the city for the festivals. Whatever the truth of that nostalgic claim, the clear implication is that in the fourth century countrymen did attend the city rites. Here the image of the deme as a mini *polis* is exposed as a fiction, since the citizens of one city did not attend the rites of another en masse. But does this mean that none of the best-known festivals were celebrated in the demes? We need to differentiate here within the loose traditional category of 'Attic' or 'Athenian' festivals: for—to anticipate a conclusion—some were held in Athens or under Athenian organization alone, others both in Athens and the demes, others again in the demes but not in Athens.[93] (Yet another group was that of festivals held in Eleusis alone.) These distinctions are not casual, but relate to the history and character of the rites themselves. By considering them we can hope to win a perspective on the development of Attic religion, and the place of Athens itself within it.

The first category is that of festivals confined to Athens. The decree of Plotheia distinguishes several types of festival to which the Plotheians as a community make contributions: those of the deme itself, of 'the Epakrians', of the Athenians, and 'quadrennial festivals'. The Epakrians are a reminder of the complexity of this Attic local religion: they were doubtless a confederation of neighbouring demes, either the trittys to which Plotheia belonged or, more probably, an older religious association of a type that is very familiar in Attica. As organizing principles alongside or around the demes, such local 'amphictyonies' (as they have been called) must never be lost from view. Perhaps it was the Epakrians who celebrated the mysterious 'quadrennial festivals' of the decree.[94] But what concerns us here is the reference to 'contributions to the Athenians' made 'on behalf of the community (τὸ κοινόν) of the Plotheians'. That shows that at this date, probably late in the fifth century, the demes or some demes provided sacrificial victims at certain central Athenian festivals. More than one interpretation of that bald fact is possible,[95] but much the most obvious is that the deme sent victims to the festival because its members attended it: this was the local contribution to the pan-Attic *eranos*. It would follow that there was no celebration of the same rites within the deme. City festivals to which the Plotheans contributed perhaps

---

[92] *Areopagiticus* 52.

[93] In this and what follows I am much indebted to Mikalson, 'Demes'.

[94] So M. Guarducci, *Historia* 9 (1935), 211: certainly the easiest interpretation if one presses the wording of the decree (*IG* I³ 258.25–31). Mikalson, 'Demes', 426, thinks of non-annual Plotheian rites; the πεντετηρίδες of the Athenian calendar (Arist. *Ath. Pol.* 54.7) are also possible. Epakrians: see *Athenian Religion*, 330. 'Amphictyonies': Humphreys, 'Demes'.

[95] One could think of merely symbolic deme participation, through an official or two, in the central celebration of a rite which was (*a*) celebrated by the deme in Plotheia; (*b*) celebrated privately in Plotheia; (*c*) not celebrated in Plotheia. But such possibilities lack clear parallels.

included the *Pandia* and the *Anakia*, but the contributory festival that we can name with most confidence is the *Diasia*, which honoured Zeus Meilichios: Thucydides records that it was celebrated πανδημεί, everyone together, at Agrai just outside Athens, and the sacrificial calendar of the deme Erchia duly lists a sheep to be sent up 'for the *Diasia* at Agrai'. This is the only festival to which the country demes are known to have made contributions, though there were surely more; and even here it is not certain that every deme, including the most distant, took part in the central rite.[96] But there is no doubt that many further festivals were celebrated in Athens alone. The *Panathenaea* was one such, very naturally, as it would have been almost a contradiction in terms for such a festival of unity to be celebrated 'by deme' in over a hundred distinct sites up and down Attica. Appropriately, the demarchs organized the great procession, and the meat of the sacrificial animals was distributed 'deme by deme, according to the number of participants sent by each'.[97] And in addition to this special case, where the demes were involved explicitly, there were many spectacular festivals, offering much to see and much to eat,[98] that were surely intended to be pan-Attic: the *Thargelia*, the *Thesea*, the *Bendidea*, the *Olympia*, the *Diisoteria* and others such as these. No local equivalent of any of these city extravaganzas is yet attested, and it would be surprising if one ever is.[99]

Festivals confined to the demes are the second category. The most popular was the *Rural Dionysia*, which was the occasion of the many dramatic performances that took place outside Athens, and is attested in roughly a dozen demes.[100] The city dramatic festivals complemented but did not replace their rustic equivalents; they were held at a different time, and drama seems to have flourished in the countryside for just as long as it flourished in the city.

[96] For πανδημεί in Thuc. 1.126.6 means in context 'en masse', not 'all the demes together'. Erchia: *LSCG* 18 A 38. The city demes are a different matter since they (and some neighbouring ones?) will doubtless have been involved in almost any festival held within the city: *IG* I³ 244, a decree of the city deme Skambonidai, mentions *Dipolieia*, *Panathenaea*, *Synoikia*, perhaps *Kronia* and an otherwise unknown *Epizephyra* (see on this text Humphreys, 'Demes', 145–6). But organizational details are thoroughly obscure. The unwillingness of men from distant demes to visit the city is stressed by Jones, *Associations*, ch. 3, perhaps too strongly (*Athenian Religion*, 77, n. 38). *Anakia* and *Pandia* of Plotheia: *IG* I³ 258.6, 9: but it is not proven that the Plothean rites of these names are those of the city; the *Apollonia* of ibid. line 8 are apparently rites of the Epakreis (*SEG* XXXII 144).

[97] Suda δ 421, *LSCG* 33 (*RO* 81) B 25–7: cf. Dem. 44. 37. It would not be surprising if earlier the demes had contributed to the *Panathenaea*, as the colonies and allies did (Deubner, *Attische Feste*, 34). Whitehead, *Demes*, 136, notes a reference to δημόται in the decree regulating the *Hephaistia* (*IG* I³ 82.12).

[98] *IG* II² 1496; cf. *Athenian Religion*, 78.

[99] The demes seem to have kept their own calendars free at such times, to let the demesmen go to the city: Mikalson, 'Demes', 428; Parke, *Festivals*, 178 (but cf. Whitehead, *Demes*, 187, n. 63 and Humphreys, 'Demes', 141, n. 27). The *Thargelia* (not in *IG* II² 1496) is the least clear case, but I infer city-only celebration from the scale and importance of the competitions. Phratries could meet at the *Thargelia* (Isae. 7.15), but that could in the particular case have been in Athens.

[100] Cf. Mikalson, 'Demes', 433; Whitehead, *Demes*, 212–22; Csapo/Slater, *Ancient Drama*, 121–38.

Another widely diffused rite was the *Proerosia*, the 'before-ploughing' offering, a form of which is now attested in five different demes. There was no equivalent celebration in the city; instead, the Athenians were invited by 'proclamation' to attend the prestigious Eleusinian rite. Three further rites of Demeter which tracked the various stages of the growth of the corn are attested here and there among the demes but not in the city.[101] It was appropriate that these two most popular country festivals should honour Dionysus and Demeter respectively. We see in them outcrops of a deeply embedded religion of farmers and farmers' wives that was more Attic than specifically Athenian.

The final category is that of festivals celebrated both in Athens and in some at least of the demes. Our information here is still tantalizingly fragmentary. The *Thesmophoria* and a group of closely related women's rites, particularly the *Skira*, probably belong to this class. It is not, indeed, decisive that administrative preparations for the *Thesmophoria* were made in the demes,[102] because local organization does not entail local celebration; and the fact that all the demes seem to have administered the *Thesmophoria* in the same way could be thought to hint at centralization. But, to take the strongest cases, it is all but certain that the women of Piraeus had their own *Thesmophoria* and *Skira*, and the women of Paiania their own *Skira*; *Thesmophoria* at Halimus too are attested, which only modern combinations have made into a subordinate part of the city festival.[103] Probably, then, local *Thesmophoria* were quite common. In the case of women's rites the pressure for local celebration would have been strong, given the suspicions of Greek husbands.

The basis for discussion of mixed or men's festivals in this group was transformed by the publication of the calendar from Thorikos. It mentions five Athenian festivals by name, and lists two further offerings that from their date and recipient are very probably to be associated with known festivals.[104] At first sight then we have evidence for six Athenian festivals that were also celebrated in at least one deme. Unfortunately the calendar does not specify where the offerings are to be made, and so the possibility is open that they

---

[101] On all this see p. 195 below. Proclamation: *LSCG* 7 A 6.

[102] Isae. 3. 80, 8.19–20, *IG* II² 1184 = *LSS* 124. These texts are commonly taken to prove celebration in the demes, but without close argument (see however A. Tsakmakis' comments on Isae. 8.20 in *Orthodoxe Theologie zwischen Ost und West, Festschrift T. Nikolaou*, Frankfurt 2002, 164). Contra, O. Broneer, *Hesperia* 11 (1942), 270–2. The city rite was well attended (Ar. *Thesm.* 281); participants from Oe and probably Kephisia are attested (Lys. 1.20; Isae. 6.49–50). But the implication in Alciphr. 2.37 that *Thesmophoria* were confined to the city is worth little (see Appendix 2).

[103] *IG* II² 1177 (*LSCG* 36); *IG* I³ 250 A 6. Halimus: Plut. *Sol.* 8.4 with Paus. 1.31.1 and Σ Ar. *Thesm.* 80: see Clinton, 'Thesmophorion', 115–17. For the case for Eleusinian *Thesmophoria* see ibid. 114–15. For Marathon the calendar entry πρὸ Σκίρων (A col. 2, line 30, in *ZPE* 130, 2000, 45–47) proves nothing: cf. πρὸ μυστηρίων ibid. line 5.

[104] Line 33 implies *Anthesteria* and line 40 *Mounichia*. An explicit reference to the *Panathenaea* (right side, near line 2) was first detected by Jameson, 'The spectacular and the obscure', 330, n. 32. Many further possible connections between entries in deme calendars and the state festival programme are discussed by Humphreys, 'Demes', 159, n. 73.

were contributions destined for a central celebration. And such is very probably the case with the offering at the *Diasia* (35), since as we saw earlier there is independent evidence that this was a central festival based on contributions from the demes; much the same considerations will apply to the one 'at the *Panathenaea*' added on the right side of the stone by a second hand. It is very plausible too that the offering for Artemis Mounichia (40) was intended for her great festival at Mounichia, as no trace of local filials of the cult survives. (An animal was also sent out of the deme to what may have been the meeting of a regional 'amphictyony' at Sunium (19).) On the other hand, two of the offerings were certainly made in Thorikos. For the *Hieros Gamos* (32) we can infer this confidently from the analogy of Erchia, where the rite was celebrated locally.[105] And it appears certain that the Thorikians held their own *Plynteria* (53–4), because the offering falls a month too late for the Athenian rite.[106]

For the final two festivals, therefore, the *Pyanopsia* and *Anthesteria* (27, 33), the analogies leave both possibilities open. There is a hint, not quite conclusive, that the *Pyanopsia* of the calendar differs in date from the Athenian rite.[107] However that may be, the character of the ceremonies themselves suggests (or at least allows) local celebration in both cases. The central core of the *Anthesteria* is a drinking party; for the *Pyanopsia*, the women prepare a special bean-stew, and children roam around with branches and beg food. These are surely in essence rites of the individual household or at most of the village. Where would a Thorikian hold his drinking party, if he went to the city for the *Anthesteria*? What was there to see or eat or do in the city at the *Pyanopsia*? The *Diasia*, it is true, was centrally celebrated though not spectacular; but rites of purification perhaps by their nature demand the participation of as large a group as possible. Perhaps then the offerings at *Pyanopsia* and *Anthesteria* in the Thorikos calendar are a modest public supplement to festivities being conducted privately throughout the deme.[108] The *Hieros Gamos* too, which as we have seen was held locally, was a rite of the household. It celebrated the household's very basis, the institution of marriage, through its prototype in the union of Zeus and Hera; the central mystery indeed seems to have been for husband to stay at home and spend an evening with wife.[109] One of the most interesting gains from the new

---

[105] See F. Salviat, *BCH* 88 (1964), 647–54. The rite is not named, but recipients of offerings made in the deme on the relevant day identify it beyond question. For an attractive suggestion that Erchian *Genesia* can be similarly identified see S. D. Lambert, *ZPE* 139 (2002), 75–82.

[106] Cf. N. Robertson, *HSCP* 87 (1983), 280–4. He also postulates *Plynteria* for Erchia, more contestably (n. 69 above).

[107] If Daux's supplement 'on the sixteenth' in 26 (ἕκτηι ἐ[πὶ δέκα]) is correct (but Humphreys, 'Demes', suggests ἐ[φ’ ἁλῆι]), then either the *Pyanopsia* (held on the 7th of Pyanopsion in Athens) fell after the 16th in Thorikos, or the calendar does not strictly observe sequence within the month.

[108] But for the other view in relation to the *Anthesteria* see Henrichs, 'Between Country and City', 260–1. On the character of the *Anthesteria* see p. 290.

[109] See p. 42.

calendars has been the indication of how important this ritual of domestic devotion was throughout Attica.

We find then at least two of the so-called Athenian festivals also celebrated in Thorikos, and very possibly four. A question of priority arises, in this and in analogous cases. Is the convergence to be explained by the demes' well-known tendency to imitate the ways of the city? Or is it rather a case of independent development from a common origin? So far as it goes, the evidence from Thorikos suggests common origin. The rites in question are all demonstrably old Ionian;[110] no case has yet been found of any deme taking up a specifically Athenian rite of recent origin, as the hypothesis of imitation would make one expect. And there is reason to think that in their unusual dating of the *Plynteria* the Thorikians may have been following an old Ionian tradition.[111] The festival calendar of Thorikos can therefore be seen as an independent descendant of that of an Ionian *polis*.

Much more evidence would be needed before this conclusion, which is far from certain even for Thorikos, could be safely transferred to the demes en masse. Outside Thorikos many of the old Ionian rites remain elusive. The opposition between 'independent development' and 'imitation' is anyway too stark: even if the Thorikians continued to celebrate their *Plynteria* a few weeks later than the Athenians, they none the less made an offering at the festival to Aglaurus, a heroine closely associated with the Athenian acropolis.[112] But let us speculatively generalize the conclusion, and see what follows. On this hypothesis the festival calendars of both Athens and the demes were built upon roughly the same substratum of old Ionian rites. Some of these were 'diffused rites' celebrated throughout Attica, but there may always have been some which brought together all the inhabitants of the region in one place.[113] Perhaps as Athens grew in importance local celebrations were to some degree supplanted by those of the city, but this was not a very conspicuous tendency, and certain old rites of Dionysus and Demeter continued to flourish in the demes, more than in the city. The city asserted itself as a centre of all Attica not so much by taking over and building up old rites as by setting up a series of spectacular new ones, of general appeal: the *Panathenaea*, *City Dionysia*, *Theseia*, *Hephaisteia* and the rest. The demes meanwhile maintained and perhaps developed the restricted local cults that expressed and emphasized

---

[110] See the index to Nilsson, *Griechische Feste*. Of rites found in other demes, there is no Ionian evidence for *Skira* (perhaps by chance).

[111] See N. Robertson, *HSCP* 88 (1983), 283, and now C. Trümpy, *Untersuchungen zu den altgriechischen Monatsnamen und Monatsfolgen* (Heidelberg 1997), 71–2: the Parian/Thasian month Plynterion probably coincides with Attic Skirophorion, in which the Thorikian but not the Athenian *Plynteria* fell.

[112] I owe this point to Professor Burkert. I am not very inclined to appeal against it to the Cypriot Aglaurus of Porph. *Abst.* 2.54. Note too Kearns's argument about the Erchian acropolis, n. 69 above.

[113] Both *Diasia* and *Thargelia* were centrally celebrated despite being old Ionian (cf. e.g. *LSS* 69 and Hipponax fr. 104.49 West).

their distinctive identity: the festivals of local heroes, of gods under distinctive titles and the like. The demes seem not to have taken up more modern and universal deities such as Asclepius or Democracy or Good Fortune or Peace. Demesmen were no doubt interested in these powers, but it was not at this level that their interest was expressed. In this as in much else there was complementarity between deme and polis.

The religion of the demes described in this chapter flourished above all in the fifth and fourth centuries, the great period of deme activity in general. The Clisthenic reforms did not evoke it out of nothing. But by granting political status to the demes Clisthenes doubtless also gave an important stimulus to their religious life. In the third and second centuries evidence for religious as for political life in the demes declines sharply in quantity. As late as the second century AD there were still, to judge from Pausanias,[114] distinctive local cults in Attica, but that need not mean that a religious life as bustling, varied and organized as that revealed by the calendars still persisted. What was lost, with this decline of traditional deme religion? As we have seen, this religion had great imaginative appeal: it associated the familiar world of the deme with that of myth, and lent interest and significance to the banal landmarks of everyday life. It also had great social and affective importance. The deme was what Aristotle would have called a grouping for community (κοινωνία) and friendship (φιλία), and very many passages in oratory and comedy illustrate the bond that was supposed to exist between fellow-demesmen.[115] The fellow-demesman comes next in the widening circle of relationships after 'friends' and 'kin'. The cement of such communal feeling and friendship must have been in large measure the shared ritual programme of the deme. The last word can therefore go to a client of Isaeus: he is in fact taking his fellow-demesmen to court en masse, but he stresses by way of preface how deeply painful it is to himself to be forced into such action against, of all people, his fellow-demesmen, 'those men with whom I share sacrifices and common festivities'.[116]

---

[114] 1.31. For the earlier books about the demes that may have influenced Pausanias see Jacoby, n. 30 to commentary on Philochorus, *FGrH* 328 F 94. Rustic shrines mark, a little paradoxically, an exception to the gloomy post-classical archaeological picture of Attica: Lohmann, *Atene*, 293. On the history of deme cults see *Athenian Religion*, 114–15; 264.

[115] Mutual aid in a crisis: Ar. *Lys.* 333, 685, *Nub.* 1321. Undesirability of enmity with demesman or wronging him: Ar. *Nub.* 1219; Dem. 52. 28. Subventions to help demesmen buy military equipment: Lys. 16.14, 31.16. Quality of being χρηστὸς περὶ τοὺς δημότας: Lys. 20.2. Importance of praise/mockery before demesmen: Ar. *Eq.* 320; Isae. 2.18, 36. Cf. Whitehead, *Demes*, 230–4.

[116] Fr. 4 Scheibe ap. Dion. Hal. *Isae.* 10.

4

International Religion

Not even at the level of practice, still less of the imagination, was Athenian religion restricted within the confines of Attica. This 'international' dimension of Athenian religion has four overlapping aspects. The first is the participation of Athens, as of almost all other Greek states, at the festivals held at the four great panhellenic sanctuaries (and, from the fourth century, at some others too). The festival and the associated truce were 'announced' at Athens, and the Athenians then dispatched an official delegation (*theoria*) to bring a sacrifice on behalf of the city. These routine procedures usually only break through into our sources when they are disturbed in some way. Thucydides tells us explicitly that the Isthmian games of 412 were announced in Athens to cancel any expectation that might have existed that, in time of war, they would not have been; we hear of the showy gold vessels used by the official delegates at the Olympic games because in 416, scandalously, Alcibiades borrowed them and pretended they were his own; the Athenians were so disgusted that the Pythian games of 346 were to be held under the presidency of Philip that they 'sent neither the *theoroi* from the boule nor the *thesmothetai*, but renounced the traditional *theoria*'.[1] (That last passage provides our only information on the normal composition of such a *theoria*, though we also know that the post of '*theoria*-leader', *architheoros*, was a liturgy; the leader probably meant the expenses of the whole mission.) *Theoria* is, indeed, a feature of happy normality, which is why the personified Theoria is handed over to the boule as a blessing of peace in Aristophanes' play; participation in *theoriai* must have been a valued perk of bouleutic service.[2] Many Athenians will also have attended unofficially. It was one of the many eccentricities of

[1] Thuc. 8.10.1; [Andoc.] 4.29; Dem. 19.128; for Delphic *theoroi* cf. Solon fr. 79 Ruschenbusch. For the post of *architheoros* see Lys. 21.5; Andoc. 1.132; [Andoc.] 4. 29 (which uses a plural, of Olympia); Dem. 21.115; Din. 1. 81–2; Arist. *EN* 1122a 24–5 (an inexpensive liturgy); *IG* II² 365 (*SEG* XXX 66); *SEG* XXV 177. 26–7. *IG* IV² 1.94.3 implies *theoriai* to the Asclepieia at Epidaurus already by 360 (P. Perlman, *City and Sanctuary in Ancient Greece*, Göttingen 2000, 67–97); *theoriai* go to Boeotian festivals too from the 3rd c.: Moretti 15, *IG* II² 971. 29–35, 1054 (*IG* II² 1534. 170–1 is unclear: Aleshire, *Asklepieion*, 310), and cf. *IG* II² 993 (*Lykaia*). On Athenian *theoriai* cf. I. Rutherford in P. Murray and P. Wilson (eds.), *Music and the Muses* (Oxford 2004), 67–90; on 'international' religion in general see M. P. Dillon, *Pilgrims and Pilgrimage in Ancient Greece* (London 1997).

[2] Ar. *Pax* 713–15 (correctly explained by the Σ vet. on 714, followed by Sommerstein but not Olson); 887–90. For *theoria* as a privilege not generally available see Ar. *Vesp.* 1188 and the fraudulent boasting of Philocleon, ibid. 1382–5.

Socrates that he had 'never once left the city for *theoria*, except once to the Isthmus'. The Isthmus was the nearest of the four sites, readily accessible by sea, and may have been the one most visited by ordinary Athenians; a claim existed that the games had been founded by Theseus, and that he had required the Corinthians to provide 'front row seating for Athenians who attended, of the area covered by the sail of the delegation ship when spread out'.[3]

The second international aspect was Athens' membership of Amphictyonies. She belonged to at least three.[4] The Amphictyonies of the classical period are a survival, some vestigial, some very tenacious, of a form of religious and political organization that pre-dates the city in the form in which we know it. Groups of neighbouring 'tribes' (*ethne*) came together at sanctuaries controlled by none of them to celebrate a common festival and debate matters of common interest, including the administration of the sanctuary. So, through Amphictyonies, Athens had joint proprietary rights in cults located outside Attica. In the case of Poseidon of Kalaureia (an island off the east coast of the Argolid) and of the second deity worshipped by the Delphic Amphictyony, Demeter of Anthela (near Thermopylai), this meant, by the historical period, very little. Apollo of Delphi, by contrast, had not faded into insignificance, but, since all Greeks could now consult the oracle and attend the Pythian games, the Athenians' access to him did not depend on their place in the Amphictyony. They were, however, the only city apart from Delphi itself to have a guaranteed place on the Amphictyonic council,[5] and this ancient involvement must have been one of the factors underpinning the huge general reverence felt for Apollo Pythios, who in Demosthenes' words was 'ancestral to the city'.[6]

The Delian Amphictyony, by the time that we can observe it, is organizationally moribund, with representatives provided by Athens alone apart from a brief and slight intrusion of Andrians. But a festival of model amphictyonic

---

[3] Pl. *Crito* 52b (for popularity cf. perhaps Ar. *Pax* 879); Plut. *Thes.* 25.7, citing Andron *FGrH* 10 F 6, Hellanicus *FGrH* 323a F 15. Plato in *Laws* (950e) wants his state to send ὅτι πλείστους ἅμα καὶ καλλίστους τε καὶ ἀρίστους to 'participate in the sacrifices and competitions' at the four panhellenic games.

[4] For these, and for other possibilities, see *Athenian Religion*, 28. On the archaic amphictyonies see now W. G. Forrest, 'The Pre-polis Polis', in R. Brock and S. Hodkinson, *Alternatives to Athens* (Oxford 2000), 280–92; on that of Delphi F. Lefèvre, *L'Amphictionie pyléo-delphique: Histoire et institutions* (Paris 1998); P. Sánchez, *L'Amphictionie des Pyles et de Delphes* (Stuttgart 2001).

[5] See Lefèvre, op. cit., 63–9. For 5th-c. allusions to the Athenian representatives see Ar. *Nub.* 624; fr. 335; for the 4th c. Aeschin. 3.106–29 is a prime if erratic source. *Hieromnemones* performed various sacrifices both at the sanctuary of Demeter at Anthela and in Delphi, and in that modest sense extended Athens' religious representation abroad: see Lefèvre, op. cit. 206; Sánchez, op. cit., 476; note e.g. *Syll.*[3] 539a 14–15, *SEG* XXXVII 92. 16–23 and perhaps Dem. *Epist.* 3.30 (with J. A. Goldstein, *The Letters of Demosthenes*, New York 1968, 50–2).

[6] 18.141; cf. *LSS* 14. 8–9. I note with bafflement the unorthodox tradition which made 'the Apollo who protected Athens' a child of Athena and Hephaestus: Cic. *Nat. D.* 3. 55 (cf. 57, 59), Clem. Al. *Protr.* 2.28.3 ('Aristotle': not apparently in Rose's edition of the fragments).

type had existed in the archaic period, and was restored to its former splendour by the Athenians in 426. And whereas at the panhellenic games the official *theoriai* from the cities merely sacrificed and watched, to the *Delia* the participating states also sent choruses.[7] Theseus had landed at Delos with the Twice Seven on the way home from Crete, and the dispatch of a chorus to the *Delia* was seen (though from what date we cannot say) as a reminiscence and a re-enactment of that event. An archaic/poetic/hieratic word ἤθεοι ('unwed youths') which is routinely applied to the Twice Seven (or at least the boys among them) in accounts of the adventure is also used to describe the chorus sent to Delos in the *Athenaion Politeia*: the exquisite word would not have found its way into the drab prose text were it not a quite standard designation for the chorus.[8] There is also the matter of the theoric boat. Philosophers in the hellenistic schools disputed whether the vessel which was still, in Demetrius of Phaleron's day, pointed out as the triakonter of Theseus was rightly so described, given that no individual plank touched by the hero survived. The reason they chose the example is that just that claim was being made: not only did Theseus' boat survive but it was still in use, the very boat used to ferry the modern ἤθεοι to Delos for the festival.[9] No more vivid example can be quoted of historical Greeks becoming, for the duration of the ritual, their mythical forebears. Perfect imitation would have required the dispatch of a mixed chorus of seven youths and seven maids. But neither a mixed chorus nor a chorus of fourteen finds a parallel at Athens, and in aetiology things can be different without ceasing therewith to be the same.[10]

The great amphictyonic festival on Delos happened every four years (there was also a celebration every six years of which nothing further is known). But the Twice Seven had vowed that, if they were saved, they would send a *theoria* to the island every year; and, from the moment that the priest of Apollo garlanded the stern of Theseus' ship for the annual voyage, the time was so sacred and so hallowed that no execution could occur until the ship's return. (We learn all this because, by chance, the stern was garlanded on the day

---

[7] See *Athenian Religion*, 86–8, 150–1, 222–3; Wilson, *Khoregia*, 44–6. Pindar, *Paean* 5 was perhaps written for an Athenian chorus dispatched to Delos.

[8] Arist. *Ath. Pol.* 56.3; for ἤθεοι in relation to the Twice Seven see Bacch. 17 *passim*; Plut. *Thes.* 15.1, 17. 1, 23.1. The aetiological connection appears first in Pl. *Phaed.* 58a–b; on Theseus and Delos see *Athenian Religion*, 86, n. 79.

[9] These connections have often been missed but are certain (and in fact explicit both in Pl. *Phaed.* 58a and Plut. *An Sen. Ger. Reipub.* 6, 786f): see Arist. *Ath. Pol.* 56.3 with Plut. *Thes.* 23.1.

[10] In normal usage ἤθεοι refers to youths only, which might seem to settle the matter. But in Bacchylides 17, which treats the myth of the Twice Seven, ἤθεοι is thrice used collectively to cover the whole group (43, 93, 128). Bacchylides 17 would have been the ideal poem for performance by Athenians on Delos but was in fact, as its envoi shows, so performed by Keans. Whether the explanation lies in independent Kean enthusiasm for Theseus or Athenian influence of some kind (cf. Wilson, *Khoregia*, 46; Mills, *Theseus*, 39, n. 170), the poem vividly illustrates the Thesean aura of early 5th-c. Delos.

before Socrates' trial; because of contrary winds, the philosopher was free to contemplate his death, and to converse, for thirty days.)[11] Delian Apollo was a very important figure in Athens, as emerges from several tantalizing testimonia. Certain tablets of Solon's sacrifical code were devoted to 'the Deliasts'; one of these specified that two members of the *genos* of *Kerykes* were to 'serve as fellow diners (παρασιτεῖν) in the Delion for a year'. Presumably these 'Deliasts' had a role in the great *theoria* to Delos and were assisted in it by the two *Kerykes*; we must, it seems, postulate a Delion in Athens at which they dined for a year, in elaborate preparation for the solemn event. This same Delion would be a possible location for the activities of a prestigious group of 'Dancers' who 'danced around the temple of Delian Apollo wearing Theran cloaks'; they were waited on by the young Euripides (but a variant tradition associates him with a different cult of Apollo, that at Cape Zoster). A separate small temple of Delian Apollo was probably built at Phaleron in the 430s. Different again is a Delion at Marathon, associated with what appears to have been an entirely separate *theoria* dispatched to Delos, with unknown frequency, by the Marathonian Tetrapolis. Prasiae too on the east coast of Attica had a temple of the god, and it was said that the mysterious 'Hyperborean offerings' made the last leg of their journey from the distant north, under Attic escort, from Prasiae to Delos. Perhaps one of the *theoriai* (of the city, or of the Tetrapolis) set out from there; or perhaps the association worked in some quite different way. These data defy assemblage into a single picture, but still collectively bear witness to the greatness of the god.[12]

At the Panhellenic games and at amphictyonic festivals the Athenians participated along with other states. But there were also certain religious activities which they undertook at Delphi either alone or in association only with the Delphians. This is the third international dimension of Athenian religion. (But this type overlaps with type two, since the annual, unlike the penteteric, *theoria* to Delos was perhaps exclusive to Athens; so too the *theoria* sent by the Marathonian Tetrapolis.) About one practice we can say little, since it is known only from a passing reference in Pausanias; and seldom are we more acutely frustrated by the drawing of a curtain on a briefly glimpsed scene. Pausanias could not understand, he tells us, why Homer honoured Panopeus in Phokis, a dingy townlet if ever there was one, with the epithet 'of

---

[11] Pl. *Phaed.* 58a–c; Xen. *Mem.* 4.8.2. For the *penteteris* and *hepteteris* see Arist. *Ath. Pol.* 54.7. The place within the calendar of these *theoriai* is uncertain: see P. Bruneau, *Recheches sur les cultes de Délos* (Paris 1970), 81–93.

[12] Deliasts: Polemon fr. 78 Preller ap Ath. 234e–f (= Solon fr. 88 Ruschenbusch); cf. Harpocration δ 26 Δηλιασταί· οἱ εἰς Δῆλον ἐξελθόντες θεωροί· Λυκοῦργος Κατὰ Μενεσαίχμου (F 87 Conomis). 'Dancers': Theophr. fr. 119 Wimmel (576 Fortenbaugh) ap. Ath. 424e–f (for the Apollo Zosterios variant see the *Vita Euripidis* p. 2.4 in E. Schwartz, *Scholia in Euripidem*, I, Berlin 1887). Phaleron: D. M. Lewis, *BSA* 55 (1960), 190–4 (questioned by H. B. Mattingly, *ZPE* 83, 1990, 112–13). Marathon: Philochorus FGrH 328 F 75. Prasiae: Paus. 1.31.2: *Athenian Religion*, 224–5, with more details (add O. Kakovogianni, *ArchDelt* 38, 1984, *Chron.* 45 for a possible identification of the site).

fair choruses', until he learnt that it was one of the places en route to Delphi at which the Thyiades paused to dance; the Thyiades, he explains, are Attic women who go every other year to Parnassus and, along with Delphic women, perform rites for Dionysus. A Delphic college of Thyiades which is evidently the one whose rites the Athenian women shared is mentioned by Plutarch; its leader was his friend Clea, a woman of standing. One year a party had to be sent out to rescue the Thyiades, cut off by strong winds and snow; it was on the very heights of Parnassus that they 'raved for Dionysus and Apollo'.[13] What is implied is a typical Dionysiac rite for women, performed in midwinter in alternate years in a distant mountain setting. But why and in what numbers the Athenian women forsook the many mountains of Attica and went to Delphi for their revels is quite obscure. No text apart from Pausanias mentions the Athenian delegation. That silence should doubtless be taken as yet another illustration of the invisibility to us of important aspects of women's lives. But the possibility that we are dealing with an innovation of the Roman period cannot quite be ruled out.

No single Athenian Thyias can we name. Pythaïsts and associated persons, by contrast, can be identified ad nauseam; and, though it is not easy to imagine more than thirty Thyiades (at the outside) taking the long road to Delphi, more than five hundred Athenians attended the *Pythaïs* of 106/5 in various capacities. (The only women in all that crowd, however, were eleven basket-bearers, a fire-bearer and the priestess of Athena.[14]) That *Pythaïs* is the most magnificent of four celebrations (the others were in 138/7, 128/7 and 98/7) all conducted on a very ample scale. These remarkable testimonia to the wealth and confidence of late hellenistic Athens are a product, it is generally agreed, not of continuity but of revival, and of revival after a very long interval; we have no reason to think that any *Pythaïs* was dispatched from Athens between the 320s and 138 BC, though the Marathonian Tetrapolis sent its own independent *theoria* to Delphi and may have continued to do so right down until the revival of the state *Pythaïs* in 138 (into which it may have merged).[15]

---

[13] Paus. 10.4.3 (ibid. 10.32.7 for 'raving for Dionysus and Apollo'); Plut. *De Is.et Os.* 35, 364e; id. *De primo frigido* 18, 953c–d. On the Delphic Thyiades, attested from the 5th c., see M. Villaneuva Pueg in *L'Association dionysiaque dans les sociétés anciennes* (Rome 1986), 31–51; on the Athenian participation, ibid. 35–6.

[14] For the two latter see *Syll.*[3] 711 D [1] 22, 711 K; cf. G. Colin, 'Les Femmes dans la Pythaïde', *FD* III.2, 37–40; on participants in general see S. V. Tracy, *BCH* 99 (1975), 215–18 (tiny modification by J. F. Bommelaer, in *Études delphiques*, *BCH* Suppl. iv 1977, 156–7). Tracy's figures for the four celebrations are 124, 315–19, 511–15, 298–9 participants. Daux, *Delphes*, 540–3, 718, warns that a block relating to the first celebration may be lost; if he is right, our picture of the groups involved at that date might be significantly affected, but the broad numerical picture only modestly.

[15] See Boethius, *Pythaïs*, 53; Daux, *Delphes*, 531–40, 549–50. Boethius' admirable dissertation remains the basic study; see too Daux, op. cit., 521–67, 708–29, which corrects confusions created by misdating of the last *Pythaïs* and by misreading of *FD* III.2 no. 54 and warns (see previous note) against *ex silentio* arguments; S. V. Tracy, I.G. *II*² 2336. *Contributors of First Fruits for the Pythaïs* (Meisenheim 1982), which shows that *IG II*² 2336 (which he re-edits: see *SEG* XXXII 218) relates to a Delphic and not an otherwise unattested Delian *Pythaïs* (see too 169–82 on the political context); I. Rutherford, *Pindar's Paeans* (Oxford 2001), 33–5.

Obviously we cannot take the opulent late hellenistic *Pythaïdes* as a simple replica of their supposed models. But the ten *hieropoioi* who led a *Pythaïs* of the Lycurgan period were among the chief public figures of the day,[16] and we must surely suppose that many lesser Athenians went with them.

What was a *Pythaïs*? It was an Athenian delegation, not tied to any Delphic festival, which at irregular intervals took sacrificial victims, 'first fruits' (commuted into money in the late hellenistic period) and perhaps a tripod to Apollo at Delphi. It brought back a 'sacred tripod' and a female 'fire bearer' (the fire perhaps carried in the tripod).[17] (None of these details are attested early, but they are likely to be traditional.) The time of dispatch of the *Pythaïs* varied, traditionally at least, over a period of three months, which were apparently the last three of the official year:[18] this was a not unsuitable time for the sending of first fruits, and for the reception in return of (we suppose) clean 'new fire'. The hellenistic *Pythaïdes* were occasions for hymns, literary and dramatic performances courtesy of the Athenian guild of actors of Dionysus, and horse races between members of the Athenian cavalry. All this amounted to the paradox of what has been called an Athenian festival celebrated at Delphi.[19] The plays and the horse-races are probably hellenistic elaborations (both are absent in 138), but a fine votive relief of the fourth century already attests 'boy Pythaïsts' who are likely to have performed in choirs (as did their successors in 138).[20] Adult Pythaïsts (precise duties unknown) are also found in the fourth century.[21] In the hellenistic *Pythaïdes* a special place was reserved for the representatives of four *gene*, a privilege which is unlikely to rest wholly on invented tradition. But an unexpected connection with demes too appears in the note in the Erchian calendar that

[16] *Syll.*[3] 296 and 297 (for the latter cf. M. A. Zagdoun, *FD* IV. 6 1977, 49–57, no. 14). The date of this *Pythaïs* remains very uncertain: see D. M. Lewis, *Hesperia* 37 (1968), 377, n. 29; Zagdoun, loc. cit. A famous Delphic monument, the Dancing Women on the acanthus column, is now known to be an Athenian dedication of this period: see *FD* III.4, no. 462; *Guide de Delphes. Le musée* (Paris 1991), 84–90; U. Kron, *LIMC* s.v. Aglauros, 292, no. 42 [+].

[17] ἀπαρχαί: e.g. *Syll.*[3] 711 D[1] 43, 728 B 3; with sacrifice and procession ibid. 711 L 9–12. Commuted: *IG* II[2] 2336 (above, n. 15), *passim*. Tripod and fire-bearer: the only texts are *Syll.*[3] 697 L 3, 711 D[1] 22, 728 I; on their interpretation, which is controversial, see Daux, *Delphes*, 718–21.

[18] See Boethius, *Pythaïs*, 13–23. The key data, in association with the passage of Strabo cited in the text which mentions the three-month period, are that (1) the *Pythaïs* mentioned in Isae. 7.27 fell between the *Thargelia* and the elections in the speaker's deme, assigned by Boethius to the last month of the official year (ibid. 27–8); (2) all honorary decrees relating to the hellenistic *Pythaïdes* fall in the Delphic 'second six months', which corresponded to the second six months of the Attic year. Deme elections could probably happen later than Boethius supposed (*SEG* XXVIII 103. 27–28), but (if we admit hellenistic evidence) criterion (2) discourages us from supposing that the three months straddled two archontic years.

[19] So Boethius, *Pythaïs*, *passim*.

[20] *IG* II[2] 2816, Boethius, *Pythaïs*, pl. 2. The four dedicators describe themselves merely as *Pythaïstai*, but four boys (and an adult) are shown in the relief. Boy chorus in 138: *Syll.*[3] 696 B, with Daux, *Delphes*, 718. In later *Pythaïdes* much cultic singing was performed by Artists of Dionysus (*Syll.*[3] 698 A 9, etc.). Simonides 519 fr. 35 was perhaps composed for a 5th-c. *Pythaïs*: I. Rutherford, *HSCP* 93 (1990), 171.

[21] By the dedication from Icaria, *IG* II[2] 2817, Boethius, *Pythaïs*, fig. 1; and by the obscure fragment of the Nicomachus calendar *BSA* 97 (2002), 364, fr. 6. 11 (see too next note).

certain offerings made to Apollo under various titles are 'to be handed over to the Pythaïsts'. These entries are, it is true, enigmatic (what did the Erchian Pythaïsts do in the years, decades even, of inactivity between *Pythaïdes?*), and it has been supposed that there existed also a distinct, local institution.[22] But prima facie it is more attractive to suppose that some kind of dispersed or localized recruiting of Pythaïsts may have operated at this date. Both the surviving dedications made by Pythaïsts appear to come from the Python of the deme Icaria.[23] Apollo Pythios, we noted earlier, was 'ancestral to the city'. *Pythaïdes* may have been one of the institutions by which he established a moral ascendancy (there are Pythia everywhere) over the demes too. As we have seen, the Tetrapolis of Marathon even dispatched a *Pythaïs* of its own.[24]

What was most picturesque about a traditional *Pythaïs* was the means of determining its time of departure. The proverbial expression 'when lightning flashes through Harma', roughly equivalent to English 'once in a blue moon', arose according to Strabo because:

in accord with an oracle the so-called Pythaïsts took a flash of lightning as a sign: they looked towards Harma [a mountain saddle in Attica near Phyle] and dispatched the sacrifice to Delphi when they saw a flash of lightning. They watched for three months, for three days and nights each month, from the hearth of Zeus of Lightning, which is in the wall between the Python and the Olympieion.[25]

The missions sent by the Marathonian Tetrapolis too were initiated by divination, though the technique was inspection of entrails in this case.[26] Whether the watch at the hearth of Zeus of Lightning occurred every year, or only in years when on other grounds it seemed desirable to think of a *Pythaïs*, is not explained; but the precise location of a flash of lightning is beyond objective verification, and on either view the result must have been that, while the

---

[22] So J. Bousquet, *BCH* 88 (1964), 666, n. 4, on *LSCG* 18 B 51, *Γ* 36, E 36–7. *Gene: Syll.*[3] 696 A, 697 B, 711 D[1] 30, 728 C; Boethius, *Pythaïs*, 105–6; *Athenian Religion*, 308 (for a further *genos* of unknown name see Daux, *Delphes*, 713).

[23] See E. Voutiras, *AJA* 86 (1982), 229–33, on *IG* II[2] 2816–17. I cannot associate the Hebdomaists of the dedication which he there publishes (perhaps from the same Python) with the *Pythaïs*.

[24] Philochorus *FGrH* 328 F 75, with *FD* III.2.18–22 (18 = *Syll.*[3] 541 A; 19 = 541 C; 20 = 637); *FD* III.2. 21 as restored by Daux, *Delphes*, 535, attests continued performance of a Tetrapolitan *Pythaïs* (so named, here only) in the 2nd and c. Thereafter representatives of the Tetrapolis have a place in the state *Pythaïs*, but no independent *theoriai* are attested (Daux, 549–50). Jacoby (n. 5 to comm. on Philochorus loc cit.) considers it possible that the Marathonian *theoria*, unlike that of Athens, attended a specific Delphian festival. Representatives of an unnamed *genos* had a privileged place in the Marathonian *theoria* too (Philoch. loc cit.; Jacoby, n. 4 ad loc.).

[25] Strabo 9.2.11, 404; for the proverb see Boethius, *Pythaïs*, 145–6. On the topography, Wycherley, *Stones of Athens*, 167, n. 29, 177, n. 9 [+] seems to me in the right.

[26] Philochorus, *FGrH* 328 F 75. This text appears to say that, once the relevant signs have been secured and the *theoria* has been dispatched, a seer continues to sacrifice daily in the Python at Oinoe (so Boethius, *Pythaïs*, 39–42; Daux, *Delphes*, 533, n. 1; Jacoby on Philoch. loc cit.). This is an odd procedure (the suspension of execution during the state *theoria* to Delos which Jacoby compares is scarcely an exact parallel): sacrifice may be appropriate, but why need a seer perform it, if the relevant omens have already been secured?.

Athenians believed themselves in each case to be sending a *Pythaïs* at Zeus'
bidding, they were in effect doing so when they themselves saw fit.[27] We know
for certain of two *Pythaïdes* of the fourth century, one of the Lycurgan period
and one sent (as a gesture of support to Athens' Phocian allies, now in control
of Delphi?) in or near 355; the dedication by 'boy *Pythaïsts*' mentioned above
probably attests one earlier celebration. The proverbial use of 'lightning
through Harma' implies that *Pythaïdes* were infrequent events. But the symbolic importance of being attached to Delphi by a special institution did not
depend on regular performance. A fourth-century *horos* in the agora marked
out 'the sacred road through which the *Pythaïs* journeys to Delphi', little used
for that purpose though the road can have been.[28]

   A poet of (surely) the old comedy made a word play on the 'lightning
through Harma' proverb. A passage in Aeschylus is probably a still earlier
allusion to the institution: in the prologue to *Eumenides* we are told that
Apollo travelled from Delos to Delphi via Attica, and that he was 'escorted
and greatly honoured by the road-building children of Hephaestus [the
Athenians], who made a savage land tame'. An ancient commentator on
the passage notes that 'it was out of favour to the Athenians that Aeschylus
says that Apollo landed in Attica and went round from there; Pindar says it
was from Tanagra'. Ephorus makes explicit a point which was no doubt
obvious to Aeschylus' audience, that the route followed by Apollo to Delphi
was 'the one on which now the Athenians send the *Pythaïs*'; again here, as in
Aeschylus and in the *horos* from the agora, the ideas of route and road are
stressed. Where Aeschylus spoke of the Athenians, as they escorted Apollo,
'making a savage land tame', Ephorus gives credit for a similar civilizing
activity to Apollo himself. The commentary on Aeschylus, by contrast,
ascribes the cleansing of the land to Theseus, and adds 'when they send a
theoria to Delphi, men holding axes walk ahead as though intending to tame
the land'. We acquire here both a striking new ritual detail, the axes, and a
rich nugget of fifth-century ideology. As they walk to Delphi in the *Pythaïs*,
the Athenians are celebrating and re-enacting a civilizing moment, and one
the credit for which somehow belongs jointly to themselves and to Apollo.[29]

---

[27] So Boethius, *Pythaïs*, 6. The consensus is that the elaborately planned hellenistic *Pythaïdes*,
which were eventually fixed to an ennaeteric cycle, cannot still have been set in motion by the
erratic old method of observation. This does not seem to me certain. But if the argument has
force, one must doubt whether the traditional method could have been used for the Lycurgan
Pythaïs either.

[28] On the *Pythaïs* of c.355 (Isae. 7.27) see H. W. Parke, *JHS* 59 (1939), 80–3. One of the boy
Pythaïsts of *IG* II² 2816 was at least 30 in 341/0 (*Agora* XV 38.26); it is implausible if not
impossible that the *Pythaïs* in which he served as a boy occurred as late as c. 355. *IG* II² 2817 can
be associated with the Lycurgan *Pythaïs* (so Voutiras, loc. cit.). *Horos: Agora* XIX, H 34.

[29] Com. Adesp. fr. 288; Aesch. *Eum.* 9–14, with the scholia ad loc.; Ephorus, *FGrH* 70 F 31 ap.
Strabo 9.3.12, 422; cf. Boethius, *Pythaïs*, 35–7; C. Gülke, *Mythos und Zeitgeschichte bei Aischylos*
(Meisenheim 1969), 41–56. Boethius, op. cit, 32–3, speculates that the axes were an offering to
Apollo. 'The sacral function of the ax-carriers cannot be certainly established', says Deubner,
Attische Feste 203. But what the scholion tells us makes excellent sense! In all essentials, this
apart, I take my interpretation from Boethius.

And the original journey which they repeat is one which established that their land of Attica was a middle point between two supremely sacred places, Delos and Delphi. In a païan composed to be performed at the *Pythaïs* of 128/7 Limenius still told how Apollo 'leaving the Cynthian isle set foot in famous Attica, origin of crops, on the [ ] ridge of Tritonis';[30] indeed it was on that momentous occasion that the païan was first heard. In no other city but Athens was the *Pythaïs* traditional, asserts flattering Aristides. The claim is not quite true: the little island of Telos may provide a second case.[31] But the point stands that dispatch of the *Pythaïs* was distinctive in a way that participation in panhellenic games or in an Amphictyony could not be. The gods wished, continues Aristides in a phrase perhaps more appropriate than he intended, that Athens should 'be pre-eminent and as it were lay hands on everything fine'.

The Athenians looked east to Delos and west to Delphi, and in both directions they saw Apollo. It was the same great god they saw, though in different aspects. Circumstances might occasionally force them to seem to favour Apollo Pythios more than Apollo Delios or vice versa, but their basic instinct was to revere both and to insist on their connection: the Tetrapolitans, like the city, sent *theoriai* in both directions, and a place of honour in the *Pythaïs* was assigned to *gene* which had strong connections also with Delos.[32] But, despite all this attention, Apollo remained at a distance, and delegations had to be dispatched to his truly favoured abodes. The Athenian relation with no other god was quite like this, so dependent on foreign missions. Even in his mythological persona, Apollo is a god who works from afar, a god of distance;[33] the duties of the Athenian Deliasts and *Pythaïsts* illustrate that proposition very clearly at a level of cult practice.

The final international dimension of Athenian religion need not detain us long. Individuals made offerings, attended festivals and sought healing at foreign sanctuaries; they were initiated too in Mysteries (such as those of the Great Gods of Samothrace).[34] And the state consulted and cultivated two foreign oracular gods, Zeus of Dodona and Ammon, in addition to Apollo of Delphi. We hear once of a *theoria* to Dodona,[35] while the renaming of one of the sacred triremes Ammonias implies regular contacts. These practices were usually too routine to invite notice, but an incident of the 330s known from Hyperides shows that tension could occasionally arise. The Athenians had adorned the statue of Dione at Dodona, and Queen Olympias had complained indignantly at what she saw as meddling. 'But the god himself by his oracle

---

[30] *DAGM* 21. 13–14.

[31] *Panath.* 363. Telos: the inscription *ArchDelt* 16 (1960) A 97 with pl. 93 gives πυθασταὶ τοὶ πυθάξαντες (cf. *IG* xii.3. 34–35): what this entailed is unknown.

[32] *Athenian Religion*, 289, 308 (on *Erysichthonidai* and *Pyrrakhidai*).

[33] An often-quoted characterization of the god by W. F. Otto (in *Die Götter Griechenlands*, Bonn 1929).

[34] Ar. *Pax* 277, Alexis fr. 183.5, Com. Adesp. fr. 1063.15.

[35] Dem. 21.53. On Dodona and Ammon see p. 111.

instructed us to do so!', answers Hyperides robustly. And had not Olympias herself done exactly the same, *mutatis mutandis*, by dedicating a *phiale* on the statue of Health in Athens? Olympias was perhaps being over-sensitive, but the point of complaint was not the consultation of Dodona by the Athenians. On the contrary, the incident neatly illustrates how surprisingly self-evident it was that Olympias too might have dealings with an Athenian healing god. The objection was that the Athenians were behaving as if it were their right and duty to take thought for the well-being of the shrine. Even piety became offensive if it came to seem proprietorial.[36]

Such resentments were rare. The correlate to Athenian travel to shrines abroad is non-Athenian travel to shrines in Attica, and this was in many cases not just tolerated but solicited. From at least the fifth century 'truce-bearers' went out from Eleusis to proclaim the 'Mystic truce' which allowed pilgrims from all Greece to attend the Mysteries without molestation; by the third century the *Panathenaea* and the *Eleusinia* too were 'proclaimed' throughout Greece.[37] It was this two-way process which fitted Athenian cults within the cults of Greece.

---

[36] Cf. my *Cleomenes on the Acropolis* (Oxford 1998), 24–6. Hyperides: *Eux.* 19–26. Most scholars suppose the statue of Health in question to be the Hygieia or the Athena Hygieia on the acropolis (for both see Paus. 1.23.4): see P. Themelis in *Macedonians in Athens*, 163, n. 14 [+].

[37] *IG* I³ 6 (*LSS* 3) B; B. Helly, *Gonnoi, 2, Les inscriptions* (Amsterdam 1973), no. 109. For *spondophoroi* and (by supplement) *theoroi* in Seleuceia in Pieria see *IG* II² 785. 19–20 (196–195 BC).

5

Who Prays for Athens? Religion in Civic Life

A special treatment of the city as a context of religious life would be redundant; this whole book is about little else. This chapter will consider instead some particular aspects of public religion. It will treat first religious decision-making and authority, the power and influence therefore of priests and priestesses, magistrates, othexr religious specialists and of the council and assembly. The priests and priestesses in question here are those appointed by the city, by the *gene* traditionally so empowered on behalf of the city, or by the demes, to serve particular gods in particular sanctuaries; the sacred officials of the Eleusinian cult, who were regularly treated as functionally equivalent to priests, belong in the same class, but not the priests and priestesses of private *thiasoi*. These are, therefore, the priests and priestesses who served bodies which had both a civic and a religious identity. (The position of phratry priest is *mutatis mutandis* the same, but about them there is little to be said.) The chapter will then turn to the place of religion in the main public domains of Athenian life. This question has two aspects. We will look first at behaviour, at the role of religious practices within the procedures of the assembly, the courts and the army; then at words, at the types of religious argument and evidence that might and might not be explicitly deployed in those contexts.

I start with religious decision-making. If we ignore here issues of influence and authority and look merely at the formal right to legislate, the matter is very simple: during the period open to our observation, power lies in the council and assembly and in no other place.[1] The people decides what gods are to be worshipped by what rituals at what times and places and at what expense; it regulates too the duties and terms of office of priests and priestesses, and creates new priesthoods at need. Persons claiming special expertise are free to contribute to debate and to suggest new measures, and may be invited to bring proposals on specific topics to the assembly.[2] Their voice will

---

[1] See Jacoby, *Atthis*, 257, n. 119; R. Garland, 'Religious Authority in Archaic and Classical Athens', *BSA* 79 (1984), 75–123 (revised and abbreviated version in M. Beard and J. North, *Pagan Priests*, London 1990); *Athenian Religion*, 123–4; for the whole chapter C. Sourvinou-Inwood, 'What is polis religion?' (*Oxford Readings*, 13–37) is fundamental. A study of the Athenian priesthoods which would bring order to the rather abundant material remains a desideratum. The only existing monograph was declared outdated by a reviewer at the time of publication, which was 1882 (Wilamowitz, *Deutsche Literaturzeitung* 1883, 262–3 = *Kl. Schr.* V.i, 239–41, on J. Martha, *Les Sacerdoces athéniens*, Paris).

often be listened to with respect, but they have no power to enforce what they advise. On many such topics the assembly decided to seek the guidance of an oracle, and a clear oracular answer on a matter of cult was always treated as binding. But a formal motion to accept the advice of the god was still required; and, more important, the decision to take the problem to the god was itself made by the assembly. Binding and enforceable religious rules emanated only from there. Doubtless there were other religious principles which a pious person might wish to observe, rules of purity above all. But breaches of such rules (about which the exegetes gave unenforceable advice) were apparently punishable only by the gods.[3] An exception to the exclusive role of the assembly would have to be allowed if it were true that at Eleusis the Eumolpids claimed a right to determine religious laws and to punish violations of them. The possibility cannot be ruled out, but it is raised by rhetorical assertions that are vague and perhaps fraudulent.[4] It is at all events very unlikely that the writ of the Eumolpids ran beyond the confines of the sanctuary at Eleusis.

It follows, to put the matter crudely, that priests do not give orders to the assembly, but the assembly to priests. Priests are in a sense officers of the state, and, if Aristotle in *Politics*[5] hesitates to class them among the regular magistrates and in *Constitution of the Athenians* largely ignores them, this is because their duties (and sometimes terms of service) differ from those of ordinary magistrates, not because they serve an institution, the Church, that

---

[2] *IG* I³ 78 (ML 73) 59–61; cf. n. 11 on Euthydemus of Eleusis.

[3] Cf. my 'What are Sacred Laws?' in E. Harris and L. Rubinstein (eds.), *The Law and the Courts in Ancient Greece* (London 2004), 57–70. Sacred laws relating to purity seem normally to have been admonitory rather than legally enforceable; they thus differ from sacred laws relating e.g. to protection of the sanctuary, priestly perquisites and good order at festivals, which were backed by enforcement procedures and fines. In Attica, in contrast to other parts of Greece, purity laws were apparently not even written down, not at least on stone. It would be unusual if courts obeyed Pericles' supposed injunction to apply 'the unwritten laws in accord with which the Eumolpids expound' ([Lys.] 6. 10) against offenders.

[4] See *Athenian Religion*, 296. The Athenians became involved in the Second Macedonian War in 200 because two Acarnanians who inadvertently entered the sanctuary at Eleusis uninitiated were summarily executed by the *antistites templi* (Livy 31.14.6–9). But this act of violence, which created scandal, against foreigners is scarcely proof of a recognized right, still less of one valid among citizens.

[5] For instructions given by deme assemblies to deme priests see Whitehead, *Demes*, 182; a conspicuous instance at city level is the instruction to the Eleusinian personnel in 415 to curse the violators of the *Mysteries* (Plut. *Alc.* 22.5, 33.3). B. Dignas in an important monograph (*Economy of the Sacred in Hellenistic and Roman Asia Minor*, Oxford 2002, esp. 1–35) challenges the consensus that sees priests as subservient to state. But the kinds of examples which she finds in Asia Minor of priesthoods standing up for their god against the city in financial affairs lack Attic parallels: no priest, to our knowledge, protested against the use of Athena's monies to finance the Peloponnesian war. (Perhaps an attempt on the monies of Demeter of Eleusis might have provoked more resistance ...) Aristotle's classification: Arist. *Pol.* 1299a 15–19: priesthoods are 'different from the political *archai*'; cf. 1322b 18–29, 1331b 4–5. For an institutional historian, priesthoods are not *archai* because *dokimasia* for them is not attested, they can be combined with other *archai*, and women can hold them (M. R. Hansen, *GRBS* 21, 1980, 170); but, by being made subject to *euthyna* (*IG* II² 354.21–22, 410.22; Aeschin. 3.18), they were certainly being pushed towards the ordinary magistracies.

is separate from the city. No such institution existed anywhere in Greece. Were it sensible to talk in such terms at all, one would have to say that Church was part of State. The individual who had the highest responsibility in religious affairs was a magistrate, the *basileus*.[6]

Similarly, trials with a religious element were held before the same courts as heard cases of other kinds. The distinctive character of such cases was, it is true, recognized in some degree. Those involving sacred olive-trees were heard before the Areopagus, disputes over priesthoods at the court of the *basileus*; slave evidence could set in motion prosecutions for impiety, temple-robbing, and harm to the sacred olive-trees, and a special jury of initiates was empanelled in 415 to try those charged of profaning the *Mysteries*.[7] The last of these provisions represents an obvious special case; the only procedure regularly admitted in religious but not in secular cases appears to be the initiation of action through denunciation by slaves. In jurisdiction as in legislation the general principle is that sacred matters no less than profane are handled through the normal institutions of the city. When in 352/1 disputes about the boundaries of the 'Sacred *Orgas*' at Eleusis had to be adjudicated, the assembly appointed a commission of fifteen men, five to be drawn from the council and ten from the Athenians at large, to look into this most sensitive of religious issues. They also invited the *basileus*, all the male Eleusinian cultic dignitaries, and 'any Athenian who wishes', to attend, to ensure that the 'boundary stones were placed as piously and as justly as possible'.[8] The commissioners would be reminded of the solemnity of their task by the presence of representatives of religion in such numbers. Yet they, the lay persons, would cast the votes. A certain general obligation to supervise the religious affairs of Athens was vested in the Areopagus, and represents a modest restriction on the authority of assembly and courts. But the Areopagus was made up of citizens, not of religious specialists.

Formal power in religious matters was diffused (with the exception just mentioned) among all those who had the right to vote; priestesses, therefore, lacked it entirely. But there is also the matter of influence and authority. We do not know for sure whose were the authoritative and influential voices when the assembly debated sacred topics. The most striking single document is the decree which proposed the summoning of first fruits to Eleusis from all

---

[6] On his functions see P. Carlier, *La Royauté en Grèce avant Alexandre* (Strasburg 1984), 325–52.

[7] See D. M. MacDowell, *The Law in Classical Athens* (London 1978), 192–202; Todd, *Athenian Law*, 307–15, or in brief my comments in M. Gagarin and E. Cohen, *The Cambridge Companion to Greek Law* (forthcoming). That slave denunciation was allowed in religious cases and them alone is strongly argued by R. Osborne in V. Hunter and J. Edmonson (eds.), *Law and Social Status in Classical Athens* (Oxford 2000), 76–92. Disputes over priesthoods: Arist. *Ath. Pol.* 57.2, with the note of P. J. Rhodes ad loc.: the existence of speeches by logographers in such cases (*Athenian Religion*, 302–3) seems to imply trial before a court. Courts where cases concerning the *Mysteries* were tried were roped off: Pollux 8.141.

[8] *IG* II² 204 (RO 58) 1–16. On the Areopagus see *Athenian Religion*, 130–1.

Greece. The seer Lampon proposed a long amendment, in which he began by tidying a few details in the decree, but went on to present three new substantive proposals on religious matter—the intercalation of a month, restrictions on altars in the Pelargikon, and a new proposal for collecting first fruits of olive oil.[9] Here is one instance of a seer of established position taking a lead in such debates. Since oracles from oracle collections could also bear on technical religious issues, figures such as the *chresmologos* Hierocles too were doubtless often heard.[10] It was another *chresmologos*, Diopeithes 'the mad', who supposedly sought to make 'those who do not acknowledge the divine' and 'teach about things in the air' liable to prosecution. Once we find mention of a priest: a decree makes provision for the performance of 'preliminary sacrifices to Asclepius as expounded by Euthydemus of Eleusis', who was the priest of Asclepius in the Piraeus.[11] Whether it was on his own initiative or by prior invitation of the council or assembly that Euthydemus had drafted his sacrificial menu is unclear; there was no expectation that a priest should raise his voice about the ritual of his sanctuary, but one who did so had an obvious claim to be heard. The same can be said of the official exegetes within their area of special competence, though no interventions by them are in fact attested. But ordinary politicians too must often have had their say. The fourth-century rhetorical handbook *Rhetorica ad Alexandrum* assumes that they would need to speak regularly on the financial aspects of cult (but why on these alone?); it provides indeed a highly instructive account of the various arguments by which one can prove the piety of increasing expenditure on sacrifices, or decreasing it, or keeping it the same. In 333 the merchants of Citium approached the boule with a request for special permission to buy land on which to build a temple of Aphrodite. The boule referred the request to the assembly without making a recommendation, and in the assembly it was the leading politician of the day, Lycurgus, who stood up to propose that the Citian request be granted. Aeschines assumes that it might fall to any ordin-

---

[9] *IG* I³ 78 (ML 73).   [10] See pp. 112–13 below.

[11] Diopeithes: Plut. *Per.* 32.2; cf. *Athenian Religion* 208. On Diopeithes see Bowden, 'Oracles for Sale', 268–9. Ameipsias fr. 10 makes the Athenian Diopeithes a *chresmologos*, which surely renders the identification with the *chresmologos* Diopeithes later active at Sparta (Xen. *Hell.* 3.3.3 and Plut. *Lys.*22.10–12, *Ages.* 3.6–7) almost irresistible. It is generally believed that he also proposed an important secular decree (*IG* I³ 61 = ML 65); but the crucial letter trace, the bottom bar of the Δ in Δ[ιοπεί]θης in *IG* I³ 61.4, was seen only by Kirchhoff (who marks _ in the relevant space in the majuscule transcr. in *IG* I but gives [Διοπεί]θης in the text); earlier editors saw nothing, which shows that deterioration of the stone is not at issue, and later editors seem merely to have followed Kirchhoff. Nothing is visible on published photos or on an Oxford squeeze. Stephen Lambert kindly reports from autopsy that a bottom bar is not visible (though not impossible); a very faint trace of a left diagonal (of Δ, A or M) can perhaps be detected. If the Δ is disallowed, several other restorations become possible. 'Mad': Ameipsias fr. 10, Teleklides fr. 7; he is associated with τύμπανα in Phrynichus fr. 9. Whether Stilbides, the other famous religious professional of the period (Ar. *Pax* 1031 with the commentators: another 'name' was Amphoteros, Eupolis fr. 225), was active in the assembly is not recorded. Euthydemus: *IG* II² 47 (*LSS* 11). For priestly figures being invited to 'expound' appropriate offerings cf. *IG* I³ 78 (ML 73) 36–7 (of the Eumolpids). Euthydemus' own interest is clear from *IG* II² 4962 (*LSCG* 21).

ary politician to 'draft vows in his decrees to the Semnai Theai on behalf of the city'. The task of revising Solon's sacrificial calendar fell neither to a politician nor to a religious specialist but to the under-secretary Nicomachus.[12]

In the year 411, when the dissolution of the democracy and the recall of the impious Alcibiades were under discussion, members of the two sacred *gene* of Eleusis were among many who protested. Others objected on other grounds, but they spoke for piety: they 'testified about the matters concerning the *Mysteries* which had caused Alcibiades' banishment and appealed in the name of the gods (ἐπιθειάζω) not to recall him'. This incident is the only collective intervention by a kind of 'religious interest' known to us in Athenian history. All the other most conspicuous examples of priestly influence and commitment that can be cited also relate to members of the great *gene* of Eleusis. It was, for instance, the great-grandson of a hierophant (and so a Eumolpid himself, unless the link was maternal) who joined in the prosecution of Andocides, another offender against the *Mysteries*, in 399, and wrote the speech, replete with arguments from religion, that survives as Lysias 6.[13] The quasi-priests of Eleusis embody the limiting case of priestly authority, the extreme beyond which it never grew. But even at this extreme the members of the two *gene* were speaking in the name not of religion but of the particular gods whose cults they served. And their other interventions were, certainly or probably, similarly restricted, with the exception of the role that the hierophant Eurymedon perhaps played in the prosecution of Aristotle for 'impiety'. If the last detail is historical, there were perhaps special contexts in which a hierophant could profess to speak in the name of a generalized piety. But earlier in the century a hierophant who performed a sacrifice which belonged by right to the priestess of Demeter had the offence brought up against him in court;[14] the religious authority even of the most eminent priestly figure was strictly delimited. As a general rule, if a priest could speak with authority in the assembly, it was only on the affairs of his own sanctuary; to offer advice on those of another would very likely have been perceived as an intrusion. It was a *chresmologos*, Diopeithes, who supposedly sought to bring atheists to book.

Priesthood brought a certain respect owed to the office, no doubt. Reliefs attached to decrees that honour priests show them with distinctive attributes—the temple key for women, the sacrificial knife for men—which, reappearing on funerary monuments, prove that both sexes could be proud of having held such office. We would like to know whether those who served

---

[12] [Arist.] *Rh. Al.* 1423a20–1424a8 (but the case for reducing sacrifices is invidious, ibid. 1437b21); Aeschin. 1.188; for the merchants of Citium see *IG* II² 337 (RO 91), and for Nicomachus Lys. 30 *passim*. One would like to know how e.g. the συγγραφεῖς responsible for *IG* I³ 78 (ML 73) were selected.

[13] [Lys.] 6. 54. Events of 411: Thuc. 8.53.2.

[14] Apollod. *Neaer.* 116. Other interventions of Eumolpids: see *Athenian Religion*, 297. The case mentioned in [Lys.] 6. 54 very likely related to the *Mysteries*.

Fig. 7. Document relief (late fourth-century) showing a hero (probably Antiochos) crowning a mortal who is marked out by his short-sleeved tunic and the knife he carries as (probably) the tribal priest.

just for a year might have been so represented on their tombstones. Lysimache, priestess of Athena Polias for sixty-four years, must have been something of a national monument, but those whom accident of birth debarred from the life priesthoods may still have been proud to have served for a term.[15] Knife-bearers, i.e. priests, on funerary monuments wear a distinctive long, unbelted, short-sleeved tunic worn also by the mature male who helps in folding Athena's *peplos* in the central scene of the Parthenon frieze. In dress too then the priest is marked out, at least on ceremonial occasions.[16] The priests and priestesses of the main public cults sat in reserved seats in the theatre of Dionysus, and at least one deme (Piraeus) honoured its own priests similarly.[17] This was an enviable and conspicuous honour. But, if the sacred personnel of the city came together as a group in the theatre at the *Dionysia*, this was the only occasion in the year at which they normally did so. For all these reasons it is generally recognized that the priesthood was not so much politically impotent—for that might imply ambitions which could not be satisfied—as politically disengaged. The influential voices in the assembly were those of the free agents, the seers and oracle-interpreters.

If religious policy was not determined by the priests, it becomes natural to suppose, since they must have done something, that their role was to carry it out. On this view priests prayed and sacrificed on behalf of the Athenians, within guidelines determined by the assembly; and they alone could do so. Yet quite the opposite case has been advocated with considerable force.[18] Authoritative prayer and sacrifice on behalf of the Athenians could be made only, it has been argued, by magistrates or other appointees of the city. Priests might assist, but their participation was not essential; a priest without a magistrate, by contrast, could not represent the city of Athens before the gods. That claim is doubtless extreme, but serves to bring the question 'who prays for Athens?' into sharp focus.

The concept of 'praying and sacrificing' or just 'sacrificing' 'on behalf of the Athenians' is not an anachronistic one. Priests and boards of officials were regularly voted honours by council and assembly in recognition of their services (this is another index of the prestige available to priests),[19] and the sacrifices that they had performed 'on behalf of the Athenians' or 'for the health and safety of the Athenians' or something of the kind are commonly the first item included in the list; the formal occasion for the vote of honours is

---

[15] Key and knife: see A. G. Mantis, Προβλήματα της εικονογραφίας των ιερειών και των ιερέων στην αρχαία Ελληνική τέχνη (Athens 1990), 40–51, 82–96; Lawton, *Document Reliefs*, nos. 145 and 164; J. B. Connelly, *Portrait of a Priestess: Women and Ritual in Ancient Grece* (forthcoming), ch. 3. A woman shown with a key is explicitly attested as a priestess in two Attic cases (IG II² 3477 with 6398; *CEG* 566); the link between knife and priesthood appears to be circumstantial only, but very strong. Lysimache: IG II² 3453, Pliny HN 34.76; it is not clear whether the woman commemorated in her epitaph as first priestess of Athena Nike served for life or a year (*Athenian Religion*, 126, n. 20).

[16] Mantis, op. cit., 82–96; figure E 34 on the Parthenon. For the special dress of the main Eleusinian officiants see Clinton, *Sacred Officials*, 32–3, 48, 116. For non-Attic evidence see P. Stengel, *Die griechischen Kultusaltertümer*, ed. 3 (Munich 1920), 47–8; *Chiron* 30 (2000), 425.

[17] IG II² 1214. 23. *Proedria* was normal in deme theatres (Whitehead, *Demes*, 220), and it is very likely that priests were always among the beneficiaries. Priests might also come out en masse on great public occasions such as the return of Demosthenes (Plut. *Dem.* 27.7).

[18] By Kahrstedt, *Magistratur*, 286–90.

[19] Annual priests in this case certainly included.

often a 'report' by the honorand on the good omens (which the council then resolves to 'accept') that he or she has secured in a particular sacrifice. On the basis of this evidence not only numerous priests but also the eponymous archon, the generals, the hipparchs, the taxiarchs, the *prytaneis*, various kinds of *epimeletai* and *hieropoioi* and, in the hellenistic period, the *agonothetai* and the *kosmetes* of the ephebes all sacrifice for Athens or for segments of it. Honorary decrees of the demes reveal just the same pattern; a new text from Acharnae has unexpectedly given us even the 'treasurer', *tamias*, 'performing all the sacrifices'. And references to sacrifices performed by magistrates such as the *basileus* and the polemarch are quite common in other types of source too.[20]

The difficulty lies in the intriguing imprecision of the Greek verb 'to sacrifice'. There are various grades or types of involvement in a given sacrifice, each of which can quite properly be indicated by the verb θύειν: the sponsor who buys the animal 'sacrifices', as does the individual who places the god's portion on the altar;[21] but so too do all those who participate in the sacrifice and share the meat. It is then theoretically possible to understand the 'X sacrifices' of the decrees as meaning in fact 'X participates in a sacrifice [the chief officiant at which is Y, not here mentioned because irrelevant to the person or group honoured]'; and we can go on to postulate that at every rite apparently conducted by a magistrate the 'real' sacrificer was a priest—or vice versa.[22] But it is very hard to deny entirely to either category the capacity to pray for the city. To deny it to priests is implausible in the light of texts which identify the special competence of priests as expertise in sacrifice and prayer.[23] As for magistrates and other representatives of the city, consider for instance the following passage. Demosthenes protests that Midias pretends to regard him as polluted by murder and yet:

he allowed me [as a member of the boule] to conduct the entry rites on behalf of the boule and to sacrifice and initiate the offerings on behalf of you all and the whole city, he allowed me as chief *theoros* to take the collective offering on behalf of the city to Nemean Zeus, he overlooked my being chosen from all the Athenians as chief of the three *hieropoioi* for the Semnai and initiating the offerings   (Dem. 21.114–15).

The solemn tone is found in several other passages where the responsibility of representing the city before the gods is described.[24] Both that tone and specific

---

[20] For this abundant material see Kahrstedt, *Magistratur*, 288; Rhodes, *Boule*, 43 and 132, and nn. 24 and 31 below. For the demes see e.g. Dem. 57.47; *SEG* XLIII 26 A 3–4; *ZPE* 130 (2000), 45–7, col. 2, 1–2, 23. Athenaeus 234 f. gives us cultic parasites as sacrificers.

[21] M. Mauss and H. Hubert in their influential 'Essai sur la nature et la fonction de la sacrifice' (*L'Année Sociologique* 2, 1899) distinguished the first of these functions as belonging to 'le sacrifiant' and the second to 'le sacrificateur'. But the distinction is helpful precisely because it is not one that most languages draw.

[22] The honorary decrees occasionally mention that the honorand sacrificed 'with' other persons: so e.g. *IG* II² 676 and *SEG* XVI 63.14, where *epimeletai* sacrifice with the priest, or Moretti 18, taxiarchs with generals.

[23] e.g. Pl. *Polit.* 290c–d.

details are extraordinary if the speech's auditors believed that, in reality, the true representative of the city was an unmentioned priest. It is much easier simply to accept the functional equivalence between priest and magistrate/ general/hipparch (or whomsoever) suggested by the language of the decrees, and allow that both categories could indeed sacrifice for the city. In that case there was no special mode of communication with the divine only operable by priest (or by magistrate): either could perform the same central acts[25] with the same results, though tradition may have insisted that one or the other should do so in a particular case. Aristotle in fact, in a passage which should be decisive, recognizes two types of 'public sacrifice', those 'assigned by convention to priests' and those performed by officials who 'derive their position from the common hearth'.[26]

The conclusion that has just been reached is scarcely controversial; many casual remarks which imply it could doubtless be assembled. But it is not an obvious truth, and it deserves more attention than a fleeting acknowledgement. This functional equipollence of magistrate with priest as representatives of the city before the gods is central to the embeddedness of religion within the city, to what Weber quaintly and somewhat misleadingly termed the 'Caesaropapism' of the ancient city.[27] In recent studies of the political antiquities of Attica one seldom finds great emphasis laid on the crown worn by the nine archons and the members of the council; yet to enter on office was to receive the crown, to be expelled from office was to be deprived of it, and, according to Aeschines, candidates for the nine archonships had to be sexually uncontaminated 'because these are crown-wearing offices'.[28] The only other permanent wearers of crowns were priests; private persons donned them in various contexts, religious rituals chief among them. Aristotle's

---

[24] Cf. Antiph. 6.45 (*bouleutai*); Xen. *Mem.* 2.2.13 (*archontes*); Aeschin. 1.188 (drafters of decrees in the assembly), 3.18 (priests); Apollod. *Neaer.* 73 (wife of *basileus*).

[25] Chief among them no doubt the 'initiation' of the sacrifice (κατάρχεσθαι), probably by cutting a lock of the victim's hair; the prayer; and, above all, the placing of the god's portion on the altar. For the importance of the last see van Straten, *Hierà kalá*, 118–33; *LSS* 14.33 (Attica, 2nd c. BC); *Chiron* 30 (2000), 425 (these epigraphic texts associate the act with priests). One may wonder why Demosthenes in the passage cited speaks twice of 'initiating the sacrifice' and never of 'putting the god's portion on the altar'. Could these acts be performed by different individuals? Or does the one imply the other?

[26] *Pol.* 1322b 26–9.

[27] M. Weber, in G. Roth and C. Wittich (eds.), *Economy and Society* (Berkeley 1978), ii. 1159–63.

[28] Archons: Lys. 26.8; Dem. 21.17, 32–3; [Dem.] 26.5, 58.27; Aeschin. 1.19; Arist. *Ath. Pol.* 57.4; *CEG* 570. 4 (two brothers who claim to have held 'crown-bearing office' four times). Council: Lycurg. *Leoc.* 122. For the later lexicographical allusions see D. M. MacDowell's note on Dem. 21.17. Apollodorus *FGrH* 244 F 140 says that the crowns of the *thesmothetai* were made of myrtle because of its association with 'the goddesses', and he need not be referring—so MacDowell—to special crowns worn at the *Mysteries*, since *thesmothetai* could be seen as permanently associated with Demeter Thesmophoros. Aeschin. 1.19 goes against the suggestion of Kahrstedt, *Magistratur*, 300 (the phenomenon is first mentioned on the penultimate page of the book!), that all ἀρχαί wore the crown; Σ vet. Ar. *Eq.* 59a, which mentions the generals, is not very trustworthy. The archons' crown is mentioned only in passing by M. Blech, *Studien zum Kranz bei den Griechen* (Berlin 1982), 319, n. 8.

phrase quoted above about magistrates 'who derive their office from the common hearth' again implies, if to us a little obscurely, a religious grounding of secular office. Of a board of officials outside the nine archons, the protectors of the laws (*nomophylakes*), we happen to know that they wore not crowns but headbands (*strophia*): the *strophion* too was a priestly emblem.[29] *Archontes*, *bouleutai* and *nomophylakes* bore these emblems of their partly sacred functions throughout the year; other representatives of the city are likely to have assumed them at need.

The very division between priest and magistrate is somewhat artificial, as the various boards of *hieropoioi* show: institutionally *hieropoioi* are simply one more board of minor magistrates, but, as their name indicates, their duties are confined to the performance of rites.[30] Priests and magistrates on assumption of their office seem alike to have made 'entry sacrifices'.[31] The phenomenon can perhaps be seen as one of distinct but converging responsibilities.[32] Priest and magistrates come at the same job from different angles: the magistrates represent the city, before the gods as in other spheres; the priest communicates with the divine, for the city as for other clients. But the point remains that there is no concern to preserve or enhance or underline any such functional differentiation. Both priest and magistrate are simply said to pray and sacrifice for the city.

Which sacrifices were performed by magistrates, which by priests, which by both together, what functions were discharged by the many boards variously concerned with sacred affairs, some on the ritual side, some on the administrative, some on the financial: we will not enter this spider's web

---

[29] Philochorus *FGrH* 328 F 64(b); cf. Clinton, *Sacred Officials*, index s.v. *strophion*. Philochorus seems to imply that the distinction in headwear between *nomophylakes* and *archontes* was part of a deliberate symbolic opposition between the 'protectors of the laws' and the magistrates against whom they protected them.

[30] For both Kahrstedt, *Magistratur*, 289, and M. H. Hansen, *GRBS* 21 (1980), 170, they are magistrates; but in Arist. *Pol.* 1322b 18–25 they fall, along with priests (n. 5), outside the *politikai archai*.

[31] The many allusions to εἰσιτητήρια (cf. A. P. Matthaiou, *Horos* 10–12, 1992–8, 44–5) can confuse because it is usually not specified what 'entry' is in question. For those of *archontes* and *bouleutai* see Lys. 26.8 (archons); Thuc. 8.70.1; Dem. 19.190, 21.114 (boule); for those of hipparchs *Agora* XVI 270 (offered to Demos and Charites and to Poseidon). The priest of Demos and the Charites and the exegetes were involved in the εἰσιτητήρια of the ephebes, a separate event on a separate date (*IG* II² 1011.5 and often). Other priests who sacrificed εἰσιτητήρια are the priest of Zeus Soter (*IG* II² 689+ Mus. Acr. 14906. 20 (cf. *Horos* 10–12, 1992–8, 44–5, p. 31), 690.3: said in *IG* II² 689 to be offered 'for the health and safety of boule and demos'), the annual priest of Asclepius (*SEG* XVIII 21, 26, 27), the (probably non-annual) priestess of Aglaurus (p. 434, n. 64), and the annual priestess in a private cult of Magna Mater (*IG* II² 1315.7). The last case appears to prove that a priest or priestess could initiate his or her own tenure of office in this way (cf. Heliod. *Aeth.* 7.2); whether the εἰσιτητήρια offered by the others were for themselves or for another body is unclear (Pritchett, *War*, iii, 65–6 and A. P. Matthaiou, *Horos* 10–12, 1992–8, 38–41 assign those of the priest of Zeus Soter to the entry of boule and *archontes*, not implausibly; but the relevance of Lys. 26.6–8 is not certain). The problem will affect our conception of the ritualization of the 'New Year' at Athens: was there a single large ceremony attended by numerous officeholders and priests? The problem of Sthorys the seer is different (p. 117, n. 7).

[32] As a reader for OUP suggests to me.

of detailed questions. The activities of the boards have a discernible logic, but it would seldom be easy to predict whether a given sacrifice at a given festival will be the responsibility of a priest, of a group of *hieropoioi*, or of a magistrate (and, if of a magistrate, then of which).[33] And since, as we have seen, no important points of religious principle were at stake, there is perhaps no need to worry too much about the issue.

It would be wrong to leave priests and priestesses without mentioning one aberrant text. Socrates in Plato's *Meno* says that he has heard the doctrine of reincarnation from 'men and women wise in religious matters' whom he then defines as 'such priests and priestesses as have made it their concern to be able to give an account of the rites they conduct'.[34] Some poets too, he continues, know of such things, and it is the testimony of a poet, Pindar, that he goes on to quote. The existence of religious specialists who offered speculative exegesis of rites does not come as a surprise. Seers who approached the doors of the rich with a hubbub of books of Orpheus and Musaeus were such in a way, for all the contempt with which Plato elsewhere speaks of them. An identifiable 'religious intellectual' at Athens may be Euthyphro of Prospalta, apparently a *chresmologos* who also advanced speculative etymological interpretations of divine names. The author of the Derveni papyrus is an aspirant philosopher deeply interested in ritual, even if his status as an actual religious practitioner is not certain.[35] But none of these figures is a 'priest'. Perhaps the text from *Meno* demands a revision of established assumptions. Or perhaps Plato is using 'priests and priestesses' in a loose way which will include religious specialists of all types.

Our second topic was to be the role of religion within the procedures of public life in Athens. We can start on the Pnyx. Attacking Timarchus, who, he maintains, should never have been permitted to raise his voice before the assembly at all, Aeschines emphasizes the orderly procedures that 'the law-giver' wished to see observed in that solemn place:

Once the purificatory offering has been taken round and the herald has pronounced the ancestral prayers, [the lawgiver] requires the presiding *prytaneis* to hold a preliminary vote on ancestral rites, and for heralds and embassies, and on secular matters, and after this the herald asks 'Who of those over fifty years of age wishes to

---

[33] Often evidence is lacking, but one can note e.g. *LSCG* 33 [RO 81] B 7–27 (*Lesser Panathenaea*), *LSS* 14.30–62 (*Thargelia*); Arist. *Ath. Pol.* 54–8; Philochorus *FGrH* 328 F 64. That the officials listed as paying the proceeds of hide-sales from various festivals in *IG* II² 1496 had also conducted the sacrifices (so Kahrstedt, *Magistratur*, 289–90, noting the variations from year to year) is not quite clear.

[34] Pl. *Men.* 81a–b.

[35] Hubbub: p. 121 below. Euthyphro: see C. H. Kahn in A. Laks and G. W. Most, *Studies on the Derveni Papyrus* (Oxford 1997), 55–63, on Pl. *Euthyphr.* 3b–c with Pl. *Cra.* 396d and *passim*, esp. 399e–400b; but note the doubts of E. Hussey, *Oxford Studies in Ancient Philosophy* 17 (1999), 303–24, at 311–15. Derveni papyrus: for a good introduction to new thought on this text see E. Hussey, loc. cit. The stress on women in the *Meno* passage has often led Pythagoreanism to be mentioned. But we could remember too the kinds of 'priestess' discussed on p. 121 below.

speak?' When all these have spoken, only then does he instruct any other Athenian who wishes, among those permitted to do so, to speak.   (Aeschin. 1.23)

We see here how the religious rituals that initiate meetings of the assembly are only part of a broader ritualization that characterized much of Athenian public procedure; the point could be made in other ways, even if Aeschines' claim that elderly speakers still had priority in the late fourth century is in fact a fraud.[36] But our concern here is with the religious elements. The assembly is first purified by blood; the herald then pronounces a combined curse and prayer best known to us from a splendid burlesque in Aristophanes' *Thesmo-phoriazusae*, from which it emerges that the herald invited all those attending the assembly to 'join in praying' that the meeting should prove successful, but traitors, deceitful speakers and the like should suffer perdition.[37] The business then opens with the matter of 'sacred rites', given respectful first place on the agenda.

Aeschines does not mention the sacrifices performed to Apollo Prostaterios and other gods by the *prytaneis* before every meeting; the good omens secured at such sacrifices were apparently then reported to the assembly, and the citizens were urged to 'accept' them.[38] When the outcome of sacrifices was reported to the council and assembly, the news seems always to have been good. Peisetairos in Aristophanes duly reports to the assembly of the Birds that 'the sacrifices are fair'. If sacrifices had sometimes to be repeated, if meetings could even be cancelled through failure to secure good omens, such cases have eluded our sources. We know that meetings could be abandoned while in progress in consequence of 'signs from Zeus' (διοσημίαι) such as earthquakes and, no doubt, storms. The delicate and sometimes controversial judgement of what constituted a διοσημία perhaps lay with the presiding *prytaneis*.[39] But the possibility that a meeting could not be opened at all (or perhaps rather that particular business could not be brought to a meeting) because of divine warnings is mentioned only in regard to elections to the

---

[36] See the note ad loc. of N. Fisher in his commentary (Oxford 2001). Broader ritualization: see R. Osborne's introduction to *Ritual, Finance, Politics*. Halfway between secular and religious is the practice of donning a crown before addressing the assembly (Arist. *Av.* 463; *Thes.* 380; *Eccl.* 131, 148).

[37] Ar. *Thesm.* 295–371; for further sources on all this see M. H. Hansen, *The Athenian Assembly* (Oxford 1987), 90–1; Rhodes, *Boule*, 36–7 (who argues that the whole introductory procedure was the same in the boule: the curse certainly was, Dem. 19.70); and cf. p. 405 below. On 'joining in praying' see Pulleyn, *Prayer*, 173–8; is a refusal to do so the failure of Theophrastus' mulish man who is δεινὸς δὲ καὶ τοῖς θεοῖς μὴ ἐπεύχεσθαι (*Char.* 15.11)? On religious procedures within the boule see esp. Ant. 6.45.

[38] Agenda: Arist. *Ath. Pol.* 43.6, with Rhodes. On the phrase μετὰ τὰ ἱερά see P. J. Rhodes in *Chiron* 25 (1995), 194–5. Sacrifice by *prytaneis*: p. 404. n. 70 below; cf. Peisetairos' positive report to the Birds, Ar. *Av.* 1118. For the possibility of the assembly contracting *vota publica* (twice attested in the 4th c.) see p. 406 below. Large general assertions about Athenian reliance on divination in state affairs are made by Quintus Cicero in Cic. *Div.* 1.95, 122; they are too vague to be helpful.

[39] For abandonments see Ar. *Ach.* 169–71; Thuc. 5.45.4.; for a controversial non-abandonment see Ar. *Nub.* 581–7 (election of Cleon as general). Pollux 8.124 states that the courts were

military offices: these took place in the first prytany, after the sixth, 'in which good omens (εὐσημία) occurred'. The task of electing those on whose competence the safety of the city depended was, it seems, approached with particular caution. And it was in this way, we note, not by use of the lot, that the gods were given the opportunity to influence these crucial appointments.[40] But it is not clear how to reconcile the special care taken in this case with the reports supposedly brought to every meeting of the assembly that 'the sacrifices are propitious'. Perhaps a different and more exacting mode of testing divine favour was applied. But, as so often in matters of divination, the 'how it really was' eludes us. Some inconvenience must have arisen from the possibility of crucial elections being postponed at short notice by a month or more. It may be for this reason that in the second century BC 'election meetings in accord with the oracle of the god' start to be attested on fixed dates.[41] If so, it was only after seeking Delphic sanction, 'the oracle of the god', that the Athenians rationalized their procedures in this way.

The courts illustrate the paradoxes of Athenian rationalism rather vividly. Inside, the advocates insist with often tortuous logic that reason alone, guided by probability, can pull out the darkest events from the cupboard of the past and expose what must have happened to the light of day. Though speakers regularly impute impiety to their opponents, and threaten the jurors with divine vengeance should they disregard their oath, it is exceptional when a defendant on a murder charge appeals to 'divine signs' as actual proof of his innocence ('ships on which murderers sail sink; all my voyages have been fair'[42]). Yet many clients who commissioned speeches in this vein from professional speechwriters also sought to bind the speeches of their opponents, again no doubt with professional aid, by use of *katadesmoi*. The city of words was also, it has often been noted, the city of curses. As for procedures, purifications and preparatory divination are not attested, though 'omens from Zeus' (διοσημίαι) could cause sessions to be suspended. The Areopagus sat only on three 'impure days' at the end of the month appropriate to its

---

dissolved in the event of a διοσημία and adds that 'those who taught about διοσημίαι and other sacred matters were called exegetes'; Hesychius ε 3830 defines an exegete as an 'expounder about sacred matters and διοσημίαι'. Jacoby, *Atthis*, 47, apparently accepts that the exegetes fulfilled this function for assembly and courts. But it is possible that Pollux has brought two distinct things together: the exegetes could well have been consulted about occasional portents, such as the 'sign in the sky' of [Dem.] 43.66, without being involved in day-to-day decisions (demanding constant attendance, and snap judgements) about courts and assembly. In Ar. *Ach.* loc. cit. the *prytaneis* dissolve the assembly. On the other side is the observation (Jacoby, 251, n. 64) that in Pollux 'the mention of the *exegetai* occurs among the δικανικὰ ὀνόματα', which implies that a serious source linked exegetes and courts.

[40] It was possible (Pl. *Leg.* 759b) to interpret use of the lot as a form of divine selection. But the lot was also seen as a randomizing device, and the contexts of actual use show this understanding to have been the prevalent one (M. H. Hansen, *The Athenian Democracy in the Age of Demosthenes*, Oxford 1991, 49–52). εὐσημία: Arist. *Ath. Pol.* 44.4.

[41] So P. Gauthier, *CRAI* 1998, 63–75, on *IG* II² 892, 954a, 955.

[42] Antiph. 5. 81–4.

potentially deadly business; homicide courts in general sat in the open air, in order, it was said, to protect the jurors from pollution and 'so that the prosecutor should not share a roof with his kinsman's slayer'. Those acquitted at the Areopagus made a sacrifice to the Semnai at their shrine just by the court (in Pausanias' day at least).[43] The homicide procedures are barnacled with archaic-seeming rules of this type which Athenians sometimes explained by the danger of pollution and which scholarship has often accepted, indeed played up, as responses to that ancient terror. They are better seen as a kind of ritual theatre that became necessary when prosecution was substituted for self-help as the proper response to homicide.[44] The victim's kin no longer took direct action, but, in exchange, the suspected killer became an internal exile until the time of the trial, excluded from the life of the community, polluted.

The courts were one of the various contexts of Athenian life where the swearing of oaths was routine. As an ephebe, as a councillor, as a magistrate, as an arbitrator, as member of the panel of jurors for a year, one swore to do one's duty. After the revolt of Chalkis in (probably) 446 the 'council and jurors' swore on the side of Athens to the terms of settlement; after the oligarchic revolution of 411–410 the decree of Demophantus required the citizens to swear en masse 'by tribes and demes' to 'kill by word and deed and vote and hand' any person subverting the democracy in future. 'The oath is what holds the democracy together', says Lycurgus.[45] These rituals of public commitment to the values of the community must in some cases have been striking ceremonial occasions. As evidence of Athenian piety one should perhaps not press them too hard, though speakers in court sometimes sought to scare jurors with the dangerous consequences of neglecting their oath.[46] The uses of the oath within the legal system itself were elaborate enough to require the simple verb 'to swear' (ὀμνύναι) to be afforced, to the bewilderment of posterity, by four distinct prefixes (ὑπ-, δι-, ἐξ, ἀντ-). These complexities cannot be laid out here. In brief, before any action both parties were required to swear to the justice of their case (to the disgust of Plato, who noted that

---

[43] Impure days: *Etym. Magn.* (131.13–19), *Etym. Gud.* s.v. ἀποφράδες (Pritchett, *War*, iii, 210). Open air: Antiph. 5.11; cf. Arist. *Ath. Pol.* 57.4; Parker, *Miasma*, 122. Semnai: Paus. 1.28.6. Curses: see Ch. 6.

[44] See E. Carawan, *Rhetoric and the Law of Draco* (Oxford 1998), 17–19 [+]; on the evidence of Antiphon B. Williams, *Shame and Necessity* (Berkeley 1993), 189, n. 28 and Carawan, 192–8.

[45] *IG* I³ 40 (ML 52) 3–4; Andoc. *Myst.* 1.97; Lycurg. *Leoc.* 79; on the oaths of ephebes and the rest see R. J. Bonner and G. Smith, *The Administration of Justice from Homer to Aristotle*, ii (Chicago 1938), 145–91. Oaths of this type (where perjury brings no benefit) are allowed by Plato in *Laws* (948e–949a). See in general S. G. Cole, 'Oath Ritual and the Male Community at Athens', in J. Ober and C. Hedrick (eds.), *Demokratia* (Princeton 1996), 227–48.

[46] See Parker, *Miasma*, 128, n. 90; 187, n. 241. Voting was sometimes rendered more solemn by fetching the ballots from an altar (Boegehold, *Lawcourts*, 46, n. 17), but only exceptionally was this done in the courts (see the proposal of Drakontides in Plut. *Per.* 32.3; other instances: Dem. 18.134, a non-judicial decision of the Areopagus; [Dem.] 43.14; *IG* II² 1237. 17–18, phratry admission).

perjury was thereby institutionalized[47]). Only in homicide trials were witnesses required to testify on oath, though in other cases they might do so
voluntarily. The oaths in homicide trials were of especial solemnity, being
taken 'standing over the cut pieces of a boar, a ram and a bull, slaughtered by
the proper persons on the proper days'. Another singularity of the homicide
courts was the requirement placed on a successful defendant to swear that
'those who voted for him had voted for what was true and just, and that he
had spoken no falsehood'; he was required 'to invoke destruction on himself
and his household if this was not so, and pray for many blessings for the
jurors'.[48] So the juror who had been lured by a defendant's deceitful wiles
into leaving a murder unavenged was not to have to bear the religious guilt
on his own head. But there were no situations at Athens in which, as in the
Gortynian code, one party to a dispute was entitled to settle it finally in his
own favour by an oath that he had, or had not, done a particular thing.
Litigants occasionally offered one another the opportunity to swear an oath
about particular points of fact, but seem normally to have done so as a
rhetorical ploy only in circumstances where they knew that the offer would
be refused.[49] So the many oaths sworn in and around the Athenian courts
decided nothing. And if they were false, it was left to the gods to punish them;
'false witness' was an actionable offence, but not perjury.

Because Thucydides did not care to expand on them, the ritual preliminaries to Athenian warfare are not well known. But enough survives to show
that before embarking on a campaign, perhaps even before mustering forces,
it was normal to secure 'good omens'; so too before engaging in battle by land
or sea. One of the duties of a cavalry commander was to 'sacrifice with good
outcome (καλλιερεῖν) on behalf of the cavalry'.[50] In the field, it was the
general's decision when to take omens and how to respond to them. But
Aeschines can accuse the politician Demosthenes of sending an army out to
face Philip 'with sacrifices unperformed, good omens unsecured'; and a
passage of Eupolis too attacks a rhetor for forcing the generals to lead a

---

[47] *Leg.* 948b–949a. On legal oaths see Bonner and Smith, loc. cit.; D. M. MacDowell, *Athenian Homicide Law in the Age of the Orators* (Manchester 1963), 90–100; Harrison, *Law*, ii, 99–100; Carawan, op. cit., 138–43.

[48] Dem. 23.67; Aeschin. 2.87.

[49] See Harrison, *Law*, ii. 130–3; D. Mirhady, 'The Oath-Challenge in Athens', *CQ* 41 (1991), 78–83 (who thinks that such oaths may have had a real, action-resolving role in some arbitration cases); M. Gagarin, 'Oaths and Oath-Challenges in Greek Law', in *Symposion 1995*, 125–34. A difficult fragment of Solon (F 42 Ruschenbusch) suggests that dispute-resolving oaths may have been admitted in early Athenian law in the absence of evidence: see Gagarin, op. cit., 127, and K. Latte, *Heiliges Recht* (Tübingen 1920), 24–5.

[50] Before a campaign: see Xen. *Hell.* 6.5.49; IG I³ 93.23 (ML 78 c 14), money set aside in connection with the Sicilian expedition ἐς καλλιέρησιν. Before battle: Thuc. 6.69.2; Diod. Sic. 13.97.5 and 7; Plut. *Nic.* 25.1. Note too Thuc. 6.32.1 for 'the customary prayers' before departure of a fleet. Pre-campaign propitiation (ἐξαρέσκω) and divination are closely linked by Xen. *Oik.* 5.19. See in general my 'Sacrifice and battle', in H. van Wees (ed.), *War and Violence in Ancient Greece* (London 2000), 299–314; and cf. p. 399, n. 48 below. Cavalry commander: Xen. *Eq. mag.* 3.3.1; cf. n. 31 above (entry sacrifices), Hesych. ι 786.

force to Mantinea in 418 in defiance of warning claps of thunder.[51] It seems unlikely that a politician could have argued in the assembly that a situation was too urgent even to permit the customary religious precautions to be observed. But one could doubtless threaten to prosecute any general who made the gods a pretext for cowardice, or treachery.

The incidents just mentioned allow an easy transition to this chapter's final topic. We have been looking at the religious procedures of assembly, courts and army. In large measure they can be seen as soothing background music of religious reassurance. Fair signs initiated our meeting for the election of generals, and it is under fair omens that we venture out on campaign. 'It is by trust in signs from the gods that you conduct the public business of the city in safety, both perilous undertakings and those free from peril' declares a speaker in the fifth century.[52] These procedures imply a society in which religious observance is embedded, and taken for granted. But they do not imply that members of that society were notably guided in their decision-making, collective or individual, by religious motives or anxieties. Embedded religion is comfortable, familiar, and easy to live with; it is in the background of awareness. We must look now also at the foreground, at the kinds of arguments from the gods' will that could be used in deliberative assemblies. The topic is forbiddingly large. Much of what we believe we know about Athenian religious attitudes derives from speeches made in courts or in assembly. Much will need to be passed over, in favour of a few key topics.

I begin with a few generalities. The tone adopted in matters of religion is one of absolute respect. Aeschylus' Agamemnon condemns himself, many readers have supposed, by the second line that he speaks in his play, in which he pays tribute to the gods as being 'jointly responsible' with himself for the sack of Troy. The cliché he should have used appears, for instance, in Demosthenes, when he explains a decisive change of heart by the Thebans as having occurred 'above all by the favour of some god, but secondly, in as far as one individual deserves the credit, because of me'.[53] One may boast as much as one pleases vis-à-vis other humans, but one must always assign first credit to the gods. The cliché 'first after the gods' is commonly used in relation to a saving intervention of some kind, and the presumption that, if the gods intervene, it will be to the benefit of the speaker's group is universal. The gods of oratory support, counsel and cherish Athens. Negative interventions occur only in the form of a divine madness which occasionally seizes the wicked, that is to say the enemies of Athens or one's political opponents.[54]

---

[51] Aeschin. 3.131, 152; Eupolis, *Demoi*, fr. 99. 29–32.
[52] Antiph. 5.81.
[53] Aesch. *Ag*. 811; Dem. 18. 153; cf. Dem. 24.7, 135; [Dem.] 25.21; Dem. 32.8; Aeschin. 3.1; also [Aesch.] Sept. 1074–5; Hdt. 7.139.5; Eur. *El*. 890–92; Xen. *Anab*. 7.7.22. Cf. Mikalson, *Athenian Popular Religion*, ch. 2, 'The Priority of the Divine'.

Athens was publicly committed to the most scrupulous piety, but circumstances sometimes pushed the Athenians into questionable behaviour. It would be interesting to learn more of the justifications deployed in such cases, which tend to be known from narrative rather than from oratorical sources; we do not know, for instance, how the Athenians defended to themselves their continued support for the Phocian cause in the Third Sacred War, after the Phocians had laid hands on the temple treasures of Delphi. The Athenian representatives in Thucydides' Melian debate declare grimly that amoral use of force is sanctioned by the example of the gods. But they are speaking behind closed doors, and no such tone is struck in any public speech even in Thucydides, let alone in reality. An incident of the 370s is intriguing, but inconclusive. According to one account, the general Iphicrates chanced to capture a vessel which contained treasure sent by the tyrant Dionysius of Syracuse for dedication at Olympia and Delphi. He sent a message to the assembly at Athens asking for guidance, and was told 'not to investigate the concerns of the gods (ἐξετάζειν τὰ τῶν θεῶν) but to consider how to feed his troops'. He duly then exploited the windfall for that purpose, very sacrilegiously in the view of the reporting source. So blunt a dismissal of the claims of the gods surprises. Or was the tone rather 'question not the ways of the providence which has put this treasure in your hands at an hour of need'? The controversial act is anyway absent from other, discrepant accounts of the same incident.[55]

Orators claim little skill at 'investigating the concerns of the gods'. 'The gods' of oratory are normally an anonymous collective quite different from the individual figures of myth and cult. Speakers do not profess to be able to describe the doings and motives of particular gods, nor even of the nameless group except in rather vague and general terms.[56] It is not that the orators are positioning themselves at a fastidious distance from the mythologized anthropomorphism of popular cult. On the contrary, they are speaking the language of ordinary experience, which knows nothing of direct interventions by individual, tangible Olympians. Only a poet or a seer can identify what god has been at work in a particular case. For this reason, our question about the role of religious arguments in public debate becomes largely a question about the role of divination and prophecy. Politicians have no more insight into the ways of the gods than any ordinary Athenian. No inspired texts exist from which guidance might be elicited by authoritative exegesis. This is the permanent condition of a religion without original revelation: partial revelations have constantly to be sought instead, through divination, about particular cases. The issue becomes that of the Athenians' attitude to such ad hoc enlightenment.[57]

[54] Supporting gods: see Mikalson, *Athenian Popular Religion*, 18, 58–60; and my 'Gods Cruel and Kind', 143–60; madness: ibid. 152.

[55] Diod. Sic. 16.57.2–3; cf. Xen. *Hell.* 6.2.33–6; Diod. 15.47.7; Ephorus *FGrH* 70 F 211; Giuliani, *Oracolo*, 181–3, who suspects an anti-Athenian invention.

[56] See Mikalson, *Athenian Popular Religion*, 66–8, 112–14.

In ordinary court cases it was ruled out entirely.[58] For obvious reasons, no individual could adduce a dream, or even an oracular response tendered to himself, as proof: there was no way of controlling the authenticity of such reported revelations. And courts did not refer cases to oracles for decision. In public deliberation the situation is more complicated, and interesting. When decisions had to be made about matters of cult, the assembly very regularly decided to put the question to an oracle. Sometimes it looks as if a decision that had already been made was merely sent for approval: the god seems, for example, to have been asked to confirm that Demon should consecrate his house and garden to Asclepius and become priest of Asclepius himself, and that it was advantageous for the deme of Acharnae to build altars of Ares and Athena Areia (we note that here the procedure extends down to deme level). About the first priestess of Bendis a genuine choice was offered, though lacunas on the stone obscure the exact terms (perhaps 'should she be Athenian or Thracian?'). Sometimes the stipulation in a sacred law that such and such is to be done 'in accord with the oracle of the god' implies a specific consultation without allowing us to recover the exact question posed; small local concerns were not below the god's notice, as we see from a text from Lamptrai which prescribes the offerings to be made to the Nymphs of a particular spring 'in accord with the oracle of the god'. The ten or so surviving examples of such routine questions are likely to be only a tiny fraction of those actually posed. Plato's Socrates declares that Apollo of Delphi should be consulted about all issues relating to 'the establishment of shrines, sacrifices, and other forms of cult for gods and *daimones* and heroes; and also the graves of the dead and the service we must do them to have their favour.'[59] Nominees for one public religious office had actually to be approved by Apollo, as is indicated by their very title of 'Pytho-ordained exegete'.[60]

One enquiry on a cultic matter is very singular. In 352/1 the Athenians determined to ask the god whether (probably) land just outside the marked

---

[57] Some years ago I had the opportunity to read an early version of H. Bowden, *Classical Athens and the Delphic Oracle: Divination and Democracy* (Cambridge, forthcoming). I acknowledge one debt below (n. 62), but I fear others may escape my memory.

[58] Mikalson, *Athenian Popular Religion*, 48. He is not quite right to say that private divination lacked respectability: the point is that it lacked probative force.

[59] Demon: *IG* II² 4969 (cf. *Athenian Religion*, 250, n. 112). Acharnae: *SEG* XXI 519. Bendis: *IG* I³ 136.29; whether *IG* II² 1283.6 refers to a different consultation or the same is uncertain (*Athenian Religion*, 172–3). Lamptrai: *IG* I³ 256 (*LSCG* 178). Other cases are *IG* I³ 7 (concerning the duties of the *Praxiergidai*); *IG* II² 137 (fragmentary: a ἵδρυσις is mentioned); several projects of the Lycurgan period (cf. *Athenian Religion*, 244–5): *IG* II² 333 ('should we make the *kosmos* of Artemis, of Demeter and Kore, and of other gods larger and fairer, or leave it as it is?': the question is asked separately in each case); ibid. 1993–4 (preparing a couch and adorning a table for Plouton); [Plut.] *X Orat.* 843f ('gilding the altar of Apollo in the agora'). Apollo had in some sense chosen the tribal heroes of Clisthenes: *Athenian Religion*, 118. Plato: *Resp.* 427b–c; cf. 469a, 540b (Delphi to be consulted on heroization of patriots); 461e (and on the legitimacy of brother–sister cohabitation).

[60] Jacoby, *Atthis*, 28–30, supposes by analogy with Pl. *Leg.* 759c–e (there being no direct evidence) that for each vacancy the Athenians sent three names to Delphi, from which Apollo chose one.

boundaries of the sacred *orgas* at Eleusis could be leased out for cultivation or should be 'left surrendered to the goddesses'. They resolved that two tin tablets should be prepared, one bearing a response in favour of cultivation and one against. These were to be wrapped separately in wool and placed in a bronze hydria. A gold and a silver hydria were to be brought; the two tablets were to be shaken out of the bronze hydria, and put one each in the gold and silver hydria, which were then to be sealed and taken to the acropolis. A commission of three was then to go to Delphi to ask whether the Athenians should act in accord with the response in the gold or the silver hydria. Every stage of these proceedings was to be conducted 'in front of the people', and the god's answer was to be read out 'to the people'. No one but a god could know, it is clear, whether the response which allowed or which banned cultivation was being chosen. Delphi was at this date under the controversial control of the Phocians, and the singular procedure adopted has regularly been seen as designed to put the outcome beyond all possibility or suspicion of Phocian influence.[61] But the issue of cultivating the sacred *orgas* or land abutting it was a sensitive one in other ways. Decisions that were made about it would have serious consequences both for Athenians living in the region, and for Megarians; from independent evidence we learn that the oracular consultation either arose from a dispute with Megara over demarcation of the sacred *orgas*, or led to such a dispute. There is a strong element of theatre about the transaction with the two hydriai; it is an ostentatious acting-out of incorruptible procedure, and the climax of the drama is performed in Athens itself, in front of the people.[62] The message conveyed is that the final verdict will be beyond all religious reproach, and it seems to be addressed above all to a domestic audience.

A somewhat similar problem about the demarcation of sacred land arose in the 330s. Territory newly acquired from Oropus had been distributed among the tribes, but some believed that part of the portion assigned to Akamantis and Hippothoontis had in an earlier division been granted to 'the god' Amphiaraus. A three-man commission was sent to consult Amphiaraus himself by incubation in his shrine. One member of the commission, Euxenippos, reported back the revelation that he claimed to have received in a

---

[61] So most recently Giuliani, *Oracolo*, 235. The text is *IG* II² 204.23–54 (RO 58; *LSCG* 32); on the problem of connecting Dem. 13.32 and the Atthidographic fragments (Androtion *FGrH* 324 F 30 and Philochorus *FGrH* 328 F 155) quoted by Didymus in his commentary ad loc. with the decree see now RO, pp. 277–9. Apart from the Megarians, there may have been Athenian losers too by the evidently controversial remarking of the boundaries of the *orgas* prescribed in lines 1–23 of *IG* II² 204.

[62] I owe this observation to Bowden (n. 57 above). P. Harding, by contrast, *Androtion and the Atthis* (Oxford 1994), 126, speaks of 'an elaborate procedure that displayed an amazing combination of credulity and cynicism'; Rhodes, *Boule*, 131, of 'the *naïveté* of Athenian public life even in the fourth century'.

dream. Such was Amphiaraus' way of rendering oracles, and a very adequate one in uncontroversial cases. But, perhaps predictably given the interests that hung on the verdict, Euxenippos was in due course accused of falsifying the god's will, and prosecuted. If there was doubt about Euxenippos' testimony, said Hyperides speaking in his defence, what should have been done was to send to Delphi to learn the truth from the god ...[63]

Cases such as these were problematic because, formally religious and therefore demanding religious modes of resolution, they yet had important secular implications. A probably traditional theme of consultation that will, by contrast, normally have been uncontroversial was that of irregular happenings and omens. It was the task of a special board of *hieropoioi* to conduct 'rites prescribed by oracle', presumably in cases such as these. A Delphic response to a question about 'the sign in the sky' is preserved in the Demosthenic corpus; the god fails to reveal what the 'sign' might actually signify, but prescribes certain rituals to be performed. That is the only clear instance of a question of that type, but several similar responses recommending ritual action may well have originally been issued in similar circumstances; oracles, like jewels, were carefully conserved and could be given new settings, and we encounter the ones in question only when redeployed. 'The luck of Athens is good' and 'beware your leaders' are two adaptable sayings of the god of Dodona which were quoted by orators respectfully. They too probably originated as part of responses to questions about portents or, more vaguely, the well-being of the state.[64] Thucydides mentions, though he does not describe, the many supplications and oracular consultations vainly undertaken at the time of the Plague.[65]

In the year 339, a shocking portent marred the preliminaries to the *Mysteries*. It appears that a prospective initiate was eaten by a shark while undergoing the preparatory purification in the sea. One Ameiniades advised

---

[63] Hyp. *Eux.* 14–18; on an important unclarity in section 15 see D. Whitehead, *Hypereides* (Oxford 2000), 201–3.

[64] Sign in the sky: [Dem.] 43.66. Similar responses: Dem. 21.52–3 (one of the Dodona responses there cited has a more specific occasion, omission by the Athenians of a *theoria* to Dodona); cf. Hyp. *Eux.* 24. Hieropoioi: Arist. *Ath. Pol.* 54.6. Dodona: Dem. 18.253; 19.298–9; Din. 1. 78, 98; for another Dodonaean response from this period ('protect the heights of Artemis, lest others capture them') see Plut. *Phoc.* 28.4 (with the doubts of Parke, *Oracles of Zeus*, 143). Parke, op. cit., 141, supposes these Dodonaean responses to have been made to questions about general welfare (on the type see Parker, 'States and Oracles', 83). A fragmentary document relief of this period showing Zeus Naios and Dione certainly reflects these connections (Athens Acr. Mus. 4887; Walter, *Akropolismuseum*, 89, no. 183; *LIMC* s.v. *Zeus*, 341 no. 201a); a fine chair (for a priestess?) dedicated not much later to Dione (Acr. Mus. 4047; *IG* II² 4643) may do so too, though the existence of what may be a separate indigenous cult of Dione (*IG* I³ 476.195.223-4 etc.; *IG* II² 5113) is a complication. *IG* II² 4707 attests a σύνοδος of Zeus Naios in the late 2nd c. (Mikalson, *Hellenistic Athens*, 278). For all this archaeological evidence see the full study by O. Palagia in *Αφιέρωμα στη μνήμη του γλύπτη Στέλιου Τριάντη* (Athens 2002), 171–80.

[65] Thuc. 2.47.4. Paus. 1.3.4 assigns the origin of the cult of Apollo Alexikakos to a Delphic response delivered at this time, but ascribes the statue to a sculptor who seems to have been active earlier (see commentaries ad loc.).

the city 'to take heed and send a mission to Delphi to ask the god what should be done', but 'Demosthenes opposed the proposal, saying that the Pythia was philippizing'.[66] We cannot know Ameiniades' motives, but there is no reason to doubt that he was merely responding, in a traditional way, to an omen which conventional piety was bound to find deeply disturbing. But Demosthenes evidently feared an untraditional response: not a list of gods to sacrifice to, but a dire political warning which would undermine Athenian morale. There was an uncontrollability about oracular consultation which meant that the barrier between religious and political concerns was never unbreakable. Religion was itself political, in a certain sense. We do not know in what circumstances or in response to what question the oracle at Delphi first underwrote the idea that all Greek states should send first fruits of corn and barley to Eleusis. But there is no mistaking the enthusiasm with which the Athenians took up this endorsement of their claim to have exercised, from of old, a civilizing mission in Greece. The phrase 'in accord with tradition and the oracle of the god' appears three times in the great decree in which they set up arrangements for collection of the first fruits.[67]

All this notwithstanding, the Athenians divided the agenda at certain meetings of the assembly into sacred and other topics. The decision to approach the god in the cases discussed so far would probably have been made during the sacred part of the meeting; it was then too that the replies of the god would have been read out and analysed, though they might later have been redeployed in quite different contexts ('just hear the good advice of Apollo which Midias flouted'). Might an Athenian ever have proposed consulting a god on topics discussed in the non-sacred part of the meeting? Herodotus, a connoisseur of Athens, never doubts it. His account of the consultation of 481 or 480 and of the subsequent debate at Athens, in the crisis of the Persian invasion, is one of the classic narratives of world history.[68] According to Plutarch, Aristides sought oracular advice before the Plataea campaign of 479, and Cimon may have done the same before invading Skyros during that same decade; but no subsequent consultation of any oracle on a military topic is reliably recorded.[69] ('Reliably' there needs to be emphasized: late sources tell of approaches made to several oracles at the

---

[66] Aeschin. 3.130. Shark: so *Σ* Aeschin. 3.130. An identical incident is ascribed to the year 322 (Plut. *Phoc.* 28.6). The easiest explanation is that it occurred in 339 and was transferred to 322 in later tradition. An alternative is that what happened in 339 was different (Aeschines speaks of 'the death of the *mystai*' (plural)) and the scholion wrongly explained Aeschines' remark by reference to the later incident.

[67] *IG* I³ 78 (ML 73). On the date see p. 330, n. 15; on the implications for Athenian relations with Delphi, Cavanaugh, *Eleusis and Athens*, 87–8; Giuliani, *Oracolo*, 116 (who still favours a date in the late 20s).

[68] 7.140–4. The essential historicity of the episode is widely but not universally accepted: see Giuliani, *Oracolo*, 55–69.

[69] I here summarize Parker, 'States and Oracles', 85–8, where problematic cases are briefly discussed; see now Giuliani, 79–109, who is yet more sceptical. Aristides: see p. 401, n. 55. Scyros: by implication Paus. 3.3.7 (cf. A. J. Podlecki, *JHS* 91, 1971, 141–3).

time of the Sicilian expedition in 415,[70] but the picturesque details they include invite suspicion, and Thucydides in a detailed narrative knows nothing of such consultations.) As for Athens' various colonizing ventures of the fifth and fourth centuries, the picture is unclear: there are quite strong grounds for supposing (on the basis of late evidence) that Delphi was consulted in 444 about Thurii and in 437 about Amphipolis, but contemporary texts that refer to two lesser ventures make no allusion to Apollo, though they mention divine guidance of other kinds.[71] Consultation seems to have been, at most, occasional. The situation with issues of internal finance, politics and legislation is more clear. To say that no one ever thought of consulting an oracle on such matters would be to go too far: Xenophon suggested doing just this when presenting a scheme for financial reform in his pamphlet *Poroi*, and punctiliously and instructively marked out three stages: if his fellow-citizens approved his proposals (stage 1), they should then approach Delphi and Dodona to ask first whether these were advantageous (stage 2), and second which gods they should cultivate in order to carry them through successfully (stage 3).[72] But many major and minor constitutional reforms from the fifth and fourth centuries are quite well documented, and never is there the least trace of such a proceeding. Xenophon here writes as a dreamer.

In Thucydides the Spartans twice, unambiguously, consult Apollo about major issues of public policy.[73] We have met no certain case on the Athenian side at any date after 479. Just once in Thucydides do the Athenians act in obedience to a specific oracular command. In 422 they expelled the Delians from their island, but in 421 after completion of the Peace of Nicias they restored them, 'mindful of their misfortunes in battles and because the god at Delphi ordained it'.[74] This notice is unfortunately so brief as to leave open several possibilities: the Athenians may have asked Apollo about their misfortunes in battle, or 'whether they should restore the Delians to their island', or Apollo may have answered crossly in these terms to a question about something quite different. So that incident is not a clear exception to the

---

[70] Plut. *De Pyth.or.* 19, 403b (cf. *Nic.* 13.6) reports that Delphi told the Athenians 'to fetch (ἄγειν) the priestess of Athena from Erythrai'; the woman's name was Hesychia, so the advice was ἡσυχίαν ἄγειν, to do nothing. Plut. *Nic.* 13.2 has Alcibiades told by Ammon that 'the Athenians would capture all the Syracusans'; they subsequently captured a list of them all, ibid. 14.7. Paus. 8.11.12 has Dodona instructing the Athenians to 'settle Sicily' (what was meant was a small hill of that name near Athens). We are dealing with narrative motifs of a familiar and evidently unhistorical type. Parke, *Oracles of Zeus*, 136, 216–17, suggests, however, that actual consultations may underly the picturesque narrative elaborations. Thucydides' treatment of religious issues is extremely selective, as Simon Hornblower has well shown (*HSCP* 94, 1992, 169–97). But he mentions oracular consultations elsewhere and he mentions the role of other forms of divination in this case (8.1.1), so the argument from silence here has considerable though not decisive force.

[71] Thurii and Amphipolis: see the sources cited in Fontenrose, *Delphic Oracle*, 329, under Q 186–8. Lesser ventures: *IG* I³ 40. 64–7 (Euboea); ibid. 46.9 (Brea); cf. *Ritual, Finance, Politics*, 339–340.

[72] Xen. *Poroi* 6.2–3.   [73] Thuc. 1.118.3, 3.92.5.

[74] Thuc. 5.1, 5.32.1 (cf. *Athenian Religion*, 151).

proposition that after 479 the Athenians never consulted Apollo about political issues; that claim can still be defended, if with some difficulty. One might more moderately argue that such consultations were exceptional. Even major decisions such as that to invade Sicily were apparently taken without formal recourse to the advice of an oracular shrine, though there were certainly many prophecies in the air. What is at issue, it should be stressed, is the dispatch of a delegation with a political question to a fixed oracle, not necessarily to Delphi. The failure to approach Delphi at a particular period may always have a particular explanation: danger or impossibility of access, suspicion that the prophetess may be disposed to laconize, or thebize, or philippize.[75] But alternatives to Delphi were available. Dodona, it has often been argued, became popular for cultic enquiries at the start of the Peloponnesian war, and again in the Demosthenic period, because Delphi then was inaccessible or unpopular. Whether the explanation is correct or not, the possibility of consulting authorities other than Apollo certainly existed. Regular *theoriai* to the oracle of Ammon (with his *paredroi* Hera Ammonia and Parammon) seem already to be attested in the late 360s. But if cultic enquiries could be taken to Dodona and to Siwa, so too could political; yet they were not, to our knowledge.[76]

Yet there were other forms of prophecy which could influence political debate. *Chresmologoi*,[77] purveyors of verse oracles that did not derive directly from an oracular shrine, are victims of much abuse in Greek texts, but the name itself is perfectly innocent, and the standard rendering 'oracle monger' should be dropped in favour of 'oracle collector', which (or the equally innocent 'oracle speaker') is all that the word means. We most commonly meet them presenting and interpreting pre-existent verses, of which they might have a collection not available to others. But Plato often mentions

---

[75] Giuliani, *Oracolo*, is a sensible analysis of Atheno-Delphian relations conducted principally in these terms.

[76] On Ammon see *Athenian Religion*, 195–6, with the important modifications by G. Petzl in G. Hellenkemper Salies and others (eds.), *Das Wrack* (Cologne 1994), 381–6; specific enquiries are unfortunately not known. For Dodona in the 340s and 330s see n. 64. *IG* I³ 1462 (*Syll.*³ 73), an Athenian dedication at Dodona in Attic script 'from the Peloponnesians after victory in a sea-battle', attests Attic interest in Dodona before (no doubt) 421, but the precise dating usually favoured to 429 is unreliable if plausible (S. Hornblower, *HSCP* 94, 1992, 192). A question about Bendis *may* have been put during the same period (*Athenian Religion*, 172). The assumption that Delphi was inaccessible has, however, been strongly challenged (Hornblower, 192–4; cf. Giuliani, *Oracolo*, 120–3).

[77] On them see Fontenrose, *Delphic Oracle*, 145–65; Bowden, 'Oracles for Sale'. '*Chresmologoi* and seers' are mentioned together in Thuc. 8.1.1 and elsewhere, and are often identified by moderns (for a survey of opinions see Bowden, 257, n. 5, who favours identification); on the basis of Ar. *Pax* 1046–7 (and Paus. 1.34.4) I am still disposed to distinguish the two functions at least as ideal types, though as Bowden argues some crossover doubtless occurred (Ar. *Av.* 988, Lampon mentioned in a context of chresmology; Pl. *Resp.* 364b–65a, seers with books of oracles of Orpheus and Musaeus; the Platonic passages cited in the following note). Different again from *manteis* and *chresmologoi* are exegetes: Eupolis fr. 319 describes the seer Lampon as an exegete, but if he means this literally (Jacoby on Philochorus *FGrH* 328 T 2, p. 257 is doubtful) then Lampon exercised two functions (which is quite possible).

'inspired prophets and oracle singers' (οἱ θεομάντεις καὶ οἱ χρησμῳδοί) as speaking well by inspiration and not by understanding. 'Oracle singer' and 'oracle collector' are interchangeable terms, and Herodotus quotes two famous oracles apparently improvised by *chresmologoi*. So *chresmologoi* could also in principle create oracles of their own under direct divine inspiration.[78] Books of oracles and the *chresmologoi* who interpreted them were already politically influential in the circle of Pisistratus. They reappear in Herodotus' account of the debate at Athens in 481 or 480 at which Apollo's advice to seek protection from a 'wooden wall' was discussed.[79] The oracle's reference to Salamis 'destroying the children of women' is doom-laden, the *chresmologoi* argue; Apollo counsels not resistance, but flight. Not so, counters Themistocles; the oracle speaks of Persian and not Greek deaths, for otherwise it would have addressed Salamis not as 'sacred' but as 'cruel'. And Themistocles' view prevails. Three important points emerge, whether the incident is historical or not: *chresmologoi*, as a group, have a recognized title to advise the assembly on certain issues; the assembly is free to reject the views of the *chresmologoi*, religious specialists though they are;[80] but, in this case at least, the politician who leads the resistance to the *chresmologoi* tackles them on their own ground: Apollo is wise, it is his interpreters who err.

As we have seen, responses may not thereafter have been very often brought back from Delphi or Dodona on which the *chresmologoi* could exercise their skill. But they retain a conspicuous role. In (probably) 446 the assembly, regulating the affairs of Chalkis after a revolt, decrees that 'three men chosen by the boule from its number shall, together with Hierocles, make the sacrifices from the oracles (χρησμοί) for Euboea as soon as possible'. Hierocles was a *chresmologos*, and had doubtless brought to the assembly's attention certain oracles promising success to an Athenian settlement on the island. An anonymous *chresmologos* ridiculed in Aristophanes' *Birds* has similar concerns: it is not just the thought of sacrificial meat (the standard comic joke against religious specialists) but the foundation of a new city that has drawn him. 'There is an oracle of Bakis bearing directly on Cloudcuckooland', he declares on arrival. The proposal to refound Thurii in 444 aroused so much interest from diviners that 'Thurii-seers' were still in the repertoire of charlatans known to Aristophanes twenty years later. Hierocles apparently

---

[78] Pl. *Apol.* 22c, *Men.* 99c, *Ion* 534c; Hdt. 1.62.4, 8.96.2. (Oracles or supposed oracles of the Amphilytus mentioned in Hdt. 1.62.4 may have been recorded and re-used for centuries: Pl. *Theag.* 124d, which also shows that he had been claimed as an Athenian.) The sharp distinction drawn by E. R. Dodds, *The Greeks and the Irrational* (Berkeley 1951), 88, n. 46, between *chresmologoi* (mere interpreters) and inspired *chresmodoi* seems to me artificial; both words are used of Hierokles (Ar. *Pax* 1047; Eupolis fr. 231), and cf. Thuc. 2.8.2 πολλὰ χρησμολόγοι ᾖδον; similarly 2.21.3. -*logos* compounds can reflect either the 'speak' (*pseudologos*) or 'gather' (*dasmologos*) sense of λέγω (Fontenrose, *Delphic Oracle*, 153).

[79] Hdt. 7.140–4. On Pisistratus see *Athenian Religion*, 87.

[80] Nothing, alas, is known of the content of Lycurgus' speech 'About' or 'Against' the Oracles' (XIII Conomis). Another instance of Themistocles arguing within a religious framework is Hdt. 8.60 γ, where he adduces a *logion* in support of a tactical argument.

acquired land in the cleruchy on Euboea for which he had performed the sacrifices; in Aristophanes' *Peace*, where he makes an extended appearance, he is introduced as 'Hierocles from Oreus' (in Euboea). Aristophanes shows him quoting oracles in opposition to peace. Here then the religious specialist intervenes in a directly political issue. Aristophanes' attack testifies to his prominence within the state; we learn incidentally that he enjoyed, occasionally or permanently, the honour of dining in the prytaneum. 'Mad' Diopeithes, another *chresmologos*, is actually credited with proposing a famous decree attacking atheistical teachings.[81]

Thucydides thrice mentions the influence exercised by *chresmologoi* during the Peloponnesian war. He does not indicate where they sang their oracles, and in one case the context envisaged is clearly one of informal groupings of men. Yet the case of Hierocles shows that a *chresmologos* could find a hearing in the assembly.[82] In *Knights* the Paphlagonian slave who represents Cleon is said to 'sing oracles' to the people, and the play goes on to represent oracle-brandishing as, in fact, a principal technique of demagogy. The Paphlagonian quotes oracles of Bakis, while the sausage-seller trumps them with oracles of 'Bakis' elder brother Glanis'; the two even compete in accounts of the blessings which they have seen Athena pouring over the city in a dream. Even when allowance has been made for probably massive comic exaggeration, some hint of the notes that could be struck in the assembly must remain. Oracles could help men to dream dreams; a favourite to which Aristophanes three times alludes was the promise to Athens that 'you will become an eagle in the clouds for all time'.[83]

Dreams can lead to grim awakenings, and Thucydides in a famous passage tells how, after the total failure of the Sicilian expedition, the Athenians were enraged both against the politicians who had advocated it and against 'the *chresmologoi* and *manteis* and all those who by religious arguments (θειάσαντες) had led them to hope that they would capture Sicily'.[84] *Chresmologoi* drop largely out of view henceforth, discredited, it has been supposed, by the failure of their Sicilian predictions. Certainly, Euripides' *Helen*, produced in the year after the disaster, contains the most general denunciation of seers to

---

[81] *IG* I³ 40 (ML 52) 64–7; Ar. *Av.* 962; *Nub.* 332; *Pax* 1043–126. For the Athenian settlement at Oreus in the territory of Hestiaea established in consequence of the Euboean revolts of 446 see Thuc. 1.114.3, 8.95.7; Theopompus *FGrH* 115 F 387. Prytaneum: see p. 117, n. 4. The political edge to Aristophanes' attacks on diviners is stressed by N. D. Smith, 'Diviners and divination in Aristophanic Comedy', *ClAnt* 8 (1989), 140–58. Diopeithes: cf. n. 11.

[82] Thuc. 2.8.2; 2.21.3 (informal: cf. 2.22.1); 8.1.1.

[83] Ar. *Eq.* 61, 116–17, 797–9, 961–1089, 1229–330; dreams: 1090–5. Eagle: Ar. *Av.* 978; *Eq.* 1012–13 ('my favourite', says the demos); 1086–7. This oracle is probably chresmodic by origin, not Delphic: Fontenrose, *Delphic Oracle*, 150.

[84] Thuc. 8.1.1. Much of this was orchestrated by Alcibiades, according to Plut. *Nic.* 13.1–2. But Alcibiades' individual consultation of Ammon on this matter of public policy (ibid.) would if authentic (cf. n. 70) be unexampled: the decision to collect a fixed oracle was normally collective (P. E. Legrand, *Quo animo Graeci divinationem adhibuerint*, Paris 1898, 72–3). Alcibiades knew how to break rules, but a response so secured could only have had limited authority.

be found in Attic literature, and one not obviously demanded by the internal economy of the play. But, in the long term, false prophecies usually create an appetite for true ones, not a wholesale rejection of the institution. Oracles of the Sibyl and of Musaeus ascribing Athenian failures to bad leadership were applied to the disastrous defeat at Aegospotami in 405, presumably near the time of the event.[85] The evidence of Plato's *Euthyphro*,[86] which has a firm dramatic date of 399, is somewhat double-edged. Learning that Socrates' religious attitudes have made him unpopular with the Athenians, Euthyphro becomes patronizingly sympathetic. 'Such things can easily be used against one before the people. Even in my own case, when I speak in the assembly on religious matters, predicting the future to them, they laugh at me as if I were mad. Every one of my predictions has been true, but people like us are always resented.' Plato can still envisage a *chresmologos* (for that, it seems, is what Euthyphro is) addressing the assembly in 399. The risk of mockery is also mentioned; but it is surely likely that some *chresmologoi* were sometimes laughed at even before (*ex hypothesi*) the Sicilian disaster brought them into disrepute.

The oracles that are mentioned in surviving fourth-century oratory are cultic responses from Delphi or Dodona; there is no trace of Bakis or the Sibyl. Lycurgus in the speech *Against Leocrates* quotes poetry and tragedy at length, but not oracles. On the other hand, Demosthenes according to Aeschines was not above recounting dreams to the assembly, one of his own in which Zeus and Athena brought him the glorious news of Philip's assassination, one of a Sicilian priestess apparently relating to the villainies of the tyrant Dionysius.[87] We noted above that old Delphic responses could be recycled years after they were issued and used to warn the Athenians against a political opponent, or to tar him with a taint of impiety.[88] There is also an instructive passage in a speech of the 350s in which Demosthenes discusses the extreme unwillingness of the rich to make contributions for defence against Philip on the basis of mere words; they would not pay, he says, even 'if all the speakers made terrifying speeches that the great king will come, that he is here, that the thing cannot be changed, and even if along with the speakers an equal number chanted prophecies'.[89] This is suggestive in two ways: it may imply that oracle-singers have their place not in day-to-day politics but in extreme situations, whether of hope (as before the Sicilian expedition) or of fear; and

[85] Eur. *Hel.* 744–60. Discredited: so e.g. Mikalson, *Athenian Popular Religion*, 40. Sibyl: Paus. 10.9.11; cf. H.W. Parke, *Sibyls and Sibylline Prophecy in Classical Antiquity* (London 1988), 105–6.
[86] 3b–c; cf. Pl. *Crat.* 396d, 428c, and n. 35.
[87] Aeschin. 2.10 (no such passage appears in the surviving text of Dem. 19, to which Aeschines 2 is a response: see D. M. MacDowell's ed. of Dem. 19, Oxford 2000, 25); 3. 77, 219. This is like Aristophanes' Cleon (n. 83).
[88] See p. 108, n. 64. For deployment against an opponent see Dem. 19. 298–9; 21.51–5: Din. 1.78, 98.
[89] Dem. 14.25, a text brought into the discussion by D. M. Lewis (ap. H. W. Parke, ZPE 60, 1985, 96, n. 11).

it implants the thought that Demosthenes denouncing Philip in the way familiar to us might have been followed on the rostrum by an oracle-singer who warned against him in a quite different way. Demosthenes' neglect of such arguments would not then prove anything, if there was a division of functions. A stone has been found on the acropolis bearing in fragmentary form a hexameter oracle of more than twenty lines, almost certainly too long to derive from Delphi or Dodona. Experts assign the letter forms to the second half of the fourth century; the attractive conjecture has been made that the oracle was designed, or at least understood, as a caution against Philip.[90] How such an *ex parte* prophecy could have earned public recognition on stone is, it must be allowed, mysterious. But that it is at least an inscribed chresmodic oracle (whatever its precise thrust) is hard to deny.

If the preceding arguments are sound, the Athenians seldom, after 479, sent delegations to the fixed shrines except with questions about cult, but even in the fourth century allowed *chresmologoi* a voice in public debates. The case underlying both strands of argument is a case about the autonomy of the assembly.[91] The dire warnings or alluring hopes offered by *chresmologoi* do not erode that autonomy. The *chresmologoi* tempt and threaten, but the people still decide; the prophecies adduced are on the same footing as all the other arguments and techniques of persuasion used in debate. But formal consultation of an oracle transfers the final burden of decision elsewhere; for an oracular verdict leaves scope for further discussion only if, like the 'wooden walls' oracle, it is itself unclear. One traditional function of oracular consultation had probably been to create consensus about the rightness of a decision affecting a group. But procedurally, for the Athenians, a decision was right if it had been taken in the democratic assembly; further guarantees were not needed. And politicians were probably increasingly reluctant to see decisions removed from the sphere of their own influence. The Athenians never consciously resolved, we may be sure, to cease consulting Apollo or Zeus about warfare and colonization. It just came to seem less necessary and appropriate to do so.

[90] See H. W. Parke. *ZPE* 60 (1985), 93–6, discussing Peek's revised text of *IG* II² 4968.
[91] For a fuller statement see Parker, 'States and Oracles', 76–7, 103–5.

6

'Those Who Make a Profession out of Rites': Unlicensed Religion, and Magic

The Greek expression paraphrased in the title to this chapter occurs in a non-Attic text, the Derveni papyrus,[1] but there were religious professionals in Attica as throughout Greece. And in Attica as everywhere else the paradox obtained that, though 'the things of the gods' had to be spoken of with utmost respect, religious professionals were always subject to suspicion and often to insult. The word of the Derveni author here rendered 'profession' is τέχνη, craft or expertise; but the author goes on at once to emphasize that this is an expertise deployed for payment, a way of making a living. It is their claim to possess an expertise accessible only on payment that makes the religious professionals of Greece such ambiguous figures. 'Clear-sighted only about gain, blind in his art' is Oedipus' verdict in Sophocles (*OT* 388-9) on the prophet Tiresias, and similar insults are very common. Priests and priestesses in public cults also profited from traditional fees and perquisites, perhaps very substantially in the most popular cults, and may in these cases have devoted many of their waking hours to ritual matters. But they did not tout for custom on the basis of arcane knowledge, and 'priestess' remained a title of respect.[2] The best religion, it appears, is amateur religion. The respectability of the priests and priestesses of the public cults is also owed to the respectability of 'ancestral tradition' as embodied in those cults. It extended even to exegetes, despite their specialized knowledge, because exegetes were official and permanent appointees of the city.[3] The shadiness by contrast of the religious professionals is also the shadiness of unlicensed, free-enterprise religion.

Doubtless the claims just made are a little extreme. It was possible for a religious professional to acquire prestige and influence in Athens; the prime example is the *mantis* Lampon, friend of Pericles, oikist of Thourioi, first signatory to the Peace of Nicias. If Lampon enjoyed the right of permanent entertainment in the prytaneum, as is generally supposed, he had received

---

[1] Col. xx (*olim* xvi) 3-4, in the edition of R. Janko, ZPE 141 (2002), 1-62 (παρὰ τοῦ τέχνην ποιουμένου τὰ ἱερά).

[2] Men. *Dysc.* 496. On all this see Gordon, 'Imagining Magic', 212-13.

[3] About their remuneration nothing is known.

the highest honour that the Athenians could bestow. The *chresmologos* Hierocles too was, as we saw in the last chapter, a figure of some authority, though there is room for doubt as to whether he can properly be counted a religious professional.[4] And other seers can be identified who were proud of their calling and reasonably prosperous: the epitaph of the maternal uncle of the orator Aeschines celebrates him as both *mantis* and warrior,[5] and another epitaph commemorates a 'seer son of a seer' belonging to a flourishing Myrrhinuntian family who, unusually, were buried together over five or six generations.[6] The distinguished Atthidographer Philochorus was scholar, patriot and *mantis*. Armies needed seers, who were noted as such on casualty lists and probably received a regular wage during a given campaigning season; a Thasian *mantis* Sthorys was actually granted Athenian citizenship, partly in consequence (it seems) of successful prophecies made by him in connection with the battle of Cnidus in 394.[7]

Regularly paid and serving the city's military needs, such practitioners had no need to lure clients by offering religious services not available within ancestral tradition. And there were other functions such as 'securing good omens' for which the state needed seers and may have engaged them for an

---

[4] See n. 16 below. Lampon in the prytaneum: the only sources are *Σ* vet. Ar. *Av.* 521b, ἔτυχε δὲ καὶ τῆς ἐν πρυτανείῳ σιτήσεως, and very similar remarks in *Σ* vet. Ar. *Pax* 1084. They presumably derive from a lost comic allusion like that to Hierocles dining in the prytaneum in Ar. *Pax* 1084. But I see no reason to conclude from Ar. *Pax* 1084 that Hierocles was a permanent as opposed to an occasional guest in the prytaneum, and the same might have been true of Lampon. Permanent guests in the prytaneum were such either because they belonged to a class so marked out, or in virtue of a personal grant (see M. J. Osborne, *ZPE* 41, 1981, 153–70). Lampon and Hierocles seem barely of a level of achievement to have merited a personal grant (though it must be allowed that in the case of religious specialists we do not know the level required); but if they belonged to an honoured category, what was it? The lacunae in *IG* I³ 131, where the categories were specified, leave the matter uncertain.

[5] *CEG* 519; the relief too (*BCH* 82, 1958, 365: an eagle carrying a snake) appears to allude to prophecy (cf. Hom. *Il.* 12. 200–9). Aeschines mentions only the military activity of his uncle, 2.78, claiming that along with Demainetos the Bouzyges he συγκατεναυμάχησε the Spartan nauarch Chilon. Only the discovery of *CEG* 519 has allowed us to understand the ingenuity of that expression, which has deceived many eminent scholars since Beloch (*Die attische Politik seit Perikles*, Leipzig 1884, 315) into crediting the uncle with generalship: it will have been as Demainetos' seer that he 'jointly defeated' the Spartan.

[6] *CEG* 473; cf. n. 12 below.

[7] Casualty lists: *IG* I³ 1147 (ML 33) 129. Sthorys: see M. J. Osborne, *Naturalization in Athens*, i (Brussels 1983), D8 (improved text of *IG* II² 17), with Osborne's good discussion of the religious issues in *BSA* 65 (1970), 164–8. Osborne concludes that we are probably dealing with pre-battle sacrifices interpreted by Sthorys while serving on Conon's staff, unprecedented though the term εἰσιτητήρια is in this context. He considers but rejects more exciting scenarios whereby e.g. Sthorys might, from Athens, have encouraged more aggressive policies by his prophecies. As the text shows, Sthorys came from a traditionally philo-Athenian family, and his achievements need not objectively have been huge. The text contains a unique reference to the seer's μισθός; Osborne suggests (166, n. 81) that there may already have existed a post or posts as seer(s) to the generals, as certainly later (*IG* II² 1708; *AM* 67, 1942, no. 25.19; cf. *IG* II² 2858. 9). The decision to display one copy of the decree in the Pythion should relate to Sthorys' function as a seer.

extended period (by the year?).[8] This was seercraft at its most respectable, though there was still the risk of unpopularity created by failure: Sthorys would doubtless not have gained his citizenship if the battle of Cnidus had been lost. Tales were even told of the heroism of *manteis*, like the one who saw in the pre-battle omens the need for 'one death in place of many', and decided that it should be his own. So it was quite possible for *manteis* to be successful and even to be admired. There was nothing pejorative about the name: to be rude to a *mantis* one called him something else, 'begging priest' or '*magos*' or the like.[9] Yet we should not forget the outburst of Sophocles' Oedipus against Tiresias. Tiresias enters the scene as 'the sacred seer, who alone of mortals has access by nature to truth'. But within a few lines Oedipus, crossed by him, is fitting this greatest of all religious professionals known to story into the stereotype of a charlatan on the make. In a little list given by Aristotle of those who are 'charlatans for profit' seers have first place.[10]

The seer is the most obvious type of religious professional and warfare is, for us, much the most conspicuous context for divination, but there must have been many others. There was no local oracle to turn to at Athens with the kind of worries about marriage and journeys and investments and offspring and thefts which the people of north-west Greece put before Zeus at Dodona. Perhaps Athenians sometimes took such questions to Delphi, but this was a time-consuming procedure and divinatory methods available locally must often have been preferred. A character in Plato speaks of the seer as being concerned with 'signs of the future' in relation to death, disease, loss of money, defeat or victory whether in war or in 'other crises' (ἄλλη ἀγωνία).[11] Of all this the literary sources reveal very little; but they reveal very little too of

---

[8] Arist. *Ath. Pol.* 54.6. Jacoby, n. 28 to commentary on Philochorus FGrH 328 T 2, notes Kahrstedt's view, *Magistratur*, 308, that '*μάντεις* were as a rule engaged ad hoc' and comments 'which may, or may not, be so, as we know nothing about the way in which they were appointed'. Kahrstedt is in my view probably right (though commanders could certainly take favourite seers with them: having secured their appointment by the city?—see Pritchett, *Greek State at War*, iii, 62–3), but what is clear is that Jacoby's own assertion (commentary on Philochorus T 2, p. 259) that *manteis* unlike other religious functionaries 'held office for life', is a bizarre and uncharacteristic anachronism: what he means is that they might be active as *manteis* for life. Talk of *manteis* as 'regular and permanent advisers of the state' (ibid. 260) is equally misleading; even the phrase 'the official *mantis*' (n. 33 ibid.) is open to question.

[9] Heroism: Xen. *Hell.* 2.4.18–19. 'Begging priest': Aesch. *Ag.* 1273; Soph. *OT* 387–9; Dickie, *Magicians*, 66. Dickie, *Magicians*, 47–95, is full of important matter on the religious professionals of Athens.

[10] Soph. *OT* 298–9 with 387–9; Arist. *EN* 1127b 20. Anaxandrides fr. 50 from Φαρμακόμαντις introduces a character, who is likely to be the φαρμακόμαντις, boasting of his ἀλαζόνεια. The attacks on Lampon in comedy for gluttony and dishonesty (Ar. *Av.* 521 with N. Dunbar's note; Cratinus fr. 62 with K/A's note; Adespota fr. 1105.98) may merely reflect his public prominence; those on Hierocles the *chresmologos*, by contrast (p. 113, n. 81), are clearly shaped by the stereotype.

[11] Pl. *Lach.* 195e. For areas of consultation cf. Ar. *Av.* 593–7: mines, trading opportunities, voyages; ibid. 718, trade, βιότου κτῆσις, marriage (Ter. *Phorm.* 705–10 lists the religious excuses available for breaking a marriage engagement). *IG* II² 4602, a dedication made κατὰ μαντείαν, may reflect private consultation of an oracle; *IG* I³ 773 (CEG 243) seems to have been made 'at the saying of seers'.

other practices such as the writing of curse tablets, which we know on other grounds to have been common. As is clear above all from Xenophon's *Anabasis*, exactly the kinds of question that were put to oracles—'is it better and more advantageous for me to marry the woman I have in mind?', as it might be—could also be put, with the aid of a seer, to the entrails of a sacrificial animal; that is why seers are credited with especial expertise in sacrificial procedures.[12] Individuals regularly 'sought good omens' (καλλιερεῖσθαι) for private enterprises, according to Aristophanes; this is something closely akin to sacrificial divination, under a slightly different name. Where normal individuals would hire a seer ad hoc, wealthy Nicias sacrificed every day and had a personal seer permanently employed; he claimed, according to Plutarch's source, to be concerned about public affairs, but the obscurities about which he really wanted illumination concerned his mines.[13] It is not certain that every person described as a seer in our sources made his living by the craft, but many surely did, and for them 'private practice' is likely to have been of central importance. Some touted for custom door-to-door, and for this reason the rude term *agyrtes*, literally 'collector' but in effect 'beggar', can be applied to them as well as to the priests and priestesses who begged in the name of particular gods. 'Am I a false prophetess, a babbler who bangs at doors?' asks Aeschylus' Cassandra poignantly.[14]

There were also 'bird-observers' at Athens, while 'sieve-seers' and mirror divination are very briefly mentioned in comedy; not requiring the expense of an animal victim, these may have been poor men's techniques. And no doubt there was much else besides. The grandson of Aristides the Just, a man too just to enrich his descendants, was forced to make a very humble living with a 'dream-interpreting tablet'.[15] We hear of the activities of *chresmologoi*

---

[12] See e.g. Xen. *Anab.* 6.1.22–4, 6.2.15, 7.6.44 and my essay in R. Lane Fox (ed.), *The Long March: Xenophon and the Ten Thousand* (New Haven 2004), 131–53. Expertise: Ar. *Pax* 1026, 1032. Philochorus was a 'seer and ἱεροσκόπος' (*FGrH* 328 T 1). One of only five attested bearers of the name Hieroptes (apparently exclusive to Attica) belongs (as noted by Humphreys, 'Family Tombs', 121) to the Myrrhinuntian mantic family mentioned above (n. 6).

[13] καλλιερεῖσθαι: Ar. *Plut.* 1181. The professional called in aid is in this case a priest, but surely might easily have been a seer. Nicias: Plut. *Nic.* 4.2; the source is one of the Socratic dialogues of Pasiphon of Eretria (fr. 2 in the ed. of G. Giannantoni, *Socratis et Socraticorum Reliquiae*, Naples 1990, i, III c).

[14] *Ag.* 1195; cf. ἀγύρτρια, 1273; and on *agyrtai* Dickie, *Magicians*, 60–74, esp. 65. Very little is know about the antecedents, except sometimes their place of origin, and 'career patterns' of seers; we see even Lampon only when he is already eminent. On Thrasyllus, the landless man who with the aid of mantic books became the richest of the Siphnians, see Isoc. 19.5–9 with Dickie, *Magicians*, 68–71 (but I do not think that the books in question are books of prophecies). Poverty was one incentive to practise the art; family tradition another (see n. 12 on a Myrrhinuntian family).

[15] Theophr. *Char.* 16.11, 19.8 (birds); Philippides fr. 38 (sieves); Ar. *Ach.* 1128–9 (mirrors); Plut. *Arist.* 27.4 (dream tablet). Doubtless some of the other compounds with -*mantis* as second element listed in Pollux 7.188 also derive from comedy. Aesch. *PV* 485–99 is a panorama of types of augury, reduced in Eur. *Supp.* 211–13 to the two basics, ornithomancy and inspection of entrails. On the relation of these last two types see Aesch. *Sept.* 24–9 with Hutchinson's note; doubtless some seers practised both.

exclusively in public political contexts. Whether they also offered their services to private individuals is uncertain; if they did not, there will scarcely have been a living to be made from chresmology, which will therefore have to be viewed as an expertise rather than as a profession.[16]

Chresmologoi aside, inspired prophets are very difficult to identify in Athens. One group are the 'belly-talkers' from within whom emerged, hoarsely, the prophecies of one Eurykles.[17] Doubtless there is a danger here of crude positivism and reductivism; the ancients derived *mantis* from μαίνομαι, 'I am mad', and, even if 'technical' prophecy from entrails and omens was the norm, inspired prophecies may have been uttered by more practitioners than we can pin down. The Tiresias of tragedy, master though he is of technical prophecy, speaks also with an authority and insight that lies beyond it. Even so, it would be hard to deny the generalization that the most influential domestic forms of divination depended on inspection of entrails and the like. For inspiration one looked abroad, to Delphi.

'Initiators' are another class of religious professionals (or perhaps one should say that initiation is another of the activities which such professionals performed). In their male form they are very scantly attested in Attica, no certain cases being known apart from the 'Orpheus initiators' mentioned by Theophrastus and perhaps by Plato. Commoner are women who led revel bands which were often entered by 'initiation': we can identify three by name, as well as whole classes such as the women who conducted corybantic initiations. The fullest account is that given by Demosthenes of the supposed activities of Aeschines' mother Glaukothea; however little trust the details may deserve, we can doubtless accept the central point that Glaukothea was a religious professional, like her brother the seer. The activities of revel-band leaders and initiators were perhaps not hugely different from those of the men and women who collected money (obviously taking some for themselves) in the name of gods, Mother above all.[18] A name sometimes given to women who led revel-bands is 'priestess', and one or two further texts introduce women so described who do not sound like priestesses in any of the cults of

[16] So Bowden, 'Oracles for Sale'.

[17] Ar. *Vesp.* 1019; Pl. *Soph.* 252c. A. H. Sommerstein in his note on Ar. *Vesp.* 1019 and Ogden, *Necromancy*, 112–13, seem to me the only scholars (even Dodds nodded, *The Greeks and the Irrational*, Berkeley 1951, 88, n. 45) to have seen the best view about Eurykles: Eurykles is the name of the spirit who spoke through belly-speakers (Pl. *Soph.* 252c is decisive), and has nothing to do (a guess of the scholia on the two passages cited) with a hypothetical human 'belly-speaker' so named. Nympholepsy (Pl. *Phaedr.* 238d; W. R. Connor, *ClAnt* 7, 1988, 155–89) is slightly different, a possession that might seize an individual but not apparently a way of making a living.

[18] Orpheus initiators: Theophr. *Char.* 16.12, and perhaps Pl. *Resp.* 364b–365a (but cf. Dickie, *Magicians*, 331, n. 65). Revel-band leaders: for Phryne and Nino see *Athenian Religion*, 163, n. 34; for Glaukothea see E. Harris, *Aeschines and Athenian Politics* (Oxford 1995), 21–8. Corybantic initiations: *Athenian Religion* 194, n. 151. That both men and women performed Corybantic initiations, even if only women are attested (Pl. *Leg.* 790d), is very plausible given the double priesthood attested for their cult in Erythrae (see most recently P. Herrmann, *Chiron* 32, 2002, 157–72). Agyrtai: Dickie, 65–6.

the city. Of the complicated plot of Menander's lost play *Priestess*, known from a papyrus summary, the salient point is that a man pretends to be possessed (θεοφορεῖσθαι) and is taken to the priestess of the title to be treated. One does not envisage the priestess of any public cult of Athens being expected to perform exorcism *ex officio*. The Superstitious Man of Theophrastus, on encountering what he judges a bad omen, summons 'priestesses' to purify him. Details remain vague, but it seems that, as 'seer' is the main generic term for a male religious professional, so 'priestess' is its female equivalent. Such a priestess, though functionally very distinct from the priestesses of the public cults, shares their respectable title. But to her as not to them less pleasant names are also applied.[19]

It is time to introduce the most celebrated text that relates to unlicensed religion in Athens. According to Plato in the *Republic*, collectors and seers (ἀγύρται καὶ μάντεις) go to the doors of the rich and offer them two services: on the one hand, purifications and initiations, conducted in accord with books of Orpheus and Musaeus, which claim to efface the consequences of misdeeds in this life and the next; on the other, bewitchments and binding spells (ἐπαγωγαί τινες καὶ καταδέσμοι) for use against enemies.[20] Orphic purifications may sound like one thing, magical attacks like quite another, and one might suspect Plato of conflating two different threats to public morals purveyed by two different types of religious specialist. But perhaps we should recognize late survivors of the kind of charismatic all-purpose man of god best illustrated for us by Empedocles, in his actions a wonder-worker and in his writings a prophet of metempsychosis.[21] However that may be, what matters for us is the association established by Plato between 'collectors and seers' and 'bewitchments and binding spells'. Students of surviving curse tablets debate whether particular examples have been composed by the person actually laying the curse, or by an expert; Plato in the *Laws* recognizes both

---

[19] Priestess applied to revel-band leaders: Dem. 19.281; Plut. *Dem.* 14.6 (Philochorus *FGrH* 328 F 60 calls the same woman Theoris a seer, a term not otherwise to my knowledge used of women except prophetesses such as the Pythia or Cassandra). Menander's Ἱέρεια: see e.g. the OCT of Menander, 305–6. Of the play of the same name by Apollodorus Carystius nothing is known, nor of the Ἱέρειαι of Aeschylus. Superstitious Man: Theophr. *Char.* 16.14. I am uncertain of the relation between the priestesses who concern us here and those who served in permanently established private associations such as those of Mother in the Piraeus. From the decrees of these latter (*IG* II² 1298, 1314–16, 1328–9, 1334) the priestesses sound like mere calques of civic priestesses (annual tenure, limited duties—but *IG* II² 1328.11, 1329.15 mention collections).

[20] Pl. *Resp.* 364b–365a.

[21] The '*magoi*, purifiers, begging priests and charlatans' attacked in Hippocrates, *On the Sacred Disease* (1.10–46 Grensemann; chs. ii–iv in the Loeb Hippocrates of W. H. S. Jones) are also involved with both purification and wonder-working, but their purifications as described are directed merely against physical sickness. On all this see Dickie, *Magicians*, ch. 1. In the related passage in *Laws* (908d–909d) Plato again associates μαγγανεία with seers, but defines their offences as the pretence to be able to summon up the dead and the claim to be able to persuade the gods; he speaks of them as γοητεύοντες by sacrifice and prayer and incantations. We have no other evidence for necromancy as a living practice at Athens (for literature and for other parts of Greece see Dickie, *Magicians*, 30–1, 77–8; Ogden, *Necromancy*).

possibilities, and prescribes different penalties in the two cases. There were therefore amateurs of cursing as well as professionals and semi-professionals. But it is the professionals who disseminate and popularize and as it were drive the practice.[22] Of all the religious activities conducted in Attica, those of bewitchment and cursing are at the furthest extreme from civic norms. And (at least for Plato) it is in the knapsack of a religious specialist that black magic enters the cities.

The dangerous word 'magic' has been spoken, and a few defensive remarks are required. Magic, it is generally agreed today, refers to no objective reality; magic differs from religion as weeds differ from flowers, merely by negative social evaluation. The study of magic is a study of the religious practices disapproved of in a given society, or a particular set of them; for 'bad religion' has different forms,[23] some activities being laughed at as merely silly ('super-stition'), others condemned as wicked and dangerous. All we can do is to analyse what practices are censured on what grounds, and then to seek explanations for these choices. Some practices so censured may turn out to be ones which we would not think of classifying as magical (not that 'our' unreflective use of the term magic is at all stable; varying explicit or implicit binary oppositions—to science, to religion, to everyday reality—push it this way and that). A key Greek concept is that of *pharmakeia* (φαρμακεία); in it is contained almost everything that is bad about magic in the Greek view.[24] *Pharmakeia* is the attempt to interfere with a person's motivations or physical condition by covert means: to drive mad with love or to kill, for instance. Whether the effect is achieved by drugs/poisons or by spells makes no difference to the diagnosis, and the woman who accuses another of destroy-ing the fruit of her womb 'by *pharmaka*'[25] may well not be clear which form of attack she has in mind; for her, the consequences are visible, the precise method invisible and irrelevant. We, however, see an important distinction here, and do not classify the wife-poisoner Crippen as a magician. Again, what matters to the woman is the damage done. It is not her concern to police the boundaries of religious behaviour; her objection to *pharmakeia* is not that

---

[22] See Gager, *Curse Tablets* 20; Ogden, 'Binding Spells', 54–60; Dickie, *Magicians*, 48–9. Plato: *Leg.* 933e: the professional envisaged here is a μάντις ἢ τερατοσκόπος, and incurs an automatic death penalty; against amateurs the court has discretion. Old tablets are collected in *DTA* and *DT*; later discoveries are listed, but not reproduced in full, in Jordan's invaluable *SGD* and *NGCT*. Many of these new texts are printed, but only in the form of photocopies from the original publications, in M. A. López Jimeno, *Nuevas tabellae defixionis áticas* (Amsterdam 1999).

[23] Cf. Gordon, 'Imagining Magic', 192. See ibid. 165 for the probable universality in this sense of 'magic before magic' : all societies disapprove of certain religious practices, even if they lack a fixed term or terms to condemn them with.

[24] The locus classicus is Pl. *Leg.* 932e–933e. On the ancient terms *magoi/mageia* and also on the emergence of the magic–religion antithesis in late 19th-c. scholarship see J. N. Bremmer in Bremmer and J. R. Veenstra (eds.), *The Metamorphosis of Magic* (Leeuven 2002), 1–11, 267–71 (updated reprint from *ZPE* 126, 1999, 1–12).

[25] Eur. *Andr.* 157–60, cf. 205–8.

it is bad religion but that it is bad behaviour.[26] Even a definition of magic as 'socially condemned religious practices' does not create a category which can then be superimposed on Greek attitudes without some friction.

There is anyway dispute as to whether techniques such as *defixio* were subject to strong social disapproval, Plato being no reliable representative of general attitudes. Direct evidence is scarce, for a reason that is slightly paradoxical; for, though it has rightly been seen that magic is a matter of imaginings even more than it is of actions[27]—the magician's dreams of power, the fears of those who suspect magical attack against themselves— in Athens we have abundant evidence for magical actions, very little for thought about magic (except at the level of mythological representations such as those clustered around the figure of Medea). The concept of 'strong social disapproval' is also a slippery one: is one speaking of the real abomin- ation felt today for paedophilia, or the mere public unmentionability of adultery and tax evasion? Respectable women in tragedy, it has been pointed out, are horrified by the idea of using love philtres, but may do so *in extremis*.[28] As for curse tablets, the number of surviving examples proves the use of them to have been no rarity. But the practice, all but invariable in the Attic instances,[29] of depositing curse tablets in graves and even in the corpse's right hand was surely a gross offence against the dead person upon whom this intrusion was made. The obscenity of such an action may have been part of the point, one of the sources of power. Men deployed such shameful methods against their enemies, it has been suggested, because they perceived life as a bitter and ruthless struggle. But they would never have boasted of them.[30]

'Bad religion', we noted, divides into that which is perceived as silly and excessive and that which is evil. A single word to stigmatize the former emerged in the fourth century, *deisidaimonia*, 'superstition',[31] and some

---

[26] Only in this sense is Faraone, *Love Magic*, 18, right that 'Nor would most Greeks dismiss magical practices as a form of "bad" (i.e. unorthodox) religion'. The badness of many such practices is very clear (cf. n. 30).

[27] Gordon, 'Imagining Magic', *passim*.

[28] See Dickie, *Magicians*, 36–8, and cf. 88 on Antiphon, *Against the Step-mother*. This is one area where we have a little evidence for values.

[29] For the normal practice see D. R. Jordan, *AM* 95 (1980), 231, n.23. Corpse's hand: W. Peek, *Kerameikos* III (Berlin 1941), 89. For the first clear exception (a curse from the sanctuary of Pankrates) see *NGCT* 14. Curses found in a well in the agora have been supposed to come from a nearby sanctuary (D. R. Jordan *ap.* Boegehold, *Lawcourts*, 55, n. 3).

[30] So Versnel, 'Beyond Cursing', 62, arguing against the view of Faraone and Winkler that cursing was socially condoned; cf. Pulleyn, *Prayer*, 90–5.

[31] See *Athenian Religion*, 278. The pejorative sense of δεισιδαίμων, originally a good quality, 'god-fearing' (e.g. Xen. *Ages.* 11.8, *Cyrop.* 3.3.58 and so still in Aristotle, *Pol.* 1315a 1), first appears in Theophr. *Char.* 16 and in Menander's play of that title. The revaluation may have occurred in the Peripatos (Theophrastus, *On Piety?*): Plutarch regularly (e.g. in *De superst.*) sees piety as a mean between atheism and superstition, and a hint of this conception, though without the word *deisidaimonia*, is found in Theophrastus as cited in Porph. *Abst.* 2.7.3–8.3 Bouffartigue (p. 138.10–139.19 Nauck); note, however, that a 'middle way' conception of piety already appears in Xen. *Mem.* 1.1.14 (a text which also shows that practices could be stigmatized as

redrawing of the boundaries between prudence and what was now accounted superstition no doubt took place; traditional practices such as the attempt to 'wipe off' diseases are treated in New Comedy, a self-consciously enlightened genre, with contempt. But it was your own affair if you chose to spend money on magic rings to cure digestive pains or, like the dying Pericles, allowed the women of your entourage to fasten an amulet round your neck.[32] What offended society was *pharmakeia* directed against others. Charms and potions designed to create love would doubtless have been viewed as forms of *pharmakeia*,[33] but receive no special attention from Plato, our main source. In *Republic* he mentions 'bewitchments' and 'binding spells'. Reverting to binding spells in *Laws*, he speaks of the fear inspired by the sight of wax figurines 'at doors or crossroads or on the tombs of parents'. The two passages remind us how partial, if concrete, is the evidence of the surviving curse tablets. Bewitchments, or conjurings of Hecate against a person or place, have left no further trace except a few tantalizing literary fragments.[34] As for Plato's wax figurines, they surprise not just by the choice of location (otherwise unattested in this context) but more strongly by the hint that practitioners of the secret art of magic may have wished, after all, that their victims should be aware that they were under attack. The deposition of such figurines at the doors or on the tombs of parents of the target will have been a kind of anonymous message designed to terrify; it does not necessarily conflict with the proposition that magic was an art that no one admitted to practising.[35] But nothing remains for us to study except the curses inscribed on lead tablets and often 'bound' with a nail driven through them, and the lead figurines that

excessively religious even before the term 'superstitious' existed: cf. Thuc. 7.50.4 and Arist. *Pol.* 1315a 3–4). For the lexicographic history see P. J. Koets, Δεισιδαιμονία (Purmerend 1929), who ascribes the development to the Socratic schools. To a considerable extent the new value term was used to stigmatize practices or excesses, sometimes associated with religious professionals and outside civic norms, that had always been viewed with suspicion; the enlightened were in this sense merely conservative. Plutarch is particularly prone to detect superstition in foreign religious practices, and Xenophon (loc. cit.) and Menander perhaps preceded him (fr. 631 (754 Koerte)). Many titles of middle/new comedy reveal an interest in religious phenomena (see Arnott, *Alexis*, 312–13, 440–41; n. 19 above; Antiphanes, Οἰωνιστής; Men. Θετταλή; Aristomenes, Γόητες); the tenor of the treatment is usually lost, but see the following note and note the frequency with which haunting or possession is feigned or wrongly assumed (Men. Ἱέρεια, Φάσμα; Plaut. *Mostellaria*: the case of Men. Θεοφορουμένη is unclear); note too titles such as Δεισιδαίμων (Menander), Γόητες (Aristomenes).

[32] Wiping off diseases: Men. *Phasm.* 50–6; Diphilus fr. 125; for Menander's tone cf. fr. 106 (97 Koerte), 156 (178), 188 (210), 844 (620), 631 (754); and cf. Com Adesp. fr. 141. Rings: Antiphanes fr. 175; cf. Ar. *Plut.* 883–5 with the notes of A. H. Sommerstein ad loc. Pericles: Plut. *Per.* 38.2; Plutarch's source, revealingly, is enlightened Theophrastus (F463, Fortenbaugh *et al.*), and there may be anachronism here. The wearing of such *periapta* by small children was all but universal (Hamilton, *Choes*, 83–111). Other protective devices included squills buried at the threshold (Ar. fr. 266) and the 'Ephesian letters' (Anaxilas fr. 18.7; Men. fr. 274 (313 Koerte)). Plato classifies such things as products of ἡ μαγευτικὴ ἡ περὶ τὰ ἀλεξιφάρμακα, *Polit.* 280e, cf. 279c.

[33] For the Attic evidence on such things see Faraone, *Love Magic*, 1–10, 110–19.

[34] See Parker, *Miasma*, 222–24.

[35] This in modification of Gager, *Curse Tablets*, 21.

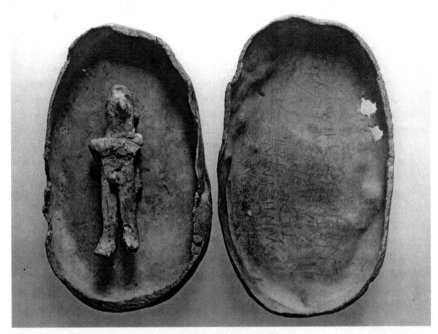

Fig. 8. A judical *defixio*. A curse against nine participants in a court case, among them Mnesimachus, is inscribed on the box; the name Mnesimachus is scratched on the figurine's right leg. Early fourth century, found with an adult's skeleton in the Ceramicus.

sometimes accompany them; vivid Attic examples of such 'voodoo dolls' are one that has been bound head and foot, pierced, and decapitated, and a cache of three enclosed in their own little lead coffins (in this case the coffin/doll assemblages themselves bear the inscribed curse).[36] About accompanying rituals and incantations we can merely note the high probability that they took place.

The question of how these practices worked could be tackled at many levels. I consider here merely that of the language of the tablets themselves. The fundamental idiom is that of 'binding'; the possibility of a form of magical binding, if not the precise form familiar from the curse tablets, is apparently an ancient one, already implied by such Homeric expressions as 'tell me which god has fastened and bound me on my journey'.[37] Many tablets simply list the name or names of the persons to be bound, with or without an introductory performative 'I bind'. Specific body parts that are to be bound ('tongue, mind, speech, hands' and so on) are often listed, and activities or

[36] See items 6 and 7 in C. A. Faraone's catalogue of voodoo dolls, *ClAnt* 10 (1991) 200–5. Both are illustrated in Gager, *Curse Tablets*, 16–17 (for another instance, 128); for many good illustrations of such material see also F. Costabile, 'Defixiones dal *Kerameikos* di Atene', *Minima Epigraphica et Papyrologica* 4 (2000), 17–122.

[37] Hom. *Od.* 4. 380; cf. e.g. ibid. 11.292, 18.155; *Il.* 4. 517, 14.73.

spheres of activity such as 'the workshop/tavern of X' or 'the speech that X is preparing against me'. Often the binding formula is expanded to introduce one or several gods; much the commonest is Hermes Katochos, Hermes who holds down (he also appears under other epithets, such as Chthonios, 'of the Earth', or Dolios, 'of Cunning'). The formula used, literally 'I bind before/to/ towards Hermes' (καταδῶ πρὸς τὸν Ἑρμῆν), may hint at cases registered or heard before a magistrate, but probably also suggests motion towards the underworld power to whom the grave provides access.[38] Just occasionally there is talk of the tablet as a 'letter' or a 'gift'.[39] Hermes and other gods can also be asked, with no apparent change of religious timbre, to 'hold down' the victim.

The powers deployed, in whichever of these ways, are always associated with earth and the underworld, and it is in the curse tablets that the problematic category of 'chthonian gods' for once comes into quite sharp if one-sided focus (for their power to benefit mortals is in this context forgotten). The main gods named apart from Hermes are Earth, Hecate and Persephone; Hades, Palaimon, the 'Exacters of Vengeance' (Praxidikai), Lethe, Tethys and (?) 'she with Persephone' appear once or twice each; once we have a general 'those below', once 'the chthonian daimon and the (female) chthonian (daimon) and all the chthonians', once 'the chthonians'.[40] Two categories of the unfulfilled dead, 'unmarried youths' and (?) 'the uninitiated' (ἀτέλεστοι), also appear once each; the familiar role in later magic of the 'untimely dead' is here anticipated.[41] There may be one example of a named dead man, the occupant of the grave which has received the tablet, being urged along with Hermes to 'hold down' an enemy; but reading and interpretation are disputed.[42] 'Persuasive analogies' referring to the tablets themselves are sometimes added: 'as these letters are cold [a reference to the

[38] A binding 'to Palaimon' has now been found within a sanctuary of that god (*NGCT* 14); note too 'if anyone has bound me anywhere whatsoever' in *NGCT* 24. Παρα+ dative is a rare alternative to πρός with accusative (*DT* 52; *SGD* 1); I see no difference in meaning. καταγράφω, 'I write down', occasionally replaces καταδῶ, 'I bind down'.

[39] *DTA* 99, 102.

[40] Hades: *SGD* 44, *DTA* 102. Palaimon: *NGCT* 14. Praxidikai: *DTA* 109, cf. the unpublished item mentioned after *SGD* 14. Lethe: *NGCT* 9. Tethys: *DT* 68. 'She with Persephone': *DT* 68. Then, respectively, *SGD* 20; *DTA* 99; *NGCT* 3. In *DTA* 72 Hermes and Hecate are followed by 'all the gods and the Mother of the Gods': the appearance of Mother here is unique and aberrant. On the problem of chthonian gods see p. 424.

[41] *SEG* XLIX 321 (= *DT* 52); *DT* 68. The 1996 supplement to LSJ cites two inscriptions of the Roman period (correct *MUB* 13.26 to 13.33) for a sense of ἀτέλεστος 'of children cut off before reaching maturity'. Such is the application of the word in both cases, but not necessarily its meaning.

[42] See *DTA* 100, as reinterpreted against Wünsch (with some misrepresentation of his position) by E. Rohde in the last appendix to *Psyche* (ed. 2, Heidelberg 1897). Wünsch's interpretation (accepted by Versnel, 'Beyond Cursing', 65) in turn introduces a rarity, self-naming by the writer of a curse. In the best discussion of the role of the dead in curse tablets (in *Poikilia. Études offertes à J.P. Vernant*, Paris 1987, 185–218), B. Bravo unnecessarily detects a use of *daimon* = dead man in adjusted texts of *DTA* 99 and 102. A good new example of a named dead man actively involved in a (non-Attic) curse is now provided by *SEG* XLIII 434 = *NGCT* 31.

coldness of lead] and back to front [backward writing and more complicated scramblings of normal letter order are common], so may his speech be cold and back to front.'[43] New twists to such formulae could be devised: thus a tablet which binds its victim 'with the unmarried youths' cruelly asks that the victim recover the power of speech when the unmarried youths read the tablet (i.e. never).[44] 'I bind them all in lead and in wax and in magic threads (?) and in idleness and in obscurity and in ingloriousness and in defeat and among tombs' blurs procedures ('in lead and in wax') with desired consequences such as 'in obscurity'.[45] Many tablets are marked by a grim infernal rhetoric of assonance and repetition.[46] But few call *expressis verbis* for the death of their targets, an extreme consequence unnecessary, it has been argued, in order to achieve the limited goal of, say, success in a particular law-suit.[47]

The rationale implied by these procedures (but it is surely not a chain of reasoning consciously followed by curse-makers) is something like the following: (1) Human capacities can in certain circumstances be 'bound'. (2) The most powerful agents of such binding are the frightening and dangerous powers of the underworld. (3) Deposition of tablets in graves 'delivers' them to these powers. (4) Binding can be ensured/reinforced by speech, both 'performative utterances' and persuasive analogies. It would be a mistake to contrast (2) with (4) on the grounds that (2) appeals to gods whereas (4) does not: the many tablets that do not name underworld powers are none the less deposited in graves, in accord with principle 3. The role of the dead in this play of power is somewhat ambiguous. Attic tablets seldom if ever allude to the particular occupant of the grave in which they are deposited. The two tablets which bind victims 'before the uninitiated' and 'with the unmarried youths' refer to classes, not to particular occupants of particular graves. Even in these two cases, any idea of exploiting, as a source of power, the anger felt by those two categories of embittered dead stays below the surface. It is rather their impotence that is stressed: we saw this above in relation to the 'unmarried youths', and the tablet that mentions the 'uninitiated/unfulfilled' (ἀτέλεστοι) wishes that its intended victims' designs remain equally

---

[43] *DTA* 67, and quite often. On forms of scrambling see E. G. Kagarow, *Griechische Fluchtafeln* (*Eos* suppl. 4, Leopoli 1929), 17.

[44] See M. W. Dickie, *Tyche* 14 (1999), 57–63, discussing D. R. Jordan's improved text of *DT* 52; *DT* 68 and (non-Attic) 43–4 are similar. On the creativity (if within strict limits) of magical language F. Graf well observes, *Magic in the Ancient World* (tr. F. Philip, Harvard 1997), 134. 'This permanent search for new combinations of meaning seems characteristic of the sorcerer's world'.

[45] *DTA* 55. 'Magic threads' (ἐμ [μί]τῳ) is proposed by Bravo, op.cit.

[46] See Kagarow, op. cit., 34–41; and more generally H. S. Versnel, 'The Poetics of the Magical Charm', in M. Meyer and P. Pirecki (eds.), *Magic and Ritual in the Ancient World* (Leiden 2002), 105–58. On the rhetoric of listing see R. Gordon in D. R. Jordan and others (eds.), *The World of Ancient Magic* (Bergen 1999), 239–78, and on the listing of body parts Versnel, 'An essay on anatomical curses', in F. Graf (ed.), *Ansichten griechischer Rituale* (Stuttgart and Leipzig 1998), 218–67.

[47] See Faraone, 'Agonistic Context', 8.

unfulfilled.[48] The one tablet mentioned above which may name a dead man also, if this interpretation is sound, credits him with a capacity to bind. Yet to speak of a 'capacity' to bind may put the thing too positively. Perhaps the corpse binds merely because it too now belongs to the underworld.

Most tablets assail a victim without attempting a justification. A minority request 'revenge' for wrong suffered by the author of the curse (who still, however, conceals his or her name).[49] One tablet addressed to the 'Exactors of Justice' (Praxidikai) even promises a 'good news sacrifice' once some evil befalls the target of the curse; the whole religious tone may change in such cases, to admit propitiatory supplications such as 'dear Earth, help me'. Such tablets blur the distinction generally and plausibly taken to exist between 'binding', an amoral technique directed against enemies, and whatever forms of supernatural redress are available to the victims of injustice. The wronged heroes of tragedy speak out their curses (for curse they do) in daylight without having recourse to lead and nails and tombs; the city itself curses those who threaten its welfare. At some times and places in antiquity the 'prayer for justice' had an institutionalized form, and inscribed curses against, say, thieves could reveal their author and be displayed to the light of day. Victims of injustice had no such symbolically powerful but still socially approved forms of action available to them at Athens. Having invoked the gods, they were normally left to reflect on the delays of divine vengeance. (We once hear of a mother wronged by her son who sat as a suppliant in the temple of Eileithyia,[50] but this was surely an extreme case and exceptional behaviour.) Those who then turned to binding might have said, with Virgil's Juno, that it was because they could not sway the gods above that they were stirring up Acheron.[51]

This is not the place to ask in detail who at Athens binds whom, and for what reasons.[52] Fundamental questions about the tensions, pressures and fears of Athenian society are involved. And, though we are abundantly informed about the 'whom?' in 'who binds whom?', 'who?' can never be

---

[48] *DT* 68. On the role of the dead in curse tablets contrast B. Bravo, op. cit. in n. 42, and Johnston, *Restless Dead*, 71–80. The possibility that the graves of *aoroi* were favoured for the deposition of *defixiones* is compatible with the available archaeological evidence, but that evidence is very scanty (of these two observations of D. R. Jordan, *GRBS* 26, 1985, 152–53, only the former has, misleadingly, been widely quoted). Whatever evidence about the activity of the dead may be found in sources of other type, in curse tablets their defining characteristic is, almost without exception (but see *SGD* 173, from Olbia), their deadness.

[49] *DTA* 98 ('dear earth'), 100 (note κολάζετε, line 12), 102, 109 ('good news'), 158; *NGCT* 3, 14. The readings of Wilhelm (n. 55 below) remove 103 from this class. The study which first identified this type is Versnel, 'Beyond Cursing', now taken further in his 'An essay on anatomical curses' (n. 46).

[50] Isae. 5.39. Such 'protest supplication' may occasionally have occurred, but it was institutionalized at Athens only in favour of slaves, who could take sanctuary in the Theseum: see Philochorus *FGrH* 328 F 177, with Jacoby's notes.

[51] *Aen.* 7. 312.

[52] I have learnt much from the work on this topic of my doctoral supervisee Esther Eidinow.

answered except by deduction and in very general terms, since with one or two very doubtful exceptions Attic curse tablets are always anonymous. It can be hard to disentangle the tensions that underly love curses when even the gender of the tablet's author is a matter of inference. In brief, the occasion par excellence for commissioning a curse is an impending law-suit.[53] Not only is this the context of a majority of those surviving curses which contain clues about the circumstances of their composition (in contrast to mere lists of names); literary allusions too imply that the practice was very familiar. One rare item of evidence for 'imagined magic' at Athens is the 'binding song' of the Furies in Aeschylus' *Eumenides*, which is sung over Orestes not long before he is tried at the Areopagus. And Aristophanes' joke about the politician Thucydides being struck dumb when a defendant in court is likely to have aroused thoughts of bewitchment in his audience.[54]

Not surprisingly, no curse can be certainly connected with that tiny proportion known to us of the cases brought to court in Athens. But, when a Lycurgus and a Demosthenes appear among eight 'accusers' bound on a tablet of the fourth century,[55] they are very likely to be the famous orators: the names were common, but not so many bearers of them were competent to speak in court. Theozotides by contrast is a rare name; and the Theozotides whose name appears, with others, on a little voodoo doll (and on its associated coffin) found in the Ceramicus is surely the politician against whom Lysias made a speech (possibly reinforced by this very curse).[56] Another judicial tablet has seventeen legible names, of which seven are borne by attested trierarchs of the period 325-322 and two by persons otherwise involved with naval affairs in that period: we descry here the type of dispute that must have provoked the curse, one concerning the fleet and most

---

[53] Not a past one: on this issue see the Attic texts cited by F. Costabile, *Minima Epigraphica et Papyrologica* 4 (2001) 193–208, and note that the Locrian text which he cites as an exception has been differently read by Jordan (*NGCT* 83); on the earlier debate C. A. Faraone, *JHS* 105 (1985), 151, n. 9.

[54] See C.A. Faraone, *JHS* 105 (1985), 150–4 (on Aesch. *Eum.* 307–96; the word δέσμιος is used in 306 and 332) and *TAPA* 119 (1989), 149–61 (on Ar. *Vesp.* 946–8); for evidence from later antiquity see Faraone, 'Binding Spells', 15–16. The victim is the defendant in both these cases: I see no reason to deny (with Gager, *Curse Tablets*, 117–18) that either side in a case might curse.

[55] *DT* 60. On a new tablet (F. Willemsen in *Kerameikos* XIV, 1990, 148–9; *NGCT* 5) the co-presence of Lycurgus and Hyperides supports the identification of each with the orator, even though this is a plain list without reference to legal procedures. On the presence of identifiable politicians see (with further examples) Habicht, 'Fluchtafeln', which builds on what he rightly calls the epoch-making article of A. Wilhelm, *JÖAI* 7 (1904), 105–26 (*Abhandlungen und Beiträge zur griechishen Inschriftenkunde*, Leipzig 1984, I, 197–218). Wilhelm's association of *DTA* 24 with deme imbroglios is rightly questioned by Davies, *Propertied Families*, 197, but texts such as *SGD* 1 and 12 cursing numerous members of a deme may well have such a basis.

[56] On this and other possible Lysianic connections see D. R. Jordan, Πρακτικὰ τοῦ XII Διεθνοῦς Συνεδρίου Κλασσικῆς Ἀρχαιολογίας (Athens 1988), 273–7. The Smindyrides cursed in *NGCT* 9 and *SGD* 6 is likely to be the profaner of the Mysteries known from Andoc. 1.15 (F. Costabile, *Minima Epigraphica et Papyrologica* 1, 1998, 36–9).

probably its finances, though not the details.[57] The listing of a large number
of names is very characteristic of the judicial curses. From them more clearly
than from any other source we can gain a sense of the large-scale mobiliza-
tion of support that might precede any actual appearance in court.[58]

It is easy to see why one might curse before a trial. The hopes and fears of
the protagonists were focused at a single point: a few hours in court would
have a decisive influence on an individual's wealth, prestige, perhaps even on
his right to reside in Athens or in the world of the living at all. The persons
commissioning the curses in such cases were surely the persons most affected
or imperilled; and this will mean, since the majority of litigation at Athens
was undertaken by persons of some wealth, that 'middle citizens' and above
were among the most important clients of curse-sellers—which is exactly
what Plato says. The few curses relating to dramatic competitions go along in
this respect with the judicial, even if the risks involved here related exclusively
to the honour of victory.[59] It is not always so easy to identify a concrete
stimulus for the creation of other types of curse. There is one recently
published example to which in one sense we can give a context with unique
precision, since four of the five persons assailed can be identified with absolute
confidence (the name of the fifth is lost): they are Cassander the successor, his
brother Pleistarchus, his general Eupolemus, and Demetrius of Phaleron who
governed Athens in Cassander's interest from 317 until the liberation of 307.
But we need to know not just the political attitude of the commissioner of the
tablet, which is obvious, but also the context in which he saw fit to act on it
through the precise medium of a curse. A force under Pleistarchus, for
instance, apparently came close to recovering Athens for Cassander (and
Demetrius?) in 304; but, if it was against a military threat such as this that
the curse was deployed, the case is unique.[60] The most comprehensive of
Attic *defixiones* dates from not much earlier and raises a related problem.[61] It
begins 'I bind, bury, cause to vanish from men' and goes on to list over a
hundred names, not a few of them identifiable (demotics being present) as
politicians of broadly anti-Macedonian sympathies. The curse-commissioner

---

[57] *DTA* 103, as revised and interpreted by Wilhelm, loc. cit., 122–5 (tr. of the unrevised text in
Gager, *Curse Tablets*, no. 38). *NGCT* 9 (on which see now D. R. Jordan in A. Matthaiou (ed.),
Ἀττικαί Ἐπιγραφαί. Συμπόσιον εἰς μνήμην Adolf Wilhelm, Athens 2004, pp. 291–302) gives for
the first time a precise court, that of the polemarch; the polemarch himself is cursed.

[58] As noted by Faraone, 'Agonistic Context', 16. In regard to the presence of women on
judicial curses (note now *NGCT* 9) a very revealing text is *DT* 49, which binds various attributes
of nine males including in every case 'the speech which he is preparing' *vel. sim.*; it also binds
various attributes of the wife of one of them, but in her case alone omits all reference to a speech
or testimony.

[59] See Wilson, *Khoregia*, 155–6. Plato: *Resp.* 364b–365a.

[60] The curse (*SGD* 14) was first identified as such by D. R. Jordan, *AM* 95 (1980), 229–36; the
case for 304 is made by C. Habicht, *Pausanias' Guide to Greece* (Berkeley 1985), 77–82, and cf. id,
Athens from Alexander, 74–5. The proposition that Cassander could only be cursed when physically close to Athens seems to me unreliable.

[61] *SGD* 48: cf. Habicht, 'Fluchtafeln'. Ziebarth's edition is apparently misleading not merely on
details (Jordan in Gager, *Curse Tablets*, 146).

is attacking his political enemies, it has been suggested (though near the end appear also four women labelled with a very gross term, λαικάστρια). But such a 'political curse' becomes easier to understand if one can associate it with a particular crisis that the writer hoped to influence. Surely few Greeks were so optimistic or naïve as merely to curse all the individuals who most vexed them at a given moment.

Attraction magic ('make her mad for me') probably tended to use a different idiom, and so largely escapes our view.[62] But one or two tablets survive which apparently bind a sexual partner in order to prevent a transfer of love or lust elsewhere.[63] They are likely to have been commissioned by women threatened with abandonment, like a tragic heroine (Sophocles' Deianeira) and the concubine known from the first speech of Antiphon, who both in such circumstances had recourse to love potions or charms. If so, it was a real sense of imperilment that caused the turn to magic. The matter is less clear with the many curses that relate to small businesses, workshops, taverns and the like; these are the largest group after the judicial, and derive from a quite different social milieu. Some attack members of a single profession—tavern-keepers as it might be—and them alone; and here commercial rivalry is a plausible motive. But others mix targets with different livelihoods in a way that suggests a list of enemies rather than of business rivals.[64] There is often a feeling of 'scatter shot' about such curses, yet even the apparently random shooting takes place within what must have been implicit social conventions. Some activities escape the attention of curse-writers. Fields and farmers, for instance, are not attacked; no more are ships and traders.

An even more remarkable circumscription is the chronological, on received views at least. Attic curse tablets begin in the fifth century and reach their highest density in the fourth, remaining very frequent right down to its end.[65] They then come close to disappearing, and their recurrence in good numbers in the second century AD looks like a new start. According to the ancients, rhetoric was created by jury courts; we might extend the causal chain, and

---

[62] Cf. n. 33. A new text from Akanthos has shown that even 'attraction magic' could in fact be encompassed within a variant of the 'binding' formula (*NGCT* 44), but other methods may have been preferred.

[63] *DTA* 78 and *DT* 68; *DT* 86, and *SGD* 57 are non-Attic comparanda, while a new text from Pella (*SEG* XLIII 434 = *NGCT* 31) is a very poignant document of this type.

[64] I owe this point to Esther Eidinow. On the milieu of these tablets see Dickie, *Magicians*, 85–7.

[65] Many of the tablets originally assigned by Wünsch to the 3rd c. were moved to the 4th by Wilhelm (n. 55), while W. Rabehl, *De sermone defixionum atticarum* (diss. Berlin 1906), esp. 40, went on to argue that they could almost all be located there; Wünsch in a review of Rabehl accepted the conclusion (*BPW* 27, 1907, 1574–9). All this was pointed out by L. Robert, *Collection Froehner, I, Inscriptions grecques* (Paris 1936), 13, and the conclusion and bibliography have often been repeated, without it seems much further study; Threatte, *Grammar*, I, 7–8, is non-committal, and H. Immerwahr, *Attic Script* (Oxford 1990), 125–6, discusses only the top end of the time span. Wilhelm and Rabehl have shown that it is unnecessary to assign a significant number of tablets to the 3rd c.: the question is whether they have also shown that it is implausible.

say that cursing was created by the need to counter the rhetoric so created. The same two places, Sicily and Athens, saw an early flourishing of all three elements, courts, rhetoric and cursing.[66] Naturally then, the argument would go on, cursing declined once Antipater abolished the Athenian democracy and thus the democratic courts in 322. But there are fallacies both of fact and logic here. Suppression of the courts could not directly explain the disappearance of curses relating to the life of the tavern. Nor does it seem that the courts were in fact suppressed for long.[67] 'But they changed in character', it might be countered. Possibly so (the matter is almost wholly obscure); but, if we adduce the decline in judicial curses as proof, the argument will be circular. The wandering seers who prepared the curse tablets may have found the impoverished Athens of the early third century unattractive. Yet, if there was a will to curse, it should have been possible to find a way. The problem is unresolved.

A tablet has very recently been published which 'curses back' (ἀντικατα-δεσμεύω) anyone, of any identity, who in any way or before any form of Hermes (possibilities are thoroughly listed in each case) has cursed the writer; on the reverse the writer apparently assails two enemies on his own account.[68] 'Cursing back' was one form of redress against magical attack, but it is disputed whether there were any others.[69] A difficult passage of Plato's *Meno* shows that in some Greek cities, Athens probably included, anyone adjudged a sorcerer (γοής) was exposed to legal action, perhaps in the form of direct arrest. But sorcerers did not advertise themselves as such, and the question remains of the charge and proof appropriate in such a case. The only explicit testimony, unfortunately, is that of Plato in *Laws*. He there distinguishes between two forms of damage through *pharmakeia*, that by poison and that by spell. He leaves open the question whether the second method can inflict real damage, but legislates against it none the less because of the fear and suspicion that belief in such practices generates. Private citizens convicted of such sorcery are to be subject to the discretion of the court; but for professional sorcerers ('seers or portent inspectors') there is to be an automatic death penalty.[70] Plato was certainly capable of legislating against forms of bad religion which the city shrugged off, but, given that popular thought did not distinguish between *pharmakeia* by poisoning and

[66] On Sicilian curses see J. M. Curbera, 'Defixiones', in M. I. Gulletta (ed.), *Sicilia Epigraphica* (Pisa 1999), 159–86.

[67] Habicht, *Athens from Alexander*, 5, has the courts functioning as before throughout the Hellenistic period; see too Boegehold, *Lawcourts*, 41–2.

[68] NGCT 24 (= *SEG* XLIX 320). Cf. Ogden, 'Binding spells', 51–4 on what he terms the 'magical arms race'.

[69] See C. R. Phillips III, '*Nullum crimen sine lege*: Socioreligious Sanctions on Magic', in *Magika Hiera*, 260–76; Gordon, 'Imagining Magic', 247–52; Dickie, *Magicians*, 50–9; D. Collins, 'Theoris of Lemnos and the Criminalization of Magic in Fourth Century Athens', *CQ* 51 (2001), 477–93. On the *Meno* passage (80a2–b7) see the very careful analysis of Dickie, 57.

[70] Pl. *Leg.* 932e–933e. The 'damage' under discussion here is non-fatal injury: for fatal injuries Plato refers back to his discussion in book 9, where unfortunately he fails to make the important distinction he makes here between the two types of φαρμακεία.

pharmakeia by spell, at Athens too harm done by spells should have been actionable under the same law as covered poison.[71] Yet we would surely have more concrete evidence if prosecutions on such a charge had been commonplace. Only where there is a strong collective preoccupation with the threat of sorcery does it make sense to seek to prove sorcery in court, because only then can the difficulty of bringing proof in such a matter be overlooked. The inner demons of Athenian society were not, we infer, those who cast binding spells at night against their private enemies.

Amateur use of love potions appears not even to have been legally actionable. Such at any rate is the conclusion that seems to follow from the case of the woman who was arraigned before the Areopagus on a charge of murdering her husband, but was successfully defended by the plea that she believed herself to be administering a love potion. The case is surprising, as one might expect any unsolicited use of *pharmaka* against another for whatever motive to be highly objectionable. But there is no sign that, acquitted of murder, the woman could then have fallen victim to a charge of *pharmakeia*.[72]

Two women cunning in spells were, however, executed in the fourth century; but the full scope of the case against them is uncertain. The Lemnian Theoris, who dealt in drugs and charms, was also according to the scholarly Philochorus a seer, and was condemned for impiety; there is also mention of arousing slaves against their masters. The priestess Nino was a leader of *thiasoi*, as well perhaps as a purveyor of love philtres to young men. The charge against her too is likely to have been impiety. Both these women were religious professionals, at the centre of groups of clients whom they could be seen as corrupting. In both cases the expertise in spells or philtres may have been a symptom of a broader impiety rather than the core of the case. What is puzzling is that no male seer is ever known to have been convicted on a similar charge.[73]

With Theoris and Nino we have returned to the starting-point of this chapter, 'those who make a living out of rites'. The execution of these two unfortunates illustrates graphically the suspicion which unlicensed religious professionals could arouse. That generalization, we saw earlier, requires

[71] I follow Gordon and Dickie here rather than Collins (n. 69 above). Harpocr. κ 19 καταδεδέσθαι· ἀντὶ τοῦ πεφαρμακεῦσθαι καὶ δεδέσθαι φαρμάκοις. Δείναρχος ἐν τῇ κατὰ Πυθέου εἰσαγγελίᾳ (VI.8 Conomis) is unlikely to attest an instance: this was a political case, and Dinarchus' usage was very likely metaphorical.

[72] Such must have been the defence (see 9) of the 'stepmother' attacked in Antiph. 1; it was successful if Arist. *Magn. Mor.* 1188b29–38 refers to the same incident, and the speaker of Antiph. 1 never attempts the argument 'even if she had given the drug as a love potion she would still have deserved to die'. A slave woman also involved had earlier been subjected to summary execution (20): perhaps the status differential of killer and victim would have led to this result even if it had been realized at the time that she had no intent to kill, but we cannot be sure.

[73] For the sources see in brief *Athenian Religion*, 163, n. 34, and for a good discussion Dickie, *Magicians*, 50–4. On the predominance of women among 4th-c. victims of impiety charges see M. Jameson, 'Women and Democracy in Fourth-century Athens', in P. Brulé and J. Oulhen (eds.), *Esclavage, guerre, économie en Grèce ancienne*, Hommages à Yvon Garlan (Rennes 1997), 95–107.

qualification and nuance. The city did not merely tolerate seers, but actually needed and employed them. Many no doubt were wholly respectable. And few claimed very subversive powers; charismatic inspired prophecy was a rarity. Yet Plato is insistent that the purveyors of black magic were seers and no other group. (Would he have allowed us to add 'and priestesses, their female equivalent'? The cases of Theoris and Nino certainly make it tempting to do so.[74]) Nobody admitted to being a γόης or a μάγος: the profession entered in the passport was always 'seer', and even a purveyor of curses doubtless did much work that was indistinguishable from ordinary seercraft. This poly-morphousness of the seer had two contrasting consequences. Seers were not, like the astrologers of imperial Rome, a class of men 'who will always be expelled and will always return'. Nobody ever dreamt of getting rid of such necessary persons en masse. But they were subject as a group not just to the periodic resentment created by failed prophecies, but also to a permanent lurking suspicion of charlatanism, and worse.

Wandering seers with spells in their bags knocked at doors only because those doors were sometimes opened. The buying of curses is just as important, and much more interesting, than the selling of them. By framing a discussion of magic within a discussion of religious professionals I have not wished to deny these evident truths. The point is one about structure and tradition (for magic too has traditions). On the one side we have the cults of the city, administered by publicly appointed priests. On the other side we have elective religion in all its forms. Elective religion is more directly responsive to the wishes of the individual than are the cults of the city, but it too is not and could not be a wholly spontaneous growth. What priests, magistrates, exe-getes, assembly and the rest are to the cults of the city, that the religious professionals are to informal or elective religion.

Disapproving remarks about the religion of the city are almost unknown. About almost every form of elective religion they are commonplace. Regular disparagement is a form of mild control, but such disparagement was not often the prelude to an attempt to suppress more rigorously. Much about the informal cult of Mother, for instance, was regularly criticized—its begging priests, its tambourines—but the continuing existence of the cult, which was very popular, seems not to have been questioned. A Demosthenic speaker can attack an adversary for pretending to treat epilepsy by *pharmaka* and incan-tations,[75] but there is no sign and no probability that even a wish was ever widely felt to eliminate such religio-medical healing methods, which were doubtless much commoner than our sources reveal. The example is an interesting one, because the Hippocratic writer *On the Sacred Disease* criticized

---

[74] It is probably not coincidence that the only fragment of Menander's *Priestess* (fr. 188 (210 Koerte)) is an attack on attempts to constrain a god by use of cymbals: that is to say, it is a rare and important example of an attack, on theological grounds, on what are construed as magical practices.

[75] [Dem.] 25.79–80.

such techniques as not merely fraudulent and ineffectual but impious. But, as far as we can tell, in the city's eyes bad religion only became substantially and threateningly impious when it brought with it what were perceived as dangerous social practices.

The Aesopic fable of the old woman before the Areopagus will bring the issue into focus.[76] An old woman who made a good living from incantations and the 'laying to rest' of divine anger was denounced by certain, doubtless envious, persons (τινες—the most convincingly authentic touch in the whole story) before the Areopagus for 'religious innovation'. She was condemned to death, and a cruel spectator asked her why, if she could appease gods, she could not also appease the jurors. With its Attic colour, the story might well derive from the first collection of Aesop's fables, made by the Athenian statesman Demetrius of Phaleron. But, were we to accept the story as historically accurate in its details, the religious implications would be startling. In the form recounted, the woman's offence is wholly theoretical and theological. She has assembled no disorderly *thiasos*, cast no binding spells, dispensed no dangerous *pharmaka*. All she has done is (it seems) to encourage lax notions about the gods by making it seem too easy to buy off divine anger. The randomizing elements in the Athenian legal system make it hard to state categorically that a given case could not have been brought or could not have been successful. (Lycurgus' prosecution of Leocrates would be obviously impossible, had it not occurred.) The malice of τινες is beyond prediction; 'impiety' is merely what on a given day a prosecutor can make it seem to be. But we can certainly say that this case is unlike any other known to us. We can also note that, though the Areopagus was responsible for certain forms of religious supervision, it was not the court before which cases of impiety were normally heard.[77] The story can become, a little precariously, an emblem of the kind of measures against unlicensed religion which the Athenians did not take, and of the limits of their suspicion of religious professionals.

---

[76] No. 56 Hausrath, usefully discussed by Dickie, *Magicians*, 51–2.
[77] R. W. Wallace, *The Areopagos Council, to 307 B.C.* (Baltimore 1989), 106–12.

7

Religion in the Theatre

It is well known that, in England in the sixteenth and seventeenth centuries, the godly looked at the theatre askance;[1] in 1606 an act was passed to 'prevent and avoyde the greate abuse of the Holy Name of God in Stageplayes, Interludes, Maygames, Shewes and such like'.[2] Greek plays were performed at a public religious festival, and there are few tragedies that do not contain a reference to a god or gods in the first twenty lines. The cultural context of the two forms of drama is clearly very different; and in the case of Attic as not perhaps of Elizabethan theatre it is sensible and even obligatory to ask what relation exists between the plays and public religion. The more important genre here is tragedy, because it treats of the gods more extensively; but comedy too will receive some glancing attention. At a mundane level, one can study the extent to which the religious world of tragedy resembles that of contemporary Athens, and can thus be exploited by the historian as a source. The literary converse to this question is one about the kinds of realism that the tragedians sought to achieve. But there is also a larger issue: the tragedies can scarcely merely have reflected, but must also have shaped, the religious experience of the citizens, of which they formed a part. The theatre, it can be argued, was the most important arena in Athenian life in which reflection on theological issues was publicly expressed.

First, however, a word needs to be said about the context of performance of the plays. The modern reader is sometimes urged by critics 'never to forget' that they were written for presentation at a religious festival. But is this ceaseless vigilance really necessary? There may be a danger of over-correcting our modern secular understanding of the theatre; for though in the modern world a play performed in a religious context would necessarily be religious in content also, the embeddedness of ancient religion entailed that certain activities, most obviously athletics, found their proper home at

---

[1] This chapter can be only a sketch; for much fuller studies see J. D. Mikalson, *Honor Thy Gods* (Chapel Hill 1991) and Sourvinou-Inwood, *Tragedy and Religion*. Amid much else, I say nothing of the ways in which the tragedians derive effects from the exploitation of religious and ritual motifs; for the many modern studies on this theme see P. E. Easterling, 'Tragedy and Ritual', in R. Scodel (ed.), *Theater and Society in the Classical World* (Ann Arbor 1993), 7–23, and in *Metis* 3 (1988), 87–109.

[2] See E. K. Chambers, *The Elizabethan Stage*, iv (Oxford 1923), 338–9; app. C ibid., 184–258, cites many contemporary criticisms of the stage.

festivals simply because they were of strong group appeal. (By parallel reasoning, performance at festivals of the polis does not entail that the problems of the polis were the playwrights' prime concern.[3]) Doubtless a Euripides who was as openly atheistical as Aristophanes pretended him to be would not have been tolerated in such a context, but perhaps not in any other public gathering either. Beyond this negative point, an influence of context on content can only be established from the content itself, not a priori. The mythological content of tragedy is undeniably important, but we cannot see the genre as simply re-enacting year by year central sacred stories, as did the medieval Mystery plays or certain forms of Japanese religious drama. 'Archmyths' underpinning the whole structure of Greek religion did exist, but they were more likely to be the subject of comedies than of tragedy, which showed a marked and revealing preference for 'heroic' over 'divine' and 'theogonic' mythology.[4] If the tragedians felt able to introduce gods on stage, that is surely as much because they were heirs to a mythological and epic tradition that freely commingled gods and men, as because they were composing works for performance at a public religious festival. It has been suggested that the preoccupation of pre-Euripidean tragedy, at least, with the relation between human action and a divine order is a heritage from the tradition of lyric 'cult-poetry' which the new genre develops.[5] There is some truth in that; but it would be hard to show that there is a stronger theological impulse in Sophocles than in, say, the *Odyssey*; and it must always be by contrast with other forms of high poetry of secular origin that the distinctively religious character of tragedy (if such there is) is identified. Perhaps by that criterion the very density of ritual allusion and religious concern in Aeschylus gives him a special place, close to proto-tragic ritual.[6] But the feature which most clearly divides tragedy from heroic (though not from theogonic) epic is its taste for explaining the origin of cults. That generic tendency (which is, however, far from being a generic rule) gives tragedy its feeling of being rooted in a particular religious landscape.

---

[3] The unacceptable alternative to this position is that there was, in effect, no imaginative literature at Athens which was not primarily concerned with the problems of the polis; for there was no context for performance other than polis festivals. Critics struggle to rescue the poets from this closed room of the imagination in various ways (poets subvert the ideology of the polis; the personal is the political ...), but it is easier just to open the door.

[4] Archmyths: for the term see J. S. Clay, *The Politics of Olympus* (Princeton 1989), 12–13. Preference: B. Knox, *Word and Action* (Baltimore 1979), 8–9. On Japanese religious drama see C. Dunn in *Drama and Religion* (= *Themes in Drama*, ed. R. Redmond, 5, Cambridge 1983), 225–37; on Mystery plays L. R. Muir, *The Biblical Drama of Mediaeval Europe* (Cambridge 1995).

[5] H. Patzer, *Die Anfänge der griechischen Tragödie* (Wiesbaden 1962), 137–73; id., *Poetica* 15 (1983), 15–17.

[6] So Sourvinou-Inwood, *Tragedy and Religion*, 201–64. The older debate on ritual origins is reviewed by R. Friedrich in *Drama and Religion* (n. 4 above), 159–223 and in *Tragedy and the Tragic*, 257–83.

There is another difference between epic and drama which should not be ignored merely because it is very obvious.[7] 'Song and dance', the chorus, is, until the fourth century, a constitutive feature of all Greek drama, one absent from epic but manifestly and pervasively present in ritual. And Athenians sometimes spoke as if drama was a matter of 'choruses for Dionysus' in just the same sense as a Spartan chorus singing a hymn to Apollo was a chorus for Apollo. Certainly no spectator could have been insensible of the continuity in this area between drama and ritual. In listening to the moving prayers for the well-being of Athens sung by the chorus at the end of Aeschylus' *Eumenides*, one may well feel that drama has, as it were, dissolved into worship.[8] Yet formally they remain imitated, not actual, prayers to the gods, just like the little less impressive prayers for the good of the foreign city Argos in the same Aeschylus' *Supplices*. The charming hymns to various gods sung by the choruses in many (though not all) Aristophanic comedies are even, unlike those of tragedy, set in present time; yet they are always recognizably hymns sung by a particular chorus in a particular play, not a voice speaking for Athens. The Clouds in their play, for instance, 'summon to the chorus' first Zeus and Poseidon, two gods important to any Athenian, but then address their own especial concerns by adding Aither and the Sun.[9] Rigorous logic may be inappropriate in this area: in the experience of spectators the logical barrier between imitated and actual prayers may well have been 'permeable'.[10] But there was, again, no generic necessity for such momentary blendings of fictive and actual worlds to occur. The choruses of drama recall, but are not, ritual choruses.

The relation between tragedy and the cult of Dionysus is a notorious problem. The problem is mitigated, it has been well emphasized of late, if we take as our unit of consideration not tragedy alone, but, as the playwrights themselves were long obliged to do, tragedy plus satyr play; for satyrs, no one

[7] See esp. P. Wilson and O. Taplin, *PCPS* 39 (1993), 170–4; A. Henrichs, ' "Why should I dance?": choral self-referentiality in Greek tragedy', *Arion* series 3, 3.1 (1994–5), 56–111; id., '*Warum soll ich denn tanzen?*': dionysisches im Chor der griechischen Tragödie (*Lectio Teubneriana* 4, Stuttgart and Leipzig 1996). For present purposes there is no need to connect the choral aspect of tragedy specifically with Dionysus, nor to enter on the debate about self-referentiality.

[8] For the possible influence of actual cult songs on Aeschylus see E. Fraenkel, *Philologus* 86 (1931), 7–11 = *Kleine Beiträge zur klassischen Philologie* (Rome 1964), 359–63.

[9] Aesch. *Supp.* 625–709; Ar. *Nub.* 563–74.

[10] To use Sourvinou-Inwood's expression, *Tragedy and Religion*, 50–3; cf. (on *Eumenides*) P. E. Easterling, *Metis* 3 (1988), 109; B. Gredley in *Tragedy and the Tragic*, 211–12. In respect of the comic chorus, A. Bierl, *Der Chor in der Alten Komödie* (Leipzig 2001), boldly argues that 'der Chor im Gegensatz zu den Schauspielern letzlich vorrangig er selbst, nämlich die theatralische Instanz "Chor", bleibt und die rollenspezifische Charakterisierung nur sekundär beigefügt wird' (18) and 'der komische Chor des Aristophanes ist weitgehend eine rituelle Äußerung und als ausdruck einer lebendigen Chorkultur zu verstehen, die traditionelle, auf dem Mythos und Ritual basierende Gesellschaften kennzeichnet' (362): at least to the second proposition in the second quotation one will unhesitatingly assent.

would dispute, have everything to do with Dionysus.[11] Two other genres performed at the *Dionysia* also have easily discerned connections with the cult of the god. Dithyramb was for Archilochus a 'song of Dionysus'; as for comedy, a link between the *phalloi* of comedy and of Dionysiac ritual is hard to doubt, for all that the *phalloi* of comedy droop while those of ritual are erect. But much more interesting is the parallel between the abuse hurled against leading citizens 'from the wagons' at Dionysiac festivals and the abusiveness of Old Comedy itself. The line of division between festival and play is here in a sense dissolved; for the de facto exemption which Old Comedy enjoyed from Athenian laws of libel is surely continuous with the ritual licence exercised by the young men on the wagons.[12]

Some seek a similar broad continuity, *mutatis mutandis*, between tragedy and a different aspect of the Dionysiac mood. Though Homer was in one sense the first tragedian, in another sense tragedy's world of polluting, inter-familial violence is the very antipodes of epic, where violence is gloriously displayed upon the battlefield. There is no glory in tragedy; there is, however, destructive madness (again alien to surviving epic). Tragic man accordingly will wish, not that he could live for ever, but that he had never been born.[13] Are not these forces of madness and lawlessness and destruction that haunt tragedy precisely 'Dionysus'? Was it not profoundly appropriate to evoke them at a festival of the disruptive god?[14] The suggestion is intriguing, because it picks out a central and extraordinary feature of tragic mythmaking. But we are not entitled to name that feature 'Dionysus'. The many-sided god cannot be reduced to the worst excesses committed by the mythical

---

[11] P. E. Easterling, 'A show for Dionysus', in ead. (ed.), *The Cambridge Companion to Greek Tragedy* (Cambridge 1997), 36–53; for a review of the debate see too Bierl, *Dionysos*, 1–20, and add now the extreme anti-Dionysiac case of S. Scullion, *CQ* 52 (2002), 102–37, which denies the Dionysiac associations even of dithyramb and comedy.

[12] Archilochus fr. 120 West. Wilson's suggestion, *Khoregia*, 322 , n. 115, that the 'cyclic choruses' honouring Apollo at the *Thargelia* need not be dithyrambs simplifies the early history of the genre desirably. 'From the wagons': see p. 297, and on the continuity between such rituals and comedy Halliwell, 'Le Rire rituel'. Exemption: S. Halliwell, *JHS* 111 (1991), 48–70; on the social implications see esp. J. Henderson, 'The Demos and Comic Competition', in J. Winkler and F. Zeitlin (eds.), *Nothing to Do with Dionysus?* (Princeton 1990), 271–314 (for more see *Ritual, Finance, Politics*, 69, n. 1).

[13] Soph. *OT* 1186–222; *OC* 1224–38; contrast Hom. *Il.* 12. 322–8, and for a confrontation of the two attitudes see Hdt. 7.46; on the difference between Homer and tragedy see Seaford, *Reciprocity and Ritual*, 11–13, or in *Masks of Dionysus*, 138–42; specifically on kin-killing E. Belfiore, *Murder among Friends* (New York and Oxford 2000), esp. 121–2.

[14] So R. Schlesier, *Poetica* 17 (1985), 20, 40; F. I. Zeitlin in P. Burian (ed.), *Directions in Euripidean Criticism* (Durham 1985), 60–1; S. Goldhill, *JHS* 107 (1987), 76; R. Schlesier in *Masks of Dionysus*, 89–114, with further references on p. 90. In the background is Nietzsche. Vernant, by contrast, sees the tragic Dionysus as the god of illusion, of 'tragic fiction' (in J. P. Vernant and P. Vidal-Naquet, *Mythe et tragédie en Grèce ancienne, Deux* (Paris 1986), 17–24 (181–8 in the Engl. tr.)); similarly C. Segal, *Dionysiac Poetics and Euripides' Bacchae* (Princeton 1982), ch. 7. But the use of masks in Dionysiac cult is quite unlike the theatrical, and it is not clear that Dionysiac delusion and theatrical illusion are comparable.

maenads; and Dionysus is by no means the only source of tragic madness.[15] If one operates with a Greek rather than a Nietzschean Dionysus, tragedy remains obstinately difficult to associate with the god.[16]

This cautious (excessively cautious, many may feel) survey has kept drama separate from the ritual life of the city while acknowledging several points of contact. But, in a quite different way, drama, tragedy in particular, could scarcely avoid having a profound influence on Athenian religious perception. In daily life, experience of the gods was muted and anonymous. One might suspect a divine element in many aspects of life, but one never or hardly ever saw an identifiable god at work. In ordinary speech accordingly one normally spoke of 'the divine' or 'the gods' or an unspecified 'god/the god/some god', not of named Olympians. This is the usage both in oratory[17] and also, with some exceptions, in the dialogue parts of both tragedy and comedy. But the distinction between these vaguely described powers and the plastic figures familiar from art and myth is not a simple distinction between real religion and an artificial variant confected by artists and poets; for in cult too gods have names and shapes and histories. Myth was integral to Greek religion because it was through myth that the gods of cult were revealed. And, though myths were told and depicted in many contexts in Greek life, the single most influential medium in classical Athens was surely drama.

We can move a little beyond these generalities, and consider the importance of tragedy's mythological setting more closely. Mythological time is special time.[18] Those few generations that led up to the Trojan war were of profound significance, because it was then that the foundations of Greek life were laid, by heroes close to the gods. This is the conception that underlies virtually the whole corpus of aitiological myth; and in religious terms the mythological period has a 'reality' and a contemporary significance that the present lacks. (For religious time has in a sense stopped: a fifth-century Athenian would have been amazed to learn, it has been well noted, that Hephaestus had just decided to get remarried.[19]) Tragedy's portrayal of the heroic age is much more complex. The tragedians have to some extent 'disenchanted' it, treating the heroes in a realistic and even critical, not a celebratory, spirit. (And, in general, their achievement in regard to the myths is to have thought them through in detail, and so to have uncovered the sufferings that they imply once they are translated back into the terms of actual human experience.[20]) In most parts of most plays, the heroes belie

---

[15] On the application of Dionysiac language to madness sent by other gods, I agree with S. Scullion, *CQ* 52 (2002), 111, n. 24, in seeing simple metaphor.

[16] Cf. Bierl, *Dionysos*, 1–20. Seaford's version of this approach (in *Masks of Dionysus*, 115–46, and his *Reciprocity and Ritual*, Oxford, 1994 235–367) escapes the charge of presenting too one-sided a Dionysus, because his Dionysus destroys in order to rebuild. But there is nothing Dionysiac about, say, the restoration of order in *Eumenides*.

[17] Cf. p. 105.   [18] Cf. p. 375.

[19] See Veyne, *Mythes*, 29.

[20] See B. Vickers, *Towards Greek Tragedy* (London 1973), ch. 6, esp. the splendid formulation on pp. 336–7.

their divine associations and descent. In watching *Agamemnon*, for instance, it seldom seems appropriate to remember that this graceless king wields a sceptre fashioned by Hephaestus and passed to his grandfather by Hermes from Zeus himself. Yet the characteristic manner of tragedy is not a simple reduction of the heroic to the contemporary but a complex and perpetual oscillation between perspectives.[21] Tragic heroes are admired as being unlike contemporary Athenians; for the same reason, on occasion, feared and condemned; felt to resemble Athenians in the most important respects (and sometimes even deliberately presented as if they were men of the fifth century); felt to exist outside time. The *Oresteia*, for instance, which has set the war against Troy in a grim and unheroic light, yet ends with the establishment of two of Athens' most important institutions and cults through the intercession of her patron goddess; that is to say, it ends in special, institution-grounding, mythological time. And, as the grateful Orestes departs, he promises that even when dead he will prevent any future Argive invasion of Attica, by sending dire omens from the tomb.[22] He expects, therefore, to exercise the special powers of a cult hero.

Throughout tragedy, the foundation of both types of cult, heroic and divine, quite often occurs or is predicted. And, since the heroes of cult acquired their honours because of their experiences while alive as men, tragedy sometimes depicted their sacred stories; in this restricted sense it can be compared to other forms of sacred drama. For any participant, for instance, in one of the several cults of the descendants of Heracles in east Attica, the justification for honouring these individuals in this place must have lain in the myth dramatized by Euripides in *Heraclidae*. The portrayal of Heracles himself in tragedy is shaped in various ways by his immense popularity in cult.[23] *Heraclidae* also shows how the evil Argive Eurystheus came to be a protecting hero of Attica: here as elsewhere tragedy seeks to provide an interpretation, through narrative, of the paradoxes of hero-cult.[24] Myth indeed is the soil in which Greek hero-cult grows; and, since the most important mythological genre in the fifth century was tragedy, tragedy too gave it nurture. It is symbolically appropriate that in his last play, *Oedipus at*

---

[21] Cf. P. E. Easterling, *JHS* 105 (1985), 3 (on tragic kings); C. Sourvinou-Inwood, *JHS* 109 (1989), 136; ead., *Tragedy and Religion*, 15–25. On tragedy's attitude to heroic myth see the influential remarks of J. P. Vernant in id. and P. Vidal-Naquet, *Mythe et tragédie en Grèce ancienne* (Paris 1973), 14, 25 (24 and 33 in the Engl. tr.), where Nestle's formulation that tragedy sees myth from the perspective of the city is approvingly cited.

[22] *Eumenides* 763–71.

[23] See M. S. Silk, *GR* 32 (1985), 1–22, at p. 4, on the (mostly lost) tragedies that illustrate Heracles in his important cult role as 'Saviour'. Silk also shows the influence on other tragedies (Soph. *Tr.*; Eur. *HF*) of his anomalous god/man status.

[24] *Heracl.* 1026–44. Here, as in Aesch. *Eum.* 762–74, and Soph. *OC passim*, a foreigner will side with Athens *post mortem* against his own people (cf. M. Visser, 'Worship your enemies', *HTR* 75, 1982, 403–28). In each case the play explains that the hero is perpetuating friendships and enmities that he formed while still alive.

Colonus, Sophocles should have shown the transformation of his greatest literary hero into a hero of cult.

But, it may be objected, have we not the testimony of his contemporary Aristophanes that Euripides brought tragedy finally down to earth? Does not its association with an enchanted time of special religious value dissolve before our eyes? Of his characters, we might adapt a line of his own and ask, 'Who would pray to such a hero?' But in fact, despite his reputation, Euripides tends to insist, more strongly than Aeschylus or Sophocles, on the close genealogical links between his characters and gods or demi-gods. In *Iphigeneia in Aulis* Achilles is described, insistently, as 'child of a goddess',[25] and his mother Thetis is a constant presence in a play that treats her descendants' fortunes, *Andromache*. We are reminded no less insistently in several plays that Helen and Clytemnestra are sisters, Orestes and Electra therefore nephew and niece, to the divine Dioscuri.[26] 'What mortal has not heard of him whose bed Zeus shared, Argive Amphitryon?' asks Amphitryon in the first line of *Hercules Furens*; and further examples are easy to find. The world of tragedy had always, as we have noted, been simultaneously mythical and contemporary; and it is much more accurate to say of Euripides that he made the traditional polarity more extreme, by pushing both sides of it to the limit, than to agree with Aristophanes that he simply eliminated the mythological pole. Mythological time remains for Euripides the time when cults are founded; and explicit aitiology, scarcely found in Sophocles though perhaps quite common in Aeschylus, becomes in him a standard element.[27]

Aitiology seems in tragedy to have two, related, grounds.[28] It is one way of bringing myth into the present, which as we have seen is always one of tragedy's concerns. And, since the institutions and practices of which the

---

[25] 901, 903, 976.

[26] *El.* 312–13, 990–3; *Or.* 465 (cf. 476); *Hec.* 441 (if genuine), 944.

[27] Attested cult *aitia* in Aeschylus, in addition to those in *Eumenides*, are *Supp.* 268–70 (apparently, an Argive hero-cult of Apis); fr. 6 (the name of the Sicilian Palici), fr. 202 (the wearing of crowns in commemoration of Prometheus' chains); those in frs. 312–13 are of a different kind. The establishment of the cult of Prometheus at Athens was probably predicted in *Prometheus Luomenos* (cf. M. Griffith's edition of *PV*, Cambridge 1983, 303), and *Ixion* perhaps depicted the first purification (cf. E. Müller, *De Graecorum deorum partibus tragicis*, Giessen 1910, 22–3); various *aitia* have also been proposed for *Danaides* (see A. F. Garvie, *Aeschylus' 'Supplices': Play and Trilogy*, Cambridge 1969, 227, 230), and *Nemea* perhaps showed the foundation of the games. Plays depicting myths on which Attic cults were based are *Eleusinioi* (?), *Herakleidai* (?), *Oreithuia*. On Sophocles see n. 30 below. For *aitia* in Euripides see the list in W. Schmid (and O. Stählin), *Geschichte der griechischen Literatur*, i.3 (Munich 1940), 705, n. 7, adding *HF* 1326–37, *Med.* 1378–1383, *Phoen.* 1703–9, *Hipp.* 29–33, *Erechtheus* fr. 65 Austin (370 Kannicht) lines 55–117; W. S. Barrett's note on Eur. *Hipp.* 1423–30.

[28] Aitiological predictions also have a narratological function, as a device of closure. I would regard this as a complementary rather than conflicting explanation. That the link between myth and cultic fact was sometimes invented by the poet is quite conceivable. But invention of actual cult facts (F. Dunn, *Tragedy's End: Closure and Innovation in Euripidean Drama*, New York 1996; S. Scullion, 'Tradition and Invention in Euripidean Aitiology', *Illinois Classical Studies* 24–5, 1999–2000, 217–33) would seem to undermine the aition's function of tying the past to a known present.

origins are shown tend to be Athenian, the aitiological poet is the civic poet whose audience is the citizen body. Euripides' *Erechtheus*, for instance, 'founds', in mythological time, a series of cults that were of particular importance in the last quarter of the fifth century BC; his *Ion* likewise founds Athens' position as mother-city of Ionia. Several plays remind the audience of talismans—corpses of heroes or other relics from the mythological period—that still keep Athens safe from foreign invasion.[29]

True generalizations about tragedy are elusive; and one must certainly stress that many plays lack an explicit aitiological element entirely. But explicit aitiological allusions are not the only or most important aspect of the phenomenon we are considering. Although Oedipus alone among Sophocles' characters is presented as a future hero, several others—Ajax, Hercules, Theseus (and others in lost plays)—did in fact receive cult in Attica.[30] The point is not that the relevant plays take on a new meaning once one recognizes the status of these characters as heroes of cult.[31] The point is rather that this is not the point. Since the mythological world on which the plays are based is also the basis of heroic cult, it is only to be expected that characters who appear in tragedy might also be honoured outside the theatre. The point is the absolute naturalness with which the two spheres criss-cross and interpenetrate one another.

Tragedy's mythological subject-matter is important for religion in another way. The myths could be made to display fundamental problems in the relations of gods and men with absolute clarity. The central question of practical theology for the Greeks was whether it was possible to establish a relation of friendship, *philia*, with the gods, in which piety and offerings were rewarded according to the normal principles of reciprocity, *charis*. The heroes of myth are, in Aeschylus' words, 'those close in stock to the gods, those near to Zeus ... (in whom) the divine blood is not yet extinct'.[32] The problem of divine friendship could therefore be dramatized, with an immediacy and lucidity unknown in real life, by depicting the sufferings of sons and lovers of the gods, mortals bound to them by the closest of all ties of *philia*. Such myths of sexual contact between man and god were by origin myths of a kind of grace, an ennobling contact between the perishable and the divine. The tragedians transformed them; Zeus' dear and much-travailed son Hercules,

[29] Cf. n. 24; also Eur. *Supp.* 1197–1210, *Erechtheus* fr. 65. 64–89 Austin. Note too the oblique references to Athenian interests or claims in Aesch. *Eum.* 12–14 (cf. p. 86), 399–402 (cf. Sommerstein's notes *ad loc.*); Soph. *Aj.* 201–2.

[30] 'Others': Procris (and Cephalus, if he appeared in *Procris*); Triptolemus in *Triptolemos* (which dramatized an important Attic cult myth); for details see Kearns, *Heroes of Attica*, s.vv. Note too how in *Trach.* 238, 753–4, cf. 993–5, Heracles founds the important Euboean cult (which had an Attic filial: *IG* I³ 383. 131) of Zeus Kenaios; the *aition* is present but remains implicit.

[31] Cf., on *Ajax*, R. P. Winnington-Ingram, *Sophocles. An Interpretation* (Cambridge 1980), 57, n. 2. Allusions to Ajax's future hero-cult have been detected in the play, but are far from clear (see the works cited by J. Griffin in *Sophocles Revisited*, 87–8).

[32] Fr. 162. On *charis* in cult and in tragedy see H. Yunis, *A New Creed* (Göttingen, 1988), 101–11, and my essay in C. Gill and others (eds.), *Reciprocity in Ancient Greece* (Oxford 1998), 105–25.

Apollo's abandoned bride Creusa, and many another god-raped maid, become in their hands living and breathing problems in theology.[33]

Mythological time is, finally, a time when the relations of gods and men had not yet been fixed in their final, historical mould. Greeks of the historical period told how several of their rites had their origin in practices of human sacrifice, commuted subsequently into gentler forms. In tragedy, accordingly, gods are still liable to issue hideous demands for human victims. And this is only the most conspicuous case; one has in principle no reason to expect that any religious institution presupposed by the tragedians bears any direct relation to the beliefs or practices of fifth-century Athens. The seduction of mortal women by gods, for instance, is a common occurrence in the world of tragedy; but men and gods subsequently drew apart, and a disgraced Athenian wife or daughter had little chance of calming her menfolk's rage by any such interpretation of her state.[34] (In *Ion*, Euripides plays with a double perspective: the plot postulates that such seductions occur, the characters tend to react with fifth-century incredulity or disapproval.[35]) Tragedy's mythological world is effectively untouched by rationalism, and Euripides in particular exploits with gusto its most outlandish aspects: Aeolus' sons and daughters mate incestuously, Pasiphae seduces a bull, Bellerophon mounts to heaven and Phaethon drives the chariot of the sun.... And to these elements of mythological fantasy are to be added other fantastic elements that derive from the narrative patterns that tragedy exploits. The 'threatening oracle', for instance, is a motif on which several tragedies are based. But it is very unlikely that any historical Greek was ever warned that he would kill his father and marry his mother or be killed by his grandson or anything of the kind.[36]

Were the religious world of tragedy in its entirety as remote from contemporary reality as this, it would still not lose its power to raise issues of actual religious concern. Gods no longer raped maidens in contemporary Athens;

---

[33] Cf. the portrayal of Io in Aesch. *PV*; Aesch. *Suppl.* 167–75. *Dictyulci* fr. 47a 782–4 (Danae); Soph. *Tr.* 1264–9, cf. 139–40; Eur. *Antiope*, 11–14 (Page, *GLP*, p. 62); *HF* 344–7, 497–501, 1087–8, 1127; *Ion* 252–4, 355–8, 425–8, 436–51, 881–922, etc; *Tro.* 820–59; *Phaethon* 45–8 Diggle. Such themes were doubtless prominent in the many lost plays, particularly by Euripides, treating such heroines as Alope, Danae, Melanippe, Tyro (on the story type, the so-called 'maiden's tragedy', see Bremmer/Horsfall, *Roman Myth*, 28–9).

[34] Contrast e.g. Europa's lovely speech in Aeschylus fr. 99, 5–6: γυνὴ θεῷ μειχθεῖσα παρθένον σέβας | ἤμειψε, or the chorus' speculations in Soph. *OT* 1098–1109, with Men. *Samia* 589–608, where the possibility of divine seduction, known from tragedy (590), becomes comic when applied to a contemporary situation. Hyginus *Fab.* 121 tells how Chryseis bore a child to Agamemnon and pretended it was Apollo's; if this story derives from a tragedy (it is F 10c in *TGrF* 2, *Fragmenta Adespota*), the old convention had been undermined by the date it was composed.

[35] See e.g. 338–341, 436 ff. and the whimsically anachronistic observation in 1541–3 that a god's child lacks a recognizable social status (cf. Ar. *Av.* 1650).

[36] Such oracles were given e.g. to Laius, Aleus, father of Auge, Acrisius. Note, however, that stories of this type were also told about historical figures (such as Astyages, grandfather of Cyrus). Thus here the narrative pattern forces even the perception of historical events into a 'mythical' mould. This means that a Greek might not have found such features of tragedy unrealistic.

but the question raised by such stories about the reliability of the gods, their willingness to repay favours received, remained, as we have seen, at the heart of practical religion. In fact the condition does not obtain; very numerous practices, turns of phrase, assumptions about religion found in tragedy have parallels outside the theatre.[37] In a rough way it might be said that, while the political world of tragedy is 'pre-historic, with contemporary intrusions', its religious world is 'contemporary, with pre-historic intrusions'. The issue of tragedy's relation to its religious environment becomes, however, especially intricate if we turn from practices and institutions to beliefs. We can take as an example beliefs about the influence of the living on the dead. In *Choephori*, Orestes and Electra perform an elaborate invocation at their father's grave, confident (if we believe their words) that he has the power 'to send support from below' to their plot against Clytemnestra. In *Persae*, a similar lament causes the dead king Darius actually to appear and prophesy. In *Eumenides*, we see the 'image' of murdered Clytemnestra urge on the Erinyes to vengeance; and in Euripides we hear how Achilles appeared above his tomb to demand the sacrifice of Polyxena.[38]

Are the powers here ascribed to the dead any more than enabling fictions to which the audience gives credence only for as long as it is seated in the theatre? No simple answer is possible. On the one hand, the predicted intervention of Agamemnon in *Choephori*, and Darius' actual epiphany in *Persae*, are responses to funerary cult of the kind that was regularly performed by every Athenian household; and the dead who received such cult were urged to send up good things, as if they had the power to do so. Statements too can be cited from non-dramatic texts that the murdered have power to afflict their killers; and 'soul-raisers' were still active here and there in the Greek world in the fifth century.[39] On the other hand, even within tragedy itself one can document the view that 'the dead are nothing'; and a character in Euripides can assert that the only point in invoking the dead is as a form of indirect appeal to the living.[40] It seems doubtful whether a sample of Athenians, if pressed (unnaturally) to say whether they found Aeschylus' portrayal of the powers of the dead credible, would have agreed among themselves, or would individually have found the question easy to answer. Again, did Athenians believe that heroes could influence their military fortunes from the grave, as is postulated in *Oedipus Coloneus* and in several further passages of tragedy? They certainly acted as if they did, on several occasions and in several ways.[41]

---

[37] For details see Parker, 'Gods Cruel and Kind', 146–7.

[38] Aesch. *Cho.* 306–509, probably (and significantly) 583–84 (cf. Taplin, *Stagecraft*. 339 n. 3: aliter A. F. Garvie ad loc.), 722–5, *Eum.* 598; *Pers.* 633–842; *Eum.* 94–139; Eur. *Hec.* 107–15, cf. *Tro.* 622–5 and Sophocles, *Polyxena*. Similar appeals to Agamemnon are found in Soph. *El.* (e.g. 453–60, 1417–21). Eur. *El.* (677–84) and (ironically tinged) Eur. *Or.* (674–6; 1225–39).

[39] The murdered: Xen. *Cyr.* 8.7.18; Parker, *Miasma*, 107. Soul-raisers: Ogden, *Necromancy*, 52–3, 95–110 (who cites a supposedly 5th-c question tablet from Dodona enquiring whether to employ one).

[40] Eur. *Hel.* 962–8; cf. p. 366 below.   [41] See Kearns, *Heroes of Attica*, 44–63.

But they could not share that absolute confidence which Sophocles' Oedipus—a dramatic character endowed with prophetic insight—feels in his own future powers as a protecting hero. In the literary exploitation of such a belief, all the reservations and uncertainties of actual belief are liable to fall away.

It is not by distinguishing realistic from non-realistic features in tragic religion that we can usefully compare it with civic religion, but by accepting the total dramatic fiction and considering what image of the divine it creates. The world of tragedy is a world of angry gods; of mortals afflicted by inherited guilt, and punished for ancestral crimes; of individuals and even whole cities faced with the absolute desolation of being 'hated by the gods'; of terrible divine revenges. At moments, it can even seem close to that of Verdi's Iago, who sings 'io credo in un dio crudele' (though the projected sadism of that conception is in fact very un-Greek). One can scarcely stress enough that no Athenian ever spoke about the gods in public in anything like these terms. In official parlance the gods love, support and protect Athens; all threats to the city are posed by the folly and deficient patriotism of its citizens. Tragedy extends our awareness of what it was possible to think and imagine and fear about the gods (and so about the ultimate reality of the world) in Athens in the fifth century; it may have extended the actual possibilities of thought and imagination and fear. It does so not only by presenting the gods as, on occasion, grimmer and fiercer than civic orthodoxy allowed. It can also treat them—or characters in tragedy can do so at least—as less important, less powerful, less perceptible than it was normal to suppose.[42] We noted earlier in respect of funerary cult that the extremes both of credulity and of doubt can be documented from within tragedy, and the point is rather characteristic. The palette contains almost every colour, and the diversity is not due simply to the contrast (in the old stereotype) between pious Aeschylus and sceptical Euripides.

The questioning of divine benevolence and justice found in tragedy is never or hardly ever final. Diverse forms of 'theodicy', a concept that is only partially anachronistic, are deployed, implicitly and explicitly; a complaint against the gods is never a thing that simply falls to the ground unregarded.[43] One form which we should note is the justification spoken by an actual god in epiphany: here was the directest 'theology' to which Athenians were ever exposed. Gods in this situation issue repeat warnings against 'impiety' (that is, vaunting words or sacrilegious acts);[44] they insist, individually, on their desire for due honour from mortals, and rejoice in the affliction of those who deny them

---

[42] See Parker, 'Gods Cruel and Kind', 157, n. 51. That article discusses at length the contrast between tragic and civic theology touched on here.

[43] I have discussed tragic theodicy in *Sophocles Revisited*, 11–30.

[44] Soph. *Aj.* 127–33; *Phil.* 1440–4; Eur. *El.* 1354–6; *Tro.* 85–6; cf. *Hipp.* 1339–41; cf. Pl. *Clit.* 407a on Socrates ἐπιτιμῶν τοῖς ἀνθρώποις ὥσπερ ἐπὶ μηχανῆς τραγικῆς θεός. On the modalities of epiphany see Sourvinou-Inwood, *Tragedy and Religion*, 459–511.

it;[45] but they 'take no pleasure' or 'feel pity' when the pious die.[46] Hard cases can be explained by reference to a broader rule: Artemis is powerless to rescue Hippolytus, her virtuous favourite, from the anger of Aphrodite, since 'this is the rule among gods. None of us chooses to counter another's will, but we always stand back.' Often, as here, the god appeals back to Zeus' will or law as an ultimate explanation against which there is no appeal.[47] It can scarcely be a coincidence that Zeus himself apparently never 'theologizes' in tragedy (though he made a remarkable appearance in Aeschylus' *Psychostasia*[48]); the ultimate explanation cannot itself be dragged on stage and required to give an account of itself.

The obvious next step is to ask whether the gods are successful in justifying their ways to man. But we must back off from a topic which demands a book of its own.[49] I turn briefly instead to one which has been less reflected on, the treatment of religion in comedy. 'Comedy' here will mean Old and Middle Comedy. About New Comedy there is much less to be said. In this faux-realist genre, the role of the gods is as in everyday life: they are taken for granted, honoured from time to time, not much thought about. It is true that characters are shown responding to the religious situations of everyday life, and doing so often sententiously and amply. At this level, as an index to the possible religious sentiments of the age, the poets of New Comedy are an important source; and, despite Menander's fame as a 'mirror of life', he doubtless also shaped it; for there is a strong moralizing, normative strand under the surface realism. In the late fourth century the nature of piety, for instance, was a topic of interest in educated circles, and the fragments of Menander appear both to reflect and to take a stance in that debate. Menandrean man is hostile to anything he conceives as magic, contemptuous of superstition;[50] and, since Menandrean comedy was an immensely powerful vehicle of cultural values, its influence on the religious life of the city should

---

[45] Eur. *Hipp.* 7–8, 21–23, 1402; *Bacch.* 1340–7, 1377–8; *Tro.* 69–86.

[46] Eur. *El.* 1329–30; *Hel.* 1678; *Hipp.* 1339–41.

[47] Eur. *Hipp.* 1329–31; cf. Soph. *Phil.* 1415; Eur. *Hel.* 1660–1, 1669; *Or.* 1634; *Bacch.* 1333, 1349; *Andr.* 1268–9; *El.* 1248. For 'necessity' or 'fate' (sometimes associated with Zeus) in similar contexts see Eur. *El.* 1248, 1301; *IT* 1438; *Ion* 1582; *Andr.* 1268–9; *Or.* 1654, 1656; *Hel.* 1660–1. In Eur. *Andr.* 1270–2 Thetis deprecates mourning on the grounds that all men have to die.

[48] See the testimonia, p. 375 Radt. Taplin, *Stagecraft*, 431–5, queries this, but has to explain away two independent testimonia: see, contra, Sourvinou Inwood, *Tragedy and Religion*, 463–4. It is not, however, certain that Zeus spoke in the play. He could certainly appear in comedy (p. 151 below), and Plaut. *Amph.* 93 claims that he also appeared *in tragoedia*. T. B. L. Webster, *The Tragedies of Euripides* (London 1967), 93, supposed that Eur. *Alcmena* ended like Plaut. *Amph.* with an epiphany of Zeus.

[49] A discussion of divine justice in Euripides forms the core of Sourvinou-Inwood, *Tragedy and Religion*; on Euripidean religion there is also now C. Wildberg, *Hyperesie und Epiphanie* (*Zetemata* 109, Munich 2002; shorter version in *Illinois Classical Studies* 24–5, 1999–2000 (= M. Cropp and others, *Euripides and Tragic Theatre in the Late Fifth Century*), 235–56).

[50] See p. 123, n. 31; 124, n. 32.

not be underestimated. But the gods are much less immediate presences in New Comedy than they are in either Old Comedy or in tragedy.[51]

To Old and Middle Comedy therefore I revert. From Aristophanes much more clearly than from any other source we see how important the festivals were within the texture of Attic life. Old Comedy swarms with allusions to them; some plays symptomatically take their names from them, and the personifications of particular festival days twice speak a prologue.[52] The general tenor of references to the gods in Aristophanes is positive, even affectionate. The late play *Plutus* constitutes a not very emphatic exception, but in general the role of the Aristophanic gods, like those of oratory, is to try to save the citizens from themselves.[53] Trygaeus in *Peace* does indeed complain that Zeus is bringing Greece to ruin through war, but Hermes explains that in truth 'you (mortals) chose to fight though they (the gods) kept arranging truces'.[54] The plays abound with light and graceful hymns, and the finest of all cameos of Attic piety is a chorus where the Clouds urge one another to come to the land of Pallas, the land of the *Mysteries*, of gifts to the gods of heaven, of temples, statues, processions, of fair-crowned sacrifices to the gods and festivals at all seasons, and in spring the crowning grace of the Dionysiac choruses.[55]

It is against this background that we must set the treatment of named gods as characters in the plays. This has at first sight more than one form. On the one hand there is mythological burlesque, already found in Old Comedy but apparently attaining an acme of popularity in the first half of the fourth century. Such plays made use of myths of every type, primarily as recreated by comedy's sister genre of tragedy. These myths might or might not bring gods with them; but a popular subgenre which treated births of gods necessarily gave them a place.[56] There were even a few comic versions of the *deus ex machina*. The other comic way with the gods, seen for instance in four plays of Aristophanes,[57] was to remove them from mythological plots and mythological time altogether. The poets of the Old Comedy treated Dionysus not

[51] I have not forgotten the deified abstractions who speak Menandrean prologues, nor the role of Pan in *Dyscolus*. But I note that N. Zagagi, *The Comedy of Menander* (London 1994), both (142–68) stresses the narratological importance of these motifs and also (167) warns against assigning too much weight to them at a level of belief.
[52] Names: see A. M. Bowie in D. Harvey and J. Wilkins (eds.), *The Rivals of Aristophanes* (London 2000), 327; personifications: Kalligeneia (final day of the *Thesmophoria*) in *Thesmophoriazusae* II of Aristophanes (fr. 331), Dorpia (first day of the *Apatouria*) in Philyllios, *Heracles* (fr. 7).
[53] Ar. *Nub.* 587–9; *Eccl.* 473–5; for benevolence cf. *Eq.* 1090–5, 1168–89. Exception: Ar. *Plut.* 87, 1117.
[54] 58–9, 62–3, 105–9, 203–12.   [55] Ar. *Nub.* 299–313.
[56] On mythological burlesque see above all Nesselrath, *Mittlere Komödie*, 188–240; on the 'birth of gods' sub-genre id. in G. Dobrov (ed.), *Beyond Aristophanes* (1995), 1–27 (the only important surviving fr. is Page, *GLP*, no. 47 = Com. Adesp. fr. 1062 K/A). *Deus ex machina*: Eubulus frs. 9, 33: Nesselrath, *Mittlere Komödie*, 235.
[57] *Peace* (Hermes); *Birds* (Iris, Prometheus, Poseidon); *Frogs* (Heracles, Dionysus); *Wealth* (Hermes). For a list of 'divine comedies' (of both types) by other poets of Old Comedy see Bowie, op. cit., 319–20.

merely as capable of acting in the Athenian present, but even as if he were an ordinary Athenian who did his military service like any member of the audience.[58] But the mythological burlesque of Middle Comedy seems to have perpetrated such a systematic embourgeoisement of myth that the distinction between plays set in mythical and contemporary time is blurred. The formula was to take a mythological plot sequence, pretend that it was taking place in a social environment like that of contemporary Athens, and let the comic incongruities begin. Such was the technique of Plautus' *Amphitruo*, the one (indirect) surviving example of the genre. Even Cratinus' *Dionysalexandros*, though set in mythological time, contained transparent allegories of current events.[59]

The indignities to which Aristophanes exposes his gods are well known. Moderns though not ancients have sometimes seen what he does to the gods as irreligious and subversive of traditional religion, whether designedly or no.[60] But such views were always in discord, not so much with the apparent conservatism of Aristophanes' general outlook (which might not go very deep), as with the general atmosphere of affection for the gods of Athens which pervades the plays. No one apparently defends such a position any longer; instead the view that it is all a matter of festival licence has won a complete and rather easy victory.[61] And it is surely correct that Greeks felt able to cheek the gods precisely because they did not doubt their power. Often the very absurdity of the comic postulate of divine weakness is itself a source of humour. Peisetairos in *Birds* convinces Heracles that under Athenian law he is a bastard and will inherit nothing when Zeus dies. Once this truth sinks in, the slow-witted demi god is appalled, and joins the rebellion of the birds against his father's rule. There is humour of embourgeoisement here, with Peisetairos applying Attic laws to Olympus and asking Heracles whether Zeus has registered him in a phratry. But underlying it is the more fundamental

[58] Ar. *Ran.* 48–54; Eupolis, *Taxiarchoi*, fr. 274.

[59] On embourgeoisement see Nesselrath, *Mittlere Komödie*, 236, 240; Arnott, *Alexis*, 19–20. The source of Plautus' *Amphitruo* is unknown, and some suppose that it is Plautus himself who has burlesqued a tragic model, after the manner of Middle Comedy: see the ed. by D. M. Christenson (Cambridge 2000), 50–5.

[60] Nilsson, *Geschichte*, 779–83 (and W. Nestle as there cited); V. Ehrenberg, *The People of Aristophanes* (Oxford 1951), 267; I know G. Keller, *Die Komödien des Aristophanes und die athenische Volksreligion seiner Zeit* (Tübingen 1931) only from K. J. Dover, *Greek and the Greeks* (Oxford 1987), 195. The 18th- and 19th-c. reception of 'Aristophanes impunitus deorum gentilium irrisor' (title of a work by C. A. Böttiger, Leipzig, 1790) can be traced through the works cited by H. Kleinknecht, *Die Gebetsparodie in der Antike* (Stuttgart 1937), 117, n.1. Ancients occasionally noted the facts, without comment: Σ vet. Ar. *Pax* 741e (cf. 741b and c), ἐπεπόλαζε γὰρ τότε ταῦτα · Ἡρακλῆς πεινῶν, Διόνυσος δειλὸς καὶ μοιχὸς Ζεύς; Julian, *Misopogon*, 366c (attacks of comic poets on Dionysus and Heracles).

[61] See already Wilamowitz, *Glaube*, ii, 95: 'Die Götter aber sind lebendige Götter, denen tut es nichts, wie viel die Menschen in der Maskenfreiheit sich gegen sie erlauben, denn das ist ja Spiel, das mit dem Festjubel verklingt'; cf. i, 41–2. I speak of 'easy victory' because I have not encountered a comparative study which locates the Greek material clearly and firmly. It is not enough to know that in various religious traditions (e.g. medieval Christianity) laughter is permitted about sacred subjects; one needs a clear view of what may and may not be laughed at.

absurdity of the postulated death of Zeus.[62] *Birds* ends with Zeus forced to surrender his sceptre to the birds; at the end of *Wealth*, the gods are starving for lack of sacrifices and Wealth has been installed on the acropolis in their place. Modern taste might expect a more conciliatory ending, whereby the traditional gods were restored at least to a share of their traditional prerogatives. But for the Athenians such a compromise was unnecessary, we may assume, because reality itself provided the necessary corrective. Of course one would continue sacrificing to the usual gods as usual.

Yet we should not allow the simple formula of festival unreality or festival licence to pre-empt all further questions about the phenomenon. It is, for instance, interesting that in more narrowly ritual contexts, though much licensed raillery certainly occurred, it was directed against mortals rather than against gods. In so far as there existed a tradition of laughing at the gods, its vehicle was epic verse.[63] Again, we must ask whether boundaries were set to festival licence. If it is true that 'there are limits, even for Aristophanes: no essential levity touches the Maiden of the Acropolis or Demeter',[64] two interesting conclusions follow. Demeter was the goddess whose cult, along with that of Dionysus, was most hospitable to ritual abuse. Yet *ex hypothesi* she herself remained untouched by it. But much more important is the way in which the case invalidates any simple 'release of inhibition' or 'getting back at authority' account of Comedy's divine comedies. If ever there was, in Athenian culture, a strong and, one might think, oppressive taboo, it was that which enjoined silence or reverent and guarded speech in relation to the Eleusinian cult. Perhaps festival licence provides release from all bonds except the ones which bind one most.

One might adopt a quite different approach, and argue that comedy ridiculed those gods who were normally seen as the less dignified, figures close to man with whom worshippers sustained what anthropologists call a 'joking relationship'. The gluttony of Heracles, a standard comic theme, was deeply embedded in his mythology and found an echo in the many cult societies which met to dine in his honour. The comic Hermes is a merry rogue always eager for offerings; such is he too in the *Homeric Hymn to Hermes* and perhaps even, if very discreetly, in his meeting with Calypso in book 5 of the *Odyssey*. The Poseidon of *Birds* is a stiff and haughty but not a notably ridiculous figure; the Prometheus who in the same play cowers behind a parasol for fear

---

[62] Ar. *Av.* 1641–75.

[63] J. Griffin, *Homer on Life and Death* (Oxford 1980), 198–202; there is playfulness too in *Hymn. Hom. Del.* and especially *Hymn. Hom. Herm.*

[64] Nock, *Essays*, ii, 543. A footnote adds 'jokes about Apollo's oracles relate to their political production and use rather than to the god; and the Birth of Athena by Hermippus was probably a satire on the myth about Zeus rather than on the goddess as worshipped' (this last probably directed against Wilamowitz, *Glaube*, ii, 95 'des Hermippos Ἀθηνᾶς γοναί, des Platon Ζεὺς κακούμενος deuten darauf, daß die Komödie von den heiligsten Personen nicht zurückhielt').

of Zeus is, like Hermes, a minor deity, and a friend to man.[65] Apollo, Artemis, Demeter, Hera and arguably Athena are spared so far as our extant evidence goes (though some of them must certainly have had some role in mythological comedies[66]). Then there is Zeus. Aristophanes, as we have seen, constructs plots which undermine his kingship, but does not in those plays expose him to visible humiliation or indeed to view at all. Mythological burlesque by contrast seems regularly to have brought him on stage in search of women, or boys: we see him so engaged in Plautus' *Amphitruo*, and a scholion mentions 'adulterous Zeus' as a standard comic theme.[67] As it happens, the treatment of Zeus in *Amphitruo* is not disrespectful; but in the *Danae* of Sannyrio, pondering the possibility of reaching his beloved through a drainage conduit, he is not a dignified figure. So even the highest god is probably not spared absurd adventures. But perhaps none but the strictest moralists ever thought the worse of Zeus for his enviable adulteries. No mortal could enter upon a joking relationship with Zeus himself. But his comprehensible lusts made him a less forbidding figure.

There remains Dionysus, the coward and braggart who in *Frogs* soils himself in fear. An ancient commentator mentions the 'cowardly Dionysus' as a stock comic theme.[68] As we noted above, Dionysus was not only made subject to human emotions, but was also treated as a kind of honorary Athenian who served in the ranks in the Peloponnesian war. It is tempting to suppose that here too a god who was regularly treated playfully was treated extra playfully in the comic theatre. Yet the Dionysus of myth is a serious and often terrifying figure; here for once the 'safety valve' or 'laughter as a refuge from awe' interpretation of the comic god has force. Dionysus fought valiantly in the Battle of the Gods against the Giants;[69] his cowardice was no doubt suggested by the effeminacy which is already his in Aeschylus, but the effeminate Dionysus of *Bacchae* is no coward. The god of the soiled tunic seems essentially to be a creation of the comic stage. It can scarcely be coincidence that the god whom comedy has reshaped most drastically is the patron of the festival. Comedy brings its presiding genius down to its own level.[70]

---

[65] Hermes: Ar. *Pax* 192–4; *Plut.* 1099–1170; *Hymn. Hom. Herm. passim*, esp. 130–2; Hom. *Od.* 5. 100–2. Note too his 'friendliness to man', Ar. *Pax*. 392–3. Prometheus: see esp. Ar. *Av.* 1504, 1545.

[66] See O. P. Taplin, *Comic Angels* (Oxford 1993), 66, n. 11; on Artemis in Amphis' *Kallisto*, Nesselrath, *Mittlere Komödie*, 234–5.

[67] Other examples included the *Daidalos* of Aristophanes (see esp. fr. 198); the *Nemesis* of Cratinus; the *Danae* of Sannyrio; the *Ganymede* of Antiphanes; cf. Ar. *Av.* 558–9. Note too the fine 'phlyax' bell-krater ascribed to Asteas, W. Beare, *The Roman Stage*, ed. 3 (London 1964), fig. iv; A. D. Trendall, *Red Figure Vases of South Italy and Sicily* (London 1989), fig. 364.

[68] See n. 60 above. Occasions for cowardice were available in Cratinus' *Dionysalexandros* and in Eupolis' *Taxiarchoi*; for other comedies where he had a role see Bierl, *Dionysos*, 29, n.14.

[69] See e.g. Carpenter, *Fifth-Century Dionysian Imagery*, 15–34.

[70] Various critics (listed in Bierl, *Dionysos*, 29, n. 10) detect a rehabilitation of Dionysus in the second half of *Frogs*. But this claim is too strong: he becomes less absurd, but his sense of humour remains that of an Aristophanic buffoon (e.g. 1477–8), and the mildly serious closing remarks are assigned to other characters; Dionysus' last thoughts are of a good dinner (1480–1).

We rejected earlier the claim that Old Comedy was irreligious. A counter-claim can be advanced, that Aristophanes was positively good for piety. The gods of Old Comedy altogether lack the fearfulness of those of tragedy. The heroes of Old Comedy, despite and even because of their failings, are amiable figures. The same is true *mutatis mutandis* of its gods. Old Comedy enabled the Athenians to like their gods a little more than they might otherwise have done.[71]

Tragedy and comedy bear a relation of some kind to ritual. Their choruses derive from, and resemble, those that in a more straightforward way dance for the gods. The abusiveness of Old Comedy is the abusiveness of young men 'from the wagons' at Dionysiac festivals. Tragic poets differ from epic in their disposition to explain the origins of the cults of the city. But these are not the most important contributions of the dramatic genres to Athenian religious life. Tragedy rendered the world of myth more palpable, one might almost say, than it had ever been. And both genres extended the varieties of religious experience. One god in the city might play many parts, and the Dionysus of, say, *Bacchae* or *Frogs* was part of an Athenian's experience of Dionysus no less than was the Dionysus of the *Anthesteria*. The omnipresence of the divine in drama may have something to do with ritual origins. But the richness and diversity of the images of the divine presented in drama, the intellectual and emotional challenge, were possible because the poets saw their primary task as one of exploring human experience, not of honouring the gods.[72]

---

[71] 'Nothing popularizes like genial ridicule': G. Lowes Dickinson, *The Greek View of Life*, ed. 8 (London 1912), 46.
[72] See S. Scullion, *CQ* 52 (2002), 134–5.

II

8

Festivals and Their Celebrants

The tradition of studying 'Athenian festivals' is one that goes back to antiquity. One aim of this book is to break with that tradition, in so far as it isolated the festivals from all the other activities and imaginings relating to the gods that took place in Athens. But the festivals cannot simply be ignored. The best introduction to the subject is not to survey the dry assemblage of antiquarian facts that dimly illustrate the goings on at this or that festival, but to note the many contexts in which festivals are mentioned in Aristophanes, sometimes at length, as in *Acharnians* and *Thesmophoriazousai*, sometimes, still more revealingly, in glancing and casual allusions.[1] No careful reader of the comic poet can doubt how central the festivals were to the shared religious experience of the Athenians.

But how are they to be treated? We are familiar, from the standard handbooks, with a way of presenting Athenian festivals that in many respects derives from the ancient scholars who wrote on the same subject. The festivals are treated one by one (whether they are listed month by month or god by god). Each is dated and assigned to a god. The ritual activities are described, and an attempt is made to identify their purpose. The sum of the accounts of the individual festivals constitutes the sum of available knowledge about Attic festivals. This convenient principle of arrangement has its limitations. To take an easy illustration, ancient scholars were uncertain what god two festivals (*Skira, Oschophoria*) belonged to, and the controversy has continued into modern times. But in both cases it seems that it is the principle of 'one god per festival' that is at fault. More generally, in this tradition of study, festivals tend to be seen as a set of ritual actions directed to a goal. The question of who performs these actions, and where, is of very subordinate interest. Ancient sources, at least in the form in which they reach us, often present actors in rituals with maddening imprecision as 'they'; and moderns are much less maddened by the imprecision than they should be. But rituals are not machines, the handles of which anyone can pull in any place to achieve a desired result. The traditional arrangement, one festival after another, also tends to discourage thought about the Athenian festivals as a class, whether about interrelations between individual festivals or about the social functions of the whole set. Even the question of what constitutes a

---

[1] Two examples from many: the allusions to the *Diasia* in *Nub.* 408 and 864.

festival tends not to be posed. And this neglect affects not only the concept of 'festival' itself but also what one might call the forms of festal action. A large number of Athenian festivals included, for instance, a παννυχίς, an 'all night' celebration in which women were the main participants. Everyone in the ancient world knew what a *pannychis* was, but we moderns need to think about the institution systematically.

A different topic on which we need to reflect is, alas, the randomness of the evidence that is available to us for Attic festivals. Presented in book upon book and article upon article, the familiar festivals come to masquerade as a canon,[2] as if they were indeed not 'some' but 'the' festivals of the Athenians. Doubtless, thanks to comedy and oratory, no genuinely popular festivals have vanished wholly from the record, and in that sense we have much fuller knowledge about Attic festivals than about those of any other Greek state. But it is striking that an early text, a decree of the deme Skambonidai of about 460 BC, appears to name four festivals of which three are familiar (*Dipolieia*, *Panathenaea*, *Synoikia*) and the fourth (*Epizephyra*—partly supplemented) otherwise quite unknown. A string of festivals of Demeter (*Chloïa, Kalamaia, Antheia*) appear only in inscriptions, and the deme calendar of Erchia quite recently revealed an unknown *Erosouria* at which Athena received a sacrifice; a number of other festivals appear in single lexicographical notices alone. A *penteteris*—a rather grand kind of celebration—held at Sunium and attended by 'the leading Athenians' appears only in Herodotus' account of a political incident of the sixth century.[3] *Metageitnia, Boedromia*, and *Pandia* are festivals, no doubt once great, that survived into the classical period as little more than names. Some of these shadowy rites had perhaps ceased to be celebrated by the fourth century, some may have been of local significance only, some may have been short-lived. But we are reminded if so that the festival programme constantly varied in ways that our handbooks, with their picture of a fixed set of rites repeated unchangingly in perpetuity, constantly disguise. Written calendars may have had the effect that practices were in reality somewhat more stable in the fourth century than they had been in the seventh: the *Proerosia*, a rite that varies in spelling, date and even chief honorand from deme to deme, counts by then as an exception.[4] But a further quite factitious impression of stability—in the festivals that were celebrated,

---

[2] There is a different sense in which the canon of the Athenian festivals became more firmly fixed in the 20th c. Much that now counts as a fact was still controversial in the 19th c., as one can see, for instance, from the first part of Nilsson, *Studia*, which has still to argue that the various Dionysiac festivals which we take for granted were all distinct one from another. The separation of *Eleusinia* from Eleusinian *Mysteries* was not finally proved correct until later than that (see p. 201). The stability of the canon in the 20th c. reflects partly real progress (for such a thing exists in scholarship, in some senses), partly the authority of Deubner, *Attische Feste*. Some modest adjustments will be proposed here and there in what follows.

[3] Skambonidai: *IG* I[3] 244; *Chloïa* etc.: p. 195 below; *Erosouria*: *LSCG* 18 β 26–31; *penteteris*: Hdt. 6.87.

[4] See p. 196, n. 14.

and in the ways in which they were celebrated—is a product of our static sources. The celebration of festivals is a form of social activity and society changes from day to day; despite the ideal of 'in accord with tradition' festivals too had to be replanned before each celebration (are two 'Royal Weddings' ever identical?), and it is inconceivable that they should have escaped from the law of perpetual change.[5]

The most important festivals, we noted above, are doubtless all known; and some impression of their relative popularity can be gained from the number and character of allusions that are made to them. (But even here contingent factors play a part. Athletic festivals such as the *Eleusinia* and the *Herakleia* at Marathon are visible in Pindar, invisible in comedy, though they certainly had not all ceased to be held; only the discovery of a play of Menander revealed that the *Tauropolia* could attract participants from Athens itself; the survival of actual prize vases shows the *Anakeia* to have been less obscure than the absence of literary allusions suggests....[6]) But as to what actually took place, except at the athletic and dramatic festivals, almost any information that is preserved is preserved by chance. At the *Tauropolia*, a mock human sacrifice was enacted; stuff fetched from under the earth at the *Thesmophoria* was mixed with the seed corn; the Athenians performed three 'sacred ploughings', at different sites; here are three items of evidence prominent in any account of Attic festivals, each one of which is mentioned in a single source that might well not have mentioned it or might well not have been preserved.[7] Had Pausanias not chanced to hear and proudly recount facts not widely known, the doings of the *arrephoroi* would have been about as obscure as those of the *aletrides* with whom they are mentioned in a famous passage of Aristophanes; even about the 'bears' of Brauron who appear in the same passage there was little to be said, until the excavation of their sanctuary revealed an unexpected new world.[8] If one allows the mind to play on the many no less important items of evidence that are, no doubt, lost, it is hard not to despair. But we must abandon the illusion that the debris of facts which have come to rest on the pages of the handbooks necessarily suffice, by a happy chance, to allow us to interpret whatever festival may be in question. As an illustration and a cautionary tale, the example of the *Skira* is discussed in detail in an annexe to this chapter.

Even if the ritual actions performed at many festivals were much more fully known than they are, would it be possible, after describing the programme of a given festival, as it were to add up the sum and state its meaning or purpose

[5] See Bell, *Ritual*, ch. 7, 'Ritual change'. The hellenistic *Pythaïs* is a festival which changes before our eyes from celebration to celebration: pp. 83–5.

[6] See Men. *Epit*. 1119–20; *Athenian Religion*, 97, n. 124, and for the newly discovered prize from a festival of Poseidon p. 59, n. 36. Wilamowitz's remark (*GöttNachr* 1896, 165 = *Kl. Schr*. V I, 108) that 'Die städtische Zentralisation Athens hat alle lokalen Feste schon während des 5. Jahrhunderts degradiert' is much too extreme, as Arist. *Ath. Pol*. 54.7 shows.

[7] Eur. *IT* 1449–61; p. 157 below; Plut. *Praecepta Coniugalia* 42, 144a–b.

[8] On all this see Ch. 11 below.

in simple words? Such is the assumption, in part again inherited from the ancients, that underlies most older accounts of Attic festivals.[9] But few modern students of ritual would find it at all plausible.[10] In a certain sense, doubtless, rituals are performed for a purpose. At the broadest level, the well-being of the state depends on the celebration of all the traditional rituals at the proper times. Every individual festival has the same highly important goal: to give the god concerned his or her due meed of honour. More narrowly, a particular rite might be conducted on a particular occasion for a particular purpose: to bring rain, to quell winds, to avert a plague. And one imagines that some (though perhaps not all) participants in some (though perhaps not all) the annually recurrent rites might have been able to identify practical goals that it was hoped they might achieve; such goal-directed explanations, however, would always have had to compete with others that appealed to tradition or spoke of 'imitation' or 'commemoration' of past events.

The real objection to a goal-directed or 'instrumental' explanation of rituals,[11] an explanation that looks above all for an effect in the external world that they are supposedly designed to achieve, lies in the contrast between the simplicity and generality of the goals and the complexity and specificity of the rituals that, it is said, are straining towards them: too much is being explained in terms of too little. To take a simple but striking example, the *Thesmophoria*, celebrated at the time of ploughing, was doubtless under-stood to have something to do with the fertility of the fields. But those who see this as the main goal of the festival need to explain why the married women of Athens had to leave their homes and camp out for three days en masse in order to achieve it. Had Anacharsis asked an Athenian, 'What are the *Thesmophoria*?', what answer might he have received? 'The rite our wives perform to make the crops grow'? Or rather, 'the festival at which women gather for three days on their own'? Festivals are, above all, forms of collective activity, but those who interpret them in terms of goals are hard put to it to explain why this should be so, or why they constitute, in fact, the most important form of festivity for societies that take them seriously. The *Myster-ies*, says Aristotle (fr. 15), were an experience (πάθημα), not a form of learning

---

[9] J. G. Frazer's view of most ritual as 'magic', which he understood as goal-directed action based on mistaken scientific premises, has left many traces in the works of Deubner, Parke, Simon (both heavily dependent on Deubner) and recently of Robertson on Athenian ritual. Important studies embodying different approaches include Jeanmaire, *Couroi* (1939); Brelich, *Paides e Parthenoi* (1969); Burkert, *Homo Necans* (German original 1972); Calame, *Thésée* (1990); Versnel, *Transition and Reversal* (1993).

[10] The literature is vast. Outstanding recent studies include G. Lewis, *Day of Shining Red. An Essay on Understanding Ritual* (Cambridge 1980); Bell, *Ritual Theory*; ead. *Ritual*; Humphrey/Laidlaw, *Archetypal Actions*. Each of these works surveys the available approaches. Note too Rappaport's discursive but interesting *Ritual and Religion*, and E. Muir, *Ritual in Early Modern Europe* (Cambridge 1997).

[11] For a rejection of 'instrumental' views of ritual see e.g. J. Beattie, 'On understanding ritual', in B. R. Wilson (ed.), *Rationality* (Oxford 1970), 240–68, and the works discussed by Bell, *Ritual Theory*, 143, n. 6.

($\mu\acute{a}\theta\eta\mu a$): he thus emerges as a precursor (if in relation to just one festival) of the modern theoreticians who see ritual, surely rightly, not as goal-directed action nor yet primarily as cognition but as, perhaps, a specialized form of drama and at all events a performance, one in which the identity of the actors is just as important as the acts which they are called on to perform. The meaning of such a performance cannot be squeezed out into a formulation in a few words any more than can that of a play or other work of art; and labels such as 'rites of passages' or 'calendrical rites' are legitimate only for use in crude preliminary sorting, not by way of final explanation. Unfortunately, if this approach to the understanding of ritual is sound, the vast gaps in our knowledge become all the more damaging. One might with luck be able to grasp the main aim of an action many details of which were obscure. But fragments of a performance mean little, and the quality of an experience can emerge only from a continuous description.

Is the best policy then in regard to the festivals to give up? Ought centuries of enquiry to be terminated? The situation is not quite that desperate. No Attic festival, it is true, and probably no Greek festival can be studied with that close attention to the complexities of symbolic evocation, that sense of the developing drama of the long procedures, that alertness to the ways in which rituals reflect, shape, distort the order of the surrounding society which are to be found in the richest anthropological studies. But the main elements of a fair number of the major festivals are known. What we should perhaps back off from is the attempt to make sense of every minor festival and every little known rite. We can try instead to answer some broader questions about what might be called the shape of Attic festivals.

One basic issue has already been studied: we have distinguished between 'single site' and 'dispersed' festivals, and considered various contexts—deme, grouping of demes, phratry, city—in which festivals might take place. Smaller organizations such as orgeonic groups and *thiasoi* seem normally to have spoken of their rites as 'sacrifices', not as 'festivals'.[12] But that is a reminder of the need to look at the concept of 'festival' itself.[13] It proves difficult to catch hold of. No one perhaps will deny that the Athenians had a concept, that of *heorte*, and a set of practices that resemble English 'festival' to a considerable degree. The *Panathenaea*, for instance, is unquestionably a festival; it is a multiple sequence of ritual actions, publicly financed, involving participation (active and passive) on a large scale; other business of the city comes to a halt during it; it is spoken of as a *heorte*, and its name has the neuter plural form

---

[12] Note however $\acute{\eta}$ $\pi o\mu\pi\grave{\eta}$ $\tau\hat{\omega}\nu$ $\mathcal{A}\delta\omega\nu\acute{\iota}\omega\nu$ of *IG* II² 1261.9 and the $\mathcal{A}\tau\tau\acute{\iota}\delta\epsilon\iota a$ of 1315.10. On the $\acute{\epsilon}o\rho\tau\acute{\eta}$ of the *Mesogeioi* (*IG* II² 1247.14) see p. 472 below. For an explanation of 'orgeonic groups' see *Athenian Religion*, 109–11.

[13] As J. D. Mikalson does very provocatively in 'The Heorte of Heortology', *GRBS* 23 (1982), 213–21, though I cannot accept all his conclusions. See too C. Calame, 'La festa', in M. Vegetti (ed.), *Introduzione alle culture antiche*, iii (Turin 1992), 29–54.

in –*a* already noted by Herodotus to be characteristic of festivals.[14] The question is how many of these characteristics can be removed and still leave a festival. It has been suggested, for instance, that no gloomy rite was seen as a *heorte* by the Greeks, since the metaphorical applications of the words *heorte* and *heortazein* all concern good cheer.[15] The melancholy and ill-omened rite of *Plynteria* would therefore have to count as something (of nature unknown) other than a festival. But it may be pure chance that no extant source applies the word *heorte* to the *Plynteria*. We should perhaps rather, guided by the characteristic neuter plural name form, accept the *Plynteria* as a *heorte*, and conclude that good cheer was a common but not a defining characteristic of a festival. (The mood of the *Plynteria* may in fact have been mixed, like that of the *Diasia*.)

Even, however, if all rites with the –*a* ending are to count as festivals, it need not follow that others which lack it are to be excluded. A rite known simply, in early texts, as 'the sacrifice to Zeus Soter' was the occasion of a public holiday in the fourth century.[16] Here emerges a new and important criterion. One can sit at Athens for a year without being able to get a hearing with the council or people, said critics of the democracy: not only was the pressure of business huge, but the Athenians had 'twice as many' festivals to celebrate as any of the Greek states, during which 'it is less possible for business of the city to be conducted'. Festivals were indeed normally holidays for courts and council, and counted as periods of special, sacred time

[14] Hdt. 1.148. Herodotus in fact speaks only of endings in –*a*, thus failing to distinguish between the neuter plural ending, which is genuinely characteristic of festival names, and the feminine singular; this latter is never unambiguously used of a whole festival (unless *Aiora* is a case) but is sometimes found for individual days within one (e.g. ἡ Δορπία, last day of the *Apatouria*), as are formations of other types (e.g. *Anarrhusis*, *Choes*, *Anodos*). *Bouphonia* is a (unique?) instance of a neuter plural used not of a whole festival but of a component within one: it was, however, easily the most important element within the otherwise little known *Dipolieia*. (*Pithoigia*, day one of the *Anthesteria*, is a feminine singular in the better sources: Mommsen, *Feste*, 384, n. 3). In relation to *Arrephoria*, *Proerosia*, and apparently *Chloïa* and *Antheia* we find an oscillation between feminine singular and neuter plural forms, as if the status of the occasion as single ritual act—a 'carrying of secret things' (?), like 'basket-carrying'; a 'pre-ploughing' or 'green shoot' or 'flower' sacrifice—or as full-blown festival were ambiguous (for femine singular ἀρρηφοφία see Lys. 21.5; for the other three festivals p. 195 below). The name *Hieros Gamos* is exceptional, but is the only one to be applied to the festival in question in Attic texts (*SEG* XXXIII 147. 32; Menander fr. 225 (265 Koerte); for the term in lexicographers see Deubner, *Attische Feste*, 176, n. 11); a more conventional form *Theogamia* appears in Σ Hes. *Op.* 783–4 Pertusi.
[15] So Mikalson, op. cit. His argument that certain rites are not ἑορταί because not so described in classical sources neglects the tendency of those sources to speak of demonstrable ἑορταί as, for instance, 'the sacrifice' or 'procession' to X rather than by name (so Calame, op. cit.; see e.g. Arist. *Ath. Pol.* 56 with the summary in 56.5; Thuc. 7.73.2). Another possible word is τελετή (Ar. *Pax* 419). For grim ἑορταί in Plutarch see *De def. or.* 14, 417b–c; *De Is. et Os.* 25, 361b; ibid. 68–9, 378d–e. Cheerful sociable rites in Aristotle, by contrast, can be called σύνοδοι (*EN* 1160a 26).
[16] Lys. 26.6; cf. Arist. *Ath. Pol.*56.5, and App. 1 s.v. *Diisoteria* (a name which appears in the 2nd c.). On the 'sacrifices' to Peace, Democracy, etc. see *Athenian Religion*, 228–32: these too were surely in some sense *heortai*. The important decrees of Eleusis *SEG* XXVIII 103 speak of the same event as 'the *Herakleia*' (once), 'the sacrifice to Heracles' (four times), and 'the festival of Heracles' (once).

(*hieromenia*) during which for instance, the state could shed no blood.[17] The 'day of the sacrifice to Zeus Soter' has therefore the strongest claim to be considered a festival. But we cannot simply say that festivals and holidays at Athens always went hand in hand. It was not only on festival days but also on 'impure days' (which might or might not coincide with the former) that the courts and council did not sit; conversely, it was perhaps possible for men's business to be conducted during parts even of official women's festivals, to say nothing of unofficial events such as the *Adonia* which were certainly in some sense felt to form part of the familiar festival round. Meetings did occasionally occur during festivals, and it may be that there was no fixed holiday pro-gramme but decisions were taken (except perhaps in regard to 'impure days' and the very greatest events) year by year.[18] Above all, as a rule we simply do not know whether lesser rites such as the *Arrephoria* or *Oschophoria* earned council and courts a day off or not; but it is precisely the status as 'Athenian festivals' of the lesser rites that is in doubt.

A possibility is that our uncertainty about the scope of 'festivals' merely reproduces theirs. A Greek religious calendar was a list of publicly financed sacrifices, not of festivals;[19] we have seen that there seems to have been no fixed programme of public holidays, and that the same event could be de-scribed as either 'sacrifice' or 'festival':[20] there was probably no context in which it was relevant to press the question 'what is a festival?' very hard. If I continue to press it for a while, it is not with a view to getting a firm answer; the issue is about the contexts in which Athenians may have been rather more, or rather less, likely to apply the term.

Most festivals contained a mixture of elements specific to themselves—the offering of a robe to Athena at the *Panathenaea*, for instance, or the drinking-parties of the *Anthesteria*—with applications, again individual to themselves,

[17] [Xen.] *Ath. Pol.* 3.1–2, 8; cf. Parker, *Miasma*, 157 [+] and, for the courts, M. H. Hansen, *GRBS* 20 (1979), 245. ἀφέσιμοι ἡμέραι (an expression found in *LSS* 14. 47, apparently in reference to the *Thargelia*) are explicitly attested in relation to the *Kronia* (Dem. 24.26, the *boule*), the *Panathenaea* (Ath. 98b, courts), the sacrifice to Zeus Soter on the last day of the year (Lys. 26.6, courts), the middle day of the *Thesmophoria* (Ar. *Thesm.* 78–80, boule and courts), the *Apatouria* (Ath. 171e; the boule, 'like other Athenians'). A meeting of the assembly on the day of the 'procession and sacrifice to Asclepius' (Elaphebolion 8) is stigmatized as highly irregular (Aeschin. 3.66–7), but its occurrence also proves that there was no legal ban (so rightly Mikalson, *Calendar*, 123—Lys 26.6 suggests otherwise, tendentiously); *nomothetai* could meet on the *Kronia*, unusually, Dem. 24.26. For possible exceptions—meetings of the assembly on festival days—see Mikalson, *Calendar*, 186–204, with the comments of D. M. Lewis, *CR* 27 (1977), 215–16: in truth, only the one case attested in a literary text can count as certain (Aeschin. 3.66–7, above), since it is otherwise never absolutely clear, when an assembly meeting is attested for a 'festival day', that the festival was in fact celebrated in that year.

[18] Men's business: the attested case of an assembly held on what ought to be the first day of the *Thesmophoria* dates from 122/1 BC (*IG* II² 1006.51–2, cited by Mikalson, *Calendar*, 189: the location in the theatre is common for the period, and proves nothing), but there is a classical Theban parallel (Xen. *Hell.* 5.2.29). The *Hieros Gamos*, Mikalson's other putative instance, was not a festival confined to women. For the council voting itself five days ad hoc for the *Apatouria* see Ath. 171e. Adonia: Ar. *Lys.* 387–98, with *Pax* 420.

[19] See *Athenian Religion*, 52–3.   [20] See n. 15.

of more standard types: sacrifices, processions, competitions, 'all-nighters'. But how many such elements did a ceremony need in order to count as a festival? More than one, it might be argued; a simple sacrifice was not a festival. Undoubtedly some complexity was the norm. But a few recognized festivals appear quite simple. At the *Diasia*, little happened to our knowledge except that numerous groups of kinsmen met and sacrificed together, at Agrai, to Zeus Meilichios. It is not clear that any public spectacle accompanied the celebrations of *Kronia* and *Hieros Gamos* in private houses.[21] One can always postulate lost elements, and not at all implausibly, a procession here or a *pannychis* there that has slipped out of our sources. But it may rather be that *Diasia* and *Kronia* and *Hieros Gamos* were festivals because, simple though they were, they were observed by a great proportion of the households in Attica.

Perhaps the real mark of a festival is in fact breadth of participation: an event is a festival if large numbers of the group celebrating it (citizens, for a festival of the city; demesmen, for a deme, and so on) are involved. It would contrast with the many sacrifices 'on behalf of the Athenian people' in fact conducted by a small group in private.[22] That hypothesis deals easily with festivals widely celebrated in individual households, such as the *Kronia*, with women's festivals, and also with those that offered such obvious draws as mass sacrifices or competitions. Of the *Chalkeia*, a festival of Athena, the Suda claims that it was 'a festival of the people long ago, but later celebrated by craftsmen only' and another source speaks of it as 'common to craftsmen, particularly bronze-workers'.[23] No other festival seems to have been, as it were, a guild fair—for even the *Hephaisteia*, especially attractive though it must have been to workers with fire, contained competitions designed to give it broader appeal—and the Suda's claim that the *Chalkeia* had once been more than this is surely correct; it was at this festival, for instance, that the weaving of the panathenaic *peplos* was inaugurated.[24]

There remain some difficult cases. At one or two festivals, such as the *Plynteria* or the annual rite of the Semnai, the only public element was apparently a procession. What then is a procession? Greek processions were, both etymologically and in reality, an 'escorting' ($\pi \epsilon \mu \pi \omega$) of something somewhere; they were, therefore, strongly goal-directed.[25] But they were

---

[21] But modest public sacrifices did accompany them: *Kronia: Agora* XV 81.6; *Hieros Gamos*: F. Salviat, *BCH* 88 (1964), 647–54 (on Erchia) and *SEG* XXXIII 147. 32 (Thorikos). On the *Diasia* see App. 1 s.v. *Diasia*; a literary competition is attested, rather questionably, in Lucian. Machon dates an encounter between an aged satrap visiting Athens and a courtesan to the *Kronia* (335 Gow ap. Ath. 581a); Gow ad loc. supposes he chose *Kronia* as appropriate to the aged satrap.

[22] On them see Jameson, 'The spectacular and the obscure'.

[23] Suda χ 35 (= *Etym. Magn.* 805.43–7: whence Pausanias Atticista χ 2 Erbse); Harpocration, χ 2 (abbreviated in Suda χ 36).

[24] Suda χ 35.

[25] Kavoulaki, 'Processional Performance', 302; F. Graf, '*Pompai* in Greece', in R. Hägg (ed.), *The Role of Religion in the Early Greek Polis* (Stockholm 1996), 55–65, at 56. Graf's distinction

usually in no great hurry to arrive; and the vocabulary of 'spectacle' and 'spectators' was regularly applied to them.[26] 'What would be the use of a procession, if people had all to lie down upon their faces, so that they couldn't see it?', wondered Alice, wisely. If Alice was right that processions were designed to be viewed, even the *Plynteria* had its own positive way of drawing the public in. Negatively, they were involved perforce, since the day was one of ill-omen on which no serious business could be undertaken.[27] The *Arrephoria* was performed, in secret, by two maidens; but in its one occurrence in an early source the word is a feminine singular (Lys. 21.5), and it should perhaps be reclassified as the name of a ritual activity (like *kanephoria*, basket-bearing) rather than of a festival.[28] The only celebrants of the *Iobaccheia* and *Theoinia* of whom we know are a college of fourteen women, the *gerarai*, and certain unspecified *genos*-members; but we know very little at all of the two rites.[29] If we set them (and the equally obscure *Procharisteria*) aside as too ill attested to allow judgement, and the *Arrephoria* as probably not a festival, we are left with no clear exception to the principle of broad involvement. As proof of his devotion to the familiar gods of the state, the Socrates of Xenophon points out that everybody could see him 'sacrificing at the common festivals'.[30]

Whether they participated directly or not, Athenians seem to have thought of the festival as a part of their collective life. Xenophon speaks of the *Plynteria* as being celebrated by 'the city of Athens'. When a momentous event occurred during a festival, the coincidence was remembered: Chabrias' victory at Naxos in 376 was won during the *Great Mysteries*, but the same festival was marred in 322 by the arrival of Antipater's Macedonian garrison; Demosthenes died on the gloomiest day of the *Thesmophoria*, and the execution of Phocion stained the procession of Zeus (Olympios) with public blood.[31]

between centrifugal and centripetal processions has, therefore, only a qualified validity. Kavoulaki has excellent remarks on processing as a special, self-conscious and conspicuous, form of walking (294–5); this point works against the ingenious view that the spectator of the Parthenon frieze also 'processed'.

[26] Kavoulaki, 'Processional Performance', 294, n. 5; ead. 'Ritual Performance', 146. Jameson, 'The spectacular and the obscure', 325, notes the special category of *pompeia*, 'procession-equipment', i.e. display equipment.

[27] See esp. Xen. *Hell.* 1.4.12; Plut. *Alc.* 34.1–2; App. 1 s.v. *Plynteria*. About the associated *Kallynteria* (see ibid. s.v. *Kallynteria*) virtually nothing is known.

[28] So L van Sichelen, *AC* 56 (1987), 96–7. But his denial that the ἑορτή of Paus. 1.27.3 is the *Arrephoria* is scarcely convincing; so a change would have to be postulated. That the *Arrephoria* also had a more public side now lost is of course possible. Brulé, *Fille d' Athènes*, 92–3 associated with it the *pannychis* with which the priestess of Aglauros was involved (*SEG* XXXIII 115; cf. n. 42). On *POxy* 664 a 32 see p. 219, n. 5. Nothing firm can be extracted from a possible reference in a decree in honour of Julia Domna (*Agora* XVI 341. 38–40).

[29] Apollod. *Neaer.* 78, Harp. θ 7 s.v. Θεοίνιον; *Athenian Religion*, 299; cf. the entries in App. 1.

[30] Xen. *Apol.* 11. On private sacrifices at public festivals cf. p. 42, n. 19.

[31] Xen. *Hell.* 1.4.12; Plut. *Phoc.* 6.4–7 (cf. *Athenian Religion*, 238); ibid. 28.2–3; *Dem.* 30.5; *Phoc.* 37.2; cf. A. T. Grafton and N. M. Swerdlow, 'Calendar Dates and Ominous Dates in Ancient Historiography', *JWarb* 51 (1988), 14–42.

Most remarkably, according to Polyaenus, the great sea-battle fought at
Alyzia in 375 between the Athenians under Timotheus and the Spartans
fell on the day of the festival *Skira*.[32] 'On this day, Timotheus garlanded the
triremes with myrtle and raised the signal. He put out to sea, fought and won.
His soldiers fought with great confidence because they thought that they had
the divine as ally.' Thus the Athenian sailors off Leukas were somehow
involved with this festival celebrated by their wives at home in Attica. The
great battle of Mantinea of 362 also seems to have coincided with the *Skira*,
and, to judge from a remark of Plutarch that Athenian valour on that
occasion 'made the day more holy',[33] the festival acquired a new function
as a kind of commemoration of the battle.

A related concept that stresses breadth of participation is *panegyris*, 'assembly of everybody'. All *panegyreis* were festivals, even if not all festivals (those
celebrated principally in private houses, for instance) were *panegyreis*. The
word could be used of Attic rites no less than of the panhellenic games. To
have a lavish supply of goods for sale, says Demosthenes, is the virtue of a
market or *panegyris*, not of a city. Crowds in their festival best, swarming
around the food booths and the stalls piled with children's toys, must always
have a place in our picture of Attic festivals.[34]

So too must the phenomenon of festival food. In modern western society,
little remains of many festivals but the foodstuffs traditionally associated with
them—beliefs come and go, pancakes abide—and the principle of such an
association may be an inheritance from the ancient world; at all events the
phenomenon was very common in antiquity. Unfortunately, not every reference to a food eaten at a particular festival can be taken to prove that the two
were as closely associated as lamb and Easter. By this cautious criterion, we
will not take the consumption of sausages at the *Apatouria*, haggis at the
Diasia, barley-soup at the *Theseia*, thick soup at the *Panathenaea* to be necessarily characteristic of the festival in question, though it very probably was in
several cases.[35] But three festivals (*Pyanopsia*, *Thargelia*, and the obscure
Galaxia) contained a reference to foodstuffs in their very names. What these
festival foods may have evoked will be considered elsewhere. What matters
here is the way in which through them the festival penetrated, as it were, into
every Attic household. The domestic bustle, the anxious buying and preparation of food, so familiar from our own, very impoverished experience of
festivals needs to be included also in our picture of those of the Athenians.
Even at festivals such as the *Panathenaea*, where the main feast was publicly

---

[32] 3.10.4: ἦν ἑορτὴ Σκίρα editors: ἑορτῆς κείρα F, the archetype of the mss. of Polyaenus.

[33] *De glor. Ath.* 7, 350a.

[34] Pl. *Tim.* 21a; Dem. 10.50. Toys: Ar. *Nub.* 864; for special clothing reserved εἰς ἑορτάς Xen.
Oik. 9.6.

[35] Ar. *Ach.* 146; *Nub.* 408–9; *Plut.* 627–8; *Nub.* 386. The Σ vet. on Ar. *Plut.* 628a speaks of
the gruel being provided 'free'. But soup-kitchens are not otherwise known in Athens, and the
Aristophanic allusion works better if individuals cooked their own, richer or runnier according to
their means. For 'deer' cakes at the Elaphebolia see p. 468.

provided, many banquets took place on the margins, whether organized by groups such as the *genos* of Salaminioi or by individuals.[36]

Individuals could participate in festivals in many different ways. One could handle or come close to sacred objects, walk or ride in a procession, dance, eat sacrificial meat or simply watch. Ancients as well as moderns had the habit of speaking of 'women's festivals' but not of 'men's':[37] men are taken to reflect the norm, and do not require special labelling. But even if women's festivals, as a category, are a product of hierarchical assumptions, there were real differences in the ways in which the two sexes participated. It appears to be taken for granted that all married citizen women will normally take part in certain 'women's festivals', the *Thesmophoria* above all.[38] In a sense such festivals of all the women are simply mirror images of the many festivals in which all the men were, if not expected, at least entitled to participate. But though men were absolutely excluded from women's festivals, it is not clear that there were at Athens (though there were elsewhere in Greece) any festivals from which women were so barred; even where only one woman, the priestess, was in fact present, she establishes that the principle of exclusion was not one of gender alone. And men were never required, as were women at the *Thesmophoria*, to camp out for three days en masse, to fast, to sit on the ground on mats containing objects pertaining in some way to their sexuality. In male religious experience the closest parallel to the intensity of the *Thesmophoria* might be initiation at the *Mysteries*, which was neither obligatory nor restricted to the one sex.[39] Women then are more positively engaged as participants in women's festivals than are men in men's. More generally, at the level of festival activity which involves close contact with sacred objects, they are at least as fully engaged as men—as priestesses, as basket-bearers, as (in one case) a wife for the god Dionysus, and so on.

In the important matter of the sacrificial feast, the case is quite different. At many festivals in Athens or the Piraeus, a major attraction was a 'meat-distribution', $\kappa\rho\epsilon\alpha\nu o\mu\acute{\iota}\alpha$, on a large scale: a portion belonged by right to each person enrolled in a deme, and women—some priestesses and other active participants aside—were therefore, we assume, excluded. The case must normally have been the same with the 'common banquets of the demes'; in the calendar from Erchia one offering alone, to Dionysus, is marked as being 'for handing over to women'.[40] Only at women's festivals did women feast (and even then the food seems to have been provided by husbands of the richer women as a liturgy rather than by the deme or city). Even though the exclusion of women from these sacrificial feasts was gender-related only at

[36] See p. 268, n. 66 below.
[37] Ar. *Thesm.* 834–5; cf. IG II² 1177 (*LSCG* 36) 10–12.
[38] Men. *Epitrep.* 749–50; cf. Ar. *Thesm.* 330; IG II² 1177 (*LSCG* 36) 8–12; cf. pp. 270–1 below.
[39] For similarities between *Thesmophoria* and *Apatouria*, however, see p. 272.
[40] *LSCG* 18 a 44–50.

one remove[41] (the sign hung up was not 'no women here' but 'deme-members only'—women, however, were not members of demes), its practical implications for their participation were obviously very large. Another striking exclusion is that women had no place in any of the major athletic or literary competitions. Five hundred boys and 500 men danced in the dithyrambs at the *City Dionysia* each year, 250 at the *Thargelia*, and no single woman or girl.

In another form of festival activity, however, women unquestionably had the main part. 'All nighters', *pannychides*, are attested for at least eleven state festivals—*Panathenaea, Mysteries, Stenia, Haloa* (?), *Pyanopsia, Tauropolia, Bendidea, Epidauria, Asklepieia, Heroa*, and very probably *Brauronia*[42]—and two of demes (Aixone's sacrifice to Hebe; the *Nemesia* of Rhamnus); privately organized rites such as the *Adonia* or *Sabazia* or a sacrifice to Pan or even the tenth-day celebrations for a child could borrow the same form. At *Mysteries, Panathenaea, Tauropolia* and, surely, *Brauronia*, virgins took part in the *pannychis*, and in each case except the first may have had the chief role; from those at 'women's festivals' (which were normally de facto married women's festivals) such as the *Stenia*, however, they are likely to have been excluded. Men were present as, at most, bystanders or spectators.[43] How participants were selected is unfortunately quite unknown. The mood of a *pannychis* was often one of gaiety, but this was also a form of religious action powerful to earn a god's favour; thus in the *Homeric Hymn to Demeter* the women appeased the angry goddess by their all-night devotions (292–3). The *pannychis* was marked, according to one charming definition, by 'la bonne humeure efficace'.[44] Once again, women as a group appear to act on the gods more directly than do men.

Often men sacrificed meat by day and women danced by night. But the modalities of 'separate development' practised at festivals were probably quite

---

[41] See R. Osborne, *CQ* 43 (1993), 404 (= *Oxford Readings*, 312).

[42] For seven of these see Deubner, *Attische Feste*, 262, index s.v. *Pannychis* (that at the *Haloa* is attested by Alciphron only: cf. p. 492); add *Hymn. Hom. Dem.* 292–3; Ar. *Ran.* 371, 445–6 (*Mysteries*); *LSCG* 7 A 17 (*Pyanopsia*); Men. *Phasm.* 93–107 (*Brauronia*); *IG* II² 1199.22 (Aixone); *Ergon* 1998, 16 (*Nemesia*). *Agora* XV 253.10 mentions a *pannychis*, associated by a very uncertain supplement with the *Chalkeia;* the priestess of Aglauros also helped with one (n. 28 above), perhaps as M. H. Jameson suggests (personal communication) that of the *Panathenaea. Adonia, Sabazia* and Pan: Men. *Sam.* 46; Ar. *Horai* test. ii (Cic. *Leg.* 2.37); Men. *Dysc.* 857. Tenth-day celebrations: Eubulus fr. 2. Attic authors also envisage them in connection with Dionysus (Eur. *Bacch.* 862) and Mother (Eur. *Hel.* 1365); for *Pannychis* with Aphrodite and Dionysus on vases see A. Kossatz-Deissmann, *LIMC* s.v. *Pannychis*, nos. 1–4. See in general L. Ziehen, *RE* s.v. Παννυχίς; Pritchett, 'Παννυχίς'; Borgeaud, *Pan*, 246–52; Bravo, *Pannychis*.

[43] See esp. *Hymn. Hom. Dem.* 292–3; Ar. *Ran.* 445–6 (the male speaker's intention of joining the women is a joke: see Dover ad loc.); Men. *Dysc.* 857 τῶν γυναικῶν παννυχίδα, *Epitrep.* 452 παννυχίδος οὔσης καὶ γυναικῶν; Critias B 1.6 D/K (cf. Sappho fr. 30.3 Voigt); Eubulus fr. 2. Bystanders: Men. *Dysc.* 855–7, *Sam.* 43; Pl. *Resp.* 328a (in both the latter texts men are spectators). At private *pannychides* the separation between drinking men and dancing women—all under the same roof—was not necessarily large or lasting (note e.g. the kisses of Eubulus fr. 2 and Callim. fr. 227).

[44] Borgeaud, *Pan*, 249. Good humour: Men. *Dysc., Sam.* (previous note); Ziehen, op. cit.

various. The *Haloa*, a maddeningly obscure festival of mid-winter, is chiefly known from a remarkable scholion on Lucian:

At this festival a rite for women (γυναῖκες: perhaps 'married women') is conducted at Eleusis and there are many jokes and jibes. Women go in by themselves and are free to say whatever they want. They do in fact say the most shameful things to one another on that occasion, and the priestesses going up to the women secretly urge them to adultery, whispering in their ear as though imparting a secret. And all the women say shameful and disgusting things to one another aloud, and handle unseemly images of the body, both male and female. Here much wine is laid out and tables full of all the foods of sea and land except those subject to the mystic ban, that is pomegranate and apple and house birds and eggs and, of sea creatures, mullet, *erythinos*, *melanouros*, crayfish, and dogfish. The magistrates set out the tables and leaving them inside for the women then withdraw; they stay outside, displaying to all the visitors that civilized food was first discovered among them and shared out to all mankind from them. On the tables are also genitals of both sexes fashioned from cake.

Women therefore feasted within while men were differently employed outside;[45] inscriptions suggest that there were sacrifices and perhaps other entertainments for men too, in a festival that may have lasted more than one day. As we shall see, men apparently had some role at the *Skira*, another 'women's festival', and a public sacrifice by the prytaneis was even made on the occasion of the *Stenia*;[46] one may wonder whether the *Thesmophoria* was unusual in its rigorous exclusion of men.

Thus far the picture is not unclear. We turn now to a variety of festival contexts in which women may or may not have been free to participate alongside men. Multiple uncertainties arise at once, and vast gaps in our knowledge of the day-to-day order of Athenian society are revealed. At some festivals, the food seems largely to have been provided by the participants themselves. In contrast to festivals financed by public bodies to which they did not belong, there was no reason why women should not have taken part in these. Athenians converged on Agrai from all Attica to feast at the *Diasia* with their 'relatives'. But did they bring their wives (and unmarried daughters)? Children could attend, which must increase the likelihood that their mothers could too.[47] We looked in an earlier chapter at 'family reliefs', many of them dedicated as it happens to the god of the *Diasia*, Zeus Meilichios. Did the group sacrifices which such reliefs commemorate (at least as an ideal) occur at festivals, or was the occasion a private one? The question cannot be answered with certainty. Similar considerations and similar uncertainties apply to the meetings of the phratries at the *Apatouria*. An item of evidence that bears

---

[45] But Lowe, 'Thesmophoria and Haloa', 162, is probably right to question whether the scholion's 'displaying to all the visitors' proves a formal discourse on the part of the magistrates. On the *Haloa* see further pp. 199–201 and App. 1 s.v. *Haloa*. The source quoted is Σ Lucian p. 280.12–281.1 Rabe.

[46] *Agora* XV 78. 7.

[47] Ar. *Nub.* 864; on the *Diasia* see p. 42 and App. 1 s.v. *Diasia*.

directly on a related case is a decree passed by a group of *orgeones*—a form of association probably closely linked to the phratry—in perhaps the fifth century. At the association's annual sacrifice, 'Meat is to be distributed to the *orgeones* who are present and to [their children] a half share and to the free wives of the *orgeones* [...] an equal share and to their daughters a half-share and to a single (female) attendant a half-share. The portion of the wife is [to be handed to] the husband.'[48] Since the female attendant must surely have been present to earn her share, it is probable that the wives and children were there too, or were entitled to be. But it remains possible even so that they sat somewhat apart from the men. The same can be said about those festivals of which important parts took place in individual houses: women as well as men no doubt participated, but not necessarily in the same way. It can reasonably be doubted, for instance, whether women took part in the hectic drinking competitions of the *Anthesteria*.

Festivals were the great context for spectacle in the ancient world, and the question arises of the extent to which women were permitted to spectate. In respect of drama it has been much discussed, without a consensus emerging,[49] but there are many further aspects. Whatever conclusion is reached for drama should probably also be reached for dithyramb, for which evidence is entirely lacking. If so, and if we exclude women from the tragic and comic theatre, we must sadly conclude that the 500 Athenian mothers whose sons competed, gorgeously arrayed, in the dithyrambs each year, could do no more than wave them good luck from the door. We are no better informed about the practice at athletic competitions, whether those of the *Panathenaea* or the various local festivals. 'Often, Telesicrates, have maidens seen you victorious at the seasonal rite of Pallas and prayed that you could be their darling husband or son', says Pindar—rites in Telesicrates' homeland Cyrene, commentators assure us, and not as the scholiast supposed the Attic *Panathenaea*. But the passage at least shows that the supposed exclusion of all women except the priestess of Demeter Chamyne from the stadium at Olympia does not represent a universal Greek norm.[50] Thucydides observes that there was of old a gymnic and musical competition on Delos to which the Ionians and

---

[48] *LSS* 20.17–23 (a text of the 3rd c., but quoting an older decree). Other orgeonic decrees—*Athenian Religion*, 109, n. 28—do not give evidence either way.

[49] S. Goldhill, 'Representing democracy: women at the Great Dionysia', in *Ritual, Finance, Politics*, 347–69 [+], argues strongly for their exclusion, but has some difficulty with Pl. *Gorg.* 502d and *Leg.* 817a–c (ibid. 658d need have no reference to performance). Though the *Laws* passage explicitly only debars tragedians from 'making public speeches to children and women and the whole mob' in the agora of Plato's Magnesia, it only needs to do so because, by implication, tragedy addresses such a promiscuous audience in the real world; this passage confirms that it is artificial to dissociate the mixed audience of *Gorg.* 502d5–6 from the ποιηταὶ ἐν τοῖς θεάτροις of *Gorg.* 502d3. See now, against Goldhill's position, Sourvinou-Inwood, *Tragedy and Religion*, 177–96.

[50] Telesicrates: Pind. *Pyth.* 9.97–100; Olympia: Paus. 5.6.7, 6.20.9 (the latter passage in fact seems to state that *parthenoi* were admitted: cf. M. Dillon, *Hermes* 128, 2000, 457–80), Men. Rhet. 364.5–6 Russell-Wilson.

neighbouring islanders went as spectators 'with their wives and children' (he knows all this from the *Homeric Hymn*, which he quotes), 'as the Ionians do now to Ephesus' (3.104). The passage certainly shows that family outings could occur in the Greek world; but does it also show that they looked a little strange to Athenian eyes?

Women's attendance at events such as these was no doubt governed by rules. Their freedom to watch the great processions can scarcely have been regulated so rigorously, but may have been restricted by social convention. We hear of a debauchee, a descendant of Demetrius of Phaleron, who built a scaffold of presumptuous height to allow a courtesan to watch the Panathenaic procession.[51] Dikaiopolis in Aristophanes, by contrast, urges his wife to watch his rural Dionysiac procession 'from the roof'.[52] Possibly respectable women could only enjoy the spectacle if they had access to a secluded roof or balcony. But evidence is too scarce for the issue to be pressed.

We have this far in the main treated men and women as undifferentiated groups. The most important ritual subgroups within both sexes, the young, will receive separate treatment in later chapters. Subsets within the classes of married women and adult men are only rarely identified ritually, but 'women married to their first husband' ($\pi\rho\omega\tau o\pi\acute{o}\sigma\epsilon\iota s$) had a special role in the rites of Athena Pallenis;[53] and the imbalance whereby old men, but not old women, had an honorific role at the *Panathenaea* deserves to be signalled.

I turn now from distinctions within the citizen body to that between it and outsiders. The case of slaves is easy: within the context of publicly financed rites of the city, they did not exist. No role was reserved for them, no meat was assigned to them, no prayers were offered on their behalf. Only at festivals celebrated within private households (*Anthesteria, Kronia*) did slaves have a certain acknowledged place.[54] This ideological exclusion is not affected by the likelihood that they were in fact needed at many festivals to perform menial services. And there was no ideological bar to their being initiated into the *Mysteries*; the best attested cases are those of slaves belonging to the sanctuary itself who 'had' to be initiated—remarkable intertwining of practical and

[51] See Hegesander of Delphi in Ath. 167f. and on such scaffolds Camp, *Agora*, 46 with *AR* 1994/5. 3. For a man sighted by a woman during the lesser Panathenaic procession see Men. fr. 384 (428 Koerte). Menander fr. 337 (382 Koerte, from the *Synaristosae*), telling of a courtesan's daughter picked up on the way home from watching the Dionysiac procession, is generally supposed to derive from a play set, like Plautus' adaptation *Cistellaria*, in Sicyon; but P. G. McC. Brown in a forthcoming study will argue from the Lemnian references in *Cistellaria* that the Menandrean original was perhaps set in Athens.

[52] *Ach.* 262 ; cf. N. Hopkinson's note on Call. *Hymn. Dem.* 4. and now *SEG* XLII 785 30–1 (Thasos, 5th c.): ἐπὶ τὸ τέγεος τῶν κατοικιῶν τῶν δημοσίων τῶν ἐν τῆι ὁδῶι ταύτηι θῆς ἕνεκεν μηδὲς ἀναβαινέτω μηδὲ γυνὴ δ᾽ ἐκ τῶν θυρίδων θήσθω (differently interpreted by A. J. Graham, *JHS* 118, 1998, 22–40).

[53] Ath. 235a, cf. *Athenian Religion*, 331; on the Panathenaea see Ch. 12 below. The posts of *gerarai* and (probably) *deipnophoroi* were reserved for married women (pp. 304 and 215 below). The only position confined to old women known to us was guardian of Athena's sacred lamp (Plut. *Num.* 9.11; Parker, *Miasma*, 88, n. 58).

[54] See pp. 294 and 202; on private rites see p. 16, n. 33.

symbolic constraints!—in order to do works within its secret parts, but a comic fragment probably also presents a favourite slave introduced by his master.[55]

The situation with metics and other free non-citizens is a little more complicated. A group of metics and a group of unmarried metic women (the principle of selection is unknown in both cases) marched in the Panathenaic procession, the men wearing purple tunics and carrying sacrificial trays known as *skaphai*, the girls serving as attendants to the citizen *kanephoroi*. A number of sources vaguely associate this practice of differentiated marching with 'the processions' or 'the public processions' in general, while one cluster speaks of 'the Dionysiac processions'.[56] The difficulty in accepting the claim in its more general forms is that it is always made in connection with a ritual object, the *skaphe*, which is very unlikely to have had a role at a wide range of festivals and was very possibly confined to the *Panathenaea*. Representatives of the allied cities are linked with both *Panathenaea* and *City Dionysia*, even if the right or obligation of sending (and presumably escorting) 'cow and panoply' to the *Panathenaea* is much more frequently attested than that of sending a phallus to the *Dionysia*.[57] A place for metics in 'the Dionysiac processions' is not impossible, therefore, but some doubt subsists. Metics were included in the *Panathenaea*, we may assume, because this was the festival of 'all Athens'; their role 'in the Dionysiac processions' (if reliably reported) strikingly illustrates the civic and unifying tone of those festivals too, though it might also be seen as acknowledging the financial contribution they were required to make to one of those festivals (the *Lenaea*) as liturgists. As for their possible participation in yet further processions, all is speculation.[58]

A different role for non-citizens is specifically attested at two further festivals. At the *Bendidea* in the fifth century a procession of native Athenians was matched by another of Thracians, presumably the Thracian residents of Athens. Bendis was a Thracian goddess, but such a joint Thraco-Athenian production of a festival is unparalleled and only imperfectly understood; an oracle was even approached to ask (very probably) whether the priestess of Bendis should be an Athenian or a Thracian woman. We also learn from an

---

[55] *IG* II² 1672.207; 1673.24; Theophilos fr. 1; cf. Foucart, *Les Mystères*, 273–4.

[56] Specific association with *Panathenaea*: Hesych. s.v. σκαφηφόροι, Phot. s.v. σκάφας and the emended text of [Ammon.] *Diff.* 247 Nickau ἐν τῇ τῶν Ἀθηναίων (Παναθηναίων Meier) πομπῇ. That the primary if not exclusive association was with the *Panathenaea* is clear from Dinarch. fr. XVI.5 Conomis, cited in Harp. σ 21 (D. Whitehead, *The Ideology of the Athenian Metic*, *PCPS* suppl. vol. 4, 1977, 88, takes the association to be exclusive). General association with 'processions': Demetrius of Phaleron, *FGrH* 228 F 5 ap. Harp. σ 21, Ael. *VH* 6.1, and various sources explaining the proverb συστομώτερος σκάφης (see the test. to Men fr. 147 (166 Koerte) and Paus. Att. σ 31 Erbse). Dionysiac processions: Suda α 4177 (from the same source *Anecd. Bekk.* 1.214.3–8; *Etym. Magn.* 155.8–15).

[57] Cow and phallus: *Athenian Religion*, 142; Panathenaic and Dionysiac processions: pp. 170 and 317 below.

[58] I hesitate to base any inference on Aesch. *Eum.* 1011 with 1027–8 (cf. *Athenian Religion*, 298–9).

inscription that at the *Hephaisteia* 'three oxen' were assigned to metics. Hephaestus was a god of crafts, and many metic craftsmen were active in Athens. Their role at his festival may represent a special case, therefore, rather than an instance preserved by chance of a more general inclusiveness.[59]

Whether metic (and foreign) wives could participate in publicly funded festivals at Athens is a question that has seldom if ever been posed, our silent sources not stimulating curiousity. The prevalent assumption is probably that they could not. But it is also quite widely assumed that to one festival, the *Haloa* at Eleusis, courtesans thronged; and they were not normally of citizen status. The assumption about the *Haloa* is perhaps the one that should yield,[60] at least if it is taken to imply that the courtesans participated fully in the rites (if we take the other view, the 'internationalism' of the Eleusinian cult may provide an explanation.) But the possibility that to some cult, somewhere, metic wives were admitted cannot be ruled out.

Metics were probably excluded from formal participation in most Athenian festivals. But they could be spectators, both of processions and of athletic and dramatic competitions. And, like citizens, they could organize their own private parties on the margins of public festivals.[61] If a group of metic kinsmen had tried to join the Athenians picnicking together at Agrai at the *Diasia*, would they have been driven away as intruders? It scarcely seems likely. Festivals were the blood of life to Greeks, and it is hard to understand how metics survived away from their ancestral gods. But the problem becomes less acute if we imagine them caught up in the festival atmosphere on the great occasions of the host state.[62]

In a rough, broad way we have reviewed the celebrants of Attic festivals. A general issue about the relation of festivals to the social order can be raised in conclusion. It is a familiar idea that the norms of behaviour at festivals have a complicated relation to the ordinary social norms: 'festival licence' is a concept which has 'native' equivalents, and 'festival of reversal' too is a familiar slogan. But the idea can be given very different twists. Some see festival licence as a cathartic mechanism which allows tensions to be released and the everyday order of society to be preserved. Others allow it a more radical political force, as a mechanism whereby real resentments that need to

---

[59] For the other view see Wilamowitz, *Hermes* 22 (1887), 220 (*Kl. Schr.* V.1. 303), stressing also the role of metics in the cults of the deme Skambonidai (cf. p. 67). *Hephaisteia*: *IG* I³ 82.23–4; on the *Bendidea* see *Athenian Religion*, 170–5.

[60] See p. 283.

[61] Note for instance the sacrifice performed by the metic Cephalus during the *Bendidea* in Plato's *Republic* (327a–328c). Non-citizens were surely present on the margins of many Athenian festivals: see p. 254, n. 5, on visitors to the *Panathenaea*, and note Dinarchus 1.23 for a Rhodian cithara-player who suffered an unspecified *hybris* from a male citizen at the *Eleusinia*.

[62] 'Die Götter Athens sind die Götter der Metoeken', Wilamowitz, *Hermes* 22 (1887), 221 (*Kl. Schr.* V.1. 304). For the other, doubtless complementary, option (private associations), see *Athenian Religion*, 337–42.

be addressed are brought into the open.[63] Somewhat related to the former idea is the postulate, as an ideal type, of a single annual 'great feast' at which the order of the world is dissolved in order to be renewed. But one must analyse the sense in which festival licence or festival abnormality are realities before seeking to apply general theories. All major festival days were holidays, for adults and for children; no criminal could be executed during them, and no debtor seized.[64] As a time of leisure, harmony and community, the festival is thus distinguished, not indeed from the ideals of the city, but from its everyday practices. Thus far all festival days differ from all business days. But, since few will suppose that the Panathenaic procession challenged, even in sport, the order of the city, distinctions still need to be drawn in the extent to which different festivals reflect or reverse ordinary social norms. A preliminary might be to refine the notion of 'reversal'. Reversal in the strict sense is a rarity: the clearest instance is that of the *Kronia*, if we accept the claim of one Latin source that masters 'waited on their slaves' as at the Roman *Saturnalia*. What by contrast is extremely common is irregular behaviour of various types. Women secede to form their own society, at the various 'women's festivals'; during them they may exchange obscenities, handle sexual objects, and, in one case, be urged by respectable priestesses to commit adultery; at *pannychides* they and their daughters stay up all night, free from close supervision. The dream analyst Artemidorus states that to dream of *pannychides* threatens adulterers of both sexes with discovery but not with punishment, since 'what takes place at *pannychides* is known to fellow participants, even if it is licentious, but is in a certain sense permitted'.[65] The social world familiar to Artemidorus in the second century AD was far removed, one must allow, from that of classical Athens, but his comment might none the less help to understand how 'rape at a *pannychis*' came to be a literary motif.[66]

As for the irregular behaviour of men, at various festivals they (young men in particular) threw abuse at passers by, sang obscene songs, carried giant phalluses in procession, and drank to excess. Comedy made these various transgressions into a literary genre.[67] At the *Anthesteria* men drank in

---

[63] See for references Bell, *Ritual*, 38–40, 52–5; below p. 203, n. 48. 'Native equivalents': see Hor. *Sat.* 2.7.4–5 for *libertas Decembri*; Strabo 10.3.9, 467, for ἄνεσις ἑορταστική.

[64] Parker, *Miasma*, 157–8; according to the Σ (170b) on Dem. 22.68 prisoners were released during the *Panathenaea* and *Dionysia* on provision of guarantors. Two rhetoricians of the imperial period build cases round a law requiring those bound to be released also at the *Thesmophoria*; in their example the individual concerned is not a state prisoner but a slave informally bound by his master (Herm. *Stat.* p. 58.4 Rabe, Sopat. Rh. in Walz, *Rhetores Graeci*, vol. 8.67. 4–8). But the rhetoricians invent too many laws for this to have much weight without confirmation.

[65] 3.61 p. 231 Pack (adduced by Brulé, *Fille d' Athènes*, 311). One thinks of discussions by anthropologists of the Mediterranean of licensed deviations from society's supposed norms (p. 279, n. 40). *Kronia*: p. 202 below.

[66] Rape at a *pannychis*: Men. *Sam.* 38–49; *Epit.* 1118–20, probably *Phasma* 93–107; note too the testimonia to Eur. *Auge*. 'Nocturnae pervigilationes' were a particular target of Aristophanes in the play in which he showed foreign gods expelled from the state (Cic. *Leg.* 2.37; Ar. *Horai* test. ii).

[67] See in particular Halliwell, 'Le Rire rituel'.

isolation from one another but in communion with their slaves. At the *Oskhophoria* two youths dressed as women.

These forms of behaviour have in common that they were all permissible only at festivals; conversely, festivals were the only licensed context, except perhaps the symposium, for irregular behaviour. But the character of the irregularity varies from case to case, and the concept of 'festival licence' has only weak and general explanatory force. As for 'festivals of reversal', a good number of festivals are touched by reversal; these elements cluster at festivals of Demeter and, still more, of Dionysus (who can plausibly be seen as the god of abnormal consciousness and behaviour), but are not confined to them. Again, though some festivals show a high concentration of such elements, there is none that consists of nothing else. Even the *Kronia* cannot be seen as a topsy-turvy world and nothing more. The label only obscures the individual phenomenon.

ANNEXE: THE FESTIVAL *SKIRA*

A festival 'Skira' (τὰ Σκίρα) is mentioned in three passages of comedy and in two, perhaps three, inscriptions of the fifth and fourth centuries. It was important enough to be used as a point of reference in the deme-calendar of Marathon, where certain sacrifices are required to be performed 'before the Skira';[68] the same text confirms its placing in, predictably, the month Skirophorion. In almost all the other allusions it appears as a festival 'at which women come together in accord with tradition',[69] one of those which 'we conduct'[70] (the speakers are women) and at which, in comic fantasy, subversive decrees can be passed by the women meeting in secret conclave. In a different comic perspective, keeping both a wife and a mistress (the latter disguised as a wife?) spells financial ruin: 'the extravagance! reckon the *Thesmophoria* twice, the *Skira* twice!'[71] It seems to follow that, like the *Thesmophoria*, this was a festival in principle attended by all married women. Local celebrations of the rite are attested for Piraeus and apparently also for the deme Paiania. Probably then the festival was one held, again like the *Thesmophoria*, at a number of sites throughout Attica. It is named along with the *Stenia* in Aristophanes and with the *Thesmophoria* in Menander, rites of Demeter both, and in the Piraeus it actually took place in the Thesmophorion.[72] Demeter and Kore must have been, to speak cautiously, among the

---

[68] ZPE 130 (2000), 45–7, col. 2. 30, 51. The only other time indication of this type in this text is πρὸ μυστηρίων, col. 2. 5 (cf. Jameson, *Selinous*, 26).

[69] IG II² 1177 (*LSCG* 36) 10–12 (Piraeus).

[70] Ar. *Thesm.* 834–5.

[71] Ar. *Eccl.* 18, 59; Men. *Epitr.* 750. Note too the fantasy of awarding προεδρία to meritorious women at the *Stenia* and Skira, Ar. *Thesm.* 834–5.

[72] Ar. *Thesm.* 834; Men. *Epitr.* 750; IG II² 1177 (*LSCG* 36: Piraeus) 10; for Paiania see IG I³ 250 A 5–9.

chief honorands. As for the actual rites, a late source which had access to good material saw them as analogous in symbolism and purpose to the Thesmophoria.[73] But almost the only detail we know is that 'they ate garlic in order to abstain from sex, so that they would not smell of perfume'.[74]

Such is the account of the festival that the contemporary sources allow us to give: one regrettably lacking in content, no doubt, but wholly coherent and comprehensible so far as it goes. Even the name always appears in the same form, as *Skira* (with a short vowel assured by metre), never *Skirophoria*, though the month name Skirophorion proves the antiquity of the longer form. Once the testimony of late sources is admitted, everything changes. Much of what they offer is a product of confusion or conflation between the several words and names containing the element *skir-*, but not everything can be dismissed. Harpocration writes under Σκίρον:

Lycurgus in the Speech *About the Priestess*. *Skira* is a festival of the Athenians, from which comes the month Skirophorion. Writers on Athenian months and festivals, among them Lysimachides, say that the *skiron* is a large sun-shade (σκιάδιον), under which the priestess of Athena and the priest of Poseidon and the priest of Sun walk as it is carried from the acropolis to a place called Skiron. It is carried by the *Eteoboutadai*. It is a token (σύμβολον) of the need to build and make shelters, since this is the best season for building.[75]

A different source adds that 'those who organize the procession of the *Skirophoria*' make use of the kind of fleece, normally associated with purification, known as a fleece of Zeus (Διὸς κῴδιον).[76] None of this could have been predicted: new personnel, including a mysterious 'Priest of the Sun', enter the picture, new gods, and the location switches from sanctuaries of Demeter at different sites throughout Attica to a particular place on the road to Eleusis.[77] We are used both to rites such as the *Thesmophoria* celebrated simultaneously at a variety of shrines and to those such as the *Panathenaea* focused on a single sacred place. The *Skira* appears to be unique in combining the two forms. Yet the facts recorded by Lysimachides and probably by Lycurgus before him can scarcely have been invented; nor can they be associated with any festival other than the *Skira* save by the postulate of a bizarre coincidence.[78]

[73] Σ Lucian p. 275.24 Rabe. But Deubner's thesis, *Attische Feste*, 40–5, that part of the scholion's detailed description actually refers to the *Skira*, and that in the scholion's view the pigs recovered at the Thesmophoria had been deposited at the *Skira*, is untenable (see Jacoby, notes to comm. on Philochorus FGrH 328 F 14–16, n. 56 and p. 203; Burkert, *Homo Necans*, 257, n. 5): Clem. Al. *Protr.* 2.17.1, from the same source, unambiguously (though it might be erroneously) associates the μεγαρίζειν rite itself with the *Thesmophoria*. Brumfield's more practical objection, that nothing except bones would be left of a pig after five months in the ground (*Agricultural Year*, 160–1), may underestimate the power of imagination in ritual.

[74] Philochorus FGrH 328 F 89.

[75] Lysimachides: FGrH 366 F 3, dated by Jacoby '50 B.C.–50 A.D. ?'.   [76] Suda δ 1210.

[77] On the location of Skiron see Paus. 1.36.4; Judeich, *Topographie*, 177.

[78] Namely that the month Skirophorion contained independently a festival *Skira* and a procession at which an object supposedly called *skiron* was carried. The procession is in fact associated with the festival by Σ Ar. *Eccl.* 18 (but that might be combination). Lycurgus: the

We seek at once to make sense of the discordant detail. The procession was heading, it is suggested, for an attested sanctuary west of Athens at which Demeter, Athena and Poseidon all received honours in common.[79] The idea has its attractions, but our only source for this sanctuary locates it at a place near indeed to Skiron but definitely distinct from it. Perhaps the rite rather reflects a historical compromise between the powerful priesthoods of the originally independent communities of Athens and Eleusis[80]—but a look at a map explodes the idea that Skiron, a suburb of Athens, represents a middle point between the two places. In yet more thrilling vein it is suggested that the *Skira* enacts the collapse of society at the end of the year: women leave their husbands, the priests of the city's two most prominent cults leave the acropolis.[81] But this is to suppose that the mere departure of the priest and priestess from their familiar place mattered more than whatever they may have done or seen on arrival at Skiron. The picture will change if we accept the assertion of a small group of late sources[82] that Skiron was site of a sanctuary of Athena Skiras, a goddess more securely located at Phaleron and on Salamis. If it existed, the shrine has a good claim to be considered destination of the procession led by the priestess of Athena Polias (there being little force in the objection that a ceremony which involved Athena under the one title could not also have involved her under the other). But in all probability it is a paper sanctuary, an almost inevitable product of multiple confusions between a puzzling festival, a puzzling word (σκιράφεια) and the goddess Athena Skiras. It is likely to be relevant in some way that Skiron was location of one of the three sacred ploughings mentioned by Plutarch.[83] But even here there is a

---

fragments of the speech *On the Priestess* make repeated reference to the cult of Athena on the acropolis (N. C. Conomis, *Klio* 39, 1961, 107–20). Surely then it was in reference to the role of the priestess of Athena in the procession described by Lysimachides that, in this same speech, Lycurgus used the word σκίρον (fr. 46 Bl., VI.19 Conomis).

[79] Paus. 1.37.2, adduced by Deubner, *Attische Feste*, 47; criticized by Jacoby, notes to comm. on Philochorus *FGrH* 328 F 14–16, n. 77, bottom of p. 204.

[80] See p. 198, n. 24 (C. Robert). According to Pausanias (1.38.1), the ancient boundary between Athens and Eleusis was at a quite different place.

[81] Burkert, *Homo Necans*, 143–9.

[82] Poll. 9. 96 and other sources (E. Gjerstad, *ARW* 27, 1929, 224) seeking to explain the word σκιράφεια (contrast Harp. σ 30, which speaks of Skiron but not of Athena Skiras): cf. Σ Ar. *Eccl.* 18 Σκίρα ἑορτή ἐστι τῆς Σκιράδος Ἀθηνᾶς, Σκιροφοριῶνος ιβ. οἱ δὲ Δήμητρος καὶ Κόρης (the only direct source for the date). But Paus. 1.36.4, speaking of Skiros of Skiron, strikingly credits him with the foundation of a temple of Athena Skiras at Phaleron, not at Skiron. Athena Skiras was first extruded from Skiron by C. Robert, *Hermes* 20 (1885), 349–79; cf. A. R. van der Loeff, *Mnemosyne* NS 44 (1916), 102–6; Gjerstad, op. cit., 224–6; protest (in my view unjustified) in E. Rohde, *Hermes* 21 (1886), 119–22 (= *Kleine Schriften*, ii, 373–7) and especially Jacoby, comm. on Philochorus *FGrH* 328 F 14–16, pp. 290–1.

[83] *Praecepta Coniugalia* 42, 144a–b. Gjerstad, op. cit., 216–20, associated the festival and the sacred ploughing (an instance therefore *ex hypothesi* of summer ploughing) directly (for criticism see Brumfield, *Agricultural Year*, 168–9); van Loeff, op. cit., 328 thought of a 'sacred harvesting' of the crop sown at the sacred ploughing.

difficulty, one that sits on the surface of Lysimachides' text. The *skiron*-bearing procession has as its destination a place named—o wonder!—Skiron. We seem to be confronted with two different and incompatible explanations for the name of the festival. Can we then be sure that the procession of the *Skira* was a procession to Skiron? The fragments of evidence reassemble at every turn of the kaleidoscope, but never form a clear picture.

This is an ancillary problem: the root of our difficulty with Harpocration's report of Lysimachides is that we are told just enough about the mysterious Skirophoric procession to justify the etymology that is being proposed for the month name Skirophorion, and no more. What the participants did on arrival, what other priests or priestesses may have joined them there, who else accompanied them, what strange spectacle may there have met their eyes: none of this is Harpocration's concern. All that matters to him is the sunshade which, he asserts—but not everyone believes him[84]—was called a *skiron*. We are given not even enough to be altogether certain that the procession belonged to the festival *Skira*. We have merely scraps of information torn away from the larger context which alone would have revealed their meaning.

Not every ancient view about the festival has been mentioned thus far. Some heard a reference to plaster,[85] *skiros*, in the festival's name, and spoke somewhat quaintly of a plaster image of Athena fashioned and carried by Theseus on his return from Crete.[86] (Surprisingly, the same etymology has been taken up in modern times, and the festival has been connected to marling of the fields or the use of lime as a preservative for the seed-corn or the plastering of the threshing-floors that were about to be put to use.[87] But the -i—of the festival is known to be short and that of the words for lime and plaster long.[88]) It might seem tempting to abandon the search for a true account of the festival and play instead with a juxtaposition of the various

[84] For scepticism see Gjerstad, op. cit., 204–5, 223; Deubner, *Attische Feste*, 47; Jacoby, notes to comm. on Philochorus *FGrH* 328 F 14–16, n. 71: the source is perhaps postulating an ancient word and practice, not attesting a contemporary one. But the claim is likely to go back to Lycurgus (n. 78 above). Pfuhl, *De Pompis*, 92–5, made the sunshade the key to his interpretation of the festival: it symbolized that protection from the heat of the sun which the rite besought.

[85] The best evidence for this meaning of σκίρος/σκίρρος, for which dictionaries only cite lexicographers, is the pun in Ar. *Vesp.* 925–6. The building material fetched ἀπὸ Σκιράδος (*IG* I³ 463.32, 39; cf. *IG* II² 1672.196, a payment for γῆς Σκίραδος ἀγωγαὶ τρεῖς) was presumably earth used for making plaster, fetched from the region named therefrom (cf. γῆ Λουσιάς in *IG* II² 1672.195, Lemnian earth, and so on: Dioscorid. *Mat. Med.* 5.97, 152–60). On σκίρος/σκίρρος and related toponyms see Ellinger, *Légende nationale phocidienne*, 76–88.

[86] Sud. σ 624, Phot. s.v. Σκῖρος; similarly Σ Paus. 1.1.4, *Etym. Magn.* 718.7. This is probably just guesswork (aliter Jacoby, notes to comm. on Philochorus *FGrH* 328 F 14–16, n. 15 and p. 202); if the facts are genuine, they might rather relate to the *Oschophoria*, as the *aition* in Sud./Phot. suggests (Gjerstad, op. cit., 229–30).

[87] See Mommsen, *Feste*, 313–14 (criticized by Brumfield, *Agricultural Year*, 169–72); Brumfield, *Agricultural Year*, 172–4; Foxhall, 'Women's ritual', 105.

[88] For the vowel length of the festival see e.g. Ar. *Eccl.* 18; for σκῖρον Ar. *Vesp.* 925. Burkert's attempt to meet the difficulty, *Homo Necans*, 146, n. 44, does not satisfy me.

'stories that were told' about it in antiquity. But such a post-modern move, entirely appropriate in some contexts, would be vacuous in this one. Had we access to the 'stories that were told' about the *Skira* by those who participated in it, there would indeed be little point in looking elsewhere for a more valid account. But all we have access to is the speculation of antiquarians who inhabited a different world.

9

Things Done at Festivals

The ritual action at Attic festivals is, for the most part, a series of variations on familiar themes. Sometimes the variation is imperceptible to us, and all we can see is the very standard element such as 'procession' or 'sacrifice'. A comprehensive cataloguing of those elements would be tedious, a comprehensive discussion out of place. This chapter will, after a brief overview, indicate something of the range of variations on common themes, and pick out a few areas where there are singularities to be noted or problems to be discussed.

Demosthenes accused his fellow-citizens of caring more about processions than about preparations for war.[1] Much time and worry must certainly have been expended on this commonest of all ritual forms, and supervision of this or that procession occurs regularly when the duties of different magistrates are listed in the Aristotelian *Constitution of the Athenians*. About many of the well over twenty attested processions little more unfortunately is known than that they occurred.[2] No Athenian equivalents survive to the informative decrees which give some clues as to how participation in two great processions at Eretria was organized.[3] In most cases we should probably envisage the commonest form, that whereby sacrificial animals were led ceremonially

---

[1] Dem. 4.26; cf. the *mot* of Stratonikos in Plut. *Lyc.* 30.6 on the Athenians as the experts among Greeks at 'processions and Mysteries'.

[2] Processions are attested (an asterisk marks cases lacking early attestation) for *Panathenaea*, *City Dionysia*, *Great Mysteries*, *Piraeus Dionysia* (IG II² 380.20–1), *Lenaea* (Arist. *Ath. Pol.* 57.1; Dem. 21.10), *Epidauria* (Arist. *Ath. Pol.* 56.4; ? cf. IG II² 704.13), *Piraeus Asklepieia* (IG II² 47. 32–8), *Eleusinia* (IG II² 930.8, cf. 3554.14–18), *Hephaisteia* (IG I³ 82.24), *Diisoteria* (Arist. *Ath. Pol.* 56.5; IG II² 380.20–1), *Haloa* (*Anecd. Bekk.* 1.385.2—in honour of Poseidon, not the main honorand of the festival), *Plynteria* (Philochorus *FGrH* 328 F 64b; *Athenian Religion*, 307–8), *Bendidea* (Pl. *Resp.* 327a; IG II² 1283.6), apparently *Boedromia* (Dem. 3.31), *Mounichia* (IG II² 1028.20 and often; cf. following note), *Oschophoria* and *Thargelia* (see n. 5), *Skira/Skirophoria* (Suda δ 1210), ? *Dipolieia* (*Agora* XVI 67 (*LSCG* 179)), ? *Olympieia* (Plut. *Phoc.* 37.1, cf. Mikalson, *Calendar*, 145: a cavalry procession), *Theseia* (IG II² 957.3 and often), *Aianteia* (IG II² 1008.23 and often), and in honour of Artemis Agrotera (Plut. *De malignitate Herodoti* 26, 862a; IG II² 1006.8–9, and often; cf. Xen. *Anab.* 3.2.12), the Semnai (*Athenian Religion*, 298–9), Aphrodite Pandemos (IG II² 659.22), *Great Gods* (IG II² 1006.29, and often); at a sub-polis level *Rural Dionysia* (Ar. *Ach.* 241–62), the *Kalamaia* at Eleusis (IG II² 949.9), and the *Herakleia* of the Mesogeioi (IG II² 1245 and 1247: perhaps—p. 472 below—to be identified with the polis festival *Herakleia* at Diomeia). A procession is even attested, surprisingly, for the women's festival *Thesmophoria* (Isae. 6.50); Philoch. *FGrH* 328 F 101 (*kanephoroi*) may imply one for the *Brauronia*. The funeral procession of the *Epitaphia* (Thuc. 2.34) is of different character.

[3] IG XII 9 189 (*LSCG* 92; RO 73), where see esp. 35–40; ibid. 194 (*LSCG* 93).

to the god's main altar, sometimes as at the *Panathenaea* from an appreciable distance. But constant variations will surely have been played on the standard form; the identity of the main participants, what they wore and carried and how they behaved en route, were crucial variables. Only at the *Panathenaea* do we hear that some participants processed in arms; but the procession to Agrai, where the polemarch conducted a large sacrifice to Artemis Agrotera in commemoration of the victory at Marathon, is one of several little-known events which might appropriately have acquired a military colour.[4]

The procession at the *Great Panathenaea* also brought Athena a durable gift, the *peplos*; and there are several cases where natural objects or products were taken to a shrine alongside or perhaps in some cases in place of animal victims. Children are often found as bearers of these bloodless offerings.[5] Most elaborate was the 'procession for the Sun and the Seasons' (perhaps an element of the *Thargelia*) at which a long list of vegetable products were carried. What mattered was normally point of arrival, but point of departure could sometimes be significant: the procession at the *Bendidea* was permitted to start from the prytaneum-hearth, in a striking gesture of acceptance of a foreign cult,[6] while that at the *Oschophoria* moved from a temple of Dionysus to one of Athena.

A different type of procession was that which escorted a god, as symbolized in a statue or other sacred object, who was on the move. This form could be combined with the other, as when a statue of Dionysus was 'brought in' in the sacrificial procession at the *City Dionysia*,[7] but it also occurs in isolation, as when 'Pallas' was taken to the sea to be washed, probably at the *Plynteria*, or sacred objects were sent from Eleusis to Athens in advance of the *Mysteries*.[8] Probably a statue was never moved in a ritual without an accompanying procession (different is the carrying of secret objects at the *Arrephoria*, which took place at night and in secret).[9]

All Athenian *pompai* appear therefore to have remained what they were etymologically, sendings or escortings:[10] they brought an offering to the god, or took the god itself somewhere. The conflux of worshippers to the outlying shrine of Brauron for the *Brauronia* was not strictly a procession, because

---

[4] See App. 1 s.v. Artemis Agrotera, *Boedromia* and *Mounichia*. Arms at the *Panathenaea*: p. 260, n. 27.

[5] So at the *Oschophoria* (p. 206 below) and the 'supplication to the Delphinion' (Plut. *Thes.* 18.1–2). Very likely the boy who took an *eiresione* to Apollo at the *Pyanopsia* (pp. 204–6 below) did so in a form of procession. 'Sun and Seasons': pp. 203–4 below (for the attested *pompe* at the *Thargelia* see Arist. *Ath. Pol.* 56.5). A fig cake called ἡγητηρία was supposedly carried in the procession at the *Plynteria* (Hesych. η 68, Phot. η 37), but the rationale is unclear and there may be some confusion with the procession 'for Sun and Seasons' probably held in the same month, at which one was also carried. At the *Mounichia* cakes ringed with small torches were carried to the shrine of Artemis Mounichia (Philochorus *FGrH* 328 F 86, with Jacoby's parallels).

[6] *IG* II² 1283.6. The prytaneum is far distant from the Bendideum in the Piraeus: presumably this was not a sacrificial procession, not all the way at least.

[7] Note too Dionysus in his ship cart (p. 302). Cf. G. Hedreen, *JHS* 124 (2004), 38–64.

[8] See pp. 478 and 346. [9] See p. 221. [10] See p. 162, n. 25.

nothing was escorted; the proper name is rather *theoria*.[11] But even if emphasis lay formally on the thing actually taken to a place and left there, other objects that were carried in processions could have great importance. Processional vessels (πομπεῖα) were symbols of wealth put to good use in the service of the gods. Athens required her colonies to send phalloi to be carried at the *City Dionysia*, even though such phalloi were not to our knowledge given to the god as offerings. What mattered was their ceremonial display, and it is far from incredible that phallagogy might sometimes have occurred independently of a sacrificial procession. We can reasonably mention here the humping from door to door by boys of an *eiresione*, an olive branch hung with symbols of the seasons; they asked for money or foods 'for' the *eiresione*.[12]

At two festivals objects were expelled or driven out: human scapegoats at the *Thargelia*, purificatory offscourings at the *Pompaia*.[13] As the name *Pompaia* shows, even such an expulsion could be seen as a form of 'sending'.

The importance of sacrifice at festivals is too obvious to need emphasis. An inscription which records the receipts from the sale of skins allows us to estimate the number of animals sacrificed at numerous named festivals of the Lycurgan period, and the totals can be very large. This is why Isaeus can speak of 'the festivals at which the Athenians banquet'.[14] These skin-sale records encourage us to think in merely quantitative terms, as if the problem were simply that of providing a portion of meat for every citizen who desired one. That must indeed have been a problem, and large numbers of bovines were often sacrificed to a single recipient. But a law which prescribes sacrifice to nine different recipients before and during an Eleusinian festival reveals the kinds of subsidiary offerings that might accompany every major one. The scale of animal sacrifice varied greatly from festival to festival, though it was seldom if ever absent completely. It is attested (by a deme calendar) even for the *Diasia*, despite Thucydides' statement that the typical offering there was 'not animal victims but offerings of the local type'. At some hellenistic festivals the ephebes 'lifted the oxen', apparently so that their throats could be slit directly over the altar; the same remarkable feat of co-ordination and strength was performed by 200 chosen men at the classical *Hephaisteia*. One exceptional festival, the *Dipolieia*, treated the sacrifice of an ox as problematic; we will revert to it at the end of this chapter.[15] Libations normally accompanied

---

[11] See p. 44, nn. 28–9. The journey to Eleusis was essentially similar and was sometimes described as a *theoria* ([Lys.] 8.5), but it could also be seen as a 'sending' of Iacchus or of the sacred objects (see p. 348).

[12] Phallagogy: see M. P. Nilsson, *Archäologisches Jahrbuch* 31 (1916), 322 = *Op. Sel.* I, 186–7. *Eiresione*: see pp. 204–5.

[13] See pp. 482 and 479.

[14] Skin sales: *IG* II² 1496; cf. *Athenian Religion*, 228, n. 38. Isaeus: 9.21.

[15] Eleusinian festival: *IG* I³ 5 (*LSCG* 4), cf. p. 328. *Diasia*: p. 466; 'bull-lifting' by ephebes: van Straten, *Hierà kalá*, 109–13; *Hephaisteia*: p. 471 below, and cf. Eur. *Hel.* 1560–4, where the lifting of a bull 'on youthful backs' (νεανίαις ὤμοισι) is a Ἑλλήνων νόμος.

Fig. 9. Black figure amphora, showing bull-lifting, *c.*550 BC.

sacrifice, but could also occur independently. One ill-known rite was named 'Water-bringing' and another *Plemochoai*, from a type of libation vessel.[16]

Choral dancing is a third basic mode of group ritual action, and the Athenian treatment of it raises most interesting issues, in relation to both sexes. Hymning the god and dancing for the god are fundamental forms of Greek worship, and yet it is remarkably hard to find Athenian men engaging in them in their simple form in the classical period. One or two instances are known in what may be rather aristocratic backwaters (certain top Athenians who served as 'Dancers' for Delian Apollo, specially clad, or the youths who sang the 'Oschophoric songs'[17]), but in the main, amid the innumerable male choruses active in Athens, none any longer stepped forward simply to accompany ritual action or hymn the god. Either they competed against other choruses, with songs not necessarily very religious in theme, or they even, as the choruses of tragedy or comedy, assumed dramatic roles. The 'cyclic

[16] 'Water-bringing': p. 296; *plemochoai*: p. 350.
[17] Theophr. fr. 119 Wimmel (576 Fortenbaugh) ap. Ath. 424e–f; for Oschophoric songs see p. 212. The 'boy pythaists' sent to Delphi and the 'youths' sent to Delos (pp. 84 and 81) also seem to have performed non-competitively, but outside Athens.

choruses' at the *Thargelia* were perhaps the closest to the old model, if we accept the attractive suggestion that these performed not dithyrambs, as has normally been supposed by analogy with those of the *Dionysia*, but (more appropriately to Apollo) paeans.[18] However that may be, the great gap that emerged between Athens and, say, Sparta in the fifth century concerned not just the presence in Athens of a new cultural element absent from Sparta, drama, but also the transformation undergone there by a traditional religious element, choral song, which lived on in Sparta in more or less its old form.

As for women, the elaborate competitions, publicly financed, between highly trained choruses of men and boys at the *Thargelia* and the *Dionysia* certainly had no female equivalent. Though generalized allusions to choirs of girls and women are frequent in tragedy, concrete evidence is almost confined to two passages. In the exodus of Euripides' *Erechtheus*, Athena instructs the Athenians to honour the king's daughters, now to be known as Hyakinthids, by sacrifices and 'with sacred dances of maidens'. And the chorus in Euripides' *Herakleidai* remind Athena that on 'the month's waning day' the 'windy hill' rings with 'the all-night beat of maiden's feet': they refer, it is generally assumed, to the *pannychis* of the *Panathenaea*, a festival the chief day of which fell on Hekatombaion 28.[19] The central importance of the *pannychis* within women's religion in Attica was noted in Chapter 8. The question must be what songs and lovely dances, and of what type, may have vanished from our sight in the darkness of the *pannychis*. Of the activities that filled the long hours on these occasions, much the most commonly mentioned is dancing. (At a festival of Demeter, ritual abuse is also attested, and of course there were also pauses for refreshment.[20]) If maidens participated at a fair number of the many attested *pannychides*, and if when they did so they danced formally in choruses, then Attic maiden choruses have emerged in good number. But how formal were the dancing and the choruses at a *pannychis*? Was it more like a performance or more like a party? One possibility is illustrated by Socrates and his companions at the start of *Republic*, when they decide to stay for a *pannychis* of Bendis 'which will be worth watching'. But one of the many rapes imagined in New Comedy to have occurred on such occasions took place when the women were 'dancing and holding the *pannychis*, scattered'. The festival in question is a private one, but this less organized

[18] Wilson, *Khoregia*, 314, n. 22, 322, n. 115.
[19] *Erechtheus* fr. 65.79–80 Austin; *Heraklid.* 777–83. The context of the rites for the Hyakinthids is unknown; as for the *Heraklid.* passage, Wilamowitz supposed a monthly sacred day, but that makes better sense linguistically than in reality (*Hermes* 17, 1882, 356 = *Kl. Schr.* 1.101; Wilamowitz's other views on this passage are generally rejected—see G. Zuntz, *The Political Plays of Euripides*, Manchester 1955, 121 [+]). For the 28th, the last day on which the moon is briefly visible (Sotion ap. *Geoponica* 1.13.2, 5.10.4), as 'the month's waning day' see Mommsen, *Feste*, 105, 150. See too p. 257.
[20] Dancing: Eur. *Heraklid.* 777–83, *Bacch.* 862; Men. *Dysc.* 950–3, *Epitrep.* 1119–20, *Sam.* 46, *Phasma* 95. Abuse: Phot. s.v. Στήνια. Refreshment: Ath. 668c, quoting Eubulus fr. 1.

form of dancing was not necessarily confined to such contexts. Pamphile was raped when she 'got detached from the choruses' at the *Tauropolia*; that gives us both the potentially formal 'choruses' but also the possibility of a participant becoming 'detached'.[21]

The issue has broader implications. We have become used to the idea that, for Greek girls, the world of the chorus was a large part of the world of education.[22] To train the male choruses which competed at festivals was expensive in time and money. Girls' choruses did not compete and conceivably did not even sing,[23] but formal choral dancing of its nature can surely not be performed impromptu. Yet no single text (if we exclude Plato's *Laws*, the models for which in the real world are seldom clear) appears to reveal an Attic equivalent to Sappho or Hagesichora, choir-mistresses (if that indeed is what they were) to the maidens on Lesbos and of Sparta. We know of only one institutional framework, the *arkteia*, within which it is possible to imagine girls being trained up for the chorus. The other structures that must surely be postulated, if one is also to postulate extensive activities by maiden choruses, have simply vanished; and it is perhaps more probable that they never existed.[24] The conclusion is rather startling. The idea that *parthenoi* learnt by learning to dance is, it seems, appropriate only to certain areas of the Greek world. All Athenian girls danced, no doubt. But, except for the minority who served as *arktoi*, there was perhaps no organized world of the chorus. Nor was there for them when they became married women.

The final recurrent component of Attic festivals is the competition (athletic, equestrian, musical). The race between 'dismounters' (*apobatai*) was almost unique to the *Panathenaea*, of which it came to serve as a marker. It was as members of the tribal relay-teams which contested the torch-races at the *Promethia*, *Panathenaea*, and *Hephaisteia* that ephebes were most conspicuously involved in the festivals of the classical period.[25]

A small number of festival activities fall outside the standard rubrics. At the *Aiora*, of uncertain date, young women swung on swings in commemoration

---

[21] Pl. *Resp.* 328a; Men. *Sam.* 46, *Epit.* 1119–20. *Phasma* 93–107 is likely to have had a similar context. For *Pannychis* as a play title in New Comedy see R. L. Hunter, *Eubulus. The Fragments* (Cambridge 1983), 175; note too Naevius, *Agrypnuntes*. On rape at festivals see p. 172.

[22] See Calame, *Choeurs*, I, *passim*, esp. ch. 4; cf. E. Stehle, *Performance and Gender in Ancient Greece* (Princeton 1997), esp. ch. 2. Stehle notes, p. 117, the paucity of relevant evidence from Athens.

[23] So Wilamowitz, *Griechische Verskunst* (Berlin 1921), commenting on the ὀλολύγματα of Eur. *Heraclid.* 782: 'es gibt in Athen keine bürgerlichen Sängerinnen, geschweige Dichterinnen'. Against this can be set Critias fr. 1.6 D/K, where the poetry of Anacreon is linked to female choruses at *pannychides*, and Ar. *Ran.* 370–1 (μολπή and παννυχίς). But the generally accepted working assumption that *choreia* implies *molpe* (Calame, op. cit., II, 130) may be too undifferentiated.

[24] Michael Jameson once told me that he preferred the other solution: a network of choral training now to us invisible.

[25] On competitions in general see *Athenian Religion*, 96–7, with notes; ibid. 103, n.5; R. Osborne in A. H. Sommerstein and others (eds.), *Tragedy, Comedy and the Polis* (Bari 1993), 21–38. 'Dismounters': pp. 254–5; torch-races: *Athenian Religion*, 254, n. 127, and p. 472 below.

of the suicide, by hanging, of a variously identified Erigone; a traditional song, 'wandering woman' (*Aletis*), was associated with the rite in some way. Various explanations of the meaning of this rite were offered, in the era when rites still had clear meanings,[26] but despite the gloomy character of the day the best answer might be 'fun'. The designation of a particular day as one on which everybody is to perform a particular activity (or eat a particular food) which they could in principle perform (or eat) individually at any time is one of ritual's characteristic devices for patterning the year, and bonding society. This patterning effect remains crucial whatever additional symbolism may have been associated with the activity.[27] The Erigone festival means collective swinging, and collective swinging means the Erigone festival; there need be no more to the ritual form than this marking out of Erigone's day, and this is certainly its primary meaning. (Whether Athenian girls also swung for fun at other times is not known; vase-paintings might suggest it, but these are commonly taken to illustrate the festival and we find ourselves in a circular argument.) A competition in jumping onto slippery inflated wineskins has been recognized for what it is, a game loosely associated with Dionysus through the wine-skin; perhaps it could be played at any Dionysiac festival, perhaps it was connected with a particular one.[28] There was a chase of some kind at the *Thesmophoria*, a mock battle at an Eleusinian festival: we cannot judge their seriousness.[29] Much more of this type must certainly elude us.

Many further particularities relate, in different ways, to foodstuffs and to feasting. A detailed study would be out of place; we can merely register such cult titles as 'parasites' and 'pre-tasters' and 'wine-choosers' and 'dinner-bearers',[30] noting that many singular practices have no doubt vanished from the record in this area too. But it is worth reverting to the whole phenomenon of festival food. One point of festival foods lies simply in their role as markers. In the anglophone world, the unfailing recurrence of turkey is one of the things that gives Christmas its recurrent distinctiveness; and, for many consumers of Christmas turkey, there is doubtless no more to be said about the matter than that. To put it in another way, the predetermined menu is an aspect of the fussiness of ritualization; what you eat must be

---

[26] See Deubner, *Attische Feste*, 118–20. J. E. Harrison, *Mythology and Monuments of Ancient Athens* (London 1890), pp. xxxix–xlv, has interesting parallels from 19th-c. Greece. On the *Aiora* see pp. 301–2; for swinging on vases see p. 302, n. 50.

[27] Cf. D. Gellner, *Monk, Householder and Tantric Priest: Newar Buddhism and its Hierarchy of Ritual* (Cambridge 1992), 135–6, on the kite-flying prescribed for a particular festival.

[28] Eubulus fr. 7 (8 Hunter); the name ἀσκωλιασμός for this game, and the supposed festival *Askolia*, were exposed by K. Latte as products of bad scholarship in antiquity (*Hermes* 85, 1957, 385–91 = *Kl. Schr.* 700–7).

[29] Semos of Delos, *FGrH* 396 F 21 (Hesych. δ 2036, Suda χ 43 s.v. Χαλκιδικὸν δίωγμα); Ath. 406d, Hesych. β 167 s.v. βαλλητύς; cf. p. 301 and p. 329.

[30] Parasites: Schmitt Pantel, *Cité au banquet*, 100–4; 'pre-tasters' (προτένθαι) and 'wine-choosers' (οἰνόπται) Ath. 171c–e, ibid. 425a–b, Didymus ap. Phot. s.v. οἰνόπται (both associated with the *Apatouria*); 'dinner-bearers': pp. 213, 215, 216–17.

prescribed, though it may not matter what the prescription is. But we must certainly allow for the possibility that festival foods bore more meaning for many Athenians than this. First therefore we need some facts about the festivals that spoke of food in their very names.

Pyanopsia/Pyanepsia was interpreted (*inter alia*) as deriving from the roasting (ἕψω) of πύανα, which are said to be 'all the edible pulses, which they bring together and boil in pots, making a porridge';[31] modern etymologists in fact accept πύανος as an allomorph of one particular pulse, κύαμος, bean. The dish in question seems to be what was often described as an 'all seed' or πανσπερμία, made up of peas, beans, lentils and the like (these being the 'seeds' of pulses). What the θάργηλος was that gave its name to Thargelia is not fully clear: different lexicographers speak of a 'pot full of seeds', 'all the produce of the earth', 'first fruits of the crops that have appeared', and one specialist even referred to 'the first bread made from the harvest'.[32] The possibilities thus range from an 'all seed' of pulses identical to that of the *Pyanopsia*, through the same with corn seeds added, to an actual baked loaf. *Galaxia*, which gave its name to a little-known festival of 'Mother', was 'a barley porridge from milk'.[33] We also hear that the last day of the *Anthesteria* was named Pots because 'the survivors from the flood boiled pots of mixed seeds (πανσπερμία)', and so now in commemoration does everyone in the city. A doubt has been raised whether the householders who prepared these foods also ate them, on the grounds that one source speaks of a θάργηλος being taken as an offering to Apollo.[34] But a rude joke in a comic fragment that links the *Pyanopsia* with flatulence implies consumption, and the πανσπερμία of the *Anthesteria* too was eaten, though not by priests. As for the θάργηλοι, the most that can be said is that the fact that some were offered does not make it impossible that others were eaten.[35]

If a θάργηλος was in fact a loaf made from the first wheat to ripen, the seasonal reference is obvious; this was a ritualized early sampling. The seasonal pattern of pulse growing is more complicated, and it does not seem likely that the *Pyanopsia* (held in autumn) can be seen as a celebration of

---

[31] So e.g. Harp. π 120, Poll. 6.61, Phot. s.v. Πύανοι κύαμοι, ἀφ᾽ ὧν καὶ Πυανόψια.

[32] See p. 481. One specialist: 'Krates in book 2 on the Attic dialect' ap. Ath. 114a, where an identification of θάργηλος with θαλύσιος is also mentioned. I wonder how realistic Krates' idea is. Could the main harvest be anticipated in this way? And would enough of this early wheat have been available for every household (if every household prepared a *thargelos*)? To judge from the ingredients provided by the deme of Cholargi for its women at their *Thesmophoria* (*IG* II² 1184 = *LSS* 124), it is possible that a *panspermia* was prepared there too. For funerary use of an 'all-seed' see p. 296, n. 32. Somewhat different from a *panspermia* are the contents of a *kernos*, as defined in Ath. 476f and 478d (the latter a citation of Polemon), since the *kernos* contains cereals in addition to pulses.

[33] *Anecd. Bekk.* 1.229.25–7 (cf. Hesych. γ 80) πόλτος κρίθινος ἐκ γάλακτος: a runny version of a 'milk' barley cake (on which see T. Braun in *Food in Antiquity*, 29)?

[34] By L. Bruit, in O. Murray (ed.), *Sympotica* (Oxford 1990), 168–9, adducing Phot. θ 22.

[35] Rude joke: Com. Adesp. fr. 118 ap. Ath. 408a, after a nest of citations from Timocles. The *aition* in Plut. *Thes.* 22.5 also implies eating of the *panspermia* at the *Pyanopsia*. *Anthesteria*: p. 295.

the 'new beans'; beans could be sown either in autumn or in spring, but the autumn sowing was apparently the main one.[36] A different approach is needed, therefore. A structuralist paradigm is available which would, *inter alia*, locate foods on an axis leading from 'primeval' to 'civilized'—an axis of the imagination, of course, not of historical reality. The ancients themselves occasionally saw peculiarities in the religious use of foodstuffs as imitations or commemorations of an ancient lifestyle, just as they sometimes saw the whole ethos of a festival in these terms.[37] Changing diet also had an important place in Greek speculations about the development of civilized life. But both these ways of thinking had a history, to which philosophical speculation in the fourth century and later made an important contribution. We cannot assume that ordinary celebrants of the *Pyanopsia* sat down to their bean stew with any such thoughts in mind. Nor can we suppose that the *Pyanopsia* had an emphatic vegetarian ethos; minor sacrifices appear to be attested, even if most households will not have eaten meat.[38] The primary organizing category for Athenian thought about food is likely to have been the opposition between simple, cheap, everyday food and more exotic fare. What is immediately clear if we think about the festival foods in these terms is that they are closer to the pole of simplicity than of luxury. The *panspermia* sounds like a variant on a well-loved staple, that pulse soup so dear to Heracles; the adaptation lay in including a multiplicity of ingredients and so stressing the idea of abundance. The 'barley porridge' of the little-known *Galaxia* was plain enough too. Doubtless a simple dish would also have been felt to be a traditional and perhaps a rustic dish. But, even if 'traditional', it was not a fragment of the past but a dietetic option still available in the present, and, which may be crucial, one accessible to almost anybody.[39] In the ancient much more than in the modern western world, luxurious eating was one of the key benefits and symbols of wealth. Festivals aspired to be vehicles of social harmony, and the unelaborate traditional festival foods were an expression of that aspiration. That is not an explanation for the choice of beans at, precisely, the *Pyanopsia*, but it may be a broader truth.

---

[36] Theophr. *Hist. pl.* 8.1.3–4. For the much more abundant Roman evidence see Olck in *RE* s.v. *Bohne*, 614–17.

[37] See Ath. 137e, with citation of Chionides fr. 7 (diet); Diod. Sic. 5.4.7 (ethos); cf. Ath. 74d, Paus. Att. η 1 on the fig. Different if related are explanations of features of festival diet or cooking by reference to particular mythical events, as in Plut. *Qu. Gr.* 31, 298b–c; Ap. Rhod. 1.1070–7, and the *aitia* for *Pyanopsia* and *Chytroi* (pp. 382 and 296). The view that fragments of ancient practice 'survive' (not 'are imitated') in sacrificial customs is also found, in Theophrastus (main text Porph. *Abst.* 2.6.2, p. 137.3–7 Nauck): see D. Obbink, 'The Origin of Greek Sacrifice: Theophrastus on Religion and Cultural History', in W. W. Fortenbaugh and R. W. Sharples (eds.), *Theophrastean Studies* (New Brunswick and London, 988), 272–95, at 276. Structuralist paradigm: see Calame, *Thésée*, ch. 5.

[38] *LSCG* 7. 8–10; *SEG* XXXIII 147. 27, and right side by 31.

[39] Cf. Theophrastus ap. Porph. *Abst.* 2. 14. 3 (p. 144. 12–14 Nauck). On the simplicity of ritual foods see J. Wilkins, *The Boastful Chef* (Oxford 2000), 267, 277, 307; on expensive food as a key expression of upper-class indulgence see Wilkins, op. cit., ch. 6; J. Davidson, 'Fish, Sex and Revolution', *CQ* 43 (1993), 53–66.

I end this chapter with a festival which displays a form of ritual action of altogether singular type, and which embodies reflection, again of altogether singular type, on the most basic of all forms of ritual action, sacrifice. The festival is the high summer festival of Zeus Polieus, *Dipolieia*, celebrated on the acropolis. Virtually all that is known of it[40] is a ritual which had a name of its own shaped like a festival name, *Bouphonia*, Ox-killing (not Ox-murder as it is often mistranslated).[41] A long account of it by Theophrastus, combining the myth of origin with a description of the ritual, is preserved, probably more or less verbatim, by the proselytizing vegetarian Porphyry; as the richest written document relating to an Attic festival it deserves to be quoted in full.

We should take the rule still observed in Athens as a rule for our whole lives. It is said that once of old, when, as was explained earlier, men sacrificed crops but not animals to the gods (nor did they exploit these to feed themselves), a *pelanos* [a kind of savoury cake] and cakes were placed on the altar in open view ready to be sacrificed to the gods during a public festival at Athens, and one of the oxen coming in from working ate some of them and trampled others. A certain Diomos or Sopater,[42] who farmed in Attica though not a native, flew into a rage at this occurrence and, seizing an axe which was being whetted nearby, struck the ox. The ox died, and when (Sopater) recovered from his rage and realized what he had done, he buried the ox and, condemning himself to voluntary exile for his act of impiety, fled to Crete. Drought and terrible crop failure seized Attica, and when they sent a public enquiry to the god the Pythia told them that the exile in Crete would bring release from all this, and that if they punished the killer and restored the victim at the festival at which he died, and tasted of the dead animal and did not hold back, things would go better for them. They made enquiries and identified Sopater as responsible for the deed. Sopater thought that he would be freed from the distaste they felt for him as for one polluted if everyone performed this act together, and he told those who had come for him that an ox must be struck down by the city. They were at a loss as to who should strike the blow, but he undertook to do this for them, if they would make him a citizen and participate in the killing. These terms were agreed, and when they returned to the city, they organized the matter as follows, and it remains so among them even now. They chose water-bearing maidens, who bring water,[43] so that (the appropriate persons) can whet the axe and the knife. After the whetting, one man passed on the axe, and another struck the ox, and another cut its throat. Others then skinned it, and all participants tasted of the ox. When this had been done, they stitched up the skin of the ox and stuffed it

---

[40] But S. Scullion, *ClAnt* 13 (1994), 85, suggests on the basis of a Coan analogy that the entry in the Nicomachus calendar (*BSA* 97, 2002, 365, face B, fr. 1 col. 2) attests a holocaust of piglets performed by heralds.

[41] See A. Henrichs, 'Gott, Mensch, Tier: antike Daseinsstruktur und religiöses Verhalten im Denken Karl Meulis', in F. Graf (ed.), *Klassiche Antike und neue Wege der Wissenschaften. Symposium Karl Meuli* (Basle 1992), 129–67, at 153–5; for bibliography on the *Bouphonia* see ibid. 153, n. 75.

[42] Porphyry elsewhere briefly recounts a slightly different myth of origin of the *Bouphonia* in which the errant ox is slain by one Diomos, said to be priest of Zeus Polieus (*De Abst.* 2. 10). It has long been recognized that Theophrastus' account had Sopater as protagonist; Porphyry has added 'Diomos or' to blur the inconsistency.

[43] Erratic tense use reflects that of the original.

with hay and set it up, looking as it did when still alive, and yoked a plough to it as if it were at work. And holding a trial for the killing they summoned all those who had been involved in the deed to defend themselves. The water-bringers blamed the whetters rather than themselves, and the whetters the man who handed over the axe, and <this man the one who struck the ox>,[44] and this man the one who then cut its throat, and the one who did this blamed the knife, and the knife, being speechless, they condemned for the killing. Ever since until the present at the *Dipolieia* on the acropolis in Athens the persons mentioned have performed the sacrifice of the ox in the same way. They put a *pelanos* and cakes on the bronze table and drive the oxen assigned for this role around it; whichever ox takes a taste is struck. Families of those who perform these acts still exist. The descendants of Sopater who struck the blow are all called 'ox-smiters' (*Boutupoi*), and the descendants of the driver 'goad men' (*Kentriadai*). They name the descendants of the slayer 'carvers' (*Daitroi*) because of the banquet that follows after the division of the meat. They stuff the skin, and when they are brought to the trial they throw the knife in the sea. And so, in the past it was unholy to kill the animals that collaborate with us in gaining our livelihood, and we must still shun doing it. (Porph. *Abst.* 2. 28.4–31.1, pp. 158.14–160.24 Nauck).

Dipolieia and *Bouphonia* were already symbols of the old-fashioned for Aristophanes, but a version of the ritual was still being performed in the time of Pausanias, in a remarkable attestation of continuity. We have a number of other, much briefer allusions to both myth and ritual which not only lack much of the detail of Theophrastus/Porphyry's account but also differ from it in various ways.[45] The name and civic role of the protagonist, for instance, vary (only Theophrastus/Porphyry makes him by origin a non-citizen), and in Pausanias the flight of the ox-smiter is a feature not just of the myth but also of the ritual. In consequence an inanimate object (Pausanias has axe in lieu of Theophrastus/Porphyry's knife) becomes subject to accusation not because human agents deny culpability, but because the human killer cannot be apprehended. But the central plot of all these variants remains that of exculpation of humans from the guilt of sacrifice. The ox always incriminates itself by eating consecrated vegetarian offerings, and Pausanias and Aelian both know of a trial at which guilt is transferred to an inanimate object. We cannot reconstruct every detail of the ritual, still less recover a pristine form of the myth of origin, but the central thrust of both is clear.[46]

---

[44] Not in Porphyry, but a necessary addition for the coherence of the narrative.

[45] Ar. *Nub.* 984; Paus. 1.24.4 (cf. 1.28.10); Ael. *VH* 8.3; in a tradition going back to Androtion, *FGrH* 324 F 13, the killer is Thaulon (Σ vet. Ar. *Nub.* 985c = Hesych. β 1004, Suda β 474, θ 67). The date of the festival (Skirophorion 14) comes from Phot. β 249 (and parallel texts), Σ vet. Ar. *Pax* 420b (Mikalson, *Calendar*, 171). An ox sacrifice to Zeus Polieus on that day now appears in the perhaps Attic calendar (see p. 484) *IMiletupolis* 1.8.

[46] The older scholarship tortured itself analysing and seeking to discredit Porphyry's account. W. F. Otto, 'Ein griechischer Kultmythos vom Ursprung der Pflugkultur', in his *Das Wort der Antike* (Darmstadt 1962), 140–61 (first in *Paideuma* 4, 1950, 111 ff.) rightly huffed all this aside, under the influence of K. Meuli. The monograph of Durand, *Sacrifice et labour*, is centred on a reading of the Sopater myth as depicting the emergence of civic institutions in Attica. I cannot see this: a city exists from the start, but Sopater is outside it.

In Theophrastus/Porphyry the eventual victim is one of a group of oxen which are driven around the altar, a procedure briefly alluded to also in the state sacrificial calendar as republished by Nicomachus late in the fifth century and possibly also in four black figure vases by the Gela painter (*c.* 500 BC).[47] A new text from Bargylia has joined a long-known one from Cos to confirm the importance of ox selection as a ritual procedure, one which could involve segments of the city such as tribes by requiring them to provide the candidates.[48] The point of the Attic ritual for Theophrastus/Porphyry was to involve 'everybody'. (But this 'everybody' need not include more than 'all male citizens'.) The ox selection perhaps gave a symbolic role to wider groups than the 'families'[49] (*Boutupoi*, *Kentriadai* and the rest) so prominent in Theophrastus/Porphyry's account. But the details are hidden from us by a vague phrase in Porphyry,[50] and by Pausanias' time (if we can trust him in this) just one animal was brought to sniff the cakes on the altar.

Theophrastus and Porphyry, it is generally agreed, have misinterpreted the ritual to make it support their own vegetarian ideals. Their own description shows that the *Bouphonia* served to license at least one act of ox-slaying, not to forbid it: to bring the drought that afflicted Attica to an end, the Pythia required 'everybody' to taste of the slaughtered ox. But both myth and ritual flirt with the idea that ox-slaying might be seen as ox-murdering before they reject it, and interpreters differ over the weight to allow to that flirtation; for some it serves only to give the final rejection more force, whereas for others it is an expression of real unease which Theophrastus and Porphyry were not wholly wrong to highlight.[51] The festival certainly relates to animal sacrifice in its most controversial form; for, whether the ox actually sacrificed had been a working animal or not, both myth and ritual treat it as such: the animal originally killed by Sopater had come in 'from working', and at the festival the resurrected animal was yoked to a plough. One way of viewing the relation between men and animals was in terms of exchange of services, and in that perspective to slaughter the partner of one's labours was a criminal act. Aratus treated sacrifice of the ploughing ox as one of the crimes of men of the Bronze Age which persuaded Justice to abandon the earth. Doubtless Aratus is a suspect witness, since the myth of a golden age without animal

---

[47] Nicomachus: n. 40 above; there may be a further allusion in *Agora* XVI 67 (*LSCG* 179), which also mentions a μάχαιρα. Gela painter: see Simon, *Festivals*, 9–10, with pl. 6; van Straten, *Hierà kalá*, 51–2 (+), with fig. 55; Durand, *Sacrifice et labour*, 95–103. The vases show oxen around an altar-like structure, on which one appears actually to stand (but Durand argues that it is behind the altar); on three of the four a further ox appears in white in front of the altar (so Durand; previous scholarship took it as a painting or relief on the front of the altar).

[48] See W. Blümel, *EpigAnat* 25 (1995), 35–9; ibid. 28 (1997), 153–6 (*SEG* XLV 1508A and B); ibid. 32 (2000), 89–93. Cos: *LSCG* 151a = RO 62A (with Burkert, *Homo Necans*, 138, n. 100).

[49] On them see *Athenian Religion*, 299, 320–1.

[50] 'The oxen assigned for this role' (τοὺς κατανεμηθέντας βοῦς): the principle of assignation is not revealed.

[51] For references on this large debate see Bremmer, *Greek Religion*, 41–2; on 'hiding the knife' see now the sceptical study of P. Bonnechere, *REA* 101 (1999), 21–35.

sacrifice spread in the hellenistic period outside the vegetarian circles in which it originated.[52] But one of the curses ritually pronounced each year by a member of the *Bouzygai* was supposedly directed against anyone who sacrificed a ploughing ox.[53]

I set that issue aside for the moment, and raise a related one. Some view the *Bouphonia* as a dramatization of the issues inherent in all animal sacrifice. It presents in an extreme form the 'comedy of innocence' (in Karl Meuli's famous phrase) that Greeks played out whenever they offered an animal. It will represent a justification not just *a fortiori* but *a fortissimo* (because it takes the hardest case) of the whole sacrificial system.[54] In the perspective suggested by Aratus, it would embody a re-enactment of the events which locked us into the present condition of the world. Others stress its absolute singularity.[55] The accepted myth of the origin of sacrifice is quite distinct. On this view, the *Bouphonia* tells us nothing about the morality of sacrificing goats or sheep or even ordinary cattle from the pasture. It relates to working oxen, and perhaps not even to them in general, but on a particular day in a particular cult in high summer.

Those who take this second view stress the ban in Attica, reinforced by a Bouzygean curse, on the sacrifice of working oxen. It is hard to see the *Bouphonia* as normative, if the norm that it supposedly established (the right to sacrifice the ploughing ox) is not in fact one that was generally accepted. Perhaps the *Bouphonia* is not a legitimation of anything, but a powerful transgressive action (to what purpose?) on a particular occasion.[56] Or perhaps there is something wrong with the sources that appear to attest a ban on sacrificing the working ox. Not to sacrifice the working ox, once its useful life was past, would have been economically very wasteful. (The option of eating but not sacrificing[57] would not have met the moral objection, and seems never to be envisaged.) Possibly the ritual provided a justification for this

---

[52] Aratus, *Phaen.* 129–36; cf. Empedocles B 128.8 D/K, Pl. *Leg.* 782c; B. Gatz, *Weltalter, goldene Zeit und sinnverwandte Vorstellungen* (Hildesheim 1967), 230, s.v. *abstinentia animalium/bovis* (ox sacrifice is typically picked out as the mark of our fallen world, as in Virg. *Georg.* 2. 536–8). For Pythagoras tolerating all meats except ram and plough-ox see Aristoxenus fr. 29a Wehrli ap. Diog. Laert. 8. 20.

[53] Aelian *VH* 5.14 (Buzyges is not mentioned, but cf. Σ Soph. *Ant.* 255), with Varro *R.R.* 2.5.3–4 (mentioning Buzyges, and wildly claiming a death penalty); cf. Σ B Hom. *Od.* 12. 353.

[54] This assumption is shared, despite fundamental disagreement on the conclusions to be drawn from it, by Burkert, *Homo Necans*, 141 (citing Meuli) and J. P. Vernant, 'Théorie générale du sacrifice et mise à mort dans la *Thusia* grecque', in *Sacrifice*, 1–21, at 15–18 (English version in Vernant, *Mortals and Immortals*, 290–302).

[55] So Jameson, 'Sacrifice and husbandry', 87; D. Obbink, 'The origin of Greek sacrifice' (n. 37 above), 284; Bremmer, *Greek Religion*, 42.

[56] So the scholars cited in the previous note. Christiane Sourvinou-Inwood mentions to me the ritual modality whereby a taboo is reinforced by selective violation. But at the *Bouphonia* we have not just a violation but an extended defence of that violation, which seems pointlessly elaborate if it relates merely to the ceremony itself.

[57] So Jameson, op. cit.

most morally problematic, but still economically desirable, sacrificial form.[58] Yet to be economically useful the justification would need to extend to all the cults of the state, not just the one, and there is no sign that the sacrificial system of any Greek state was governed by economic rationality in this area. Working oxen were sacrificed in Thebes to Apollo Spodios (or perhaps originally rather to Heracles) and in Lindos to Heracles;[59] but in both cases the sacrifice was marked out by myth of origin or by ritual action or by both as no less exceptional than the practice of the *Bouphonia* itself.

In times of civil war every citizen must take sides, decreed Solon. To conclude a discussion of the *Bouphonia* in agnosticism seems very feeble. But what Theophrastus/Porphyry gives us is a very brilliantly illuminated central scene. The broader setting is in absolute darkness. The skin of the sacrificed ox is stuffed with straw and attached to a plough, and some suppose that the whole ritual speaks not only of killing but also of labour; we must plough and we must sacrifice, and, if we do so in the right way, the continuity of civilized society is assured.[60] Given the ancient city's absolute dependence on agriculture, Zeus Polieus, Zeus of the City, could readily also be viewed as guardian of the fields. But the plough yoked to the stuffed ox can be explained, as by Theophrastus/Porphyry, as merely part of the making good of the ox's death; the relation of the festival to agricultural concerns is quite unclear.[61] The issue of the morality of sacrifice is so elaborately emphasized that the ritual ought to be trying to say something of broad significance. But why is the most morally dubious of all forms of sacrifice picked out for attention? Should Theophrastus have realized that, if even the sacrifice of the ploughing ox could on occasion serve the needs of the city, it was foolish indeed to nurture scruples about less problematic forms? That is a comfortable conclusion at which to arrive, but not indubitably a right one.

---

[58] So Rosivach, *Public Sacrifice*, 162–3. Rosivach believes that he can reconcile this interpretation with our sources by the postulate that Aelian and Varro's ban on sacrificing plough oxen (n. 53 above) refers to a mythical period prior to the institution of the *Dipolieia*. This is also, if I understand him, the position of Durand, *Sacrifice et labour*, 175–7. But the ban appears to have been embodied in a (continuing) Bouzygean curse; and, even if one doubts the rather unclear evidence of Aelian and Varro on this point, the Theban and Lindian cases mentioned in the text speak in favour of a general Greek inhibition.

[59] Thebes: Paus. 9.12.1, with Schachter, *Cults*, 2, 21; Rhodes: e.g. Philostr. *Imag.* 2. 24 (Durand, *Sacrifice et labour*, 145–52); cf. P. Stengel, *Die griechischen Kultusaltertümer*, ed. 3 (Munich 1920), 123.

[60] So Durand, *Sacrifice et labour*, passim; and cf. Otto (n. 46 above).

[61] Durand, *Sacrifice et labour*, 184 points out that the season of the festival, summer, was one (but only one) of the appropriate times for fallow ploughing (on which see Hes. *Op.* 462 with M. L. West's note). For the relation of a civic Zeus to agriculture, the cult of Zeus Sosipolis in Magnesia, where a bull was displayed to Zeus Sosipolis ἀρχομένου σπόρου (*LSA* 32 = *Syll*³ 589. 14) and later sacrificed to him, has often been compared, as recently by S. Scullion, *ClAnt* 13 (1994), 86–7.

10

The Festival Year

It seems to be of the nature of festivals that they should occur at a particular time: not necessarily on a particular day (though in Athens even this had become the norm by the fifth century), but certainly within a particular period and, no doubt, in a particular order.[1] The Greeks had three calendars in their informal experience of time. There was the succession of the months, all but for slight differences of length identical to one another, determined by the moon. Then there were the changing seasons, which shaped the cycle of natural growth and of activities in many spheres (agriculture, stock rearing, seafaring and warfare, for instance). Since the seasons depend on the sun, the solstices are significant moments in this calendar; so are other astronomical phenomena such as the rising or setting of the Pleiades which can be taken to indicate the right moment for human activities. And finally there was the sequence of the festivals. We need to ask what relation existed between the third of these ways of experiencing time and the other two.

Formally the festivals were tied to the calendar of the months (which were often named from festivals), and they could be associated in ways that were not merely formal with individual days within the month: gods had sacred days (Apollo's seventh, for instance) on which their festivals commonly fell. Indeed the internal structure of the month was a vehicle of religious meaning, the new moon, for instance, being an occasion when individuals regularly 'went up to the acropolis and prayed to the gods to grant blessings to the city and to themselves'. When calendar months and the actual lunar cycle got out of step, time was felt to be out of joint. Many major festivals were held near the middle of the month, perhaps in order to allow the full moon to shed light on their *pannychides*.[2] But what mattered was the positioning of a festival at a particular point within the lunar month, not in a particular month. The close symbolic interweaving of twelve gods, twelve tribes and twelve months that Plato proposed in *Laws* is quite unlike the practice of any actual Greek city.[3] The more important if less formal connection was doubtless that between festivals and the calendar of seasons.

---

[1] For rites that are listed in calendars as to be performed before other rites, see Jameson *et al.*, *Selinous*, 25–6.

[2] New moon: Dem. 25.99 (cf. p. 20, n. 55); on this and on monthly days see Mikalson, *Calendar*, 13–24. Out of joint: Ar. *Nub.* 608–26. Full moon: C. Trümpy. ZPE 121 (1998), 109–15.

[3] O. Reverdin, *La Religion de la cité platonicienne* (Paris 1945), 62–5.

Festivals, it was felt, had a proper and even a 'natural' relation to the cycle of the stars and seasons, and it was the job of civic calendars to ensure that they were indeed celebrated at the proper time, that consecrated by tradition and pleasing to the gods. The pious Plato of *Laws* wants young citizens to be educated in astronomy for this purpose.[4] But the relation between the festival calendar and the cycle of the stars was always somewhat uncertain, for more than one reason. The Greek calendar was 'lunisolar', that is to say the discrepancy between a year of twelve moons or *c.*354 days and a solar year of *c.*365 days was removed by periodic intercalation of an extra month (the norm was probably thrice every eight years, but the controversial details need not concern us here). In consequence the relation between, say, the calendar date Hekatombaion 1 and an astronomical phenomenon such as the solstice will have varied at different moments within the cycle of intercalation: Hekatombaion 1 could fall at different points within a span of slightly more than twenty days in the Julian solar calendar. Such fluctuation is inherent within the lunisolar system.[5] But the Athenians (like it seems other Greeks) also added and subtracted days ad hoc from individual months, so that time might stop on Hekatombaion 25 for eight days (to take an extreme but attested case) whereas another month or months would forfeit days in compensation. The double dating found in hellenistic inscriptions whereby an event occurs on Thargelion 11 'in accord with the archon' but Thargelion 18 'in accord with the god' reflects this phenomenon: addition of days has created a seven-day discrepancy between official time (that of the archon, who presumably made the relevant decisions to add or subtract days) and the actual point reached in a lunar cycle ('the god'). One main motive for the addition of days may have been to allow more time to prepare for festivals, which could still occur on what was nominally their proper day. But in extreme cases, where the two calendars were running well over a month apart, the relation of festivals to the agricultural year will have been much disordered. Whether archons brought the two calendars back into harmony as soon as they conveniently could is controversial; on another view discrepancies could be carried on, so that (for instance) official and real new moon, once dislocated, may have diverged for the rest of the year (with implications about which we can only guess for the public and private new moon rites). We know from a famous passage of Aristophanes that irregularities already occurred in the fifth century. We learn from the same passage that they were resented; but this is not a completely reliable guarantee that

---

[4] Pl. *Leg.* 809c; cf. an instructive passage from an introduction to astronomy by Geminus (*c.*50 AD?), *Eisagoge*, 8.6–9; both texts are quoted by W. K. Pritchett, *Athenian Calendars and Ekklesias* (Amsterdam 2001), 31–2. In this paragraph I have attempted to extract what is needed for heortological purposes on a complex and hugely controversial topic (see Pritchett, op. cit., *passim*) on which I am an amateur.

[5] See Follet, *Athènes*, 351–62, a very clear introduction. For documentation on what follows see Pritchett, op. cit., esp. 1–40.

they were allowed less often, and rectified sooner, than in the hellenistic period, from which almost all our evidence dates.[6]

I revert, with these warnings, to the festival year. It might seem obvious to begin at the beginning with the New Year. But that would be to presuppose that the Athenians or the Greeks recognized such a thing. Years are 'natural' in the sense that every society perceives the recurrence of the seasons; but the notion that the year begins and ends at a particular point is an arbitrary one,[7] which may or may not exist in a particular culture. Even a society, such as the Athenian, in which tenure of certain offices is for a year is not necessarily committed to the belief that years have beginnings and ends. When one set of officials gives way to another, it may simply be that the magistrates have changed, not that a year has come to an end. As it happens, that radical claim would be too strong in the case of Athens; Lysias once speaks of Skirophorion 30, the day before the change of magistrates, as the last of the year, and Plato casually assumes that in his Magnesia the 'new year' will begin with the first new moon after the summer solstice.[8] The concept therefore existed; but there is little sign that it brought with it the fantasy of a decisive annual caesura between old and new or was festooned with symbolic meaning. In modern English-speaking societies a variety of administrative 'years' (school, academic, legal, tax) co-exist with a quite distinct calendar year, the change in which alone is ritualized, in some regions very emphatically. In Athens, there are several administrative years (of archons, of *bouleutai*, of ephebes, of 'treasurers of Athena') of which the most important, the archontic, is identical with the calendar year. But as to ritualization, the most that can be said is that a festival of Zeus Soter fell on the last day of the calendar year early in the fourth century (but apparently was relocated later!), and that the incoming magistrates made 'entry sacrifices' on (presumably) the next day.[9] More loosely, one can note that festivals of major civic importance (*Dipolieia, Synoikia, Panathenaea*) clustered in the last and first months of the calendar/

---

[6] Ar. *Nub.* 608–26; for the view that the 5th-c. calendar was not hugely irregular see K. J. Dover in id., A.W. Gomme, A. Andrewes, *A Historical Commentary on Thucydides,* iv (Oxford 1970), 269. For the controversy whether correction of irregularities was rapid see Pritchett, op. cit., 9–13.

[7] Against Burkert, *Homo Necans,* 142, see M. P. Nilsson, *Primitive Time-Reckoning* (Lund 1920), 267–8 ('Of the Kiwai Papuans Landtman writes to me:-"The year has no beginning, since there is no term to describe this, and it cannot be said that one season more than another marks an occasion of greater importance" '); id. *Die Entstehung und Religiöse Bedeutung des griechischen Kalenders,* ed. 2 (Lund 1962), 54–5; M. Camp-Gaset, *L'Année des grecs* (Paris 1994), 147–62 (despite concessions on 157–60). Not even the concept of 'year' is a universal: see the striking study of A. Itéanu, 'Synchronisations among the Orokaiva', *Social Anthropology* 7 (1999), 265–78 (with reference to the anthropological literature).

[8] Lys. 26.6; Pl. *Leg.* 767c. Plato doubtless reflects an Attic ideal; how often it was achieved depends on heavily controversial questions about calendric cycles.

[9] Zeus Soter: see App. 1 s.v. *Diisoteria*; entry sacrifices: see p. 98, n. 31. Some scholars (most recently A. P. Matthaiou, *Horos* 10–12, 1992–8, 37–41) identify the rites of Skirophorion 30 with the entry sacrifices. Administrative years: see Rhodes, *Boule,* 24–9 and *Commentary* Ath. *Pol.,* 406–7. The ephebic year apparently began in Boedromion (Pélékidis, *Éphébie,* 175).

archontic year. But all this is a far cry from specific ritualization of a 'New Year'. As has often been noted, the calendar year changed in different seasons in different *poleis*, in a way hard to explain if anyone cared much about this New Year.

We are deprived of a natural starting point. We can begin instead with the small number of festivals that by their names suggest an association with the agricultural year. Here evidence from two demes combines usefully. A law from Paeania regulates the offerings that are to be made, apparently at two sites, one inside and one outside the deme,[10] at three festivals, the *Prerosia* ('pre-ploughing'), the *Chloïa* ('green shoots'), and *Antheia* ('flowering'). Similarly named sacrifices appear in the same order in a calendar from Thorikos, and at Thorikos, where they are given dates, we can see how they combine to form a cycle connected with the planting and growth of the corn. It starts in autumn with the pre-ploughing sacrifice; in spring when the green shoots are due to put up stems there follows the *Chloïa*, the festival of χλόη, green shoots; in late spring comes the *Antheia*, a festival not of flowers in general but of the flowers of the corn, which open about forty days before the harvest. (The Roman Flora too, Botticelli's Flora, was according to Varro an unromantic guardian of the flowering corn.) Theophrastus in the *Historia Plantarum* carefully chronicles these stages in the life-cycle of the corn, and his chronology fits quite well with the dates in the calendar.[11] A further stage had its own festival, the *Kalamaia*, celebrated by at least two demes and probably, as it gave its name to the Ionian month name Kalamaion, of great antiquity. The καλάμη is the stem of the corn both before and after it has been cut, but the month name *Kalamaion* apparently falls in high summer; probably then the festival relates to gleaning rather than to the intermediate stage between shoots and flowering, the formation of the stem.[12] The occurrence of the cycle *Prerosia–Chloïa–Antheia* in two widely separated demes, and of related rites elsewhere, suggests deeply rooted traditions.

Some reservations are necessary here. These are not 'Attic festivals' celebrated in the same form in every community. The *Antheia* is not found outside

---

[10] So Humphreys, 'Demes'. On the Paeania text (*IG* I³ 250) see M. P. Nilsson, *Eranos* 42 (1944), 70–6 = *Opuscula Selecta* 3 (Lund 1960), 92–8, who rightly associated the *Antheia* with Demeter. For *Chloïa* at Eleusis see n. 13; note too the priestess of Demeter Chloe in the deme Aixone in *IG* II² 1356.16 (*LSCG* 28). The presence of these festivals at Thorikos (*SEG* XXXIII 147) was first detected by G. Daux, *L'Antiquité classique* 52 (1983), 150–74; I diverge from him slightly in understanding the syntax as, 38, ἡ Χλοῖα (θυσία), cf. ἡ προηροσία (n. 14), and, 44, 'a pregnant sheep as "the flower offering" '; cf. perhaps πρεροσιάδον χριθόν in *IG* I³ 250 A 21–2 or the πρεροσίον τέλεον of ibid. 18, ὁδὸς θαλυσιάς (Theocr. 7.31). The close link of these festivals with the corn cycle is disputed by S. Georgoudi in S. Castignone and G. Lanata (eds.), *Filosofi e animali nel mondo antico* (Pisa 1994), 177–81.

[11] 8.2.4–7. For Theophrastus wheat matures in eight-plus months after sowing, and flowering comes forty days before maturity. The Thorikian *Antheia* comes in the seventh month after their *Prerosia* (which will have immediately preceded sowing). Varro: ap. August. *De civ. D.* 4.8; cf. K. Latte, *Römische Religionsgeschichte* (Munich 1960), 73.

[12] So rightly Brumfield, *Agricultural Year*, 151–2.

these two inscriptions, the *Chloïa* in only one further text (but there are also some references to sacrifices to Demeter Chloe).[13] Indeed the full cycle of all four festivals is nowhere attested, though it is a fair guess that most agricultural demes would have celebrated some of them. The *Proerosia*, much the most widely attested of these rites, proves intriguingly elusive. The name, the date and even the honorand of the rite all vary: the name shifts from *Proerosia* to *Prerosia* to *Plerosia* like a philological exhibit (even *Proeresia* occurs), at least two different dates are found, and though it was normally a rite of Demeter, at Myrrhinus it honoured Zeus.[14] These variations suggest that the institution of the formal 'pre-ploughing' sacrifice (whoever its recipient) was well established from of old in the Attic countryside. In some of its disguises, however, the explicit connection with ploughing is obscured (*Prerosia*) or has even disappeared (*Plerosia*, which rather suggests 'filling'). In Athens itself, sacrifice was made to Demeter the Green at her shrine near the entrance to the acropolis during the month Thargelion and probably as part of Apollo's festival, the *Thargelia*;[15] by then the fields had long ceased to be green in reality.

An ill-attested sacrifice or festival known as 'Thanks in advance' (*Procharisteria*: variant form *Proschaireteria*) is said to have been conducted by 'all the magistrates' (οἱ ἐν τῇ ἀρχῇ πάντες) 'at the end of winter, when crops were beginning to grow'. The lexicographical sources from which alone we know the *Procharisteria* speak of it as being offered to Athena, and it has long been a principal exhibit for those who see Athena as having been once a multipurpose goddess associated even with agriculture. But one of the lexicographers quotes a fragment of Lycurgus which describes it as 'the most ancient sacrifice on account of the coming up (ἄνοδος) of the goddess'. Only one

---

[13] *IG* II² 949.7 (Eleusis), between *Haloa* and *Kalamaia*: note too *ZPE* 130 (2000), 45–7, col. 2, 49 (Marathon), sacrifices to Chloe in Anthesterion; Cornutus, *Theol. Graec.* 28 p. 55.14 Lang ('in spring'). On the greening of the fields see Brumfield, *Agricultural Year*, 133, 136.

[14] See *IG* I³ 250 (*LSS* 18: Paiania) A 8, 18, B 4: Demeter, date unclear, Πρη-; *SEG* XXXIII 147.5 (Thorikos) recipient unclear, Hekatombaion; ibid. line 13: recipient either Zeus Polieus or unspecified, Boedromion, Πρη-; *IG* II² 1177.9 (Piraeus): probably Demeter, date unspecified, Πλη-; ibid. 1183 (RO 63) 33 (Myrrhinus or Hagnous): Zeus, date unclear (cf. L. Ziehen in *RE* s.v. *Πληροσία*, 234; aliter Whitehead, *Demes*, 197, n. 112), Πλη-; ibid. 1363.6 (*LSCG* 7: Eleusis): (Demeter), Pyanopsion, Προη-; *IG* II² 1028.28, etc., τὰ Προηρέσια at Eleusis (ephebic decrees). For the association of Zeus Chthonios (Polieus at Thorikos would be a little surprising) with Demeter in a ploughing context see Hes. *Op.* 465–7. As to the name, discovery on stone of the intermediate Πρη- form triumphantly vindicated philological speculation: cf. Ziehen, *RE* s.v. *Πληροσία*. ἡ προηροσία (sc. θυσία) vel sim. is commoner than τὰ Προηροσία (except at Eleusis). Cf. Threatte, *Grammar*, i, 479–80 (who however dissociates the Πλη- and Πρη- forms on mistaken chronological grounds). Plut. *Conv. Sept. Sap.* 15, 158d, speaks of Proerosia Demeter.

[15] For the shrine see Ar. *Lys.* 835; Paus 1.22. 3; cf. *IG* II² 1472. 39 (a dedication to Demeter Chloe in an inventory), 5129 (theatre seat for her priestess); for the sacrifice see Philochorus *FGrH* 328 F 61 (= Σ R Ar. *Lys.* 835), Σ Soph. *OC* 1600 (which cites Eupolis fr. 196): both texts give Thargelion as date, the latter 'the sixth of Thargelion', but as the book of Philochorus in question is 'the sixth', confusion is not impossible (see Jacoby *ad loc*). The shrine was associated with a first appearance of corn (absolutely, or in Athens as opposed to Eleusis?) in a Delphic oracle recorded in *IG* II² 5006 ('*aetate Hadriani*': Fontenrose, *Delphic Oracle*, 173–4, 189).

goddess has a 'coming up', and that is Persephone. Would the magistrates have given thanks to Athena for the coming up of Persephone? It is perhaps more likely that the lexicographers have mistaken one 'the goddess' for another. In that event *Procharisteria* will be yet another seasonal rite of Demeter, though one whose relation to the functionally similar Green Shoot offerings (*Chloïa*) is unclear.[16]

Little is known of the ritual of these corn-related festivals except that they involved sacrifice (for the Eleusinian *Kalamaia* a procession is found too)[17] and that at two of them, at least, the women of the Piraeus 'came together in accordance with tradition'.[18] So even here the direct benefits perhaps sought for the crops by the ritual go the indirect route, by way of women who are not themselves the principal cultivators. At Paiania a distinction seems to be drawn between 'pre-ploughing commencement offerings' and the 'pre-ploughing offerings' themselves (προερόαρχος[19] and προερόσιον), and at Thorikos too the festival is mentioned in a fragmentary context two months prior to the main celebration.

The *Proerosia* is a group expression of the kind of concern seen in Hesiod's advice to the farmer to 'pray to Zeus of the earth and reverend Demeter that the sacred grain of Demeter may come to full growth, when you first begin ploughing, when you take the end of the plough-handle in your hand and come down on the back of your oxen with the goad'. It must have been principally at this time that farmers thought of the Marathonian hero Echetlaeus, 'plough-handle man', known to us only because he appeared in his normal rustic guise at the battle of Marathon and laid about him with his plough.[20] Another transfer to communal level of the concerns of individual farmers is seen in the institution attested by a single passage of Plutarch: 'the Athenians perform three sacred ploughings, first at Skiron, a commemoration of the most ancient sowing (τοῦ παλαιοτάτου τῶν σπόρων ὑπόμνημα), the second at Rharia, the third the so-called Bouzygean below the acropolis'. (The continuation, which is Plutarch's only reason to give us this precious nugget of information, is seldom added: 'but the most sacred of all is sowing at

---

[16] Suda π 2928 s.v. Προχαριστήρια, with citation of Lycurg. fr. 50 Blass, VII. 1a Conomis; *Anecd. Bekk.* 1.295.3; cf. Harpoc. π 114 s.v. Προσχαιρητήρια, citing Lycurg. VII. 1b Conomis (probably the same festival despite the difference in name). For οἱ ἐν τῇ ἀρχῇ πάντες in this sense cf. Suda ει 273. The postulate of error by the lexicographers goes back to Sauppe (see Conomis' app. crit.), but is not considered by Mommsen, *Feste*, 420, Deubner, *Attische Feste*, 17 or Bérard, *Anodoi*, 24.

[17] Brumfield, *Agricultural Year*, 184, unpersuasively disassociates the πομπή of IG II² 949.9 from the *Kalamaia*.

[18] IG II² 1177, Piraeus: 'Plerosia' and *Kalamaia*.

[19] On the interpretation of this word I follow N. Robertson, *GRBS* 37 (1996), 351–2, against Nilsson, *Op. Sel.* 3, 95. Thorikos: n. 14 above.

[20] See M. H. Jameson, 'The Hero Echetlaeus', *TAPA* 82 (1951), 49–61, on Paus.1.15.3, 1.32.4–5 (a rich discussion of pre-ploughing practices in all their aspects). Hesiod: *Op.* 465–9.

marriage and ploughing for the procreation of children'.[21]) A bell krater of
the Hephaestus painter (*c*.425) seems to depict a mythical prototype of the
rite: it shows a bearded hero ploughing in the presence of a goddess who holds
a sheaf of corn (Demeter or Athena?) and an elder who might be Cecrops.[22]
'Pre-ploughing sacrifice' and 'sacred ploughing' might perhaps have combined as a single ceremony, just as Hesiod's farmer remembers the goddess
moments before touching the plough handle. But that is apparently not the
case, and the relation of the two rituals is not clear.[23] The rationale for the
triplication of the ceremony also escapes us.[24] One might have expected
either one sacred ploughing for the whole of Attica, like that performed in the
past by the minister of agriculture in Siam, and by the emperor himself in
China,[25] or a series conducted at different points throughout the countryside.
As there was no agreed best time to start the sowing, and conditions varied
slightly in different parts of Attica, it has been suggested that the three sacred
ploughings were spread out through the extended sowing season.[26] (We cannot
strictly even exclude the view that one was performed in spring or summer.) But
would ritual take account of the contingencies of the actual in quite that way?[27]

[21] *Praec. Conj.* 42, 144 a–b. Proclus on Hes. *Op.* 389 quotes a scrap of verse (*PMG* 877) 'from the
Eleusinian rites' to show that the ancients sowed early: it was presumably sung at the *Mysteries*
rather than the *Proerosia* or Sacred Ploughing, if Proclus' argument about earliness is to stand up.

[22] Cambridge, Mass., Fogg Coll. 60. 345 (*ARV*² 1115. 30 A: Simon, *Festivals*, pl. 7.2; Durand,
Sacrifice et labour, 178, fig. 86; *LIMC* s.v. *Bouzyges*, no. 2 [+] (C. Bérard, who reviews the debate
and favours Demeter)).

[23] Plutarch mentions sacred ploughing at three places, at only one of which the festival
Proerosia is attested, while the *Proerosia* was celebrated in a number of demes unaccompanied, to
our knowledge, by sacred ploughing. It is, however, conceivable that the staggered series of sacred
ploughings did not begin until the prestigious Eleusinian *Proerosia* had been duly performed.

[24] The commonest explanation (going back to C. Robert, *Hermes* 20, 1885, 378) has been in
terms of a reconciliation between the traditions of Athens itself and a once independent Eleusis:
both cities had originally claimed to be site of 'the most ancient sowing', but surrendered their
title in favour of a compromise candidate, Skiron, conveniently located en route between the two
(though far closer in fact to Athens than to her presumptive rival). But if Athens had ever wished
to dispute Eleusis' special title of glory, she had certainly ceased to do so, had begun indeed
enthusiastically to promote the Eleusinian claim, a good half-millennium before the date at which
our only source mentions these sacred ploughings as being performed. I would think it possible by
contrast that an Athenian custom was extended to Eleusis at quite a late date (perhaps in the
hellenistic or Roman period, if it is true that the *Bouzygai* were involved). Various traditions are
found in later sources about the 'inventor' of the plough—Triptolemus (e.g. Virg., *Georg.* 1.19;
F. Jacoby, *Das Marmor Parium*, Berlin 1904, 67—so shown in early art only on one Boeotian
skyphos: G. Schwarz in *LIMC* s.v. *Triptolemos*, no. 26, cf. ibid. p. 67) or Bouzyges (*Σ* Aeschin. 2.78
no. 168 Dilts; sources cited as Aristotle fr. 386 R) or Demeter or Athena (*Hymn. Orph.* 40.8; *Serv.
Dan.* on *Aen.* 4.402; cf. Detienne/Vernant, *Mètis*, 170–1), but it is not clear that one should speak
in terms of rivalry (Smarzyck, *Religionspolitik*, 190, n. 95).

[25] Jameson, op. cit., 55. For older writings on 'first ploughing' rites see A. Dieterich, *Mutter
Erde*, ed. 3 (Leipzig and Berlin 1925), 97.

[26] Brumfield, *Agricultural Year*, 19–23.

[27] J. Z. Smith, *To Take Place* (Chicago 1987), 109: 'Ritual is a means of performing the way
things ought to be in conscious tension to the way things are'. Spring or summer: E. Gjerstad,
ARW 27 (1929), 240, associates the ploughing at Skiron with the festival *Skira*. But see Brumfield, *Agricultural Year*, 168–9.

The *Thesmophoria* was celebrated in the sowing season, shortly after the *Proerosia*, and served to produce a compost-like substance that, mixed with the seed corn, would ensure an abundant harvest the following year.[28] In this case, an appeal to the agricultural cycle tells us something about the festival, but far from everything; about some other festivals of Demeter it does not obviously tell us anything, though it may be the fault of the gaps in our sources that the crucial points of contact fail to appear. The *Haloa*, an Eleusinian festival of Demeter and Kore at which Dionysus and Poseidon[29] also had some role, bears a satisfyingly Demetrian name: it very obviously evokes ἅλως, 'threshing-floor', or less clearly ἀλωή, 'cultivated plot, vine-yard'.[30] But it was held in the month Posideon (December–January), when threshing floors were damp and idle. An attractive explanation makes a strength of the apparent difficulty. Ever since November the farmer has been hectically engaged with ploughing and sowing cereals, pruning and digging round the vines and other trees; only now can he pause, in the brief space before the spring vine-pruning and digging begins, to celebrate the two gods with whom he has been practically engaged without a break for the past two months.[31] The date would depend, then, on the cycle of men's activities, not women's, despite the prominence of women at the festival. One source in fact relates the festival to 'the pruning of the vine and the tasting of the wine which has been stored'. The new wine of the autumn would have been drinkable by now,[32] and Dionysus was sufficiently prominent at the festival for a fourth-century orator to be able to represent an illicit sacrifice made during it as an act of impiety against him.[33] The source's claim is none the less problematic, because it would entail that the ceremonial 'Opening of the

---

[28] See p. 273.

[29] On Dionysus see n. 33. The *Haloa* fell in Poseidon's month, *Posideon*, season of many a festival of the god in other parts of the Greek world (see esp. N. Robertson, 'Poseidon's Festival at the Winter Solstice', *CQ* 34, 1984, 1–16; the date of *Haloa*, Posideon 26, is given by Phot. a 1080; cf. Mikalson, *Calendar*, 94). At Athens, Poseidon's place in the festival calendar is extraordinarily reduced, and all he receives in his own month is a procession said to form part of the *Haloa* (Paus. Att. a 76 Erbse: the doubts of Brumfield, *Agricultural Year*, 106–7, are scarcely justified), presum-ably therefore conducted at Eleusis. The relations of Demeter to Poseidon are tangled and mysterious. Poseidon was honoured at Eleusis as 'father' (Paus. 1.38.6; Robertson, op. cit., 3), but perhaps as other things as well (he probably receives sacrifice at the *Eleusinia*, IG I³ 5. 4); in Arcadia, he made himself Demeter's undesired husband (Paus. 8.25.4–10; Burkert, *Greek Reli-gion*, 138 with 403, n. 35). Plutarch speaks of Poseidon Phytalmios and Demeter Prerosia as powers presiding over the farmer's art. Plut. *Conv. Sept. Sap.* 15, 158d (cf. *Quaest. Conv.* 5.3.1, 675f; Robertson, 13). What specific aspect of this complex was evoked at the *Haloa* we can only guess. For a possible joint festival of Poseidon and Dionysus see App. 1 s.v. *Protrugaia*.

[30] For the ancient etymologies see Jacoby's note on Philochorus *FGrH* 328 F 83.

[31] Foxhall, 'Women's ritual', 104. She notes the absence of attested assembly meetings and virtual absence of festivals for the month Maimakterion.

[32] Brumfield, *Agricultural Year*, 25–6. One source: Σ Lucian 279. 25–6 Rabe; consequently it claims (281.2–3) ἀλωαὶ ... αἱ τῶν ἀμπέλων φυτεῖαι.

[33] Apollod. *Neaer.* 116–17, the importance of which was already stressed by Clinton, *Sacred Officials*, 17, n. 41 (my note making the same point, *Hermes* 107, 1979, 256–7, was unneces-sary). Deubner, *Attische Feste*, 64, had disputed the authority of the sources (Paus. Att. a 76 Erbse; Σ Lucian p. 279.25 Rabe, cf. 281.1–3) which associated the festival with Dionysus.

Casks' at the start of the *Anthesteria*, most popular of all festivals and a festival
of Dionysus, had been anticipated at a ceremony the primary honorand of
which was Demeter. Demeter's gift itself lay in the furrow inert and endan-
gered by frost at this time, after sprouting in the late autumn. Perhaps that is
precisely why it needed ritual protection;[34] at all events the people of Mykonos performed a whole series of sacrifices to Demeter in what seem to be this
month and the following, one explicitly 'for the crops' and one in association
with 'a song for the crops'.

As was noted earlier,[35] this festival of many gods was also quite elaborate
structurally, with the two sexes participating in different ways. Huge entries
in the Eleusinian accounts to supply firewood and kindling for the *Haloa* attest
a further element; almost three tons of wood were burnt, perhaps in the form
of a single spectacular bonfire. (If such a bonfire took place on the 'threshing
floor of Triptolemos', as has been ingeniously suggested, the festival's name
would find an explanation[36]). The festival will then have extended into the
night.[37] Possibly the great bonfire illumined the year's gloom at the time of
the least light, the winter solstice.[38] But other Greek fire festivals are very
miscellaneous and it is not established that the later European custom of
marking seasonal change in this way has ancient analogues. The women at
the *Haloa* handled sexual objects, and were urged by priestesses to commit
adultery. Is there a special link between ritual licence and particular times of
the year? Has bawdy privileged seasons?[39] The questions rest.

The festival is mentioned only twice in the classical period but appears in a
cluster of hellenistic decrees. There was now a citizen garrison stationed at
Eleusis, and the soldiers regularly resolved to proclaim the honours that they
conferred on their officers at what they called 'the ancestral meeting of the
Haloa' (πάτριος ἀγών). One general made sacrifices at his own expense at
the festival and invited all the citizens stationed at Eleusis to participate. For
the garrison, the *Haloa* had evidently become the great event of the year.
Normal usage at this date would suggest that the 'ancestral meeting' was an

---

[34] So Brumfield, *Agricultural Year*, 121. Mykonos: *LSCG* 96. 11–26, in the months *Posideon* and
Lenaion (cf. Trümpy, *Monatsnamen*, 64–5).

[35] See p. 167; on the Haloa see too pp. 279 and 283.

[36] So Robertson, *CQ* 34 (1984), 5, on *IG* II² 1672. 124–5, 143–4 (for Triptolemos see Paus.
1.38.6); he compares the Delphic fire-festival *Septerion* performed 'round the threshing floor'
(Plut. *De def. or.* 15, 418a–b).

[37] A woman's *pannychis* is mentioned by the unreliable Alciphron, 4.6.3. Possibly the festival
lasted two days. A neat two-day scheme (day one: *pompe*, ending at the shrine of Poseidon in the
entrance court of the Eleusinian sanctuary; night of day one: *pannychis* (for women) and bonfire
party (for men); day two: 'ancestral *agon*') is suggested by Robertson, op. cit., 6.

[38] So Brumfield, *Agricultural Year*, 117–18. 'Jahresfeuer' has various entries in the index to
Nilsson, *Griechische Feste*, but the use of the term is not defended as far as I can see: the concept is
not discussed by W. P. Furley, *Studies in the Use of Fire in Ancient Greek Religion* (Salem 1981).

[39] Cf. Brumfield, *Agricultural Year*, 121–6 (who floats but backs off from the view that
'earthiness' is deployed to revive the dead earth in winter).

otherwise unattested competition, probably in athletics.[40] The detail illustrates in exemplary fashion the limitation of any attempt to explain festivals in terms of their explicit functions. The only set of celebrants at the *Haloa* whom we can identify with any precision at any date are those revealed by the inscriptions. And what we find at this agricultural festival are soldiers (citizen soldiers admittedly) assembled to watch sport.

Three main festivals of Demeter remain. The *Mysteries* are a special case, and we can accept the formulation that they evoke the idea of corn without relating to any particular stage in the agricultural year.[41] The enigma of the *Skira* has been discussed elsewhere. All that can confidently be said is that this was a festival of Demeter celebrated early in high summer, perhaps in the interval between harvesting and threshing. A final Eleusinian festival which some would associate closely with the agricultural year is the *Eleusinia*. Though sometimes confused by non-Athenian authors of late antiquity with the *Mysteries*, this was a distinct festival, as was finally put quite beyond doubt by a decree of the late third century BC which speaks of the 'treaty-bearers who announce the *Eleusinia* and *Panathenaea* and *Mysteries*'. The *Eleusinia* included competitions in 'athletics, music, and horse-racing' as well as 'the ancestral competition', and the third-century decree, found at Gonnoi in Thessaly, is one of a number of proofs of the festival's lasting place within the panhellenic competitive circuit: clients of Pindar won victories at it in the fifth century BC, and at least half a dozen further successes are recorded on dedications found in various parts of the Greek world and dating from the hellenistic to the late imperial period. From the middle of the third century Athenians regularly honoured worthy citizens and benefactors by proclamation 'at the athletic competition of the *Eleusinia*', and the decree just mentioned shows that it was protected by a sacred truce. It was also, in the fourth century, occasion for abundant sacrifices at the expense of the city.[42]

Like most festivals with an athletic element, it was not celebrated in the same form every year, but the cycle has proved hard to define. The question is more intricate than important except in one regard. Victors at the *Eleusinia* received as prize an allocation of corn from the Rarian field, and the festival is

---

[40] So Moretti (a specialist in these matters) on his no. 20.14–15 (*IG* II² 1304b): 'gare ginniche'; cf. *IG* II² 1299. 29, 77; *IG* II² 1304. 46–7. *Aliter* Robertson, op. cit., 4: 'another bout of merry-making'. But a somewhat organized context is necessary for the proclamation. One general: *IG* II² 1299.9–14. The festival makes a late and unexplained appearance in *IG* II² 3559 (1st/2nd c. AD.)

[41] So Foxhall, 'Women's ritual', 102–3; on the placement of *Skira* see ibid. 105.

[42] Treaty-bearers: B. Helly, *Gonnoi* (Amsterdam 1973), ii, 120 no. 109. 24–38 (= *ArchEph* 1914, 167–72, no. 232); cf. P. Foucart, *REG* 32 (1919) 190–207, and for the earlier debate (in which Mommsen, Foucart, and van der Loeff had already seen the truth) van der Loeff, *De ludis eleusiniis*, 3–12. On the Athenians'concern attested by the decree to promote their festival abroad see Helly, op. cit., ii, 126–7. Competitions: *IG* II² 1672. 258–61 (details of the athletic competition emerge from the individual victor dedications, for which see the index to L. Moretti, *Iscrizioni agonistiche greche*, Rome 1953; on Pindar's clients see *Athenian Religion*, 97, n. 124). Proclamation: *IG* II² 851.13, and often. Sacrifices: *IG* II² 1496.130, 138. See too pp. 328–9.

said to have been established as a thank-offering to Demeter for the crops or even 'after the harvest'. It has therefore been identified as an item that on the surface appears to be absent from the Attic festival year, a true harvest festival.[43] The imagination can play with pleasure on a primitive *Eleusinia* at which, the harvest in, the labourers competed in the goddess's presence for choice samples of her gifts. But it falls rather late in the summer for that function, and, what is more serious, it may be that until the third century the *Eleusinia* was not held every year.[44] A harvest festival celebrated in alternate years would be a curious thing.

A festival said explicitly by an ancient source to attend the bringing in of the harvest is the *Kronia*. Macrobius reports that 'Philochorus says that Cecrops first set up an altar in Attica to Saturn and Ops [i.e. Kronos and Rhea] and honoured those gods in lieu of [before?][45] Zeus and earth, and established the custom that in all households when the crops and fruits were brought in the masters should feast on them with their slaves, with whom they had shared the hard labour of cultivating the land.' Accius in the late second century BC goes further and has masters actually waiting on their slaves; he is inevitably under suspicion of transferring too much of the *Saturnalia*, the origin of which he is explaining, back onto Greece, but Greek parallels for the thoroughgoing reversal do exist.[46] Nothing of substance is known of the festival beyond this. Even so, it is remarkable as perhaps the clearest example of a festival that embodies, that puts into action, a myth.[47] In the 'life in the time of Kronos' (a proverbial expression) there was no slavery; at the *Kronia* the difference between slave and master is effaced or even reversed. But the suspension of status differences cannot outlast the festival, because we live now under Zeus. Oppressive social relations that entail a certain proximity and even intimacy between oppressor and oppressed appear to create a need for reversal rituals of this type, however

---

[43] Corn as prize: Aristid. *Panath.* 38 with the Σ ad loc. (3.55.31–33 Dindorf); id. *Eleusinios* 4; Σ Pind. *Ol.* 9. 150 b and c; cf. *IG* II² 1672. 258–60; Healey, *Eleusinian Sacrifices*, 25. The prize allocation was large: as for the *Panathenaea*, transport home must have been a problem. Thank offering: see sources cited as Arist. fr. 637 Rose; Σ Pind. *Ol.* 9. 150 c; Aristid. *Panath.* 38 with Σ. Harvest festival: see R. M. Simms, *GRBS* 16 (1975), 269–79, and the hyperspeculative article of G. Baudy in *Food in Antiquity*, 177–95.

[44] For the date (Metageitnion or early Boedromion) and periodicity of the festival see App. 1 s.v. *Eleusinia*. Brumfield, *Agricultural Year*, says that the *Eleusinia* comes 'three months after the harvest was finished' (p. 187). But that ignores the period of up to two months which she allows elsewhere for threshing (41–2).

[45] Macr. *Sat.* 1.10.22 = Philochorus *FGrH* 328 F 97. 'In lieu of' translates the Latin 'pro'; Jacoby (on Philoch. loc. cit.) supposes Philochorus' original claim to have been that the cult of Kronos and Rhea pre-dated that of Zeus and Earth. A date in high summer (Hekatombaion 12) is independently attested (Dem. 24.6).

[46] Accius fr. 3 in Courtney, *FLP* (ap. Macr. *Sat.* 1.7.36); parallels: Versnel, *Transition and Reversal*, 103–4; suspicion: Deubner, *Attische Feste*, 152 [+]. I see no way of deciding the matter.

[47] See the admirable study 'Kronos and the Kronia' in Versnel, *Transition and Reversal*, 89–135.

precisely one analyses their effects.[48] (In that sense even the myth is second-ary.) Such rituals can find a place in festivals of different types—the other such suspension of the master–slave relation in Attica occurred at the *Anthes-teria*—but there must always be something about the festival to make it an appropriate niche. In this case the appropriate context was created, as Phi-lochorus saw, by the heavy and obviously significant labour of harvesting (and threshing, we must add, to get the timing right) undergone jointly in the preceding months. But this is not exactly a harvest festival; nor need Kronos its patron have any intrinsic connection with agriculture.[49]

We have looked at festivals of Demeter, and at one of Kronos. Rites of other gods evoke the seasons or seasonal produce in various ways. Two festivals of Apollo, *Thargelia* and *Pyanopsia*, make complex play with natural symbolism. The former honoured Apollo Pythios (though Apollo Delios is also mentioned in a reliable source); the Apollo honoured by the latter is unknown, but Apollo Delphinios is a good candidate.[50] The parallels between them are rather striking. Both take their name from a distinctive festival food, and both are said by sources to involve the consumption or display of the year's produce. Thus both are associated with agriculture in a way that for festivals of Apollo is paradoxical. In a sense they mark the beginning of high summer and of winter respectively. *Thargelia* was a festival of purification and propiti-ation which also bore a relation to the ripening corn and to agriculture more generally. The notorious sending out of two scapegoats relates to the first aspect; so too perhaps does the competition for 'cyclic choruses', if what they sung were paeans. To the second aspect relate the *thargeloi* presented and perhaps eaten at the festival, and a sacrifice to Demeter Chloe which probably formed a part of it.[51] A remarkable assemblage of natural products was displayed at the festival, if, as we probably should,[52] we identify a 'procession for the Sun and the Seasons' at which they were carried with the procession (details not specified) which is independently attested for the *Thargelia*; a recently published decree of the third century which mentions offerings to 'Sun, Seasons and Apollo' shows how readily the three powers

---

[48] For the standard dichotomy (do 'rituals of reversal' express a real or only a dreamtime vision of a different world?) see p. 172, n. 63. In a richly documented discussion Versnel, *Transition and Reversal*, 115–21, answers 'in the ancient world, dreamtime only' and distinguishes two distinct counter-revolutionary functions of such rituals: they may be safety valves, but they may also, by enacting a reversed world, demonstrate its impossibility.

[49] On this matter see Versnel, *Transition and Reversal*, 100 [+].

[50] Pythios/Delios: *Athenian Religion*, 96, n. 120; Delphinios: Calame, *Thésée*, 229, 319–22, building on F. Graf, *MusHelv* 36 (1979), 13–19.

[51] On all this see pp. 185, 196.

[52] So Deubner, *Attische Feste* 190; this association is countenanced by Calame, *Thesée*, 381–82, n. 43, end. *Σ* vet. Ar. *Eq.* 729a II (= Suda ε 184) and *Σ* vet. Ar. *Plut.* 1054c treat the *Thargelia* (and *Pyanopsia*) as festivals of Sun and Seasons. One could on that basis equally well link the Sun and Seasons procession with *Pyanopsia*, but it is neater to identify it with the attested *Thargelia* procession and leave the *Pyanopsia* free for the boys' roamings with the *eiresione* (see n. 57 and Calame, loc. cit.). New decree: *SEG* XXXIII 115.

could be associated, and *Thargelia* fell at the time when the intense heats of high summer were just beginning. (On the other view we are still left with a notable procession for Sun and the Seasons, though not at the *Thargelia*.) Our source is Porphyry, who is making more or less verbatim use of Theophrastus.[53] The objects carried were εἰλυσπόα (unexplained), *agrostis* (a reed eaten by animals, conventionally identified as dog's tooth grass), ? small nuts in some form and one other object (the text is in chaos), pulses, 'oak', arbutus berries, barley grains, wheat grains, fig cake, cake of wheat and barley meal, 'pillar' (a type of ritual bread), a large pot (full of an 'allseed'?). 'Mud and grass' (ἰλύς, πόα) have been proposed in lieu of εἰλυσπόα,[54] with the justification that, according to Plutarch, primitive man fed on mud: in terms both of palaeography and cultural history this is admirably neat, but pompologically very hard to envisage. This procession does not neglect the cereal harvest, but also digresses from it to introduce non-cereal and even primeval or animal foods (perhaps 'oak' stands for acorn); these were all no doubt dependent for ripening on 'Sun and Seasons' (this is an argument against introducing 'mud'), but not at the specific time of the festival. Analogy makes it plausible that children, who like plants required the aid of powers such as the Sun and Seasons for growth, will have had an important place in the procession, but nothing is recorded.

'The Seasons' (Horai) had a sanctuary of their own at Athens, containing among other things an altar of 'Upright Dionysus', since (we are told) the fruit of the vine too is 'nurtured' by the Seasons. Philochorus records that at sacrifices to the Seasons the meat was boiled and not roasted as a way of 'supplicating the goddesses to avert excessive heat and drought', as symbolized by roasting.[55] At normal sacrifices, roasting of entrails was followed by boiling of the remaining meat; the point must be that at sacrifices to the Seasons the first of these two stages was omitted. Philochorus' language is general, but the detail would well suit the *Thargelia* celebrated at the start of the heats of summer.

One source speaks of first fruits being 'carried round' (as though from door to door) at the *Thargelia*.[56] Such carrying round was certainly characteristic of the other Apolline festival, *Pyanopsia*. The object carried was an *eiresione*. According to the Atticist grammarian Pausanias, an *eiresione* was 'an olive branch garlanded with wool, with fruits of the earth of various kinds hanging from it. A boy with both parents alive carries it out and places it in front of the temple of Apollo at the *Pyanopsia*.' (This and other clear statements in good sources, linking the *eiresione* with the *Pyanopsia* only, should prevail over two

---

[53] *Abst.* 2.7.1 Bouffartigue (p. 137.16–138.2 Nauck); procession at *Thargelia*: Arist. *Ath. Pol.* 56.5.

[54] So J. Bouffartigue in the Budé Porphyry, citing Plut. *De esu carnium* 2.993e–f.

[55] 328 FGrH F 173; for the sanctuary see id. F 5. A lost dedication to 'Seasons and Nymphs' (*IG* II² 4877) is undatable.

[56] Hesych. θ 104.

scholia which provide a loose amalgamated description of *Thargelia* and *Pyanopsia* and associate the *eiresione* with both.[57]) There were many private *eiresionai* in addition to this official one, as emerges for instance from several passages of Aristophanes which show that any normal house in Athens might be expected to have one outside the front door all year round; rather surprisingly we also once find an *eiresione* dedicated by members of the boule.[58] The orator Lycurgus associates the origin of the custom with an ancient famine, and says 'decorating a large olive branch with everything that the seasons produce at that time they dedicated it to Apollo in front of their doors, calling it *eiresione*, making first fruit offerings of all the products of the earth, because the suppliant branch placed with Apollo ended the famine in our land.' 'Everything' is the key word for Lycurgus; he even claimed that other Greeks called the festival '*Panopsia*', because at it 'they saw all crops'. What 'everything' might entail is harder to define (and we should certainly not expect every *eiresione* to have been identical). Lycurgus implies raw natural products only, but a respectable hellenistic scholar mentions shaped cakes. Late sources speak of *akrodrua*, a vague term that sometimes designates nuts but can be extended to almost any produce that grows on branches such as figs and grapes. A humorous little hexameter poem sung by those who carried the *eiresione* is quoted in several places:

> *Eiresione* brings figs and rich loaves
> and honey in a cup and olive oil to wipe oneself with
> and an unmixed wine bowl, so that she can go to sleep drunk[59]

Some suppose that the components of a typical *eiresione* are here described.[60] But if the song is a begging song—an obol for the *eiresione*—the figs and rich

---

[57] So Calame, *Thesée*, 291 with 376, n. 2 [+], taking up the argument of Deubner, *Attische Feste* 191–2 (which I wrongly rejected in *Miasma*, 25) about the scholia cited in n. 52 above. But I think Calame is wrong to say that the sources speak explicitly of use once a year only. Paus. Att.: ε 17 Erbse, cited with Crates FGrH 362 F 1 in Eust. *Il.* 22.496, p. 1283.7. The *eiresione/Pyanopsia* link is implicit also in Lycurg. fr. XIV. 2a Conomis (cf. XIV. 3: frs. 82–3 Blass), Plut. *Thes.* 22.4–7, and explicit e.g. in *Anecd. Bekk.* 1.246.27. Two scholia: n. 52 above. The 'boy with both parents alive' (ἀμφιθαλής) was perhaps recruited from the *Erysichthonidai* (IG II² 4991); in the Roman period a title of ἠρεσιώνης emerges (*Agora* XV. 399.5, etc.: S. Follet, *RPhil* 48, 1974, 30–2): cf. N. Robertson, *AJP* 105 (1984), 389–90, who points out that the two such boys who can be given an age were about 7, or less.

[58] Aristophanes: *Eq.* 729, cf. *Vesp.* 399, *Plut.* 1054. Boule: *Agora* XV 240.12.

[59] Cited e.g. in Plut. *Thes.* 22.7. Lycurgus: see n. 57. Hellenistic scholar: Menekles of Barka, FGrH 270 F 8 (cakes also in Σ vet. Ar. *Plut.* 1054b). Akrodrua: Σ vet. Ar. *Eq.* 729a (1). *Etym. Magn.* 303.18–20.

[60] So Calame, *Thesée*, 296–301. For Calame the *Pyanopsia* (in what is eaten and what is carried) relate to 'un premier menu civilisé'. But on his own showing (i.e. accepting the foodstuffs listed in the little song as of central importance at the festival) the menu is actually, in terms of imagined cultural history, quite a broad one, extending from figs, 'the first civilized food' (Ath. 74d) but one eaten raw, via beans, which require fire but not grinding, to the actual expression of the 'ground life', bread, and even, if we believe Menekles, cakes, which are already for Plato a stage beyond primeval simplicity (*Resp.* 373a). What then among vegetable products is excluded?

loaves and so on may rather be the blessings that are promised to those who give generously. On either view the song associates the *eiresione* with varied abundance.

Whatever an *eiresione* was usually hung with, the grounds for carrying it in procession at just this time of year are a little puzzling. There are difficulties in the attempt to see the *Pyanopsia* as a kind of 'harvest home', initiated by Lycurgus though it is. The festival occurred well on in autumn, close in time to the pre-ploughing (*Proerosia*) with which Lycurgus in fact associated it aetiologically. The grape harvest aside, agricultural activity at this time all looked forward to the next year. The only newly available fruits of the season were of slight importance. Perhaps the point was that these were the very last products to be collected: the *eiresione* ritual looked back over the whole summer and all its produce from the end.[61] If that is so, the rite was a marker of the seasons rather than a simple ritual transposition of agricultural concerns.

Two of the various festivals of Dionysus explicitly evoke particular stages in the life-cycle of the grape.[62] The first day of *Anthesteria* in February/March was *Pithoigia*, the 'opening of the jars' of the new wine. But it was a cultural decision to broach the wine at just this time. *Oschophoria* fell in the season of the vintage, and took its name from the carrying in procession of *oschoi*, vine branches carrying clusters of grapes. Yet this festival, which, almost more than any other, one might have expected to be diffused through every village of Attica, was conducted over a particular route by a restricted group of participants, the members of a particular *genos* chief among them; and the ritual details, which include cross-dressing by two youths, altogether resist reduction to simple viticultural concerns. This strangest of Attic festivals must have a treatment on its own.[63]

In regard to none of the festivals surveyed so far has the claim been that they are explicable without residue as 'farmers' festivals', but that this was one level at which they must have been understood by participants. The place

---

Calame mentions (302) fresh fruit, but even fresh fruit is surely a product of that ripening which he plausibly sees (317) as of importance for the festival.

[61] Calame, *Thesée*, 310 (cf. 317) writes: 'Récolte anticipée et récolte achevée placent Thargélies et Pyanopsies ... dans la perspective du même thème de l'alimentation civilisée'. *Pyanopsia* will have fallen roughly in the middle of the 'after harvest season' (μετόπωρον or φθινόπωρον), the season when 'hunger is light' (Bion fr. 2.4 in the edition of J. D. Reed, Cambridge 1997, from Stob. 1.8.39) because food is abundant (contrast Alcman *PMG* 20 on spring hunger). On the dating of seasons A. W. Gomme, *A Historical Commentary on Thucydides*, III (Oxford 1956), 699–721 is still useful, though his Thucydidean conclusions are disputed (Hornblower, *Commentary*, ii, 491–2).

[62] The ancients also so associated *Lenaia* (cf. ληνός, winepress), but the connection with λῆναι, bacchantes, is generally preferred today. Linguistically the connection with the feminine is easier but both are possible (Pickard-Cambridge, *Dramatic Festivals*[2], 29–30). The fact that Lenaion and *Lenaea* come too late for the vintage does not of itself exclude the 'winepress' etymology, such an anomaly being not unparallelled (cf. p. 199 on *Haloa*); but it does exclude a simple connection of the festival with actual wine-producing activities.

[63] See the Annexe to this chapter. For *Pithoigia* see p. 291.

of a great number of other festivals in the calendar cannot be even partially explained by criteria of this kind. We must look for others.

Hieros Gamos is easy: it falls in winter, the season generally favoured for marriage in Greece according to Aristotle, and in a month actually named Gamelion. Another dictum of Aristotle is that 'the old-established sacrifices and assemblies seem to occur after the harvest, as a kind of first-fruit offering. For that was when people had most time to spare.'[64] The peripatetic Stagirite was doubtless taking a panhellenic view, and we can apply his insight to Attica only with some glosses. We have seen that festivals of 'harvest home' type, like that so opulently evoked by Theocritus in the last lines of the seventh *Idyll*, are hard to find in Attica; the *Kronia* is a rather stronger claimant than the *Eleusinia*.[65] The *Mysteries* fell in Boedromion (September/October), and if participants thought of them in direct relation to the agricultural year at all, they are surely more likely to have looked forward to the impending ploughing and sowing than back to the now quite distant harvest.

Important festivals of other types, however, crowd into the high summer period. In the months of Skirophorion and Hekatombaion we find the *Dipolieia*, the festival of Zeus Soter, the *Synoikia*, the *Panathenaea* and probably the *Herakleia* of Marathon. The rites that gravitate hither are therefore those of Zeus and Athena. In particular it is noticeable that the only three festivals for which good numbers of celebrants climbed to the acropolis itself—the *Dipolieia*, *Synoikia*, *Panathenaea*—are all bunched in this period. High summer, it seems, was less the time when harvesters relaxed after their labours than when Attica looked inwards to its centre, a time of civic consciousness. Festivals of Athena are entirely absent, by contrast, from the six months stretching from Maimakterion to Munichion (November/December to April/May) and the case is almost the same for Apollo; in the three central winter months Zeus appears only as the husband of Hera, at the *Hieros Gamos*, and in a specialized form as Zeus Meilichios at the gloomy *Diasia*. The great god of that period is Dionysus, who has major festivals in three successive months. Indeed Dionysus on the one side and the major Olympians on the other come close to making a 1 : 3 division of the year at Athens, much as, according to the ancients, Dionysus and Apollo did at Delphi.[66] (The parallel becomes closer if in the Delphic case we see in Apollo simply the chief local representative of the Olympians.)

To some extent groups of festivals can be seen as gaining meaning by pairing, contrast, association. A case which is perhaps unique in the whole Greek world is the formal coupling of a festival of Mother at Agrai with one of Demeter and Kore at Eleusis to constitute *Lesser* and *Greater Mysteries*. There is an explicit link again between the *Chalkeia*, at which the weaving of

---

[64] *EN* 1160a 25–8: αἱ γὰρ ἀρχαῖαι θυσίαι καὶ σύνοδοι φαίνονται γίνεσθαι μετὰ τὰς τῶν καρπῶν συγκομιδὰς οἷον ἀπαρχαί· μάλιστα γὰρ ἐν τούτοις ἐσχόλαζον τοῖς καιροῖς. Marriage: Arist. *Pol.* 1335a 35–8. On *Hieros Gamos* see the entry in App. 1.

[65] See pp. 201–3.   [66] Plut. *E.Delph.* 9, 389 b–c ; Jeanmaire, *Couroi*, 246.

Athena's robe was begun, and the *Panathenaea* at which the lovely finished object was presented. Asclepius was unusual in having two festivals addressed to him under the same title at the same sanctuary. But they were held six months apart, and fell within or next to major festivals of two other saving or liberating gods, Dionysus and Demeter. This placement of the new god's festivals is likely to have been carefully planned.[67]

The women who prepared the *archon basileus'* wife for her marriage to Dionysus (at the *Anthesteria?*) had to swear that they had duly celebrated two lesser Dionysiac festivals, the *Theoinia* and *Iobaccheia*. And we could have guessed that the 'women's festivals' echoed one another even without the claim of a learned scholion that the underlying mythology and symbolism of *Thesmophoria*, *Skirophoria* and even '*Arretophoria*' were 'the same'.[68] The points of similarity between Apollo's two main festivals, *Pyanopsia* and *Thargelia*, are striking, as we have seen. It may even not be coincidence, though festivals of different gods are here concerned, that *Thesmophoria* with its third day 'Fair Birth' fell in the ninth month after *Hieros Gamos*, 'Sacred Marriage'.

A bold and elegant theory postulates a connection of this type between the festivals of two different months.[69] If correct, the theory would set the relation between the cycle of festivals and the year in a quite new light. It takes its start from the festivals of the month Pyanopsion. This was probably the period of the most intensive ritual activity in the whole year. The month is crowded with festivals of Demeter: *Proerosia*, *Stenia*, *Thesmophoria*. The other great theme of the month is young men. Boys were the main celebrants of the *Pyanopsia* on the 7th, 'youths' and 'ephebes' of the *Oschophoria* which fell about this time,[70] and it was at the *Apatouria* near the end of the month that young men were admitted definitively to the phratries by the haircut sacrifice, and left childhood behind along with their youthful locks. The Thorikos calendar registers an offering to be made to a hero 'Young Man' during Pyanopsion, possibly at or just before the *Pyanopsia* itself.[71] Both *Pyanopsia* and *Oschophoria* were associated aetiologically with Theseus, a young man who led a group of unmarried boys and girls on a perilous adventure. His own festival the *Theseia* apparently fell on the eighth of the month.[72] *Pyanopsia* and *Oschophoria* commemorated events relating to the hero's safe return from Crete: before his departure, he had gone with the twice seven from the Prytaneum to the Delphinion and there deposited a suppliant branch cut 'from the sacred olive tree', whence even now on Mounichion 7 'they send the maidens to perform propitiation'.[73] Most unfortunately, that rite is known

---

[67] See p. 344 (*Mysteries*); p. 227, n. 41 (*Chalkeia*); p. 462 (*Asklepieia*).

[68] Apollod. *Neaer*. 78; Σ Lucian p. 275.22–276 Rabe (cf. pp. 474 and 273).

[69] Jeanmaire, *Couroi*, 228–376, accepted e.g. by Calame, *Choeurs*, I, 228–30 (but not by id., *Thesée*, 432–5).

[70] On all this see the relevant entries in App. 1.

[71] *SEG* XXXIII 147. 26–7; cf. *Gifts for the Gods*, 146.

[72] Plut. *Thes*. 22–3; Mikalson, *Calendar*, 70 (on Plut. *Thes*. 36.4 and *IG* II² 1496.133–6).

[73] Plut. *Thes*. 18.1–2.

only from the single phrase of Plutarch just quoted. But the olive suppliant bough taken (we infer) by maidens to the Delphinion in the month Mounichion recalls the olive-wood *eiresione* (associated by Lycurgus with supplication) that boys carried at the *Pyanopsia* five months later.[74] Mounichion took its name from what must have been a great and ancient festival of Artemis Mounichia celebrated during it, one which doubtless marked the 'graduation' of the young girls who served in the sanctuary of Mounichion as 'bears'. At Marathon, a sacrifice was made to 'Young Man' in Mounichion.[75] Mounichion and Pyanopsion thus emerge, on the evidence of the festivals celebrated during them, as intimately associated with the young; and in myth Theseus and his companions are said to have set out during one, returned during the other. The hypothesis arises that the myth provides a model for the actual practices by which the young of Athens had once been brought to maturity: in Mounichion, still children, they left society, like the twice seven, for a period of seclusion, to return in Pyanopsion as adults. The myth in short reflects the ritual cycle by which—the difficult concept can no longer be avoided—the young were initiated.[76]

The theory has real attractions. The procession at the *Oschophoria* was led by two youths dressed as maidens: transvestism is often found in rites of passage, as a way, it seems, of dramatizing the transition that the rite exists to create, in this case that from girl-like boy to true man.[77] And the dinners brought by certain 'dinner bearers' at the same festival were said to commemorate those fetched for the twice seven by their mothers when in seclusion before departure: we note the 'initiatory motif' of seclusion.[78] There was a tribal race for ephebes at the *Oschophoria*: 'runner' in Crete was the standard expression for 'adult'. More radically, if the *Pyanopsia* can be detached from the maturing of crops and attached to the maturing of young men, its association with Apollo becomes very much easier to understand.

Parts of this theory work better than others. Rigorous criteria need to be met before it is appropriate to speak of 'initiation'.[79] Initiation is a rite of

[74] See above pp. 204–5.

[75] ZPE 130 (2000), 45–7, col. 2. 21; on the *Mounichia* see p. 231, n. 59.

[76] Jeanmaire, *Couroi*, 257, 277.

[77] See P. Vidal-Naquet, *Chasseur noir* 168 with n. 67 (116 with n. 56 in the Engl. tr.); J. Bremmer, 'Dionysos Travesti', in *L'Initiation. Actes du colloque international de Montpellier, 11–14 Avril 1991* (1992), I, 189–98; revised English version in *The Bucknell Review* 43 (1999), 183–200; D. D. Leitao, *AntCl* 14 (1995), 130–63. For this view of the *Oschophoria* see Jeanmaire, *Couroi*, 344–58; Calame, *Choeurs*, I, 228–32; Vidal-Naquet, *Chasseur Noir*, 164–9 (114–17 in the Engl. tr.).

[78] For details of the *Oschophoria* see the Annexe to this chapter; with the 'dinner-bearers' cf. the Samian ritual of Hdt. 3.48, with C. Sourvinou-Inwood, *OpAth* 17 (1988), 167–82 = ead. *Reading Greek Culture* (Oxford 1991), 244–84.

[79] For salutary scepticism on the whole subject see Price, *Religions*, 17, 94; for excellent historiographical reviews W. Burkert in *Le orse*, 13–27; F. Graf in *Initiation*, 3–24. One source of unclarity in the literature has been a failure to distinguish between strict rites of passage and rituals, such as choral dancing, which had a broader function within the socializing of children. The latter are much commoner in Greece than the former.

passage through which one moves from one social status to another. A rite that does not bring a change in status is not an initiation; conversely, the status change in question must not be realizable except by initiation (except in rare cases of 'representative' initiation, where a select group stands for a whole age-class). *Pyanopsia* surely did not constitute a rite of passage of the type in question. Large numbers of boys no doubt took part in it, but there is no reason to doubt that they could participate several years running if they chose. In the attested cases the central figure, the 'boy with both parents alive' who carried the official *eiresione*, was quite a youngster (7 or less).[80] The *Oschophoria* is rather more promising, since it did at least deploy a particular age-class, 'ephebes' (just how many is unknown). As for the ritual cycle extending from Mounichion to Pyanopsion, the rites of Mounichion do not concern boys at all.

Rites of passage certainly did exist for young men in classical Athens. There is nothing arcane or unfamiliar about them. A boy was admitted to a phratry (or his prior admission was confirmed), probably around the age 16, by the 'hair-cutting' sacrifice and a wine-offering for Heracles; at 18 he entered a deme, served as an ephebe (at least if he was of hoplite status or above), and then at last 'counted with the others'. As an ephebe he participated in a number of festivals of the city. These and these alone are the rites or processes of passage of the classical city. 'But once it had been different', the argument runs. Yet there is little independent reason to think so.[81] The best that can be claimed is that the *Oschophoria* may have had a special importance for those undergoing the 'proto-ephebate' which, we assume, existed prior to the reform of the institution by the law of Epicrates in the 330s.[82] It would not have been a rite de passage *stricto sensu*, but it would have encapsulated and condensed symbolically some of what the ephebate as a whole, the true transitional process or initiation, sought to achieve. As for the *Pyanopsia*, it was doubtless seen as a festival at which young boys—young shoots—were given their head, were allowed a place within the festival year, in a way appropriate to a festival of Apollo.

I revert, in conclusion, to the concept of 'New Year'. The concept of a single annual rejuvenation of things is, it was argued, alien to the Greek experience of time. But New Years need not come once in the year only, it has been

---

[80] See p. 205, n. 57.

[81] Phratry registration is certainly not a young institution, though deme registration postdates Clisthenes. As for the classical ephebate, there is no good reason to see it, with Jeanmaire, as a new, purpose-built form of military training which supplanted older ritual forms; most scholars would now with Vidal-Naquet see it as a transposition of older practices into a more modern context. On phratry admission see p. 458.

[82] See *Athenian Religion*, 253–5. Inscriptions attest the vastly increased range of festivals in which the ephebes of hellenistic Athens were involved, beginning with *SEG* XXIX 116 of 214/3; for tr. of a typical specimen (*IG* II² 1006) see Mikalson, *Hellenistic Athens*, 243–6.

suggested.[83] The formulation is rather quaint, but, if we substitute for 'New Year' the vocabulary of 'incision festivals' or 'festivals of renewal' or something of the kind, the concept may be helpful. We must not reify the concept, as if, any more than the rite of reversal, the thing had a fixed and firm and definitely recognizable shape. But some festivals, not necessarily the most important, suggest the idea of purification or fresh beginning more emphatically than others. The dispatch of scapegoats at the *Thargelia* 'cleansed the city'; the image of Athena was cleansed at *Plynteria* and *Kallynteria* in the same month. *Thargelia* was perhaps associated with bread made from the new wheat, and the festival of new wine, *Anthesteria*, seems likewise to have been treated as a new beginning of a broader kind. The day of *Plynteria* was a 'polluted day', as was the central day of *Anthesteria*, by contrast perhaps with the purified time that was to follow. The *Anthesteria* fell just before the start of spring, the month Thargelion with its several purifications at the start of summer. It is natural to look for a similar ritual incision in late summer or autumn.[84] The month Pyanopsion, during which the new agricultural cycle began, was also as we have seen a month of perpetual ritual activity; but the festivals in question lack to our knowledge explicit symbols of purification. *Pyanopsia* mirrors *Thargelia* in many ways, but as a festival of purification *Thargelia* is mirrored rather by the little-known *Pompaia* (honouring a different god, Zeus) in the following month. Even 'festivals of incision', therefore, prove a little ragged. We should anyway beware of excessive claims about the power of festivals to shape experience of time, to steer it through channels of stagnation and renewal. One does not need to proceed far into the new year to discover that it remains much like the old. In speaking of a festival of renewal one is speaking, above all, of an experience that is undergone at the festival itself.

ANNEXE: THE *OSCHOPHORIA*

The main literary sources are some aetiological passages in Plutarch's *Life of Theseus*, and an extract from Proclus' encyclopaedia which treats 'oschophoric songs'. We can begin with the latter:

Oschophoric songs were sung by the Athenians. The chorus at the festival was led by two youths, dressed as women, carrying a vine branch covered with healthy bunches of grapes (and this was called *osche*, whence the name of the songs). They say Theseus originated the practice. After he had voluntarily undertaken the voyage to Crete and

---

[83] See Versnel, *Transition and Reversal*, 119. He also speaks on the same page of 'incision ceremonies'.

[84] But one cannot tie these ritual incisions at all closely to Greek views about 'seasons' (whether two, three or four: on seasons see n. 61). It is misleading of Camps-Gaset, *L'Année des Grecs*, to entitle a chapter on *Anthesteria*, *Thargelia* and *Pyanopsia*, 'Les limites des trois saisons'. On Thargelion as a month of purifications (and on the *Pompaia*) see Parker, *Miasma*, 24–9; on *Anthesteria*, p. 315 below.

freed his homeland from the disaster of the tribute, he performed this rite as an expression of gratitude to Athena and Dionysus, who had both appeared to him on the island of Dia, using as assistants two youths who had been kept indoors in the shade. The Athenians' procession went from the Dionysiac shrine to the precinct of Athena Skiras. The chorus followed the youths and sang the songs.[85] [We will omit for the moment a final sentence.]

The festival included, therefore, a procession from one shrine to another; ahead walked the two 'youths dressed as women', behind followed a chorus singing oschophoric songs and, no doubt, performing the oschophoric dances that chance also to be attested.[86] The shrine of Athena Skiras was at Phaleron and evidently stood in close relation to a precinct there called 'the Oschophorion'.[87] If the vaguely identified starting point[88] was one of the Dionysiac shrines in Athens (as is generally assumed), then the procession covered some 7 kilometres. The 'oschophoric songs' can be compared with, for instance, the 'daphnephoric songs' that accompanied the ceremony of 'laurel-bearing' at Thebes. From a papyrus we learn that Pindar, who wrote *daphnephorika* in his home town, also composed at least one *oschophorikon* for '[lost name] the Athenian'; in the ancient edition it seems to have stood in or near the victory odes.[89] Pindar's poem cannot literally have been a victory ode, even though there was a race at the *Oschophoria*: *oschophorika* were performed at the festival itself and could not, unless improvised, celebrate victories won at the same festival. It must rather have honoured one of the two *oschophoroi*,[90] who were chosen, we are told independently, 'from those pre-eminent in birth and wealth'.[91] But it may well have dilated on the athletic prowess of the young *oschophoros* or his kin, in a way familiar from *Nemean* 11, a poem classed among the epinicians by the ancient editors even though formally written on the occasion of the installation of Aristagoras as *prytanis* of Tenedos; still more striking is the glorification of the various excellences of Agasicles and his family apparently occasioned by his service as *daphnephoros* in the Theban cult.[92]

---

[85] Procl. *Chrest.* ap. Phot. *Bibl.* 239, p. 322a.

[86] Aristocles ap. Ath. 631b, with the comments of Latte, *De saltationibus*, 76.

[87] Athena Skiras at Phaleron: Paus. 1.1.4, 1.36.4 (cf. *FGrH* 115 F 228 with Jacoby); cf. Hesych. s.v. 'Ωσχοφόριον. Deubner initially supposed that the Oschophorion was a subdivision of the precinct of Athena Skiras (*Attische Feste*, 143), later the reverse ('Weinlesefest', 4–5).

[88] All the sources are as vague as Proclus.

[89] See I. Rutherford and J. A. D. Irvine, *ZPE* 72 (1988), 43–51, on *POxy* 2451 fr. 17b = Pindar fr. 6c S/M. E. Knauer, *AA* 111 (1996), 239–46, associates a very fragmentary cup by the Triptolemus painter with the race.

[90] Irvine and Rutherford (see previous note) deny that Pindar could have written for one *oschophoros* out of two. The objections to the other view seem to me stronger; cf. Kavoulaki, 'Ritual Performance', 153.

[91] Istros *FGrH* 334 F 8; cf. Hesych. s.v. ὠσχοφόρια, *Anecd. Bekk.* 1.285.29–32.

[92] Pindar fr. 94b S/M (surely a *daphnephorikon* despite the doubts of Schachter, *Cults*, i, 85: see L. Lehnus, *BICS* 31, 1984, 77). According to Proclus, *Chrestomathy* (ap. Phot. *Bibl.* 320a 3–6) *parthenika, daphnephorika, tripodephorika, oschophorika* and *euktika* are mixed genres containing praise of men though addressed to gods. So they could be described as written for a named mortal (cf. Lehnus, op. cit., 78, on Pind. Fr. 94c).

From Pindar's involvement we get a taste of the social flavour of the occasion, in the mid-fifth century at least.

The aetiological connection with Theseus touched on by Proclus is more fully developed by Plutarch, on the authority of the Atthidographer Demon.[93] To increase the number of his male companions Theseus had disguised two girlish-looking but doughty friends as maidens; thus the famous expedition of the twice seven consisted, in fact, of five maidens, seven youths and two transvestites. On their return from Crete, Theseus processed along with the two singular youths, 'dressed as are now those who carry the *oschoi*. And they carry them as an expression of gratitude to Dionysus and Ariadne because of the myth, or perhaps rather because they came home while the fruit harvest (*opora*) was being got in.'[94] A new detail follows. 'The dinner-bearers are included and share in the sacrifice to imitate the mothers of the children on whom the lot fell. For they used to go to them with bread and relishes. And myths are told'—possibly the sole attestation in all Greek heortology of the telling of myths at a festival—'because the mothers told myths to their children to cheer them up and console them.' Other sources explain that the original 'dinner-bearing' was necessary because the twice seven were shut up in the temple of Athena 'in order to be sent to the Minotaur'.

In a different context Plutarch mentions a separate detail, the blend of joy and sadness that characterized Theseus' return. 'And so even now at the *Oschophoria* they say that it is not the herald but the herald's staff that is crowned, and the participants chant over the libations *eleleu, eleleu, iou, iou*, though the one cry expresses enthusiastic hope, the other shock and consternation (*Thes.* 22. 4).' (This emotional ambiguity or tension is also characteristic of another Dionysiac festival, the *Anthesteria*.) Finally we learn from the sentence of Proclus that immediately follows the passage quoted that 'ephebes from each tribe competed in racing with one another. And the winner drank of the so-called pentaple cup (πενταπλόα), which was mixed from olive oil and wine and honey and cheese and barley.' How many ephebes competed per tribe, and whether individually or as a team, we do not learn.[95] Two further sources that mention the race assert that the runners carried vine-boughs and that their course too was 'from the precinct of Dionysus to the temple of

---

[93] *Thes.*23.2–4 = Demon FGrH 327 F 6.

[94] Word order imposes this translation (so Jacoby, comm. on Philochorus FGrH 328 F 14–16, p. 295), as against 'they bring the *oschoi* to Dionysus out of gratitude' (Deubner, 'Weinlesefest').

[95] The other references to the race (following notes) are no clearer. For old speculations see the references in E. Kadletz, *GRBS* 21 (1980), 370, n. 23; note especially Jacoby, n. 170 to comm. on Philochorus FGrH 328 F 14–16. Analogy and references to 'the winner' certainly suggest that there was just one race, not as is sometimes supposed one per tribe. On the other hand the mention of a single winner does not absolutely exclude racing by teams, if we allow the possibility that the last runner in a relay could count as winner on behalf of his team. Very strangely, the festival is not mentioned in the prolix ephebic decrees (Pélékidis, *Éphébie*, 226–8); nor is there evidence that the teams were financed by liturgists.

Athena Skiras'; one adds that their parents had still to be alive. All these details seem more appropriate to the actual two *oschophoroi*—it is independently attested that they carried vine boughs and followed this route—and the attribution of them to runners is likely to be a product of confusion.[96] But a claim that the winner, after drinking the pentaple drink, 'revels with a chorus',[97] cannot be explained away so easily—unless it represents an ill-informed guess about the nature of the 'oschophoric songs'. More drastically, one source, Aristodemus, assigns what is evidently the same race not to the *Oschophoria* but to a different festival, the *Skira*. Conciliation is impossible, and we have to choose. A 'competition' at the *Oschophoria* chances to be attested also in an inscription, and for this and other reasons much the most plausible view is that Aristodemus erred—as was easy to do, given the role of Athena Skiras at the *Oschophoria*.[98]

If these analyses are correct, a credible programme for the day can be established:[99] first, the procession to Phaleron, headed by the *oschophoroi* and accompanied by oschophoric singing; then, various activities at Phaleron— the libations, the 'dinner-bringing', the race; finally, perhaps, a *komos* escorting the victor back to Athens. The chorus that sang during the procession could on this account have dissolved itself into the ephebes who competed in the races later in the day.

A new dimension was added in 1938 by the publication of the arbitration of the *Salaminioi*. A connection between the festival and a specific *genos* had not hitherto been suspected; but the role of the *Salaminioi* at the *Oschophoria* has been, ever since, a paradigm case of such an association. The priestess of Athena Skiras, it emerged, was a 'Salaminian', and the *genos* used the

---

[96] So Deubner, *Attische Feste*, 145 (on Aristodemos *FGrH* 383 F 9, Σ Nic. *Alex.* 109).

[97] Aristodemos *FGrH* 383 F 9, accepted by Deubner, *Attische Feste*, 145-6.

[98] The other view was taken by Jacoby, commentary on Philochorus *FGrH* 328 F 14–16, pp. 294–5, 300–5 (accepted, but misrepresented, by Parke, *Festivals*, 77–80, 160–1). On this view the goal of the race was not the temple of Athena Skiras at Phaleron, but another, only doubtfully attested (p. 175, n. 82), at Skiron west of Athens; and the *Oschophoria* itself was enacted wholly at Phaleron and had no connection with a shrine of Dionysus. Jacoby had to postulate the coexistence of two festivals at which *oschophoroi* were active, one of them taking place early in the summer, long before the grape harvest (Jacoby's appeal to stored grapes, notes to comm. on Philoch. loc. cit., p. 220, scarcely meets the difficulty), and to issue 'an impressive warning' (he meant 'emphatic') against being swayed by the epigraphic evidence for a competition (*LSS* 19.61) mentioned in the text. All this is pointless masochism. E. Kadletz suggests (*GRBS* 21, 1980, 363–71) that the *oschophoros* of the Hagios Eleutherios calendar (Deubner, *Attische Feste*, pl. 35, the third figure) is portrayed as a victor (but it is uncertain, as we have seen, that actual competitors carried grape-clusters).

[99] So in effect Deubner, *Attische Feste*, 142–6, and L. Ziehen, *RE* s.v. *Oskophoria*, 1537–43. Deubner's vindication of the authority of Proclus seems to me uniformly convincing. If one doubts the testimony of Proclus everything becomes uncertain, and it becomes possible to postulate (e.g.) a race to Phaleron in the morning followed by a procession back to Athens later in the day (this old reconstruction was revived, against Pfohl and Deubner, by Jeanmaire, *Couroi*, 346, n. 1). E. Kadletz, *GRBS* 21 (1980), 371, suggests that both race and procession went from Athens to Phaleron. No source attests a procession from Phaleron to Athens, and Proclus speaks of the contrary; it would however fit the *aition* of Plut. *Thes.* 22–3.

goddess' shrine as a place of meeting and display; the Salaminians appointed a special *archon* whose job it was to choose the *oschophoroi* and 'dinner-bearers', *deipnophoroi*, very possibly from within the *genos* itself; and ordinary members of the *genos* feasted at the festival, in part no doubt on the 'loaves in the shrine of Skiras' (put there probably by the 'dinner-bearers') to a share of which they were entitled.[100] Extra portions of the Skiras loaves went to the various Salaminian priests and priestesses, and to certain officiants who are likely to have had a role at the *Oschophoria* itself: a herald (already familiar from Plutarch), a basket-bearer (*kalathephoros*), and certain women mysteriously termed 'Handles' (Κῶπαι).[101] But we still do not know how the chorus that sung the oschophoric songs was recruited, nor even with full confidence the gender of its members. Again, it is scarcely certain that, since the 'dinner-bearers' were 'imitating' actions performed by the mothers of the twice seven, they must themselves have been married women.[102]

The inscription did not even resolve a long-standing controversy about the chief honorand of the festival.[103] The procession moved, unusually, from a precinct of Dionysus to one of Athena. As far as explicit testimony goes, two lexicographers speak of a festival of Athena Skiras, but Plutarch treats the rite as, in part at least, an act of gratitude to Dionysus for mythical services rendered. The peculiarities of the ritual—the transvestism, the vine-branch, the cry of *eleleu*, the concluding revel—are, it seems, exclusively Dionysiac,[104] but the main setting is unquestionably a temple of Athena. We should surely assign the festival to both gods. Even if the combination were a product of the contingencies of history, through the takeover of a Dionysiac rite by a *genos* devoted to the cult of Athena Skiras as it might be, it would remain important that, within the logic of polytheism, the graft of Dionysus onto Athena was one that could take.

---

[100] *LSS* 19 *passim*, esp. 20–4, 41–50, 61–2; cf. *Athenian Religion*, 309–11. Lines 21–4 and 61–2 suggest that meat was available as well as bread.

[101] W. S. Ferguson, *Hesperia* 7 (1938), 51–2, unpersuasively suggested that they turned the handles of the mills that ground sacred corn for the Skiras loaves (cf. *aletrides*). *Kopo* is a term for a sacred olive-branch used in the Theban *daphnephoria*: Procl. *Chrest.* ap. Phot. *Bibl.* 239, 321b. The *kalathos* is distinct from the familiar *kanoun*; what it might have contained in a given case is unknowable (cf. N. Hopkinson, *Callimachus*, Hymn to Demeter, Cambridge 1984, 41–2; Latte, *De saltationibus*, 81–2). There may well be a connection with the *deipnophoria*.

[102] As is assumed by Deubner, 'Weinlesefest', 7, and Calame, *Thésée*, 338. The chorus are generally supposed to be male, but the consensus is challenged by Calame, *Choeurs*, i, 231; *Thésée*, 335 (where he postulates a mixed chorus); he is wrong, however, to say that Procl. *Chrest.* ap. Phot. *Bibl.* 239, 321a 33–322 a 30 treats *oschophorika* as a subdivision of *partheneia*, though he does so treat *daphnephorika*.

[103] See still, for Athena, Jacoby, comm. on Philochorus *FGrH* 328 F 14–16, pp. 294–6; for Dionysus, Deubner, 'Weinlesefest', 10–11.

[104] Calame, *Thésée*, 335. Note too the association between *oschophoroi* and bacchic dances in Ath. 631b. Vidal-Naquet, *Chasseur noir*, 166 (115 in the Engl. tr.), suggests an association between transvestism and Athena Skiras; but his case is much weakened if no connection exists between the festival Skira and Athena Skiras (see p. 175). Plutarch: n. 94 above. Lexicographers: Suda ω 256; *Anecd. Bekk.* 1.318.25.

Strangely enough, the interpretation of the festival by the earlier critics was not much affected by the debate about its main honorand, energetically though this was conducted. The *Oschophoria* related, it was clear, to the gathering of the grapes and the cycle of the year, and if Athena Skiras was its recipient then Athena Skiras would have to be brought into association with the life of the fields.[105] Inconvenient details were simply smoothed away. The two *oschophoroi* were not dressed, shockingly, in women's clothes, but in the old-fashioned Ionic chiton which as good traditional ritualists they continued to wear long after it had come to seem effeminate. As for the 'dinner-bearers', what more useful provision during a long day's ritual away from home than a lunch box brought by a devoted female?[106]

These details, by contrast, are, as we have seen, central for a more recent 'initiatory' interpretation.[107] Further details have been added in support. If persons undergoing initiation are marginal in one sense, so too in another are the site of the festival—the coastline—and the presiding *genos*, the immigrant *Salaminioi*; and does not the goddess's very name evoke the substance *skiron*, a white clay known to a late source as 'mystic clay' because of its regular use, smeared on the face, as a ritual disguise?[108] But it is not so clear that the *Salaminioi* were perceived as 'marginal', and on these points it may be unwise to insist. Perhaps one can find stronger support in the gods of the festival. On the one hand, new evidence from Macedonia has made the association between 'Dionysus False Man' (Pseudanor) and rites of passage much firmer.[109] On the other, a case can be made for linking with the festival the daughters of Cecrops, powers as closely associated with the growth of children and with ephebes as it is possible to be. We know that the *Salaminioi* controlled a priesthood of Aglauros, Pandrosos and Kourotrophos. The new Photius has given us an expanded version of a long-known article on the subject of 'dinner-bearing'. It runs: 'the dinners brought to the daughters of Cecrops, Herse and Aglauros and Pandrosos. They were brought at considerable expense in accord with a mystic doctrine by ambitious and free-spending individuals.' Perhaps this 'dinner-bearing', which is usually taken to be a quite distinct rite, celebrated on the acropolis,[110] should rather be identified with that of the *Oschophoria*; these 'ambitious and free-spending

---

[105] So W. S. Ferguson, *Hesperia* 7 (1938), 40, and Jacoby, commentary on Philochorus F 14–16, p. 303. Pfuhl, *De Pompis*, 50, and Deubner (*Attische Feste*, 143–4, and 'Weinlesefest', *passim*), by contrast, treated her relation to the festival as contingent and trivial.

[106] Deubner, *Attische Feste*, 144.

[107] See p. 209.

[108] Γύψος μυστιπόλος, Nonn. *Dion.* 27. 228 (cf. Jeanmaire, *Couroi*, 355–6; Ellinger, *Légende nationale phocidienne*, 174–9). Vidal-Naquet, *Chasseur noir*, 165 (115 in the Engl. tr.), notes an association between places named Skiras *vel sim.* and 'localités marginales' (cf. Ellinger, loc. cit., 76–88); see ibid. for the *Salaminioi* as 'un génos marginal, frontière'.

[109] M. B. Hatzopoulos, *Rites de passage*, 63–85, with Bremmer (n. 77 above).

[110] Jacoby, comm. on Philochorus 328 *FGrH* F 183: 'The deipnophoria is a rite which by its nature is not confined to a particular festival or a particular deity'; but he goes on to note that there are only the two instances which I am now considering. Jacoby contrasted the selected

individuals' would be at home in the Pindaric world of oschophoric songs, though doubtless not there alone. In that event the three Cecropids would acquire a place in the festival, and its distinctive relation to ephebes would become very hard to doubt. An 'ephebes' rite' is perhaps what we should call it, since both 'rite of passage' and 'initiation', as we have seen, are misleading.

A problem for most interpretations of the festival is its geographical specificity. A mere celebration of the vintage ought to take place in Athens, or in a vinous region such as the deme Icaria, or throughout Attica. But the *Oschophoroi* and company leave Athens along a precisely defined route to a particular and unusual destination. The interpretation as an 'ephebes' rite' can embrace this withdrawal of the young men from the centre with relish. And the arrival of the future citizens in a sanctuary of the civic goddess is not an embarrassment. To make this interpretation work, one must doubtless exclude young women from the oschophoric chorus, which is not hard to do. The female presence in the rite is as providers of food, *deipnophoroi*, for young men. And, which is crucial, one must look beyond the two *oschophoroi* to the chorus who follow them and, more specifically, to the many ephebes who conduct the tribal foot-race. If, under the guise of celebrating the maturation of grapes, the ritual more centrally concerns the growth of effeminate-seeming young men to bearded manhood, the two festival transvestites must stand for their whole age-class.[111]

deipnophoroi of the *Oschophoria* with the mass offerings to the Cecropids attested by the lexicographical notice in the corrupt form (*Anecd. Bekk.* 1.239.7 = Philoch. loc. cit.) in which he read it; the version preserved in Photius δ 138 (quoted in the text) removes the contrast. A vague reference in Athenagoras, *Leg.* 1 adds nothing. For the link of the Cecropids with maturation see pp. 433–4 below. Salaminian priesthood: *Athenian Religion*, 309, 311.

[111] For a different approach see Calame, *Thésée*, 128–9; 143–8; 324–7; 338–9. Calame focuses on the various foodstuffs associated with the festival: grape-clusters, a raw fruit; the *pentaploa*, a prepared food but one made from the ingredients used, in Greek perception, by primitive man, and finally 'Skiras loaves', preferred food of modern civilized humanity. This mixing of values in the alimentary code reflects the character of a rite in which (on his view) youths, maidens and mature women all participate (it is not therefore an initiation) and which has as recipients two seldom associated gods. The fundamental movement is from Dionysus to Athena, from disorder to civilization.

11

Parthenoi in Ritual

The ritual roles of boys have come up here and there in previous chapters, and we have tackled the question of rites of passage for boys, which exist, and initiation, which does not (except in the sense that this is what the ephebate is). An annexe to this chapter will treat the rituals in which boys of the upper classes participated during their education prior to the ephebate. Girls earn a chapter of their own.[1] The main justification for this asymmetrical treatment is that, in contrast to boys, many girls went through a ritual process which involved a period of seclusion and can reasonably be seen as a form of initiation. But there is also rather more to be said about other ritual roles assigned to *parthenoi*. This may be partly due to chances of documentation, and the question whether in reality boys or girls had a larger role in the ritual life of the city is too bound up with questions of definition to be worth pursuing. What is certain is that *parthenoi* were in some ways[2] put forward in ritual contexts. The clearest expression of this is the necessary presence of a *parthenos* as 'basket-bearer' in every sacrificial procession. The most crucial ritual role of married women, at festivals such as the *Thesmophoria*, was separate, and secret. In visible rituals it fell to a large extent to *parthenoi* to embody the feminine presence in the city.

Like every other discussion of the topic, this too will start from a famous passage of Aristophanes' *Lysistrata*, in which the chorus explain why they will now offer good advice to the city.[3] It is, they say, because the city has reared them up in comfort and renown (χλιδῶσαν ἀγλαῶς ἔθρεψέ με), and they now owe wise advice in return. To illustrate the advantages that they have enjoyed, they list four religious functions that they claim to have discharged. They thus provide rare 'native' testimony[4] to the idea, familiar to outside observers, that it was 'cultic citizenship' above all that gave women a sense of

---

[1] They have earned an interesting book, Brulé, *Fille d'Athènes*.

[2] But contrast pp. 182–3 on the effacement of 'maiden choruses' at Athens. And there were to our knowledge no 'virgin priestesses' at Athens (Parker, *Miasma*, 90): even the priestess of Artemis at Brauron could be a mother (Hyp. fr. 199 Blass). I speak generically of unmarried girls as *parthenoi*, but strictly *parthenoi* are unmarried girls of marriageable age, girls ripe for marriage (Redfield, *Locrian Maidens*, passim).

[3] 638–47. M. B. Walbank's attempt to relate all these offices to the cult of Artemis at Brauron (*CQ* 31, 1981, 276–81) overlooks Lys. 21.5, which defends the reading ἠρρηφόρουν and so the reference to Athena in 641.

[4] Cf. Eur. *Melanippe Desmotis*, fr. 660.12–22 Mette.

belonging to that city from whose political deliberations they were excluded. They also, rather surprisingly, treat their religious services not as contributions that they have made to the life of the city but as privileges that have been granted to them, ways in which they were reared up in comfort and renown. An internal contradiction in the chorus's position perhaps emerges here: they profess to speak as everywoman, but most of the offices that they list were occupied only by a small number of members of a social elite. In the resolutely unrealistic genre of comedy, the distortion can pass muster.

The chorus begin 'Straightaway when I was 7 I was an *arrephoros*'. They are claiming to have served at the youngest possible age, the permissible range being from 7 to 11.[5] There are many further references to such *arrephoroi* or *errephoroi* or later even *ersephoroi*—the variants are puzzling, the etymology beyond recovery, but we are certainly dealing with a single office.[6] The many statues of *arrephoroi* known from the third century onwards illustrate the pride taken in their young kinswomen's office by the evidently prosperous men and women who set them up.[7] The statues were dedicated either to Athena or to Athena and Pandrosos, the latter being that daughter of Cecrops who had a temple on the acropolis just next to the Erechtheum.[8] Pandrosos (probably: but 'Pandora' is a variant) was 'along with her sisters the first to prepare woollen clothing for mortals', and the *arrephoroi* along with the priestess 'warped the loom for' the *peplos* of Athena at the *Chalkeia*. Many suppose that they are accordingly shown holding the *peplos* on the Parthenon frieze.[9]

---

[5] *Etym. Magn.* 149.18–20 (= *Anecd. Bekk.* I. 202.3–5). L. van Sichelen, 'Nouvelles orientations dans l'étude de l'arréphorie attique', *AntCl* 56 (1987), 88–102, raises the possibility that the *arrephoria* only took place in Panathenaic years (whence the age range). The story in *POxy* 664 a 32, which implies a nubile (and publicly visible) *arrephoros*, is better told in reference to a *kanephoros* in Diod. 9.37.1 (cf. Brulé, *Fille d'Athènes*, 287–8).

[6] Against Deubner, *Attische Feste*, 13–15, see especially W. Burkert, 'Kekropidensage und Arrephoria', *Hermes* 94 (1966), 1–25, at 6 (cf. *Homo Necans*, 150, n. 62). Burkert makes the decisive point that the ancient grammarians who discuss the variants never doubt that only one ceremony is in question; their 'procession in honour of Herse' (even, Moeris s.v. ἑρρηφόροι, 'dew-bringing to Herse') is, pace Deubner and Jacoby, comm. to *FGrH* 334 F 27, nothing other than the Arrephoria (G. Donnay accordingly assigns Herse a role at the Arrephoria, 'L'arréphorie: initiation ou rite civique?', *Kernos* 10, 1997, 177–206, at 196: for a listing of all sources for the rite see ibid. 203–5; cf. Mansfield, *Robe of Athena*, ch. 5). Epigraphic documents of otherwise absolutely comparable type may display either form (Threatte, *Grammar*, I, 127–8, who discusses the etymology). No dissent from Burkert in Brulé, *Fille d'Athènes*, 79–82, or N. Robertson, 'The Riddle of the Arrephoria at Athens', *HSCP* 87 (1983), 241–88, at 244–50.

[7] *IG* II[2] 3461, 3465–6, 3470–3, 3482, 3486 (?), 3488, 3496–7, 3515–16, 3528, 3554–6, 3634. Some of the later instances were dedicated by 'council and people'. For reference in other contexts to quondam service as *arrephoros* see *IG* II[2] 3960, *AJA* 45 (1941), 541. *IG* II[2] 3472, 3488 and 3515 include Pandrosos. See Kirchner's notes on 3473 and 3488, with Tracy, *Attic Letter-Cutters*, 60, for prosopographical connections.

[8] See Paus. 1.27.2; Philoch. *FGrH* 328 F 67; cf. Travlos, *Pictorial Dictionary*, figs. 91, 281; Kron, *Phylenheroen*, 41, n. 149. For her association with Athena see further Philoch. F 10 and ? *PMG* 888. The claim of ΣRΓ Ar. *Lys.* 439a that 'Athena is called Pandrosos' does not seem to me reliable.

[9] Cf. p. 227, n. 41. A different image of the *arrephoros* or something similar is detected by M. Schmidt, *AM* 83 (1968) 203–4, with pl. 76, on the alabastron Athens NM 17917 = *ARV*[2] 735/107: a human girl fleeing from Athena like a frightened Cecropid. Woollen clothing: Suda π 2892.

About the manner of selection for the various honorific posts open to children we usually have no more information than snobbish statements by the lexicographers that they were filled by 'the well born'. One exception is the 'hearth-initiate': according to a lexicographer he or she was chosen by 'sortition from pre-selected candidates', but a fourth-century inscription ordains that nomination for this symbolically most potent office could be made by 'anyone who wishes' and that the *basileus* should (merely) draw lots among the candidates so proposed.[10] (But a small doubt remains. The stone is fragmentary, and the gaps are large enough to have contained some restriction on this apparently most egalitarian provision.) As for the *arrephoroi*, an anonymous fragment preserved in a lexicographer speaks of the *basileus* 'selecting' them (the word used is the ancient hieratic verb, ἐπιώψατο). Such selection of cult functionaries at a priest or magistrate's inclination is found in other contexts, and can readily be envisaged as the standard archaic practice. But according to Harpocration 'four *arrephoroi* were elected by show of hands because of good birth, and two were chosen to start the weaving of the *peplos* and do other jobs concerning it.'[11] Did practice change? Or was it the *basileus* who selected two *arrephoroi* from a list of four elected by the people,[12] in a compromise between civic and hieratic principle? This latter hypothesis is neat, though evidently not certain. It is interesting to let the mind play on the postulated 'election' of four little *arrephoroi*. It did not embody the full principle of the radical democracy, since the girls were elected, not chosen by lot, and supposedly on grounds of good birth. And, more striking, this would be the only context in which the assembly voted among persons of that gender. That anomaly is accompanied by another. There was a doubtless rather minor liturgy (for it appears only once) called *arrephoria*, which probably required the liturgist to feed and clothe the white-dressed maidens during their period of service.[13] This would make it the only known liturgy at state level of which the beneficiaries were females.

---

[10] *Anecd. Bekk.* 1.204.19–20; *Agora* XVI 56. 41–2; Clinton, *Sacred Officials*, 99–100. On this post see p. 343 below.

[11] Anonymous fragment: Suda ε 2504; cf. *Athenian Religion*, 250, and, on the functionaries recruited by festival archons, 309, 331. Usage of the verb ἐπιώψατο recommends the supplement ἐς at the end of line 3 in *IG* I³ 3 (so E. Vanderpool in *Studies Presented to Sterling Dow*, GRB Monograph 10, 1984, 295–6) rather than the δέ accepted in IG. Harpocration: α 239.

[12] So e.g. W. Burkert, *Hermes* 94 (1994), 4 [+]. Others suppose that the *basileus'* choice was ratified by vote of the assembly (Parke, *Festivals*, 141; Mansfield, *Robe of Athena*, 270), or that the assembly voted on a shortlist made by him (Brulé, *Fille d'Athènes*, 83). The separate question arises whether the unsuccessful two became second-class *arrephoroi* with different duties (Deubner, *Attische Feste*, 11–12; N. Robertson, *HSCP* 87, 1983, 276–7; cf. Mansfield, *Robe of Athena*, 271; why then a single name, wonders Brelich, *Paides e Parthenoi*, 231), including perhaps the ritual described by Pausanias, or, more plausibly, were not confirmed in the function at all (W. Burkert, *Hermes* 94, 1966, 3–4).

[13] Lys. 21.5, with J. K. Davies, *JHS* 87 (1967), 37.

Apart from their involvement with Athena's *peplos*, all that we know of the ritual activities of the *arrephoroi* comes from Pausanias:

Two maidens known by the Athenians as *arrephoroi* dwell not far from the temple of Athena Polias. For a period they live with the goddess, and when the festival comes they do the following at night. They place on their heads objects which the priestess of Athena gives them to carry; neither she who gives it knows what kind of thing she is giving, nor do those who carry it understand. There is an enclosure in the city [*or* 'on the acropolis'] not far from the so-called Aphrodite in Gardens, and through it a natural underground passage downwards. The maidens descend by this. They leave below what they were carrying and bring back another covered object which they get there. Then they are dismissed and other maidens are brought to the acropolis in their place.[14]

The topography of the passage has been much discussed. When a sanctuary of Aphrodite was discovered on the north slope of the acropolis in 1931, it became very tempting to suppose that the maidens went down an originally Mycenaean stairway that led inside the rock of the acropolis from the top to a point quite close to the newly excavated precinct. A consequence was that the maidens were descending, literally and metaphorically, from Athena to Aphrodite.[15] But this appealingly concrete and dramatic vision does not quite fit the words of Pausanias, whose precinct of 'Aphrodite in the Gardens' (which he mentions anyway as a landmark, not a destination) ought to be the attested one in the lower town, not that of an Aphrodite below the acropolis whose cult title is otherwise unknown. The matter is not resolved—Pausanias might be slightly unclear, our information might be deficient—but there is no firm ground here to build on.

A muddled scholion on Lucian apparently says that the objects brought up by the *arrephoroi* were 'secret sacred objects made from dough: imitations of snakes and of male genitals'.[16] And it is very generally believed that the ritual relates in some way to a central Athenian myth: Athena entrusted the baby Erichthonius/Erechtheus to the three daughters of Cecrops to guard, hidden in a basket which they were instructed not to open; they, or two among them, disobeyed, and, terrified by the huge snake wrapped around the babe that they found inside, leapt to their death from the acropolis. Pandrosus, the

---

[14] Paus. 1.27.3. For the translation of the phrase ἔστι δὲ περίβολος ἐν τῇ πόλει τῆς καλουμένης Ἀφροδίτης οὐ πόρρω see E. Kadletz, *AJA* 86 (1982), 445–6, who argues (and a check with *TLG* has confirmed) that πόρρω in Pausanias is never adverbial except when used in first position to connect with what precedes. The *peribolos* here encloses a religious passageway, just as places where in myth gods or heroes entered or left the underworld could be bounded by a *peribolos* (Paus. 2.36.7, 9.8.3); there is no need therefore to associate the *peribolos* with a divine owner in the genitive (as C. Calame argues against Kadletz, *I greci e l'eros*, Rome/Bari 1992, 201, n. 27).

[15] So Burkert, *Homo Necans*, 150–4. See contra e.g. N. Robertson, *HSCP* 87 (1983), 251–3; for subsequent discussion see Brulé, *Fille d'Athènes*, 89–91; Pirenne-Delforge, *Aphrodite*, 54–9.

[16] Σ Lucian p. 276.15–17 Rabe; cf. p. 273 below, N. Robertson, *HSCP* 87 (1983), 255–7.

honorand of the *Arrephoria*, was also a Cecropid, and in many versions the one good sister who obeyed the goddess.[17]

Between myth and rite there are, therefore, clear similarities—and differences no less clear. Myths and rituals, it is sometimes said, have the same structure, but myths dramatize what cults present in more mundane terms. But in this case the ritual moves to an ending—the bringing back to the acropolis of new sacred objects—quite absent from the story. The relation will rather have to be seen as one in which the real *arrephoroi* pass a test which their mythical prototypes have failed.[18] In the myth, the daughters of Cecrops briefly had charge of the baby Erichthonius, who was a kind of prototype of all Athenian children. They proved but sorry nurses; yet two of them appear associated in cult with Kourotrophos, 'child-rearer'.[19] Were the *arrephoroi* too, then, anticipating in play their future duties to their own children? Their attested ritual actions do not obviously evoke anything of that kind.

Everything about the *Arrephoria* is obscure, even its status as a festival.[20] Is it possible both to study Greek religion, and to retain a measure of everyday canniness and caution? If it is, it will be well not to attempt to solve 'the riddle of the *Arrephoria*'.[21] Two important points can, however, be extracted from Pausanias' account. First, since a new pair of *arrephoroi* were 'brought to the acropolis' at the same festival which saw their predecessors discharged, there was always a team in post, and the term of service was annual. Second, 'for a certain period' the two maidens lived 'with the goddess'. They lodged, it is

[17] So e.g. Paus.1.18.2; Apollod. 3.14.6; a different tradition in Amelasagoras *FGrH* 330 F 1 (see Jacoby ad loc.). See in general U. Kron in *LIMC* s.v. *Aglauros, Herse, Pandrosos*, 283–98; Brulé, *Fille d'Athènes*, 28–79. The link between rite and myth goes back to F. G. Welcker, *Griechische Götterlehre*, III (Göttingen 1862), 105–6; note too J. E. Harrison in Harrison and M. de G. Verrall, *Mythology and Monuments of Ancient Athens* (London, 1890), pp. xxxiii–xxxvi; ead. *Prolegomena*, 133–4. No ancient source (not even Pausanias, *pace* Mansfield, *Robe of Athena*, 322, n. 51) explains the ritual by reference to the myth; the *Arrephoria* was, however, associated with Herse as well as with Pandrosus (whence doubtless, not vice versa, the form *hersephoros*: Jacoby on *FGrH* 334 F 27), and thus by implication with the sisters as a group. On the other hand, the supposed reference to semen as 'dew' in Callimachus' account of the Erichthonius myth has vanished from A. S. Hollis' edition of *Hecale* (Oxford 1990: his fr. 70.4). Brulé, *Fille d'Athènes*, 108, revives the old conjecture (Palmer, as cited in Alberti's ed. of Hesych.) Μοῖραι in the corrupt gloss of Hesych. α 611: Ἀγλαυρίδες · †μυραι † παρ᾽ Ἀθηναίοις (νύμφαι or κόραι have also been conjectured). Given that the Aglaurids were not worshipped as a group (despite Eur. *Ion* 23 Ἀγλαυρίδες παρθένοι) this seems to me too bold.

[18] So Redfield, *Locrian Maidens*, 120.

[19] Note especially the Salaminian joint priesthood of Aglauros, Pandrosos and Kourotrophos (*LSS* 19 (RO 37) 12; *Athenian Religion*, 309); cf. *IG* II² 1039.58, a sacrifice by ephebes to Athena Polias, Kourotrophos and Pandrosos; Kearns, *Heroes of Attica*, 24–5; Brulé, *Fille d'Athènes*, 38. Erichthonius as prototype: for the gold snakes put in cradles by human Athenian mothers which commemorated Erichthonius' snake see Eur. *Ion* 20–6, 1427–9; Parker, 'Myths', 196.

[20] See p. 163, n. 28.

[21] Some recent views (for Burkert see n. 15 above): the *arrephoroi* take down food for a sacred snake and bring back a sacred stone (Robertson, *HSCP* 87, 1983, 241–88); a symbolic encounter with sexuality (the snake), with a hint of a virginity ordeal (Brulé, *Fille d'Athènes*, 95–7); magical strengthening of the olive trees by the dew-sisters (Simon, *Festivals*, 46); 'magical fertility ritual' (Parke, *Festivals*, 141). Redfield, *Locrian Maidens*, 118–27, links the ritual through the myth of Erichthonius with the ideal of autochthony.

assumed, in a special building to which 'the ball court of the *Arrephoroi*' (attested by chance in a literary source) was attached.[22] Whether or not the 'certain period' of residence away from their families lasted throughout the full year of their service, being an *arrephoros* evidently entailed much more than the brief though no doubt terrifying culmination recorded by Pausanias. The most interesting detail recorded about their life is that they dressed in white and were forbidden the use of gold ornaments, which like coloured clothes were seen as instruments of sexual attraction.[23] Thus their status as servants of the asexual goddess was underlined.

We move to the next stages in the progression that the chorus of *Lysistrata* claim to have passed through. The punctuation of the following line is in dispute; they either claim 'I was a corn-grinder' (*aletris*) or 'I was a corn-grinder at age 10 for the goddess who leads'. With the first punctuation the chorus will have ground corn in the service of, no doubt, Demeter ('the goddess who leads', *archegetis*, now attached to the following line, will be Artemis); with the second the *archegetis* will be Athena.[24] The function was apparently one seldom mentioned in literature, as the ancient commentators on Aristophanes quote no parallels; it looks as if they knew no more of it than we do.[25] The chorus's third office (performed at or after the age of 10) was as a 'bear at the *Brauronia*': we will pass over this important cult for the moment. They claim finally 'and once, as a beautiful girl, I bore a basket, wearing a necklace of figs'. Basket-bearing took place in the open air, in the light of day, in fully public space, and this function can be discussed much less tentatively than the others considered so far. Basket-bearers were *parthenoi* who walked at the front of sacrificial processions, carrying on their heads the *kanoun*, a characteristic three-handled basket which contained the vital prerequisites,

[22] [Plut.] *XOrat.* 839c. For the building commonly identified as an (unattested) 'house of the *Arrephoroi*' see Travlos, *Topographical Dictionary*, 71, fig. 91, and the scepticism of N. Robertson, *HSCP* 87 (1983), 253.

[23] Harpoc. a 239 (Harpocration says that any gold they wore became sacred, which is correctly understood as entailing a prohibition by Mansfield, *Robe of Athena*, 272); on gold and coloured clothes see Parker, *Miasma*, 83, n. 36. The special loaves known as 'risers' (ἀνάστατοι) which were made for the *arrephoroi* (Ath. 114a; Sud. a 2082; Paus. Att. a 116 Erbse) have sometimes been given a phallic interpretation. Were that correct, the play between emphasis on sexuality and its symbolic suppression in their lives would be complex; but dough too rises. The risers might have a connection with the '*deipnophoria* for Herse, Aglauros and Pandrosos', in which the *arrephoroi* are likely to have been involved if it related to cults of the acropolis. But on p. 216 I have associated it rather with the *Oschophoria*.

[24] In Attica Archegetis is an attested title only of Athena (not before the 3rd c.: *SEG* XXVIII 60.65; *IG* II² 674.16; cf. Shear, *Kallias*, 36, n. 88 and *Athenian Religion*, 120–1). Context is crucial (so rightly Sourvinou-Inwood, *Girls' Transitions*, 140–6), and in the right context Artemis could doubtless be *archegetis*; but I hesitate to give her this title in a context involving both goddesses. For the debate on these lines see n. 74 below.

[25] See the scholia ad loc., Hesych. a 2892; Paus. Att. a 63 Erbse ap. Eust. 1885.16 on Hom. *Od.* 20.105 (who speaks of 'well-born maidens' and a 'sacred grinding'). Cf. Brelich, *Parthenoi e Paides*, 238–40 (who compares the similar work of the Roman Vestals, Serv. *Ecl.* 8.82), Brulé, *Fille d'Athènes*, 114–16; Sourvinou-Inwood, *Girls' Transitions*, 142–6 (who like Brelich suggests a link with the ritual, p. 197 above, of 'sacred ploughing').

practical and symbolic, for the sacrifice: knife and barley grains. They are often clearly to be seen on vases and reliefs,[26] where they must be distinguished from *kistophoroi*, young women again but in all appearance of subordinate status, who carry large round baskets of miscellaneous equipment at the rear. The most celebrated *kanephoroi* were those of the *Panathenaea*, who walked in splendid state followed by metic maidens carrying stools and parasols for their use.[27] But Dikaiopolis' daughter acts as *kanephoros* at his private celebration of the *Rural Dionysia*,[28] and very probably every sacrificial procession contained one. For a simple ceremony a single *kanephoros* sufficed, and even at a procession on the scale of that at the *City Dionysia* only one, surprisingly, seems to have served.[29] At the Panathenaea there were more—an inscription proves it, even if the identification of *kanephoroi* on the Parthenon frieze is disallowed—but we can scarcely believe that the 'gold ornaments for a hundred *kanephoroi*' which provident Lycurgus had made for the goddess were intended for use on a single occasion.[30] Rather this was magnificent, overflowing abundance, far in excess of any practical need. The largest attested numbers are those of the *kanephoroi* who accompanied the Pythaids that went to Delphi in the late second century, eleven for instance in $138/7$.[31]

'Parthenoi of distinction' were chosen to be *kanephoroi*, according to Philochorus. The events leading up to the assassination of Hipparchus suggest that, under the tyranny, distinction lay in the eye of the tyrants.[32] How these prestigious positions were assigned under the democracy is not recorded. Nor does any text say how old *kanephoroi* might be expected to be, except one scholion which speaks of a *kanephoria* to Artemis by 'those of an age for marriage'. That source is unreliable in itself, but the age mentioned is likely

---

[26] See e.g. figs. 2, 3, 8, 11, 12, 13 (a magnificent example), 17, 19, 114 and (non-Attic) 14–16, 56 in van Straten, *Hierà kalá*, with his discussion, 10–24, 162–4 (for *kanephoroi* in art also L. J. Roccos, *AJA* 99, 1995, 641–52); in general, J. Schelp, *Das Kanoun. Der griechische Opferkorb* (Würzburg 1975). κανᾶ, including heavy silver ones, are often listed in temple inventories: Aleshire, *Asklepieion*, 242; Harris, *Treasures*, index p. 300 s.v. basket.

[27] See p. 258 and, for the *kanephoroi* as the only female recipients of honorific cuts of meat, p. 266. For the Panathenaic *kanephoroi* as the paradigm see Men. *Epit.* 440, Philoch. *FGrH* 328 F 8.

[28] Ar. *Ach.* 242. For the *City Dionysia* see IG II^2 668.32 (of 266/5); cf. IG II^2 896.1–28, 3489, Suda κ 318 and Σ vet. Ar. *Ach.* 242a (Pickard-Cambridge, *Dramatic Festivals*^{2}, 61, n. 5) (which does not inspire great trust). For the *Brauronia* see p. 248; note too (2nd c.) IG II^2 3483 (*Diisoteria*); IG II^2 4456 (Aleshire, *Asklepios* 191), with 3457 and 3554 (*Epidauria*: further references in Aleshire, *Asklepieion*, 90–2). Later attestations include *Eleusinia* (IG II^2 3554), festivals for 'Mother of the Gods' and Aphrodite at Alopeke (IG II^2 3220, 3489, 3636). Note too those of the *Pythaïs* (p. 83), and the κανηφόροι ἀπὸ Παλλαδίου of IG II^2 5118, and in general the 'other processions' of Philochorus *FGrH* 328 F 8 and πομπή τις in Thuc. 6.56.1. From art van Straten, *Hierà kalá*, 13–21, identifies *kanephoroi* in Attic cults of Athena, probably Dionysus, ? the Eleusinian goddesses, and Apollo (*Pythaïs*? *Thargelia*? p. 21).

[29] IG II^2 668.32, 896.1–28 (cf. Pickard-Cambridge, *Dramatic Festivals*^{2}, 61, n. 5); so too it seems at the *Epidauria* (IG II^2 4456). Or was this the 'chief *kanephoros*' in each case?

[30] [Plut.] *XOrat.* 852b (*Athenian Religion*, 244), with the sceptical comment of Schelp, op. cit., 19.

[31] See p. 83, n. 14.

[32] Philochorus *FGrH* 328 F 8; Thuc. 6. 56.1, and p. 258.

Fig. 10. *Kanephoros* in sacrificial procession, by the Kleophon Painter (440–420 BC).

to have been close to the norm. It fits the size and bodily development of the *kanephoroi* shown in art;[33] it fits too a recurrent emphasis found in the literary sources on the *kanephoros* as a potential object of desire. '(Perform your task) fair one, fairly (καλὴ καλῶς)', *kanephoroi* are urged by two separate characters in separate contexts in Aristophanes, who must therefore be using a ritual formula.[34] Allusions in comedy seem also to show that the Panathenaic *kanephoroi* were expected to enhance their alluring pallor by the application of a kind of white make-up;[35] and gold ornaments, forbidden to the little *arrephoroi*, were provided for the older group by Lycurgus, the responsible statesman. Fathers 'adorned' their daughters before 'sending them up to the

[33] See n. 26, and Sourvinou-Inwood, *Girls' Transitions*, 54–7. One scholion: on Theocr. 2.66b (cf. Annexe I to this Ch.).

[34] Arist. *Ach.* 253, *Eccl.* 730, cf. *Lys.* 646. My remarks are largely based on Brulé, *Fille d'Athènes*, 287–310.

[35] See Ar. *Eccl.* 732 with Hermippus fr. 25. The two texts together guarantee the use of a white application, though perhaps not one made of ἄλφιτα, which might drive from a burlesque context in Hermippus. (ἐντρίβω is the *vox propria* for the application of cosmetics—Ar. *Lys.* 149, *Eccl.* 904; B. Guillet, *Les Femmes et les fards dans l'antiquité grecque*, Lyon 1975, 27—and the white ψιμύθιον was very common, Guillet 33–5.) 'Respectable' women often, it seems, painted to attract their husbands, though the practice could also be stigmatized as ἑταιρικός (for both points see Xen. *Oec.* 10.2–9; for the former e.g. Ar. *Lys.* 149, for the latter Eubulus fr. 97 K/A, 98 Hunter with Hunter's note; Sud. ψ 108; Guillet, 93–111). Guillet wonders whether they showed themselves out of doors so adorned: if he is right, the display of the *kanephoroi* becomes remarkable. Perhaps the ceremonial whiteness in part evoked the ideal of σκιατροφία (cf. the role of the σκιαδηφόροι), i.e. good upbringing. Burkert's appeal to ritual disguise, *Homo Necans*, 170, is hard to credit in the context of the *Panathenaea*.

acropolis' as *kanephoroi*.[36] There were stories of men falling in love with *kanephoroi*, and even carrying them off, as Boreas did Orithyia in an early source.[37] The *kanephoria*, it has been suggested,[38] constituted a kind of beauty parade, at which maidens ready for marriage emerged briefly from seclusion to display their ripened charms. Too few girls served as *kanephoroi* for the institution to have had quite that function in a general way. But the few *kanephoroi* there were must indeed have stood, in the festival showcase, as symbols for all the nubile maidens of the year.

When bearing the basket as beautiful girls, the chorus of *Lysistrata* claim to have worn—gold ornaments? No, a necklace of dried figs. This is very surprising. A possible association between figs and nubile girls can, no doubt, be imagined, but the *Panathenaea* was scarcely the place for such earthy symbolism. Was it rather at the *Dionysia* that the chorus pretend to have served?[39] Even in that context, it is a little strange to imagine a '*parthenos* of distinction' dressed in a ritual accoutrement worn otherwise, to our knowledge, only by the scapegoats at the *Thargelia*.

The passage in *Lysistrata* is not an encyclopaedic survey of ritual functions available to *parthenoi*. The chorus do not claim to have been *loutrides* or *plyntrides*, the *parthenoi* who cleansed Athena's ancient image at the *Plynteria*; if, as is likely, the office was restricted to two girls of the *genos* of *Praxiergidai*, it was too specialized for their argument. Nor have they been 'hearth-initiates', a position again unsuitable for their argument because it was open to only one child each year, who could, very unusually, be of either sex. They have not been among the maidens who were sent each year to the Delphinion to propitiate Apollo.[40] Nor, since as *arrephoroi* they have held the most honorific of functions associated with the *peplos* of Athena, do they mention a lesser office which in the late hellenistic period, at least, was open to *parthenoi* in much greater numbers. Honorary decrees of the late second century reveal to us 'the maidens who worked the wool for Athena for her robe', and they are very numerous. They are listed by tribe, and the total

---

[36] Acusilaus *FGrH* 2 F 30, cf. Ar. *Lys.* 1193. The *kanephoros* on a volute krater in Ferrara by the Kleophon Painter (Ferrara T 57; van Straten, *Hierà kalá*, fig. 13; here Fig. 10) wears a dress of gorgeous elaboration. Gold: n. 30. At the *Mysteries* of Andania make-up and gold were banned together (*LSCG* 65.22).

[37] Diod. Sic. 9.37.1; Boreas: Acusilaus *FGrH* 2 F 30; Ov. *Met.* 2. 708–25 (Hermes and Herse); cf. p. 248, n. 132 (Brauron).

[38] So Brulé, *Fille d'Athènes*, 308, who compares Restif de la Bretonne, *Monsieur Nicholas* (on Bourgogne in the 18th c.) 'Les grands fêtes, toutes les filles au dessus de quinze ans vont à l'offerte ... c'est une sorte de montre.'

[39] So L. Deubner in J. Hastings (ed.), *Encyclopaedia of Religion and Ethics*, s.v. baskets, 444 (rejected by Brelich, *Paides e Parthenoi*, 286, n. 114, without comment on the figs.; the problem has gone largely unobserved, but C. Calame in *Le orse*, 48, supposes an earthy joke). Scapegoats: Helladius ap. Phot. *Bibl.* 279 p. 534a 2–7; cf. J. Bremmer, *HSCP* 87 (1983), 312–13.

[40] *Loutrides*: Ar. fr. 849, cf. Mansfield, *Robe of Athena*, 367–8; *Athenian Religion*, 307. Hearth initiates: see Clinton, *Sacred Officials*, 98–114 (first attested by a plausible supplement in *IG* I³ 6 C 25). Delphinion: Plut. *Thes.* 18.1–2.

seems to have been of the order of 115.[41] The decrees mention also that they marched in procession, presumably at the *Panathenaea*. 'Working the wool' was not a rite of passage, because some girls did it on two occasions five years apart (the age requirement must have been elastic). But it was in all appearance the main context in which the unmarried daughters of the social elite of late hellenistic Athens— the sisters of the ephebes—acted as a group. Preparing the wool was a time-consuming process which could have occupied many hands, if scarcely 230 all at once, for a number of days. The practice of the classical city is unattested, but an allusion in Aristophanes[42] suggests that 'carding the wool for the *peplos*' was already then a collective activity.

The abundance of ritual roles assigned to *parthenoi* is striking. It is often argued that some of them represent survivals from a system of initiation, in which girls were prepared symbolically, and in some measure practically, for women's tasks: childcare, sexuality and weaving (the *arrephoroi*), food preparation (the *aletrides*).[43] The *arrephoroi* lived away from their families for an extended period, which came to an end with a terrifying ordeal; during this period, they were required to dress in a particular way and to eat distinctive foods. The great and obvious objection is that two, or even four, *arrephoroi* do not constitute an age-set. The problematic concept of symbolic or representative initiation has therefore to be introduced,[44] probably in association with the claim that participation had 'originally' been much more general. The ultimate origin of these rites is beyond our knowledge. But the data that we observe can perhaps be better explained from a combination of two motives. One is the need to fuss over the gods, to accord them special attention. It is not

---

[41] See S. B. Aleshire and S. D. Lambert, ZPE 142 (2003), 68–70 (re-edition of *IG* II² 1036 + 1060) of 108/7; *IG* II² 1034 +1943 (Tracy, *Attic Letter-Cutters*, 217–19), of 103/2; ibid. 1942, of c.100. For totals, and girls who served twice, see Tracy, 219; for their social niveau Lambert, loc. cit., 85–6. Procession: ZPE 142 (2003), 68–70 fr. b 14 (but there is no explicit indication that the procession was that of the *Panathenaea*). Mansfield has stressed that 'working the wool' is a different function from weaving the *peplos* (279), and, if the former is what the *parthenoi* of the honorary decrees did, the question arises who actually wove. The *arrephoroi* to our knowledge merely 'warped the loom with the priestesses' at the *Chalkeia* (Suda χ 35 = *Etym. Magn.* 805.43–7; identified as Pausanias Att. χ 2 Erbse). Passages in tragedy that imply that any Attic woman might weave (Eur. *Hec.* 466–74, *IT* 222–4) help little; nor does the vague notice of Hesych. ε 5653 ἐργαστῖναι · αἱ τὸν πέπλον ὑφαίνουσαι. Σ Eur. *Hek.* 467 writes (with reference to the peplos) οὐ μόνον γὰρ παρθένοι ὕφαινον, ὡς φησιν Ἀπολλόδωρος ἐν τῷ περὶ θεῶν (*FGrH* 244 F 105), ἀλλὰ καὶ τέλειαι γυναῖκες, ὡς Φερεκράτης ἐν Δουλοδιδασκάλῳ (fr. 51); but we cannot control his evidence. Mansfield, 277–81, has the *arrephoroi* weave; Aleshire/Lambert, loc. cit., 75–7, assign this job too to the *parthenoi* of the decrees.

[42] *Av.* 827. Time-consuming: see E. J. W. Barber in *Goddess and Polis*, 110.

[43] See (for the *arrephoroi*) Jeanmaire, *Couroi*, 264–7; Brelich, Paides e Parthenoi, 236; Burkert, *Hermes* 94 (1966), 13–21, *Homo Necans*, 152; for the *aletrides* Brulé, *Fille d'Athènes*, 116. That the *aletrides*, like the *arrephoroi*, lived with the goddess for a period (Brelich, 239) is conceivable, but not more. See contra S. Price, *Religions* 17, 94.

[44] See Brelich, Paides e Parthenoi, 238; Burkert, *Hermes* 94 (1966), 19–21. It is known from antiquity, but only in relation to a special case, the 'hearth-initiate' (Porph. *Abst.* 4.5.4 Bouffartigue (p. 235.20–2 Nauck)). 'I cannot be initiated for someone else any more than another can take a bath for me': Redfield, *Locrian Maidens*, 91.

quite correct to say that the *aletrides* are preparing themselves for the tasks that as mature women they will have to perform. Women of the class from which *aletrides* were drawn are unlikely to have spent much time grinding their own corn.[45] The effect of the ritual was to exalt the goddess, in whose service even the humblest tasks could only be performed by persons of quality. (There may also have been some ancillary concern for the purity of food-stuffs.) The other reason is that rituals are a display-cabinet for what society considers most important. Children are the 'soul' of mortals. A festival pro-gramme that failed to give them a prominent place would be the phenomenon that required a special explanation. The *arrephoroi* stand for their age-class in the sense that they present an ideal image of it.[46]

The *Brauronia*, however (at which the *Lysistrata* chorus served as 'bears') is different. We will need to pause and consider not just a festival but a sanctu-ary and a whole cult. For the study of Greek religion there is none more important.[47] The *arkteia* which took place at the sanctuaries of Artemis at Brauron and Mounichia is the only maturation ritual for young girls that we can to some extent observe from close to, and is one that some and perhaps all our sources claim was undergone by all Attic girls before marriage.

Brauron and Mounichia belong to a string of sanctuaries of Artemis sited along the coastlines of Attica and its neighbours, secluded places highly appropriate for the ritual retreat of young girls; Euripides speaks of Halai Araphenides, close to Brauron and site of a perhaps related cult of Artemis, as being 'at the extreme limits of Attica'.[48] The sanctuary at Brauron was uncovered in a brilliantly successful excavation that lasted, with a five-year interval, from 1945 to 1962. Some broad outlines of the site's history are established:[49] cult use goes back to geometric or even protogeometric times; a

[45] On the humble status of corn grinders see Hom. *Od.* 7.103–4, 20.105; *Adesp. Iamb.* fr. 37 West; Call. *Hymn* 4. 242; cf. Thuc. 2.78.3.

[46] 'Those selected represent the cohort in the sense that the ritual represents something about the meaning of that age-class to the wider community': Redfield, *Locrian Maidens*, 91, cf. 117. 'Soul' of mortals: Eur. *Andr.* 419, cf. *HF* 634–6.

[47] For the large bibliography see Travlos, *Bildlexikon*, 56–7; P. Brulé, 'Retour à Brauron', *DHA* 16.2 (1990), 61–90; R. L. Fowler in *Oxford Readings*, 326, n. 28 (= *ICS* 20, 1995, 9, n. 28); J. Mylonopoulos and F. Bubenheimer, *AA* 1996, 8, n. 13; add now Giuman, *Dea, Vergine, Sangue*; Ferrari, *Figures of Speech*, 166–81; C. A. Faraone in *Initiation*, 43–68; Redfield, *Locrian Maidens*, 98–110, and the collective *Le orse*. I have not seen A. I. Antoniou, Βραυρών (Athens 1990).

[48] *IT* 1450–1; on the site see Travlos, *Bildlexikon*, 211–15 [+]; on the cult see p. 241 below. 'String of sanctuaries': see Brulé, *Fille d'Athènes*, 186–95.

[49] The excavator published a summary just before his death: J. Papadimitriou, 'The sanctuary of Artemis at Brauron', *Scientific American* 208 (1963), 111–20 (p. 115 speaks of a temple built 'a short time before 500' and 'parts of its interior pavement and fragments of pottery indicating that it was preceded by an older shrine'); cf. *Athenian Religion*, 18, 74; I. Kontis, 'Artemis Brauronia', *ArchDelt* 22 (1967), *Mel.* 156–206, at 166–9; Boersma, *Building Policy*, 131; M. B. Hollinshead, *AJA* 89 (1985), 432; and now P. G. Themelis in *Le orse*, 103–6. Law: finally published by P. G. Themelis in *Le orse*, 112–13. For other unpublished inscriptions see *SEG* XXXVII 30–31, 34–5; for superb photos of four votive plaques see *Mesogaia*, 124–7.

temple of moderate size was built, possibly over a predecessor, in or near the
Pisistratean period; and a large stoa was begun but not quite completed in the
last quarter of the fifth century. The site was still in use in the late fourth or
third century, when a 'law of the *nomothetai*' provided for a regular programme of inspection and repair, but probably became unusable through
flooding not long after. But the excavation broke off with the death of the
excavator in 1963. No final reports appeared, large proportions of the finds
remain unpublished, and, worst of all, a substantial area of the site remains
unexplored.[50] In these circumstances, questions about the identification and
function of buildings remain inevitably in a state of flux. The most intriguing
concerns 'the old temple' and 'the Parthenon' which have long been known
from inventories as the main places of storage for Artemis' property; they are
not, it is now clear, the homonymous buildings on the Athenian acropolis but
located at Brauron itself.[51] The opposition 'old temple–Parthenon' tends to
suggest that the Parthenon too was a (newer) temple.[52] If this is so, the
Brauronian Parthenon was the first temple demonstrably to bear that problematic name, at a time (c.416) when the masterpiece of Ictinus on the
acropolis was still 'the hundred-footed temple' or something similar and the

[50] See *Ergon* 1962, 29–31. The 'law of the *nomothetai*' (previous note) that attests various
undiscovered buildings proves the same.

[51] 'Old temple' and 'Parthenon': so first *IG* I³ 403 and *SEG* XXXVII 30; for later references see
Linders, *Temple Records*, 70 (given the exact parallel with the later texts there is no need to doubt
that the Parthenon of the two 5th-c. texts is that at Brauron: such Brauronian treasures as came
to Athens in 416/15 seem to have gone to the Opisthodomos: D. Peppas-Delmousou in *Comptes et
inventaires*, 335). The published inventories (listed in Linders, *Temple Records*, 3, nn. 11–12 (*IG*
I³403–4), 5) were all found on or near the acropolis. But duplicates of several have since been
uncovered at Brauron (see Linders, 3, n. 18, 20–1, 72–3, nn. 34–6) and a Parthenon is now
attested there; the old view that the temple and Parthenon of the inventories were those of the
acropolis leads to several anomalies (Linders, 70–3), not least that dedications made to Artemis
would have been worn by statues of Athena, and is to be rejected (so first J. Papadimitriou, *Prakt*
1950, 187; C. Calame's tentative revival of the old view in *Le orse*, 55–7, does not convince). For
the property of Artemis Brauronia that was in fact stored on the acropolis see Osborne, *Demos*,
160.

[52] At all events, whatever the Parthenon was, there ought to be a new temple (but why then is
it unknown to the inventories?) for the old temple to contrast with. The view of several scholars
(so recently J. Mylonopoulos and F. Bubenheimer, *AA* 1996, 7–23) that the Parthenon was part
of the old temple fails to address this point; and, for inventorying purposes, it would be odd if not
impossible to contrast old temple and Parthenon if one was part of the other. The difficulty is that
suitable candidates for an old and a new, ergo doubtless larger, temple cannot be found on the
ground; the principal temple is probably in fact older than the 'small temple/tomb of Iphigeneia'
identified as the 'old temple' by M. B. Hollinshead, *AJA* 89 (1985), 434–45, who makes the bigger
temple the Parthenon. It seems to follow that either old or new temple/Parthenon has not yet
been identified, perhaps lying in an unexcavated part of the sanctuary: P. G. Themelis, *Magna
Graecia* xxi, 11–12 (Nov./Dec. 1986), 6–11, locates the old temple on the spot where the chapel
of St George now stands. The main temple is put somewhere in the period late 6th—mid-5th c.,
but its relation to earlier buildings on the site, and the number of phases to be recognized, are very
obscure issues (see the cautious remarks of I. Kontis, *ArchDelt* 22 (1967), *Mel.* 168; cf. Boersma,
Building Policy, 175, Hollinshead, op. cit., 432, n. 63). Three cult statues located indoors are
known from the inventories (Linders, *Temple Records*, 14): Mylonopoulos and Bubenheimer, op.
cit., propose to locate them in the three aisles of the main temple.

Parthenon merely a room within it. A *parthenon* is a 'room for maidens', not a 'temple of a virgin goddess' (which would be Parthene(i)on),[53] and if any cult might reasonably have included within a temple a 'room for maidens' important enough to give its name to the whole building (and set a precedent) it was surely that at Brauron.[54] But these are not more than exciting possibilities.

Again, a third-century inscription reveals, among the buildings dedicated to the goddess by 'the city for the safety of the people of Athens', a gymnasium and *palaistra*. Perhaps young men had or acquired a greater place in the life of the sanctuary than most other evidence suggests; we also in fact hear of a 'sacred hunt' and of 'stables'. Otherwise this must be a unique Attic example of what Propertius calls, in reference to Sparta, a *virgineum gymnasium*.[55] The most plausible correlation between buildings known from texts and those uncovered on the site concerns the most striking monument visible today, the three-sided stoa of the late fifth century which doubtless contained the 'rooms' known from the same third century inscription. For an exciting period the nine main 'rooms', each equipped with eleven couches, were identified as dormitories for the little bears. But it is now agreed, on the basis of numerous analogies, that they are dining-rooms for the use of men; the bears did not enter them, unless we rather wildly suppose that, like Aeschylus' Iphigeneia, they might be called before their fathers to sing 'in the fair-tabled men's chambers'.[56] Such ritual dining-rooms are likely to have been used by cult officials on the occasion of major festivals, and the scale of this VIPs' dining complex, as large as any in Attica, is an index of the civic importance of the cult.

The great moment in the life of the sanctuary was unquestionably the four-yearly *penteteris*, the *Brauronia*. Aristophanes implies that in times of peace numerous Athenians made the cheerful and perhaps drunken pilgrimage (*theoria*) to watch the festival. The performance at it by the little bears[57] is very likely to have been the culmination of their period of service. Was it also the chief attraction of the *penteteris* for adult spectators from Athens? That

---

[53] See Th. Reinach, '*Παρθένων*', BCH 32 (1908), 499–513; J. Tréheux, 'Pourquoi le Parthénon?', REG 98 (1985), 233–42, esp. 241, n. 40. The first use of Parthenon for the whole acropolis building is Dem. 22.13, 76 of 354/3, but Lycurgus later can still speak of it as 'the Hekatompedon' (frs. 3 and 58 Blass, I.3 and IX.2 Conomis), which is the name used for the whole building in inventories.
[54] On the *adyton* in the Mounichia *aition* see p. 238.
[55] Prop. 3.14.2. Gymnasium, *palaistra* (and stables): *Le orse* 112–13, lines 5–6. Hunt: hypothesis to Dem. 25, sec. 1. For discussion of the location of the stables see O. Kakovoyianni, ArchDelt 39 (1984) [1989], B, 45; J. Mylonopoulos and F. Bubenheimer, AA 1996, 19, and especially P. G. Themelis in *Le orse*, 105–7; Men occasionally dedicated metal objects to the goddess, not it seems clothing (Linders, *Temple Records*, 38, 40); for a ἱππικὸς κεκρύφαλος and ἐχήνια dedicated by Xenotimos son of Karkinos (the tragic poet) see IG II² 1388.73–4, etc., Linders, 74, n. 48; Harris, *Treasures*, 50 (ii 31).
[56] Aesch. Ag. 244. On the 'rooms' see B. Bergquist, in O. Murray, Sympotica (Oxford 1990), 38 [+]. Note the dining equipment listed in SEG XXXVII 34.
[57] Ar. Lys. 645.

hypothesis fits well with what can be read in ethnographers about the element of public display often to be found in initiations, less well with our common assumptions about the relations between the sexes in Attica. Good grounds could doubtless be given for seeing precisely this case as exceptional. If display by the girls was not the centrepiece of the festival, one may reasonably ask what was. The *penteteris* must surely have been the context for the rhapsodic performances of the *Iliad*—in a competition doubtless attributable to the Pisistratids, enthusiasts for Homer as their father was for Brauron— said by one lexicographer to have been held at the site. But a festival of Artemis cannot have been built around recitations of Homer. Whether the 'sacred hunt' was part of this festival, and what form it took, we can only guess. There was also, as at so many festivals, a *pannychis* centred on dancing by woman (and perhaps providing the context of the little girls' performance).[58] It is possible that unattested 'lesser *Brauronia*' took place in the non-penteteric years; certainly there seems to have been an annual festival at the shrine of Artemis Mounichia, the other site where girls 'played the bear'.[59]

However that may be, many activities demonstrably took place in the long intervals between *penteterides*. The 'family reliefs' dedicated at Brauron were mentioned in Chapter 2. The excavations also revealed, to our delight, numerous marble statues of children, the earliest dating from the fourth century.[60] The girls among them are as it happens of an age to be 'bears', but boys predominate and many, perhaps most, are portrayed as toddlers or even crawlers. It seems that Artemis protected children of both sexes independently of the *arkteia*. A famous passage of Euripides tells how 'the

---

[58] Rhapsodic performances: Hesych. β 1067. Sacred hunt: n. 55. *Pannychis*: see p. 166.

[59] Little unfortunately is known of the *Mounichia* (see IG II² 1006.29 and the late 2130.49) of Mounichion 16, and none of that little except perhaps a vague phrase of Libanius (n. 103 below) illuminates the role of the *arktoi*: a procession (IG II² 1028.20, and often) taking to the shrine the cakes ringed with small torches known as ἀμφιφῶντες (Philochorus FGrH 328 F 86, with Jacoby); an association with the battle of Salamis (*Athenian Religion*, 187, n. 124); a naval ἄμιλλα by ephebes in the harbour, doubtless in commemoration—so Deubner, *Attische Feste*, 205—of Salamis (e.g. IG II² 1006. 29; even ναυμαχήσαντες Μουνίχια appears in the late IG II² 2130.49); perhaps some participation by demes (p. 76). Deubner even denied (loc. cit.) that a form of *arkteia* occurred at Mounichia (it is attested only by Harpoc. a 235 (not very clear), ΣΓ Ar. Lys. 645a and the aitiological legend discussed below), but the discovery of numerous *krateriskoi* at the shrine (n. 76) refuted him.

[60] Much material, though visible in the Brauron museum, remains unpublished, but see S. Karusu, ArchEph 1957, 68–83; I. Kontis, ArchDelt 22 (1967), Mel. 190, n. 120; T. H. Price, BSA 64 (1969), 97 (on such 'temple-boys' cf. C. Beer in *Gifts to the Gods*, 21–9); K. Rühfel, *Das Kind in der griechischen Kunst* (Mainz 1984), 216–22. For a fine 'kourotrophos' statuette from the shrine see CRAI 1988 803 fig. 1 or LIMC, Artemis, no. 721 (there are five pressings from the same mould). For similarities between the votive material from Brauron and from other 'kourotrophic' sanctuaries see Giuman, *Dea, Vergine, Sangue*, 47–8. Against seeing the girls as necessarily bears see P. C. Bol, AA 1981, 645–6; Sourvinou-Inwood, *Girls' Transitions*, 40. One, remarkably, appears to be portrayed as blind (see Karusu). On Artemis as *kourotrophos* see Diod. Sic. 5.73.5, Nilsson, GGR, 493–4 and e.g. Anth. Pal. 6.271 (Phaedimus I in Gow/Page, HE), where the function is seen as an extension of her concern with childbirth; but cf. Anth. Pal. 7. 743 (Antipater Thessal. LXVII in Gow/Page, GP) which fails to make this extension.

fine-woven robes left behind in their houses by women whose souls break in childbirth' will be dedicated to Iphigeneia, buried at the site.[61] Above all there is the testimony of the inventories, since these register the 'new accessions' of each year. The reasons for which particular dedications were made are never discernible, and totals fluctuate between years in ways which we cannot explain. Three dedications of garments were made in 349–348, only one in the following year, six in 346-345, but twelve in 347–346 and twenty-five in 345-344.[62] The smallest totals[63] do not suggest a flood of devotees, but there was at least a trickle every year. The three cult-statues were all festooned in garments dedicated by the faithful.[64]

I turn to the *arkteia*.[65] A fierce sisterhood of questions at once confronts us. How many *arktoi* were there, of what age, and for how long did they serve? To the third question it is generally agreed[66] that we can answer 'not for the period of the festival alone', because the bears are said to be 'consecrated to Artemis' and to 'tend the shrine', both expressions which imply a service of some duration; less decisive, since the vital word is a supplement, is a reference to 'the *amphipoleion* in which live [the bears?]'. If we look for parallels for groups of children living in temple precincts for a period, we find that seven youths and maidens of Corinth served Hera Akraia for a year, two Locrian maidens Athena Ilias probably for the same time; how long the *arrephoroi* spent on the acropolis is unknown.[67] But the Locrian and Corinthian cases are not closely comparable to that of Brauron—there an annual succession of small groups of children, here a festival held every four years probably involving much larger numbers—and the question remains open.

---

[61] Eur. *IT* 1464–7. Garment dedications after successful childbirth are widely attested (e.g. *Anth. Pal.* 6.202 = Leonidas of Tarentum I in Gow/Page, *HE*). The variant here is unique (C. Wolff, *ClAnt* 11, 1992, 320), but not necessarily inauthentic: Artemis may have received normal post-childbirth dedications, Iphigeneia those from the dead. The inventories do not know Iphigeneia, however.

[62] Some items are dedicated 'half-finished' (because of death?—Brulé, *Fille d'Athènes*, 230), often with 'woof and wool' to go with them: see e.g. *IG* II^2 1514. 53–4, with Linders, *Temple Records*, 17–19. The marble bases interpreted in the earlier literature as bases of racks for the display of dedicated clothing supported mangers, according to Themelis, *Le orse*, 105–6; *alii alia*. On garment dedications for Artemis see in general Cole, *Ritual Space*, 214–25.

[63] Small totals for early years might reflect 'de-accessioning' due to decay (cf. W. Günther in *Comptes et inventaires*, 229–32). There will also have been minor dedications in other materials. A four-yearly cycle of high totals, to be linked with the *penteteris*, is not observable.

[64] See Linders, *Temple Records*, 14 [+].

[65] The contribution of C. Sourvinou-Inwood in various works, culminating in *Girls' Transitions* (supplemented by 'Lire l'arkteia', *DHA* 16.2, 1990, 45–60), has been outstanding.

[66] See e.g. Deubner, *Attische Feste*, 207–8 (on Harpoc. α 235, Σ Ar. *Lys.* 645c); Brelich, *Paides e Parthenoi*, 258–9 (but his archaeological argument is now rejected); the only recent dissenter to my knowledge is Ferrari, *Figures of Speech*, 168. Amphipoleion: *Le orse*, 112–13, lines 3–4.

[67] Parmeniskos in Σ Eur. *Med.* 264; Strabo 13.1.40 (600), etc. The nine Coan ἀγρεταί (Hesych. α 769; *LSCG* 156 B 6) served Athena for a year, but we do not know where they lived. If we accept that there was an annual 'graduation' of bears the gap between these cases and the *arkteia* closes up.

On the number of the *arktoi* our late sources appear to differ.[68] Most state or imply that all Athenian girls imitated the bear prior to marriage; one, in the form preserved to us, speaks of 'chosen girls' , but probably only through corruption from 'girls called bears'.[69] But constraints of space and of cost render this very unlikely.[70] If we suppose that Brauronian bears could 'graduate' only at four-yearly intervals, then we have to imagine at least half (for some went to Mounichia) of four years' crop of girls busy tending the shrine at Brauron for an unspecified period: about a thousand girls, in one sanctuary of moderate size? And, since no liturgists were told off to finance the bears, there were also constraints of costs for the individual families, particularly if the period of service was extensive.

One tiny scrap of early testimony may assist us. Didymus believed that the word 'to tithe' (δεκατεῦσαι) could be used in the sense of 'to be a bear', and in this connection a few words were adduced from a lost speech of Demosthenes: 'not to tithe her nor to initiate her' (οὐ δεκατεῦσαι ταύτην οὐδὲ μυῆσαι).[71] The case seems to have concerned an heiress, and the phrase recalls passages in the speeches of Isaeus about disputed inheritances where the attitude of A to B is illustrated by the rites he did or not introduce him to. It looks as if the orator was speaking of someone who cannot have recognized the legitimacy of a daughter because he failed to 'consecrate her <to serve as a bear> as a tithe'. If that is so, the linking 'to tithe or to initiate' is very interesting. An easy inference is that a man was free, but not obliged, to tithe a dependent girl at Brauron just as he was to have her initiated at Eleusis. The resultant hypothesis of 'universal right of access (among citizens) but restricted actual participation' perhaps accounts as well as any other for the problematic claim of the sources that participation was universal. It was apparently on the same basis—their parents' willingness to meet the attendant costs—that youths were 'selected' for ephebic service before and after the short-lived

---

[68] See Sourvinou-Inwood, *Girls' Transitions*, 111–17, and for various views the references in P. Perlman, *GRBS* 24 (1983), 128, n. 75; Dowden, *Death and the Maiden*, 27–8; n. 70 below (E. Simon).

[69] ΣΓ Ar. *Lys.* 645a ἐπιλεγόμεναι < ἄρκτοι added by Wilamowitz ap. G. Stein, *Scholia in Aristophanis Lysistratam*, diss. Göttingen 1891, 28> παρθένοι. Everything else about this scholion so resembles the rest of the tradition which speaks of general participation (Suda α 3958; Σ Ar. *Lys.* 645c; *Anecd. Bekk.* 1.445.11–12) that a divergence on this point is unlikely; the tense of ἐπιλεγόμεναι too supports the change.

[70] See Vidal-Naquet, *Chasseur noir*, 199 (146 in the Engl. tr.), and Sourvinou-Inwood, *Girls' Transitions*, 116. There is no literary support for the idea (Simon, *Festivals*, 86) that the *arkteia* was performed at all the sites where *krateriskoi* have been found, and in the case e.g. of the urban shrine of Artemis Aristoboule at Melite the hypothesis is very implausible (Sourvinou-Inwood, 116–17). W. Burkert in *Le orse*, 25, suggests that the *proteleia* on the Athenian acropolis known from Suda (p. 440, n. 88) served as a substitute in families unwilling or unable to put their daughters through the full *arkteia*.

[71] Harpoc. δ 16. The fragment is crucially important in showing that δεκατεύω in this as in other usages is a transitive verb, with the young woman as object. The other fragment (Pollux 8.53) of the speech in question (*Against Medon*) speaks of an heiress: R. Clavaud, *Démosthène. Lettres et fragments* (Paris 1987), 132. In Isaeus see e.g. 9.30.

state-financed ephebate of the Lycurgan period. For what it is worth, numbers undergoing the voluntary year-long ephebate of the third and second centuries ranged from about twenty to about forty-five per year.[72] If we applied the higher figure to the bears (to allow for the depopulation of the third century), multiplied it by four, and detached half for Mounichia, we would have ninety bears at each *penteteris*, or, if we postulated unattested annual graduations, about twenty-three a year. But there are too many uncertainties for such calculations to be much more than the fantasies of an idle hour. The krateriskoi, to be mentioned below, introduce a complication: cheap and numerous, they can be taken to imply large-scale participation by families with little money to spare. But it has also been suggested that they could be bought and used, as a form of token participation, precisely by those who were unable to put their daughters through the rites.[73]

In regard to the second problem, the age of the bears, new evidence and new analyses have brought real progress, and the uncertainty that remains is quite limited. The chorus in *Lysistrata* claim to have been bears at Brauron either 'when 10 years old' or, on a less well-attested but linguistically perhaps easier reading, 'after' their service as *aletrides* which was performed at age 10.[74] One scholion on the same passage says that the bears were not younger than 5 and not older than 10. Other scholia and lexicographers agree that the rite had to be undergone 'before marriage'.[75] New evidence came with the identification[76] of a type of vase, the so-called *krateriskos*, that seems, most unusually, to have had a special association with this particular ritual. The krateriskoi in question date, on accepted views, from the late sixth to the end of the fifth century. They show—to give a simplified account—groups of girls who dance vigorously,[77] run or move in procession, usually near an altar (often shown with fire) that is regularly associated with a palm-tree. The girls often carry crowns, or torches, or branches; numerous varieties of dress

---

[72] Pélékidis, *Éphébie*, 165.

[73] Arrigoni, 'Donne e sport', 103; Dowden, *Death and the Maiden*, 28. Finer *krateriskoi* did exist: L. Kahil, *AntK* 20 (1977), 89. The equation 'cheap vases = impoverished purchasers' is anyway unreliable.

[74] Ar. *Lys.* 644–5. For the debate on these lines initiated by her brilliant article in *CQ* 21 (1971), 339–42, see Sourvinou-Inwood, *Girls' Transitions*, 68, n. 1, 136–48, and in brief the commentaries of J. Henderson and A. Sommerstein ad loc. Two recent articles (S. Grebe, *MusHelv* 4, 1999, 194–203; F. Perusino in *Le orse*, 167–74), advocate a return to the old reading κᾆτ' ἔχουσα in 645 without unfortunately considering seriously Stinton's mediating proposal (*CQ* 26, 1976, 11–13) καὶ χέουσα.

[75] *ΣΓ* Ar. *Lys.* 645a; cf. Suda α 3958; *Σ* Ar. *Lys.* 645c; *Anecd. Bekk.* 1.445.12.

[76] By L. Kahil in numerous studies (see Sourvinou-Inwood, *Girls' Transitions*, 116, also *CRAI* 1988, 799–813); see above all *AntK* 8 (1965), 20–33; ibid. 20 (1977), 86–98; *Hesperia* 50 (1981), 253–63; for further material from Mounichia see Palaiokrassa, *Ἱερό*, 74–82, 147–68, and ead. *AM* 104 (1989), 38–39. On dating see Kahil, *AntK* (1965), 22; (1977), 93; *Hesperia* (1981), 259 and the tentative suggestion of Palaiokrassa that they persist into the 4th c. For a recent inventory see T. F. Scanlon, *Nikephoros* 3 (1990), 109–20; the best plates (colour) are in Reeder, *Pandora*, 321–8 (see too Sourvinou-Inwood, *Girls' Transitions*; *Le orse*).

[77] Lonsdale, *Dance*, 187.

appear,[78] and in a significant number of examples the girls—who in this case are with one exception at the top of the age range—are shown naked. Deer appear occasionally. Examples of such krateriskoi have been found in both the sanctuaries associated with the *arkteia*, in large numbers, and in at least two further shrines of Artemis,[79] but not to a significant degree in any other context. One precious example shows a bear—the animal—amid what we can thus take to be the human bears whose emblem she is. On another, krateriskoi appear as it were in action, tilted as if to pour a libation. Rigorous analysis of the age of the girls shown on the krateriskoi puts the youngest between 5 and 7 and the oldest somewhere in the range from 10 to 11½ or 12.[80] This is already a notable gain. The statement of the scholiast on Aristophanes that the bears came from a broad age-band is confirmed, but the possibility that the band reached up to the age of marriage is disallowed. The oldest girls are shown with breasts just beginning to swell, a process that the ancients believed to occur shortly before menarchy. The only doubt that remains is whether the scholiast was right to set the age of 10 as a strict upper limit.[81]

If the *Brauronia* only occurred every fourth year, it is easy to see why girls of differing ages had to be included.[82] But one may wonder why the bears on the krateriskoi fall into two groups, one at either end of the age band. Either this is polar representation, with the whole of a range indicated by its two extreme points, or our very inadequate literary sources have obscured a nuance.

A separate role at the festival for older girls (we presume) as *kanephoroi* is rather weakly attested.[83]

---

[78] See Sourvinou-Inwood, *Girls' Transitions*, 119–24.

[79] The shrines of Artemis Tauropolos at Halai Araphenides and of Artemis Aristoboule at Melite. Other sites that have yielded small amounts of material are the acropolis (presumably from the sanctuary of Artemis Brauronia), the cave of the Nymphs at Eleusis, and the agora: see Kahil, *AntK* (1977), 87–8 and (acropolis) *Hesperia* 50 (1981), 253–63.

[80] Bear: Kahil, *AntK* (1977), 90–1 with pl. 19 = Sourvinou-Inwood, *Girls' Transitions*, pl. 2 (discussed p. 63) = Reeder, *Pandora*, 324–7, no. 99; here Fig. 12. On Kahil, op. cit., pl. 20, see n. 121 below. Tilted krateriskoi: Kahil, *AntK* (1965), pl. 8.8 (= Sourvinou-Inwood, *Girls' Transitions*, pl. 3); cf. Sourvinou-Inwood, *BICS* 37 (1990), 13; for the possibility suggested by traces of burning that the krateriskoi served also as *thymiateria* see Kahil, *AntK* (1965), 24–5; *AntK* (1977), 88; Palaiokrassa, Ἱερό, 80. Age: Sourvinou-Inwood, *Girls' Transitions*, 39–67. The inference that the girls on the *krateriskoi* are bears is rejected by Ferrari, *Figures of Speech*, 166–81, and N. Marinatos in *Le orse*, 29–42.

[81] Breasts and menarchy: Arist. *HA* 581a 32–581b 6; cf. Sourvinou-Inwood, *Girls' Transitions*, 25; L. Dean-Jones, *Womens' Bodies in Classical Greek Science* (Oxford 1994), 47–55 (who cite D. W. Amundsen and C. J. Diers, 'The age of menarche in classical Greece', *Human Biology* 41, 1969, 125–32). (But offerings relating to menstruation are not attested: P. Brulé, *DHA* 16.2, 1990, 75.) For a powerful argument that the scholiast was right see Sourvinou-Inwood, 28–30, 61–2: the very oldest bears are those, aged 10, who are just entering a recognized 'pre-menarche' age-band, and the iconographic signs that designate that band—above all breasts just starting to swell—are used even for its youngest members. That may well be the answer. But is it certain that strict limits in terms of year of birth were set ? T. F. Scanlon (*Nikephoros* 3, 1990, 99) points out that in men's athletics eligibility for the classes boys, youths, men was determined ad hoc by local judges, and could lead to disputes.

[82] See Brelich, *Paides e Parthenoi*, 169–71; Bonnechere, *Sacrifice humain*, 28, n. 22 [+].

[83] See Annexe 1 to this Ch.

Fig. 11. Red figure krateriskos from Brauron (430–420 BC) showing clothed 'bears'.

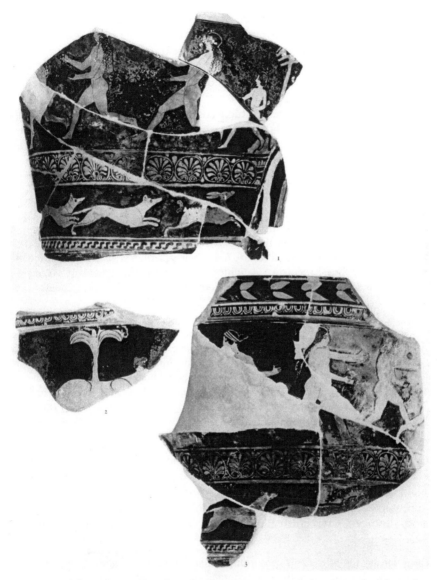

Fig. 12. Red figure krateriskos from Brauron (430–420 BC) showing naked 'bears'.

Why be a bear? The scholiasts offer an explanation in terms both of myth and of function: the rite owes its origin to a variously described offence against Artemis, and every maiden must undergo it before marriage. The function is on the surface only weakly accounted for by the myth, since the myths relate to maidens but not to marriage.[84] We must look at the two kinds of explanation separately, initially at least.

We will start with myth,[85] which comes in three forms. Very unfortunately, all are known from late lexicographical sources only, and only in one case can we guess where the lexicographers got their story from. According to one form (called 'Brauron' in what follows):

A wild she-bear used to come and spend its days in the deme of Philaidai [where the sanctuary of Brauron was located]. It grew tame and lived with humans, and a maiden played with it, but when the little girl went too far the she-bear grew angry and scratched the girl. Her brothers were enraged at this and shot the bear down, and in consequence a plague beset the Athenians. When they consulted the oracle they were told that they would get a release from their sufferings if in recompense for the dead bear they forced their own daughters to be bears. The Athenians voted that maidens should not cohabit with men without first being bears for the goddess.

The second form ('Mounichia') runs:

A she-bear appeared in it [the sanctuary of Artemis at Mounichia] and was slain by the Athenians. A plague ensued, and the god prophesied release from it if somebody sacrificed his daughter to Artemis. One Baros or Embaros was the only person to undertake to do it, on condition that his family should hold the priesthood for life: he adorned his daughter and then hid her in the *adyton* and sacrificed a goat which he had dressed up as if it were his daughter. And so there arose a proverb 'You're no Embaros', for those out of their senses, mad.

One source alone gives the necessary continuation, in a corrupt form the gist of which seems to be that when an oracle told the inhabitants to continue sacrificing in the same way, Embaros revealed his trick, 'and from then on the maidens were not afraid to be bears before marriage, as though making appeasement for the events of the hunt (?)'. The third and most intriguing story ('Iphigeneia') is curtly recorded as a variant in a scholion to Aristophanes.

But some say that the events concerning Iphigeneia happened at Brauron, not Aulis. Euphorion: 'Brauron near the sea, cenotaph of Iphigeneia'. It is thought that Agamemnon sacrificed Iphigeneia at Brauron, not at Aulis, and that a bear, not a deer, was slaughtered in her place.

---

[84] But C. A. Faraone goes much too far (in *Initiation*, 43–68) in postulating two distinct sets of ritual practices.

[85] See Brelich, Paides *e* Parthenoi, 247–63; T. Sale, *RhM* 118 (1975), 265–84; Brulé, *Fille d'Athènes*, 179–86, 200–22; Dowden, *Death and the Maiden*, 9–47; note too Bonnechere, *Sacrifice humain*, 31–6, and the works cited in n. 92 below.

'Some' is evidently the Atthidographer Phanodemus, who is independently said to have recorded that a bear died in Iphigeneia's stead.[86]

All three stories probably start from the same *primum mobile*, Artemis' anger at the killing of an animal or animals.[87] In 'Brauron' and 'Mounichia' the motif is explicit; as for 'Iphigeneia', most versions of the story of her sacrifice begin so, and even amid the magnificent and terrifying obscurity of Aeschylus' narrative of the myth in *Agamemnon* it is clear that Artemis is angry on just these grounds, however hard it may be to see what precisely the offence against her may have been.[88] According to 'Mounichia' and 'Iphigeneia' the goddess sought or seemed to seek the life of a virgin in exchange for that of the animal; but, by different mechanisms in the two stories, a further animal was substituted for the girl.[89] The little bears thus 'imitate' the original or, in 'Iphigeneia', the substituted animal; but they also surely, in a different sense, imitate the original girl whose life was owed to the goddess. No story presents the imitation of bear by girl as a product of likeness between them; on the contrary, the relation of man and bear is one of potential or actual hostility, even if the claim of one source that a virgin was to be sacrificed 'to the bear' is too extreme. At least one ritual practice is evidently implied by 'Mounichia', the sacrifice of a goat, and as it happens just such a sacrifice is attested for the *Brauronia*.[90] The hiding of Embaros' daughter in the *adyton* in 'Mounichia' might reflect the seclusion of the bears during their term of service;[91] and it is conceivable that a ritual hunt by young male relatives of the 'bears' lies behind the killing of the sacred animal, in 'Brauron' and 'Mounichia', by a 'brother' or 'young men'.

Can analysis of these stories be taken further? 'Brauron' presents a bear that becomes tame and a girl who provokes it by what is called ἀσέλγεια, indecorous or disrespectful behaviour. Is the bear an illustration of the power of acculturation, the girl by contrast a negative example of conduct unbecoming a maiden?[92] The issue is difficult, and we will revert to it. For the

---

[86] 'Brauron': Suda α 3958; 'Mounichia': Paus. Att. ε 35 Erbse ap. Eust. *Il.* 2.732 (p. 331.25), with the continuation in *Anecd. Bekk.* 1.445.1–13; 'Iphigeneia': Σ Ar. *Lys.* 645a–b, cf. Phanodemus *FGrH* 325 F 14. The texts are printed (with some parallel texts that add little) in Brelich, *Paides e Parthenoi*, 248–9. For the possibility that the 'Relief of the gods' at Brauron depicted Iphigeneia with Artemis see most recently Themelis in *Le orse*, 110–11.

[87] The stories intersect, but I do not think it is right to seek a single template for all three, with Sale, followed by Brulé, Dowden and Bonnechere as quoted in n. 85. Certainly, 'Brauron' shares elements with 'Mounichia' (the bear at the sanctuary) and 'Mounichia' with 'Iphigeneia' (the commuted maiden sacrifice). But it is equally true that 'Iphigeneia' is far removed from 'Brauron', and differs from both the others in its relation to Panhellenic myth.

[88] e.g. Proclus' summary of the *Cypria*, p. 32.55–63 Davies (combined with the motif of Agamemnon's boasting). Aeschylus: *Ag.* 134–44.

[89] Cf. A. Henrichs in *Sacrifice* 198–208; Vernant, *Figures, idoles, masques* 197–201; *Mortals and Immortals*, 214–16.

[90] Hesych. β 1067; cf. Brulé, *Fille d'Athènes*, 196. 'To the bear': *Anecd. Bekk.* 1.445.4.

[91] So Brelich, *Paides e Parthenoi*, 257–8, and cf. p. 232 above. For the 'sacred hunt' see n. 55.

[92] So Vernant, *Figures, idoles, masques*, 201–6; *Mortals and Immortals*, 217–19; Osborne, *Demos*, 165–70. See too n. 125.

moment let it be said that the bear of 'Mounichia' remains wild and even that of 'Brauron' reverts to savagery; as for the little girl, we really do not know whether she behaved lewdly in front of the bear, or pulled its tail. The verbal formulations in the Byzantine sources which are all we have for these stories cannot be pressed for their nuances as if they were the text of Aeschylus.

What are we to make of Iphigeneia's association with the bears? Is this an authentic instance of that rare phenomenon, a major myth that has its origins in an identifiable local cult? The matter is complicated, and two-sided. On the one hand, Iphigeneia is inextricably associated with the world of cult in a way that her 'mother' Clytemnestra, for instance, is not. She had a tomb which received cult at Brauron, another supposedly at Megara, and at Hermione was even combined with her goddess as Artemis Iphigeneia.[93] The very myth which makes her famous in literature also points back repeatedly to her cultic associations with Artemis. While no stress is laid on the identity of the powers to whom other maidens in myth, such as the Erechtheids, are sacrificed, in the case of Iphigeneia there is never doubt that it is Artemis who demands her death, or seems to. And even in the earliest versions the victim is always in fact an animal substitute, and Iphigeneia (or Iphimede) herself is snatched away to serve her goddess in a foreign land, or even transformed into Artemis Einodia/Hekate.[94] Whatever the actual etymology of her name may be,[95] Greeks must certainly have heard an allusion in it to the function with which she was associated in cult, 'strong birth'. But even though the myth itself of Iphigeneia points back to cult repeatedly, it cannot be explained simply in terms of ritual practices. Service of girls is attested in the sanctuaries of Artemis at Brauron and Mounichia, but the myth in its earliest form is set at Aulis, site indeed of yet another sanctuary of the goddess but not one at which any such service is known to have occurred.[96] Iphigeneia received worship at Brauron, but in a function associated with childbirth that has no

[93] Eur. *IT* 1462–67; Paus. 1.43.1, 2.35.1 (but these 'tombs of Iphigeneia' were only so identified late, according to J. N. Bremmer, 'Sacrificing a child in ancient Greece: the case of Iphigeneia', in E. Noort and E. Tigchelaar, eds., *The Sacrifice of Isaac*, Leiden 2002, 21–43, which is relevant to all aspects of Iphigeneia; for radical scepticism about Iphigeneia's role at Brauron see too G. Ekroth, *Kernos* 16, 2003, 59–118). Note too Paus. 1.43.4 (Iphinoe), 7.26.5, both showing links with *parthenoi*. On Iphigeneia's parentage see Stesichoros fr. 191 *PMG* ap. Paus. 2.22.7 (daughter of Helen and Theseus); P. H. J. Lloyd-Jones, 'Artemis and Iphigeneia', *JHS* 103 (1983), 87–102 (= id., *Greek Comedy, Hellenistic Literature, Greek Religion and Miscellanea*, Oxford 1990, 306–30), at 95.

[94] Hes. fr. 23a 13–26: 'Iphimede' becomes Artemis Einodia (I do not see that the passage implies two versions, true death and substitution, as argued by F. Solmsen, *AJP* 102, 1981, 353–8); Stesichorus fr. 215 *PMG* (p. 209 Davies): she becomes Hekate; Proclus' summary of the *Cypria*, p. 32.55–63 Davies (perhaps a contamination: M. B. Hollinshead, *AJA* 89, 1985, 422): she is carried off to Tauris and made immortal. On all this see Bonnechere, *Sacrifice humain*, 38–48. On the relation of Artemis Hekate to birth see Aesch. *Supp.* 676; Pingiatoglou, *Eileithyia*, 93.

[95] See Lloyd-Jones, *JHS* 103 (1983), 95, n.48; Dowden, *Death and the Maiden*, 46.

[96] Unless we accept an archaeological argument by Travlos about Aulis which M. B. Hollinshead attacks (*AJA* 89, 1985, 430–2). The old postulate that a rite of 'being the fawn' was celebrated in Thessaly and at Aulis has been exploded by new data: see Hatzopoulos, *Rites de passage*, 26–34.

correlate in her myth.[97] Most serious of all, it is only to a limited degree that Iphigeneia can be seen as a 'role-model'[98] for the maidens of Attica. Her death, it is often said, is a prototype of the symbolic death that in their initiation those maidens undergo. That parallel can in fact become much sharper if put in the form 'as Agamemnon sacrifices Iphigeneia to Artemis, so Attic fathers tithe their daughters to Artemis'; the crucial similarity (which depends on a proper understanding of the four words of Demosthenes discussed on page 233) is that in both cases father acts upon daughter. But in other respects the destiny of Iphigeneia and the bears differs greatly. Iphigeneia is sacrificed, supposedly, for a collective good. So too, in terms of the founding myth, are the bears, to avert a plague. But in a different sense they are tithed, as it were, for their own good, to pre-empt hostility on the part of Artemis against themselves. They look forward to marriage and childbirth, both of which are denied to Iphigeneia. The careers of Iphigeneia and the bears run initially in parallel (Iphigeneia sacrificed to Artemis, the bears tithed to her), but then move apart. That the little bears and their relatives may often have had the story of Iphigeneia in mind is very plausible. The Iphigeneia of Aeschylus in her saffron dress may well evoke the typical uniform of the bears.[99] But the myth could not interpret for them the whole of their experience in the way that the 'initiatory myth' hypothesis needs to postulate. Stories such as that of Iphigeneia seem to explain not so much what happens to the young worshippers as the paradoxical status of the unmarried heroes (such as Hippolytus) or heroines who are so often associated with them. Dead or transformed before marriage, these heroes and heroines are fixed for ever in what for their charges is a temporary condition.[100]

At Halai Araphenides, only about 6 kilometres up the coast from Brauron, Artemis was honoured as Tauropolos, 'bull-ranger'. A votive plaque from Brauron shows her as a 'bull-ranger' there too, and Euripides in *Iphigeneia in Tauris* provides a joint *aition* for the two cults. It sounds as if they were related or analogous. We know almost nothing of the *Tauropolia* held at Halai—there are few more grievous gaps in our knowledge of Attic festivals—but Athena in Euripides instructs that it be set up in consequence of Orestes' escape from the sacrificial knife among the Taurians: 'when the people holds festival, in compensation for your slaying, let someone hold a knife by a man's neck and

---

[97] Brelich, Paides *e* Parthenoi, 273–75.

[98] So Brelich, Paides *e* Parthenoi, 263; Bonnechere, *Sacrifice humain*, 36, and Dowden, *Death and the Maiden, passim*; for qualifications/reservations see Sourvinou-Inwood, *DHA* 16.2 (1990), 52; I. Clark, *International Journal of Moral and Social Studies* 5 (1990), 263–73 (review of Dowden).

[99] *Ag.* 239. The first critic to adduce Brauron in connection with Aeschylus was perhaps J. J. Peradotto, *Phoenix* 23 (1969), 243–6, soon followed independently by Sourvinou-Inwood, *CQ* 21 (1971), 339–42; cf. *Girls' Transitions*, 132–3.

[100] Cf. R. Seaford, *JHS* 108 (1988), 124; Redfield, *Locrian Maidens*, 114.

cause blood to fall, for the sake of the rite and to honour the goddess'.[101] As at Brauron, Artemis is therefore a goddess to whom life may be owed, a killer goddess.

I turn back from the mythical to the functional answer to the question 'why be a bear?' All the sources agree that it was a rite to be performed 'before marriage', and one even claims with high improbability that 'the Athenians voted that maidens should not cohabit with men without first being bears for the goddess'.[102] Libanius in his mannered way says that 'in another month, Mounichion I think' the Athenians 'introduce their maidens to Artemis, so that having first cultivated Artemis they may approach the works of Aphrodite'. We learn from a fragment of Menander that pregnant women invoked Artemis to forgive them for their loss of virginity.[103] There is no direct reference here to Brauron, but we see why the future bride must propitiate the virgin goddess. And Artemis' concern with virginity leads on, it is easy to suppose, to her concern with childbirth: if a young bride has propitiated the goddess successfully, she gives birth with ease, if not, with an anguish that may prove deadly. Many of the items of clothing listed in the Brauronian inventories are doubtless thank-offerings for successful birth.[104]

Thus far the *arkteia* echoes, in a new key, practices and attitudes familiar throughout Greece. Offerings, often of hair, to be made before marriage are common, and the typical recipient was Artemis or a virginal figure such as Hippolytus closely associated with her.[105] To Artemis was offered the girdle of maidenhood—whatever precisely that may have been—and her association with childbirth is very familiar; in parts of the Greek world 'Artemis Eileithyia' stood in for plain Artemis. Cyrenean women were required to approach Artemis before marriage, in pregnancy and after childbirth.[106] The *arkteia* is

[101] *IT* 1458–61; plaque: *Mesogaia*, 127. For a competition in *pyrriche* probably held at the *Tauropolia* see Ceccarelli, *Pirrica*, 83–5 (on *SEG* XXXIV 103); for the *pannychis* Men. *Epit.* 1118–20, and cf. p. 183, n. 21. P. H. J. Lloyd-Jones, *JHS* 103 (1983), 87–102, at 96–7, suggests that the *Tauropolia* were a kind of masculine equivalent to *Brauronia*. The problem is to see how such a rite would fit with other evidence for men's maturation rites.

[102] Suda α 3958. Craterus the collector of decrees spoke of the *arkteia* (*FGrH* 342 F 9 in Harpoc. α 235), which suggests that a decree spoke of the institution; it does not prove the decree wildly postulated by the lexicographers genuine.

[103] Lib. 5.29–30 Foerster (he goes on to associate Artemis with the Piraeus); Men. fr 38 (35 Koerte). For finds of *lebetes gamikoi* at Brauron and Mounichia see Palaiokrassa, Ἱερό, 67–73, 94, 134–37; *AM* 104 (1989), 11.

[104] For the practice see Σ Call. *Hymn* 1.77b (on the Artemis Chitone there mentioned see W. Günther in *Comptes et inventaires*, 232–7), G. Ekroth, *Kernos* 16 (2003), 71, n. 58; cf. *Anth. Pal.* 6.271 (Phaedimus I Gow/Page, *HE*); *Anth. Pal.* 6.202 (Leonidas I Gow/Page, *HE*); *Anth. Pal.* 6.272 (Perses II Gow/Page, *HE*); note too *Anth. Pal.* 6.273 (Nossis XII Gow/Page, *HE*). The epigram by Phaedimus relates to a well-known Attic family (Habicht, *Studien*, 194–7).

[105] See e.g. Hdt. 4.34; Eur. *Hipp.* 1425–30 (Paus. 2.32.1); Paus. 1.43.4; Plut. *Arist.* 20.7–8; Stat. *Theb.* 2. 253–6 'huic (Athena) more parentum | Iasides, thalamis ubi casta adolesceret aetas, | virgineas libare comas primosque solebant | excusare toros'.

[106] Girdle: Sud. λ 859 s.v. λυσίζωνος γυνή (but at Troizen Athena Apatouria got it, Paus. 2.33.1); cf. *Anth. Pal.* 6.358, and on the sense Brulé, *Fille d'Athènes*, 234, 277, n. 309. An r.f. lekythos by the Achilles Painter in Syracuse (21186: Oakley/Sinos, *Wedding*, fig. 9) appears to

distinctive in that the future brides propitiated the goddess not by gifts alone but also, it seems, by a period of service in her shrine; and the service, unlike the gifts, preceded the marriage by several years. But the analogies are so great that the lexicographers were evidently right or right in part to treat the *arkteia* as a 'pre-marriage' practice like the others.

What, in the practices of the *arkteia*, might serve this premarital function? From literary sources we learn only that the bears wore, and perhaps at a certain point shed, the saffron robe or κροκωτός. In Athenian eyes the *krokotos* was primarily the dress of the married woman, viewed particularly as an object of sexual desire.[107] For the bears the *krokotos* meant dressing up; for their elders it was an evocation, in some ways piquant and paradoxical, of the little girls' future role. For further evidence on the rites we look to the krateriskoi. They reveal among the bears numerous permutations of age and dress and activities and attributes, but three broad themes stand out, those of choral dancing (and processions), races and nakedness.

Dancing is easy: learning to sing and dance under the supervision of older women was, we know, a fundamental element in the socialization of Greek girls throughout the archaic and classical periods,[108] and here, for once, we can identify an Attic context in which the process could take place. The role of running is less familiar.[109] Races between unmarried girls are known from Elis, from Sparta and now perhaps from various places in Thessaly and Macedonia.[110] They tend to be interpreted as rites of passage, even though there is no sign except perhaps in the North Greek cases that all the girls of a given age-group were required, at a specific moment, to run their way through to the next. Such an interpretation focuses on the single moment of performance of the ritual race. But the torch-races run by ephebes were the

---

show a young woman ceremonially untying her girdle for Artemis. For other dedications to Artemis at marriage see *Anth. Pal.* 6.280 (Anon. XLI Gow/Page, *HE*); *Anth. Pal.* 6.276 (Antipater of Sidon LI Gow/Page, *HE*). On Artemis and childbirth see e.g. Pl. *Tht.* 149b–c; S. G. Cole, *ZPE* 55 (1984), 243, n. 62, and *Ritual Space*, 212–13; W. Günther in *Comptes et inventaires*, 233; Pingiatoglou, *Eileithyia*, 98–119, 153–72. Cyrene: *LSS* 115 B 1–23 (RO 97.83–105); cf. Parker, *Miasma*, 344–6, and on this cult, the priestess in which was called 'bear', P. Perlman, *Arethusa* 22 (1989), 127–30.

[107] Literary sources: Ar. *Lys.* 645, cf. perhaps Aesch. *Ag.* 239. Sexual desire: see e.g. Ar. *Lys.* 219, and L. Bodson, *'IEPA ZΩIA* (Brussels 1978), 132–3; Brulé, *Fille d'Athènes*, 240–5 [+]; Sourvinou-Inwood, *Girls' Transitions*, 127–9. Vernant, *Figures, idoles, masques*, 182, speaks of 'la prime jeunesse et sa seduction', a somewhat different claim.

[108] Calame, *Choeurs, passim*; Vernant, *Figures, idoles, masques*, 205, cites Pl. *Leg.* 653d–654a on the socializing function of the chorus (but the primary reference there is to boys).

[109] L. Kahil, *AntK* 8 (1965), 30, draws attention to a race scene very reminiscent of the krateriskoi on a b.f. lekythos (Athens NM 548, her pls. 10.6, 7) attributed to the Beldam painter. I doubt the suggestion of T. F. Scanlon, *Nikephoros* 3 (1990), 109–20, that the Brauronian girls are not in fact racing but chasing one another, in a kind of tag.

[110] If Hatzopoulos is right so to interpret the νεβεύσασα *vel sim.* of the very important inscriptions he publishes and studies (*Rites de passage*, 25–40), in what is now a fundamental work for any enquiry into female rites of passage. Elis: Paus. 5.16.2–4; Sparta ibid. 3.13.7, cf. Hesych ε 2823. I allow that it is likely that all Spartan girls ran (cf. Theocr. 18.22–4), but a specific race that constituted a rite of passage for them all is not known.

culmination of a process of training, and perhaps we should envisage regular physical exercise for the girls too. (Girls are in fact occasionally shown running with torches on the *krateriskoi*, in an interesting echo of the ephebic rite par excellence.) It was famous in antiquity that girls did such things in Sparta, where 'sport that brought no shame' was engaged in, according to cheeky Propertius, by 'naked girls amid grappling men'.[111] But we have noted the presence at Brauron of a gymnasium and a *palaistra*, and some suppose that Attic vases which show mature females in a state of après-sport undress attest such activities even among married women.[112] Xenophon says that Lycurgus established contests for women no less than for men in the belief that 'the offspring of two strong parents are themselves more sturdy'; Plutarch echoes the claim, and adds that women were also prepared thereby for the ordeal of childbirth.[113] Perhaps the parents of the bears had similar beliefs and hopes.

The nakedness in which many bears are shown on the krateriskoi could scarcely have been predicted. The effect must above all have been to underline the effect of 'not yet'[114]attaching to the bears: not yet bound by the code of adult female propriety, not yet ready for a man. But, since change of dress is something close to a 'natural symbol' for change of status, it is very plausible that a prelude to the nakedness was a ritual disrobing like that performed, for instance, at the Cretan *Ekdysia*, 'Stripping';[115] one reading of the doubtful passage in *Lysistrata* in fact makes the chorus speak of 'shedding the *krokotos*' ('wearing the *krokotos*' is the alternative) when a bear. Unfortunately it is not quite clear which bears went naked and in what circumstances, since no activity or age-group is invariably associated with nudity on the krateriskoi (though frequent associations exist). Plato in *Laws*[116] recommends that girls should compete in races naked up to the age of 12, 'in fitting attire' from then on. As the only allusion in an Attic author to races and nakedness for girls the text is noteworthy; but it fails to illuminate the world of the bears, who are all very probably under 12 and who are more likely to be naked the older they

---

[111] 3.14.3–4. *(quod) non infames exercet corpore ludos | inter luctantis nuda puella viros*: for *luctari* of sexual activity see id. 2.1.13, 2.15.5, *TLL* s.v. *luctari*, 1731. Cf. Arrigoni, 'Donne e sport', 70–95 (but her distinction between 'political-eugenic' and ritual athletics seems misguided); T. F. Scanlon, 'Virgineum Gymnasium: Spartan Females and Early Greek Athletics', in W. J. Raschke (ed.), *The Archaeology of the Olympics* (Madison, Wis. 1988), 185–216.

[112] See C. Bérard, *AION* 8 (1986) 195–202, disputing the argument that the implied setting of the scenes is Sparta. On the whole issue see Arrigoni, 'Donne e sport'.

[113] Xen. *Lac.* 1.4 (cf. already Critias 88 DK B 32); Plut. *Lyc.* 14.3.

[114] 'Nondum', first word of an ode of Horace (2.5) that is based on the treatment of such themes in Greek lyric.

[115] Ant. Lib. *Met.* 17.6 (Phaistos); *IC* I.ix.1.98–100 (Dreros) τὰν ἀγέλαν τοὺς τόκα ἐγδυομένους and *IC* I.xix.1.17–18 (Malla) τὰν ἀγέλαν τὰν τόκα ἐσδυομέναν are compared. See Brelich, Paides e Parthenoi, 200–2; Sourvinou-Inwood, *Girls' Transitions*, 127–34.

[116] 833c–d. Doubtful passage: n. 74 above.

are. We are left to speculate about the specific place of nakedness in the sequence of ritual actions.[117]

No krateriskos shows bears engaged in quieter pursuits. But objects relating to the world of weaving—spindle whorls, loom weights, thigh-protectors used in carding wool—have been found at the site in good numbers.[118] Envisaged as expressions of craft, such activites were in the protection of Athena; but it seems they could be seen as belonging also to maidenhood and so become congenial to Artemis. Whether actual training or competitions in these works of women took place we cannot know.

Does all this amount to justification for speaking of the *arkteia* as an 'initiation'? Those who wish to do so will stress the claims (however exaggerated) that all Athenian girls were required to undergo it; the probability that the bears lived for a period in the shrine, and the possibility that they underwent a form of training for grown-up female activities; the secluded location of the sanctuary (but it is countered that female initiations, where attested, normally occur in central rather than marginal space). On the other side it is urged that female initiations in a society which lacks a male equivalent are an oddity; that several of the positive indications are uncertain or inconclusive; and, above all, that even the sources which present the *arkteia* as obligatory see it as a means to propitiate Artemis or as a premarital rite of passage rather than as one associated with the growing up of adolescent and pre-adolescent girls.[119] But one has only to separate out these functions (girls' maturation; preparation for marriage; propitiation of Artemis) to see ways in which it is wrong or unnecessary to do so. Girls' maturation even from a young age is seen by the Greeks as a growing towards marriage; and what on the human level is preparation for marriage, on the divine level is propitiation of the goddess. All reservations having been made, the *arkteia* looks more like a kind of initiation than like any other form of Greek ritual activity.

But a further crucial question remains. Why were the 'bears' bears? A sceptic might urge that there is no substantial phenomenon here to be explained; for names can be traditional, and we do not know how seriously the idea of beardom was evoked in the rites.[120] The aitiological stories speak

[117] For sensible hypotheses see Sourvinou-Inwood, *Girls' Transitions*, 62–6, 131–2; agnosticism in Palaiokrassa, Ἱερό, 93.

[118] For a good summary see S. G. Cole, *ZPE* 55 (1984), 239–40; cf. Linders, *Temple Records*, 19, Brulé, *Fille d'Athènes*, 226–231 and *DHA* 16.2 (1990), 76–80 (where he cites the 6th-c. graffito of a woman of Taranto: Μελόσας ἐμὶ νικατέριον· ξαίνοσα τὰς κόρας ἐνίκη, *LSAG* 280, 283, no. 1). The relief Brauron Mus. 1183, *LIMC* s.v. *Artemis* no. 724 has been taken to show a goddess weaving, but L. Kahil in *LIMC* ad loc. is sceptical.

[119] See C. A. Faraone in *Initiation*, 43–68; Ferrari, *Figures of Speech*, 166–81; also R. L. Fowler in *Oxford Readings*, 326–30 (from *ICS* 20 (1995), 9 ff.). Ferrari's own suggestion, 176–7, that the *arkteia* relates above all to citizenship seems to require a proof that all citizen girls underwent it, and none but them.

[120] Brulé, *Fille d'Athènes*, 225, warns against overestimating the importance of the *aitia* for 'la religion vécue'.

of bears, but that is predictable, it might be said, and scarcely revealing; the bear that appears on a krateriskos could be seen as merely a symbol of the *arkteia*, and one fragmentary vase which does indeed show humans disguised as bears or transformed into them is not necessarily a krateriskos and might have nothing to do with Brauron.[121] The sceptic would be right that we must engage imaginatively with situations, not play with words. But it is far from established that 'bear' was a word and no more in this context.

The great shaggy beast that walks and copulates like a man has a richer mythology in northern Eurasia than perhaps any other. Much of it relates to the experience of the hunter, his terrors and his guilts. Doubtless this is one reason why Artemis is, of all Greek gods, much the most closely associated with the bear. There was bear to be taken, along with wild boar, on Attica's highest peak M. Parnes, according to Pausanias.[122] But religious thought puts old symbols to new uses, and the bizarre phenomenon that we have to explain is that at Brauron the ancient adversary of hunters became a matter of concern, and on the surface an object of imitation, for little girls. Young girls, preparing for marriage and childbirth in the service of Artemis, are associated with a wild animal. We are dealing with a particular instance of the broader paradox whereby the 'mistress of animals' is also closely associated with the birth pangs of women. The sharpness of the antithesis is sometimes blurred by middle terms. 'Virginity' provides a bridge between Artemis' role as huntress and as mistress of women, but only by way of an association, which is itself problematic, between hunting and virginity. Images can function in the same way, as when Artemis turns her arrows against women, or by contrast lays them aside and permits easy birth.[123] Is there a deeper unity? The antithesis of wild and tame, it is plausibly suggested,[124] is fundamental: the uncontrollable physical trauma of childbirth is an eruption of wild nature into the social world. The Greeks perhaps said something similar in their own way when they called Artemis a 'lion to women'.

---

[121] *AntK* 20 (1977), 92–3, with foldout C and pl. 20 (= Simon, *Festivals*, pl. 25; Brulé, *Fille d'Athènes*, 252, fig. 33; and, in colour, Reeder, *Pandora*, 327, n. 100). For the uncertainty whether the vase is a krateriskos see ibid. 89; its provenance is unknown, but it belongs to a private collection which contains important *krateriskoi*. If Simon is right (*Festivals*, 88) to interpret the scene depicted as Kallisto and Arkas and if the vase is indeed a Brauronian krateriskos, the remarkable possibility arises of evocation of this myth in the ritual (so A. Henrichs in J. Bremmer (ed.), *Interpretations of Greek Mythology*, London 1987, 265).

[122] On the mythology of the bear see P. H. J. Lloyd-Jones, *JHS* 103 (1983), 97–8; Brulé, *Fille d'Athènes*, 215–16, 257–9; *DHA* 16.2 (1990), 9–27; P. Leveque, *REA* 91.3–4 (1989), 60–4. On dedications of bear statues in Greek sanctuaries see E. R. Bevan, *BSA* 82 (1987), 17–21; P. Perlman, *Arethusa* 22 (1989), 115. Artemis is much the commonest recipient. H. G. Buchholz, 'Zum Bären in Syrien und Griechenland', *Act. Praeh. Arch.* 5/6 (1974/5), 175–85, does little more than refer to myth in regard to Greece. Mt Parnes: Paus. 1.32.1; cf. Brulé, *Fille d'Athènes*, 271, nn. 160–1.

[123] See the epigrams of Phaedimus and Nossis cited in n. 104 above.

[124] See p. 239, n. 92.

What of the more specific problem of the bears? A popular approach has been through the Greek habit of speaking of children, girls in particular, as if they were animals. Maidens are fawns or fillies who must in due time be tamed and 'yoked' to a man.[125] Being a bear is therefore a playing out, by intensification, of that natural wildness of the young girl which it is, none the less, one function of the *arkteia* to overcome. The 'tamed' bear of the Brauron *aition* becomes on this reading the model for the young girls to imitate. But the animals with which girls are otherwise associated are the ones that fear and flee from men, that shun, initially at least, the yoke. The obvious animal emblem for the unyoked, but yokable, maiden would be the filly. The bear is wild in a very different sense. In Greek stories, attempts to tame bears, like lions, prove delusive; the animal bursts forth more savage than before. As types of savagery, bear and lion are in fact not seldom associated.[126] As for the trouble famously taken by the mother bear to 'lick her cubs into shape', this maternal devotion was necessary only because what she gave birth to was an unformed mass of matter, scarcely a creature at all; according to a late didactic poet (pseudo-Oppian, in the third century AD), it was mad desire for intercourse that caused her to void her womb untimely.[127] The whole point, it will be countered, is that the image of 'bear' represents the potential wildness of the human in extreme form. But could a resemblance of any kind have been perceived between the future Athenian mothers and this 'wildest and grimmest of beasts', as Plutarch calls it?

The association of the strongest and most brutal of animals with one of the weakest and timidest forms of human life was surely perceived to be a paradox. A famous simile of the *Odyssey*[128] plays wittily with the juxtaposition of a mountain lion and girls just turning their thoughts to marriage. The bear was probably still a terror figure to girls who played the bear: we mentioned earlier a scholion's talk of maidens sacrificed 'to the bear', and the one krateriskos which shows the beast also shows maidens who are perhaps in flight from it. If the myth of Kallisto, the unchaste servant of

---

[125] For such imagery see Calame, *Choeurs*, ii, 411–15; J. Gould, *JHS* 100 (1980), 53; the note of Nisbet/Hubbard on Hor. *Od.* 1.23.1 For variants of this approach see Vernant, *Figures, idoles, masques*, 201–6; Vidal-Naquet, *Chasseur noir*, 199 (146 in the Engl. tr.); Osborne, *Demos*, 165–70; Sourvinou-Inwood, *DHA* 16.2 (1990), 54–60; Seaford, *Reciprocity and Ritual*, 306–7. Differently Kearns, *Heroes*, 30–1, sees an equivalence between shot bear and deflowered girl: two offences against Artemis.

[126] Failed taming: see Aesch. *Ag.* 716–36, with Fraenkel's note on 736, and the extraordinary story given by Eudemos ap. Ael. *NA* 4.45. Bear and lion: Hom. *Od.* 11.611, *Hom Hymn.* 4.223, 5.159. On the almost wholly negative ancient view of the bear see P. M. C. Forbes Irving, *Metamorphosis in Greek Myths* (Oxford 1990), 46, 73–5.

[127] See Arist. *Hist. an.* 579a 18–30; Plut. *De amore prolis* 2, 494c; Oppian *Cyn.* 3. 139–69; Aelian *NA* 2.19 ('the bear does not know how to give birth'); only in Philost. *Ap. Ty.* 2.14 (p. 152 in the Loeb) to my knowledge is the maternal love of the she-bear ('most savage of creatures') stressed. P. Perlman, *Arethusa* 22 (1989), 111–33, makes the case for the bear as 'an ancient symbol of motherhood', but ignores the negative traits.

[128] 6.130–6.

Artemis who was transformed into a bear, was evoked during the ritual, her fate was doubtless presented as an awful warning.[129] Can we identify a particular terror embodied in the bear, that for instance of the forthcoming first sexual encounter?[130] But the one or two myths that tell of women mating with bears do not suffice to make the animal a symbol of devouring male sexuality. The matter must be left in rather more general terms. The bear embodied the extreme limit of the world of Artemis, that aspect of the goddess which was most alien and savage and terrifying. The girls imitate the bear neither to encourage good bearish qualities in themselves nor yet to exorcize bad ones; for the bear is outside the human world altogether. But, though bearishness was outside them, it was also, as an expression of the wildness of Artemis who might kill them, very close to their future lives. What pretends to be 'imitation' is really appeasement, exorcism. By becoming bears, by encasing the savage force in their own weak frames, they rendered it familiar and tame.

ANNEXE I: *KANEPHOROI* AT BRAURON?

According to a myth first attested in Herodotus, the Pelasgians of Lemnos avenged an old insult by descending on Brauron while 'the women (i.e. wives) of the Athenians' were conducting a festival, and carrying off many of them to keep as concubines. Philochorus told the same myth, but of two reports of his account (both in scholia) one says that he identified the victims as 'bears' (a tradition very likely found also in Aristophanes' *Lemniai* and Euripides' *Hypsipyle*),[131] one as 'basket-bearers' (*kanephoroi*).[132] For our purposes the question is whether anything here presupposes ritual practices at Brauron other than the *arkteia*. 'Nubility' characterizes the victims in all three variants, if in different ways; with 'bears' the Pelasgians would have had to wait a little. Herodotus may have blurred the distinctive Attic details in favour of the familiar story type, 'married women seized during a festival'. The *kanephoros* version too might be owed to the familiar association between *kanephoroi* and sexual allure. A different scholion claims that 'Athenian girls of an age for marriage were basket-bearers for Artemis' (locale unidentified). Do the two reports confirm one another? If so, older girls—ex-bears as it were—

[129] Krateriskos with bear: see Sourvinou-Inwood, *Girls' Transitions*, 63; Lonsdale, *Dance*, 191–3; here Fig. 12. Kallisto: n. 121 above.

[130] So Brulé, *Fille d'Athènes*, 260–1; DHA 16.2 (1990), 25–7; cf. Lonsdale, *Dance*, 183–5. Myths: those of Polyphonte and Egesta (Brulé, 215).

[131] Harpocr. α 235 ὅτι δὲ αἱ ἀρκτευόμεναι παρθένοι ἄρκτοι καλοῦνται Εὐριπίδης Ὑψιπύλῃ (fr. 767 Nauck), Ἀριστοφάνης Λημνίαις (fr. 386) καὶ Λυσιστράτῃ. G. W. Bond in his edition of *Hypsipyle* (Oxford 1963), 139, supposes that the heroine told the story to the chorus, but according to the chronology of Hdt. 6.138 the relevant event would not by then have occurred: did Dionysus prophesy it in the *exodos*?

[132] Hdt. 6.138, cf. 4.145.2; Philochorus FGrH 328 F 100 and 101.

participated at the *Brauronia* as a distinct group.[133] But basket-bearers did not normally hunt in packs, and it is more likely that we have coincidence in error.

ANNEXE 2: FESTIVALS FOR BOYS: THE RELIGIOUS WORLD OF
THE GYMNASIUM

There was, we have seen, no male equivalent to the *arkteia*. But if the *arkteia* was a blend of socialization and involvement in cult for girls, there was also a context where for boys and young men general training intersected with ritual activity. Since studies of Greek religion seldom say much about the gymnasium, a few words of introduction may be helpful.

In most Greek cities in the hellenistic period, the gymnasium was one important focus of religious life. One 'gymnasium religious calendar' survives, and almost all gymnasia must have had such calendars in effect, even if they were not inscribed on stone. The various categories of youth who trained and studied in the gymnasia went out from them to participate, as groups, in the public festivals; the public often came in for sacrificial feasts held, conveniently, in the large open space of the gymnasium, and the young had festivals of their own within the walls.[134] The role of the gymnasium was formalized in the early hellenistic period, when in many cities the office of gymnasiarch became one of the most onerous and prestigious to which the publicly spirited rich could aspire.[135] For the early period by contrast our picture of the workings of the gymnasium, important though it certainly already was as a social institution, must be a little blurred.

The sites of the three great gymnasia of Athens—Academy, Lyceum, and 'at Kynosarges'—had a variety of functions.[136] Academy and Lyceum were

---

[133] Different scholion: *Σ* Theocr. 2.66–8b. Deubner, *Attische Feste*, 208; Brelich, Paides *e* Parthenoi, 241, 280, 283; Brulé, *Fille d' Athènes*, 315, all accept the presence of *kanephoroi* at Brauron, without discussing the discrepancy between the two reports of Philochorus. Pfuhl, *De pompis*, 82, supposed that the bears also served as basket-bearers. Deubner, *Attische Feste*, 208, n.3, and Brelich, Paides *e* Parthenoi, 286–90, uneconomically fail to connect the *Σ* Theocr. notice with Brauron. This *Σ* may represent an attempt to reconcile the details of Theocritus' text (whence come the *kanephoroi*) with a tradition also reported ibid. about Attic attitudes to Artemis. For the unreliability of the Theocritean *Σ* in matters of Attic cult see *Σ* 4.25c with Deubner, 53, n.9.

[134] *IG* II² 1227 is a good brief illustration, from the Athenian cleruchy of Salamis (131/0 BC). An inventory from an Athenian gymnasium of about that period survives (*SEG* xxvi 139: the Ptolemaeum? Travlos, *Pictorial Dictionary*, 233–41): numerous statues of gods are listed. See in general E. Ziebarth, *Aus dem griechischen Schulwesen*, ed. 2 (Leipzig, 1914), 40–4, 136–68; M. P. Nilsson, *Die hellenistische Schule* (Munich, 1955), 61–75, 78–80; Nilsson, *Geschichte*, ii, 61–7. Calendar: *Syll.*³ 1028 (*LSCG* 165; Cos).

[135] See above all Gauthier/Hatzopoulos, *Loi gymnasiarchique*.

[136] See J. Delorme, *Gymnasion* (Paris, 1960), 33–50; on the Lyceum also J. P. Lynch, *Aristotle's School* (Berkeley, 1972), 9–16; below p. 402; on Kynosarges M.-F. Billot in M.-O. Goulet-Cazé and R. Goulet (eds.), *Le Cynisme ancien* (Paris 1993), 69–116. Delorme finds γυμνάζεσθαι as a pattern of life first attested in Theogn. 1335–6.

places of training and display for the cavalry, Lyceum also for footsoldiers; all three contained or abutted sanctuaries and may in fact have grown up around them. The existence of, say, 'the Lyceum' at a given date does not prove that it already functioned as a gymnasium. All that can be said is that all three were so used late in the fifth century, the Academy it seems already in the sixth, when a friend of the tyrants, Charmus, founded an altar to Eros 'at the shady limits of the gymnasium'.[137] According to lexicographers, an expensive wall was built 'around the Academy' by the Pisistratid Hipparchus, and according to Theopompus the Lyceum was founded by Pisistratus. If either of these last two details can be trusted, the provision of gymnasia was already an object of public concern and expenditure in the archaic period; that was certainly the case in the fifth century, when Pericles 'supervised' works of an unspecified nature in the Lyceum.[138]

Public laws prescribed what might and might not be done both in these official gymnasia and in the numerous private *palaistrai* that had also sprung up by the time of Plato, our prime source for this whole world; there were fixed hours of opening and closing, and only the free were permitted to train.[139] Most striking perhaps are the assumptions behind the rule that bastards should 'be registered at' or 'contribute to'[140] the gymnasium of Heracles at Kynosarges. Whatever the precise scope and context of that problematic regulation may have been, it was apparently a way of giving to a group that was partially excluded, but not despised, a niche in Athenian society; and the means adopted was to associate them with a gymnasium.

But what took place in the gymnasia and *palaistrai*? Young men of various ages went there to train (γυμνάζεσθαι), though boys seem normally, as later, to have been separated from predatory 'youths'.[141] By the late fifth century the gymnasia had already become typical contexts for informal higher

[137] Academy: Page, *FGE* Anonymous XCVI ap. Ath. 609c; cf. Paus. 1.30.1; Plut. *Sol.* 1.7; *Athenian Religion*, 74. The next attestation of athletics there is Ar. *Nub.* 1002–8. For the Lyceum see e.g. Pl. *Euthd.* 271–2, Xen. *Hell.* 1.1.33, Aeschines of Sphettos fr. 2 Dittmar, fr. 43 Giannantoni (cf. Lynch, op. cit. 15); for Kynosarges Plut. *Them.* 1.3 with Dem. 23.213 and Ath. 234d–e. On the role of Lyceum and Academy in military training see Ar. *Pax* 356; Hesych λ 1380; Xen. *Eq. mag.* 3.1 and 6.
[138] Academy wall: e.g. Suda τ 733, but see the doubts raised by J. P. Lynch in K. J. Rigsby (ed.), *Studies Presented to Sterling Dow* (*GRBM* 10, 1984), 173–9. For Cimon's role see Plut. *Cim.* 13.7. Lyceum: associated with Pisistratus by Theopompus 115 *FGrH* F 136 but with Pericles by Philochorus 328 *FGrH* F 37, both known from Harpocration λ 30. Both men could have had a hand, as later Lycurgus (who was also credited with its 'foundation': [Plut.] *X orat.* 841c–d, 843f, 852c).
[139] Aeschin. 1.10, 138: for the exclusions at Beroia see Gauthier/Hatzopoulos, *Loi gymnasiarchique*, 78–87. Private *palaistrai*: e.g. Pl. *Chrm.* 153a, *Lysis* 204a.
[140] συντελεῖν ἐς Κυνόσαργες, Dem. 23.213: the many lexicographers' interpretations of the phrase probably derive from here (see in detail Billot, op. cit., 89) and have no real authority. The main sources are Plut. *Them.* 1.3 and Ath. 234d–e; see D. Ogden, *Greek Bastardy* (Oxford, 1996), 199–203 [+]. Plutarch associates the choice of Heracles with Heracles' own supposed illegitimacy (cf. Ar. *Av.* 1649–50).
[141] Pl. *Lysis* 206c–d; for later practice see B 13–15 of the Beroia law (Gauthier/Hatzopoulos, *Loi gymnasiarchique*).

education—debate, sophistic display—[142] though to learn their letters boys still went to separate establishments. How regularly individuals might attend, and on what organizational basis, is unclear; one text apparently of the fourth century contains a vague but characteristic allusion to 'those who frequent' a given gymnasium, an anticipation of the groups of 'those who anoint themselves' or 'those who strip'[143] often found in hellenistic decrees. A little more precision would be possible in one area if we knew more of the 'proto-ephebate' that existed before the institution was formalized by the law of Epicrates in the 330s; for it was doubtless in gymnasia, though not necessarily those of Athens itself, that the young volunteers underwent much of their training. There too they will have prepared, probably over substantial periods of time, for the great torch-races that were contested at least three times a year between the ephebes of the different tribes.[144]

It is at all events clear that the gymnasia already had their own festivals or at least their own festival, one which remained central to gymnasium life in the hellenistic period, the *Hermaia*.[145] Aeschines assumes that *Hermaia* take place in every gymnasium, and an offering to 'Hermes in the Lyceum' listed in the calendar of Nicomachus surely relates to such a festival. Plato's *Lysis* takes place on the fringe of a celebration of the *Hermaia* at a newly opened private *palaistra*. No details emerge—all analogy suggests that it consisted of athletic competitions—but we learn something more important, that the young celebrants provided their own 'performers of rites', *hieropoioi*, and could be said to sacrifice on their own account.[146] The ephebate prepared the young for a role in the city by granting them 'cadet magistracies' within the corps of ephebes. Similarly it was at the festivals of the gymnasia that, probably for the first time, they could become subjects of the verb 'to sacrifice'.

Possibly, however, that initiation occurred even earlier. The 'cult of the Muses' practised in the Academy and the Lyceum was a transposition to a higher level of what took place in elementary schools, for which *Mouseia*, festivals of the Muses, were what *Hermaia* were to gymnasia. Schools were associated with the Muses because choral dancing, lyre-playing and a concern for rhythm had been central to Greek education from the earliest times; by the late fifth century a character in Euripides could say 'I have been not ill mused (οὐ μεμούσωμαι κακῶς)' to mean 'my education has been good'. The

---

[142] See e.g. the openings of Pl. *Lysis* and *Euthydemos*.

[143] *IG* II² 1250. 6, οἱ φοιτῶντες; cf. the Beroia law (Gauthier/Hatzopoulos, *Loi gymnasiarchique*), B 7–8, 83, with the comments of the editors, 57–8, and for the verb Ar. *Eq.* 988 (of schooling). Organization: see S. C. Humphreys, *JHS* 94 (1974), 91.

[144] See p. 472.

[145] See Gauthier/Hatzopoulos, *Loi gymnasiarchique*, 95–6, who cite *Bull. épig.* 1962, 248: 'une fête qui existe en tout gymnase, en chaque ville'.

[146] Aeschin. 1.10; Nicomachus: *BSA* 97 (2002), 364, fr. 6.4; Pl. *Lysis* 206c–207a, 207d. Analogy: see e.g. the Beroia law (Gauthier/Hatzopoulos, *Loi gymnasiarchique*), B 45–87; for the hellenistic period in Athens see *IG* II² 1227 (131/0, on Salamis). For a probably different type of *Hermaia* in Athens see App. 1 s.v.

association persisted—there were jokes about unsuccessful schools that contained more muses than pupils—and in the first century BC it was still a norm
for groups of 'mellephebes' (those about to complete their elementary education) to make a dedication to the Muses. No source unfortunately describes
the conduct of a Muse festival in a school.[147]

---

[147] *Mouseia* in schools: Aeschin. 1.10; cf. Lynch, op. cit., 113–16. Euripides: *Melanippe Sophe*
fr. 483.4 Nauck ap. Ar. *Lys.* 1127; cf. e.g. Ar. *Eq.* 188–93; A. Queyrel in *LIMC* s.v. *Mousa/Mousai*,
658. Jokes: Ath. 348d, D.L. 6. 69: such teachers have, σὺν θεοῖς, many pupils. Outside Athens see
e.g. *Syll.*[3] 577.36 and *passim*, 578.57, Herondas 3.1, 71, 97. Mellephebes: *IG* II[2] 2986, 2991,
2991a; cf. Pélékidis, *Éphébie*, 208–9 and *IG* II[2] 2994 (dedication by a lampadarch). The character
by contrast of the public cult or cults of the Muses (*IG* I[3] 369.66, 86), not necessarily identical
with the cults of the 'Muses of Ilissus' (Pl. *Phaedr.* 278b; Apollod 244 *FGrH* F 145; Paus. 1.19.5),
is not known.

12

The *Panathenaea*

Four Attic festivals stand out for the frequency with which they are mentioned and the abundance of evidence that survives in relation to them. The following chapters will treat them in turn. And where should we begin but with the *Greater Panathenaea*, doubtless the best known of all Greek festivals of the pre-Christian period, with the single exception of the Eleusinian *Mysteries*? Indeed, for English speakers, Keats and the Parthenon marbles can combine to make it seem the Greek festival par excellence. Even in antiquity, its 'visibility' within the Greek world was perhaps uniquely great, through the concrete symbols of it obligingly taken home by visitors: not just the famous amphorae received by victors, but also smaller vessels evoking the larger in shape and decoration and probably sold as souvenirs.[1] Its history can be intermittently traced over a very long period.[2] Only one of the ritual symbols deployed, the famous ship on land, is out of the ordinary. But commonplace elements are combined in ways which illustrate several potentialities of the festival form with great clarity. For the competitive programme the Athenians sought, and to some extent achieved, a panhellenic prestige comparable to that of the four great festivals of the circuit. But it remained a context in which Athenians strutted their wares before Athenians, a great domestic showcase. Issues of prestige and social ranking, implicit in almost any ritual action, regularly become explicit when sources speak of the Panathenaic procession. And abundant evidence attests the festival's emotional and imaginative importance for the society in which it occurred.

To take the last point first, the prominence of the *Greater Panathenaea* in the administrative or organizational year is a demonstration of 'embedded religion' in action. The term of office of the treasurers of Athena ran 'from

---

[1] See e.g. Neils in *Goddess and Polis*, 42–6; Shear, *Polis and Panathenaia*, 432–56, on, *inter alia*, Beazley's linking of miniature Panathenaic amphorae with the perfume called 'Panathenaic'. 'Visibility': cf. D. G. Kyle in *Worshipping Athena*, 116–23 on the Panathenaic amphorae as 'self-declaratory prizes' creating 'donor-honor'.

[2] For this and much else about the festival see now the comprehensive and valuable study of Shear, *Polis and Panathenaia*. The key text relating to the final years of the *Panathenaea* is *IG* II² 3818, which honours one Plutarch for 'thrice bringing the sacred ship' to 'the temple of Athena': he is apparently identical with the Plutarch who honours Herculius in *IG* II² 4224 in the period 405–410 (see E. Sironen in P. Castrén, ed., *Post Herulian Athens*, Helsinki 1994, 46–8). The largely forgotten collection of testimonia in A. Michaelis, *Der Parthenon* (Leipzig, 1870–1), 318–33, remains basic; German translations are now available in an appendix to *Parthenon im Basel*.

Panathenaea to *Panathenaea*'; the tribute required from cities of the empire was reassessed in (greater) Panathenaic years, and it was stipulated that ambassadors should come to Athens to renew inter-state treaties 'ten days before the *Greater Panathenaea*'. In casual speech too, the festival was a natural point of reference to fix an event in time.[3] The *Panathenaea* was one of the two festivals to which in the fifth century Athens' allies were required to send delegations, and some participation by friendly cities is still attested later.[4] Individidual visitors too came to the city from all Greece, and the official programme of the festival was surrounded by a 'fringe'of social events, not just banquets held by individuals, but also such things as impromptu philosophical seminars: does not Plato imagine even the grave Parmenides visiting Athens for this occasion? According to a comic poet, a young countryman under a stern father's control would come to town once in five years only, to 'see the peplos'.[5] Comedy is full of allusions to the festival.

What are at first sight three distinct myths of its origins survive. According to the earliest attested, the festival was first celebrated by 'Erichthonius the son of Hephaestus', that is to say, as the detail 'son of Hephaestus' underlines, the autochthonous ancestor of the Athenians, the nursling of Athena. Erichthonius was the inventor of the chariot, and we are often told that it was at the first *Panathenaea* that Erichthonius first drove his invention; once it is specified that he had an armed passenger (*paraibates*), wearing like Athena a triple-crested helmet, who was imitated by the 'dismounters' (*apobatai*) in a famous competition held at the classical *Panathenaea*.[6] (The 'dismounters', clad in armour, jumped out of a chariot in motion and then raced on foot.) A black figure oinochoe of *c.*510 seems to show Athena herself running as *apobates* alongside the chariot of Erichthonius.[7] This *aition*, probably the best

[3] Treasurers: *IG* I[3] 52 A 27–9 (for accounting 'from *Panathenaea* to *Panathenaea*' cf. e.g. ibid. B 27–8, *IG* I[3] 292.1–2, 296.1–2; Arist. *Ath. Pol.* 43.1); tribute: *IG* I[3] 61.8–9; ambassadors: Thuc. 5.47.10; casual speech: e.g. Isoc. 12.17.

[4] See *Athenian Religion*, 142, 221–2. If the 'crowns' given to Athena by allied states were presented in person, there was (so Shear, *Polis and Panathenaia*, 204) more participation even in the 4th c. than is there allowed. For the *spondophoroi* who in the hellenistic period solicited participation from throughout Greece see B. Helly, *Gonnoi* (Amsterdam 1973), 2, no. 109; Polyb. 28.19.4.

[5] Visitors: Apollod. *Neaer.* 24; Pl. *Parm.* 127a; seminars: Epicrates fr. 10, cf. *POxy* 2889 = Aeschines Socraticus fr. 76 Giannantoni (from *Miltiades*); countryman: Plaut. *Merc.* 66–8 (from Philemon, *Emporos*), cf. Plaut. fr. dub. iii Lindsay 'nusquam ad civitatem venio nisi cum infertur peplum'. Plato's *Timaeus* is set at the festival (21a, 26e).

[6] [Eratosth]. *Cat.* 13; cf. e.g. Marmor Parium, *FGrH* 239, sec. 10; Shear, *Polis and Panathenaia*, 45. For other details associated with Erichthonius see: Philochorus *FGrH* 328 F 8–9; he is founder of the *Panathenaea* already for Hellanicus, *FGrH* 323A F 2. In Dion. Hal. *Ant. Rom.* 7.73.2–3 the *apobatai* simply dismount, whereas in *Anecd. Bekk.* 1.426.30–427.2 (similia in *Etym. Magn.* 124.31–6) they have previously mounted the moving chariot (cf. S. Müller, *Nikephoros* 9, 1996, 57–63).

[7] National Museum, Copenhagen, Chr. VIII. 340 (*LIMC* s.v. Erechtheus, no. 50; Neils, *Goddess and Polis*, 21, fig. 6). Shear, *Polis and Panathenaia*, 49–52 follows Vian, *Guerre*, 102–24, 248 in detecting an influence of *apobatai* iconography on Attic gigantomachies of the late 6th and early 5th centuries. Euripides' reference to Athena παρασπίζουσαν ἅρμασιν ...Ζηνὶ γηγενεῖς ἔπι is certainly suggestive (*Ion* 1528–9).

known, associates the festival with primeval, authentic, autochthonous
Athenian-ness. It also highlights a form of sport which the Athenians, and
apparently the Athenians alone,[8] had practised since ancient times, one of
the festival's trademarks. According to a second tradition (perhaps going back
to Atthidography) the festival was founded by Theseus at the time of the
synoecism of Attica. This account was made compatible with the first (though
it very likely originated separately) by the hypothesis of a change of name:
before Theseus, the festival had been called not *Panathenaea* but plain *Athenaea*.[9] It emphasizes the idea of inclusiveness inherent in the festival's name[10]
by associating it with the author of Attic unity, Theseus.

According to a third explanation, found in a work ascribed to Aristotle, the
festival was celebrated 'for the death of Aster, the giant killed by Athena'.
There may be a whiff of scholasticism here, in the attempt to give the
Panathenaea, like so many other Greek games, an origin as funeral games
celebrated 'for' (ἐπί) an identifiable dead person. We cannot be quite certain
that this *aition* was current in Attica; the choice of the obscure Aster as
Athena's victim in place of the obvious Enceladus might derive from a now
submerged Athenian tradition—or ignorance. The question arises how the
third *aition* relates to the others. One source combines it with the first, having
the festival founded in the time of Erichthonius son of Amphictyon 'for the
death of Asterios' (as he is here called).[11] The combined version is chronologically strange, since Asterios must have died long before Erichthonius was
born. Possibly it represents an attempt to reconcile discrepant versions by a
late source ignorant of Athenian traditions. In that event all talk of 'the' *aition*
of the *Panathenaea* becomes illicit, since we have more than one. But perhaps
Erichthonius was indeed imagined by the Athenians as having founded the
festival to celebrate, in retrospect, his foster-mother's ancient feat.[12] On any
view, such an *aition* could not have been proposed but for the symbolic
importance at the festival of Athena's victorious role in the battle against
the Giants. Taken as a group, the three *aitia* linked the festival with an

---

[8] See *Athenian Religion*, 90, n. 91; 146, n. 101. Conceivably in the 8th c. it had been more
widely diffused (but is it sure that the new vase from Eretria published by K. Reber, *AntK* 42,
1999, 126–41, shows sport and not war?). But for the Athenians' understanding of the game this
changes little.

[9] So Paus. 8.2.1. There is also a change of name in Istros *FGrH* 334 F 4, but in the fragment
as preserved (in Harpocration) the change is made by Erichthonius. Though this is not inconceivable (see Jacoby on Istros ad loc.), it is very likely that Istros too ascribed the change of name
to Theseus and has been misrepresented through abbreviation.

[10] For the debate on the actual etymology see n. 2 (end) to Jacoby's commentary on Istros
FGrH 334 F 4: as Jacoby observes, Athenians certainly heard in the name the word πάντες.

[11] So Σ alt. Aristid. *Panath.* 189, p. 323 Dindorf; the first Σ there (which quotes Aristotle and
appears as fr. 637 Rose) is the only other passage to associate *Panathenaea* with the death of
'Aster', but does not mention Erichthonius. On Aster/Asterios see Vian, *Guerre*, 262–5; the
importance of the aitiological link with the gigantomachy is stressed by Vian, *Guerre*, 246–64,
Pinney, 'Pallas and Panathenaea', 471, and Shear, *Polis and Panathenaia*, 31–7.

[12] Some chronological oddity was unavoidable if the festival, an institution of men, was to be
linked aitiologically to the gigantomachy, an event in the world of gods.

autochthonous Athenian king, with the unifier of Attica, and with Athena triumphant over the forces of chaos.

The procession and sacrifice occurred on Hekatombaion 28. Athena was born on the 'third' of something, as her epithet Tritogeneia declared, and by Attic backward counting the 28th was 'the third of the waning month'.[13] Thus Hekatombaion 28 could be seen as Athena's birthday; but so, since Greek birthdays were tied to days of the month and not of the year, could the 3rd, 13th and 28th of any other month. So much truth—it is rather little—is there in the popular modern claim that the festival celebrated Athena's birthday.

No source states explicitly the relation between the procession and the two other main elements of the festival, the competitions (in athletics, horseman-ship and music), and the *pannychis*. The most likely sequence is perhaps competitions (over a period of days),[14] *pannychis* (night of Hekatombaion 27), procession and sacrifice (Hekatombaion 28); certainly the competitions should come first. Among the competitions, some were open to all comers, whereas others were fought out between Athenians only, often arranged in tribal teams; the distinction reflects the double aspect of the festival as at once domestic and Hellenic. Definitely contested by tribe were the torch-race and the competitions in 'manly excellence (*euandria*)' (mysterious skill), boat-racing, and equestrian display (*anthippasia*); very probably also so organized were the cyclic choruses.[15] No other Attic festival has anything like so many tribal events. The prizes in these events (usually cattle) are said to go not to the victorious team but to the victorious tribe: more meat, therefore, at the tribal banquet which occurred during the festival. It is disputed whether the three competitions between teams of 'pyrrichists' of different ages (boys, beardless youths, men) were tribally organized;[16] even if they were not, they matched citizen against citizen in a display of war-related agility. Even amid the horse and chariot races, the nub of the programme from the point of view of crowd appeal, certain events were reserved for citizens, above all the testing *apobates*

---

[13] See Mikalson, *Calendar*, 23 (and for the date of the *Panathenaea* ibid. 34), who thinks that the sources which locate Athena's birthday on the 28th (e.g. Phot., Suda τ 1020 s.v. Τριτογενής) rather than the more predictable 3rd were in fact influenced by the *Panathenaea*. The 'birthday' theory was rightly criticized by Mommsen, *Feste*, 158 (who traces it back to Preller) and Pinney, 'Pallas and Panathenaea', 471. Pritchett, 'Παννυχίς', 183 tentatively links the crescent moon that sometimes appears with Athena on coins (*Athenian Religion*, 155, n. 10) to the timing of the festival at a time of waning moon (cf. Eur. *Heraklid.* 779).

[14] In favour of this sequence see Tracy, 'Panathenaic Festival', 135–6 (the whole study is now basic for the competitions); on the programme of the games see too Shear, *Polis and Panathenaia*, 382–4.

[15] On all this see Wilson, *Khoregia*, 36–40.

[16] Tribal performance is questioned by Ceccarelli, *Pirrica*, 33–5, with strong arguments, defended by Shear, 'Polis and Panathenaia', 322–3 [+] (cf. ead., *ZPE* 142, 2003, 90 n. 7). The tribal competitions continued to be held in the agora even when individual events were moved to the new Lycurgan stadium, according to Shear, 841. On the early 4th-c. inscription (*IG* II² 2311) from which we learn the prizes offered for the various competitions see J. Shear, *ZPE* 142 (2003), 87–108.

race.[17] On the literary side too, homeric recital by panhellenic rhapsodes was matched by tribal competition in cyclic choruses.

Like the *apobatai* race, the competition in the armed dance, the *pyrriche*, had a special association with the festival.[18] The first Pyrrhic dance was performed by Athena herself, whether immediately after her birth or to celebrate her victory over the Giants. Some suppose the latter explanation, so appropriate to the *Panathenaea*, to be distinctively Athenian.[19] The eye of the city was upon the performers in these domestic events. Lackadasaical and unathletic performance by young citizens—once in the *pyrrhiche*, once in the torchrace—is twice picked out for criticism or ridicule by Aristophanes.[20]

The *pannychis* at the *Panathenaea* all but slipped out of the record. All that we hear about its content (and even here the reference to the *Panathenaea* has been doubted) is of joyful cries (*ololygmata*) and the beat of maidens' feet heard all night long on the windy hill: maiden choruses on the acropolis, therefore, accompanied no doubt by much informal partying by other classes of the population. The date of the *pannychis* is controversial. It has been argued strongly that a Greek *pannychis* was typically not a preparatory vigil but a climactic celebration.[21] Yet a specific item of evidence points the other way in the case of the *Panathenaea* (the *Lesser Panathenaea* at least—but surely we can assume like practice in both cases). A decree of the Lycurgan period instructs the 'performers of sacred rites' who organize the annual *Panathenaea* to 'perform as fine a *pannychis* for the goddess as possible, and dispatch the procession at sunrise'. It is hard to resist the implication of that juxtaposition that the one thing led to the other. Certainly, the tribal torch-relay must have been performed early on Hekatombaion 28—though not necessarily as part of a *pannychis*—if the fire on the great altar that was lit with the victorious torch [22] was that of one of the great sacrifices celebrated on that day.

[17] Dem. 61.23–4. Commemorative monuments for victory in tribal and citizen-only events seem to have had a distinctive, rather modest form: see J. L. Shear, *JHS* 123 (2003), 171–2, 175.

[18] In Attica it is attested, at festivals, only here and at the *Tauropolia*.

[19] Victory: Dion. Hal. *Ant. Rom.* 7.72.7: see Ceccarelli, *Pirrica*, 27–30, citing important studies by E. K. Borthwick. I cannot quite believe the suggestion of Pinney, 'Pallas and Panathenaea', that the Athena shown on the Panathenaic amphorae is an Athena πυρριχίζουσα.

[20] *Nub.* 987–9; *Ran.* 1089–98; cf. fr. 459.

[21] *Ololygmata*: Eur. *Heraclid.* 777–82 (cf. p. 182, n. 19). Climactic celebration: so Pritchett, 'Παννυχίς'. Pritchett dissociates the all-night maiden choruses attested by Eur. loc. cit. from the *pannychis* proper. Given the regular association between maiden choruses and *pannychides* this is implausible; if he is right that the *pannychis* follows the sacrifice, then the maiden choruses should go there too. Deubner, *Attische Feste*, 24, combines the maiden choruses with the tribal cyclic choruses (using also the unreliable evidence of Heliodorus for a paian). This is impossible: the two things in Athens were always distinct.

[22] Herm in *Phdr.* 231e. It is often assumed that torch-races were performed by night. If so, since good numbers of Athenians evidently watched the Panathenaic torch-race, it seems economical to assign it to the *pannychis* (so e.g. Deubner, *Attische Feste*, 24), which will therefore fall before the procession. But it is not clear that torch-races did require darkness (E. Parisinou, *The Light of the Gods*, London 2000, 36–44, states no view), and in that event one can suppose the Panathenaic race held when spectators of the procession were already assembling. For the

The procession was marshalled in the outer Ceramicus at the edge of the city. The destination was the acropolis, but it was crucial that all who wished should enjoy the spectacle on the way. Stands were even erected for spectators in the agora. The route through the agora took the procession, rather slowly no doubt, through what in every sense had been since the sixth century[23] the public centre of the city. On arrival at the Eleusinion on the far side of the agora at the foot of the acropolis the Panathenaic ship and probably the charioteers peeled off; the remaining participants went up to the goddess and presented to her an embroidered robe (*peplos*), which depicted her role in the battle of Gods against Giants.[24]

I turn to the question of who marched, and in what order. In 514 the tyrant Hippias and his brother Hipparchus were personally marshalling the Panathenaic procession when Hipparchus was assassinated; the attack was launched because Hippias had humiliated the sister of one of the assassins by declaring her unfit to serve as 'basket-bearer' in (according to Aristotle) that same procession. The stakes in terms of prestige were evidently high. Conversely, the proverb 'more laconic than a tray' supposedly derived from the role of 'tray-bearer' assigned to metics in the great parade: 'tray-bearer'/'tray' became slang for 'metic', and the proverb indicated the silence and social constraint of the non-citizen surrounded by his betters. Metics were also marked out by the purple tunics that they were required to wear. More pointedly still, metic maidens served as 'parasol-bearers' and 'stool-bearers' to citizen basket-bearers (Aristophanes twice alludes to this picturesque procession within a procession), discharging what must have been seen as a servile function.[25]

Much more is recorded about inclusion and about ranking at the *Panathenaea* than at any other Greek festival. We hear explicitly of the roles assigned to metics (both girls and men), 'handsome old men' (a group of whom carried

iconographic link between torch-races and altar see Kephalidou, Νικητής, 218–25; O. Palagia, 'A gymnasiarch's dedication and the Panathenaic torch-race', in ἀγαθὸς δαίμων. *Mythes et cultes: Études d'iconographie en l'honneur de Lilly Kahil.* BCH suppl. 38, 403–6. Lycurgan decree: *LSCG* 33 B 31–4 (this important text is also *Agora* XVI 75; RO 81). For a possible role of the priestess of Aglauros at the *pannychis* see p. 166, n. 42.

[23] Though perhaps not in 566: see Jameson, 'The spectacular and the obscure', 325.
[24] Marshalling: Thuc. 6.57.1. Stands: p. 169, n. 51. Panathenaic ship and Eleusinion: Philostr. *VS* 2.1.5 (550). On the course followed by the procession on the acropolis itself see C. Löhr in *Kult und Kultbauten*, 16–21. Robe: see nn. 54 and 71.
[25] Thuc. 6.56–8; Arist. *Ath. Pol.* 18.2–4. Tray-bearers: see p. 170, n. 56. Even if one doubts the explanation of the proverb, the pejorative connotations are unambiguous in the fragment of Dinarchus *Against Agasikles* cited by Harpoc. σ 21, which contrasts 'ephebes' and 'tray-bearers' (cf. Wilson, *Khoregia*, 27). Purple: Phot. s.v. σκάφας, Suda α 4177 s.v. ἀσκοφορεῖν (? cf. Aesch. *Eum.* 1011 with 1028). 'Parasol-bearers' etc.: Ar. *Av.* 1549–52, with Σ vet. on 1551a (citing Hermippus fr. 25, Nicophon fr. 7); Ar. *Eccl.* 730–9; Demetrius of Phaleron *FGrH* 228 F 5 ap. Harpoc. σ 21; Ael. *VH* 6.1. Demetr. loc. cit. and Pollux 3.55 speak also (cf. Ar. *Eccl.* 738–9) of 'hydria-bearing' (Pollux assigning it to wives of metics, not daughters), which is not an intrinsically servile function. The sources associate these female roles with 'the processions' only, but at Athens that phrase can scarcely exclude ours; some of the roles appear in what looks like a parody of the Panathenaic procession in Ar. *Eccl.* 730–45 (cf. Shear, *Polis and Panathenaia*, 136–8).

(a)

(b)

Fig. 13(a) (b). Procession in honour of Athena on an Attic band cup of the mid-sixth century.

olive branches; there was, very characteristically, no such role for old women), 'colonists', and freedmen,[26] and several further classes of participant are attested in one way or another. Despite all this information, scholars have still in a large measure to marshal the procession in their own minds. Sources do not describe the order of the procession nor the numbers of any one class of participants involved. If a distinctive block of hoplites marched in the procession, as there is fairly good reason to suppose, we do not know how they were selected; nor is the role of the cavalry very clear, or of the ephebes.[27] Picturesque rarities such as the elderly 'branch-bearers', by contrast, needed to be explained to readers of Attic texts and received special entries in late antique dictionaries. Again, we learn from the Lycurgan decree on the *Lesser Panathenaea* that meat from the sacrifices was distributed to the demes 'in accord with the number of "escorters" [i.e. participants] provided by each deme'. But if, as seems to be implied, any demesman who chose to march could do so, what has happened to the privilege of participation? Perhaps we should imagine[28] a more formal and honorific head to the procession, in which a place was by invitation only, followed by a larger and more miscellaneous tail. In the front half will have marched the *prytaneis* and various other groups of magistrates and officials; all the something-bearers (basket-bearers, tray-bearers, and so on), including those of metic status, and perhaps girls connected with preparation of the *peplos*; musicians; perhaps victors in the contests,[29] and a selected troop of hoplites (and of cavalry? and of ephebes?); and sacrificial animals (but did they all come here? Numbers were large). In the rear will have marched any other citizens who chose, grouped probably by deme. Having reached this point, we will then have to decide whether classes of participant such as representatives of allied states, and freedmen, marched at the front or the rear. And whether hoplites who marched with their demes none the less carried 'spear and shield'. And ... at a certain point the procession dissolves into disorder, the ranks jostle and blur, in the mind.

---

[26] Old men as *thallophoroi*: Ar. *Vesp.* 540–5 with the learned Σ vet. on 544b; Xen. *Symp.* 4.17; colonists: Σ vet. Ar. *Nub.* 386a, and n. 34 below; freedmen: *Anecd. Bekk.* 1.242.3–6 δρῦν φέρειν διὰ τῆς ἀγορᾶς· τὸ τοὺς ἀπελευθερωθέντας δούλους καὶ ἄλλους βαρβάρους κλάδον δρυὸς ἕκαστον διὰ τῆς ἀγορᾶς ἐν τῇ τῶν Παναθηναίων ἑορτῇ φέρειν.

[27] Hoplites are normally accepted on the basis of a 6th-c. band cup (private coll., Basle: *LIMC* s.v. *Athena*, 1010, no. 574; here Fig. 13), Arist. *Ath. Pol.* 18.4 (which brings the evidence for marching in weapons, though not necessarily in a hoplite block, down to the 5th–4th c.) and especially Thuc. 6.58.1: doubts in Tracy, 'Panathenaic Festival', 149. For performance by the cavalry at the festival see the main text; that they actually marched in the procession is suggested only by visual evidence (the Basle band cup; Parthenon frieze). In the hellenistic period presentation of the traditional ἀριστεῖον to the goddess (see below) was apparently entrusted to the ephebes: *Hesperia* 16 (1947), 170, no. 67.27–8, with L. Robert, *BCH* 109 (1985), 472, n. 22; note too n. 25 above (Dinarchus).

[28] With Maurizio, 'Panathenaic Procession', 302. Lycurgan decree: *LSCG* 33 B 25–7.

[29] So Tracy, 'Panathenaic Festival'.

Despite the many uncertainties, it is not in doubt that some women, metics and 'colonists' walked in the procession. But the simple proposition that the *Panathenaea* is a festival of inclusiveness (of the whole population of Attica, and some foreigners) and of unity (within the citizen body) will seem bland and simplistic to politicized eyes.[30] We have already noted that metics, though certainly included, were included in a way which marked out not just their difference from citizens but also their hierarchical inferiority (the humiliating 'trays'). That they had a share in the division of publicly provided meat is very uncertain: one lexicographer presents such participation as the quid pro quo entailed by tray-bearing, but they are certainly not among the recipients of honorific cuts in a Lycurgan law (perhaps they were entitled to ordinary, non-honorific shares).[31] There may actually have been compulsion on the metics as a group to produce the appropriate number of 'tray-bearers'.[32] About the 'oak-bearing' freedmen rather little is known, but their position must have been less dignified than that of metics. Whether it is more important that these non-citizen groups were let in, or that they were separated and subordinated, is a question to which there can probably be no answer; ancient sources give different accounts of the Athenians' intentions (to humiliate the metics, to conciliate the metics), and metics' own perceptions probably varied.[33] One of the beauties of ritual as a device for the marking of status is doubtless that it can be so effortlessly ambivalent. As for allies, to receive a right of participation would have been a clear mark of friendship and honour; about the obligation to participate in fact imposed on them they may have had other feelings.[34] Slaves, finally, do not seem to have received privileges at the *Panathenaea*, let alone honour.[35]

What of unity within the citizen body? The metics, it may be urged, at least had a recognized ritual role: there was no processional block of thetes or sailors, no ceremonial recognition of the contribution to Attic life of what

---

[30] See especially Maurizio, 'Panathenaic Procession' and Wilson, *Khoregia*, 25–7, 46–8; for a Gramscian approach (the *Panathenaea* as a means of winning popular acceptance for the dominance of an elite) see V. Wohl, *ClMed* 47 (1996), 25–88 (unreliable on specifics).

[31] Hesych. s.v. σκαφηφόροι· οἱ μέτοικοι οὕτως ἐκαλοῦντο· σκάφας γὰρ ἔφερον ἐν τοῖς Παναθηναίοις, ἵνα ὡς εὖνοι ἀριθμῶνται μετέχοντες τῶν θυσιῶν. Lycurgan law: note the restriction to 'Athenian' escorters in *LSCG* 33 B 14. But some meat was provided for metics at the *Hephaisteia* (p. 171, n. 59).

[32] So Wilson, *Khoregia*, 26. But the 'metic liturgies' of Dem. 20.18–20 must primarily have been the more expensive choregic ones, and the lexicographers (Phot. and *Anecd. Bekk.* 1. 304.27–9, s.v. σκαφηφορεῖν) who neglected these and fastened instead on 'tray-bearing' (a favourite of theirs) to explain Demosthenes' phrase (which is a likely source of the language they use) were perhaps in error. That leaves only the vaguer testimony of Demetrius of Phaleron *FGrH* 228 F 5, as reported by Harpoc. σ 21, that 'the law instructed' metics to perform these services.

[33] So Wilson, *Khoregia*, 27, in an excellent discussion. Ancient sources: contrast Hesych. s.v. σκαφηφόροι (n. 31 above: a conciliatory gesture) with Ael. *VH* 6.1 (willed humiliation).

[34] Cf. *Athenian Religion*, 143; for participation as a privilege see M. Jameson in *Ritual, Finance, Politics*, 307.

[35] Dem. 61.23–4 rhetorically exalts the *apobates* competition as one not open to slaves and foreigners. But no hint survives of actual participation by slaves in other competitions.

Aristophanes called 'the ῥυπαπαῖ.'[36] They marched at the rear as demesmen if they marched at all: the select end of the procession was full of upper-class girls, empty of lower-class men. On this account, the procession reflects the social fact (reality here prevailing over ideology, or one of its strands) that rich metics mattered more in Athens than poor citizens. Or one might detect here a clash of ideologies, the ideal equality of all citizens giving way before an inherited, broadly aristocratic value-system shared by all classes which could never allow a class defined by its absence of wealth to enjoy ceremonial prominence.

But, if poverty could not be celebrated, seamanship surely could. The tribal 'ship-race' should not be forgotten, ill attested though it is.[37] Nor should we forget the famous ship up whose mast the *peplos* of Athena was 'hoisted by countless (thetic?) hands' in order to be conveyed in the procession. The ship unfortunately has no history; it first appears, by implication, in a fragment of the comedian Strattis around the end of the fifth century. Or rather, the mast of what later became the ship so appears; the ship itself is unattested until Roman times, and one view is that the mast (though already so named) was trundled along in the classical period on a float.[38] Yet the recurrent use of nautical language (mast and yard-arm) is odd if the vehicle was not already a real or at least symbolic ship. The ship-cart of Dionysus, with which that of Athena has so often been compared, bespoke the god's arrival from the sea. Athena did not visit her city thus; if her ship evoked anything (beyond the oddity and unreality of the festival world), this can only have been Athens' power at sea.[39] A ship transported the city's holiest of holies, the robe which depicted its patron goddess's victory on land.

It remains manifestly true that much of the limelight at such processions fell on the rich. Xenophon digresses in *The Cavalry Commander* to describe how 'the processions' (which must include that at the *Panathenaea*) could be made 'most pleasing to the gods and the spectators': starting from the Herms, the cavalry should go round all the shrines and images in the agora, 'honouring the gods', then ride up at speed tribe by tribe to the Eleusinion. How these cavalry manoeuvres related to the movements of the main procession is not certain and not very important,[40] nor how far Xenophon's recommendations square with normal practice (which they certainly do not simply describe);

---

[36] Ar. *Vesp.* 909; cf. Maurizio, 'Panathenaic Procession', 299.

[37] *IG* II² 2311.78–80; cf. Wilson, *Khoregia*, 48.

[38] An old view, still defended by Shear, *Polis and Panathenaia*, 143–55. On the ship see esp. Shear, *Kallias*, 39–44; Mansfield, *Robe of* Athena, 46–50. Strattis: fr. 31; for unquestionable early 3rd-c. allusions to mast and rigging see *SEG* XXVIII 60.64–70; *IG* II² 657.14–16.

[39] Those who take the ship back to the origins of the festival or beyond (Deubner, *Attische Feste*, 33) assume a mechanical borrowing of the Dionysiac model. If the point was really to evoke Athenian sea-power the ship will have been added in the 5th c. (so Parke, *Festivals*, 39); Mansfield, *Robe of Athena*, 68, imagines use of a ship captured at Salamis.

[40] Did the cavalry process from the start, and peel off on arrival at the Herms? Or wait there? Xenophon: *Eq. mag.* 3.1–4. For the ceremonial role of the cavalry see too Dem. 21.171, 174.

what matters is the presumption that cavalry displays contributed in an important way to the spectacle and the spectators' pleasure at major festivals. As a class, the cavalry at Athens were often imagined, and resented, as rich, pampered young men; but, as they wove their beautiful patterns in the agora at the festivals, we may conceive that many who were not cavalry felt that to be such was a grand thing. Athenian democracy was not committed to suppressing such admiration. What mattered was that the whole event was orchestrated not by tyrants but by democratically appointed magistrates, whom even the poorest citizens could envisage as representatives of themselves.[41] The formal places of honour at the front of the procession were assigned not to knights or other embodiments of privilege, but to officials, the democratic *prytaneis* chief among them.

As is well known, however, horsemen dominate the evocation of the Panathenaic procession on the Parthenon frieze. The problems posed by that enigmatic[42] monument can only be touched on here. One reason for the prominence of horsemen may well be an attempt to capture within the frieze the movement of the procession itself from agora to acropolis: the many horsemen at the rear evoke the stylish gyrations of the cavalry in the lower town.[43] (This is not to deny that they also embody fantasy and yearning, a delight in images of healthy and moneyed youth.) And Athena's cult title Hippia need not be wholly irrelevant, even though it was not on the acropolis that she was honoured as such.[44] The 'dismounters' (*apobatai*) who ride ahead of the horsemen are surely there because this was the form of competition that was quintessentially Panathenaic, and this will remain the truest explanation for their presence even if a 'realistic' explanation is also available, in the very plausible hypothesis that victorious *apobatai* in fact rode in the great procession.[45] We will hurry past the various differentiated groups that make up the main body of the procession on the frieze. Particular problems abound,[46] most acute the failure to include even a token group of hoplites. The broad theme is of animals (sheep and cattle)[47] led to sacrifice within a

[41] See Eur. *Supp.* 406–8. Arist. *Ath. Pol.* 7.4 is ambiguous, since it apparently attests a residual property qualification for office, but one that was disregarded.

[42] 'The Parthenon frieze is a text', says Neils, *Parthenon Frieze*, 125. Alas, no!

[43] On the problem of the placing of the scenes on the frieze—one location, many locations?— see Jenkins, *Parthenon Frieze*, 26–8. For various 'pluralist' views see the works cited by T. Schäfer, *AM* 102 (1987), 186, n. 5 and those criticized by Neils, *Parthenon Frieze*, 184–5. I doubt that we need to invoke the Periclean reorganization of the cavalry in order to understand the role of the horsemen (with J. J. Pollitt, in *Architectural Sculpture*, 51–65).

[44] Cf. n. 57.

[45] Tracy, 'Panathenaic Festival', 150 (for a chariot in a lesser Panathenaic procession see Men. fr. 384 (428 Koerte)). Some recent accounts which relate the frieze to a more general idea of 'festival' (see Hurwit, *Acropolis*, 227) underestimate the specificity of this rite.

[46] See in brief Jenkins, *Parthenon Frieze*, 25; Hurwit, *Acropolis*, 226.

[47] Sheep and cattle on the north side, cattle only on the south. This distribution has often been taken to indicate a differentiation between two distinct if related sacrifices, in one of which Athena is associated with Pandrosus, who is said by Philochorus *FGrH* 328 F 10 to receive a sheep whenever Athena receives a cow. The two sets of sacrifices attested in *LSCG* 33 B 7–27 are

designedly heterogeneous company of worshippers. A counterpoint has been observed, here and earlier, between grouping by ten on the south frieze and grouping by four on the north; the numbers refer, it is suggested, to the ten Clisthenic and the four Ionian tribes. To a student of history, rather than of iconography, so strong an emphasis on the old tribes at this date would come as a surprise.[48] The front of the procession is dominated by women. Twenty-nine female figures are currently counted at the head of the procession on the east frieze, of whom the majority are certainly unmarried girls. The point is brilliantly underlined by architectural form, with the east face of the frieze almost entirely given over to women, gods and heroes. (The argument is weakened, but not destroyed, if the controversial group of 'eponymous heroes' become, as some would have it, mortal marshals.[49]) Gods are present in a dignified abundance which is unlikely to have anything to do with actual ritual at the *Panathenaea*.[50]

How numerous the choice maidens were in reality can only be guessed. In hellenistic Athens over a hundred girls involved with working wool for Athena's *peplos* probably walked somewhere in the procession. With numbers on that scale spectators could have treated the cortège as a kind of 'Brautschau', a parade of the marriageable girls of the wealthier classes. But 'basket-bearers' (the role attested for citizen girls in the classical period) were not recruited by the hundred.[51] Tiny numbers, on the other hand, seem to be excluded by the evidence of the frieze. But one does not look to it for precise numerical information. What we can take from it is the strong emphasis on the female presence at the climactic point of the procession.

At the centre of the east frieze, framed and highlighted between the columns of the peristyle, is the quiet scene involving handling of a *peplos*:

---

often also brought in; the shrine of Pandrosus was next to the 'old temple' (Paus. 1.27.2), where one of the first set of sacrifices was probably offered, and it faced the relevant side of the Parthenon frieze. For versions of this theory see Mommsen, *Feste*, 119, 140; Pfuhl, *De Pompis*, 15–16; Deubner, *Attische Feste*, 26–7; Ziehen, 'Panathenaia', 470–4; Simon, *Festivals*, 60–1 (where Athena Parthenos is wrongly introduced as a recipient of sacrifice); T. Schäfer, *AM* 102 (1987), 186–8; Brulé, 'Panathenées', 46. This might be right (one does not need to postulate two processions, which would violate the unity of the frieze—Jenkins, *Parthenon Frieze*, 28–9 – but a single procession which branches); but the context of the fragment of Philochorus is unknown (Jacoby comments ad loc. 'the ritual prescription does not look very much like the description of a festival'), and the presence of sheep among offerings to Athena scarcely requires a special explanation (cf. the Marathon calendar, *ZPE* 130, 2000, 45–6, A col. 2. 41, and the old sacrifice to Erechtheus, Hom. *Il.* 2.550).

[48] Despite their role at the *Synoikia* (*Athenian Religion*, 14). H. Wrede, in *Parthenon im Basel*, 27–30 [+], sees the difficulty, but his solution involves an unpersuasive treatment of *LSCG* 33 B. On tens and fours see now e.g. Jenkins, *Parthenon Frieze*, 30; Neils, *Parthenon Frieze*, 54–5.

[49] On the controversy see Neils, *Parthenon Frieze*, 158–61.

[50] Though for the hypothesis of a theoxeny see Neils, *Parthenon Frieze* 198–200, citing L. R. Taylor; a similar case was argued by M. H. Jameson in a David Lewis Memorial Lecture in Oxford. For doxography see *Parthenon im Basel*, 170. The presence of so many gods seems to me the chief qualification to be made to J. H. Kroll's interesting case for 'The Parthenon Frieze as a Votive Relief', *AJA* 83 (1979), 349–52.

[51] See p. 224 and pp. 226–7 above.

Athena's *peplos* it must be,[52] given that this is the compositional keystone of the entire frieze, though all the details are uncertain. Presentation of a *peplos* to a goddess, or a *chiton* to a god, is a ritual action attested elsewhere in Greece, though not very frequently. The real life of the Athenian *peploi* has become a theme of controversy.[53] Were they offered every four years only, or was a different, smaller *peplos* also presented in the intervening 'lesser' Panathenaic years? Could a *peplos* of a size to be used as 'sail' of the Panathenaic ship really have been woven by young girls (even with the aid of older women) on domestic looms? And what happened to the *peploi* once delivered? Were they draped on a cult image of the goddess, and, if so, on which? The answers to these questions tend to elude us because the sources speak of the real life of the *peplos* only occasionally. We hear instead of what it stood for. For a young girl, to imagine being involved in its preparation was to imagine a tranquil, seemly existence. For men, embroidered as it was with the image of Athena victorious, it was a challenge and an inspiration to display like valour. And for all, as the most important of the gifts made to Athena, it was, as it were, the seal of the contract between the goddess and the city.[54]

Athena also received an 'excellence award' (*aristeion*) in the form of a crown at each celebration of the festival, presumably at this point. Perhaps it was associated with her role in the gigantomachy (though other gods too received such *aristeia*).[55] Once the *aristeion* and the *peplos* had been delivered (wherever the latter went), there remained the animals. A decree of the 330s exploits a new source of revenue to expand the existing programme of sacrifices at the *Lesser Panathenaea*; the new programme though not its predecessor is therefore known in unusual detail, and what happened at the *Greater* is likely to have been similar, if on a larger scale. Four sacrifices are mentioned, in two groups: first come 'the one sacrificed to Athena Hygieia and the one sacrificed in the [old temple]';[56] then, as many cows as can be

[52] With regret, I cannot accept Joan Connelly's brilliant interpretation (*AJA* 100, 1996, 58–80) that relates the scene and the whole frieze to the sacrifice of the daughters of Erechtheus. On the framing of the *peplos* scene see R. Stillwell, 'The Panathenaic Frieze: Optical Relations', *Hesperia* 38 (1969), 231–41, pl. 63, reproduced as Neils, *Parthenon Frieze*, 70, fig. 54. For bibliography on the scene see Neils, 268, nn. 103–18, and the formidable catalogue of disagreement in *Parthenon im Basel*, 171–4. M. Steinhart's identification of the male figure(s) as *Praxiergidai* is interesting: *AA* 1997, 475–8.
[53] Presentation: Hom. *Il.* 6. 269–311; *Od.* 3.274; Callim. *Aet.* fr. 66.2–6; Paus. 3.16.2, 5.16.2. Controversy: mostly because of the innovative study of Mansfield, *Robe of Athena*.
[54] Eur. *Hec.* 466–74; *IT* 222–4; Ar. *Eq.* 566–8; 1180. On the 'real life' questions see n. 71 below.
[55] See Shear, *Panathenaia and Polis*, 195–200; also n. 27. The *aristeion* first appears in *SEG* XXIII 82.29–31, of 402–1.
[56] According to the easiest but still puzzling (since sacrifice normally occurred outside temples) restoration in B 9–10 of the decree (*LSCG* 33 (RO 81): side B treats the sacrifices). Ziehen, 'Panathenaia', 472, and Brulé, 'Panathenées', 41–6 suppose an offering to Erechtheus, who had an altar within the Erechtheion (cf. Paus. 1.26.5); in A. Moreau (ed.), *L'Initiation* (Montpellier 1992), II. 20–6, P. Brulé stresses the texts which intimately associate the cult of Erechtheus with Athena (Hom. *Il.* 2. 550–1; Hdt. 5.82.3; the goddess promises him sacrifice of bovines in Eur. *Erechth.* fr. 65.94 Austin).

purchased with 41 minai (about 50?) are to be offered to Athena Nike and Athena Polias, one animal, 'picked from the fairest cows', to the former, the rest 'on the big altar' to the latter. So, though most of the victims go to Athena Polias, she also receives sacrifice in at least two of the other three aspects in which she was worshipped on the acropolis. The *Panathenaea*, one might say, summed up the goddess. The *peplos*, woven by girls, apprentices of Athena Ergane, embroidered with the triumph of Athena Nike, and presented to Athena of the City, was a symbol of All the Athenas.[57] And it created links with other festivals of the goddess at different points in the year: with the *Chalkeia*, at which the weaving was ritually begun, and with the *Arrephoria*, at which the girls who initiated the weaving entered on their own service.

The offerings to Athena Nike and Athena Polias are explicitly said to occur after the procession. The occasion of the other two is not specified; nor is their scale.[58] A contrast exists too between the rules for the distribution of meat in the two cases. From the offerings to Athena Hygieia and in the (old temple?) 'portions' are to be given to eight named categories of recipient (*prytaneis*, nine archons, Treasurers of the Goddess, *hieropoioi*, generals, taxiarchs, Athenian 'escorters', (basket-bearers)); each group, depending on its size and importance, receives between one and five portions, and the residue goes to 'the Athenians'. The meat from the offerings to Athena Polias and Athena Nike is to be distributed 'to the Athenian people in the Ceramicus as at the other meat distributions. Portions are to be assigned to each deme in accord with the number of participants ($[\pi\acute{\epsilon}\mu\pi o\nu]\tau\alpha s$,[59] literally "senders") provided by each.' On the one hand, then, portions of privilege, marks of recognition assigned to Athenians only (note the specification 'Athenian'

---

[57] But I cannot wholly follow H. v. Heintze, 'Athena Polias am Parthenon als Ergane, Hippia, Parthenos', *Gymnasium* 100 (1993), 385–418, 101 (1994), 289–311, 102 (1995), 193–222, who associates the east side of the building with Ergane, the west with Hippia (not a cult title on the acropolis), the north and south with Parthenos (not a cult title at all).

[58] On the common view it was modest. V. Rosivach has urged by contrast (*PP* 261, 1991, 430–42) that we have here the traditional (note the references to tradition in B 10 and 15) hecatomb, i.e. offerings on a large scale; the offerings to Athena Nike and Polias are new sacrifices created from the new resources available at the time of the law's passing. But the hecatomb must surely always have been offered 'on the great altar' (as Rosivach acknowledges, in his unpersuasive attempt to locate there the sacrifice 'in the (old temple)'). It follows that the law is not introducing new sacrifices but adjusting their funding arrangements or scale (so too Brulé, 'Panathenées', 40, n.7; cf. RO pp. 402–3). The offering to Athena Hygieia can therefore revert to the modest scale predictable in a minor cult, and take the other with it. As for occasion, these sacrifices too probably occurred on the day of the procession. A preliminary rite on (e.g.) the day before would be entirely conceivable, but how then would the distribution of spare meat to the people have worked? On the information provided by IG II² 1496.98–101 on the sacrifices of 333/2 see Shear, *Panathenaia and Polis*, 91–3; her new readings give a division between a small and a large sacrifice comparable to that found in *LSCG* 33. On these sacrifices cf. n. 47 above.

[59] The supplement is virtually guaranteed by the *stoichedon* count.

escorters),[60] including the female basket-bearers, but not to all Athenians; on the other, a mass distribution to all Athenian males (but presumably no others) who chose to participate. Why the privilege portions for *prytaneis* and the rest were taken from one set of offerings rather than the other is not explained: tradition perhaps, very probably combined with the fact that one but not the other was on a scale to permit mass distribution to the people. But the oscillation between sacrifices at which all notional beneficiaries did, and did not, eat of the sacrificial meat in person was basic to the structure of religious life even in democratic Athens. There was nothing unusual about the reserving of (probably) most of the meat from two of the offerings to a select group.[61] And the select group in this case was defined in terms of civic function, not birth and wealth, and included the *prytaneis*, among whom any Athenian might one day find himself.[62]

But, if 'having a share in the city' did not mean eating from every animal sacrificed in its name, it did in Athens increasingly mean eating from a good number. Meat from the sacrifice to Athena Polias was distributed 'in the Ceramicus as at the other meat distributions'. In the Lycurgan period there were some sixteen such, it has been calculated.[63] These events pose a challenge to the imagination. A great public picnic, but of men only (since there is no hint that portions were set aside for the wives of demesmen)? Or were the portions taken away to be consumed in private?[64] At the *Panathenaea* and the *City Dionysia* a further element has to be considered, in the civic liturgy attested for these two festivals of 'feasting one's tribe'. Either we must suppose that each citizen was entitled to feast twice at the *Panathenaea*, once as a tribesman (at an unidentifiable point in the programme), once as a demesman after the procession; or we must combine the occasions and suppose that the meat fetched from the Ceramicus was taken away to a tribal banquet put on by the liturgist.[65] On either view we see the state's concern to feed each citizen richly at the great festival. (There was also much feasting around the

---

[60] πομπ[εῦσι]ν τοῖς Ἀθηναίοις. The point holds whatever these πομπεῖς, who are distinguished from ordinary members of the procession, were. They are taken by some as those specifically designated to control the cattle (Mommsen, *Feste*, 121, n. 4; Pfuhl, *De Pompis*, 19, n. 118; L. Ziehen, *Leges Graecorum sacrae e titulis collectae*, Leipzig 1906, 94), by others as all the participants in the formal front half of the procession (Deubner, *Attische Feste*, 25; Schmitt Pantel, *Cité au banquet*, 127, n. 21; Brulé, 'Panathenées', 50–1, who envisages, p. 56, some 200.) They appear in a similar list of recipients of privilege portions at a festival of Asclepius (with *prytaneis* and archons and *hieropoioi*): *IG* II² 47. 35–8.

[61] See Jameson, 'The spectacular and the obscure', 331–4.

[62] See Schmitt Pantel, *Cité au banquet*, 126–30, for whom the festival offers two visions of the city, one egalitarian, one hierarchized, but hierarchized in terms of function within the city. She rightly questions, 128, whether the *prytaneis* and the rest ate their portions at a communal banquet, unequal as they were: they will have been for taking home.

[63] Rosivach, *Public Sacrifice*, 64; cf. *Athenian Religion*, 129.

[64] So, against orthodoxy, Jameson, 'The spectacular and the obscure', 326.

[65] So Schmitt Pantel, *Cité au banquet*, 129–30 (see ibid., 120–5 for tribal *hestiasis*).

fringes of the festival, by private individuals, by *gene* such as the Salaminians,[66] by victors in the competitions; but again here the exact context is unknown.) Here the festival ended, unless we should after all place the *pannychis* last, as a merry climax.

The author of the article on the *Panathenaea* in the great German encyclopaedia of classical antiquity,[67] after struggling for many pages as we have done with the particularities of the festival, steps back at the last to enquire into its 'religious meaning'. This he finds, rather unexpectedly, in a primeval association of Athena with the fertility of the fields. In neither turn in his argument will we follow him. The meaning of the festival resides in its particularities and nowhere else, in a process, not a result. As an emblem to set over the *Panathenaea*, the myth of Athena's victory in the gigantomachy is doubtless the best, because it brings out the triumphant self-assertion that marks the festival, the absence of discord or of concern with Dionysiac depths. The Athenians processed in arms; the allies were required to dispatch suits of armour. But that single myth sheds no more light on much of what the Athenians felt and thought at, and about, the *Panathenaea* than does any other summation of a complex experience in a few words.

As a coda a few words are required on the annual (or '*Lesser*', as they are now usually called) *Panathenaea*.[68] The *Lesser Panathenaea* were, in brief, the *Greater Panathenaea* shorn of their panhellenic dimension. The 'all comers' individual competitions were absent, but some at least of the domestic tribal competitions were held; pyrrhic dancing and dithyramb are firmly attested, torch-races only very unreliably.[69] It would be no great surprise to find one or two further components of the *Greater* games (*apobatai* above all) recurring here; but no source attests it, and the time covered by the competitive programme must have been much reduced. The *pannychis*, the procession (apparently with some involvement of non-citizens)[70] and the sacrifices all took place. But at the *Lesser* festival there was, it seems, no *peplos*. The few sources that associate the *peplos* with the *Lesser Panathenaea* are of less worth than the much larger number that associate it with the *Greater*, sometimes in

---

[66] *LSS* 19. 87 (for private individuals see Apollod. *Neaer.* 24; victors, Xen. *Symp.* 1.1–4). Victims provided by demes (attested for Skambonidai, *IG* I³ 244 A 19; Thorikos, p. 75, n. 104; perhaps Plotheia, *IG* I³ 252. 26–8) were presumably fed into the great sacrifice; animals won as prizes in tribal competitions may similarly have been added to the tribal banquet, whenever that occurred. But the *Salaminioi* can scarcely have led their pig in the great procession. It must have been sacrificed and consumed separately, probably earlier in the festival.

[67] Ziehen, 'Panathenaia'.

[68] See Shear, *Polis and Panathenaia*, 72–119.

[69] By Tzetzes, on Ar. *Ran.* 1087; some take *IG* I³ 82.30–3 to provide firm counter evidence that the torch-race was penteteric only. See Shear, *Polis and Panathenaia*, 113–14.

[70] πομπ[εύσι]ν τοῖς Ἀθηναίοις in *LSCG* 33 B 14, which refers to the *Lesser* festival, implies non-Athenian participation too.

terms that clearly imply it to have been visible only once every five years.[71]
Are familiarity and frequent contact required to fix religious symbols in the
mind? A priori one might have thought so. But one ground for the fame of the
peplos seems to have been that it was often spoken of but very seldom seen.

---

[71] See Deubner, *Attische Feste*, 29–30; Shear, *Kallias*, 36, n. 89. Note esp. that the ἐφέτειος
π[έπλος] of *IG* II² 1036.2 (*ZPE* 142, 2003, 68–9, fr. b 2) is not an 'annual' *peplos* but the '*peplos*
newly arrived this year' (Koehler *AM* 8, 1883, 58, cited by Deubner); so Shear's postulate, *Polis
and Panathenaia*, 98–102, that an annual *peplos* was introduced in late hellenistic times is
unnecessary (why such a change to such a central tradition?). The only textual evidence of
any weight that goes the other way is indirect: two inscriptions which honour *parthenoi* who
'worked the wool for Athena for the *peplos*' cannot on accepted archon datings be put in greater
Panathenaic years (S. B. Aleshire and S. D. Lambert, *ZPE* 142, 2003, 77). But the indirectness
makes them finally inconclusive, since we know so little of the stages of *peplos*-production.
Mansfield, *Robe of Athena*, 2–50 and *passim*, has argued that two *peploi* are to be distinguished,
the huge tapestry *peplos* used as sail for the Panathenaic ship every four years—professionally
produced, decorated with the Titanomachy—and the much smaller 'robe *peplos*', undecorated,
produced annually by the *arrephoroi, ergastinai*, etc. to gird the ancient image of Athena Polias.
E. J. W. Barber in *Goddess and Polis*, 103–18, accepts a modified version of this theory, which
allows both *peploi* to be decorated; this modification copes with Eur. *Hec.* 466–74 (a decorated
peplos produced by non-professionals), but blurs Mansfield's supposedly clear contrast. The
central difficulty with this theory is that not one of the numerous sources which speak of the
Panathenaic *peplos* hints at such a distinction between *peploi* of two types. (The conflict between
the sources which speak of penteteric and annual *peploi* provides no support; none speaks of two
types of *peplos*.) Mansfield argues that the 'sail *peplos*' would be far too large to drape on a statue,
or to produce on a domestic loom. No source to my knowledge actually says that the Panathenaic
robe was so worn (so too Georgoudi, 'Lisimaca', 178), though to the question 'whence then came
the clothing removed at the *Plynteria*?' I have no answer. (The fragmentary early lines of the
inscription *ZPE* 142 (2003), 68–9, merely tantalize: Mansfield's interpretation, 358–60, is over-
confident.) Mansfield also argues that the details given in Arist. *Ath. Pol.* 49.3 (cf. 60.1) imply
professional manufacture, and claims validity for the tradition which ascribes the first Panathenaic robe to a pair of professional male weavers 'Helikon and Akesas' (Zenobios 1.56, cf. *Ath.* 48b
and *RE* s.v. *Helikon* 6). Some professional involvement along with the girls is not inconceivable.

13

Women's Festivals: *Thesmophoria* and *Adonia*

It would be an exaggeration to say that Athenian men and Athenian women had different gods, but the differences between the relation of the two sexes to the gods go deep. When in Aristophanes' *Ekklesiazousai* the women are planning to appear at the assembly disguised as men and are rehearsing their roles, this point proves a stumbling block. One woman ends her speech 'I don't approve of this, by the two goddesses', and another calls out later 'well said, by Aphrodite'; both are picked up at once by the more experienced Praxagora: 'you swore by the two goddesses when [disguised as] a man!', 'you fool, you named Aphrodite. A fine thing if you had said that in the assembly!'[1] The women have remembered to refer to themselves by masculine endings, but have forgotten to swear by masculine gods. The rule is not simply that men swear by gods and women by goddesses (men swear by Athena, and, still more often, by Demeter, women by Zeus and occasionally Apollo), but the tendency is in that direction, and a woman's oath by Poseidon or Herakles or Hermes or Dionysus would doubtless be as odd as a man's by Aphrodite or the two goddesses or Artemis or Hecate. Even among goddesses, convention pushes women towards those held to have feminine concerns: no woman in extant comedy appears to swear by Athena, that masculinized figure, though her associate Aglauros does appear.[2]

Women's oaths are one expression of the separateness of the female religious sphere in Greece. Women's festivals are another; and in Athens, as in most regions of Greece,[3] much the most important member of that class was the *Thesmophoria*. For a married citizen woman, participation in the festival was, indeed, a defining experience. The rite was, it seems, celebrated by all the

---

[1] Ar. *Eccl.* 155–9, 189–91. The man disguised as a woman in Ar. *Thesm.* does rather better (517, 569) but blurs male and female at 594 (cf. E. W. Handley's note on Men. *Dysc.* 202). The male oath by Hecate at Ar. *Plut.* 1070 may be a reaction to the incongruity of the old woman's oath by Aphrodite in the previous line. Epicrates fr. 8 presents oaths by Kore, Artemis and Pherephatta as especially appropriate to (Dorian) young women. See A. H. Sommerstein, 'The language of Athenian women', in Sommerstein and F. de Martino (eds.), *Lo spettacolo delle voci* (Bari 1995), ii, at pp. 64–8.

[2] Ar. *Thesm.* 533. It must be allowed that the quantity of female speech in comedy is much less than that of male. Metrical constraints are also relevant: the male oath by Hera, quite often found in Plato, is absent from comedy, being even harder to fit in iambics than that by Demeter (which does occur).

[3] See Sfameni Gasparro, *Misteri e culti mistici*, 223–83. On female religious experience in general see now Dillon, *Girls and Women*; Goff, *Citizen Bacchae* (n. 39 below); Cole, *Ritual Space*.

wives of Athenian citizens (with their little children), and by them only.[4] Marriage made a woman, for the first time, a θεσμοφοριάζουσα; and perhaps the most public mark of the disgrace of the woman detected in adultery and put away by her husband will have been exclusion henceforth from the festival.[5] Even if not all married women in fact participated every year, the point remains that they had the right, and were apparently expected, to attend. (One passage in Menander raises the possibility of concubines also being admitted. But it is spoken by an old man in a rage: he believes that his son-in-law has fathered an illegitimate child, and he envisages him bringing the child's mother home as a kind of second wife alongside his daughter. So the exception—which anyway exists only in the mind of a querulous old man in a play—relates at least to a 'quasi-wife'.[6])

The *Thesmophoria* must have been the most striking interruption of the year in the routine of women's lives. The festival lasted three days, and though there was possibly a little 'commuting'[7] the norm was that the women camped out in booths (*skenai*). Three days away from the wool basket! It was probably a 'diffused' rite, one celebrated at numerous locations (some twenty to thirty?) throughout Attica, in specially designated *Thesmophoria* or other sanctuaries of Demeter called into service as such. No 'city Thesmophorion' is attested, and for once the argument from silence has almost overwhelming force; no such building can have existed, and the city women must have used the Thesmophorion of a city deme or a different sanctuary of Demeter (the Eleusinion has been suggested) instead.[8] Seen

---

[4] See Detienne, *Jardins*, 152 and 'Violentes "eugénies" ', 196–7; for the exclusion of *parthenoi* see Callim. fr. 63.9–12. Brumfield, *Agricultural Year*, 84–8, argues against such exclusiveness; for an ingenious variant (two distinct *Thesmophoria*, a city one open to all and local rites confined to citizen wives) see M. Sakurai in *17° Congreso Internacional de Ciencias Historicas, I. Grands thèmes. Methodologie, Sections chronologiques* (Madrid 1990), 169–72. The counter case cited by Brumfield, Lucian *Dial Meretr.* 2.1, is trumped by better sources (Ar. *Thesm.* 330, 541, supported in different ways by Isae. 3.80, 6.49–50, 8.19; *IG* II² 1184); Alciphr. 2.37 which she also cites is a 'letter from the country', not 'from a courtesan' as she says, but would anyway matter little (see Appendix 2).

[5] Apollod. *Neaer.* 85–7; Aeschin. 1.183.

[6] Menand. *Epit.* 749–50. Cf. especially 645–6 (the child), 693–4 ('the lovely wife he is bringing home'), and for the expectation that a woman in such circumstances would be freed, 538–40.

[7] So Dillon, *Girls and Women*, 119 (but his argument that in Aristophanes' play women still have to go up to the sanctuary on day two of the festival may be over-naturalistic). On *skenai* see especially Kron, 'Frauenfeste', 620, n. 50. Both *skenai* and *stibades* (see below) are seen by Versnel, *Transition and Reversal*, 242–3, as 'signals of primitivism'; he quotes Diod. Sic. 5.4.7 on Sicilian rites of Demeter which 'imitate the ancient way of life'.

[8] In all this I follow Clinton, *Thesmophorion* (dissent in Robertson, 'Proerosia', 338, 358, n. 115, and 359, n. 117). A celebration at Halimus seems to have been particularly prestigious: see Clinton, 115–17, and Philicus, *SH* 680.54 with the editors' note. Clinton suggests that the city rite was held in the deme sanctuary of Melite (known from *Agora* XVI 277) which may have been identical with the Eleusinion (but was the Eleusinion high enough to suit the language of Aristophanes, n. 11 below?) He strongly rebuts the still often repeated suggestion that the Pnyx was used. A. Tsakmakis (in *Orthodoxe Theologie zwischen Ost und West, Festschrift T. Nikolaou*, Frankfurt 2002, 166–7) proposes the Piraeus Thesmophorion.

thus, as a diffused rite with broad participation celebrated over several days, the *Thesmophoria* most resembles another ancient festival, the *Apatouria*; as the *Thesmophoria* informally identified Athenian wives, so the *Apatouria* was semi-formally concerned to register future citizens.[9]

Two days before the *Thesmophoria* itself, another 'women only' festival of Demeter, the *Stenia*, took place, this too apparently involving broad participation.[10] The accumulation of ritual activity in honour of Demeter is remarkable, but we know nothing specific about the festival except that the women exchanged insults during a night-time rite. The three days of the *Thesmophoria* were called 'Going up' (ἄνοδος), 'Fasting' (νηστεία), and 'Fair Birth' (καλλιγένεια). The first name could also be translated 'Coming up' and refer to the return of Kore from the underworld; but even if she could be envisaged as returning during this festival of autumn at all, she should surely not return on the first day, before a fast. The name refers instead to the 'Going up' of women to the sanctuary of Demeter Thesmophoros, set notionally, and often actually, on a high place; Aristophanes in *Thesmophoriazousai* repeatedly speaks of women 'going up' or 'being sent up' to the festival, and his evidence is conclusive for Athenian understanding of the name.[11] The 'Going up' received all this emphasis because it marked the separation of the women from their menfolk.

A remarkable scholion on Lucian describes what we take to be the central rite of the festival, though unfortunately without indicating where it fell within the three-day sequence. The scholion's account is one of the longest that we possess (but how short it still is!) of a Greek ritual, and perhaps the only such description of a 'mystery'; for these were things that were not to be revealed to males, though one can scarcely conceive that they were ignorant of at least the outlines. A second scholion on Lucian discusses two further festivals, the *Rural Dionysia* and the *Haloa*, and betrays the same interests and assumptions; both evidently come from the same source, and together they stand out as among the most important attempts that survive to us at exegesis of rituals.[12] What we have, unfortunately, looks like a crude abbreviation of a

---

[9] C. Rolley has argued that on Thasos the space which harboured a series of cults of *patrai* was in fact the town's Thesmophorion: *BCH* 89 (1965), 441–85.

[10] See Appendix 1 s.v. *Stenia*. Robertson, 'Proerosia', 334, n. 43, treats *Stenia* as merely day one of a five-day festival (to solve the conundrum posed by Ar. *Thesm.* 80.).

[11] Ar. *Thesm.* 281, 585, 623, 893 (all cited by Deubner, *Attische Feste*, 54, with IG II² 1177.23, display of a decree in the Piraeus πρὸς τῇ ἀναβάσει τοῦ Θεσμοφορίου). Day names: Σ Ar. *Thesm.* 80 (running from 11–13 Pyanopsion), Alciphr. 2.37.2; Phot. θ 134 s.v. Θεσμοφορίων ἡμέραι has an extra first day called *Thesmophoria* (and *Kathodos* as the name of day two). For views on the name *Anodos* see Sfameni Gasparro, *Misteri e culti mistici*, 246, n. 82. On the various possible locations of Demeter sanctuaries see S. G. Cole in S. Alcock and R. Osborne, *Placing the Gods* (1994), 199–216 (= *Oxford Readings*, 133–54). Two sources offer *Kathodos* (Phot. loc. cit; Σ Ar. *Thesm.* 585, as a variant) instead of *Anodos*. Harrison, *Prolegomena*, 123, referred the variation to the double ritual activity (deposition and recovery of remains) she postulated for the day; more probably *Kathodos* is just a slip.

[12] pp. 275.23–276.28 and pp. 279.24–281.3 Rabe. See on all this Lowe, 'Thesmophoria and Haloa' [+]; also Robertson, 'Proerosia', 365–9. On the secrecy of the *Thesmophoria* see Ar. *Eccl.* 443.

fuller and more nuanced account. It runs as follows; glosses in brackets attempt to remedy its incoherence.

Thesmophoria is a festival of the Greeks containing mysteries. These are also called *Skirophoria*. [Manifestly untrue, but the underlying proposition may be that the same rationale underlay the festival *Skirophoria*.[13]] It was performed according to the more mythical account because, when Kore was raped by Plouton while gathering flowers, a swineherd called Eubouleus was pasturing pigs on that spot and they were swallowed in the chasm along with Kore. So in honour of Eubouleus the piglets are thrown into the pits of Demeter and Kore. [The scholion speaks as if we were already familiar with these piglets and pits, which are in fact introduced later.] The rotten remains of the items thrown into the chambers are brought up by women called bailers who have kept themselves pure for three days; they go down into the secret places and bring up the remains and put them on the altars. They think that anyone who takes some of this and mixes it in when sowing will have good crops. And they say that there are snakes underground in the pits, which eat most of what is thrown in. And so they make noises when the women bail out and when they deposit those figures again [the 'figures' have not yet been explained], to make the snakes which they regard as guardians of the secret places withdraw. The same rites are also called *Arretophoria*. [Here too a distinct but, in the source's view, related festival is simply identified with the *Thesmophoria*. *Arretophoria* is apparently a 'learned' etymologizing alternative—meaning 'Carrying of secret objects'— to *Arrephoria*. How much of the detail that follows relates to the *Thesmophoria* is unclear.] They are conducted on the basis of the same rationale concerning the birth of crops and the sowing of men. Here too secret sacred objects are brought up made of wheat-dough—imitations of snakes and male genitals. They also take pine branches because of the plant's fertility. Into the secret places known as chambers are thrown these objects and piglets, as we have said already [we are back now with the *Thesmophoria*], these too [the piglets] chosen because of their abundant offspring as a token of the birth of crops and of men as a kind of thank-offering to Demeter, since she by providing Demetrian crops civilized the whole human race. The earlier account of the festival was mythical, but the one under consideration is physical. It is called *Thesmophoria* because Demeter is called Thesmophoros because she established laws or *thesmoi* by which men were to acquire and work for their food.

For the source of the scholion, therefore, the quintessence of the *Thesmophoria* lay in 'performing the chamber rite' (μεγαρίζειν). A shorter account based on the same source seems to indicate that both stages (the deposition of next year's piglets and recovery of the rotted remains of last year's) occurred at the *Thesmophoria*.[14] But all this will not have occupied three days, and we

---

[13] The references to the Attic *Skirophoria* and *Arretophoria* confirm that the author of the scholion had the Attic *Thesmophoria* in view, though this is not stated.

[14] So Burkert, *Homo Necans*, 257, n. 5. on Clem. Al. *Protr.* 2.17.1. The popular attempt to locate the deposition at a different festival of Demeter (see references in Kron, 'Frauenfeste', 616, n. 25) requires the postulate that Clement has over-compressed things. Robertson, 'Proerosia', 365–79 proposes deposition at *Thesmophoria*, retrieval at *Proerosia*. The question matters little, except in relation to the potential interconnectedness of different festivals of Demeter. The r.f. lekythos (Athens NM 1695; *ARV*[2] 1204.2; Deubner, *Attische Feste*, pl. 2) that used to be adduced as an illustration was dissociated by A. Rumpf, *BJb* 161 (1961), 208–9: the animal shown is a dog, the recipient probably therefore Hecate.

know rather little of what else filled the time. On the day of 'Fasting' the women sat on the ground, perhaps in imitation of the mourning and fasting Demeter;[15] this certainly counted as the grimmest ($\sigma\kappa\upsilon\theta\rho\omega\pi\sigma\tau\acute{a}\tau\eta$) day of the festival, one that Plutarch could pick out when seeking Greek parallels for gloomy Egyptian rites. The women sat on ad hoc mats ($\sigma\tau\iota\beta\acute{a}\delta\epsilon\varsigma$) made from plants which are explicitly said by our sources to have been chosen for their power to inhibit lust.[16] In antiquity this fast was perhaps the most unusual feature of the festival, as several allusions to it show. Recent scholarship has been more interested in the feast mentioned by Isaeus, which presumably followed the fast at the end of day two or on day three (though a three-day festival must have included several meals). If meat was eaten, then women must—or must they?—have wielded the sacrificial knife.[17] Other elements attested for the festival float vaguely without a firm context: we hear of obscene jesting and insults; of a sacrifice called 'penalty'; of (surprisingly) a procession; of a ritual called 'pursuit' or 'Chalcidic pursuit'; of taboos—on eating pomegranates which have fallen to the ground, and on wearing garlands of flowers (perhaps the offending object was rather flowered dresses).[18] Much more of this type is undoubtedly lost to us, and there is usually little to be made of such scraps of information deprived of a context.

The scholion associates the central 'chamber' rite aitiologically with the rape of Kore. The myth of the rape and of Demeter's quest was very likely often in the minds of participants, though the connection is not otherwise made explicit except in late antique sources. Demeter's fast may have been the model for that of the participants, Iambe's jokes to the grieving goddess for their rude talk.[19]

---

[15] So Harrison, *Prolegomena*, 127–8, on Plut. *De Is. et Os.* 69, 378d; id. *Dem.* 30.5; for other allusions to the fast see Ar. *Av.* 1519; Cornutus, *Theol. Graec.* 28, p. 55.7–11 Lang; Ath. 307f.

[16] Such is the unanimous and widely diffused (if only late-attested) explanation for their use at the *Thesmophoria*: see on *agnus castus* Dioscorides, *De materia medica* 1.103.3 (96.11–13 Wellmann); Ael. *NA* 9.26; Galen *SMT* 6.2 (X 808 Kühn); on κόνυζα *Σ* Theocr. 4.25b and 7.68a. It looks to be of popular, not of learned origin. Against attempts to transform *agnus castus* into a fertility symbol see Versnel, *Transition and Reversal*, 237 (with references in n. 26); see too on *agnus castus* U. Kron in R. Hägg and others (eds.), *Early Greek Cult Practice* (Stockholm 1988), 138, and on *kneoron* and *konuza* Kron, 'Frauenfeste', 622. Two of these plants are also said by Dioscorides (not in connection with the festival) to be abortefacients (*De materia medica* 3.121.2–3; 4.172.3). But I think Lucia Nixon goes too far ('The cults of Demeter and Kore', in R. Hawley and B. Levick, eds., *Women in Antiquity: New assessments*, London 1995, 75–96) in inferring a rival, female understanding of such plants, which would make the festival a celebration of women's control over their own fertility.

[17] See below. Feast: Isae. 3.80, cf. the list of foodstuffs in *IG* II² 1184 (*LSS* 124). Animal sacrifice at the Attic *Thesmophoria* is only unreliably attested (*Σ* vet. Ar. *Ran.* 338a—the passage in Aristophanes refers rather to the *Mysteries*), but is highly probable given the analogies from Delos and Eretria cited by Detienne, 'Violentes "eugénies" ', 191–4.

[18] Cleomedes, *Caelestia* (ed. R.B. Todd, Leipzig 1990), 2.1, 498–9 (also in H. Usener, *Epicurea*, Leipzig 1887, p. 89); Hesych. ζ 145; Isae. 6.50; Hesych. δ 2036 with Suda χ 43; Clem. Al. *Protr.* 2.19.3; *Σ* Soph. *OC* 681 (cf. Parker, *Miasma*, 83, n. 36). Callim. Aet. fr. 21.9–10 might link the insults to day two.

[19] See *Hymn Hom. Dem.* 198–205, with Richardson's notes. Late antique sources: see p. 383. The same myth then provides the aitiological background to both *Thesmophoria* and *Eleusinian Mysteries*, though the telling of it in *Hymn Hom. Dem.* is much more closely directed to *Mysteries* than to *Thesmophoria* (p. 340, n. 54).

Herodotus, by contrast, has the *Thesmophoria* 'introduced' to Greece from Egypt by the daughters of Danaus.[20] That is an aitiology of untraditional, 'diffusionist', type, linked with Herodotus' theory of cultural borrowings by Greece from Egypt; yet by choosing the Danaids as protagonists it points to the element of sexual politics certainly implicit in the festival.

I turn to interpretation. One can read off the twentieth century's changing paradigms for the interpretation of Greek ritual more clearly perhaps in relation to the *Thesmophoria* than in any other context.[21] Any interpretation must confront at least the following propositions:

1. The *Thesmophoria* related to the fertility of the fields. It occurred around the time of the autumn sowing, and the Lucian scholion says explicitly[22] that the chamber rite was believed to create a kind of sacred compost which would ensure abundance. This rite was not a minor ancillary: chambers are, to judge from archaeological and epigraphic evidence, almost the *sine quibus non* of a sanctuary of Demeter Thesmophoros. Prayers were made at the festival (if we may trust a passage of Aristophanes which has no traces of comic distortion) to one of the gods whose names speak of wealth derived from agriculture, Ploutos or Plouton.[23]

2. The *Thesmophoria* related to the fertility of women. The goddess 'Fair Birth' gave her name to the third day of the festival. The relation between women and Demeter was grounded in the fertility of women, which allowed them to symbolize (and seek ritually to ensure) the fertility of the fields.[24] Any woman who brought to Demeter the goddess' preferred offering, a piglet, could not forget that various words for 'pig' were the commonest slang terms for the female genitalia.[25]

---

[20] Hdt. 2.171.2–3. Some suppose that Hdt's *aition* provided the conclusion to Aeschylus' Danaid trilogy: see the refs. in A. F. Garvie, *Aeschylus' Supplices: Play and Trilogy*, 227 (he is sceptical), and now F. I. Zeitlin, *Playing the Other: Gender and Society in Classical Greek Literature* (Chicago 1996), 163–71.

[21] Even the word 'initiation' has been uttered, though less frequently than in many contexts: see the works cited, and criticized, by Sfameni Gasparro, *Misteri e culti mistici*, 281, n. 219, and Versnel, *Transition and Reversal*, 253, n. 88.

[22] Lowe, 'Thesmophoria and Haloa', 162, wonders what grounds he had for this assertion and whether we should believe him. But there is no difficulty in believing that his grounds were good, given that he is speaking of public behaviour of men.

[23] Chambers: see Kron, 'Frauenfeste', 617. Ploutos/on: Ar. *Thesm.* 297–8 (R gives Ploutos, but Clinton, *Myth and Cult*, 54, n. 131, argues plausibly for Plouton); on these gods see pp. 336–7.

[24] 'Women can (conceive), in which, as Plato says (*Menexenus* 238a), 'they imitate the earth'. At the *Thesmophoria* they tried to persuade the Earth to imitate *them*': E. R. Dodds, *The Ancient Concept of Progress and other Essays* (Oxford 1973), 147. Cf. in general C. Delaney, *The Seed and the Soil: Gender and Cosmology in Turkish Village Society* (Berkeley 1991).

[25] See M. Golden, *ECM* 7 (1988), 1–12 [+]; I reserve my position on his argument (8) that 'the use of pig words for the female vagina invokes elements of fear and hostility' created by fear of female sexuality. In the oldest of the types of 'woman carrying pig' votive found at the Thesmophorion of Bitalemi near Gela, the pig is held directly in front of the genitals: M. Sguaitamatti, *L'Offrande de porcelet dans la coroplathie géléenne* (Mainz 1984), 27, 60.

3. The *Thesmophoria* served to define the status of citizen women. We saw above the rules of participation which meant that this was necessarily so. Unlike the previous two propositions, this third is never explicit in the sources; nor could one expect it to be, not being the kind of thing that Greek sources say. But in myth and in comic fantasy the aspect of self-assertion by women is expressed with the utmost clarity. Indeed, 'defining the status of citizen women' may seem scarcely to do justice to a myth (admittedly from outside Athens) that presents the women of Cyrene dripping with the blood of their city's great founder Battus, castrated for intruding upon the rites.[26] Perhaps one should substitute 'define the status of women as opposed to men (and of citizen women as opposed to all others)'. However that may be, the myths, and Aristophanes' play, reveal a very acute awareness of a dimension of the festival which is not that of women making useful and necessary preparations for the ploughing. And surely an Athenian man, asked about the *Thesmophoria* by a Triballian, would have been likely to say that it was the time when our women go away, not the time when we prepare sacred compost for our fields. Women organized themselves for the festival, and ran it. The word *archon*, commander, magistrate, seldom appears in the feminine, but it does so occur in relation to the two organizers elected for the *Thesmophoria* by each deme. The question whether the women did or did not kill with their own hands any sacrificial victims there may have been is of minor importance by comparison.[27]

If we attempt to rank these propositions, a paradox emerges. The first proposition has the strongest support in 'native' testimony, but is the weakest in explaining the form that the festival actually takes; a handful of women could have conducted the jiggery-pokery with piglets and penis cakes, while the rest remained at home. Proposition two is needed to explain why all the Athenian wives attended, and proposition three to explain why they alone did so. But neither proposition two nor three has anything very specific to offer in relation to the chamber rite. It is better to let the three propositions co-exist without attempting to rank them hierarchically or (still worse) eliminating any entirely.[28]

Some further glosses are now required on these propositions. The chamber-rite is the key exhibit for the defence of the 'agricultural fertility' model which

[26] Aelian, fr. 44; for the husband-slaying daughters of Danaus as responsible for the introduction of the *Thesmophoria* to Greece see Hdt. 2.171. Cf. Detienne, 'Violentes "eugénies" ', *passim*, and W. Burkert, *CQ* 20 (1970), 12 (= *Oxford Readings*, 242–3). Detienne, 'Violentes "eugénies" ', 201, speaks of a 'pouvoir féminin qui hésite entre deux modèles: une cité réduite et ramassée sur sa légitimité; une gynécocratie où le droit politique au sacrifice sanglant confine à une violence dirigée contre l'espèce mâle'.

[27] Kron, 'Frauenfeste', 640–3, 650, argues against Detienne, 'Violentes "eugénies" ', that they did. But a more basic difficulty concerns the primacy assigned by Detienne's theory to killing with one's own hand. In the terminology of Hubert and Mauss, women could certainly be *sacrifiants* even if they were not *sacrificateurs*: see R. Osborne, *CQ* 43 (1993), 400–2 (= *Oxford Readings*, 306–8). *Archousai*: Isae. 8.19; *IG* II² 1184 (*LSS* 124) 3.

[28] As Versnel rightly insists, *Transition and Reversal*, 240, 260.

dominated the study of early Greek religion from the late nineteenth century until the early 1960s.[29] Here, for once, we are almost told by an ancient source that a particular rite was performed to encourage the crops to grow.[30] (What we are in fact told is that a particular rite was performed, and that the detritus left by this rite was believed to promote the growth of crops.) But the source of the scholion does not endorse, though he does not reject, the view of these activities which he reports ('they believe'). For him, piglets are used as a ' "token" of the birth of crops and of men as a thank-offering to Demeter'. Corn would ripen and wombs would swell, it seems, even without the *Thesmophoria* being celebrated. But it is just for that reason that men do and should celebrate them, from gratitude to Demeter.[31] Anthropologists sometimes contrast 'instrumentalist' and 'expressive' views of ritual.[32] The scholion reports an instrumentalist view, but himself adopts an expressive one. Yet the distinction between the two positions is perhaps clearer to the analyst than to the participant. Did the farmers who mixed the rotten remains recovered from the underground chambers with their seed-corn suppose the messy substance to be effective in just the same way as modern farmers believe fertilizers to be? Even if they did, they will not have believed it to be effective for the same reasons; the *Thesmophoria* remains worked, not because of chemistry, but because they derived from a duly performed traditional ritual imitative of deeply significant events of the mythical time. Conversely, even the source of the scholion might have felt that neglect of the *Thesmophoria* would incur Demeter's anger and, in the long term, ill consequences for farms and families. In that sense his *Thesmophoria* too would have been instrumental. This is why the very vague formula 'the *Thesmophoria* relate to the fertility of the fields' was chosen above. The fact that relation ought not to be doubted, even when quite different aspects of the festival are acknowledged; but the character of the 'relating' remains an issue.

I turn now to these different aspects. Any ritual performed by all, and only, the members of a given group will say something about what it means to belong to that group; this is almost axiomatic. According to a persuasive interpretation,[33] the ideal image of the citizen women of Athens presented by the *Thesmophoria* is an austere one. The Thesmophoriazousai are not only required to fast and sit on the ground; they are, above all, desexualized,

---

[29] On this and what follows see Lowe, 'Thesmophoria and Haloa'; on the emergence of the fertility paradigm also S. C. Humphreys, 'Historicizing Fertility', in *Aporemeta* 5. *Historicization-Historisierung* (Göttingen c. 2001), 169–200.

[30] Somewhat similar customs (e.g. conservation in a church for forty days of some seed, which is then mixed with the rest or scattered on the fields) are still found in Greece: Brumfield, *Agricultural Year*, 89; M. Lilimpaki-Akamati, *Το Θεσμοφόριο της Πέλλας* (Athens 1996), 103–4.

[31] On the gap between what the scholion reports and his own views Jane Harrison is at her rhetorical best: 'Even after he has given the true content his mind clouds over with modern associations. The festival, he says, is a "thank-offering" to Demeter. But in the sympathetic magic of the *Thesmophoria* man attempts direct compulsion, he admits no mediator between himself and nature, and he thanks no god for what no god has done' (*Prolegomena*, 124).

[32] See p. 158.   [33] Of Marcel Detienne, as cited in n. 26.

required to sit, perhaps after a period of preliminary abstinence, on a kind of 'chastity mat', forced (but this detail is not attested for Athens) to leave at home their jewels and their most alluring clothes. As a reward they receive the title 'bees', a most respectable and housewifely but also, in ancient eyes, an asexual insect.[34] Good women, the right women to bear future citizens, are women without lust.

On this view, Thesmophorian virtues were detected in his wife by the grieving husband who declared on her tombstone 'Not robes, not gold did this woman admire in life, but her own husband and modesty ....'[35] The violent harridans of some Thesmophoric myths dissolve into reassuring figures. We know that the *Thesmophoria* were conducted with the full approval of male society. There were no 'resistance to Demeter' myths. Prosperous citizens were required to 'provide the *Thesmophoria* feast' for the wives of their fellow demesmen as a liturgy. Scholars sometime speak as if the myths of violence linked with the *Thesmophoria* depicted a potentially murderous force ready to erupt into the middle of male society. But the emphasis is the opposite; trouble arises only when men seek to intrude on rites from which they are rightly excluded.[36] The *Thesmophoria* is a licensed and protected enclave for women who accept the restrictions imposed on them.

But, it has been protested,[37] this reconstruction represents, at best, a masculine ideal of the *Thesmophoria*. ('Ideal', not simply view, since a quite different masculine view is found in Aristophanes' play.) Once gathered together, for once, away from men, the bees may have shown their stings. The dirty talk attested for many Greek festivals, the *Thesmophoria* among them, has traditionally been expurgated by the claim that such talk was deemed necessary in order to promote fertility. But the image of prim matrons overcoming their distaste in order to mouth obscenities, 'a ceremonious duty steadily performed by matrons whose standards of chastity were probably as high as ours',[38] is rather absurd. A rude mood must surely be created before rude talk can flow free, even during a ritual. Perhaps the bees joked and laughed at festivals such as the *Thesmophoria* about the embarrassing details

---

[34] Apollodorus *FGrH* 244 F 89. For preliminary abstinence and the (Peloponnesian) restrictions on jewels and clothing see Parker, *Miasma*, 82, n. 33, 83, n. 36. F. I. Zeitlin, *Arethusa* 15 (1982), 149, rightly speaks of 'the inherent "double bind" under which the woman operates. This double bind demands chastity from the wife and yet insists on her sexual nature.' Versnel, *Transition and Reversal*, 245–60, speaks of the Thesmophoriazousai as being symbolically restored to (257) the 'premarital virginal existence of the *numphê*', which, in the absence of symbolism indicating such a regression, perhaps goes a little too far.

[35] *IG* II² 11162, *CEG* II, 573.

[36] To n. 26 add Hdt. 6.134.2, another myth of a male intrusion on a Thesmophorion where punishment comes from god, not woman. For this reason I resist the argument of Versnel, *Transition and Reversal*, 249, that 'the whole festival is manifestly (and necessarily) wrong'; it is, of course, unusual, as he well shows. Liturgy: Isae. 3.80.

[37] By Winkler, 'Laughter of the oppressed'. This brilliant study brings great progress but also, in the attempt to abolish necessary distinctions established by Detienne between different types of women's rite, some regress.

[38] Farnell, *Cults*, III, 104.

of sexuality and about the inadequacies (collective and individual) of their husbands; and perhaps they did so with a gusto from which it was no doubt good that men were shielded by the rule of secrecy. It was a festival of female bonding occurring, *inter alia*, through a kind of verbal taboo-breaking licensed by the ritual context.[39]

This account has immense intuitive plausibility. But it supplements the 'men's ideal' view of the festival, without necessarily contradicting it. The women might joke about sexuality at the festival but they were still symbolically desexualized, and their ticket of admission was still their standing as respectable wives. Some suppose that adultery was more easily performed and more readily tolerated in Athens than the official voice of tragedy and oratory would suggest.[40] Were we to postulate that the *Thesmophoria* was a context in which this unofficial view of adultery was aired, with women jesting about their own and others' infidelity, we would indeed have a festival divided against itself. But fantasy need not go so far. A detail reported about the *Haloa*, again by the scholion on Lucian, becomes very interesting at this point. We are told that there was much handling of obscene objects at the festival, and still worse (at some point in its transmission the scholion seems to have picked up a veneer of Christian disapproval of pagan practices), priestesses whispered in the ear of the participants, urging them to commit adultery (p. 169 above). The question 'how could the male source of the scholion know?' is very pertinent. But if we allow that he did, the detail that it was the priestesses who made the gross suggestion becomes crucial. Priestesses of Demeter, of all people, cannot have seriously set themselves up as enemies of public morals in the way described. The suggestion must have been deliberately outrageous, a comic festival reversal of an accepted norm (which was thereby confirmed). So much for the *Haloa*. At the *Thesmophoria*, ribaldry need not even have prevented the women, or some of them, from internalizing the male Thesmophoric ideal of the woman whose fertility is grounded in sexual restraint.

On the old view which saw in the festival little but agricultural magic, it was something of a puzzle that the sole participants were women. However much agricultural work citizen women in fact did,[41] in ideology farming was done by men; and the women who are most likely to have been influential at the *Thesmophoria*, the wives of rich demesmen, are the ones who are least likely to have spent much time in the fields. The puzzle vanishes once the festival is seen also to relate to gender issues and to human fertility. But it

[39] Versnel, *Transition and Reversal*, 244 and Brumfield, *Agricultural Year*, 122–6 (a good discussion) mention modern Greek parallels. Brumfield also a modern American one. Versnel sees such aischrology as a usurpation by women of male language, but it should perhaps rather be seen as an enactment of the physicality and 'earthiness' of the fertile gender (so B. Goff, *Citizen Bacchae*, Berkeley 2004, 131).

[40] So Winkler, 'Laughter of the oppressed', 201–2; cf. D. Cohen, *Law, Sexuality and Society* (Cambridge 1991), 133–70.

[41] On this see W. Scheidel, *Gymnasium* 97 (1990), 405–31; the essentials also in R. Brock, *CQ* 44 (1994), 342–44.

remains true that women performed the ritual work that helped the crops to grow. The symbolic equivalence between human (or animal) fertility and that of the earth must here be crucial. Into the pits at the *Thesmophoria* went the most prolific of animals (which also provided the slang term for 'vagina') and penis cakes; out came a substance that would benefit the fields. Women were themselves, as the Attic marriage formula indicated, a fertile field. This analogy required or empowered women to perform these rites, performance of which in turn enhanced the standing of women. Part of the work of women within the city, one of the glories of citizen wives (here the seemingly disparate elements of the festival coalesce), was to be in charge of the rites on which the fertility of the fields depended.[42]

The symbolic interdependence of the sexes in this sphere is perhaps best shown on an important Siana cup (*c.* 575–550). On one side two men, both naked, plough and sow respectively; on the reverse, Demeter sits in grief, while five women lead a naked youth to or round an altar, behind which stands another woman or goddess holding a winnowing basket (*liknon*).[43] The ritual shown cannot be given a name; the role of the youth amid the women is a particular enigma. But the division of the two sides between men who plough and sow, and women who perform ritual in the presence of the goddess, sums up a whole aspect of this religion of Demeter.

Whatever the historical origin of the name *Thesmophoria*,[44] all ancients accessible to us heard in Demeter's epithet Thesmophoros 'bringer of laws (*thesmoi*)'. The associations between Demeter and ideas of civilization and progress were deep and complex, though they are scarcely ever made explicit in early sources. Easiest to grasp is bread as a symbol of civilized diet, whether contrasted with a rough earlier diet of acorns and thistles or a brutal one of human flesh. The 'ground life', ἀληλεσμένος βίος (i.e. life using ground corn) was a proverbial expression for the easy, comfortable life.[45] There is also an association between agriculture and the norms of life in society, as if the cooperative effort required for farming were a basic form of human collaboration. It was at about the time of the *Thesmophoria* that three 'sacred ploughings' were performed. The sacred ploughing below the acropolis was performed by a member of the *genos* (if that is what it was) of *Bouzygai*; and as he ploughed—or at least on the same occasion—he uttered the proverbial

---

[42] 'Les Thesmophories instituent une cité de femmes dans l'espace d'un rituel essentiel à la reproduction de la cité des hommes': Detienne, 'Violentes "eugénies"', 201.

[43] London 1906. 12–15.1 (*ABV* 90.7; B. Ashmole, 'Kalligeneia and Hieros Arotos', *JHS* 66. 1946, 8–10; Simon, *Festivals*, pl. 7.1; Durand, *Sacrifice et Labour*, 182, fig. 88; *LIMC* s.v. *Bouzyges* no. 1); here Fig. 14.

[44] On this see Kron, 'Frauenfeste', 627, n. 34 [+]. Ancient interpretations: see e.g. Callim. *Hymn* 6.18 with N. Hopkinson's note ad loc.; Diod. Sic. 5.5.2; Σ Lucian p. 276. 25–8 Rabe; and above all the Latin calque 'legifera' for Ceres (Virg. *Aen.* 4.58).

[45] So Zen. 1.21 and parallel texts; the proverb occurs in Amphis fr. 9. The proverb οὐ γὰρ ἄκανθαι (Ar. fr. 284 and 499) was similarly explained in antiquity (Hesych. ο 1541 etc.)—wrongly, according to Kassel and Austin on Ar. fr. 284.

(a)

(b)

Fig. 14 (a). Siana cup, showing ploughing and sowing. (b) Reverse of (a), showing ritual performed by women in honour of Demeter (c. 575–550).

'Bouzygean curses': 'The *Bouzyges* at Athens who performs the sacred ploughing utters curses, particularly against those who refuse to share fire or water or to show the way to those who are lost' or, another source adds, 'who leave a corpse unburied'.[46] Why curse while ploughing? Some believe, Theophrastus tells us, that one should utter curses and abuse when sowing cumin.[47] But quirky little practices of that kind scarcely suffice to explain this solemn public ritual. The Bouzygean curses sound much more like the public curses pronounced against antisocial behaviour in many Greek states, whether at festivals or, as in Athens, before meetings of the assembly. The public curses strike at more political offences such as treason, those of the *Bouzygai* support more elementary forms of cooperation on which life in a community depends. The latter resemble those three commandments of the agricultural hero Triptolemus which, in a vague phrase of Xenocrates, 'still survive at Eleusis': revere parents, honour gods with crops, and do no harm to living creatures.[48] Bouzyges and Triptolemus are mouthpieces through whom Demeter gave her laws; the Bouzygean curses were an impressive statement of the need to collaborate made at a time of high importance in the life of the community.[49]

Demeter's relation to another institution of civilization is less certain. According to ancient scholars, at Athenian weddings a boy both of whose parents were still alive, wearing a headdress made of thistles and acorns, carried around a winnowing-basket full of loaves and recited 'I have escaped the worse, I have found the better': the symbolism indicated, they said, the change away from the savage ancient diet/life style (the ambiguity of the Greek word δίαιτα is very perceptible here).[50] We are also told by the lexicographer Pollux that at their weddings Athenian brides were required to carry a flour sieve, and a vessel for roasting barley, as symbols of their future role in the production of food.[51] These decontextualized fragments are not easy to interpret. Pollux sees in the sieve and the roasting dish a call to wifely duty; some moderns take them as betokening fertility (perhaps the wife's womb will swell like a baked loaf), others as a symbol of the association between marriage and the 'ground life'.[52] Whatever we make of sieve and roasting dish, the doings of the boy with the winnowing-basket (if correctly reported)

---

[46] *Paroem. Graec.*1.388 no. 61, Σ Soph. *Ant.* 255; cf. Jacoby on Philochorus *FGrH* 328 F 96, n. 5; *Athenian Religion*, 287. The association between *Βουζύγαι* and Eleusinian sacred ploughing made by Σ Aristid. vol. III p. 473, 25–7 Dindorf is not very reliable (M. H. Jameson, *TAPA* 82, 1951, 55, n. 13).

[47] *Hist. pl.*7.3.3 (cf. 9.8.8), καταρᾶσθαι καὶ βλαφημεῖν.

[48] Fr. 98 Heinze ap. Hermippus fr 84 Wehrli ap. Porph. *Abst.* 4. 22. 2 Bouffartigue (267.23–268.2 Nauck). F. Schwenn, in *RE* s.v. *Triptolemos*, 222, supposes that they were inscribed like the Delphic maxims. Hermippus actually associates Bouzyges and Triptolemus as primitive Athenian lawgivers: see fr 82 III (=*FGrH* 328 F 96) with fr. 84 Wehrli.

[49] Harrison, *Prolegomena*, 145; Durand, *Sacrifice et labour*, 175–87.

[50] Paus. Att. ε 87 Erbse, cited by Eust. on *Od.* 12.357; cf. e.g. Zen. 3.98.

[51] Poll. *Onom.* 1.246, 3.37.

[52] So respectively Vérilhac/Vial, *Mariage*, 352–3 and Detienne, *Jardins*, 215–17 (116–17 in the Engl. tr.).

certainly set up a contrast between thorns and bread in the context of the marriage ceremony. But the point was perhaps to stress the opulence of the occasion (the 'ground life' was above all a life of comfort) rather than to make any stronger connection between Demeter and the norms of marriage. It was Cecrops, not Demeter, who taught humans to confine their wild desires within lawful bounds.[53] Demeter seems not to have received wedding sacrifices in Athens, nor is she listed among the quite numerous gods of marriage. It is a surprise to discover that a priestess of the goddess expounded an 'ancestral ordinance' (*patrios thesmos*) to young couples on their wedding night in Plutarch's Boeotia. Scholars of the nineteenth century, starting from that text of Plutarch, actually derived the epithet Thesmophoros from a supposed association with the *thesmoi* of marriage; such an association between Roman Ceres and marriage is in fact quite explicit.[54] But the practice reported by Plutarch may be a product of speculation about the epithet, not its source. One may therefore hesitate to claim marriage too among the *thesmoi* brought by the goddess. But everything we have seen about the rules of inclusion at the *Thesmophoria* illustrates a sense in which the state of marriage (not the wedding as such) was indeed her domain.

Not all women's festivals were as austere as the *Thesmophoria*, or as exclusive. In regard to the *Haloa*, we hear not only of rich feasting but also, from a good source (Apollodorus, *Against Neaera*), of a sacrifice brought during the festival by a *hetaira*. In the *Courtesans' Letters* of Alciphron the festival has become a key event in the social diary of the demi-monde; but it seems possible that Alciphron, eager for Attic detail but knowing Attica only from a small selection of texts, spun this conception simply on the basis of the passage just mentioned in Apollodorus' speech.[55] It can at the least be doubted whether citizen and non-citizen women mingled at the festival as equals; perhaps the woman mentioned by Apollodorus brought a private sacrifice because she was excluded from offerings available by right to Athenian women. All that is sure is that she was not debarred from the shrine.

The one named festival which, beyond a doubt, women of all types were free to attend was the *Adonia*. Courtesans celebrated the *Adonia* but citizen women did so too, and Menander's *Samia* shows a citizen wife and a Samian courtesan conducting it together (38–46).[56] (Men attended if at all as spec-

---

[53] Cf. Jacoby, n. 3 to comm. on Philochorus *FGrH* 328 F 93.

[54] Plut. *Praec. conj.* 1, 138b, adduced by F. G. Welcker, *Griechische Götterlehre*, ii (Göttingen 1860), 496, still followed by O. Gruppe, *Griechische Mythologie und Religionsgeschichte*, ii (Munich 1906), 1176; they quoted uses of *thesmos* in relation to marriage in earlier texts (Hom. *Od.* 23.296; Soph. *Ant.* 799). Ceres: see e.g. Verg. *Aen.* 4.58, where *Serv. Dan.* quotes Calvus fr. 6 Morel, Plut. *Rom.* 22.3.

[55] Apollod. *Neaer.*, 116–17; cf. App. 2, and on the *Haloa* pp. 167, 171, 199–201.

[56] Contrast eg. Diphilus fr. 42, 38–40; fr. 49 (courtesans) with Ar. *Lys.* 387–98, which in context must imply citizen celebrants (or how is it relevant to the *proboulos'* situation ?) whether or not the γυνή of 392 is Demostratus' wife; on the whole issue cf. Winkler, 'Laughter of the oppressed', 200–1. Men as spectators: Men. *Sam.* 43.

tators; it was a women's festival, and Philippides wrote a 'Women holding the *Adonia*'.) This freedom was possible because the *Adonia* had no public component except that many women participated; the celebrations were privately organized in private houses. 'Women held many festivals distinct from the public ones, coming together privately', correctly writes a scholiast on the first line of Aristophanes' *Lysistrata*.[57] What is singular and remarkable about the *Adonia* is that in contrast to other such rites, usually known only from fugitive allusions and probably celebrated irregularly according to individual inclination, the *Adonia* had not just a name but also a recognized if informal place among the festivals of the state; Aristophanes can include it in a list along with *Mysteries* and *Dipolieia*,[58] and it was often mentioned in comedy. The natural inference is that it was celebrated on a fixed date or at least during a fixed period (which is, however, much debated) every year. The women of Athens who weep for Adonis resemble the women of Babylon and Palestine who weep for Tammuz. Adonis was already lamented by Sappho in the early sixth century, and it may have been over a long period that the *Adonia* acquired its paradoxical position among the festivals of Athens, both within and outside the canon.[59]

Only the briefest cameo of the rites can be presented here.[60] Seeds of quick-growing plants (lettuce and fennel) were planted on large potsherds, to create the so-called gardens of Adonis. At a certain point the women took the gardens up to the roofs of the houses and there— secluded but not hidden, nor inaudible—lamented for Adonis. The god himself was represented by little images. Different celebrations of the *Adonia* no doubt varied, but 'gardens', the little images and the accompanying lament were presumably the *sine quibus non*. Not every vase showing a woman on a ladder need relate to the *Adonia*, but one on which an Eros passes a 'garden' planted on half a pot to a woman on a ladder is perhaps the clearest illustration of a specific festival that survives to us (Fig. 15). The festival could extend into an informal *pannychis*, with dancing. After the festival the gardens were or could be carried out and

[57] The festival is not *demoteles*, notes Σ Ar. *Lys.* 389. The best parallel for such a women's celebration within the house is the party for Hecate in Ar. *Lys.* 700–1; the rites mentioned in Ar. *Lys.* 1–2 seem to have taken place in shrines.

[58] Ar. *Pax* 420.

[59] On Tammuz and others see W. Burkert, *Structure and History in Greek Mythology and Ritual* (Berkeley 1979), 105–11. For the cult of Adonis as practised by Phoenicians in Athens see *Athenian Religion*, 160, n. 29. On the date of the *Adonia* see most recently M. P. H. Dillon, *Hermes* 131 (2003), 1–16, who makes a good case for the date in late spring implied by Ar. *Lys.* 387–98 against that in early–mid-summer given by Plut. *Nic.* 13.11 and *Alc.* 18.5 (there is, as he shows, no other evidence). Even the later dating may be too early to fit the connection with the heliacal rising of Sirius known in later antiquity from Syria and Spain (J. L. Lightfoot, *Lucian. On the Syrian Goddess*, Oxford 2003, 316): see R. R. Simms, *Antichthon* 31 (1997), 45–53.

[60] For an acute and thorough study see J. D. Reed, 'The Sexuality of Adonis', *ClAnt* 14 (1995), 317–47.

Fig. 15. Eros passes an 'Adonis garden' to a women on a ladder: Athenian lekthos, early fourth century BC.

thrown into springs.[61] If left they would soon wither, but there is no sign that they were not meant to be still lush at the time of the lament. About the image of Adonis which the Athenian women had in their heads, all that is clear is that he was the dead young lover of Aphrodite. A myth whereby he moved to

[61] Gardens: Men. *Sam.* 45; Pl. *Phaedr.* 276b; *Theophr. Hist. pl.* 6.7.3; *Caus. pl.* 1.12.2; Theocr. 15.113–14; Hesych α 1231, Suda α 517; Zenob. 1.49 (Diogenian. 1.14). Hesych. and Suda speak of fennel and lettuce, Σ Theocr. 15.112–13 less plausibly of corn and barley. Little images: Plut. *Nic.* 13.11 and *Alc.* 18.5; Alciphr. 4.14.8; Hesych. α 1231. One vase: Badisches Landesmuseum, Karlsruhe, B 39; *LIMC* s.v. *Adonis*, no. 47; other vases are dissociated from the festival by C. M. Edwards, *Hesperia* 53 (1984), 59–72, but A. P. Zarkadas, *Horos* 7 (1989), 137–43, makes a case for the r.f. lekythos Ath. Acr. Mus. 6471, *ARV*² 1175.11, *LIMC* s.v. *Aphrodite* no. 210. *Pannychis*: Men. *Sam.* 46. Springs: Zenob. 1.49.

and fro between Aphrodite and Persephone (presumably post mortem), spending six months of the year with each, already existed at this date; its resonance is strikingly illustrated by the sobriquet 'Adonis' applied to an amphibious fish, like him a voyager between two normally distinct spheres.[62] But it seems certain that the Athenian ritual centered on the death of Adonis, not on any partial restoration to life.

It was evidently acceptable for Athenian men to express disapproval of 'Adoniasmos on the roofs' as a symptom of female licentiousness; and Clearchus explained the proverb 'that's nothing sacred' as originating in an angry exclamation of Heracles when confronted by an image of unmanly Adonis.[63] Whether there were other men who found such attitudes stuffy we can only guess. As in all myths telling of a goddess's amours among men, the mortal lover comes off ill (though less ill in this case than did Tithonus and Anchises), and some male fear of the dominating woman seems to be expressed in the story pattern. What women found in the cult is a different question. For as long as the festival was seen, according to the old paradigm, as a device for the control of agriculture, that issue scarcely needed to be raised.[64] Structuralism dramatically transformed the festival into a celebration of anti-agriculture (and anti-fertility), by way of a contrast between the *Thesmophoria*, conducted by legitimate wives, and the ludicrous mimicry of agriculture performed by sensual and rackety women at the *Adonia*.[65] But legitimate wives too enjoyed the *Adonia*, and Plato's contrast between the short-lived gardens of Adonis and the procedures of serious farmers cannot be taken as a key to the ritual's meaning. It is very implausible to imagine courtesans gathered together to celebrate their own sterility and negativity through the image of Adonis' doomed and futile gardens. Perhaps the short-lived gardens express rather a teasing/mocking female attitude to male sexual prowess, an assertion that the real power of control over life and generation lies elsewhere.[66] But that suggestion scarcely does justice to the luxury of the lamentations for Adonis; yet the delicious emotionalism of the rite, the revelling in a fictional bereavement, was a pleasure distinctively offered by the *Adonia* in contrast to the more ordinary women's rituals.[67]

---

[62] Clearchus fr. 101 Wehrli ap. Ath. 332b (cf. Ael. *HA* 9.36). The fish in question (ἐξώκοιτος) has in turn given its name to a sea–land missile (the exocet). On the myth see Apollod. *Bibl.* 3.14.4; Burkert, op. cit., 109–10, and on all questions relating to the 'resurrection' of Adonis, Lightfoot, op. cit., 305–11.

[63] Ar. *Lys.* 387–98, cf. Cratinus fr. 17; Clearchus fr. 66 Wehrli; note too Plato comicus fr. 3 (which makes Adonis a pathic, though also a seducer of women); for the possibility of an alternative view see J. D. Reed, *ClassAnt* 15 (1995), 332–5.

[64] Deubner, *Attische Feste*, 221.

[65] Detienne, *Jardins, passim*; the Plato passage is *Phaedr.* 276b (Plato's point was often echoed later: W. Atallah, *Adonis dans la littérature et l'art grecs*, Paris 1966, 227–8).

[66] So Winkler, 'Laughter of the oppressed'.

[67] This factor is stressed by J. D. Reed, *ClassAnt* 15 (1995), 345–6, and R. R. Simms, *CJ* 93 (1998), 121–41. Both suggest that the festival satisfied a female 'need to mourn' (Simms, 136) frustrated by the Solonian restrictions; but (other difficulties aside) a great gap yawns between Solon's legislation and the first attestation of the festival.

One pleasure of the *Adonia* was doubtless the simple opportunity that it offered to enjoy the company of other women.[68] But Theocritus' fifteenth *Idyll*, which depicts an Adonis ritual as celebrated in third-century Alexandria, suggests that the experience could be more intense than that. Alexandria is not Athens, and, beneath the mimetic guise, what the male author Theocritus offers is not a reproduction of the emotions of Alexandrian women but a speculative interpretation of them. None the less, the poem represents an attempt by a sensitive if humorous Greek to catch something of the emotional texture of the ritual; we can at the least scrutinize Theocritus' interpretation as one hypothesis among others about the source of the cult's appeal. We listen in Theocritus to a professional singer's song over what is treated as the marriage couch of Adonis; she sings, we may suppose, what the ideal participant might feel. 'Kypris holds Adonis, rosy-armed Adonis holds Kypris. The bridegroom is only eighteen or nineteen years of age. His kisses don't prick; his lips are still covered with golden down' (128–130). The 'marriage' of Venus and Adonis was, it appears, very unlike the realities of Greek marriage, where the groom was all but invariably much older than the bride, on Aristotle's recommendation indeed twice her age.[69] This inversion of roles is always clear in the Greek artistic evidence (Veronese's magnificent picture in the National Gallery in London must be forgotten here). Revealingly, Venus is often clothed, Adonis nude; it is not in doubt who the sexual plaything in the relationship is.[70] Adonis is addressed by Theocritus' singer with warm affection: 'Be favourable to us next year too, dear Adonis. You found us happy when you came this year, Adonis, and when you come again you will come as a friend' (143–4). In conclusion Theocritus points the contrast between this sugared relationship and the actual domestic lives of the women who thus drooled over Adonis. 'It's time to go home', one comments; 'Diokleidas hasn't had his lunch. He's all vinegar anyway, and when he's hungry it's best not even to go near him. Farewell, beloved Adonis; find us happy when you come again' (147–9).

What of the gardens? On the old fertility/agricultural interpretation Adonis the god was a metaphor for the natural world; his death and supposed rebirth represented the annual cycle of the plants. But in Greek sources the metaphor often goes the other way, with young humans being spoken of as if they were young shoots.[71] Whatever the origin of the gardens, such was surely their significance in Athens. They were a second embodiment of Adonis: their annual planting symbolized his annual return, their rapid growth mirrored his; by disposing of them (for fear that they would wither if left) the participants acknowledged that their brief emotional engagement with Adonis was, after all, a brief fantasy, a mere holiday from reality. Perhaps the little images

---

[68] So M. P. H. Dillon, *Hermes* 131 (2003), 1–16.
[69] *Pol.* 1335a 28–9; cf. Hes. *Op.* 695–8, with M. L. West's notes ad loc.
[70] See *LIMC* s.v. *Adonis, passim.*
[71] See e.g. Hom. *Od.* 6. 162–8; Soph. *Tr.* 144–6 with commentators.

of Adonis were at a certain point laid in the gardens, as if on a bier.[72] Such are the guesses about the emotional experience of the *Adonia* that Theocritus' poem may encourage one to make.[73]

I append here an important vase-image which must bear on some of the themes of this chapter; the difficult question is that of which themes it bears on. A woman bends over a group of phalli which emerge from the ground,

Fig. 16. Attic red figure pelike showing a Phallus garden, *c*.440–430 BC.

---

[72] So R. R. Simms, *CJ* 93 (1998), 121–41.
[73] Similar views (which may also of course have been influenced by Theocritus) are quoted with approval by J. D. Reed, *ClassAnt* 14 (1995), 345: note esp. O. Murray, *Early Greece*, ed. 2 (London 1993), 87: 'The hymns sung by women mourn forbidden fruit—the fantasy lover that society has deprived them of, and those frontiers of desire which they will never know'.

apparently in order to sprinkle seed among them; around the base of the phalli young leaves are visible.[74] The image fits neatly with the old 'agricultural fertility' model of women's cults; it could be taken to show lewd objects being manipulated not for the sake of lewdness but (note the leaves) in order to encourage the plants to grow. That interpretation cannot be excluded—it is not in doubt that Greeks in many contexts saw the fertility of humans and of fields as related—though it will not follow that such was the sole or even the dominant function of ritual obscenity. But could a vase-painter casually have depicted a secret ritual of the *Thesmophoria* or the *Haloa* in this way? (*Haloa* has been the favourite candidate,[75] because 'handling' of phalli is attested at that festival.) Yet a purely private ritual directed to the fertility of the fields would be an oddity. Old comedy is full of jokes about women's delight in the phallus, and perhaps a similar point is made visually here: 'see the kind of plant that women wish to grow in their gardens!'

[74] R. F. pelike in London, E 819; Beazley, ARV² 1137.25; Deubner, *Attische Feste*, pls. 3.1 (an important drawing) and 3.3; here Fig. 16.
[75] So Deubner, *Attische Feste*, 66, followed by Parke, *Festivals*, 99.

14

The *Anthesteria* and other Dionysiac Rites

If one had to identify an Athenian festival day that had an emotional appeal (at least for men) like that of modern western Christmas, the best candidate would be 'Beakers' (*Choes*) (middle and constantly mentioned day of the festival known to scholarship as *Anthesteria*).[1] Callimachus describes an Athenian who lived in Egypt faithfully observing it; according to the local historian Possis, it was first introduced to Magnesia on the Maeander by the great Themistocles when living there in exile. There was even a story of Timon the misanthrope forced to celebrate it, with a single companion.[2] It seems to have been, like Christmas, inescapable.

Our sources associate the festival with the Limnaion, the old temple (unidentified) of Dionysus 'in the Marshes' (a characteristically undistinguished address for this least monumental of gods).[3] That may seem to indicate a single celebration on the outskirts of Athens itself. But the central day was given over to parties held in private houses, which it is easier to imagine taking place throughout Attica. It may be better to envisage the *Anthesteria* as a diffused festival, in which case local sanctuaries of Dionysus will have stood in for the one 'in the Marshes' for those who chose to stay in their demes.[4] But the central ritual of the 'marriage of Dionysus' will have occurred in Athens only. This was not a festival of public pomp and expenditure,[5] and all three days have names associated, in an appropriately homely way, with different kinds of pot: storage jars (*pithoi*), beakers for drinking wine (*choes*), and cooking pots or, as some think,[6] water jars (*chytroi*).

---

[1] On the sparse attestation in sources relating to Athens of the name *Anthesteria* see Hamilton, *Choes*, 5; Thuc. 2.15.4 speaks of 'the older *Dionysia*'.

[2] Callim. *Aet.* fr. 178.1–5; *FGrH* 480 F 1; Plut. *Ant.* 70.3. The collection of testimonia in Hamilton, *Choes*, 149–71, is most useful.

[3] A cult epithet of this type does not speak directly of the god's nature in the way that e.g. Lysios would. But it speaks indirectly, in that the sanctuary of a different type of god (Zeus or Apollo) would probably not have been located 'in the marshes', and, had circumstances forced it to be so, would none the less have been differently identified *dignitatis causa*. On the location see Pickard-Cambridge, *Dramatic Festivals*², 19–25. The notion which crops up here and there in the modern literature that the temple in the marshes was seen as a point of access to the underworld is based on a forced reading of the *parodos* of Ar. *Ran.*, and a questionable analogy with the cult at Lerna.

[4] Cf. p. 76 above (with the different view of Henrichs in n. 108).

[5] 'It occurred largely on the level of folk custom', Burkert, *Homo Necans*, 215. As Burkert notes, it is absent from the 'skin sale records' (*Athenian Religion*, 227–8).

[6] On the meaning of *chytros* see n. 28.

The problems of reconstruction, unfortunately, are much more severe in relation to the *Anthesteria* than any other major festival. Some activities are firmly associated with particular days of the festival, while others have to be found a place; other important elements may or may not belong to it at all. And there are difficulties even with activities assigned to particular days. According to the orator Apollodorus, the temple of Dionysus in the Marshes was open 'once a year only, on the 12th of the month Anthesterion', the central day of the festival. But good sources attest activity at the temple both on the previous day and 'at the sacred *Chytroi*', which prima facie should be the day after. The most popular solution is the hypothesis that days (whether in general, or by a special archaic reckoning used for festivals) began at sunset; the activity at the temple on day one will have occurred after sunset (thus on Anthesterion 12), that 'at the sacred *Chytroi*' can be put after sunset on day two. But the postulate of a dusk to dusk festival calendar is a very insecure one[7] (and we are still left with a temple open for rather more than twenty-four hours). It might be simpler to suppose that Apollodorus exaggerates, and to allow activity at the Limnaion to spread over three full days. Other hypotheses are possible.[8] The point may seem a small one, but it is symptomatic; if one is trying to assemble the miscellaneous data into a coherent sequence, to give the festival a kind of plot, a set of small uncertainties of this type quickly multiply into very large ones. A wholly consensual account of the *Anthesteria* would begin and end with the proposition that a drinking competition took place on the second day; consensus would break down even over important details of that competition. The reconstruction that follows will need to be rather pernickety, and dry.[9] I will begin with elements that are, however problematically, assigned a date; and I will allow sources to speak for themselves where possible.

They broach the new wine at Athens on the eleventh of Anthesterion, calling the day 'Pot-opening' (*Pithoigia*). And in the past, it seems, they used to pour a libation before tasting the wine and pray that the use of this drug (φάρμακον) should prove harmless and beneficial to them.[10]

---

[7] For the festival-day theory see works cited in Hamilton, *Choes*, 45, n. 119; for criticism Mansfield, *Robe of Athena*, 434–47, and Hamilton, 47, n. 127 [+]; also W. K. Pritchett, *ZPE* 49 (1982), 262–3.

[8] Jacoby rejected the precise indication of a day in Apollodorus (*Neaer.* 76) as interpolated. In regard to the first day, some distinguish between the sanctuary (open) and the temple itself (still closed), or even locate the ceremony in the streets outside the sanctuary: see n. 13, and Hamilton, *Choes*, 45–6 (who is not sympathetic); cf. N. Robertson, 'Athens' festival of the new wine', *HSCP* 95 (1993), 197–250, at 224 and 242, for the same approach to ceremonies of day three. Hamilton, *Choes*, 42–50, revives Didymus' location of *Choes* and *Chytroi* on the same day (in Σ vet. Ar. *Ach.* 1076a (ii)), a position which is normally and in my view rightly rejected on the authority of Philochorus (*FGrH* 328 F 84). See too n. 29.

[9] 'A mere statement of the recorded facts is easy': Farnell, *Cults*, v, 214. I have not found it so. For a radical critique of existing reconstructions, see now Humphreys, *Strangeness*, Ch. 6.

[10] Plut. *Quaest. conv.* 3.7.1, 655e.

In itself that account suggests a ceremony performed in private houses, but the following is usually associated with it:[11]

> Phanodemus says that the Athenians used to bring the young wine[12] to the shrine[13] of Dionysus in the Marshes from the pots (*pithoi*) [this detail suggests the identification with '*Pithoigia*'] and mix it for the god, then sample it themselves. This is why Dionysus was called Of the Marsh, because that was the first occasion when young wine was blended with water and drunk mixed. That is why springs were called nymphs and nurses of Dionysus, because water makes wine grow when mixed in. And so, delighted by the mixture, they celebrated Dionysus in song, dancing and invoking him as Of fair Flowers and Dithyrambos and Baccheutes and Bromios.

Some at least of Phanodemus' expressions refer to the distant past ('that was the first occasion'), very likely the time of Dionysus' first arrival in Attica under king Amphictyon.[14] The point of aitiology is to explain the present, but, if certain titles of Dionysus are the feature of the present which is here being explained, it is not guaranteed that the wine-mixing at the shrine continues too. But, if we suspend doubt on this point, the two sources taken together give us a communal wine-opening at a public sanctuary, culminating (if the last sentence of the second passage still refers to the festival) in informal song and dancing. The time of day is not identified.[15] Presumably any male citizen who chose could attend, probably any free male inhabitant of Attica. A very bustling scene we must imagine if so.[16] We would like to know whether men of the outlying demes brought their *pithoi* all this way or went to local shrines (or simply opened their jars at home, reciting Plutarch's formula). Both sources stress that, on this one day of the year on which wine-drinking (a practice of every day of the year), was a subject of explicit

---

[11] Phanodemus *FGrH* 325 F 12 ap. Ath. 465a. *Aliter* Robertson, *HSCP* 95 (1993), 224–7, who puts it on *Chytroi*, and Nilsson, *Studia*, 123; id., *Geschichte*, 587, who puts it at the start of *Choes* (thus requiring the Athenians to make two trips to the Limnaion on that day); a tendency to play down the *Pithoigia* still in Hamilton, *Choes*, 9 and 50 ('the *Pithoigia* need hardly concern us'!). Nilsson's views on this matter were formed before the publication of the important Callim. fr. 178.1–2.

[12] For this sense of γλεῦκος (wrongly abolished in the 1996 supplement to LSJ) see Burkert. *Homo Necans*, 217, n. 6; cf. N. Robertson, *HSCP* 95 (1993), 211–12.

[13] This correction of Jacoby (πρὸς τὸ ἱερόν for πρὸς τῷ ἱερῷ) appears necessary, given that word order demands that the phrase be attached to φέροντας, not κιρνάναι, unless we agree with Bravo, *Pannychis*, 87, n. 32, that Athenaeus is excerpting too carelessly for arguments based on proper style to operate. If Jacoby is right, Deubner's ceremony in the vicinity of, but not in, the sanctuary ('Strassengelage', *Attische Feste*, 94, n. 5; 127–8) is ruled out.

[14] Philochorus *FGrH* 328 F 5.

[15] Burkert, *Homo Necans*, 216–18, not implausibly puts it in the evening, partly because of the supposed 'festival day' (see above).

[16] Vividly evoked by Burkert, *Homo Necans*, 218. Transport of the largest type of *pithos* would scarcely be practicable. Nilsson and Robertson (n. 11) suppose that the wine was not brought to the shrine in *pithoi* (the Greek bears either view). Σ vet. Hes. *Op.* 368 makes the *Pithoigia* (rather than the *Choes*) the occasion for treating slaves and hired hands. This would imply a setting within the house. Probably it is just a mistake. Tzetzes on Hes. *Op.* 368 speaks of the *Pithoigia* as a 'communal *symposion*', a turn of phrase of which D. Noel, 'Les Anthestéries et le vin', *Kernos* 12 (1999), 125–52, makes too much.

attention, the need for cautious and civilized drinking practices was emphasized.[17]

Phanodemus is again a main source for day two:

Phanodemus says that the festival of the Beakers (*Choes*) at Athens was founded by
king Demophon, who wanted to entertain Orestes on his arrival in Athens. But since
he did not want him to approach the shrines before his trial nor share in libations, he
ordered the temples to be closed and a beaker (*chous*) of wine to be put beside each
person, saying that a cake would be given as prize to the first to drink up. And he
instructed them, on finishing drinking, not to take the crowns they were wearing to
the temples, because they had been under the same roof as Orestes, but to put them
each around his own beaker and take the crowns ['the crowns' deleted by Meineke, to
give a vague 'and take them'] to the priestess at the shrine in the marshes, and then
sacrifice the remnants [perform the remaining sacrifices?] in the shrine.[18] And from
then the festival was called Beakers.[19]

From the version of this *aition* put in Orestes' own mouth by Euripides, we
learn further that he was seated at a separate table and that the drinking took
place in silence; both these further details are normally taken to be aitiological
too. In *Acharnians*, our most important source, Aristophanes introduces a
herald who proclaims 'Hear ye, people. In accord with ancestral tradition,
drink the *Choes* on the trumpet signal. Whoever drinks up first, will get a
wineskin ...'. The proclamation seems to be addressed to all citizens. But the
hero Dikaiopolis is then invited to what appears to be an official public *Choes*:
having won the drinking competition he claims his prize from 'the king
(archon)'. (But, though a guest, Dikaiopolis takes his own wine in his own
chous.[20]) A public ceremony, held in the mysterious Thesmotheteion, is
mentioned also by Plutarch. The contest won by Dikaiopolis was embedded—
and this was surely the norm—in a full-scale banquet.

Unlike Dikaiopolis, most Athenians must have revelled privately, with
relatives and friends; at this private level the drinking competition is not

[17] Bravo, *Pannychis, passim*, would extend the scene into the night with a mixed παννυχίς (cf.
p. 166, n. 43). But the link of such practices with the *Anthesteria* is based entirely on the
reconstruction of several very fragmentary poems.

[18] It is not clear whether the priestess received crown plus *chous* or just crown. The uncertainty remains whether or not one deletes τοὺς στεφάνους with Meineke. θύειν τὰ ἐπίλοιπα is
generally taken to refer to pouring out the remaining undrunk wine as a libation. Burkert, *Homo
Necans*, 231, objects that θύειν is not σπένδειν. But there were no 'remaining sacrifices' for
individuals to perform, as far as we know.

[19] Phanodemus *FGrH* 325 F 11 ap. Ath. 437c–d.

[20] Eur. *IT* 947–60; Ar. *Ach.* 1000–2, 1085–7; 1202. In the fragment of Eratosthenes concerning a comparable Alexandrian festival quoted in Ath. 276a–c the host is envisaged as
providing the banquet in the normal way. But even in Aristophanes the host will evidently
provide much—only not the *chous*. It is not important that in Euripides (and hence Plut. *Quaest.
conv.* 2.10.1, 643a), there is no hint of these special arrangements: Orestes could not bring his
own *chous*. Thesmotheteion: Plut. *Quaest. conv.* 1.1.2, 613b (? cf. Alciphr. 4.18.11, θεσμοθέτας ἐν
τοῖς ἱεροῖς κώμοις [Reiske: ταῖς ἱεραῖς κόμαις/κώμαις mss.] κεκισσωμένους); cf. N. Robertson, *HSCP*
95 (1993), 215.

attested, but can surely be assumed.[21] Slaves feasted too, as is confirmed even by an entry in the Eleusinian temple accounts which mentions the cost of a sacrificial victim, jugs and wine 'for public slaves for Beakers'. It was, says Callimachus, a 'white day' for slaves. If the practice of solitary drinking extended to private houses they cannot, by definition, have shared their masters' table, but they probably ate and drank in the same room.[22]

After the separate parties, the sense of collective experience was renewed when participants converged on the old temple of Dionysus to dedicate the crowns. One would like to take this as the occasion when 'the revelling-under-the- influence crowd' (κραιπαλόκωμος... λαῶν ὄχλος) mentioned by Aristophanes thronged the precinct in the marshes 'at the sacred *Chytroi*'.[23] But, as we have seen, on a plain reading 'at the sacred *Chytroi*' suggests that they came back the following day, if for no attested purpose, as 'the crowd of revellers with hangovers' (κραιπάλη can indicate either drunkenness or its aftermath).

According to Phanodemos as quoted above, when the temple of Dionysus in the Marshes was open for the *Choes*, others were closed (roped off, as we learn from other sources).[24] Hereto links a crucial detail added by a single lexicographer, Photius: 'Unclean day: at the *Choes* at Athens in the month Anthesterion, in which the souls of the dead are believed to come up, they used to chew buckthorn from morning and anoint their doors with pitch'. We have, therefore (unless we disbelieve Photius' explanation of the custom),[25] to

---

[21] Dikaiopolis won a wine-skin whereas Phanodemus speaks of a cake as prize; it has often been supposed that we have here the contrast between public and private (so e.g. Deubner, *Attische Feste*, 99). Private feasting is well attested, and if the feasting is held in private houses the drinking should be too; we cannot, then, literally imagine a single trumpet signal initiating the competition throughout Athens. But Nilsson, *Eranos* 15 (1915), 185–6 (*Op. Sel.* 1, 150–1) and Hamilton, *Choes*, 12–13, envisage a single public drinking competition breaking up into a plurality of private parties; Auffarth, *Drohende Untergang*, 211, has a mass drinking competition perhaps in the agora.

[22] This is certainly the case in the louche story (locale in Greece unrecorded) told by Ath. 437e of Dionysius the renegade Stoic. Slaves' participation: *IG* II² 1672. 204; Callim fr. 178.2. That masters waited on servants and that servants enjoyed *parrhesia*, as at the *Peloria* of Thessaly (Baton *FGrH* 268 F 5), is not stated; I doubt whether Callim. fr. 178. 2 with 19 suggests it (R. Scodel, *ZPE* 39, 1980, 37–40).

[23] The passage (Ar. *Ran.* 217–19) is so taken by Radermacher, Stanford, Dover and Sommerstein, untroubled by heortological complications, in their commentaries ad loc. I have wondered whether Ar. *Ach.* 1076, 'at the time of the *Choes* and *Chytroi*', might suggest that the festival was sometimes called '*Choes* and *Chytroi*' and that either day-name could then be used colloquially to indicate the festival as a whole. I cannot prove use of *Choes* for the whole festival in living usage, many instances being ambiguous, but Skylax, *Periplous*, 112 (T 28 in the collection of testimonia in Hamilton, *Choes*) and Dem. 39.16 are plausible cases; in scholiastic usage (e.g.) T 22–6 in Hamilton, *Choes*, 158, may well be cases. The present passage of *Frogs* is the best candidate for *Chytroi* not used specifically of the day; one might also think of the *chytrinoi agones* (n. 36).

[24] Poll. 8. 141. K. F. Johansen, 'Am Chytrentag', *ActaArch* 38 (1967), 175–98, detects such roping off illustrated on the r.f. krater *CVA* Copenhagen 4, fig. 148 1a–b (*ARV*² 1156, no. 11; Auffarth, *Drohende Untergang*, 230, fig. 10) and the r.f. sherd *CVA* Bucarest 1, fig. 32.1. I do not understand the spikes attached to the supposed ropes.

[25] As do Burkert, *Homo Necans*, 218, 220, n. 26 (with useful information on buckthorn and pitch); Bremmer, *Soul*, 111–12; N. Robertson, *HSCP* 95 (1993), 206–8. None of these shows

add the souls of the dead to the cast list. Though Photius says vaguely that they came up 'in the month Anthesterion', it was precisely 'at the *Choes*' that protective measures were taken against them. 'At the *Choes*' might refer to the festival as a whole, not the specific middle day, but it was on the middle day that we know the temples to have been closed, and it was on this day that polluted Orestes arrived. The day of the drinking competition must have been one 'polluted day', even if there were others.[26]

Most of our knowledge of the *Chytroi* comes from a paraphrase (including a short fragment) of Theopompus given in one scholion to Aristophanes, and a series of snippets quoted from the same context in Theopompus by another.[27] The paraphrase tells us that, according to Theopompus, the survivors from the flood boiled a pot (*chytra*) of mixed seeds (*panspermia*), from which the festival was named.[28] The scholion containing the verbatim extracts runs:

> Theopompus explains the origin as follows: 'So the survivors named the whole festival by the name of the day on which they returned to good spirits', then 'and they sacrifice on *Choes* (?) to none at all of the Olympian gods, but to Hermes Chthonios. From the pot which is boiled by everyone in the city none of the priests eats. They do this on the [numeral probably missing] day', and 'the survivors appeased Hermes on behalf of the dead'.

'On *Choes*' (the best reading, despite some manuscript complications)[29] is horrendous: we must simply suppose an error for 'on *Chytroi*'. Once that has been accepted, we learn that on *Chytroi* every household prepared a *panspermia* for Hermes Chthonios which had some relation to the dead (the 'sacrifice' to Hermes, the *panspermia* and the offering brought to appease Hermes on behalf of the dead being surely identical).[30] The signals that we

anything wrong with Photius' view (μ 439 s.v. μιαρὰ ἡμέρα) that I can see. Hesych. μ 1314 is slightly different: μιαραὶ ἡμέραι τοῦ Ἀνθεστηριῶνος μηνός, ἐν αἷς τὰς ψυχὰς τῶν κατοιχομένων ἀνιέναι ἐδόκουν.

[26] There is oscillation between singular and plural in the relevant lexicographical notices (see previous note). The conclusion about *Choes* itself can be avoided only by the conjoined hypotheses (countenanced by Jacoby, comm. on Philochorus *FGrH* 328 F 84, p. 365) that (1) Photius' 'at the *Choes*' is loose and (2) the closure of the temples on Anthesterion 12 has no connection with the day's impurity.

[27] Theopompus *FGrH* 115 F 347 (a) and (b).

[28] Both *chytros* and *chytra* are by etymology vessels used for pouring liquids (χέω: cf. Farnell, *Cults*, V, 219) and *chytros* may have retained that association more strongly (Nilsson, *Studia*, 135–6), but this does not warrant positing an original libation ritual (with Nilsson) in lieu of that attested, still less (with N. Robertson, *HSCP* 95 (1993), 199–205) dissociating the Theopompus material from *Chytroi* altogether. Calame, *Thésée*, 330, suggests that the secondary sense of *Chytroi* as geological 'basins' (i.e. in this case holes in the ground, points of access to the underworld) is also relevant.

[29] See the long note in Nilsson, *Geschichte*, 594, n. 7, with the addendum of Burkert, *Homo Necans*, 239, n. 4. Nilsson's solution is that the sacrifice in question occurred on the evening of day two, still *Choes* by the civil calendar but already *Chytroi* by the sacred. This is artificial, overcrowds that evening (which also, by a different application of the 'festival day', hosts the revel of Ar. *Ran.* 217–19!—n. 23), and leaves day three empty.

[30] *Aliter* Burkert, *Homo Necans*, 239.

receive from Theopompus about the character of *Chytroi* are mixed. On the one hand its mythical forerunner was the day on which the survivors of the flood 'returned to good spirits'. On the other, offerings were made to none but Hermes Chthonios, and those offerings were unsuitable food for persons bound to purity.[31]

Yet, since we are told explicitly that priests did not eat of them, it follows that ordinary people did; Hermes received only a share. These domestic offerings to Hermes are not easy to interpret. They relate, no doubt, in some way to the 'souls' who are wandering free at the festival, but (*pace* much older scholarship)[32] they are not addressed to them. The notion that they are 'the first European intercession for the dead' is charmingly anachronistic; other objections aside, whereas the dead of the *Genesia* are individuals, one's own kin, who need cult, those of the *Anthesteria* are treated as an undifferentiated swarm.[33] Hermes Chthonios is not a god of the dead, but the god who presides over passages between this world and that below.[34] The survivors of the flood in Theopompus' *aition* will have prayed to him, very appropriately, to grant an easy descent to their dead comrades. Perhaps the prayer in this case was to lead back down those souls who had come up earlier in the festival.

Theopompus associates the *Chytroi* aitiologically with the flood. The *aition* offered by the Chiot Theopompus is not guaranteed to represent 'native exegesis', but he knew Athens well, and it very probably does. A mysterious testimonium '*Hydrophoria*: a mourning festival at Athens for those who died in the flood' has often been linked with the *Chytroi*; so has an allusion in Pausanias to annual offerings of honey and barley cake made at the rift (near the temple of Zeus Olympios) where the flood waters disappeared.[35] The point must be left unresolved; if the *Hydrophoria* did indeed fall on this day, then libations of water (we assume) were poured to the dead in addition to the *panspermia* offered to Hermes Chthonios.

[31] Cf. Parker, *Miasma*, 338, on *LSCG* 154 A 23, 156 A 8.
[32] e.g. Nilsson, *Studia*, 134; id., *Geschichte*, 595; Farnell, *Cults*, v, 219; Deubner, *Attische Feste*, 112; Meuli, *Ges. Schr.*, 922, n. 5. (The case might, however, be strengthened if the rite εὔδειπνος, n. 48 below, is assigned to this day.) An association between *panspermia* and the dead is common but not invariable (cf. Burkert, *Homo Necans*, 238–9; add the testimony of an anonymous writer on *mirabilia* adduced by X. Schutter, *Kernos* 9, 1996, 341, after E. Rohde, *Acta Soc. Phil. Lips.* 1, 1871, 42, that οἱ Ἀθηναῖοι τοὺς τελευτήσαντας ἐπὶ τὸν τάφον ἄγοντες καὶ πανόσπριον ἐπέφερον, σύμβολον τῆς παρ' αὐτῶν εὑρέσεως τῶν ἁπάντων).
[33] Auffarth, *Drohende Untergang*, 234; the phrase quoted is Deubner's approving paraphrase, *Attische Feste*, 112, of L. R. Farnell, *Greek Hero Cults and Ideas of Immortality* (Oxford 1926), 346. The newly attested possibility at Cyzicus of honouring dead persons at the *Anthesteria* (*SEG* XXVIII 953, 51–56) proves little, given that living persons too could be so honoured (Michel 534.20–1).
[34] See Sourvinou-Inwood, *Death*, index s.v. Hermes Chthonios; more generally on Hermes and Hades, Farnell, *Cults*, V, 11–15; Nilsson, *Geschichte*, 508–9.
[35] So, most confidently, Nilsson, *Studia*, 136–8; id., *Geschichte*, 181; followed e.g. by Auffarth, *Drohende Untergang*, 237, on Phot. s.v. Ὑδροφόρια; Paus. 1.18.7; agnosticism in Burkert, *Homo Necans*, 242, n. 16 (more views in Hamilton, *Choes*, 38, n. 96). Nilsson's treatment of Plut. *Sulla* 14.10, which prima facie attests 'many commemorations' of the flood at other occasions in Anthesterion, is criticized by N. Robertson, *HSCP* 95 (1993), 201–2.

Despite all this, Dionysus was not wholly excluded from day three. As we have seen, 'revellers with hangovers' may have returned to his precinct on that day; and we hear of a minor dramatic competition at the *Chytroi*, for comic actors; it was 'revived' by Lycurgus. A recently restored fragment of Callimachus appears to attest a belief that the 'older *Dionysia*', as Thucydides calls the *Anthesteria*, hosted the city's 'choral festivals' until Dionysus Melanaigis, god of the city *Dionysia*, was brought in by Eleuther.[36] Despite Lycurgus' attempted revival, only faint traces of the *Chytroi* competitions appear later.

I turn to elements undated within the festival. The lexicographer Photius is again our main or sole authority for two. 'Jokes from the wagons. At Athens at the festival of *Choes* revellers on wagons mocked and abused those they met. They did the same later at the *Lenaea*.' That is clear enough: much harder is:

'Outside, Carians, it's the *Anthesteria* no longer' [an iambic trimeter]. Some say that this proverb derives from the large number of Carian slaves; during the *Anthesteria* they feasted and did not work, and when the festival was over their owners used to send them out to work and say 'outside, Carians, it's the *Anthesteria* no longer'. But some give the proverb in this form 'Outside, Demons (Κῆρες), it's the *Anthesteria* no longer', on the grounds that souls roam around the city at the *Anthesteria*.

The Carian version has a variant explanation whereby Carians once occupied part of Attica and were given hospitality by the Athenians at the festival. Much has been made of this 'proverb', in one form or the other.[37] But what we have is not a ritual formula actually used at the *Anthesteria*, but a proverb applied in quite different circumstances, 'in relation to people who always want to get the same thing' (in and out of season). There is no knowing when such a floating formula got free from whatever mooring it may have had in real ritual practice, nor what distortions it may have suffered since. As direct evidence for the *Anthesteria* this testimonium is best, however regretfully, abandoned. It tells us something of what ancient scholars knew or believed about the festival. But these beliefs (good times for slaves; open door hospitality; roaming souls) only confirm what we knew already.

Surviving *choes*, by contrast, introduce a new dimension. The antiquarian Crates speaks, a little obscurely, of a type of vessel which has been 'after a fashion consecrated and is used only at the festival' (of *Choes*). Whatever he means, it is universally agreed[38] that we can recognize a *chous* when we see

---

[36] See *Hecale* fr. 85 Hollis, as supplemented by W. S. Barrett (an important addendum to *Athenian Religion*, 94, n. 116); Thuc. 2.15.4. For testimonia on the *chytrinoi agones* see Hamilton, *Choes*, 38–4; N. Robertson, *HSCP* 95 (1993), 246, adds *ithyphalloi*, from Ath. 129d.

[37] Phot. (and Suda) s.v. τὰ ἐκ τῶν ἁμαξῶν and θύραζε Κᾶρες (the latter = Paus. Att. θ 20 Erbse); for the variant Carian explanation see e.g. Zen. 4.33. For an excellent *mise au point* see Burkert, *Homo Necans*, 226–7. Burkert's own theory that the 'Carians' are mummers disguised as primeval inhabitants of Attica has been influential (Bremmer, *Soul*, 113–20; Auffarth, *Drohende Untergang*, 233–4), but relies too heavily on analogy; and for any Athenian the primeval inhabitants of Attica, if there were any, were Pelasgians, not Carians.

[38] If on unstated grounds, as T. H. Carpenter notes, *CPh* 89 (1994), 372–5 (review of Hamilton, *Choes*). Crates: ap. Ath. 495a–c.

one, and that a good proportion of the well over 800 known examples bear some relation to the festival. On a recent count,[39] 279 small *choes* have a yet smaller *chous* depicted somewhere on themselves, as a way, surely, of evoking the *Choes*. Much the commonest subject of *choes*, 'miniature' *choes* in particular, is children. In particular, enormous numbers show chubby naked little boys, still crawling or not a great deal older, often wearing amulets, sometimes crowned; various activities are portrayed, but regular elements are tables, grapes, and little *choes*, which too are often crowned. The specialized association between a type of vessel and a type of scene evidently requires an explanation. It is usually and plausibly sought in the epigraphic and literary evidence which represents the *Choes* as an acknowledged milestone in a child's life. This evidence is late but also clear. It consists of a small boy's gravestone of the second century AD, inscribed 'Of the age of the *Choes* rites, but fate anticipated the *Choes*'; a reference, from roughly the same period, to 'marriage, birth, *Choes*, ephebate' as occasions in relation to which a member of the society of Iobacchoi was required to treat the company; and the statement of Philostratus that 'Athenian children are crowned with flowers in the month Anthesterion in the third year from birth', this event occurring in a context of drinking and sacrifice.[40] The miniature *choes* allow this late-attested function of the *Choes* as a rite of passage to be backdated to the classical period. This is doubtless why 'Pyraichme, good nurse' is shown with a *chous* at her feet on her grave relief, of the fourth century.[41]

Further details remain very unclear: when during the festival did the crowning occur? What further rituals were entailed? Did the children, now ritually removed from the perils of babyhood, discard amulets after 'their' *Choes*?[42] Is Philostratus' 'in the third year' a fixed rule, or a norm? (By realistic criteria, the children on the pots are of varying ages; but these criteria may be inappropriate.) The function of the actual *choes* is very uncertain too; the type of the miniature *chous* with predominantly child-related iconography is found only c.420–390 BC, whereas a vase with actual ritual work to do could not

[39] Hamilton, *Choes*, 88. What follows is heavily dependent on this work, in particular his strengthening of the case built up by several scholars for the view that 'for students of the Anthesteria, it is the small *choes*, not the large ones, that are meaningful' (83).

[40] IG II² 1313 9; IG II² 1368 (LSCG 51) 130; Philostr. *Her.* 35.9 de Lannoy (p. 187 Kayser). Hamilton, *Choes*, 72–3, rejects the conclusions generally drawn from these passages. But his argument, from the associated grave relief (Deubner, *Attische Feste*, pl. 16.1), that the boy who died 'of the age of the *Choes* rites' was 'considerably older than three' is misguided: my colleague R. R. R. Smith tells me that the child shares characteristics (particularly in his hairstyle) with the baby Eros and is in fact considerably younger than three. The joke in Ar. *Thesm.* 746 is also relevant, as G. L. Ham observes, 'The *Choes* and *Anthesteria* Reconsidered: Male Maturation Rites and the Peloponnesian Wars', in M. W. Padilla (ed.), *Rites of Passage in Ancient Greece* (Lewisburg 1999 = *Bucknell Review* 43, 1999), 201–18, at 204.

[41] AM 67 (1942), 222, no. 30 (SEG XXI 1064); AntK 6 (1963), 9 with pl. 3.2.

[42] Cf. Auffarth, *Drohende Untergang*, 243–4. G. L. Ham, op. cit., argues that *Choes* concluded the 'babyhood' phase, seen by Plato (*Leg.* 789e, 792a, 793e) as lasting up to the third birthday; both crawlers and toddlers can symbolize it.

Fig. 17. Chous showing a naked boy wearing amulets, with a chous: *c.*420 BC.

come and go in that way.[43] Nor is the meaning of the iconography at all obvious: what is just childish play, what by contrast evokes ritual, and in

---

[43] Ham, op. cit., supposes the population losses of these years to have caused the ritual to receive unique emphasis. She detects two main types of scene on the miniature *Choes*: banquet (= the *Choes* banquet); procession (= the procession to the Limnaion).

Fig. 18. Chous showing a naked girl wearing amulets, with a chous: *c.*420 BC. One of a pair with Fig. 17.

what ways? The most serious issue is raised by the rarity of little girls on these scenes.[44] Some suppose that a link between the rite of passage and the central themes of the festival was established by giving the little children a sup of

[44] Cf. Hamilton, *Choes*, 145, n. 68 ('virtual absence'). G. L. Ham, op. cit., supposes the ritual to have been for boys only.

much-diluted wine, as a harbinger of adulthood.[45] But drinking in the Greek world was predominantly for men. Philostratus' reference to the crowning of 'children' need not include girls. On the other hand, if girls were excluded from the ritual, it is odd that they should appear on *choes* at all. What is clear is that boys were viewed as the primary beneficiaries.

There remain elements that do not certainly belong to the *Anthesteria*. Since the discovery of a lovely fragment of Callimachus, a ceremony known as Swinging (*Aiora*) or Wandering Woman (*Aletis*, from a song that accompanied the swinging) has generally been assigned to its third day. 'Swinging' to the accompaniment of songs is also attested in Colophon,[46] and sounds like an old Ionian festival custom. In Attica the wandering woman was said to be (whether from early times we do not know; evidence begins only in the third century) a variously identified 'Erigone'. Erigone might be the daughter of Icarius, who introduced wine to Attica but was murdered by the ungrateful peasants, supposing he had poisoned them; or she might be the daughter of Aegisthus, furious over the acquittal of Orestes by the Areopagus; and still further possibilities were canvassed.[47] However it was, she had hung herself from a tree in grief, and the Athenian women (probably just *parthenoi*) were required to swing on a plank of wood hung from a tree once a year in expiation.[48] The fragment of Callimachus tells how an Athenian in Egypt remembered the customs of his home. 'He never forgot either the dawn of jar-opening nor when the Orestean Choes bring a "white day" for slaves. Celebrating too the annual rite for the child of Icarius, your day, Erigone so bemourned by Attic women, he once invited his friends to dinner ....' 'The dawn of jar-opening' and 'Orestean Choes' are the first two days of *Anthesteria*, but Callimachus could have mentioned the first two without mentioning the third; even the syntax, which links *Pithoigia* and *Choes*, detaches the third

---

[45] So e.g. Burkert, *Homo Necans*, 221 (the special association between *Choes* and children's burials there mentioned has since been refuted: Hamilton, *Choes*, 70–1); Simon, *Festivals*, 94.

[46] If, that is, the relevant fragment from Aristotle's *Constitution of the Colophonians* refers to a local custom (fr. 515 Rose ap. Ath. 618e–f). On the Attic rite cf. p. 184.

[47] *Etym. Magn.* 62.5–12 s.v. ἀλῆτις offers five; cf. Burkert, *Homo Necans*, 241–3; Kearns, *Heroes of Attica*, 167. The identification with Icarius' daughter was made famous and possibly created (but see Nilsson, *Op. Sel.* I, 425) by Eratosthenes in his poem *Erigone* (see now A. Rosokoki, *Die Erigone des Eratosthenes*, Heidelberg 1995).

[48] Hygin. *Astron.* 2.4.5: 'quod ea se suspenderat, instituerunt uti tabula interposita pendentes funibus se iactarent ... itaque et privatim et publice faciunt, et id Aletidas appellant.' Latin sources which speak of hanging masks in trees (e.g. Lact. Plac. on Stat. *Theb.* 4. 691 and 11.644) are generally supposed to be conflating *Aiora* with the Roman *oscilla*: see M. P. Nilsson, *Eranos* 15 (1915), 187–200 (*Op. Sel.* i, 152–65), at 189; Nilsson also argues against the association with the grape-harvest (*vindemia*) (the only dating a source offers) given by Hygin. *Fab.* 130: Erigone diem festum oscillationis instituerunt ... et ut per vindemiam de frugibus Icario et Erigonae primum delibarent (Icarius shares Erigone's honours, wrongly, also in Σ min. Hom. *Il.* 22.29 and Ael. *NA* 7.28, which even adds her dog). Further details of the ritual are lacking except for *Etym. Magn.*42.3 αἰώρα· ἑορτὴ Ἀθήνησιν ἦν καλοῦσιν εὔδειπνον (Hesych. ε 6751 is corrected to give a similar sense). This might suggest funerary offerings (cf. Aesch. *Cho.* 484), rather than the banquet of the living of Callim. fr. 178. 3–5.

festival a little.[49] Some but not decisive support for linking *Aiora* with *Anthesteria* can be found in the myths (which associated 'Erigone' either with a Dionysiac hero or with Orestes, source of the strange customs of Beakers) and in swinging scenes on *choes*. But a positive counter-argument is available if it is true, as once source claims, that *Aletis* was the actual name of a festival day; the day named *Aletis* cannot also be the day named *Chytroi*.[50] Whatever the answer, our picture of the *Anthesteria* is not very greatly affected, since the days are past when we could assign a 'meaning' to the ritual of swinging itself.[51] If it was on *Chytroi* that the swinging took place, the complexity and diversity of these ancient festivals is underlined; and women or at least *parthenoi* acquire a function in an otherwise very masculine festival. But *Aiora* may have been an independent minor festival, date unknown.

The ship-cart of Dionysus is more important. Some four black figure skyphoi show Dionysus riding, with flute-playing satyrs, in a ship which is also a cart with old-fashioned wheels; on a skyphos in Bologna the cart is accompanied by mortals in procession, leading a sacrificial cow or bull.[52] The usual, and not unreasonable, assumption is that an Athenian ritual is reflected, even though similar representations appear earlier outside Attica, and in Attica do not outlive the sixth century. This ship on land, unlike that of the *Panathenaea*, seems to symbolize the idea of the god's arrival from the sea; that idea in turn is a special application of the idea of Dionysus as a god of advents and epiphanies, never more than a temporary visitant to a city. The fifth-century comic poet Hermippus, in parodic mode, invites the Muses to list 'all the blessings Dionysus has brought in his black ship, since he has been a shipmaster over the wine dark sea'.[53] This advent could, therefore, be beneficent. But when did it occur? The argument for assigning it to the *Anthesteria* is partly by elimination – at the *City Dionysia*, the obvious alternative, Dionysos was carried in as a statue, not from the sea – partly by analogy with a similar ritual celebrated in Smyrna, in the second century AD, at a Dionysiac festival held in the month Anthesterion.[54] That analogy (rather perilous, given that

---

[49] Callim. fr. 178.1–5. Note the asyndeton in line 3 and tense change in line 5.

[50] So R. Pfeiffer, *Kallimachosstudien* (Munich 1922), 102–4, stressing Hesych a 2953 s.v. Ἀλῆτις· ἑορτὴ Ἀθήνῃσιν, ἡ νῦν Αἰώρα λεγομένη, καὶ ἡμέρας ὄνομα, ὡς Πλάτων ὁ κωμικός (fr. 233); cf. Hesych. a 2217 s.v. Αἰώρα· ἑορτὴ Ἀθήνῃσιν. Pfeiffer later (commentary on fr. 178. 1–5) countenanced the other view, which is widely accepted (as e.g. by Burkert, *Homo Necans*, 241–3; Burkert stresses visual evidence, but Hamilton, *Choes*, 48, n. 130, notes that only two of the six swinging scenes he adduces occur on *choes*).

[51] For a late attempt see J. Hani, *REG* 91 (1978), 107–22.

[52] See Auffarth, *Drohende Untergang*, 214, n. 4, who adds a fragment from Tübingen (and some non Attic representations) to the instances regularly adduced; his whole discussion, 213–20, is rewarding. Bologna skyphos: here fig. 19.

[53] Hermippus fr. 63. Advents: see Burkert, *Homo Necans*, 201, who cites Otto; M. Massenzio, *Cultura e crisi permanente: la 'xenia' dionisiaca* (Rome 1970); M. Detienne, *Dionysos à ciel ouvert* (Paris 1986: Engl. tr. by A. Goldhammer as *Dionysos at Large*, Cambridge, Mass. 1989), chs. 1–2.

[54] On all this contrast Burkert, *Homo Necans* 201 (Dionysia); Auffarth, *Drohende Untergang*, 213, n.3 (*Anthesteria*), both with earlier references. Smyrnaean Anthesterion doubtless corresponded to Attic Anthesterion: Trümpy, *Monatsnamen*, 102.

Fig. 19. Procession escorting Dionysus in a ship chariot, by the Theseus painter (*c.*500 BC.)

striking ritual practices of the second century AD are not usually best explained as survivals from the ancient Ionian heritage) does at the least prove that a god could arrive by ship outside the sailing season.[55] But even the winter festival *Lenaea*, for which unlike the *Anthesteria* both a procession and abundant meat sacrifices are attested,[56] might by that argument become a candidate. The problem remains unresolved.

Then there is the marriage of the god. This is, it seems, the only attested ritual enactment of a wedding between a Greek god and a mortal;[57] and it is known, a brief lexicographic notice aside, from just two texts (so unreliable is our access to what we would most like to know). The Aristotelian *Constitution of the Athenians* says briefly (3.5) 'the king used to occupy what is now the Boukoleion, near the Prytaneum. There is proof of this; even now it is here that the meeting and marriage of the wife of the king (i.e. the *archon basileus*) with Dionysus takes place.' The phrase here translated 'meeting and marriage' was long translated, sometimes with shock, sometimes with gusto, sometimes with mere puzzlement, as 'sexual intercourse and marriage'; but

---

[55] Nilsson's early claim (*ARW* 11, 1908, 401 = *Op. Sel.* I, 23) that the ship carriage ritual marked the opening of the sailing season was chronologically difficult, as he later realized (*Arch. Jahrb.* 31, 1916, 334 = *Op. Sel.* I, 205); his solution, that ritual likes to anticipate actuality, is not wholly convincing.

[56] Meat sacrifice at the *Anthesteria*, but on no large scale, is attested by *SEG* XXXIII 147.33–4. The bovine on the Bologna skyphos does not fit well our image of the *Anthesteria*.

[57] Cf. Wilamowitz, *Glaube*, II, 75–6.

it is certain that a ceremonial 'meeting' is what is spoken of.[58] There was therefore no joint marriage procession from the Limnaion to the Boukoleion (since that is where the couple first met); nor do we know for certain that sexual union was simulated. The second source is Apollodorus in his attack on Neaera:[59]

This woman performed the secret rites on behalf of the city, and saw what as a non-citizen she should not have seen, and, despite being the kind of woman she is, entered the place that none of all the many Athenians may enter except the wife of the *basileus*, and administered the oath to the Reverend Women (*Gerarai*) who help with the rite, and she was given as wife to Dionysus, and on behalf of the city performed the many sacred secret rites to the gods.

Apollodorus goes on to explain that a specific law defined what was required of the wife of the *basileus* in terms of purity of origin, and that this law was displayed beside the altar in the temple of Dionysus in the Marshes, where too, it seems, the *basileus*' wife 'administered the oath' to the Reverend Women. These details provide the only specific grounds (disputed iconographic evidence aside) for associating the marriage of Dionysus with the *Anthesteria*: the *basileus*' wife and the Reverend Women had as their headquarters the temple in the marshes, a temple only opened for the *Anthesteria*, and should therefore have had a role to play at the festival; and if the oath sworn by the Reverend Women was administered in that temple, this ceremony, which the orator implies led up to the marriage, must have occurred at the *Anthesteria*.

The chain of argument appears, just, to hold firm.[60] But it is left to our imagination to fill in many details. We can only guess how the god was represented.[61] Presumably the nuptials of gods, like those of men, occur in the

[58] See A. Wilhelm, 'ΣΓΜΜΕΙΞΙΣ', AnzWien (1937), 15–30 = *Akademieschriften zur griechischen Inschriftenkunde* II (Leipzig 1974), 582–600, who gives an intriguing survey of reactions to what he proves to be the false translation. It fitted well with the prevailing 'fertility cult' paradigm: Frickenhaus and Deubner, *Attische Feste*, 102, even proposed—but I draw a veil over the gross suggestion. The implications of Wilhelm's study have only been semi-assimilated in subsequent literature.

[59] Apollod. *Neaer.* 73.

[60] The link of Dionysus' marriage ('sacred marriage' has no authority in this context) with the *Anthesteria* has long been generally accepted (for the older scholars see Deubner, *Attische Feste*, 101). Hamilton, *Choes*, 55–6, makes a good case for scepticism, citing S. M. Peirce, 'Representations of Animal Sacrifice in Attic Vase-Painting 580–380 B.C.' (diss. Bryn Mawr 1984) (*non vidi*), 149: 'If the *basilinna* and the *gerarai* can celebrate rites other than on the twelfth of Anthesterion or in the Limnaion [as they can], then there is no reason to assume that the rites they celebrated [i.e. the marriage to Dionysus] *must* have been in the Limnaion on the twelfth of Anthesterion.' My emphasis on the oath taking place during the *Anthesteria* is an attempt to circumvent that point; it depends on the assumption that the same altar is referred to in chs. 76 and 78 of Apollod. *Neaer.*

[61] See Auffarth, *Drohende Untergang*, 222.

evening;[62] but the evening of which day?[63] A procession which escorted the god to his bride[64] would have made the extraordinary event vivid to many more Athenians. We might associate with it the 'jests from the wagons', and the ship-cart ... Processional scenes on actual *choes* used to be adduced in support (one even shows Dionysus with a personified 'Pompe', identified by inscription);[65] but that support broke when Andreas Rumpf, in a golden article of six pages important also for the *Thesmophoria*, pressed home the implications of the truth that between *choes* and *Choes* there existed no necessary iconographic connection. Anything can appear on a *chous*, even, for instance, the races between 'dismounters' held at the *Panathenaea*.[66] Many *choes* do relate in a reflexive way to the festival, no doubt, but the scholar wishing to use them to extend our knowledge of it is trapped in a double bind: reference to the festival can only be secure if what is shown is something we already know. Such references as there are are likely to be impressionistic, not documentary.[67] The interesting suggestion has been made that in certain scenes depicting the union of Dionysus and Ariadne we should detect something like 'Ariadne as the wife of the *archon basileus*' or 'the wife of the *archon basileus* as Ariadne'; on this view, an interference takes place between the continuing ritual and its mythical model. But that is to assume that Ariadne (who never set foot in Attica) is indeed the relevant mythical model in this context. We seem rather to need a myth of quite different shape, an Attic equivalent to the myth of Dionysus' arrival (for an arrival is surely what is needed) in Aetolia; king Oeneus loaned his wife to the amorous god, and was granted a vine in return.[68]

---

[62] So Burkert, *Homo Necans*, 233, against Deubner, *Attische Feste*, 109. But the assumption is far from certain.

[63] A wedding on day two is *communis opinio*. But the only objection I can see to day one is the possibility that the Limnaion was not then open for the preliminaries (Apollod. *Neaer*. 76: see above). Burkert's argument, *Homo Necans*, 233, that an impure day had to be avoided may not be reliable in relation to so extraordinary a wedding; if sound, it commends the evening of day two only if we accept the postulate of a sacral evening-to-evening calendar (whereby the evening of day two belongs to day three).

[64] So Simon, *Festivals*, 92.

[65] Metropolitan Museum 25.190; G. van Hoorn, *Choes and Anthesteria* (Leiden 1951), no. 759; Metzger, *Représentations*, pl. 45.1 (*Recherches*, 60, no. 18).

[66] 'Attische Feste—Attische Vasen', *BJb* 161 (1961), 208–14; cf. Hamilton, *Choes*, 67–9. That even the treatment of Dionysiac themes on *Choes* usually finds parallels on other vessel types was shown by Metzger, *Recherches*, 55–76. The object shown on the *chous* New York MMA 24.97.34 (Deubner, *Attische Feste*, pl. 11.2–4; Parke, *Festivals*, pl. 44) which is often interpreted as 'children enacting the Basilinna's marriage procession' (so Parke) (it also appears on the krater Copenhagen NM 13.817), is convincingly explained as a kottabos stand by J. Reilly, *AA* 1994, 499–505.

[67] Metzger, *Recherches*, 68–9.

[68] Main source Hyginus, *Fab*. 129; see R. Seaford's note on Eur. *Cycl*. 9. Basilinna as Ariadne: E. Simon, *AntK* 6 (1963), 6–22, and *Festivals*, 97–9; followed e.g. by Burkert, *Homo Necans*, 233, Seaford, *Reciprocity and Ritual*, 267–9; doubted by Schöne, *Thiasos*, 66; M. H. Jameson in *Masks of Dionysus*, 55; and the ever-sceptical Carpenter, *Fifth-Century Dionysian Imagery*, 66–7. It is argued that the proto-king Theseus surrenders Ariadne to the god on Athena's orders (Pherecydes *FGH* 3 F 148) just as the *basileus* surrenders his wife. But the *Anthesteria* ritual seems to relate crucially

These sceptical conclusions can serve to introduce 'Mask of Dionysus' vases, as it will be better to call them in place of their hotly contested traditional name '*Lenaea* vases'; for the accepted criterion for membership in this class of vases is simply the presence of a mask of Dionysos suspended on a pillar, around which women perform ritual actions. According to an authoritative recent study, the seventy or so vases in question fall into three groups: one of twenty-eight black figure lekythoi of the period 490–480, one of twenty-five red figure stamnoi predominantly of the period 460–440, and a third of related vases not falling into either of these classes.

The unity of both of these series [the black figure lekythoi and red figure stamnoi] is defined by typology of vases, attribution to a restricted number of painters, and the formal structure of the image. In the first case, the composition is organised in relation to a central pillar bearing one or two masks seen in profile and shows women, exceptionally satyrs, walking or dancing, playing the aulos, and making gestures of greeting to the god. In the second case, the mask, still in the centre of the composition, is seen frontally, behind a table from which women make use of containers of wine.[69]

The women who draw wine from the vessels on the red figure stamnoi are often accompanied, around the back of the vase, by women in movement, who in the latest example are dancing excitedly. The two series differ in important respects, but it is argued that vases from the miscellaneous group bridge the divide: though wine is wholly absent from the canonical group of black figure lekythoi, for instance, it appears on several related scenes on vessels of other shapes which, like the lekythoi, present the pillar Dionysus not frontally but in profile.

With a few isolated exceptions, scholars long assumed that these vases constituted a more or less documentary record of an identifiable public ritual; but was it one performed at the *Lenaea*, or at the *Anthesteria*? Ecstatic dancing (emphasized on the black figure lekythoi) argued for the *Lenaea*; the manipulation of wine which dominates the red figure stamnoi made the case for the *Anthesteria*, though there was always an unacknowledged difficulty in supposing that a secret (and in fact unattested) wine-mixing ritual performed by the Reverend Women was exposed to the eyes of anyone who chose to purchase a stamnos.[70] A few scholars thought that informal, private

to Dionysus' presence in Athens; the fortunes of a non-Athenian woman on Naxos are not relevant. The Oineus parallel is inexact too, because Dionysus' union with Oineus' wife is unofficial, whereas Apollodorus unambiguously attests for Athens the vocabulary of marriage (ἐξεδόθη). But it seems closer.

[69] Englished from Frontisi-Ducroux, *Le Dieu-masque*, 67–8; this study reviews earlier writings very thoroughly. For a useful summary of the data see R. Osborne in *Tragedy and the Historian*, 204–5. A remarkable and enigmatic new *chous* ascribed to the Eretria painter (published by O Tzachou-Alexandri in J. H. Oakley and others, *Athenian Potters and Painters*, Oxford 1997, 473–90) offers a mask of Dionysus, attached to a stepped structure, and much else (a table bearing a *liknon*, flanked by a young man named Epimetheus, who drinks, and an older Prometheus). Our uncertainties increase …

[70] On the fact that all surviving 'Mask of Dionysus' stamnoi, like a majority of *stamnoi* of all types, were found in Etruria see Frontisi-Ducroux, *Le Dieu-masque*, 69–70.

(a)

Fig. 20. Dancing around the column Dionysus, on a black figure lekythos; c.490 BC.

festivities might be portrayed.[71] A much more cautious attitude prevails today. The author of the very fine study just quoted stresses that these images are products not of documentary realism but of the 'social imagination'. What the historian can derive from them is a set of representations created by the social imagination of Athens: a representation of Dionysus as the god of the gazing mask, the god of a gaze towards which the dancing women on the black figure lekythoi invariably turn and which confronts the user of the red figure stamnoi directly; a representation of ritual possibilities, in particular of ways of exploiting space around a fixed central point, the gazing god; a

[71] e.g. C. Robert, *GGA* (1913), 366–73, cited by Frontisi-Ducroux, *Le Dieu-masque*, 41.

(b)

Fig. 20. *Continued.*

representation of women's relation to wine and to Dionysus, one which
stresses the continuity between the grave and eminently respectable ladies
who manipulate wine on the *stamnoi* and the dancing Maenad.[72]

Yet these formulations would permit a relation, if a complicated one, to
actual rituals. The hugely varied images presented to us each year on Christmas cards are unquestionably products of a social imagination, but it is a
social imagination of Christmas, not of Easter. Gods are not easily separated in

[72] Frontisi-Ducroux, *Le dieu-masque, passim,* esp. 167–74. S. Peirce, *AntCl* 17 (1998), 59–95,
argues that the women are definitely portrayed as drinking (not merely distributing) wine, but
that iconographical schemata are deployed which mark them as still respectable.

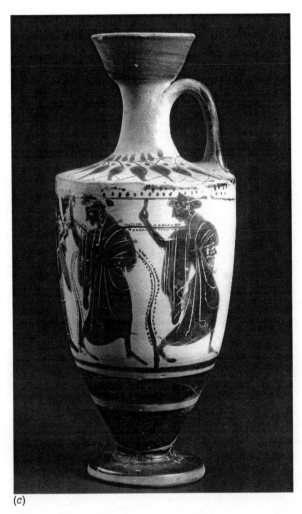

(c)

Fig. 20. *Continued.*

Greece from their instantiations in particular shrines and epithets and festivals; it is not clear that the starting point for the imaginings revealed on the 'Mask of Dionysus' vases is 'Dionysus' as opposed to 'Dionysus as worshipped in a particular ritual context'. The ground becomes slippier if the unity of the corpus of 'Mask of Dionysus' vases comes into question. The differences between the black figure lekythoi and the red figure stamnoi are just as notable as the similarities, it can be argued. And why separate off the 'Mask of Dionysus' vases among the many Dionysiac scenes painted by the artists

(a)

Fig. 21(*a*). Ritual around the column Dionysus, *c.*460 BC. Museum of Fine Arts, Boston. Gift of Edward Perry Warren. Photograph © 2004 Museum of Fine Arts, Boston.

who created the red figure stamnoi?[73] No one has yet deconstructed the mask of Dionysus hung on its pole: this, it is agreed, is so specific and singular an image that we can be sure of its real existence out there. But many are the ways in which it might have been deployed. Can we at least hold on to the association between the pillar Dionysus and women? Something very

[73] For both points see R. Osborne in *Tragedy and the Historian*, 206–7; for the latter T. H. Carpenter, *JHS* 103 (1993), 203–5 (but see now, contra, R. Hamilton, in E. Csapo and M. C. Miller, eds., *Poetry, Theory, Praxis. Essays in Honour of William J. Slater*, Oxford 2003, 43–68). Carpenter stresses that we are dealing with the work of a small number of painters only.

(b)

Fig. 21(b). Reverse of Fig. 21(a). © 2004 Museum of Fine Arts, Boston.

important remains if so, a form of domesticated Athenian maenadism.[74] Yet even this has been questioned. On the latest of the red figure stamnoi the women have turned into full-blown dancing maenads with inscribed maenadic names—Dione, Mainas, Choreia, Thaleia. Perhaps those figures on the earlier stamnoi who look so much like respectable Athenian ladies are in fact nymphs ...[75] Yet the distinctive and down-to-earth image of the mask on a

---

[74] So Osborne, op. cit. Note *IG* I³ 1030 *bis*, a stone mask of Dionysus dedicated by two women.
[75] Carpenter, *Dionysian Imagery*, 60, 80–2; for Carpenter we are dealing with 'unspecific Dionysian scenes composed of stock Dionysian elements' (81).

pole, combined with the gravity of the women on the earlier stamnoi, does not encourage us to view the scenes as just a medley from the mythological repertoire.

We can hold on, provisionally, to the idea of domestic Athenian maenad-ism. But we lack a context for it. And that lack is not a matter of a missing antiquarian detail of small interest. We would like to know whether these rituals were performed by thirty Athenian women, so to speak, or by thirty thousand. There is some attraction in supposing that these were widespread domestic rituals, something within the direct experience of the male drinkers who used the vases.[76] Such domestic rituals could have occurred at the *Anthesteria*, among other occasions. But we can go no further than this.

This inescapable uncertainty is particularly unfortunate for a reason which has seldom been noticed. While much has been said in what precedes of the *Anthesteria* pleasures of men, slaves and children, the only women mentioned have been the priestess of Dionysus, the wife of the *archon basileus* and her fourteen assistants, and (with a question mark) the girls swinging for Erigone. On that showing, the *Anthesteria* emerges, for a major three-day festival, as remarkably woman-unfriendly, even by Athenian standards. (The *Apatouria* was probably woman-unfriendly too, but that is less surprising given its fundamental concern with phratry-membership and thus with citizenship.) If associated with the *Anthesteria*, the 'Mask of Dionysus' vases might have given women a larger place, if not in the sun, at least in a secluded place.[77]

I turn to interpretation—or rather, from smaller problems of interpretation to larger ones. The festival is, at a first glance, made up of disparate elements; most obviously, days one and two honour Dionysus, day three (for the most part) honours Hermes Chthonios. The older interpreters tended to accept that it was, indeed, a composite. On the one side there was a festival of new wine, designed, as they put it in language borrowed from the anthropology of the day, to break the taboo on the new vintage; on the other, a form of 'All Souls'. These had, as a matter of historical chance, coalesced. Thence derived the mixed character of the festival, part joyful, part polluted. Occasionally a point of contact between the two aspects was sought, tentatively, in the dominion of the underworld gods over both death and growth.[78]

More recently,[79] it has come to be generally and surely rightly believed that the mix of fair and foul in the festival is intrinsic and uneliminable. According

---

[76] Frontisi-Ducroux, in Bravo, *Pannychis*, 123–34, is sympathetic to Bravo's 'mixed *panny-chides*' (n. 17 above) as one possible context.

[77] This would apply particularly if one imagined many separate groups of women active in this way (masks being easy to secure). But for Nilsson, the main proponent of the association with the *Anthesteria*, the women of the vases were simply the Reverend Women of Apollod. *Neaer.* 73 (p. 304 above). All we would get then would be public interest in their role.

[78] Nilsson, *Studia*, 130–1: 'Chytri *quodammodo* cum illis sacris Choum cohaerent ...'.

[79] Largely in consequence of the important treatment in Burkert, *Homo Necans*, 213–47. But Hamilton, *Choes*, 14–15, and N. Robertson, *HSCP* 95 (1993), 197–250, still seek to minimize gloomy elements.

to the sources, the 'polluted day' when the temples in general were closed and people chewed buckthorn for protection against ghosts was day two, the day of the drinking competition, not day three, the day of sacrifice to Hermes Chthonios. (The main point stands even though not every detail is quite certain.) About the drinking competition itself there is an irreducible abnormality which is not confined to the aitiological derivation from polluted Orestes—this silent, competitive drinking from separate cups at separate tables, in violation of all the norms of sharing and sociability governing the Greek symposium, in flagrant violation too of the norms of civilized drinking affirmed at the *Pithoigia* the previous day.[80] We can grant, on the good evidence of Aristophanes' *Acharnians*, that the competition was but one element within a doubtless hugely enjoyable banquet which will not have been conducted in silence. But it was an element, and formally it set the tone. Wakes do not cease to be commemorations of the dead however riotous they may prove.[81] One can provide the festival with a plot whereby, in strong contrast to the old model, day two is the time of maximum crisis, abnormality and pollution (but is the 'marriage' part of it, or part of a putting right?); normality returns on day three, the day when the survivors of the flood recovered their spirits.[82] But this return to normality is at best a gradual one, since the offerings on day three are still touched with impurity.

So the *Anthesteria* has become a festival of oppositions and of paradox. It is a festival at which some social norms are overturned—slaves dine with their masters, young men insult their betters from wagons—and even (so to speak) some cosmic norms: the dead roam the streets, a god visits the city (arriving from the sea?) to take a mortal bride. Wine is consumed with caution on day one, with abandon on day two. On day three (in aitiology) the flood waters withdraw, and the world is revealed anew. All this confusion is initiated by the opening of the jars of new wine.[83] The festival can be seen as an instance of a 'reversal ritual accompanying a critical passage in the agricultural or social year', an ideal type of which there exist very many further examples

[80] The quantity drunk at the drinking competition is usually supposed to be the measure of a *chous*, i.e. 3.28 litres (Hamilton, *Choes*, 84, n. 1). High-speed draining of such a quantity is surely Scythian drinking, even if Dikaiopolis' claim to have taken it unmixed (Ar. *Ach.* 1229) is a comic impossibility.

[81] On the other hand, this possibility of dissonance between formal occasion and actual experience is in all seeming a regular phenomenon which any theory of ritual needs to accommodate. There is nothing frightening about having the dead around the house at Christmas, says Nilsson from childhood experience (*Eranos* 15, 1915, 182 = *Op. Sel.* I, 147).

[82] So Burkert, *Homo Necans*, 213–47, who relates the ambivalent mood of the festival to his general theory of sacrifice, which is seen as a guilt-producing act which participants make good by symbolic means. He sees the *Choes* as a kind of eating of the god (embodied in wine), who is then re-assembled (as the 'pillar Dionysus' of the 'Mask of Dionysus' vases) and given a bride. Auffarth, *Drohende Untergang*, 241, goes too far in declaring sacrifice itself to have been suspended on day two: contrast n. 56.

[83] Jane Harrison's charming old theory (*Prolegomena*, 40–5) that the *Pithoigia* related to jars though which souls escaped from the underworld, as on a well-known amphora in Jena (Jena Univ. 338; *ARV*² 760.41; *LIMC* s.v. *Hermes*, no. 630), has a certain symbolic truth.

more or less (here lies the rub) resembling one another and the *Anthesteria*.[84] But there are theoretical difficulties in the comparativism that underlies the appeal to an ideal type. What exactly do we learn, other than that similar things are found elsewhere too?[85] We learn, it may be answered, about recurrent linkages: the association found in Athens, say, between a new wine festival and return of the dead is not a unique but a widely observable phenomenon. That is indeed worth learning; what is not clear is what comparison can contribute to explaining such linkages, unless it is to risk perilously general claims about how societies of certain types necessarily ritualize the year. And if the ideal type becomes categorized as a 'régénération totale du temps',[86] as a moment of return to the primeval, and we then claim that our festival too has these characteristics, we are in danger of substituting a synthetic ideal type for the *Anthesteria*.

A complementary approach to the festival's complexity might be through its god. According to an influential modern view,[87] Dionysus' essence lies in the power to complicate reality, to dissolve the culturally constructed world by breaking down the oppositions that define it. A master of illusions, he produces drunkenness and madness; he destroys the barriers between man and animal, male and female, young and old, free and slave, city and country, man and god. No ritual form other than a ritual of reversal would be appropriate to such a god. And it is precisely at the *Anthesteria* that the paradox inherent in his relation to the city finds its richest expression.[88] In myth he is the god who lures the women to the mountains in defiance of the established authorities of the masculine world; yet his cult is in fact as deeply embedded as any other in the religion of the city. At the *Anthesteria* he may have been represented, through the ship-cart, as a visitant from abroad. But to this stranger the 'king' yields up his wife as bride.

The marvel of this ritual, its authentic mystery, was long obscured by reductive classification as 'fertility magic'. At the centre of our vision of the

---

[84] See already H. Jeanmaire, *Dionysus* (Paris 1951), 48–56, and Meuli, *Ges. Schrift.*, 296–8; the approach has been developed by Versnel in several works, most recently *Transition and Reversal*, 115–21 (whence the quotation); Bremmer, *Soul*, 117–23; Auffarth, *Drohende Untergang*, 1–37 (who gives the theoretical and comparative context—Eliade, Lanternari, *et al.*) and *passim*.

[85] My concern is with the explanatory power of comparison. I do not doubt that comparison often has a valuable heuristic role, in suggesting questions to put to the sources; but the answer given by the sources is then crucial. Comparison can also suggest phenomena likely to have occurred even if not (for understandable reasons) attested in sources. But in the present case I would not import (e.g.) 'periods of sexual licence' to the *Anthesteria* from rituals of reversal known elsewhere.

[86] This phrase of Eliade is taken up by Meuli, *Ges. Schrift.*, 297, n. 2.

[87] The 'archaeologies' of modern views of Dionysus by Albert Henrichs (*HSCP* 88, 1984, 205–40; *Masks of Dionysus*, 13–43) are an indispensable orientation. On the recent fortunes of 'Otto's polar Dionysus', most appealing to postmoderns, see *Masks of Dionysus*, 29–36 (and on the similar language of the ancients *HSCP* 88, 1984, 235). The rhetoric of this approach can fly out of control, but for a particularly powerful application in relation to a specific area (sexuality) see Csapo's study (n. 105 below).

[88] See Seaford, *Reciprocity and Ritual*, 235–80, 'Dionysus and the polis'.

Anthesteria must be the very presence of Dionysus, as new wine, and as god.[89]
Whatever its further implications, the giving of the *archon basileus*' wife to
Dionysus is a supreme gesture of hospitality, the god's acceptance of her a
supreme token of presence. Yet an old problem will remain. Dionysus habit-
ually has no dealings with the dead, death and the Dionysiac being, rather,
opposite poles of a magnet. Even when, as a god of eschatological mysteries,
he becomes powerful to aid the individual to a better lot in the afterlife, he is in
no sense a lord of the nameless dead such as roamed at this festival.[90] And in
fact, if we believe our most reliable sources, Dionysus received no offerings at
the *Chytroi* (even if some rites were still performed in his honour). One cannot
understood the *Anthesteria* without its specific god, Dionysus, nor reduce it to
him.

I conclude with a summarizing redescription of the festival. The *Anthesteria*
makes a collective event out of what might just have been an event in the life
of the individual household.[91] And this appeal to 'everybody', 'the whole city'
(women perhaps excluded), this mixing up in one celebration of the whole
citizen body, appears particularly characteristic of Dionysiac festivals and of
the place of Dionysus within the city.[92] Whether this wine-broaching was an
important event in dietetic terms (would supplies of old wine have run low?) is
hard to tell. But in a wine-drinking society the change of wines is one of the
most potent 'natural symbols' (to reapply Mary Douglas's term) of transition
that is available. The Athenians dramatized it by making it occasion for
Dionysus' marriage, the most vividly realized advent of a god attested in all
Greek cult. The *Anthesteria* is indeed a time of strange advents, of Dionysus, of
the dead, of (in myth) the polluted Orestes. The rowdy god's presence licensed
young men to cheek their elders 'from the wagons'. Wine-drinking itself was
made an object of attention (as not at other Athenian festivals), by the prayer
for safe use of wine on day one, and by the deliberately hectic use made of it
on day two (two faces of Dionysus, but both revealed within ritual bounds).
With new wine came new Athenians, the children (boys?) now ceremonially
crowned. It is frustrating that we know so little of the context of this crowning. If it happened at one of the banquets of day two, the question becomes
one of who dined with whom, which we do not know; but, if we imagine a
restricted group of often related males at each banquet, the context would

[89] The marriage receives proper emphasis from Daraki, *Dionysos*, 73–116. But her analysis is
skewed by taking Heraclitus too literally and treating Dionysus as a 'maître-des-morts'.
[90] See Nilsson, *Geschichte*, 594–8; S. G. Cole in *Masks of Dionysus*, 276–95. Opposite poles:
Parker, *Miasma*, 64.
[91] So Burkert, *Homo Necans*, 217.
[92] So Seaford, *Reciprocity and Ritual*, 246, citing *inter alia* the Delphic oracle quoted in Dem.
21.52 which urges the Athenians ἄμμιγα πάντας to honour the god. I do not accept Seaford's
correlate, that Dionysus stood for the city in opposition to its subgroups such as the *oikos* (ibid.
344–62, and in *Masks of Dionysus*, 115–46); the *Anthesteria* suggests the opposite. For I. Venturi,
Dioniso e la democrazia ateniese (Rome 1997), looking from a broad, ancient near-eastern comparative perspective, the Attic Dionysus is anti-regal and anti-gentilician.

have been more intimate than the induction to the phratry at the *Apatouria*
that followed it quite soon. At a rather domestic gathering of this kind, slaves
might readily be allowed a place of temporary equality. To the upcoming
generation (the new wine?) corresponds in a way the old wine, the generations gone. But the symmetry is imperfect, because it was not at the *Anthesteria* that families paid cult to their own forefathers. The questions why the
dead roam at the time of the New Wine and why that time is so polluted
remain tantalizing ones. Comparativism tells us, in its rough and ready way,
that societies feel the need for periodic clean sweeps and fresh starts, that fresh
starts feel fresher if pollution precedes, and that the idea of a fresh start can
readily be attached to a natural symbol of change such as the new wine.
These are regrettably vague formulae, but must serve until better are found.
The new wine festival could accordingly recall not just the first bringing of
wine to Attica, but the resumption of ordered human life after Deucalion's
flood.[93]

OTHER DIONYSIAC FESTIVALS AND RITUALS

Dionysus springs the bounds of a festival-by-festival approach. This is partly
because, as we have seen, the location at particular festivals of several
important rituals is insecure. But there are also characteristic forms of Dionysiac behaviour which occur at more than one festival or even outside the
festival context. It is not without reason that scholarship sometimes speaks of
Dionysiac, but not, say, of 'Athenaic', ritual. It is of aspects of such Dionysiac
ritual, and behaviour, that this section will treat. But first a skeleton outline
must be given of the other Dionysiac festivals, primarily the three dramatic
festivals *Lenaea, Rural Dionysia* and *City Dionysia*.[94]

In Athens as in Delphi, Dionysus is a god of the winter, and *Rural Dionysia,
Lenaea, Anthesteria* and *City Dionysia* succeed one another at intervals of
roughly a month over the period from about December to March. The part-
Dionysiac festival *Oschophoria* falls at an uncertain date in the autumn.

Seeking comic embodiments of the delights of peace, Aristophanes in *Acharnians* revealingly chooses not just one but two festivals of Dionysus. We have
already met his comic version of Beakers; and the phallic procession held earlier
in the play in honour of the eponymous god Phales (241–79) is almost our only
important source for the ritual of the *Rural Dionysia* (at which in many demes

---

[93] The relation between flood myths and festivals of new beginnings was noted by Meuli, *Ges.
Schrift.*, 299. Scholars had often, by contrast, seen the *Chytroi* myth as a re-application of a motif
first trivially suggested by the role of water in the *Hydrophoria* ritual (n. 35). Meuli's suggestion is
a nice instance of the heuristic value of comparison.

[94] For full treatment see Pickard-Cambridge, *Dramatic Festivals*[2], *passim*, and Csapo/Slater,
Ancient Drama, 103–38.

plays were also performed).[95] *Lenaea* too is rather obscure. It included a procession and many sacrifices; it was doubtless during the procession that insults were hurled 'from the wagons' as at the *Anthesteria*: one of the two Greek verbs for 'to insult in a ritual context' was in fact πομπεύω, literally 'I process'. (But πομπή also yields the sense '(empty) display'; both 'pomp' and that which punctures it come from the same root.) Nothing more to our purpose is known for certain about the *Lenaea*, except the unexpected fact that the hierophant at some point invoked Dionysus in his Eleusinian persona as Iacchus. But dancing by women had a place if the name derives, as is now generally supposed, from Λῆναι, 'maenads', rather than from those wine-presses, ληνοί, which should not have been in use at the time of the festival in mid-winter.[96]

As for the *City Dionysia*, the most spectacular ritual was a procession which culminated in the sacrifice of at least a hundred animals in the sanctuary of Dionysus. This was, after the *Panathenaea*, the greatest procession of the year, and, though the details are much less well known, here too we find graded participation: citizen 'wine-skin bearers' and (probably) 'loaf-bearers' (*obeliaphoroi*) contrast with metic 'tray-bearers' in their purple robes; the *choregoi* who finance the performances are repaid for their expense by a position of gold-clad dignity (shamelessly insulted on a famous occasion by Midias, according to the victim Demosthenes), and gold glints too from the golden sacrificial basket carried by a maiden 'basket-bearer'. All analogy suggests that the phallus which the Athenain colonists at Brea were required to send home 'for the *Dionysia*' was carried in this procession; such a requirement cannot have been imposed on the Brean settlers alone, and it will follow that numerous phalluses accompanied (perhaps) one chief one.[97] The procession apparently paused during its route through the agora for choruses to sing in honour of the Twelve Gods and of others.[98]

---

[95] A procession is also attested (along with sacrifice and competition) for the demes Acharnai, Eleusis and Piraeus: *SEG* XLIII 26 (b) 4–6; *IG* II² 949.30–4; Appendix 2 s.v. *Dionysia, τὰ ἐν Πειραιεῖ*. See further Appendix 2, s. v. *Dionysia, τὰ κατ᾿ ἀγρούς*.

[96] Procession: Arist. *Ath. Pol.* 57.1; sacrifice: *IG* II² 1496. 74, 105, 146; 'from the wagons' : see n. 37 above; hierophant: *Σ* vet. Ar. *Ran.* 479c. A sacrifice at the *Lenaea* by the Eleusinian *epistatai* is mentioned in *IG* II² 1672.182. Schöne, *Thiasos*, attributes to the *Lenaea inter alia* a procession imitating the return of Hephaestus to Olympus (45–6). But the argument that only a ritual basis can explain the scene's long-lasting appeal to painters is not compelling: it would make an odd procession in actual cult. On the 'Lenaea' vases see p. 306.

[97] See on all this Pickard-Cambridge, *Dramatic Festivals*², 61–2. Phalloi: *IG* I³ 46.15–17 (Brea); cf. *SEG* XXXI 67 (Paros, in the 370s), and Smarczyk, *Religionspolitik*, 158–61. Analogy: the *Rural Dionysia*, the Delian *Dionysia* (Pickard-Cambridge, 62, n.4), and cf. Plut. *De cupid. divit.* 8, 527d (Pickard-Cambridge, 62, n.3). What happened to the phalluses after use is not known: it does not seem to me to follow from the reference to burning something 'on 16 figwood *phaletes*' in *Com. Adesp.* fr. 154 that they were burnt, since this is a joke with a *para prosdokian* element.

[98] Xen. *Hipparch.* 3.2: Xenophon proposes that during processions the cavalry should ride round the shrines in the agora paying their respects, and adds an analogy from existing practice: ἐν τοῖς Διονυσίοις δὲ οἱ χοροὶ προσεπιχαρίζονται ἄλλοις τε θεοῖς καὶ τοῖς δώδεκα χορεύοντες. The passage puzzles me. The context in Xenophon shows that the reference cannot be to choral

Quite distinct from the procession (it is universally now agreed), which brought sacrificial victims to the god, was an earlier 'bringing in of the god' in statue form which, so to speak, renewed the first mythical coming of the god to the city. (The 'bringing in' was felt to be so integral that it was replicated in the Piraeus *Dionysia*, which, though formally just one instance among many of the *Rural Dionysia*, grew into an expensive major festival, almost a second *City Dionysia*.[99]) The god's advent was celebrated, it has been strongly argued, with rituals performed in the agora, an al fresco drinking party (the 'reception' or *xenismos* in the strict sense) in the north-west corner and, at an *eschara* (hearth altar) by the altar of the Twelve Gods, a goat-sacrifice accompanied by hymns of which a surviving dithyrambic fragment of Pindar may be a specimen.[100] The eventual destination of the god's statue was the theatre. Such a reception could have led on to the *komos* or revel-procession which is also attested.[101] Or the *komos* may be distinct, and unlocatable. On whatever day it occurred, the *komos* was probably a drunken evening event, and it is one of the rare contexts in which wearing of masks by some participants is explicitly attested.[102] We should note finally the civic rituals—display of tribute, parade of orphans, proclamation of honours—that introduced the first morning of actual performances.[103]

After this foundation-laying, I revert to Dionysiac rituals. 'The traditional festival of the *Dionysia*', writes Plutarch nostalgically, 'was conducted in a homely and cheerful way (δημοτικῶς καὶ ἱλαρῶς): an amphora of wine, a vine tendril, then someone dragging a goat, someone else following with a basket of figs, and presiding over it all [or 'finally'] the phallus (ἐπὶ πᾶσι δ' ὁ φαλλός)'.[104] The phallus is basic. What was carried was not in fact just a phallus but a phallus on a long wooden pole, which could be decorated to suggest the shaft of a very long, thin penis; the phallus itself, in this and other iconographic contexts, is normally given an eye, like an animate thing. What

performances in the theatre itself (though it could perhaps be to the *eisagoge* ritual: Pickard-Cambridge, *Dramatic Festivals*[2], 62). But are we to suppose that the choruses that were destined to perform in the theatre marched in the processions as choruses, and had also prepared hymns to render at sites en route? Or who are these 'choruses'? Pindar fr. 75 could be an instance of such a hymn, for reasons given by Sourvinou-Inwood, *Tragedy and Religion*, 96–8 (though she links it rather with the *eisagoge*).

[99] See Pickard-Cambridge, *Dramatic Festivals*[2]. 44, n. 2 ('bringing in'), 46–7.

[100] See Sourvinou-Inwood, *Tragedy and Religion*, 67–100, for this reconstruction from converging if never quite explicit indications (and for the many topographical issues relating to the *eisagoge*, which I have left vague). Pindar: fr. 75.

[101] Led on: so Sourvinou-Inwood, *Tragedy and Religion*, 89. Attested: in the law of Euegoros quoted in Dem. 21.10. The old view, revived by P. Ghiron-Bistagne, *Recherches sur les acteurs dans la Grèce antique* (Paris 1976), 226–7, that κῶμος here = χοροὶ ἀνδρῶν remains implausible (Pickard-Cambridge, *Dramatic Festivals*[2], 63, 103). Lamer's argument, in *RE* s.v. *Komos*, 1289, that a *komos* always entails movement still has force (*aliter* Ghiron-Bistagne, 231–8).

[102] See Dem. 19.287, as correctly interpreted by Sourvinou-Inwood, *Tragedy and Religion*, 70, with reference to Aeschin. 2.151. Drunkenness: Pl. *Leg.* 637a–b.

[103] Pickard-Cambridge, *Dramatic Festivals*[2], 59.

[104] Plut. *De cupid. divit.* 8, 527d.

a typical phallic procession was like it may be idle to enquire, since sportive variation was probably the norm. That in Aristophanes is very simple (but there are good plot reasons for this), a single phallus to be 'held upright' by a single carrier. An extraordinary black figure vase of the mid-sixth century in Florence shows on its two sides something very different, six naked (and sometime ithyphallic) men straining under a giant phallus, on which is perched (or fastened) a huge demonic figure, who bears in turn, on one side of the vase, a diminutive rider.[105] An extract from a Hellenistic antiquarian, Semos of Delos, describes the singular costumes and songs of two teams or troupes (*ithyphalloi* and *phallophoroi*) associated with phallic processions, but does not make plain where in the Greek world the rather precise perform-ances that he evidently has in view took place. Similar teams or troupes (the word is appropriate in order to stress that more was required than just to carry the pole) surely performed in Attica too, or Aristotle could not have derived comedy from 'the leaders of phallic rites'. But what kind of Athenians assumed the ambiguous honour (if Athenians indeed they were) we do not know.

How was a festival affected by being conducted under the presidency of a phallus? Modern westerners might react to such a symbol with a blend of embarrassment and amusement; the breach of a central convention of mod-esty might seem to demand, or at least to license, uncontrolled behaviour of many kinds. Inhabitants of a city full of herms cannot have been so embar-rassed by exposed genitalia, but comic phalli could still raise a laugh among children, and a phallic procession was surely not conducted in an atmosphere of grim solemnity. Pindar's Apollo laughs at the ithyphallic antics of the mules of the Hyperborean land.[106] The phallus probably struck an informal, uninhibited note, therefore. But it was also, above all, a symbol and a celebration, or at least an acknowledgement, of male lust.[107] The proof lies not so much in aitiological myths that explain the rite through incidents of frustrated lust, nor yet in the thoroughly lustful song with which Dikaiopolis in Aristophanes accompanies his phallic procession, as in the manifest con-tinuity between the rituals and the perpetual aching desires of Dionysus'

---

[105] On all this see the brilliant study by Csapo, 'Riding the Phallus', with pictures and detailed study of the cup Florence 3897 (here Fig. 22; Deubner, *Attische Feste*, pl. 22 (a drawing); Csapo/Slater, *Ancient Drama*, pl. 19). For a simpler phallus pole on a r.f. cup by the Sabouroff painter (Malibu 86.AE.296) see ibid. pl. 1c. Aristophanes: *Ach.* 259–60. Semos of Delos: *FGrH* 396 F 24 ap. Ath. 622a (Csapo/Slater, *Ancient Drama*, 98). For *ithyphalloi* in Attica see Demochares, *FGrH* 75 F 2, and Hyperides fr. 50 Jensen ap. Harpocr. ι 10.

[106] Pind. *Pyth.* 10.36, cited by F. Lissarrague, 'The Sexual Life of Satyrs', in *Before Sexuality*, 53–81 (a splendid account), at p. 55; G. Hedreen, *JHS* 124 (2004), 51–8. I have not been able to see A. di Nola, 'Riso e oscenità', in his *Antropologia religiosa* (Florence 1974), to which Lissarrague refers. Children: Ar. *Nub.* 539.

[107] See the remarks of A. Henrichs in *Papers on the Amasis Painter and his World* (Malibu, Calif. 1987), 94–9, who builds on Burkert, *Greek Religion*, 166. Both recognize that phalluses mean different things in different contexts (though the old explanatory tools of 'aversion' and 'fertility' seldom achieve much).

(a)

(b)

Fig. 22. Phallos poles on the two sides of an Attic black figure cup, *c.*560 BC.

companions the satyrs, so comically depicted on such a huge number of vases. The satyrs are not merely negative examples of a lust that is undiscriminating and outrageously uncontrolled; they also express, in comically transferred form, a recognition and even a complaisant acceptance of the power of desire within those who are not satyrs but men.[108] Such desire is stimulated by Dionysus in his capacity as god of wine, as the ancients often pointed out. But to be maddened by desire is also in itself a Dionysiac experience, in the sense of being a form of 'madness'. Aphrodite is patroness of love or desire when seen as a relation between two persons. Viewed merely in its effects on a desiring male subject, desire derives rather from Dionysus.[109] No ancient source, when listing the domains of Dionysus' competence, mentions 'sexuality'. Yet it is hard to dispute that issues of sex or at least gender were close to the heart of his appeal.

We must turn now to the 'Anacreontic vases', a series of vases dating from *c*.530–*c*.460 which show males ('Booners') revelling in what appears to be women's attire;[110] they take their most familiar name from a belief, no longer accepted, that they depict a fashion specifically associated with the luxurious poet Anacreon and his circle. That the figures depicted are unusually dressed men, not women in false beards, is now generally agreed; their beards, it is true, are unnaturally large, but that is an artifice of the painters to underline the paradoxical contrast between the nature of their subjects, and their garb. Bearded though they are, they wear or sport some or all of the following items: turban, long tunic, soft boots (the *kothornos*), earrings, lyre (the *barbitos*), parasol. Some items in this list had once been men's garb, or had 'oriental' associations; but taken as a whole the booners' outfit unquestionably looked effeminate to the vase-painters' eyes. The proof, or one of them, lies in two white ground lekythoi now in Paris which were evidently designed

---

[108] Myths: those relating to Ikarios and Prosymnos (Csapo, 'Riding the Phallus', 266–7, 275–6). Dikaiopolis' song: Ar. *Ach.* 261–79. Satyrs and human sexuality: cf. E. Hall in M. Wyke (ed.), *Parchments of Gender* (Oxford 1998), 13–37; Moraw, *Mänade*, 247 (identification with satyrs); Isler-Kerenyi, *Dionysos*, 105 and 227 ('essere satiri voleva dunque dire essere felici'). Negative examples: Lissarrague in *Before Sexuality*, 66. The satyrs come to express others things too not directly related to Dionysus: there is something of the child in them, and they are also an oblique way of imagining slaves (for links between their sexuality and that of slaves see Lissarrague, op. cit., 56–7; the satyrs of literature too have many servile traits, and are often depicted in temporary servitude (R. Seaford, *Euripides* Cyclops, Oxford 1984, 33–6). On their childishness see Lissarrague in *Masks of Dionysus*, 219–20).

[109] The figure of Eros does not appear with Satyrs on vases before the mid-5th c.: Lissarrague in *Before Sexuality*, 66.

[110] See especially D. C. Kurtz and J. Boardman, 'Booners', *Greek Vases in the J. Paul Getty Museum* 3 (1986), 35–70; F. Frontisi-Ducroux and F. Lissarrague, 'From ambiguity to ambivalence: a Dionysiac excursion through the "Anakreontic" vases', in *Before Sexuality*, 221–56; M. C. Miller, 'Re-examining Transvestism in Archaic and Classical Athens: the Zewadski Stamnos', *AJA* 103 (1999), 223–58 (a splendid study with much essential comparative literature on cross-dressing). On occasional forms of cross-dressing by satyrs and maenads see C. Caruso, 'Travestissements dionysiaques', in C. Bérard et al., *Images et société en Grèce ancienne* (Lausanne 1987), 103–9; Miller, op. cit., 245–6.

Fig. 23. 'Booners', with flute-girl, *c*.490–470 BC.

as a pair.[111] They depict two identically dressed figures in identical postures; but one is a booner, one a woman. With their unshaven beards, the booners are not seeking to disguise their gender; they are merely 'putting on women's clothes', a phrase and a practice quite often found in association with formal and informal Dionysiac rites up and down the Greek world. Just this is done by Pentheus in Euripides' *Bacchae*; and in that play as in Aeschylus' *Edonoi* Dionysus himself is accused of effeminacy (in *Bacchae* the effeminacy is chiefly manifested in hairstyle, but in Aeschylus also in dress). In comedy, the god's unmanliness both of dress and character has become a trope.[112]

The context of the booners' activities is for us to guess. They are regularly associated with revellers, drinking, and music, and often seem to be dancing.[113] The best view is probably that they are upper-class men amusing themselves at symposia and the *komoi* that could follow on from them, though it is certainly not excluded that such behaviour could also find a home in slightly more formal Dionysiac contexts. Why did they do it? Dionysus' own effeminate locks are, according to Euripides' Pentheus, a snare for women, and we know the image of the marriage of Dionysus and Ariadne to have been erotically charged in a way that almost no other divine amour

---

[111] See Frontisi-Ducroux/Lissarrague in *Before Sexuality*, fig. 7.18–19 (Musée du Petit Palais, Paris, 335 and 336), also figs. 7.11, 7.14–15, and their comments pp. 218–19; Miller, op. cit., 240. This point is not addressed in the critique of Miller in R. T. Neer, *Style and Politics in Athenian Vase-Painting* (Cambridge 2002), 222, n. 84. Neer may be right that Miller restricts the canon too much by excluding figures (such as his fig. 12) who have some accoutrements, but not all, of 'full dress' booners: these partial booners are oriental but not effeminate.

[112] Transvestite rites: Csapo, 'Riding the Phallus', 262–3 [+]. Pentheus: Eur. *Bacch.* 836, 852. On the dramatic representation of Dionysus (Aesch. fr. 59, 61; Eur. *Bacch.* 353, θηλύμορφος, and 453–9, long hair and pale skin; Ar. *Ran.* 46, cf. Cratinus fr. 40) see Csapo, 261–2.

[113] Drinking and revellers: see Frontisi-Ducroux/Lissarrague, op. cit; Miller, op. cit., 236–8 (ibid. 245–6 on a lekythos in Princeton which might indicate a procession). Music and dancing: S. D. Price, 'Anacreontic Vases Reconsidered', *GRBS* 31 (1990), 133–75, at 143, n. 28. M.-H. Delavaud-Raux, *RA* (1995), 227–63, goes so far as to see them as parodying the female Dionysiac dances depicted on the '*Lenaea*' vases (p. 306 above); Price too (op. cit.) sees them as performers. Symposia and *komoi*: see the texts adduced by Csapo, 'Riding the Phallus', 262.

was.[114] But the booners of the vases are not obviously interested either in women or in men; the scenes lack erotic overtones altogether, as if gender confusion has put their protagonists beyond sexuality.[115] Initiatory cross-dressing, even if still associated with Dionysus, is something quite different. The booners are upper-class Athenians, it has been suggested, who felt under threat from the emerging democracy and subconsciously chose this indirect way to assert their right to be different, to act as they pleased. At the symposia shown on pots, individuals also dressed up as Scythians, Phrygians and later as Persians. The point would be to be mildly outrageous, therefore.[116]

The suggested line of descent from the booners to the bad boys' clubs of the late fifth and early fourth centuries is intriguing and plausible, but we seem also to need some account of the attraction of this particular form of irregular behaviour. The most interesting guide is Euripides' portrayal of Pentheus' cross-dressing in *Bacchae*, even if some elements (such as Pentheus' prurient desire to spy on wild maenadic revels) are relevant only to the situation within the play. We can note, first, that the point of assuming women's clothes is to become like a maenad (915). It is as if the most authentic human followers of Dionysus are the maenads, and a man who wishes to come close to the god must imitate their condition.[117] But, second, there is a high shame-barrier that Pentheus must surmount in order to do so: 'I cannot put on women's clothes', he says at one point categorically (836). Thirdly and crucially, cross-dressing and madness are brought as close together as can be. On the level of plot, Dionysus declares that he must instil in Pentheus a 'mild frenzy' if he is to overcome his inhibitions against assuming such garb (851). But the result is that we first see Pentheus mad when we first see him in women's clothes (912 ff.); that is to say, ecstasy appears as a consequence of transvestism no less than as a precondition for it. Two of the Dionysiac madnesses, drunkenness and lust, are always available to men; cross-dressing permits a kind of access also to the third, that intoxication without wine normally reserved for women.

[114] Xen. *Symp.* 9. 2–7; cf. Daraki, *Dionysos*, 97–103, esp. 99 on how the couple of Dionysus-Ariadne 'abolishes the division which opposes marriage to desire'; M. H. Jameson, 'The Asexuality of Dionysus', in *Masks of Dionysus*, 44–64. Cratinus fr. 278 speaks of the sexual yearning of Dionysus' 'concubine' (unidentified) for the absent god. The obvious parallel for Dionysus as embodiment of a gentle sexuality attractive to women is Adonis. This is yet another aspect of the gender complexities of the cult.

[115] So Frontisi-Ducroux/Lissarrague, op. cit., 228–9 (and, on the 'transcendence of sex' of Dionysus himself, 232, n. 109); Miller, op. cit., 247, speaks of a 'sexless third gender'.

[116] So Miller, op. cit., 246–53, with reference to M. Garber, *Vested Interests: Cross-dressing and Cultural Anxiety* (London 1992), a work which associates group cross-dressing with 'category crisis'. Miller notes the offensive θηλύτητες ἐσθήτων ascribed to Alcibiades in Plut. *Alc.* 16.1. On Athenian hellfire clubs see O. Murray in id. (ed.), *Sympotica* (Oxford 1990), 149–61. Scythians etc.: see B. Cohen in I. Malkin (ed.), *Ancient Perceptions of Greek Ethnicity* (Washington 2001), 242–51.

[117] See Frontisi-Ducroux/Lissarrague, op. cit., 231: they observe that on vases from c.510–460 Dionysus is typically accompanied by satyrs and by nymphs, not mortal men (though the case is different earlier, especially in the work of the Amasis painter).

I have treated phallic processions and cross-dressing as distinct phenomena. But they converge in the ambit of the *ithyphalloi*, performers who according to Semos of Delos wear masks of drunken men and women's clothes as they escort the phallus. Semos' description mentions no particular polis, but the combination of mask (probably), cross-dressing and phallic pole is found on a red figure cup by the Sabouroff painter, now in the Getty museum.[118] The juxtaposition of sexual identities here reaches a paradoxical extreme, with the symbol of masculine desire being carried by feminized men. And at this extreme there is blurring too of the neat distinction made hitherto between phallic rites, which are about sex, and Dionysiac transvestism, which is about ecstasy. To take the extreme case as key to the whole complex may be an error. But it has been argued that a certain ambivalence often attended phallic rites conducted by men, a hinted awareness that the phallus which one brandished as if to penetrate others might also enter oneself.[119] An Argive rite in which men sat astride a phallus-pole was explained by a scandalous myth which made Dionysus himself a catamite.

That intriguing argument cannot be taken further here. I revert instead to the question of women. Women, we have seen, are the god's privileged congregation. Yet, as has often been noted, the occasions in Attica when they could certainly worship Dionysus are very few. Every two years a team was dispatched to join the Delphic Thyiads revelling in mid-winter on Parnassus. This was full-blown maenadism, but only small numbers can have been involved. Within Attica, the fourteen *gerarai* performed secret rites at the *Anthesteria*, and also participated in two further mysterious minor festivals (*Theoinia* and *Iobaccheia*). At the deme level, we find a recognition of the special status of women vis-à-vis Dionysus in the stipulation that meat from a sacrifice to Semele at Erchia was γυναιξὶ παραδόσιμος ('which may be handed over/for handing over to women').[120] The *Lenaea* is a blank sheet, on which we may inscribe whatever fancy dictates, though we must certainly stop short of a mass exodus to the mountains. But only if we allow fancy quite

[118] Malibu 86.AE.296 (Csapo, 'Riding the Phallus', plate Ic: ibid. 265–6 for the link with the *ithyphalloi*, perhaps first noted by J. R. Green, *Greek Vases in the J. Paul Getty Museum* 2, 1985, 105, n. 7). Semos: n. 105 above. Semos describes their attire without drawing attention to its femininity, but lexicographers make the obvious implication explicit (Hesych., Phot., Sud., s.v. Ἰθύφαλλοι). The passage associating ithyphallic rites with passive homosexuality quoted by Csapo, 263, from Suda β 403 lacks authority: it comes from Synesius, *Laus. Calv.* 21. But Demosthenes made a similar slur, Dem. 54.17. The figures on the Malibu cup are apparently wearing bald masks: both beards and bald masks pick out masculine traits which are in deliberate tension with feminine dress.

[119] This is the central thesis of Csapo, 'Riding the Phallus'. It depends to a large extent on a detailed exegesis, which cannot be discussed here, of the Florentine cup (Fig. 22 above). A fragment of a Clazomenian neck amphora (Csapo, pl. 8b) is unambiguous, but not necessarily representative. Wholly unconvincing is the interpretation in these terms of Pentheus' seat in a pine tree in Eur. *Bacchae*. Scandalous myth: most fully Clem. Al. *Protr.* 2.34.3; Csapo, 275–6.

[120] Parnassus: see p. 83 above; *gerarai*: see p. 304, and *Athenian Religion*, 299–300; Erchia: *LSCG* 18 a 48.

large scope will we be able to give women en masse any substantial role in the public festivals of Dionysus.

Alongside the public festivals we dimly descry, through a mist of official male disapproval, informal bacchic rites that were open to women; Aristophanes indeed represents them as very popular, but, beyond a reference to 'cymbals', reveals nothing of their content or organization (were they 'initiations'? could men attend too?).[121] The only bacchic 'initiations' that are clearly attested in Attica are a specialized form, the 'orphic-bacchic' rites administered, to both sexes, by 'orpheus-initiators'. The formal purpose of these was to secure well-being in the afterlife, but they included bacchic 'play', and some may have undergone them chiefly with a view to more immediate enjoyment. And Dionysiac experience under another name was available in the rites of Sabazius, of 'Mother' and in other elective cults.[122] It is not in his relation to women alone, unfortunately, that the unofficial Dionysus almost entirely escapes our view. Plato once speaks with disapproval of certain 'purifications and initiations' in which participants imitate drunken Nymphs, Pans, Silens and Satyrs.[123] The passage is a much-cited one, necessarily, there being no other direct evidence till much later for dressing up in such guises as part of a ritual. The popularity of such practices remains hard to judge.

But stay, it may be objected, ought we not to use our eyes, in studying this god whose blank and pitiless gaze so often still confronts ours directly?[124] Can we not exploit the uniquely abundant evidence of the vase-paintings to get beyond these frustratingly vague formulations? The material is indeed abundant, and students of Dionysus have the experience unfamiliar to hellenists of

---

[121] Ar. *Lys.* 1–3; cf. the *Dionusiazousai* of Timocles.

[122] On all this see *Athenian Religion*, 161–2, 191–4. Orphic-bacchic: Eur. *Hipp.* 953–4; Pl. *Resp.* 364e; both sexes (and the possibility of recurrent 'initiation'): Theophr. *Char.* 16.12. Little can be done with the metaphorical reference to Bacchic initiation in Ar. *Ran.* 357. There is certainly initiatory/mystic language in Eur. *Bacch.*, though opinions differ about its extent; it could in my view as well derive from orphic/bacchic rites as from separate 'Bacchic mysteries' of the type supposed by R. Seaford (CQ 31, 1981, 252–75 and in his edition of the play, Warminster 1996) and R. Schlesier, 'Die Seele im Thiasos. Zu Euripides, *Bacchae* 75', in J. Holzhausen (ed.), ψυχη-*Seele -anima. FS* Karin Alt (Stuttgart/Leipzig 1998), 37–72; cf. ead., 'Dionysos in der Unterwelt'.

[123] Pl. *Leg.* 815c; cf. Seaford, *Reciprocity and Ritual*, 266. Combinations of komasts or padded dancers with satyrs in early 6th-c. iconography are sometimes taken as evidence that the 'satyrs' are in fact men (Hedreen, *Silens*, 156, though he envisages performance rather than mere dressing up; for a different nuance see Isler-Kerenyi, *Dionysos*, 47, 83, cf. 139). The vases showing Dionysus, with satyrs, in his ship-cart (p. 302 above) may attest satyr-mimicry in public cult. The Platonic passage is central to the argument of Bérard, *Anodoi, passim,* that the vases which associate satyrs with goddesses (only once a god) emergent from the earth relate to initiations: the emergence of the deity stands for the initiate's rebirth. He takes the 'hammers' borne by the satyrs as noise-making instruments. Other difficulties aside (cf. p. 423, n. 28), the predominance of female 'initiates' appears inexplicable on this theory. C. Bron, 'Porteurs de thyrse ou bacchants', in C. Bérard (ed.), *Images et société en Grèce ancienne* (1987), 145–53 (cf. Moraw, Mänade, 197–99) detects a ritual in certain images showing a seated veiled woman with satyrs.

[124] On the special importance of seeing and being seen in Dionysiac cult (Eur. *Bacch.* 470; masks; frontal depiction already on the François vase) see Isler-Kerenyi, *Dionysos,* 180, n. 92 [+].

confronting an almost uncontrollable mass of evidence.[125] But the truths that emerge are, in the main, big and general ones about the role of Dionysus in the Greek imagination, not historical or cultic particularities.[126] The Dionysiac world of the vases is a world of, in Euripides' phase, 'congregationalized hearts'; Dionysus is seldom alone, almost always accompanied by his satyrs or maenads or both.[127] Conversely, the familiar type of votive relief which shows a procession of worshippers approaching the deity is rather rare in the cult of Dionysus; this god's place is among his worshippers, not detached from them behind an altar. The satyrs and maenads together incorporate the whole gamut of Dionysiac 'madness'; the satyrs are subject to drunkenness and sexual frenzy, the maenads undergo an ecstatic encounter with wild nature.[128] Some satyrs (though not till the mid fifth century) are almost house-trained, others very wild; maenads range across the same spectrum, though the savage extreme in their case is horrendous, whereas in that of satyrs it is mainly comic. Both sets of representations express, like Euripides' *Bacchae*, Dionysus' ambivalent potential. Mythical maenads, who tear animals limb from limb, blur into 'real' maenads, who demurely ladle wine from jars in front of an image of the god; there is no sharp line of division. There can be no such blurring of mythical into real satyrs; but masquerades in which men dressed up as satyrs (and satyr plays) to some extent provide here too a real dimension, even if the frequency of such mumming is very uncertain.

The god himself is unimaginable without his followers but does not resemble them. He is seldom drunk, seldom mad, never sexually aroused. The relationship with Ariadne, often depicted, is dignified and restrained. Even in grim situations he retains a smiling tranquillity which comes suddenly to seem sinister. (Was he a model for Plato's portrayal of Socrates?) The calmness of the god of madness is a characteristic Dionysian paradox. His followers surrender their individuality in the collective excitement. But they do not achieve union with the source of that excitement, however close they may seem to approach. Dionysus eludes them, and retains his enigmatic smile.

---

[125] See Carpenter, *Archaic Dionysiac Imagery* and *Fifth-Century Dionysiac Imagery*; Schöne, *Thiasos*; Moraw, *Mänade*; Isler-Kerenyi, *Dionysos*; p. 306 above on Lenaea vases; C. Gasparri in *LIMC* s.v. *Dionysos*.

[126] Moraw, *Mänade*, argues from iconography that maenadism first became familiar in Attica in the late Pisistratid epoch (249; 252 is more cautious), and that mixed private *thiasoi* became accepted in the 5th c. (199–200; 259); Isler-Kerenyi, *Dionysos*, 178–82, postulates Bacchic mysteries for the period *c*.540. None of these points seems to me at all secure.

[127] Schöne, *Thiasos*, 1. The mixing of genders in the 5th-c. iconographic *thiasos* is probably (but see the previous note) a non-realistic feature, in that in actual cult citizen maenads did not mix with men (for whom the satyrs stand). In 6th-c. iconography the companions of the satyrs often yield to their advances, but lack clear maenadic traits; the true maenads of later imagery repel the satyrs (S. McNally, *Arethusa* 11, 1978, 129–30; F. Lissarrague in *Before Sexuality*, 65: 'maenads are as chaste as they are sober'; Moraw, *Mänade*, 42–5). We seem to move from scenes which have the *komos* (men plus *hetairai*) as template (Schöne, 116–18) to an effective if unrealistic deployment of the prototypical worshippers of both genders.

[128] For a defence of the application of the language of 'madness' or 'possession' even to real maenads see J. N. Bremmer, 'Greek Maenadism Reconsidered', *ZPE* 55 (1984), 267–86, at 281.

15

Eleusinian Festivals

The *Mysteries* were, and are, the most famous Greek festival. Already in 480 BC, when Xerxes' army was ravaging Attica, an Athenian who was with the Persian army, Dikaios son of Theokydes, saw a cloud of dust 'as of about 30, 000 men' moving from Eleusis, and heard the sound of the 'mystic chant' (*iakchos*). Huge throngs usually went from Athens to Eleusis for the *Mysteries*, raising the *iakchos* cry on the way; what Dikaios heard was a divine equivalent going in the opposite direction, to aid the Athenians and their allies against those who were ravaging their fertile fields.[1] Dikaios explains to his Spartan companion, the ex-king Demaratus, that 'This is a festival which the Athenians celebrate each year for the Mother and the Maiden, and any Athenian or other Greek who chooses is initiated. The cry which you hear they chant at this festival.' Faithfully recounted by Herodotus of Halicarnassus, the story attests the panhellenic prestige of the *Mysteries* of Eleusis, even if for narrative purposes it postulates a Spartan king who knows nothing of them. At the other end of antiquity, though most Athenian festivals simply slip into oblivion, we have in Eunapius[2] a contemporary account of the catastrophe that overcame this one: first, the appointment of an unlawful hierophant, a non-Athenian who already held high office in the cult of Mithras; then in 395 the sacking of the sanctuary by Alaric the Goth, let in by the impiety of 'the men in black cloaks', or Christian monks. In the interim Romans had come to Eleusis to be initiated 'in a fairly steady stream'.[3]

The visitors came for the single, all-glorious festival. But the *Mysteries* need to be put in a broader context. Other festivals of Demeter and Kore were also celebrated at Eleusis, several of them with involvement of the same sacred personnel who had central roles at the *Mysteries*. When an Athenian spoke of

---

[1] Hdt. 8.65. For a collection of testimonia (unfortunately not quite comprehensive) see Scarpi, which I refer to for some of the less easily accessible texts.

[2] Eunapius *Vit. Soph.* 7.3.2–4 (pp. 475–6 Didot). The penultimate hierophant, Nestorius, supposedly predicted these disasters (cf. Burkert, *Mystery Cults*, 51); he was a figure of importance in the 4th-c. religious world, influential with Julian (Clinton, *Sacred Officials*, 43). Life for a late 4th-c. Greek would be 'unlivable' if Valentinian suppressed τὰ συνέχοντα τὸ ἀνθρώπειον γένος ἁγιώτατα μυστήρια (Zosimus 4.3.3).

[3] K. Clinton, 'Eleusis and the Romans: Late Republic to Marcus Aurelius', in M. C. Hoff and S. I. Rotroff (eds.), *The Romanization of Athens* (Oxbow monograph 94, Oxford 1997), 161–81, at 163; cf. id., 'The Eleusinian *Mysteries*: Roman Initiates and Benefactors, Second Century B.C. to A.D. 267', in *ANRW* II.18.2 (Berlin 1989), 1499–539.

'Demeter of Eleusis' he doubtless saw her in relation to the whole complex of activities associated with the great sanctuary.[4] We need to study not a single festival, but—untranslatable into Greek though the concept is—a cult. Again, there were sanctuaries of Demeter throughout Attica, some bearing the epithet 'Eleusinian', some not. Demeter of Eleusis needs to be found a place within the whole set of Attic cults of the goddess. And, though most festivals existed as rites performed and as nothing else, there was a literature too attached to this one: poems about the coming of Demeter to Eleusis, poems depicting the afterlife in ways more or less suggested by the cult. With the exception of the *Homeric Hymn to Demeter* these poems are lost, but almost any initiate's sense of the physical Eleusis will have been shaped by this Eleusis of the mind.

I begin with Eleusinian festivals. The agonistic *Eleusinia* with its competitions in 'athletics, music and horse-racing' and its 'ancestral competition' (of unknown content) was briefly mentioned in Chapter 10. This was an Eleusinian festival in the strongest sense: as its name would suggest, it was celebrated there alone, and administratively it belonged to the sanctuary rather than to the local community, the deme of Eleusis.[5] Of the content of the *Eleusinia*, the competitions aside, we know most about the sacrifices. (There are also unrevealing references to a procession and a basket-bearer.) An archaic inscription prescribes the offerings to be made before and at the festival. The recipients are a blend of powers worshipped (certainly or probably) in other contexts at the sanctuary—Plouton (?), 'the goddesses', Artemis, Poseidon, Earth (?), the Graces, and, according to a questionable supplement, Triptolemos—with others more distinctively athletic: Hermes Enagonios, Telesidromos or 'race-finisher' (otherwise unknown), and, if a plausible supplement is correct, Dolichos, who in this context will be 'Long Distance'. Indeed Dolichos, if correctly read, even slips in between Plouton and the two goddesses to share a triple sacrifice.[6] The emphases that emerge from the list are therefore 'general Eleusinian' and 'athletic'. A section of the state calendar of Nicomachus is generally supposed also to relate to the festival. It adds a row of Eleusinian heroes familiar from the *Homeric Hymn*

---

[4] On the need for us to do the same see Clinton, *Myth and Cult*, 7–8, and *passim*.

[5] Expenses are met from temple funds: see *IG* II² 1672. 258–62 . The identity of the *hieropoioi* of *IG* I³ 5 is controversial: I suppose them to be the 'Eleusinian *hieropoioi*' (*IG* I³ 78.9, and often). On the festival see pp. 201–2.

[6] With H. von Prott (*AM* 24, 1899, 248), I read προτέ]λεια in *IG* I³ 5.2 (for the spelling see now *SEG* XLI 182) and interpret as 'preliminary offerings for the *Eleusinia*'; προτό]λεια, advocated by R. M. Simms *GRBS* 16 (1975), 272 (cf. Phot. s.v. πρωτόλεια) goes less well with θύεν. For προτέλεια as preliminary offerings of any kind see *Anecd. Bekk.* 1.293.5–6. προτέλεια needs a dependent genitive whereas a connection between τὸς ἱεροποιὸς and 'Ελευσινίον is problematic: *hieropoioi* were not appointed for specific festivals (so rightly K. Clinton, *AJP* 92, 1971, 4, n. 11), but the translation '*hieropoioi* of the Eleusinians' would seem to require τὸς ἱεροποιὸς τὸς 'Ελευσινίον. The offering shared by two heroes introduced by the reading Τριπ [τολέμοι in 4 is unparalleled and the π supposedly seen by Pittakys and Lenormant very doubtful (see Kirchhoff's note in *IG* I 5): the word might be τρί[ττοιαν.

to Demeter but, to our knowledge, lacking sporting interests: Eumolpos, Poly-xenos, 'Nursling', Dioklos and Keleos.[7] Eleusinian mythology was evoked at the festival in some depth and breadth if all these figures were honoured at it. But the premise is insecure; it is possible that the list relates rather to the *Mysteries*. The intimate association of the *Eleusinia* with Eleusinian myth-ology is, however, not in doubt. It claimed to be the most ancient of all athletic festivals, founded in celebration of Demeter's gift to mankind; that was why the prize continued to take the form of grain.[8]

On some occasion during the year at Eleusis was performed the 'Pelting' (*Balletys*), a mock battle between young Eleusinians conducted probably with stones in honour of Demophon, the Eleusinian prince whom according to the *Homeric Hymn* Demeter vainly sought to make immortal. The 'ancestral competition' of the *Eleusinia* could be this.[9] But the *Haloa* too hosted an 'ancestral competition' of unknown content; indeed the event could have occurred at almost any Eleusinian festival.

The *Haloa* too was an Eleusinian festival in the strong sense: it occurred (in all seeming) at Eleusis only, the 'priestess of Demeter' was probably a main celebrant, and expenses were met from the funds of the goddesses. Foods banned to *mystai* were absent from the otherwise well-piled tables at the festival, according to one source; the same source speaks of it as a showcase for the Eleusinian claim to be the source of 'civilized food'.[10] And though both Dionysus and Poseidon had an ill-defined role at the *Haloa*, its location was certainly the sanctuary of Demeter and Kore.[11]

---

[7] *BSA* 97 (2002), 363–4, fr. 3. 60–86. The full list is: sacrifices are to be made by the Eumolpids to Themis, Zeus Herkeios, Demeter, Pherrephatte, Eumolpos, Melichos, Archegetes, Polyxenos, 'Nursling', Keleos; a further set are to be made (by the *Kerykes?*- so K. Clinton, *AJP* 100, 1979, 6–7: *aliter* N. Robertson, *JHS* 110, 1990, 69, n. 92) to Hestia, Athena, the Graces, Hermes Enagonios, and other recipients now lost. These offerings are generally associated with the *Eleusinia* (so first W. S. Ferguson, *Classical Studies presented to Edward Capps*, Princeton 1936, 155, n. 52; A. Körte, *Glossa* 25, 1936, 138–42; cf. Healey, *Eleusinian Sacrifices, passim*) on the grounds that (1) they are biennial and (2) they overlap with those listed in *IG* I[3] 5. But (1) is inconclusive given that sacrifices at the *Synoikia*, probably an annual festival, appear in this same biennial list; as for (2), the strong sporting emphasis seen in *IG* I[3] 5 is absent, Hermes Enagonios aside, from the list in the Nicomachus calendar.

[8] See p. 202, n. 43.

[9] So O. Kern, *RE* s.v. *Mysterien*, 1215, followed e.g. by G. Baudy in *Food in Antiquity*, 181; Brumfield, *Agricultural Year*, 183. Richardson, *Hymn to Demeter*, 246, thinks Athenaeus' lan-guage implies a self-standing festival; but should the language of an Athenaeus be pressed on such a matter? For earlier guesses about the πάτριος ἀγών see Healey, *Eleusinian Sacrifices*, 65, n. 55. For the 'ancestral competion' at the *Haloa* see p. 201, n. 40.

[10] Celebration at Eleusis only (*aliter* Jacoby, comm. on Philoch. *FGrH* 328 F 83, p. 363 and n. 11): only the unreliable Alciphr. 4.18.4 speaks of celebration outside Eleusis (in Athens itself: but *IG* II[2] 949 seems to exclude this). Priestess: Apollod. *Neaer.* 116–17 (cf. 'priestesses' in Σ Lucian p. 280.16 Rabe). Later the demarch appears (*IG* II[2] 949.7) , perhaps in a supplementary role (cf. ibid. line 10). Who the 'magistrates' mentioned by Σ Lucian p. 280.25 Rabe may be is unclear. Expenses: *IG* II[2] 1672.124–5, 143–4. One source: see p. 167.

[11] Where exactly the women's banquet occurred is unknown; the 'sacred house' would have been suitable (Clinton, *Myth and Cult*, 119–20), but seems to have gone out of use after the Persian invasion.

A little more complicated is the case of those festivals of Demeter and Kore which bear a close relation to the agricultural cycle even in their name. In an Athenian decree of 165/4 a demarch of the Eleusinians is thanked for the ritual acts he performed at the *Haloa, Chloïa* and *Kalamaia* (this last 'with the hierophant and priestesses') for the well-being of the Athenians. A natural conclusion is that *Chloïa* and *Kalamaia*, like *Haloa*, were not performed in Athens itself, and that the Eleusinian celebration stood in. But *Kalamaia* are attested in one other deme, and festivals of comparable type (*Antheia, Proerosia*) in several.[12] Festivals of this type were not necessarily tied to Eleusis, therefore, but the Eleusinian celebration was always likely to enjoy especial prestige.

A clear example of this phenomenon is the *Proerosia*. A 'pre-ploughing sacrifice' was celebrated in various demes of Attica, but the rite at Eleusis was the most prestigious. The hierophant went to Athens on Pyanopsion 5 to 'proclaim the *Proerosia*', and in the late hellenistic period ephebes came from Athens to 'lift the oxen' at the festival and make themselves useful in other ways.[13] If several bulls had to be lifted, the sacrifice must have been on a substantial scale; and in all seeming the Eleusinian rite served the city of Athens. Indeed, according to one account of the matter, it served the whole world. 'All mankind' or at least 'all the Greeks' (and also the Hyperboreans) were afflicted by plague and crop-failure; Apollo of Delphi decreed that the evil would cease only if the Athenians made pre-ploughing sacrifices on behalf of all, and the Athenians duly undertook the pious task—which is why 'first fruits' of the corn are now brought to Eleusis as a thank-offering by all.[14] The myth was known to the orator Lycurgus, who mentioned the mission of the arrow-bearing hyperborean Abaris, most picturesque of the ambassadors who came to Athens at that time. Does it follow that in practice as well as in myth the *Proerosia* was associated with the famous 'first fruits' summoned to Eleusis, by a decree perhaps of the 430s,[15] from the Attic demes, the allies and, ideally, the whole Greek world?[16] Was it then that the sacrifices financed from the proceeds were made? Such a practice would have stressed the endless circularity of the agricultural year, with the produce of the old season

---

[12] See pp. 195–6 above. The decree is *IG* II² 949. A hero Kalamites had long been known, but from vague notices only; Clinton, *Myth and Cult*, 106, n. 6, has now splendidly detected him, in an Eleusinian context, in the KΛΛΜΙΤΕ of an R. F. dinos in the Getty.

[13] *LSCG* 7. 2–7; *IG* II² 1028.28 etc.; Pélékidis, *Éphébie*, 224, n.3.

[14] For the myth see Lycurgus XIV. 3–5 Conomis (83–5 Blass, *FGrH* 401 (c) F 2–4), Aristid. 1 (*Panath.*) 399, Suda α 18, *Σ* Aristid. p. 55.33–56.5 Dindorf (for other lexicographical references see Jacoby on *FGrH* 323 F 23); for its association with first fruits see Suda ει 184, *Σ* vet. Ar. *Eq.* 729a. *Σ* vet. Ar. *Plut.* 1054f.

[15] *IG* I³ 78 (ML 73), so dated by Cavanaugh, *Eleusis and Athens*, 73–98, with an argument from the absence from the decree of the Eleusinian *epistatai*, a board probably set up *c.*432 (but see the effective objections of V. J. Rosivach, *BMCR* 97.2.22).

[16] See *Athenian Religion*, 143; on the link between festival and first fruits see ibid. n. 85 and especially Smarczyk, *Religionspolitik*, 184–216. The case for association with the *Proerosia* is now strongly restated by N. Robertson, *GRBS* 37 (1996), 319–25.

ceremonially received at the festival which looked forward to the first labours of the new.

But there is a complication. An earlier-attested justification for the dispatch of first fruits to Eleusis was that it was at Eleusis that corn first appeared, to be distributed thence to the rest of the world by Triptolemus; this happened in primeval time, whereas Abaris and his arrow supposedly belonged somewhere in the archaic period.[17] The myth of the plague in Abaris' time has been seen as a secondary elaboration, yet one more reason why the Greeks owed gratitude to the Athenians.[18] Perhaps the first fruits were rather received at the *Mysteries*, most splendid of all Eleusinian festivals and the one most intimately connected with the discovery of corn.[19] Yet no source connects the tribute directly with the *Mysteries*, while the *Proerosia* too could be associated with the momentous first discovery of corn: at the start of *Supplices* (produced within a decade or so of the 'first fruits' decree), Euripides shows Theseus' mother Aethra 'making preliminary sacrifice for the ploughing of the land' at the enclosure in Eleusis 'where the ear of corn first appeared bristling over this land'. A tradition according to which it was Triptolemus who first 'showed' how to perform pre-ploughing rites again takes them back to very early times.[20] Perhaps in a fuller formulation it would have become clear that what happened in Abaris' time was not the foundation of the rite but the extension of one hitherto performed 'on behalf of the Athenians' (on the advice of Triptolemus) to the whole world.[21]

The famous First Fruits decree implies that it had always been customary for Attic communities to dispatch first fruits to Eleusis. A decree of the deme Paiania dated to *c*.450 speaks, darkly, of 'pre-ploughing barley'. Probably then the first fruits decree took up an existing association between First Fruits and the Eleusinian *Proerosia* and sought to extend it to Hellas at large. If that is so, the sacrifices mentioned in the decree (to 'the two goddesses', Triptolemos, 'god' and 'goddess', Euboulos and Athena) will have been made at the

---

[17] Isocr. *Paneg.* 31. See Jacoby on Hippostratos *FGrH* 568 F 4, and on the two justifications esp. Smarczyk, *Religionspolitik*, 190–4.

[18] So Smarczyk, *Religionspolitik*, 193; but such a 'zusatzliche Legitimierung der Getreidezehntforderung' would surely have been easier if there was an existing link between *Proerosia* and first fruits.

[19] So Smarczyk, *Religionspolitik*, 196, n. 114 [+]. But his attempt to associate μυστηρίοις with ἀπάρχεσθαι in *IG* I³ 78 (ML 73) 24–5 κελεύετο δὲ ho hιεροφάντες μυστερίοις ἀπάρχεσθαι τὸς hέλλενας τὸ καρπὸ κατὰ τὰ πάτρια is certainly wrong: κελεύειν in context urgently needs a specification of occasion, whereas the modality of ἀπάρχεσθαι is contained in κατὰ τὰ πάτρια κτλ; μυστηρίοις on this view is also pointlessly emphatic. A reference to the tribute in the 4th-c. law regulating the *Mysteries* (*Agora* XVI 56 side B a 13) does not seem to me decisive, because the *spondophoroi* announcing the Mystic Truce may also have solicited contributions for the *Proerosia* (does the 'oracle' in side A 10 of that law allude to it?).

[20] Eur. *Supp.* 28–31; Triptolemus : so the *Marmor Parium* (*FGrH* 239 A 12), if persuasive supplements are accepted.

[21] So Jacoby on Clidemus *FGrH* 323 F 23.

Proerosia—and the festival will have had or claimed importance for the whole Greek world.[22]

Eleusis is very likely to have hosted its own local *Thesmophoria*. But in this case there is no indication that the Eleusinian celebration enjoyed special prestige. If we divide up the two goddesses' spheres of concern very crudely into agriculture, eschatology and the lives of women, Eleusis appears distinctively concerned with the first two more than with the third. Only the *Mysteries*, it is true, speak of the afterlife. But *Mysteries*, *Eleusinia*, *Haloa*, and *Proerosia* (to omit the minor *Chloïa* and *Kalamaia*) all treat of agriculture, and deploy shared themes and myths relating to the origins and distribution of corn; Triptolemus, for instance, is likely to have received offerings at two or three of the festivals, and was supposedly also a presence at the fourth (the *Haloa*).[23] It is legitimate to speak in this context of 'Eleusinian ideology'.

I turn to the theme of 'Eleusis within Attica'. A decree of *c.*432 attests an Eleusinion 'in the city' and one at Phaleron which were under the same administrative and financial control as that of Eleusis.[24] For sanctuaries at different places to be under the same management is, in Greek terms, a singular arrangement, for which the relation between Brauron and the city Brauronion is the clearest Attic parallel. About the Eleusinion of Phaleron nothing further is known; we now know the one in the city to go back to the seventh century.[25] An irresistible explanation for the shared control lies in the relation of all three places to the ritual of the *Mysteries*; on Boedromion 19 or 20 a procession went from the city Eleusinion to Eleusis, but on the 16th the potential *mystai* had gone en masse to Phaleron for purification. Evidently the Phaleron Eleusinion was put to use in some way on that occasion. In principle then these branch Eleusinia might have had narrowly circumscribed functions. But the city Eleusinion, at least, certainly served as a place of worship in a broader sense, because (to take the clearest case) the demesmen of Erchia made offerings there on occasion. Indeed, if the argument that the 'Plutonium' should be relocated from Eleusis to the vicinity of the city Eleusinion is sound,[26] the main shrine of a major Eleusinian god was located beside it (Triptolemus had a place there too).

The word 'Eleusinion' also occurs in documents relating to three demes, Paiania, Phrearrhioi, and Marathon.[27] Branch Eleusinia of the kind described, with a direct function in the ritual of the *Mysteries*, cannot have existed in these places. Either then the Eleusinia referred to in these docu-

---

[22] In 329/8 sale of the first fruits allowed purchase of forty-three sheep and goats and three bulls, and left over a sum for a *pelanos* (*IG* II² 1672. 288–291); if I am right, these sacrifices will have been made at the *Proerosia*. Paeania: *IG* I³ 250 A 22. B 4.

[23] For the *Proerosia* see above; for the *Eleusinia* see p. 328, for the *Haloa* p. 167; for the *Mysteries* there is no specific evidence, but a high general probability.

[24] *IG* I³ 32.   [25] See Miles, *Eleusinion*.   [26] See n. 48 below. Erchia: see n. 31.

[27] *IG* I³ 250 A 15, 17, 26, B 30; *SEG* XXXV 113. 9, 18, 23; *ZPE* 130 (2000). 45–7. col. 2. 43. 48. It is hard to do much with the corrupt notice *Anecd. Bekk.* 1. 242.14–15 Διάκρια· τόπος Ἀττικῆς ὑπὸ Βραυρῶνα Ἐλευσίνιον Δήμητρος καὶ Φερεφάττης ἱερόν.

ments are among the three already known, or there existed also a different type of Eleusinion, a sanctuary of Demeter Eleusinia that served local needs and was locally administered. In two of the instances the case against the Eleusinion being local is quite strong. The law from Paiania (of the fifth century) prescribes a series of offerings for festivals of Demeter, some to be made (probably: the Greek is ambiguous) 'here', some to be sent 'to the Eleusinion'. The Eleusinion therefore is likely to be outside the deme.[28] A fragmentary text of uncertain character found in the southern Attic deme of Phrearrhioi mentions not merely an Eleusinion but also an 'altar of Plouton', the god Iakchos, and a sacrifice to be made 'in the courtyard of the Eleusinion'.[29] If the Eleusinion in question is local, it is also a remarkably faithful replica of that at Eleusis or in the city. Those sanctuaries had important courtyards, not a usual feature of Greek shrines, in order to create a public space distinct from the area accessible only to initiates or reserved for sacred objects. Such a courtyard would have had no such function at Phearrhioi; it would have been a mere gesture to Eleusis, an attempt to recapture some of the atmosphere of the mother sanctuary. Actual revelation of mysteries occurred at Eleusis, and there alone.[30] (On the other hand, this text defines perquisites to be received by priests, which would normally imply that the issuing body controlled the sanctuary.) The Marathon text provides no strong pointers either way. New evidence is needed in order to resolve the issue. But the outcome is likely to involve either emphatic imitation of Eleusinian arrangements by the demes or actual use by them of central Eleusinia (or a mixture of both). And that is the point, the central importance of the Eleusinian cult for all inhabitants of Attica, and not just in relation to the afterlife. The Eleusinion of the Paiania law is being used for what one might call 'general agricultural' business. Offerings associated with the *Proerosia*, the *Chloïa* and perhaps the *Antheia* are sent to it.[31] Even for such business Eleusinian Demeter had especial prestige. No other *epiklesis* of the goddess, with the exception of Thesmophoros, had much currency in Attica.[32]

---

[28] So Humphreys, 'Demes', 154.

[29] R. M. Simms, *Hesperia* 67 (1998), 91–107, makes a good case for non-local celebration.

[30] Cf. Osborne, *Demos*, 178: 'all these commemorations outside Eleusis can only be alternatives by also being confirmations'. By 'actual revelation of mysteries' here I mean 'of Eleusinian mysteries'. There were also the Lycomid mysteries at Phlya (*Athenian Religion*, 305), but we know too little about them for useful discussion; it is interesting that they too were of Demeter.

[31] See Nilsson, *Op. Sel.* iii, 92–8 (from *Eranos* 42, 1944). One can imagine the gratification with which the aged Nilsson read this new text, which chimed so neatly with so many of his assumptions. At Marathon too (*ZPE* 130, 2000, 45–7), Demeter has both agricultural and 'mystic' faces: she receives an expensive pregnant animal (col. 2. 48), but the Marathonians also honour 'Telete' (col. 2.10) and are very aware of the *Mysteries* (col. 2.5). About ritual in the city Eleusinion we are it seems informed (a brief reference in the Erchia calendar aside, *LSCG* 18 β 3), only by the votives and other archaeological remains, and Perhaps by the Paiania calendar (n. 27).

[32] Demeter Azesia is known only from a *horos* in the agora (*Agora* XIX, H 16). On Demeter Achaia see *Athenian Religion*, 288. In *IG* II² 4587 *karpophoros* is a poetic, not a cult epithet of Demeter; *IG* II² 4730 is a Macedonian inscription mistakenly included in the Attic corpus (W. Peek, *AM* 67, 1942, 56, no. 92). For Demeter Phrearr(i)os see *IG* II² 5155 and perhaps lines 12–13 of the Phrearrhian lex sacra (so R. M. Simms, *Hesperia* 67, 1998, 91–2).

The deme of Teithras had an important Koreion.[33] We know no more of it than that.

I look back now to Eleusis. This is not the place to survey the administration of the great sanctuary or the functions of the many priestly personnel (drawn from 'the *gene* concerned with the goddess') who served in it. Responsibility was divided between magistrates of the city and priests drawn from *gene* in a way typical of Athenian religion; but the numbers involved and the extent of collective commitment among the relevant *gene* are unique. The hierophant and the daduch wore special 'sacred garments' (and a sacred hairstyle) which gave them a kingly dignity.[34] But our concern here is with rites and gods. Discursive accounts of the ritual of the *Mysteries* never existed,[35] but gods and heroes who had a relation to them were honoured with sacrifices and votive reliefs, and might be depicted on vases or coins with Eleusinian themes. ('Eleusinian' vases are strikingly widely distributed, but wide distribution characterizes all Attic pottery, and we cannot confidently explain them either as 'advertisement' or 'souvenirs'. The coins, however, are seen as special 'festival issues'.[36]) One indirect approach to the *Mysteries*, therefore, is to assemble from such sources a cast of Eleusinian deities,[37] and the method is not the less useful for inevitable uncertainties at the margins over whom to include. Some candidates are obvious: the 'two goddesses' Demeter and Kore (or 'Mother and Kore' or 'the elder' and 'the younger' goddess as they were sometimes called; Kore's proper name Persephone was officially not used, but occasionally slipped out even in cult documents);[38] Triptolemus, the hero who in his winged chariot distributed the gifts of Demeter throughout the world, a regular recipient of cult and subject of innumerable depictions on

---

[33] *SEG* XXIV 151. 21 (a place for display of leases).

[34] Administration: see Cavanaugh, *Eleusis and Athens*. Personnel: Clinton, *Sacred Officials*, *passim* (on dress and hair 32–3, 48; *Myth and Cult*, 70, n. 38); on the 'gene concerned with the goddesses' (*IG* II² 2944.10–11) briefly *Athenian Religion*, 293–7, 300–4, 317. On the claim of Porph. ap. Euseb. *Praep. evang.* 3.12.4 that the hierophant is dressed to represent the demiurge, the daduch the sun, the altar priest the moon and the Hierokeryx Hermes see Nilsson, *Geschichte*, II, 352 and P. Boyancé, *REG* 75 (1962), 467; they rightly recognize interpretation here, not practice. (The passage is a Greek analogy within a discussion of Egyptian gods and does not attest Eleusinian rites in Egypt: the common denominator, as emerges in what follows, is the idea of 'man representing god' in a cult.)

[35] Books 'about the *Mysteries*' at Eleusis' *vel sim.* (*FGrH* 326 F 2–4; *FGrH* 328 T 1: Burkert, *Homo Necans*, 250, n. 9) must have kept to externals. Polemon wrote a monograph on 'The Sacred Way' (Harpocr. ι 4).

[36] See most recently J. H. Kroll, *AJA* 96 (1992), 355–6, and in general K. Clinton, 'The Eleusinian Mysteries and Panhellenism in Democratic Athens', in *Athens and Attica*, 161–72.

[37] M. P. Nilsson, 'Die eleusinischen Gottheiten', *ARW* 32 (1935), 79–141 (*Op. Sel.* II, 542–623); Clinton, *Myth and Cult* (which is now easily the single most useful book about Eleusis: for some iconographic reservations see E. Simon, 'Eleusis in Athenian Vase-painting', in J. H. Oakley and others, *Athenian Potters and Painters*, Oxford 1997, 97–108).

[38] See Clinton, *Myth and Cult*, 63, nn. 199–200 (where the evidence of inscribed vases is also mentioned; for poetry, in an Eleusinian context, see e.g. Eur. *Suppl.* 271; Ar. *Ran.* 671). For the taboo see Eur. *Hel.* 1307, ἀρρήτου κούρας. 'Mother and Kore': Hdt. 8.65.4. 'Elder' and 'younger': e.g. *IG* II² 1672. 300–1 (accounts).

vases; Iacchus, the divine embodiment of the chant raised during the procession to Eleusis, a central figure in the Eleusis of the imagination, even if his place as a recipient of offerings is insecure.

Others by contrast do perhaps need some introduction. 'The god' and 'the goddess' are unattested or almost so[39] in literary texts but are known from an important small group of inscriptions and votive reliefs. They shared a priest with Euboulos, and in a crucial fourth-century relief dedicated at Eleusis by Lysimachides they are shown (identified by inscriptions) with Demeter and Kore.[40] Two identical tables appear, laden with food; at one sit Demeter and Kore, at the other 'the god' reclines, holding a vessel in his left hand and a *rhyton* in his right, with the goddess seated at his side (in the familiar 'banqueting hero with heroine' schema). A much later relief dedicated by Lakrateides includes 'god' and 'goddess' (identified by inscriptions) in a group of Eleusinian figures which also contains, among others, Plouton (identified by an inscription) and Demeter and Kore (iconographically obvious).[41] A problem arises, either solution to which is interesting. If 'god' and 'goddess' are independent figures—presumably a lord and lady of the underworld— they are also extraordinarily obscure ones; though they have *ex hypothesi* been supplanted in their main functions by named powers, they are allowed to cling to their formal honours, in a remarkable instance of cultic conservatism, for almost as long as we can trace the cult.[42] It is doubtless better to see 'god' as in some sense identical with Hades and 'goddess' with Persephone, particularly now that a new text attests a local Attic cult of a 'reverend goddess' who appears to be Persephone.[43] On this view the gods of the nether world are split at Eleusis into two aspects: as rulers of the dead they are 'god' and 'goddess', as sources of growth they are Plouton and Kore. But this view too has a surprising consequence. The phenomenon of a single god being invoked in a single prayer or oath under two different epithets is not uncommon.[44] It is also well established that the typical iconography of Zeus Basileus, say, is different from that of Zeus Meilichios. But it is hard to imagine a relief depicting Zeus Basileus seated beside a differently depicted Zeus

---

[39] See Clinton, *Myth and Cult*, 115.

[40] Athens NM 1519, *IG* II² 4683; *LIMC* s.v. *Demeter* (vol. IV.1), no. 385; here Fig. 24. Priest: *IG* I³ 78.39.

[41] Eleusis Museum 5079, *IG* II² 4701; *LIMC* s.v. *Ploutos*, no. 16; Nilsson, *Geschichte*, pl. 40; Kerényi, *Die Mysterien*, pl. 36 (*Eleusis* p. 44); Mylonas, *Mysteries*, pl. 71; Clinton, *Myth and Cult*, pls. 5–7 (with discussion pp. 51–3).

[42] For survival of the priesthood of 'God, goddess and Eubouleus' in the 2nd c. AD see Clinton, *Myth and Cult*, 56, n. 152. The independence of 'god and goddess' is an old view (e.g. Foucart, *Mystères d'Éleusis*, 90–8), revived by A. Peschlow-Bindokat, *JdI* 87 (1972), 124–7. For the other view, also old (see the survey of opinions in O. Höfer, *RML* V, 1916, s.v. *Thea*), see Clinton, *Myth and Cult*, 114–15.

[43] A new fragment of *IG* II² 1356 attests a priestess and also a priest of ἀγνὴ θεός at Aixone (Steinhauer, Ἱερὸς νόμος Αἰξωνέων); cf. already Antiphanes fr. 55.9. For this title outside Attica see L. Dubois, *Inscriptions dialectales de Sicile* (Rome 1989), no. 38; *IG* XIV 204; ἁγνή < ν > Φερ < σ > εφόνεαν in a 'gold tablet' from Thurii (G. Pugliese Carratelli, *Le lamine d' ore orfiche*, Milan 2001, 99).

[44] Cf. *OpAth* 28 (2003), 175.

Fig. 24. Two divine couples on relief dedicated by Lysimachides.

Meilichios. Yet, in the Lysimachides and Lacrateides reliefs, we have the 'same' deities visually depicted twice,[45] with different iconographies, in a single context. Even if we detect here, hypothetically, an imperfect coalescence between the originally distinct figures of, say, Kore and Persephone,[46] it remains remarkable that, while being assimilated, the deities also remained distinct. Whether Kore-Thea is product of an amalgamation or a division, the same tension between a need to combine and a need to separate is at work.[47]

Plouton, we have just seen, is another Eleusinian god. Indeed, it is at Eleusis that this euphemistic alternative (as Plato calls him)[48] to Hades is first and

---

[45] Kore and 'goddess' in the Lysimachides relief, Plouton and 'god' in Lakrateides'.

[46] See Clinton, *Myth and Cult*, 61, 114, with citation of Zuntz and Nilsson. The argument runs that, in Homer, Persephone is queen of the underworld and has no association with Demeter; Hades is king of the underworld and has no association with Plouton, or with agricultural wealth. But since, in his few references, Homer gives Persephone no genealogy different from that later familiar, the proof in her case is incomplete. As for Hades/Plouton, what is missing is evidence for the postulated Plouton who was a pure god of agricultural wealth unassociated with the underworld.

[47] The issue is at least recognized in H. von Prott's formulation, though I do not perfectly understand it, *AM* 24 (1899), 258: 'Θεός und Θεά ... sind Pluton und Kore, soweit der Mythos diese mit Hades und Persephone gleichgestezt hat und gleichsetzen musste, sie sind es nicht, insofern der Kultus die wesenhaften Unterschiede der ursprünglichen religiösen Vorstellung niemals verwischt hat'.

[48] *Crat.* 403a; for Eleusinian attestations see *IG* I³ 5.5 (but not 386.156: see Clinton, *Myth and Cult*, 21); *LSCG* 7.22; *IG* II² 4701, 4751; and on the Plutonium and associated cult (*IG* II² 1672.169, 182, 1933.2), which he locates beside the Eleusinion in the city, Clinton, 18–21. The location of the altar of Plouton mentioned in *SEG* XXXV 113.7 is uncertain (p. 333 above). On iconography see Clinton, 105–13, esp. 111–13 on 'Eleusinian scenes'.

most abundantly attested, and the case could be made that it was from Eleusis that his cult spread through the Greek world. In lieu of the horrors of the underworld, his name evokes the riches of the earth, and the bearded or even white-haired man we see on vases, sceptre in one hand, overflowing cornucopia in the other, is no kind of figure of terror. He can even be present as a benign spectator of the dispatch of Triptolemus or in other 'this world' contexts, as if he too, like Kore, could migrate peacefully between the worlds.[49]

Plouton's name inevitably associates him with another figure who is central to Eleusinian values (and iconography) even though he probably receives no actual cult. To those they love, we are told by the *Homeric Hymn to Demeter* (489), the Eleusinian goddesses send Ploutos, Wealth: Wealth is probably the naked boy who stands between Demeter and Kore in the most famous work of art with an Eleusinian theme, the 'Great Eleusinian relief', and is often shown with the goddesses; once a figure identical to him is named 'Eniautos', 'Year' or rather 'the produce of the year', in a helpful reminder of the primary source of wealth in this world of thought. Like Plouton, he commonly carries a cornucopia, and their names could even be playfully interchanged.[50]

Three figures remain whose functions are little known though their status as Eleusinian gods or heroes is secure. Euboulos, as we have seen, shared a priest and offerings with 'god' and 'goddess'.[51] Outside Attica a divine triad of Demeter, Kore and Zeus Eubouleus is rather widely attested. What Zeus Eubouleus is in the Greek world at large, it has been plausibly argued,[52] that Plouton is at Eleusis: a god of the underworld who is not, like Hades, utterly alien, but can be approached in cult. At Eleusis, therefore, Zeus Eubouleus was redundant and had to be remodelled as a hero. There emerged Euboulos, either son of Dysaules of Eleusis or simply an 'earth-born' Eleusinian, who gave

[49] On all this see Clinton, *Myth and Cult*, 105–13; Clinton tentatively supposes that an actual myth may have existed to this effect.

[50] Ar. *Plut.* 727 with the *Σ* vet. c, which cites Soph. fr. 273 and 283. On Ploutos see Clinton, *Myth and Cult*, 49–55, with strong arguments for detecting him in the Great Eleusinian Relief, here Fig.25 (E. B. Harrison, *Hesperia* 69, 2000, 267–92, now pleads for Eumolpus, but without fully explaining why that hero should be shown as a child; Clinton and O. Palagia reply, *AM* 118, 2003, 263–80); on the relation of Plouton to Ploutos K. Schauenberg, *JDAI* 68 (1953), 47–8. Different but still positively valued are the Ploutoi from the age of Kronos who formed the chorus of Cratinus' *Ploutoi* (see esp. fr. 171.12). Eniautos: J. Paul Getty Museum, Malibu, 86.AE.680, Apulian loutrophoros, Clinton, *Myth and Cult*, pl. 4a, here Fig.26. Note too the pelike Athens NM 16346 (Schauenburg, 42, fig. 5), which juxtaposes Plouton with a Demeter who holds a plough. 'They say that a field is the horn of Amaltheia': Phocylides fr. 7 Diehl.

[51] *IG* I³ 78.39, and n. 42. There is much debate about the identification of young male figures (who usually hold torches) in Eleusinian scenes, Iacchus, Eumolpus and Euboulos all having their partisans (see Clinton, *Myth and Cult*, 56–78 [+], and E. Simon, 'Eumolpos', *Festschrift für Walter Pötscher*, *Grazer Beiträge Suppl.* 5, Graz 1993, 35–42). In particular, one would like an agreed identification of the figure carrying the child Ploutos shown with the two goddesses on two votive reliefs found in the agora excavations and obviously deriving from the city Eleusinion (Clinton, *Myth and Cult*, figs. 9–10; Miles, *Eleusinion*, pl. 38). Clinton argues strongly for Euboulos; the case for Euboulos' importance in cult does not, however, depend on the point.

[52] Clinton, *Myth and Cult*, 60; on Zeus Eubouleus see ibid. 58, 60, n. 178.

Fig. 25. Ploutos (?) between Demeter and Kore on the 'Great Eleusinian Relief', c.450–440 BC.

Fig. 26. 'Eniautos' with Eleusis on an Apulian loutrophoros, *c*.330 BC.

Demeter information in her search for Kore and was rewarded, like his brother Triptolemus, with instruction in agriculture; in one version he was a swine-herd whose flock was sucked into the earth along with Kore, in an *aition* for the central ritual of the *Thesmophoria*. Was there also a myth which allowed him to perform greater services, more supernatural, more commensurate with his continuing prominence in the cult? A figure identifiable as Euboulos, runs an attractive recent argument, appears on vases in contexts which suggest that he might have guided Kore up to Eleusis from the underworld.[53]

---

[53] Clinton, *Myth and Cult*, 71–3. Theiler's conjecture in *Hymn Orph.* 41 (n. 133), whereby Demeter makes Euboulos immortal, would fit in well here. On the attested myths of Euboulos see Kearns, *Heroes of Attica*, 162.

Demophon is the son of the ancient Eleusinian king Keleos and Metaneira who, according to the *Homeric Hymn to Demeter*, the goddess nursed during her stay in Eleusis and vainly sought to make immortal. The *Hymn* itself mentions rites to be performed in his honour for ever, and he is probably the 'Nursling' who receives an offering among other Eleusinian figures in the calendar of Nicomachus. What is uncertain is the relevance to the *Mysteries* of this ambivalent story of a goddess's concern for a mortal. Some relevance one might expect there to be, given that the Demophon episode is a turning point in a poem which culminates in the foundation of the *Mysteries*; and when Sophocles speaks of the two goddesses as 'nursing their sacred rites' at Eleusis he has doubtless chosen his metaphor with care. But there is no independent evidence that the figure of Demophon was evoked in the great ceremony.[54] Still more mysterious is Daeira, an 'enemy of Demeter' whose rites at Eleusis the priestess of Demeter was required to shun (and vice versa). Some said she was the sister of Styx, some a watcher set by Plouton over Persephone, some Persephone herself; and still wilder speculations are recorded. For Aristophanes, we have recently learnt, she was mother of Semele. But at least two demes made her offerings in an Eleusinian context, and in 333/2 she shared in a national sacrifice of a certain scale.[55]

The role of two gods at Eleusis is controversial. Hecate is prominent in the *Homeric Hymn to Demeter*, has some place in Eleusinian scenes on vases, and in the deme Paiania is closely associated with the goddesses of Eleusis; at Eleusis itself, offerings to her, under that name at least, are not attested.[56]

---

[54] *Hymn. Hom. Dem.* 219–91 (promise of rites 265–7); Nicomachus calendar: *BSA* 97 (2002), 364, Face A, fr. 3 line 69; Soph. *OC* 1050. On all this contrast *G&R* 38 (1991), 8–10, and Clinton, *Myth and Cult*, 87, 97–8. Clinton has refuted, 100–2, the iconographic argument for taking back the identification of 'Nursling' with Triptolemus to the classical period. But I do not find it satisfactory (with Clinton) to view the Demophon incident, with its marked Eleusinian colour, as an *aition* for the *Thesmophoria*, a festival with no especial Eleusinian connections. (This theory now underlies A. Suter, *The Narcissus and the Pomegranate. An Archaeology of the Homeric* Hymn to Demeter, Michigan 2002.) Demophon's name seems now to have appeared on a sherd with an Eleusinian scene: *Fouilles de Xanthos* 9 (1992), 30–2 (only four letters of a name and the top of a *bacchos* are visible). But Peschlow-Bindokat, 'Demeter und Persephone', 141–2, has denied the presence of the child in the Eleusinian votive relief (*LIMC* s.v. *Demeter* (vol. IV. 1), no. 272) long taken to depict a child in a fire.

[55] *IG* I³ 250 A 16 (Paiania): an ἀμνὲ πρερόαρχος, sent 'to the Eleusinion'; N. Robertson, *GRBS* 37 (1996), 349 plausibly suggests a comparable restoration in the Thorikos calendar *SEG* XXXIII 147.5–6. Marathon calendar (*ZPE* 130, 2000, 45–7), col. 2. 12: a pregnant sheep worth 16 dr. in Gamelion (as Robertson notes, the offering suggests that she is functionally comparable to Demeter despite their mythological enmity). *IG* II² 1496. 102–4 records 229 dr. secured by sale of skins from victims sacrificed to her and other figures (lost in a lacuna) probably in Gamelion of 333/2 (the offering is absent from other years covered by the record). The main sources are Eust. on *Il*. 6. 378 p. 648.33 ff., which contains Pherecydes *FGrH* 3 F 45, Phanodemos *FGrH* 325 F 15 (where Jacoby prints the whole passage from Eust.), Aelius Dionysius δ 1 and Paus. Att. δ 1 Erbse; Serv. *Aen*. 4. 58; and Σ Ap. Rhod. 3.847, quoting Aesch. fr. 277 and Timosthenes *FGrH* 354 F 1; also *Etym. Magn*. 244.34–6; Lycophron 710 with Σ; Pollux 1. 35 (priestess); and for genealogy Paus. 1.38.7; Clem. Al. *Protr*. 3.45.1. Add now Ar. fr. 804 (from Phot. δ 5). See Nilsson, *Op. Sel*. II, 545–7; Clinton, *Sacred Officials*, 98.

[56] See Clinton, *Myth and Cult*, 116–20, and on Paiania (*IG* I³ 250) Nilsson, *Op. Sel*. iii, 97, where his former opinion on the place of Hecate is revised.

More important is the question of Dionysus. His sanctuary at Eleusis was physically distinct from that of the two goddesses, though important in its own right for the inhabitants of the town.[57] But in the fourth century he is shown in several Eleusinian scenes. Dionysus was an initiate, if a much less famous one than Heracles and the Dioscuri, and that myth will explain his presence in some cases. But he is sometimes paired on vases with Demeter as if on terms of absolute equality; and a chorus in Sophocles invoke Dionysus as one who rules 'in the vales, open to all, of Eleusinian Deo'.[58] Two further facts can be adduced, though they do not reduce our uncertainties but rather extend their scope. First, the only source which tells us anything specific about the content of the *Lesser Mysteries* at Agrai (usually described in the vaguest terms, but associated with Demeter and Kore) describes them as 'an imitation of the story of Dionysus'. Second, a religious offence committed in Demeter's precinct during the *Haloa* could be treated rhetorically as an act of impiety against Dionysus; this Eleusinian festival seems to have honoured the two gods jointly. As a minimalist interpretation it might be said that, in general Greek perception, cults, particularly mysteries, of Demeter and Dionysus were so closely associated[59] that vase-painters, orators and other persons not bound to precision could amalgamate them if they chose; in regard to Eleusis this could happen all the more easily because the famous Iacchus procession had a markedly Dionysiac character. A maximalist interpretation will introduce the 'Orphic' myth of Dionysus son of Persephone, and transfigure our picture of the cult … I shelve that issue for the moment.

We need not worry about lesser Eleusinian heroes. The place in Eleusinian iconography of Eumolpus, founder of the priestly *genos* of *Eumolpidai*, is very controversial, but nothing of religious importance hangs on the issue directly.[60] As for Eleusinian mythology, there is really only one myth that needs to be mentioned.[61] Demeter came to Eleusis in search of her daughter. At

---

[57] It was where decrees of the deme were displayed (Clinton, *Myth and Cult*, 125, n. 11: he reasonably calls it 'their most important sanctuary').

[58] See Metzger, *Représentations*, 248–58; *Recherches*, 49–53; 'Le Dionysos des images éleusiniennes du ivᵉ siècle', *RA* 1995, 3–22; Clinton, *Myth and Cult*, 123–5. The Mondragone relief (Kerényi, *Mysterien*, pl. 35 (*Eleusis*, pl. 42); n. 59 below) may also be from Eleusis. Clinton suggests that the pictures merely acknowledge the importance of the cult of Dionysus in the deme of Eleusis: we are given a joint image of two important but distinct Eleusinian cults. Dionysus the initiate: [Pl.] *Axioch*. 371e (I know no other literary source—contrast e.g. Xen. *Hell*. 6.3.6); G. Mylonas, Ἐλευσὶς καὶ Διόνυσος *ArchEph* 1960, 68–118. Sophocles: *Ant*. 1119–21.

[59] e.g. Paus. 2.11.3, 2. 37. 1, 8.25.3; Callim. *Hym. Dem*. 70 τόσσα Διώνυσον γὰρ ἃ καὶ Δάματρα χαλέπτει. For reliefs from Chalkis and Mondragone showing a similar combination see Clinton, *Myth and Cult*, 137 [+]; but in these Dionysus is linked more closely with Plouton or Hades than with the goddesses. *Lesser Mysteries*: n. 82. Dionysus at *Haloa*: p. 199.

[60] See nn. 50 and 51.

[61] I have given my views on the relation of the *Homeric Hymn to Demeter*, which tells the myth, to the Mysteries in *G&R* 38 (1991), 1–17; I should have cited there Riedweg, *Mysterienterminologie*, 51, on the link between 273–80 and 'mystic fire'. For a different view see Clinton, *Myth and Cult*, 28–37, 96–9 (cf. n. 54). See too now H. P. Foley, *The Homeric* Hymn to Demeter (Princeton 1993).

Eleusis she recovered her, perhaps with the aid of local inhabitants, and in gratitude 'showed the rites' and either restored corn to the earth, or bestowed it on mortals for the first time. J. H. Newman famously concluded a sermon in which he had spoken of Christ's passion with the words: 'Now I bid you recollect that He to Whom these things were done was Almighty God'. We must recollect that she who came to Eleusis was the goddess Demeter in person. These were the most momentous events ever to occur on Attic soil, more serious even than the dispute of Poseidon and Athena for possession of the land; indeed, they were perhaps the most momentous events in the history of the world, and they happened in a particular place, not so far from Athens. The other myths of Eleusinian propaganda (the mission of Triptolemus, the '*Proerosia*' myth) grew out of this first one.[62] We cannot recount the myth in a canonical Eleusinian recension, perhaps through ignorance, but more probably because even at the *Mysteries* the myth was not narrated sequentially and so had no need to assume a fixed form. But every worshipper had a version of it in his or her head as they entered the sanctuary. Demeter's advent at Eleusis propelled the Eleusinian cult in the same way that Christ's incarnation propels Christianity, in a way quite untypical therefore of the normal relation between story and rite in Greek polytheism.[63]

With that solemn proclamation, I turn to the *Mysteries*. Some points need first to be made about their place within the structures of religious life.[64] From the time at which we can first observe them, full participation in the *Mysteries* was open, on payment,[65] to male and female, slave and free (though not to children or non-speakers of Greek). Thus the all-welcoming vales of Eleusinian Deo hosted the most open of all Greek cults, one which illustrates one of the senses in which there was such a thing as 'Greek religion'. Every initiand was required to sacrifice a 'mystic piglet' 'on his own behalf'.[66] Individual offerings were commonplace in Greek religion, but at collective rituals one animal or group of animals was commonly brought 'on behalf of' all; the individualism of the *Mysteries* stands out by contrast, and reflects their

---

[62] The summary of 'what all poets and authors and historians' say about Eleusis in Aristid. *Or.* 22. 3–5 Keil (*Eleusinios*) illustrates this very well; Aristides also mentions the initiation of Heracles and the Dioscuri, and foundation of the *Eleusinia* with prizes from the newly emerged corn.

[63] Cf. Sfameni Gasparro, *Misteri e culti mistici*, 137–8.

[64] See above all Sourvinou-Inwood, 'Reconstructing Change'.

[65] Exact costs are unknown. A standard 15 drachmas per candidate is often deduced from *IG* II² 1672.207 (329/8), where the μύησις of two public slaves cost the Eleusinian sanctuary 30 drachmas. But, as Clinton has pointed out ('Sacrifice', 69–70), part of that sum may have gone on a sacrificial victim or victims; that was a variable cost, and prices in that year were extraordinarily high. There is also a problem over 'mystic piglets', perhaps paid for by the 30 dr. of that text but certainly not included among the προθύματα δο[θέντα εἰς μύ]ησιν in *ArchEph* 1971, 83, no. 4. 61–2. If they are a separate and subsequent offering (so Clinton), that is a further cost. There were also (*IG* I³ 6 C) fees, from which slaves working for the sanctuary were possibly exempt. For 'I initiate you' meaning 'I pay for your initiation' see Apollod. *Neaer.* 21–2.

[66] Ar. *Ach.* 747 with Σ vet. 747b; cf. Ar. *Pax* 374, Burkert, *Homo Necans*, 256–8.

character as a preparation for another individual experience, death. Foreigners too normally participated individually, not through representative delegations sent by their cities.[67] But, despite these divergences from the civic norms, the *Mysteries* remained in a strong sense an Athenian festival, and not just in organization or in the passionate sense of the Athenians that their welfare was tied up with them.[68] Though children in general were apparently excluded, one boy or girl was chosen to go through all the required ritual acts with especial precision on behalf of the initiates en masse. The child's title was 'the initiated from the hearth', and the best guess is that this hearth was the 'hearth of the city' in the Prytaneum; in the fourth century 'any Athenian who chose' could probably propose candidates for the 'hearth-child'.[69] Again, the 'Iacchus procession' from Athens to Eleusis is morphologically exactly comparable to the *theoria* to Brauron or any other symbolic linking of centre to periphery conducted by a Greek state. There was an Eleusinion in central Athens, at the foot of the acropolis, just as there was a Brauronion on its top. Foreign visitors did not go straight to Eleusis, but walked with their hosts from Athens. The *Mysteries* originated, it can be argued, as a civic cult without eschatological concerns.[70] It certainly seems to have been the norm for Athenians who could afford it to undergo initiation. Addressing a jury Andocides can say 'when we got back from Eleusis' after the *Mysteries*, as if all Athenians were involved. In the late hellenistic period the ephebes sacrificed at the *Mysteries* 'inside the sanctuary', which should imply that they were all initiates. In the Greek original of Terence's *Phormio* it seems similarly to have been assumed that a young man of good family would go through the rite.[71]

Almost our first administrative document relating to the *Mysteries*, from c.460, attests both the 'Mystic Truce' which facilitated participation from all parts of Greece, and the grade structure which, for anyone desiring initiation in its most perfect form, greatly complicated it. As an ideal, a candidate passed

---

[67] But *IG* II² 992 attests a Milesian *theoria*, in the first half of the 2nd c. BC (Tracy, *Attic Letter-Cutters*, 101).

[68] Attested above all by the events of 415 and their aftermath (cf. Isocr. 16.6 on the *Mysteries* as the most sensitive spot for Athenians). In organization note especially the role of the *archon basileus* and *epimeletai* (Arist. *Ath. Pol.* 57.1), and the special post-*Mysteries* assembly meeting supposedly instituted by Solon (Andoc. *Myst.* 111). But it is only by an uncertain supplement that the Eleusinian officials enjoyed dining rights in the prytaneum in the classical period (*IG* I³ 131. 4–5), as they were to do much later.

[69] On all this see Clinton, *Sacred Officials*, 98–114; id. *Myth and Cult*, 55, n. 145; the unpublished inscription that he cites (cf. p. 220) is now *Agora* XVI 56.

[70] See Sourvinou-Inwood, 'Reconstructing Change'.

[71] Andoc. *Myst.* 111; *IG* II² 1028.11; Ter. *Phormio* 49. Much later, the Cynic philosopher Demonax who lived in Athens was unpopular for 'alone of all' refusing to be initiated (Lucian, *Demonax*, 11). Stephen Todd observes to me that the decision during the crisis of 415 to 'exclude non-initiated' and then continue with an assembly meeting (Andoc. *Myst.* 12) must imply that good numbers would have stayed behind.

first through the *Lesser Mysteries* in Anthesterion,[72] then ordinary initiation at the *Great Mysteries* in Boedromion seven months later, and finally *epopteia* a year later again. There was certainly no admission to *epopteia* without prior initiation, and according to Plato there was no access at all to the *Great Mysteries* except by way of the *Lesser*;[73] but in the Roman period this was evidently not a formal requirement, or passing dignitaries could not have undergone initiation, and perhaps it never was. (There were hugely more initiands at the *Great* than at the *Lesser Mysteries* of 407/6, to judge from the takings registered in accounts for that year.)[74] What portion of felicity in the afterlife was available to a person who had passed through fewer than the full three stages we are not told. Demetrius Poliorketes took no chances and went the full course, but only after requiring the Athenians to adjust the calendar and allow him to get through the nineteen months in one.[75]

The *Lesser Mysteries* were celebrated in the sanctuary of 'Mother at Agrai', a figure distinct from Demeter though readily to be identified with her.[76] The pre-history of these arrangements is part of the deepest mystery of the *Mysteries*, not that of what was done or shown at Eleusis, but that of the emergence of eschatological mysteries within a society which may hitherto have lacked them. By the time that we can observe them, the *Lesser*

---

[72] *IG* I³ 6 B. Date of *Lesser Mysteries*: Plut. *Demetr.* 26.2 and *IG* I³6 B 36–47 (Burkert, *Homo Necans*, 265 n. 2 argues after Mommsen, *Feste*, 406, for Anthesterion 20). On grades see now K. Clinton, 'Stages of initiation in the Eleusinian and Samothracian *Mysteries*', in M. B. Cosmopoulos (ed.), *Greek Mysteries* (London 2003), 50–78. On the truce M. Sakurai, *Kodai* 5 (1994), 27–36, summarized in *SEG* XLVII 54.

[73] *Gorg.* 497c with Σ.

[74] So Clinton, *Sacred Officials*, 13, n. 13, commenting on *IG* I³ 386.144–6 (similarly Cavanaugh, *Eleusis and Athens*, 189). Even if the takings there registered are after deductions for expenses (cf. *IG* I³ 6 C 14–20) the discrepancy is very marked. Clinton observes (for this reason?— I know no other early evidence) that participation in the *Lesser Mysteries* was never a precondition for participation in the *Greater*. But the restoration ἐκ τ[ὸν Ἄγραι]σι μυστερίον (so Cavanaugh: τ[ὸν ἐν Ἄγραι]σι priores], though contextually hard to resist, is morphologically problematic (Threatte, *Grammar*, II, 378).

[75] Plut. *Demetr.* 26.

[76] The scanty testimonia about the shrine are printed in Milchhoefer, *Schriftquellen*, pp. xxiv–xxv (but Paus. 1.14.1 refers to the city Eleusinion). None names Rhea, whom Simon, *Festivals*, 27, adduces. Expressions referring to Agra/Agrai are linguistically odd in many ways: R. Simms, *GRBS* 43 (2002/3), 219–29, postulates a goddess Agra/Agraia to explain them. The 'temple beside the Ilissos' that used to be identified as the Metroon is now often given to Artemis Agrotera: see Travlos, *Pictorial Dictionary*, 112–19; C. Picon, *AJA* 82 (1978), 49, n. 8. M. Krumme, *AA* 1993, 213–27, and Robertson, 'Palladium Shrines', 392–408, have revived an old identification as the temple of Athena ἐπὶ Παλλαδίου. The claim in Σ vet. Ar. *Plut.* 845b that *Greater Mysteries* belonged to Demeter, *Lesser* to Kore is pure schematism (Burkert, *Homo Necans*, 265, n.3). H. Möbius, *AM* 60–1 (1935–6), 243–61 (cf. Vikela, *Pankrates-Heiligtum*, 71–2) stresses the proximity of Mother at Agrai to Zeus Meilichios in place and time (*Lesser Mysteries* and *Diasia* fell close together in Anthesterion). But it does not follow that the two cults were intimately related, still less that the cult of the Metroon at Agrai was originally a joint cult of Meter and Meilichios.

Mysteries are, both in aitiology and in practical administration, firmly associated with the *Greater*.[77]

The three stages are known from literature, but there was probably[78] a preliminary revealed only by inscriptions: before joining the group celebrating the *Mysteries*, each candidate had apparently to undergo an individual 'pre-initiation' administered at any time by a qualified member of the two priestly families of Eleusis. 'Pre-initiation' is a convenient term of scholarship: Greek confusingly uses the same term μύησις for both 'pre-initiation' and 'initiation'.[79] Part of the point of pre-initiation was doubtless a feeling that, in order to enter the secret place, one had already to be marked out from the uninitiated. Certain slaves at Eleusis received μύησις at the sanctuary's expense, not, we assume, from solicitude for their souls, but to allow them to perform repairs within the sacred precinct; Pausanias was warned by dreams to describe nothing which lay within the walls of the sanctuary at Eleusis, or even of the Eleusinion at Athens.[80] The relation between pre-initiation and participation at the *Lesser Mysteries*—was the one a precondition for the other?—is obscure. So too is the content of both sets of ceremonies. Three interrelated reliefs of the Roman period which show the initiation of Heracles—he is seated, hooded, on a fleece-covered chair, while a priestess holds a basket over his head or a torch at his side—ought to have a relation to the cult, because the *Homeric Hymn to Demeter* describes how the mourning goddess herself was persuaded to seat herself on a 'jointed seat' covered with a fleece (196). Perhaps this rite of 'seating' was 'pre-initiation', or a part of it. Or perhaps it formed part of the *Lesser Mysteries*, which were founded in some traditions specifically for Heracles.[81] This aside, almost all that we hear about the *Lesser Mysteries* is either vague—they are a

---

[77] The same *epistatai* were apparently responsible for both sets (*IG* I³ 386.144–6: cf. n. 77), and cf. *IG* I³ 6 B and C. This does not mean that the sanctuary of Mother at Agrai was controlled by Eleusis: it had a separate treasury, administered by the Treasurers of the Other Gods (*IG* I³ 383.50).

[78] Pre-initiation was first postulated by Pringsheim, *Archäologische Beiträge*, 38–41, was taken up by P. Roussel, *BCH* 54 (1930), 51–74, and has been generally accepted (see recently Clinton, 'Sacrifice'. 69–70; he promises a full treatment in the introduction to his *Eleusinian Inscriptions*). Much of the supporting evidence can be otherwise explained, as R. M. Simms argues, *GRBS* 31 (1990), 183–95. But an act performable by individual Eumolpids or Kerykes and described as μυεῖν is certainly attested by *IG* I³ 6 C. Simms suggests that μυεῖν is the early equivalent to what was later termed μυσταγωγεῖν (this is in effect a return to the position of Mommsen, *Feste*, 209–10); other difficulties aside, the act of μυεῖν could probably be performed in the city Eleusinion (*IG* I³ 6 C 45–6). The quantity and role of mystagogues (first attested at Eleusis by *LSS* 15, a very fragmentary decree of the 1st c. BC) is never clear (Nock, *Essays*, 793, n. 8).

[79] It is generally recognized (e.g. Deubner, *Attische Feste*, 78, n. 12; Clinton, *Sacred Officials*, 13, n. 15) that texts such as Ar. *Pax* 375 must refer to the rite at Eleusis, not pre-initiation only.

[80] See n. 65 above (slaves); Paus. 1.14.3, 1.38.7.

[81] Cf. Parker, *Miasma*, 284–85 [+]; Clinton, 'Stages of initiation' (n. 72 above), 59–60 (who argues for an indirect link, cf. *Myth and Cult*, 137–8, with pre-initiation). Heracles and the *Lesser*

Fig. 27. Roman funerary urn (Augustan period) depicting the initiation of Heracles at Eleusis.

purification preliminary to the *Greater*—or puzzling: they are 'an imitation of the story of Dionysus'.[82]

What cannot be doubted is that the scale of this building up to the *Mysteries* was something unique in Greek religious practice. In the process initiands also acquired some knowledge, as emerges from the counter case of two uninitiated Acarnanian youths who, in 200 BC, unwittingly entered the sanctuary during the *Mysteries*, betrayed themselves by ignorant questioning, and were summarily executed.[83] The more immediate preliminaries to the great ritual conducted in Boedromion were also rather complicated. 'Sacred objects' (the ones ultimately to be displayed to the initiates?), in baskets decorated with special fillets, were brought the fourteen miles from Eleusis to the Eleusinion in Athens on Boedromion 14, in order to be 'escorted back' on the 19th or 20th. The priestesses brought them in a wagon along the Sacred Road, a road very significant to the Athenians for this reason; the building of bridges both at Rheitoi near Eleusis and over the Cephisus near Athens (probably: but there was also a Cephisus near Eleusis) to ensure the safe passage of sacred objects and pilgrims was sufficiently important for both projects to be attested epigraphically.[84] A certain ritual fussiness predictably

Mysteries: Diod. Sic. 4.14.3; Steph. Byz. s.v. Ἄγρα καὶ Ἄγραι (and from this tradition John Tzetzes on Ar. *Plut.* 842 and *Ran.* 501a; in the latter case he muddles Agrai with Melite). Metzger sees pre-initiation in a pelike in Naples (H 3358) showing a mature figure offering a drink to two younger, seated men, with inscription ΜΥΣΤΑ (*Recherches*, 29–30).

[82] Purification: Σ Ar. *Plut.* 845; Clem. Al. *Strom.* 4.1.3.1 (p. 249.8–10 St.): schematism again, encouraged by actual attested purifications at them (see Parker, *Miasma*, 284). Story of Dionysus: Steph. Byz. s.v. Ἄγρα καὶ Ἄγραι· χωρίον ... τῆς Ἀττικῆς πρὸ τῆς πόλεως, ἐν ᾧ τὰ μικρὰ μυστήρια ἐπιτελεῖται, μίμημα τῶν περὶ τὸν Διόνυσον. Scholars have sometimes translated the phrase 'an imitation of Dionysiac rites' and supposed a reference to theatrical representations; but the usage of μίμημα and ὑπόμνημα in comparable contexts is decisive in favour of the translation given here (see *Liverpool Classical Monthly*, 14, 1989, 154–5). IG II² 661.9–10 attests a sacrifice.

[83] Livy 31.14.6–8.

[84] Bringing and escorting back: IG II² 1078 (3rd c. AD). Fillets: Plut. *Phoc.* 28.5. Rheitoi: IG I³ 79. Cephisus: IG II² 1191.15–23, cf. *Anth. Pal.* 9.147 (Antagoras II in Gow/Page, *HE*; for the

characterized these processions: there were stops at fixed points especially significant in Demetrian legend, and the 'sacred things' were 'met' on arrival at or near Athens. We hear of (but cannot interrelate) two such 'meetings': the ephebes went out to an unknown place called Echo, but there was also a significantly named hero called 'Receiver' or 'Host', Hypodektes, whose *orgeones* also seem to have met the *sacra* somewhere. Word of the arrival of the sacred things could then be sent formally to the priestess of Athena.[85]

On Boedromion 15 initiates assembled in the agora, and a proclamation was made excluding from the rites persons 'incomprehensible in speech' (i.e. unable to communicate clearly in Greek) and persons polluted by bloodguilt. Perhaps the initiates were also told to observe a fast, and to abstain from sexual contact and from certain foods.[86] On the 16th, the day of 'Initiates to the sea', they went with their mystic piglets to Phaleron for purification (of piglets and of themselves). The rite of 'sacrificial victims hither' attested for about this time may reveal the fate of the piglets (otherwise unknown);[87] less

Athenian Cephisus see Foucart, *Mystères*, 334 (with strong arguments), for the Eleusinian Mylonas, *Mysteries*, 184–5); both inscriptions express concern for the safety of the sacred objects. Wagon: IG II² 847.17–18 (cf. Cavanaugh, *Eleusis and Athens*, 135–43); the *sacra* were apparently dismounted and the wagon sent round for the crossing at Rheitoi (Foucart, *Mystères*, 337). On the 'Sacred Road' see Travlos, *Bildlexikon*, 177–89.

[85] Stops: Philostr. *VS* 2.20 (602), at the 'sacred fig' (on which cf. IG I³ 386.163, Cavanaugh, *Eleusis and Athens*, 194); cf. n. 93. Ephebes: e.g. IG II² 1011.7–9. Hypodektes: Kearns, *Heroes of Attica*, 75, on IG II² 2501.4–9. Word to priestess: IG II² 1078. 16–18 (3rd c. AD). By the 3rd c. AD the *sacra* were escorted all the way from Eleusis (IG II² 1078).

[86] Date: Hesych. a 864 ἀγυρμός· … τῶν μυστηρίων ἡμέρα πρώτη: it should therefore precede ἅλαδε μύσται on the 16th (Polyaenus, *Strat.* 3.11.2). For the possibility that ἱερεῖα δεῦρο belongs here see below. Proclamation: Ar. *Ran.* 369 with Σ, Isoc. *Paneg.* 157 (exclusion of barbarians); Suet. *Nero* 34.4 ('impii et scelerati'). The precise formula may be 'pure in hands and comprehensible (σύνετος) in speech', as found in Theo Sm. *De util. math.* p. 14. 23–4 Hiller and Celsus ap. Origen, *C. Cels.* 3.59 (so Foucart, *Mystères*, 311); Libanius, *Decl.* 13.19 has 'pure in hand and soul, and Greek in speech'. For the attested dietary restrictions (closely linked by Libanius loc. cit. with the main proclamation) see P. R. Arbesmann, *Das Fasten bei den Griechen und Römern* (Giessen 1929), 76–7; Parker, *Miasma*, 358 (cf. 283); sexual restrictions are plausible but unattested. A new testimonium, Philicus *Suppl. Hell.* 680.37, appears to link the fast with ἅλαδε μύσται.

[87] ἅλαδε μύσται: Polyaenus, *Strat.* 3.11.2 (cf. IG I³ 84.35–6; IG II² 847.20), illuminated by the incident(s) discussed on p. 109, n. 66. ἱερεῖα δεῦρο: this phrase, attested only in Philostr. *VA* 4.18 (μετὰ πρόρρησίν τε καὶ ἱερεῖα δεῦρο) but evidently a fixed formula, sounds like an instruction addressed to the initiates en masse, like ἅλαδε μύσται. Ar. *Ran.* 338 is usually taken to indicate that the piglets were eaten, and since the double entendre contained in the line could have been achieved without a reference to eating I still consider this plausible (but Deubner, *Attische Feste*, 75, and Clinton, 'Sacrifice', 77, have the initiates taking the piglets with them to Eleusis). ἱερεῖα δεῦρο would therefore follow the ἅλαδε ἐξέλασις (at which the animals were still alive), on the same day (Foucart, *Mystères*, 314–17, citing Rubensohn) or the next (Deubner, *Attische Feste*, 72—similarly Mylonas, *Mysteries*, 250–5—who finds support in the offerings to Demeter and Kore on this day in IG II² 1367.6, a private calendar of the Roman period). Foucart's view appears preferable, given that Deubner's pushes the *Epidauria* onto Boedromion 18, a day of attested assembly meetings (see Mikalson, *Calendar*, 56–7, who is agnostic). If ἱερεῖα δεῦρο has no connection with the sacrifice of the piglets, it could follow the proclamation on Boedromion 15 (Clinton in R. Hagg (ed.), *Early Greek Cult Practice from the Epigraphical Evidence*, Stockholm 1994, 18, and N. Robertson, *AJP* 119, 1998, 564–5). Of these scholars, only Foucart and Robertson link the formula with the piglets (and Robertson not with their sacrifice).

probably it refers to a quite different sacrifice. After Chabrias won a victory off Naxos on this day, a commemorative 'wine-pouring' was added to the festivities. There ensued for the initiates at least two days without attested activities; we are explicitly told that on one of them, on which was intercalated a procession for Asclepius, 'the initiates stay at home', a quiet phrase revealing an unprecedented form of preparation, abnegation or precaution.[88] On the 19th or 20th came the 'escorting out' of Iacchus, in the form of a statue it is generally supposed, from (we assume) the Iaccheion in Athens to Eleusis.[89] Perhaps the 'sacred things' had already been taken back in a separate procession composed of priestessess, dignitaries and ephebes, or perhaps they came back with Iacchus;[90] at all events the Iacchus procession was the one that mattered, the one that took the initiates to Eleusis en masse.

Herodotus' figure of '30,000' is hyperbole, but we should certainly think of several thousand participants.[91] The emblem of these sacred travellers (not

---

[88] Arist. *Ath. Pol.* 56.4: the day is Boedromion 17, except for those (see previous note) who put ἱερεῖα δεῦρο here. 'Wine-pouring': *Athenian Religion*, 238, n. 74.

[89] Plut. *Alc.* 34.4; *Phoc.* 28.2 (cf. *Camill.* 19.10); of the ephebes *IG* II[2] 1006.9, and often. The reading δι' ἀγορᾶς in the problematic line Ar. *Ran.* 320, ᾄδουσι γοῦν τὸν Ἴακχον ὅνπερ δι' ἀγορᾶς (the alternative is Διαγόρας) is topographically defensible if we suppose that the procession started from the Eleusinion (whence the *sacra* probably had to be fetched) and struck up the Iacchus on the way through the agora to the Iaccheion (Plut. *Aristid.* 27.4: generally identified with the temple of Demeter, containing a statue of Iacchus, beside the Pompeion, Paus. 1.2.4); cf. on all this Graf, *Orphische Dichtung*, 49.

[90] *IG* II[2] 1078.19–20 puts the escorting of the 'sacred objects' back to Eleusis on Boedromion 19. Plut. *Phoc.* 28.2 (and *Camill.* 19.10) puts the escorting of 'Iacchus' to Eleusis on the 20th. But it has always been assumed that 'sacred objects' and 'Iacchus' were escorted in a single great procession. The postulate of a 'dusk to dusk' festival day, questionable in itself, is no help in reconciling this discrepancy, since in both cases our sources are giving a time for the beginning of the procession (Clinton, 'Sacrifice', 70; cf. p. 291, n. 7). It has been suggested that we should acknowledge two distinct processions, one on Boedromion 19 of priests and officials taking back the sacred objects, one on Boedromion 20 of worshippers at large escorting Iacchus (so Mansfield, *Robe of Athena*, 437, followed by Clinton, loc. cit., and, in a different form, by N. Robertson, *AJP* 119, 1998, 547–72). But prima facie the ephebes are firmly associated both with the return of the sacred objects (*IG* II[2] 1078) and with the Iacchus procession (*IG* II[2] 1006. 9, and often), which should therefore be the same event (see too n. 93 below). Plutarch's date finds some support in Euripides (*Ion* 1075–7); the postulate of a change by the time of *IG* II[2] 1078 is possible (so W. K. Pritchett, *ZPE* 128, 1999, 85–6), but uncomfortably ad hoc.

[91] Hdt. 8.65. The only partly objective indicators are the size of the *Periclean telesterion*, which according to Noack could accommodate not more than 3000 (F. Noack, *Eleusis*, Berlin 1927, 235), and the receipts for 407–6 (*IG* I[3] 386.144–6), on the basis of which Cavanaugh, *Eleusis and Athens*, 189 (building on Clinton), suggests 2,200 initiates for that year; but if the receipts recorded there exclude 1600 dr. put aside to cover expenses (*IG* I[3] 6 C 14–20), as she supposes, we should by her logic add another 800 initiates. No one claims rigour for these figures, which are based on informed guesses about the sums payable per initiate in 407–6. It seems clear that fees paid by *epoptai* must be included in the receipts for 407–6, even though none such are mentioned in *IG* I[3] 6 (as noted by Nock, *Essays*, II, 793, n. 7); for if *mystai* alone amount to 2,400, the totals once *epoptai* are added become impossibly high, unless one postulates (see contra Nock, op. cit., 793, n. 8) repeated or separate sittings in the *telesterion*. Clinton suggests, *Myth and Cult*, 85, n. 118, that *mystai* numbered hundreds, *epoptai* thousands; this is to suppose that repeated *epopteia* was both permitted and common. Nock by contrast (793) envisages past *epoptai* as joining in the Iacchus procession but not re-admitted to the rites, except perhaps prior to the huge growth of the *Mysteries* in the late 5th c. Does evidence exist on the point? If Nock is right, we must add incalculable numbers of ex-initiates to the several thousand candidates present in the Iacchus procession.

'pilgrims': the word introduces quite inappropriate Christian associations) is a bundle, often seen in art, of what are usually taken to be myrtle branches; they are fastened together at several levels with rings, to form something resembling a short, fat staff.[92] Nothing is recorded about the ordering of the huge cavalcade, and over so long a route one might expect different participants necessarily to have gone at their own pace. Pauses were made, by privileged persons at least, for 'sacrifices, libations, dances, paians' at significant spots en route.[93] But enough of the character of a group procession remained for the chant of Iacchus which gave the god his name to be raised. And several crucial general features can be made out, from the glittering evocation by Aristophanes in *Frogs* above all.[94] The most important is excitement, exhilaration; the years fall away, the long journey becomes easy. These are Dionysiac motifs, and that is the reason for which in literature, though not in cult and probably not in iconography, Dionysus very regularly becomes Iacchus, and the Iacchus of Eleusis can become, though much less frequently, Dionysus.[95] Aristophanes' exhilarated initiates also engage in 'sport' and 'mockery' which they see as particularly appropriate to a festival of Demeter, and here two independent testimonia add their voices: from a different passage of Aristophanes we learn that the young were licensed to ridicule the old 'before the *Mysteries*', while the mockery hurled at those passing the bridge over the Cephisus near Athens was sufficiently famous for 'bridge'-related words to be used by Plutarch to characterize the pasquinades directed against Sulla by the Athenians.[96] A certain hostility to

[92] The crossed pairs at bottom centre of Clinton, *Myth and Cult*, frontispiece (the Ninnion pinax) and fig. 18 are very clear; they symbolize initiation. For examples in the hands of initiates see e.g. ibid. figs 21, 24, 31, 34, 35 and, in a rare 'group photo' of initiates, the Nigrinus relief, Deubner, *Attische Feste*, pl. 6.1 (Roman period). The common name for them in scholarship is βάκχοι, from Σ vet. Ar. *Eq.* 408a βάκχους ἐκάλουν...καὶ τοὺς κλάδους οὓς οἱ μύσται φέρουσιν. μέμνηται δὲ Ξενοφάνης ἐν Σίλλοις (B 17 D/K). ἑστᾶσιν δ᾽ ἐλάτης <βάκχοι> πυκινὸν περὶ δῶμα. Compare the κλῶνες promised to Demeter in Philicus, *Suppl. Hell.* 680.38. Pringsheim's point that μύσται there should refer only to Bacchic initiates may be over-scrupulous (*Archäologische Beiträge*, 16). C. Bérard (n. 99 below), 17, n. 1, interestingly adduces Himer. 41.1 (initiates bear φῶς καὶ δράγματα, ἡμέρου βίου γνωρίσματα), but does not (if I understand him) insist that the objects shown are corn sheaves (cf. Clinton, *Myth and Cult*, 49, n. 102, and for a link between branches and the rites of Proserpina, Serv. *Aen.* 6. 136). When initiates were bound with wool fillets (n. 93) is unknown.

[93] Plut. *Alc.* 34.4 and IG II² 1078. 29–30; the similarity of these texts, which on the 'two processions' hypothesis would relate to different processions, seems to me an argument against it. One can (with Foucart, *Mystères*, 325–39) try to guess the sites for stops from Paus. 1.36.3–38.7; attested is only purification at Rheitoi. Foucart (337) locates the rite of κροκοῦν (*Athenian Religion*, 303) at the palace of Krokon in Eleusis (Paus. 1.38.2), but this would perhaps not have been practicable with large numbers (Deubner, *Attische Feste*, 77).

[94] Ar. *Ran.* 316–459; note esp. 345–53, 398–403 (rejuvenation, ease); 374–5, 389–93 (mockery); cf. Graf, *Orphische Dichtung*, 40–50, and Dover, *Frogs*, 57–69.

[95] See Graf, *Orphische Dichtung*, 51–66, with Clinton, *Myth and Cult*, 64–71. For Eleusinian Iacchus as Dionysus see Graf, 51–2; Clinton, 66, n. 23.

[96] Young and old: see Ar. *Vesp.* 1362–5, as interpreted by J. S. Rusten, *HSCP* 81 (1977), 157–61 (but I find no reference here to 'bridge-abuse', which may be distinct). *Gephyrismos*: Hesychius γ 469 γεφυρίς· πόρνη τις ἐπὶ γεφύρας, ὡς Ἡρακλέων. ἄλλοι δὲ οὐ γυναῖκα, ἀλλὰ ἄνδρα ἐκεῖ καθεζόμενον <ἐπὶ> τῶν ἐν Ἐλευσῖνι μυστηρίων συγκαλυπτόμενον ἐξ ὀνόματος σκώμματα λέγειν εἰς

hierarchy seems therefore to prevail. Most participants walked beside heavily laden donkeys (whence the proverb 'donkey celebrating the *Mysteries*' for someone missing out on fun), but wealthy women rode on buggies. Inequalities of wealth were normally tolerated in Athens, and it was perhaps the communitarian/egalitarian ethos of the Iacchus procession which caused Lycurgus, in this one context, to attempt legislation in a vain effort to make the rich go on foot. In this rare joint cavalcade of the two sexes, awareness of others, including sexual awareness, was predictably acute.[97]

Aristophanes' Iacchus is the 'light-bringing star of the night-time rite' (343), and it is generally assumed that on arrival at the sanctuary at dusk the weary travellers will have continued to revel in his honour; a ceremonial 'reception of Iacchus' is attested.[98] Eleusinian iconography depicts, one might almost say, torches, torches, nothing but torches.[99] At this point the veil of secrecy descends, to be lifted only, on what is described as 'the last day of the *Mysteries*', to reveal a minor ritual of libation. ('Minor' in our perspective because we can say little of it; but the type of vessel used, the *plemochoe*, has been found in large numbers in the city Eleusinion and could be used as a symbol of the *Mysteries*; the day itself was called *Plemochoai*.)[100] The sequence of events during the mystic period is entirely a matter of speculative construction. Some things were shown to both grades of initiate, some to *epoptai* only, but only one detail is associated specifically with *epopteia* by a source. Recent accounts concentrate the crucial revelations, to both *mystai* and

---

τοὺς ἐνδόξους πολίτας (<ἐπὶ> Latte; <ὄν> των Radermacher; <πρὸ> τῶν J. S. Rusten, *HSCP* 81, 1977, 159); ibid. 470 γεφυρισταί. οἱ σκῶπται· ἐπεὶ ἐν ᾿Ελευσῖνι ἐπὶ τῆς γεφύρας τοῖς μυστηρίοις καθεζόμενοι ἔσκωπτον τοὺς παριόντας. H. Herter as cited by Rusten argues plausibly that glosses about γεφυρίς, term for 'eine gewöhnliche Brückenhure' without ritual reference, have got confused with those about γεφυρισταί. [Ammon.] *Diff.* no. 443 Nickau derives the term γεφυρισμός, wrongly, from squibs inscribed on bridges. For the location (the Athenian, not the Eleusinian Kephisos) see Strabo 9.1.24 (400)—the bridge will probably therefore be the one built by Xenokles, n. 84 above. Pasquinades: Plut. *Sull.* 2.2, 6.23, 13.1. The general testimony of Aristophanes to the character of the festival remains valid even if we decline to recognize γεφυρισμοί in *Ran.* 416–30 (Dover, *Frogs*, 247, compares Eupolis fr. 99 and argues that 'purely theatrical precedent is an adequate explanation'; H. Fluck, *Skurrile Riten in griechischen Kulten*, Endigen 1931, 57–8, stresses the absence of allusions to bridges in the context in Ar.).

[97] Donkey: Ar. *Ran.* 159, cf. Diogenian. 6.98; buggies: Ar. *Plut.* 1014; [Plut.] *XOrat.* 842a–b; sex: Ar. *Ran.* 409–15; *Plut.* 1013–4.

[98] *IG* II² 847. 21.

[99] Cf. C. Bérard, 'La lumière et le faisceau: images du rituel éleusinien', in *Recherches et documents du centre Thomas More* 48 (1985), 17–33.

[100] Rites of 'last day': Ath. 496a–b: one *plemochoe* was upturned to the east, one to the west, perhaps into 'a chasm in the earth' (as in Eur. fr. 592, which is quoted), to the accompaniment of a 'mystic utterance' (ῥῆσις μυστική). In AD 117/18 there was a 'sacred boule at Eleusis' (*IG* II² 1072.3, with Mikalson, *Calendar*, 61) on Boedromion 23, perhaps indicating that the *mystai* had not yet dispersed (for this concept see *Agora* XVI 56 side A 34 μέχρι δ ἂν μύσται λυθῶσιν); *Agora* XV 129.35–40 attests a meeting in the Eleusinion on Boedromion 24 in 222/1, probably an instance of the special post-*Mysteries* session (Andoc. 1.111). Plemochoe: see Miles, *Eleusinion*, 95–104. Symbol: see Clinton, *Myth and Cult*, 80 with fig. 18; ibid. 74–5 (after F. Brommer, 'Plemochoe', *AA* 1980, 544–49) on the three female figures with *plemochoai* on their heads on the Ninnion pinax.

epoptai, in a single night, but older reconstructions[101] spread over two cannot actually be refuted. (Alexander of Abonouteichos, who calqued his *Mysteries* on earlier models, had one preliminary and two substantive days.) Sacrifices also float unlocated.[102] There is no point in pressing for a precision that the evidence does not allow. What we have to work with are archaeological data; accounts, in general terms, of 'the extraordinary experience';[103] indications of the media through which the extraordinary experience was realized; and a small number of claims, usually controversial, about its actual content.

The archaeological data, complicated and controversial, can only be treated with utmost brevity here. Central among them is what, to avoid controversy, it is convenient to call the *telesterion*: a building designed to accommodate the faithful inside, and thus unique among the forms of Greek sacred architecture. Its size and shape changed in its many reconstructions, but from the point at which the *telesterion* form first emerged we have always to envisage a square or rectangular windowless building (single-storeyed, but with a lanterned roof) criss-crossed with internal columns; the initiates sat on stepped seats round the walls. Within the *telesterion*, it is generally now agreed, was a small rectangular enclosure; this is believed to have stayed in one place while the *telesterion* changed shape around it, so that it finished almost in the centre of the Periclean building whereas it had been against the wall of the 'Pisistratean' precursor.[104] Most scholars name the rectangular enclosure *anaktoron*, locate in it the throne of the hierophant, and suppose that from it emanated the central revelation which occurred, in Plutarch's phrase, 'when the *anaktora* were opened'. But it is also argued that *anaktoron/anaktora* refer always, as they certainly do sometimes, to the whole *telesterion*.[105] Even on this theory something will have been shown from the enclosure; but prior to this there will have been a revelation achieved by throwing open the doors of the *telesterion*. On either view, if to different extents, it is very difficult to see how the crucial display of sacred objects or depiction of sacred scenes could in fact have been visible to all the initiates in the room.[106] But here a robust and table-thumping response is in

---

[101] Foucart, *Mystères*, 357; so too Mommsen, *Feste*, 244–5. Alexander: Lucian, *Alex.* 38–9. All recent writers, I think, work with a single night; so explicitly Clinton, in his helpfully concrete day-by-day reconstruction in N. Marinatos and R. Hagg (eds.), *Greek Sanctuaries* (London 1993), 118–19.

[102] Those certainly attested are the sacrifices of bovines mentioned in ephebic decrees (e.g. *IG* II² 1028. 10–11). Clinton's argument, 'Sacrifice', 71–2, for location of the altars outside the sanctuary is persuasive in itself, but I am not clear how to explain αὐτοὶ ἐβουθύτησαν ἐν τῶι περιβόλωι τοῦ ἱεροῦ (*IG* II² loc cit.). About the προθύματα sacrificed by *epimeletai* of *IG* II² 847.16 we have no information.

[103] Title of the final chapter of Burkert, *Mystery Cults*.

[104] See in brief Mylonas, *Mysteries*, 78–88; 111–13; 117–24, with fig 26.

[105] So Clinton, *Myth and Cult*, 126–32, reviving the view of L. Deubner, 'Zum Weihehaus der eleusinischen Mysterien', *AbhBerl* 1945/46, no. 2; dissent in Sourvinou-Inwood, 'Reconstructing Change', 46, n. 14. I find Clinton's view of the key Plutarch text (*De prof. virt.* 10, 81d–e) hard.

[106] Graf, *Orphische Dichtung*, 128–9.

order: we know that the initiates did see the sacred objects, even if we do not understand how. It is illegitimate to use the problem of visibility as an argument against certain kinds of representation ('sacred drama'), when it applies equally to those representations which we know, beyond a peradventure, to have occurred.

Plutarch in a famous passage divides the mystic experience into three stages: first one of confused and weary wandering in the dark (as part of the ritual, it is implied;[107] but elsewhere he characterizes this stage as simply one of uncomfortable jostling in a crowd); then 'every kind of terror, shivering and trembling and sweat and amazement'; finally light and exultation and entry (metaphorical, we presume) into a sweet meadow landscape. The context in Plutarch is a comparison between initiation and death, and this will have shaped his emphases; but we can retain the idea that the final mood was meant to be one of exhilaration, an exhilaration which anticipated the blessedness of the afterlife.[108]

Initiation is a thing experienced, not a thing learnt, according to Aristotle's fine aphorism.[109] Yet initiates are sometimes said to know things that other people do not: only initiates may hear, Isocrates tells us, the services done for Demeter by the inhabitants of Eleusis, while according to Pausanias the grounds for the antipathy between Demeter and the bean are familiar to 'anyone who has seen the rite at Eleusis'; initiates know why certain parts of certain animals may not be eaten, adds Clement. Despite Pausanias' 'anyone who has seen the rite', not all these items could readily have been conveyed by mime. Some preparatory teaching has therefore to be supposed, though how it was conveyed (at pre-initiation?) is unclear.[110] Eumolpus, mythical ancestor of the hierophants, is etymologically 'fair singer', and an epitaph speaks of a hierophant 'pouring forth a lovely voice':[111] it is generally and plausibly supposed that within the *telesterion* there was some intoning of 'sacred cries' but little if any discourse in prose.

---

[107] Aliter Graf, *Orphische Dichtung*, 136–7.

[108] Fr. 178 Sandbach, first para.; this fragment is ascribed to Themistius by the source Stobaeus, but phrases from it are quoted by Clement of Alexandria writing long before Themistius. Style and content point to Plutarch (cf. Graf, *Orphische Dichtung*, 132, n. 26). 'Jostling': id. *De prof. virt.* 10, 81d–e.

[109] Fr. 15 Rose. But Aristotle presupposes prior learning, according to Burkert, *Mystery Cults*, 69, and Riedweg, *Mysterienterminologie*, 127–9.

[110] Isocr. *Paneg.* 28; Paus. 1.37.4; Clem. Al. *Strom.* 2.20.106.1 (p. 171.2–5 St.). Foucart, *Mystères*, 282–4, thinks of preliminary instruction imparted by mystagogues (cf. Plut. *An seni* 23, 795d, μανθάνων καὶ μνούμενος contrasted with διδάσκων καὶ μυσταγωγῶν), except for the detail about the beans, which he supposes to have been actually revealed in the *telesterion* (466). On 'teaching' as a stage in the mystic process as recognized in the platonist tradition (e.g. Clem. Al. *Strom.* 5.11.71.1 (p. 374.1–2 St.)) see Riedweg, *Mysterienterminologie*, 2–29; he argues, not to me convincingly, that a 'purification-teaching-revelation' structure already underlies Pl. *Symp.* 201e–212.

[111] *IG* II² 3639.4 (2nd c. AD).

The dominant language in early texts is of 'showing' or even just 'doing' the *Mysteries*.[112] From Lucian we learn that the slang expression of his day for the profanation of *Mysteries* was not to 'speak them out' but 'dance them out', and late texts speak repeatedly of σχήματα, perhaps gestures, perhaps more elaborate dance figures.[113] A gesticulating or dancing hierophant (or troupe consisting of hierophant, daduch, herald, priestesses) is not attested in earlier sources, but doubtless should not be ruled out. It was the central role played by this individual or small cadre of individuals that allowed the *Mysteries* to be impiously 'imitated' in private houses in 415. But in the *telesterion* itself there were also 'apparitions' (already attested in Plato), doubtless of a frightening kind; support can also be found in Plato for the showing of statues of gods.[114] One striking sound is attested, the banging of a gong by the hierophant to accompany an invocation of Kore, and there may have been many. But more expressive than sound seems to have been the hush which filled the large hall at crucial moments and perhaps even for crucial stretches of time. Above all there were light effects. Plutarch speaks of a great light at a climactic moment, Dio of 'the alternation of darkness and light' in the mystic experience, and the attestations, in literature and in art, of torches, light and 'mystic fire' are numerous indeed.[115] It would be an exhausting and perhaps a vain task to attempt to sort them into different classes—torches outside the *telesterion*, torches inside the *telesterion*, fire inside the *telesterion*, and so on. In Eleusinian symbolism, flame feeds on flame, starting with the torches carried by Demeter in her search for Kore,[116] prolonged in those of Iacchus and his worshippers, culminating in the great light revealed according to Plutarch at the 'opening of the *anaktoron*'. Kore's iconography as a torch-bearing maiden is a model instance of a deity acquiring attributes from the ritual by which she is honoured.[117]

---

[112] See Burkert, *Homo Necans*, 287, n. 63, quoting texts relating to the profanation in 415. His whole discussion of mystic media, 286–8, is most useful. Texts relating to the profanation provide positive rather than negative evidence: we cannot say that a thing did not occur at Eleusis simply because it was not imitated by the profaners; they were anything but bound by a pious obligation to reproduce every detail.

[113] Lucian, *Salt.* 15; σχήματα: see Burkert, *Homo Necans*, 288 (Cleanthes supposedly already spoke of μυστικὰ σχήματα, *SVF* I, no. 538, from Epiphanius).

[114] Apparitions: Pl. *Phaedr.* 250c, Burkert, *Homo Necans*, 288, n. 64. Statues: the soul in Pl. *Phaedr.* 254b, a context replete with mystic language, catches sight of beauty '*on a pure base*': see Riedweg, *Mysterienterminologie*, 61–2, and for a suggestion about the technology of apparitions and statue display Clinton, *Myth and Cult*, 89. On showing of statues at Eleusis (an old idea) cf. P. Boyancé, *REG* 75 (1962), 464, 469–70 (appealing to Sen. *Ep.* 90.28).

[115] Gong: Apollodorus *FGrH* 244 F 110b; this may in fact have occurred out of doors. Hush: Plut. *De liberis educandis* 14, 10 f.; *De prof. virt.* 10, 81d–e; Hipp. *Haer.* 5.8.39–40. Light: Plut. fr. 178 (first para.), Dio. Chrys. *Or.* 12.33; Riedweg, *Mysterienterminologie*, 48.

[116] It is in some ways curious that in art it is Kore, not Demeter, who is regularly shown with torches. But the two had to be differentiated, and a significant iconography was available for Demeter: her seated posture conferred dignity and might evoke mourning, particularly when she was shown on the 'mirthless rock' (discussed by Clinton, *Myth and Cult*, 14–27).

[117] For Persephone shown with a '*bacchos*' (cf. n. 92) see C. Bérard, *Recherches et documents du centre Thomas More* 48 (1985), 21, who comments 'l'imagerie est l'espace idéal dans lequel s'épanouit la transcendance religieuse'.

I come now to the content of the revelations, but first the 'password' given by Clement must be mentioned: 'I fasted, I drank the kykeon, I took from the hamper (κίστη), after working I deposited in the basket (κάλαθος) and from the basket to the hamper'.[118] So the *mystai* are required by the ritual to state that they have fasted and drunk *kykeon* like the grieving Demeter of the *Homeric Hymn*. As for the third group of acts, this is language which, as it were, plays at secrecy, omitting the grammatical object which the verbs require if they are to be understood by an outsider. If one is, none the less, to speculate what the *kiste* contained, the best guess may be those corn-grinding instruments which we know from Theophrastus to have had a role in certain secret rituals.[119] (The reference is doubtless to Eleusis even if not to this precise act.) When the initiate made his or her declaration is not recorded. But all this eager grinding cannot have formed part of the ceremony in the *telesterion*; it occurred at an earlier stage, if it occurred at all.

The goal of the *Mysteries* is eschatological; the cult's promise of a blessed afterlife is repeated with remarkable consistency over many centuries. Nineteenth-century scholarship accordingly postulated, not unreasonably, that after-death experience was somehow dramatized in the *Mysteries*.[120] The hypothesis is universally abandoned today. It is objected that a journey through the underworld of the type then postulated could not have been conducted in a *telesterion* such as archaeology has revealed.[121] But we could give up on the idea that each individual initiate pre-enacted his or her own post mortem wanderings, and still suppose that the afterlife was depicted or evoked in less elaborate ways. The weakness of the old position is that it is based on probability more than on specific testimony.[122] Yet the allusions to

---

[118] Clem. Al. *Protr.* 2.21.2 ἐνήστευσα, ἔπιον τὸν κυκεῶνα, ἔλαβον ἐκ κίστης, ἐργασάμενος ἀπεθέμην εἰς κάλαθον καὶ ἐκ καλάθου εἰς κίστην. The preceding chapter in Clem. on Baubo is widely agreed to ascribe to Eleusis an orphic expansion of the Eleusinian myth (Burkert, *Homo Necans*, 285), and some doubt even the authenticity of the formula given here (Mylonas, *Mysteries*, 200–5 and works cited by Burkert, *Homo Necans*, 270, n. 20, who dissents).

[119] In Porph. *Abst.* 2.6: once men of old learnt how to bruise and grind corn they made a secret of the instruments they used and treated them as sacred objects (κρύψαντες εἰς ἀπόρρητον ὡς ἱεροῖς αὐτοῖς ἀπήντων), as having provided a godlike assistance to human life: already linked with Eleusis by J. Bernays, *Theophrastos' Schrift über Frommigkeit* (Berlin 1866), 272; cf. Burkert, *Homo Necans*, 272. For a review and critique of the phallographic fantasies woven by scholars around Clement's password see Deubner, *Attische Feste*, 81–3 (grossest is that of Kern, reported 81, n. 5); cf. Burkert, *Homo Necans*, 269–74.

[120] See especially Foucart, *Mystères*, 389–414; on p. 392 he writes 'le voyage des mystes à travers les régions du monde inférieur, figurées dans le télestèrion, est un fait généralement admis'. Wilamowitz denied every form of 'drama' at Eleusis, but regarded it as certain that symbols of Kore's rule over both earth and underworld were displayed (*Glaube*, II, 57). On the promise see *Hymn. Hom. Dem.* 480–2, with the note of Richardson, *Hymn to Demeter*, ad loc.

[121] So Mylonas, *Mysteries*, 268–9, citing Noack, and Graf, *Orphische Dichtung*, 128–31.

[122] For this one can cite only Lucian, *Cataplus*, 22 (recently discussed by C. G. Brown, *CQ* 41, 1991, 41–50: dismissed by Burkert, *Homo Necans*, 280, n. 28) and perhaps the anonymous Hadrianic rhetorical exercise PUniv.Milan no. 20, pp. 176–7 (D63 Scarpi), which could as well imply for the *Mysteries* an underworld environment as an epiphany of Kore (which was the view of Otto and Kerényi, discussed by Burkert, *Homo Necans*, 286: on this text see now D. Colomo, *ZPE* 148, 2004, 87–98). In Idomeneus of Lampsacus *FGrH* 338 F 2 (also discussed by Brown) the

'apparitions' and, still more, to 'every kind of terror, shivering and trembling and sweat and amazement', give it some general support. The easiest answer to the question 'what were these fearsome apparitions?' is surely 'figures from the underworld', who would in the end have been revealed as mere bogeys.

That, however, is speculation; I revert to testimony. Many scholars suppose two 'sacred dramas' to have been played out at the *Mysteries*—dramas in the sense of 'mythical sequences', variously evoked, not of formal presentation on a stage. The main sources are, inevitably but problematically, Christians who felt themselves exempt from the rule of secrecy.[123] Much the better attested is Demeter's search for the lost Kore. 'Deo and Kore have become by now a mystic drama, and Eleusis holds the torch over the wanderings and the rape and the grief of the two' (Clement); 'among us Kore is not carried off, nor does Demeter wander and bring in Celeuses and Triptolemuses and snakes, and perform some acts and undergo others. I am ashamed to reveal to the day the rite of night, and make indecency a mystery! Eleusis knows of this, and those who are spectators (*epoptai*) of these acts about which silence is observed, and which truly deserve silence' (Gregory of Nazianzus); 'Proserpina is sought with lighted torches, and when she is found the whole rite concludes with celebration and throwing of torches' (Lactantius). With these texts belongs 'Why is the priestess of Ceres abducted, if Ceres was not treated in the same way?' (Tertullian), if we suppose a confusion between Ceres (Demeter) and Persephone.[124] Strong pagan underpinning for all this comes from Isocrates' statement that only initiates may hear the services performed for wandering Demeter by the inhabitants of Eleusis; and Proclus says that 'the rites have transmitted among their secrets certain sacred laments of Kore and Demeter and of the greatest goddess herself'.[125]

The 'mystic drama' of most of these texts could have been enacted indoors by a small number of cult officiants, with the initiates as spectators. But Lactantius implies an outdoor setting and initiates who participate energetically. The hunt for Kore would fit well with the first stage of Plutarch's three

subject of the phrase ἀπὸ σκοτεινῶν τόπων ἀνεφαίνετο τοῖς μυουμένοις appears to be 'Aeschines' mother', which means that the μυούμενοι will be those initiated by her in private rites, not Eleusinian candidates, despite the choice of verb. Apparitions: n. 114 above. Terrors: Plut. fr. 178.

[123] Two Christian claims about the content of the *Mysteries* (Clement on Baubo, n. 118 above; Tert. *Adv. Valent.* 1 on a phallus as object of the revelation) are too generally rejected to merit discussion in the text. But the selectivity that has gone into standard accounts of the *Mysteries* should not be forgotten. Riedweg, *Mysterienterminologie*, 116–23, argues that Clem. *Protr.* 2.12–23.1 derives in the main (13.1–21.2) from a Hellenistic handbook; Clement was not revealing secret knowledge if so.

[124] Clem. Al. *Protr.* 2.12.2; Gregory Nazianzenus *Or.* 39.4 (vol. 36 p. 337b Migne); Lactant. *Div. Inst. Epit.* 18.7; Tert. *Ad. nat.* 2.7. For an explanation of the confusion in Tertullian see Mylonas, *Mysteries*, 310–11 (followed by Sourvinou-Inwood, 'Festival and Mysteries', 29) : the Eleusinian cult was served by a joint priestess of Demeter and Kore, and 'the priestess of Demeter was abducted, *but it was in the role of Persephone* that she was abducted'. Foucart, *Mystères*, 476, referred the passage to the 'sacred marriage': Zeus' wooing was a little rough ... This passage aside, no source points to depiction of the rape itself (Clinton, *Myth and Cult*, 85, n. 113).

[125] Isocr. *Paneg.* 28; Procl. *In R.* 1.125.20–2.

stages of initiatory experience, that of confused and weary wandering. And searches by worshippers for gods are found in other Greek cults; this part of the ritual can be related to the general and pervasive desire for a deity's advent, as well as to the specific myth of Kore's return from the underworld.[126] The collective outdoor search is too good to lose. Perhaps the details in the other accounts which seem to imply an indoor setting, and spectatorship, are inauthentic. Perhaps the myth was evoked more than once, in different places.[127]

The second sacred drama postulated by scholarship is a marriage.[128] It is very much less well attested than the first. The only unambiguous statement comes from Asterius, bishop of Amaseia c.400.

> Was it not you who deified Demeter and Kore in your folly, and you built temples for two females and you honour them with sacrifices and prostrate yourself before them with all kinds of devotion? Are not the *Mysteries* at Eleusis the core of your worship, and do not the people of Attica and the whole of Greece pour together to initiate folly? Is the dark crypt not there and the solemn meeting of the hierophant with the priestess, the two alone together? Are not the torches extinguished while the whole huge crowd believes its salvation to lie in the things done by the two in the dark?

Excavation has shown the answer to Asterius' question 'is the dark crypt not there?' to be 'no'; but the one slip does not necessarily discredit the whole report.[129] Those who believe it usually take 'hierophant and priestess' to have enacted the roles of Zeus and Demeter, on the basis of a scholion to Plato which records that 'these [the *Mysteries*] were celebrated for Deo and Kore, because Plouton abducted Kore, and Zeus had intercourse with Deo.' But the scholion to Plato appears to be abbreviating a passage of Clement in which the 'Mysteries of Deo' in question are not Eleusinian at all, but Phrygian.[130] And it is hard to see what religious relevance Zeus' union with Demeter might have to the other themes of the *Mysteries*.[131] The hierophant and priestess could have

---

[126] On all this see Sourvinou-Inwood, 'Festival and Mysteries'. Clinton also defends an outdoor setting: see his (confessedly hypothetical) detailed reconstruction in *Myth and Cult*, 84–95, summarized in N. Marinatos and R. Hagg (eds.), *Greek Sanctuaries* (London 1993), 118–19.

[127] So Sourvinou-Inwood, 'Festival and Mysteries'.

[128] Foucart, *Mystères*, 475, claims to have been the discoverer of it, in his *Recherches sur l'origine et la nature des Mystères d'Eleusis* (Paris 1895), 48. Deubner, *Attische Feste*, 84–7, follows him, on the basis of Tert. *Ad nat.* 2.7 (above n. 124), Clem. *Protr.* 2.15 and *Σ* Pl. *Gorg.* 497c—suspect witnesses, for reasons given in the text. The old argument (e.g. Foucart, 481; Harrison, *Prolegomena*, 550) that the sacred marriage in the cult established by Alexander of Abonouteichos (Lucian, *Alex.* 38–39) is based on an Eleusinian model still has some force, despite the objections of Mylonas, *Mysteries*, 315–16; on Alexander's bricolage see most recently A. Chaniotis, *Electrum* 6 (2002), 67–85.

[129] Contrast Mylonas, *Mysteries*, 311–16; Burkert, *Homo Necans*, 284, n. 47. Asterius: *Homily* 10.9.1 (ed. C. Datema, Leiden 1970; D45 Scarpi); in the first sentence I read ἐδείμω δὲ δύο γυναίοις (so O: γυναίους codd. cet.) ναούς.

[130] *Σ* Pl. *Gorg.* 497c. See Mylonas, *Mysteries*, 289–91; Burkert, *Homo Necans*, 266, n. 7 (where read Clem. *Protr.* 2.15) and 283.

[131] It is sometimes seen as 'the marriage of heaven and earth', the source of growth; the mystic cry 'rain, conceive' is compared (so e.g. Deubner, *Attische Feste*, 86). But this very unanthropomorphic interpretation would be odd, in a cult which otherwise makes such use of anthropomorphic myth.

been imitating a quite different couple. Scandalous behaviour on the part of Demeter is clearly hinted at in the phrase of Gregory quoted above: among us Christians, 'nor does Demeter wander and bring in Celeuses and Triptolemuses and snakes, and perform some acts and undergo others.' According to a scholiast on Aristides, Demeter gave herself to the Eleusinian king Celeus.[132] This is doubtless the story to which Gregory alludes. To pagan Greeks it need not have been a scandal, since communities' claims to divine favour were often grounded in myths of sexual union between gods and mortals (though usually, it is true, the divine partner is male). But Christian authors sowed with the whole sack when attacking pagan mysteries, and Gregory might not have scrupled to ascribe what he judged a shameful tale about the goddess of the *Mysteries* to the rite itself, even if it was not there represented.[133]

In addition to the anonymous union, an anonymous birth is, rather more reliably, attested. It is an easy assumption that the child was born of the union, but, since we know nothing of the sequence of these events, nor of the *Mysteries*' concern for tidiness or sequential logic, not an inescapable one. The source for the birth is a Gnostic treatise from which long sections are quoted by bishop Hippolytus; it consists of a series of identifications between 'the first origin of all things' which is 'man and the son of man' and a succession of gods and religious phenomena, and uses material culled, it is argued, from a pagan commentary on a hymn to Attis. One such identification is, incidentally, with 'that great mystery of the Eleusinian rites, "rain, conceive"', but the passage that concerns us here (the only passage in our sources that refers specifically to *epopteia*) runs:

The Phrygians also call it [the first principle] a 'harvested green corn stalk', and after the Phrygians the Athenians, when they initiate in the Eleusinian rites and show to *epoptai* what is the great, marvellous, most perfect epoptic mystery there, an ear of corn harvested in silence.[134] This ear is among the Athenians too the perfect great beam of light from the undefined, just as the hierophant—not castrated, like Attis, but made a eunuch by hemlock and cut off from all fleshly procreation[135]—conducting at night in Eleusis amid many flames those great unmentionable *Mysteries* calls and cries 'the reverend goddess has born a child, Brimo Brimos', that is the strong one has born a strong child.[136]

---

[132] *Σ* in Aristid. p. 53.15–16 Dindorf.

[133] Foucart, *Mystères*, 469–70, claims that Gregory has ascribed to the *Mysteries* a myth known to him from Orphic poetry. But all he adduces is a difficult passage of the Orphic Hymns (41.8) which may (but note a neat conjecture by W. Theiler, *Philologus* 94, 1940–1, 247, accepted in G. Ricciardelli's recent ed.) make Demeter mother of Eubouleus by a mortal.

[134] Normal word order recommends this rendering, but 'showing to *epoptai* in silence' is easier sense (on the problem see Foucart, *Mystères*, 433–4).

[135] On the temporary chastity imposed on the hierophant and in late antiquity apparently reinforced by antaphrodisiac drugs see Parker, *Miasma*, 88, n. 55.

[136] Hippol. *Haer*. 5.8.39–41 (E20 Scarpi: for 'rain, conceive' see ibid. 5.7.34, D59 Scarpi); on the gnostic writer see J. Frickel, *Hellenistische Erlösung in christlicher Deutung: die gnostische Naasenerschrift* (Leiden, 1984: brief summary in Clinton, *Myth and Cult*, 94, n. 167; text and commentary in M. Simonetti, *Testi gnostici in lingua greca e latina*, Fondazione Valla 1993, 50 ff.).

Even if we accept the authenticity of the information given us by the Gnostic, we remain uncertain what he is telling us. Brimo can be Hecate or Demeter or Persephone or an independent goddess.[137] Initiates may, or may not, have known which she was in this case. A tidy suggestion is that she was Demeter and her son was (as often) Wealth.[138] The child Ploutos is a regular figure in Eleusinian iconography. The Gnostic appears, in his dark way, to associate the revelation of a silently harvested ear of corn with the loud proclamation of the birth of a child, and evidently the ear could well symbolize Wealth born of Demeter. Yet one might expect the strong child born to the strong mother to do something with his life. After his birth, Wealth has no history.

Are there other candidates for the child? 'Demeter suckling Iacchus' (whom she must also have born) was a proverbial concept in the ancient world, perhaps already hinted at on an extraordinary sherd of a bell krater from Al Mina, which shows a young Iacchus or Dionysus seated on the goddess's lap.[139] But in religious terms a 'birth of Iacchus' would have been a rather weak climax; Iacchus has nothing to offer mankind beyond the mystic experience itself. Persephone, however, is also said to be Iacchus' mother,[140] and herewith the position becomes complicated, because, on the one hand, Iacchus was often assimilated to Dionysus, and on the other Persephone was mother of that alternative Dionysus who in Orphic myth was a key eschatological figure. We duly find it said in some texts that 'Dionysus son of Persephone' is honoured at Eleusis;[141] and a famous pelike in St Petersburg, which has the child Ploutos among Eleusinian deities on one side, shows what may be the emergence from the earth of Dionysus son of Persephone on the other.[142] A representation at Eleusis of the birth of the Orphic Dionysus

[137] See Burkert, *Homo Necans*, 289, n. 71. Her recent appearance on an 'orphic' gold tablet from Pherai confirms her place among the 'mystic personnel' of the classical period, but not necessarily in that of Eleusis (Pugliese Carratelli, *Lamine d' oro*, 123; SEG 45.646).

[138] So recently Clinton, *Myth and Cult*, 91–5; this is the commonest view (see e.g. Deubner, *Attische Feste*, 85, with references).

[139] Lucr. 4.1168 (where 'Ceres ab Iaccho' is a lover's euphemism for a girl with swollen breasts), whence Arnob. 3.10; Suda ι 16 Ἴακχος. Διόνυσος ἐπὶ τῷ μαστῷ; Σ Aristid. p. 648.15–16, Ἴακχο 21–3 Dindorf (where Demeter is explicitly identified as mother); cf. Graf, *Orphische Dichtung*, 198. The sherd (Oxford 1956, 355): Metzger, *Recherches*, pl. 25.2; Nilsson, *Geschichte*, pl. 53.1; *LIMC* s.v. *Iakchos*, no. 8; cf. Clinton, *Myth and Cult*, 91, n. 146; Metzger, *RA* 1995, 10.

[140] Σ Eur. *Or.* 964 and *Tro.* 1230; Σ vet. Ar. *Ran.* 323b ('Dionysus': but the verse commented on speaks of Iacchus); O. Kern in *RE* s.v. *Iakchos*, 621–2. This Dionysus/Iacchus had intercourse with Demeter, according to Σ Ar. *Ran* loc. cit.

[141] 'Just as the Athenians reverence Dionysus the son of Zeus and Kore, a different Dionysus this one, and it is for this Dionysus, not the Theban, that the mystic Iacchus is sung' (Arr. *Anab.* 2.16.3); cf. Σ Pind. *Isth.* 7.3a, κατὰ μὲν τὸν μυστικὸν λόγον ... παρεδρεύει αὐτῇ ὁ ἐκ Περσεφόνης γεγονώς Ζαγρεὺς Διόνυσος, ὁ κατά τινας Ἴακχος. 'Kaum mehr als Frucht theologischer Systematisation', according to Graf, *Orphische Dichtung*, 75–6.

[142] On the scene see above all Graf, *Orphische Dichtung*, 66–78 (+); Bérard, *Anodoi*, 147–51; on the other face of the vase (St Petersburg, ST 1792; *ARV* 1476, 1), Clinton, *Myth and Cult*, 134. A case that the Dionysus shown is the son of Semele is still made (after C. Robert) by H. Metzger, *RA* 1995, 7–8. On the Orphic Dionysus see A. Powell (ed.), *The Greek World* (London 1995), 494–8 [+].

would be, so to speak, eschatological dynamite; it would change the whole base on which the cult's promises about the afterlife were grounded. But for that very reason it is rather hard to believe in. The Orphic Dionysus brings with him a baggage of un-Eleusinian myth which most initiates will not have known. If the *Mysteries* consisted primarily in 'showing', not teaching, it is unlikely that the hierophant set out to expound all this as one of the secret doctrines of the cult. But if the hierophant did, the Orphic writings on these subjects would have been profanations of the *Mysteries*; yet they circulated without complaint. Perhaps 'Wealth' is after all the best candidate for the child.

If such was indeed the climactic revelation, the eschatological *Mysteries* issued in reassurance relating to life in this world. An interweaving of concern for the crops and for the afterlife is already central to the *Homeric Hymn to Demeter*. To explain the association, moderns often appeal to the 'rebirth' of corn as a symbol of human survival after death:[143] 'Verily, verily, I say unto you, Except a corn of wheat fall in to the ground and die, it abideth alone: but if it die, it bringeth forth much fruit' (John 12: 24). And they remind us that the dead at Athens were known as 'Demetreioi', and that since the time of Cecrops it had been the custom to scatter corn upon the earth of the newly covered grave. The hope would have been to undo the contrast, familiar to ancient poets, between the recurrence of the seasons and the final doom of men.[144] Yet, it has been objected, what Eleusinian initiates aspired to was not a perennial cycle of living and dying, like that of the corn, but a single and final entry upon a blessed existence. That objection may press the details of a religious symbol too hard. But there is no clear metaphorical connection in Greece between the cycle of crops and ideas of death and rebirth; the dead are probably 'Demetrian' simply because they have been laid in earth, Demeter's realm.[145]

However all this may be, for the worshipper the central point of contact between agriculture and the afterlife is not a concept but a goddess. The *Mysteries* are powerful in both areas because so is Kore. Some think the 'harvested blade of corn' mentioned by the Gnostic writer as the climactic revelation is her.[146] We come back at this point to the significance of myth for

[143] Richardson, *Hymn to Demeter*, 15, with citation of an eloquent passage of Frazer and further references. Demetreioi: Plut. *De fac.* 943b; corn: Cic. *Leg.* 2. 63 (but Cicero's explanation is 'ut sinus et gremium quasi matris [i.e. the soil] mortuo tribueretur, solum autem frugibus expiatum vivis redderetur', thus markedly failing to associate the corn with rebirth). For bringing of an 'all-seed' to graves see p. 296, n. 32.
[144] [Moschus] *Epitaph. Bion.* 99–104; cf. Hor. *Od.* 1.4, with the commentary of Nisbet and Hubbard ad loc.
[145] For variations on these objections see Foucart, *Mystères*, 473; E. Rohde, *Psyche*, ed. 8 (Tübingen 1921), 292 (p. 224 in the tr. by W.B. Hillis); W. F. Otto, 'Der Sinn der eleusinischen Mysterien', in *Die Gestalt und das Sein* (Darmstadt 1959), 313–38, at 318–19. The agricultural cycle symbolizes the succession of generations, not rebirth: Eur. *Hypsipyle* fr. 60.93–6 Bond, Eur. fr. 415.
[146] So Nilsson, *Op. Sel.* ii, 606; W. F. Otto, op. cit.; Sourvinou-Inwood, 'Festival and Mysteries', 37.

the *Mysteries*. The *Mysteries* commemorated Kore's return after the rape, from which derived her unique status as a commuter between the two worlds. Such a movement between the two worlds was not what the *mystes* aspired to, but it was (we assume) as a commuter that the goddess was also a mediator, both Kore, the inoffensive maiden who could be imagined seated on her mother's lap,[147] and Persephone, who slept in the arms of the king of the dead. The return of Kore betokened the opening of communication between the two worlds and the possibility for mortals of winning the favour of the queen of the underworld. The finding of Kore, who though not reducible to the corn in some sense still was it,[148] promised fields yellow with corn. Kore's partner was Plouton, a king of the underworld with softened outlines, and one who bespoke wealth in his very name.

This survey has been full of doubts, ambiguities, failures to come clean. But there is a question that can be posed to circumscribe our uncertainties.[149] Would the secret of Eleusis, could we know it, come as a surprise? Anyone familiar only with standard panhellenic mythology would have found some parts of the Orphic poems surprising indeed. Did Eleusis offer a radically novel vision in the same way? The question is, of course, unanswerable. Some idiosyncrasies are possible. But nothing suggests that the answer would, on a large scale, have been 'yes'; this was a cult of showing, not of teaching, and the ideas that it deployed were almost necessarily those that the initiates brought with them to the *telesterion*. It worked by making familiar myth more vivid and immediate to the worshippers than did any other Greek cult. Demeter revisited Eleusis, refound her daughter, reiterated her pledge to Eleusis and to those who came to Eleusis in order to celebrate the rites which she herself had instituted. In a sense the *Mysteries* worked automatically, *ex opere operato*: even a worshipper who took nothing emotionally from the experience but an unpleasant memory of shoving and wandering in the dark was still a beneficiary of the mystic promise. But at a deeper level it was the collective emotional involvement (or at least the illusion of such) that sustained the rite.

What does one do after being granted a vision of, in Pindar's words, 'the end of life and its god-given beginning?' Some suppose that the new initiates wandered amid the meadows of Eleusis, to anticipate the pleasures of the Elysian fields.[150] Two sources say, but perhaps not in relation to Eleusis, that

---

[147] As in the famous group (from Eleusis) *LIMC* s.v. *Demeter* (vol. IV.1), no. 290.

[148] For an excellent treatment of this complicated relation see Burkert, *Homo Necans*, 260–61. Kore = grain: Eubulus fr. 75.10, Antiphanes fr. 55.9.

[149] It goes back in effect to C. A. Lobeck, *Aglaophamus* (Regimontii Prussorum 1829), which argues 'Graecorum mysteria erudiendis hominum ingeniis non instituta, neque a sacris publicis quidquam diversa fuisse' (5 and *passim*). Cf. E. Rohde, *Psyche*, ed. 8 (Tübingen 1921), 289, 'it was difficult to let out the "secret", for there was essentially no secret to let out' (p. 222 in the tr. by W.B. Hillis, which I quote). Kerényi's argument that familiar myth cannot have formed the subject of a 'mystic drama' goes against all this, unpersuasively (*Die Mysterien*, 39–40).

[150] Burkert, *Homo Necans*, 292. Pindar: fr. 137 Snell/Maehler.

it was only at this stage that the *mystes* was crowned.[151] The last day may have been a day of sacrifices, of feasting therefore, as well as of libations; but all details escape us. Some 'après mystères' conviviality is certainly attested, and groups of friends attended the *Mysteries* together.[152] Perhaps they did so year after year, though the rules for 'post-epoptic' attendance are completely unknown. On getting home, it was apparently the norm to consecrate the clothes in which one had been initiated, or to use them as lucky blankets for children. Some sanctity therefore remained from the extraordinary experience, even if the custom also developed of wearing old clothes to the *Mysteries*, to avoid the loss of new ones by consecration.[153]

In the longer term, one brought home 'sweeter hopes' for the afterlife. The 'official' Eleusinian promise as reflected in the *Homeric Hymn to Demeter* and in many later texts seems to have been similarly vague: a 'better fate' awaits initiates in the afterlife, whereas for the uninitiated 'everything there is bad'. The picture presented in the *parodos* of Aristophanes' *Frogs* differs from this vague promise in two ways. The pleasures and pains of the afterlife have become much more concrete, flowery meadows on the one side, mud and dangerous monsters on the other. And the line of division between blessed and afflicted is in part a moral one: on the edges of the underworld is a region of mud where lie those who have transgressed basic moral rules, whereas the blessed sporting in the meadows are 'we who have been initiated and have behaved properly to guests and ordinary people'.[154] On both points Aristophanes is likely to reflect some of the common understandings of his time. The depiction serves no obvious comic purpose; and, according to Plato's Adeimantus, 'Musaeus and his son' told of an afterlife in which the righteous (ὅσιοι) enjoyed a symposium while the wicked were consigned to mud and

---

[151] Plut. fr. 178 and Theo Sm. *De util. math.* p. 15.1–4 Hiller (E7 Scarpi). This claim is generally held to be demonstrably incorrect (Mylonas, *Mysteries*, 238–9; Riedweg. *Mysterienterminologie*, 125–7); but the early crowning of Roman emperors was not necessarily typical (*IG* II² 3632.19–20), and crowning in art could be 'proleptic'.

[152] Plut. *Quaest. Conv.* 2.2.1, 635a ἐν Ἐλευσῖνι μετὰ τὰ Μυστήρια τῆς πανηγύρεως ἀκμαζούσης εἱστιώμεθα; Pl. *Ep.* 7, 333e οὐκ ἐκ φιλοσοφίας γεγονότε φίλω, ἀλλ' ἐκ τῆς περιτρεχούσης ἑταιρείας ταύτης τῆς τῶν πλείστων φίλων, ἣν ἐκ τοῦ ξενίζειν τε καὶ μυεῖν καὶ ἐποπτεύειν πραγματεύονται; cf. p. 44, n. 29. But the supposed use of *adelphos* for fellow-initiate at Eleusis, rightly judged 'remarkable' by Burkert, *Mystery Cults*, 45 (cf. *Homo Necans*, 288, n. 67), depends solely on what has now emerged as a wrong reading in Sopater, *Rhet. Graec.* 8. 123.27 Walz: see D. Innes and M. Winterbottom, *Sopatros the Rhetor* (*BICS* suppl. 48, London 1988), 101.

[153] Ar. *Plut.* 845 with Σ ad loc., the former quoting Melanthius *FGrH* 326 F 4; Ar. *Ran.* 404–8; Dover, *Frogs*, 62–3.

[154] 'Official' promise: n. 120 above. 'Hopes': Isocr. 4.28, Pl. *Resp.* 331a (on the language of 'hope' in Greek religion see Parker, *Miasma*, 175, n. 173; Mikalson, *Athenian Popular Religion*, 125, n. 12; H. Versnel, *ZPE* 58, 1985, 256–7). Mud: Ar. *Ran.* 145–51, 273–311; meadows 154–58, 318–36, 372–6, 447–59 (passage quoted: 456–9). This paragraph and the next are simplifications of Graf, *Orphische Dichtung*, 40–150, which remains basic. Graf discusses the extensive collateral evidence ignored here.

forced to carry water in a sieve.[155] Musaeus' son is Eumolpus, founder of the *genos* that provided the hierophant, and the teaching ascribed to those two must have been one popularly associated with Eleusis. In the fourth century, Triptolemus occasionally joins Rhadamanthys and Minos as a judge of the underworld: a quintessentially Eleusinian figure, he can only have received this high honour if a moral judgement of souls was believed to form part of the Eleusinian vision of the afterlife.[156] As represented by Adeimantus, Musaeus and Eumolpus have in fact almost entirely substituted moral worth for initiation as the criterion for admission to different areas of the underworld. But to do so would have been to remove the *Mysteries'* raison d'être, and Aristophanes' double requirement ('we who have been initiated and have behaved properly') is much more likely to reflect their teaching. Diogenes the Cynic asked 'Will Pataikion the thief fare better after death than Epaminondas because he has been initiated?' To this the hierophant's response, had he deigned to give one, might have been that, no, villainous Pataikion had not effaced his villainy by initiation and would lie in mud; as for virtuous Epaminondas, the goddess's promise and invitation had been conveyed to him—the *Mysteries* were announced in Thebes each year—and it was his own fault if he had failed to take advantage. But in its simplified form the message conveyed to the world remained that initiation at Eleusis would improve your lot in the afterlife.[157] So even a Pataikion might think the fee worth paying.

Adeimantus mentions the teachings of 'Musaeus and his son' but fails to explain the form in which those teachings were conveyed. We must touch very briefly on the theme of the 'imagined Eleusis' created by poetry. The topic is bewilderingly complicated, but some basic points can be quite simply stated. The main written medium for eschatological speculation in archaic Greece was hexameter poetry ascribed to Orpheus or, less often, Musaeus. Adeimantus' reference to teachings of 'Musaeus and his son' (Eumolpus) suggests that poetry of that type may have been composed with specific reference to Eleusis; poems ascribed to Eumolpus are in fact attested, though they cannot be dated. By the fourth century Orpheus himself was sometimes credited with having founded the *Mysteries*; and poems by Orpheus on Eleusinian themes are attested, though again they cannot be dated. (One relevant poem ascribed

---

[155] Pl. *Resp.* 363c–d. The meaning of this passage is constantly distorted by translating συμπόσιον τῶν ὁσίων 'symposium of the pure', as though only ritual requirements were relevant. But the ideal of ὁσία bridges the ritual and moral spheres. Pl. *Phaed.* 69c, by contrast, speaks of initiation only; [Pl.] *Axioch.* 371a–e blurs ritual and moral.

[156] Pl. *Apol.* 41a, and cf. the three Apulian vases cited by Graf, *Orphische Dichtung*, 123.

[157] But it seems to me possible that an exhortation to observe the basic Greek rules of conduct was addressed to the *mystai* at some point. The lines from Frogs were inscribed on a Hellenistic altar from Rhodes: G. Pugliese Carratelli, *Dioniso* 8 (1940), 119–23. On initiation and morality cf. Dover, *Greek Popular Morality*, 264–5; Rudhardt, *Pensée religieuse*, 119, who notes that Isocrates speaks in identical language of the 'fair hopes' of the initiated (4.28) and of the just (8.34). Diogenes: Plut. *De aud. poet.* 4, 21f; a variant in Diog. Laert. 6.39.

to Orpheus in later antiquity was none other than what we call the *Homeric Hymn to Demeter*: this is pseudo pseudepigraphy.)[158] Very possibly then the underworld of flowery meadows and mud and sieve-carriers and a judgement on moral criteria was described in one or several poems ascribed to Orpheus or Musaeus or Eumolpus.[159] On the need for morality Orpheus and Eleusis could agree (for it is naïve to suppose that a cult which, without reservation, promised felicity to Pataikion could ever have achieved lasting panhellenic fame). But the more esoteric Orphic doctrines and demands (purification from inherited guilt; vegetarianism) are likely to have been played down or omitted in this context. The common understanding of the cult will have been based on a blend of the simple promise ('initiation is good for you') and elements learnt from such poems. And individuals will have made additions *ad libitum* both from the inherited conglomerate of mythological accounts and from philosophical speculation. A recently published epitaph from Thrace explains how a mime actor reached a happy old age 'because' he had been initiated at Samothrace and Eleusis. And why after all in an individual's understanding should initiation not benefit one in this life as well as the next?[160]

This is not the place to discuss Athenian beliefs and imaginings about the afterlife in detail. Numerous elements from the just-mentioned 'inherited conglomerate' occur here and there, and in genres that admit fantasy new fantasies appear.[161] But a few words are needed in order to restore Eleusis to a context. To pay cult to the dead was one of the very foundations of piety; to envisage being deprived of such cult was one of the worst of horrors. When Athenians spoke of such practices, they by no means always stressed that the dead stood in need of these attentions or would be angered if deprived of them; vaguer appeals to tradition, honour and propriety are often found. But embedded in the ritual itself was a belief or at least a formal fiction that communication between dead and living was possible, though difficult: for the dead were invoked three times (communication being difficult) and urged, in gratitude for the gifts they were being given, to 'send up good things from there'.[162]

---

[158] On all this see in brief the references in M. L. West, *The Orphic Poems* (Oxford 1983), 23–4; on the poems ascribed to Eumolpus, Graf, *Orphische Dichtung* 20. On the Orphic account of Demeter's arrival at Eleusis see *Athenian Religion*, 100–1; it is not clear that this poem exercised much influence.

[159] Cf. Graf, *Orphische Dichtung*, 139–50. Lloyd-Jones very plausibly postulated a 6th-c. epic (ascribed to Musaeus?) which described Heracles' initiation at Eleusis and descent to the underworld (*Maia* 19, 1967, 206–29 = id. *Greek Epic, Lyric and Tragedy*, Oxford 1990, 167–87); but Graf's further postulate, 145–6, that Heracles found an Eleusinian underworld awaiting him, divided into initiated and uninitiated, is very insecure. So it is hard to name a poem. The less plausible alternative to all this is that both Aristophanes and Plato derive from an oral common understanding of Eleusis.

[160] C. Karadina-Matsa and N. Dimitrova, *Chiron* 33 (2003), 335–44 (2nd c. BC or later; exact proverance unknown).

[161] See Bremmer, *Afterlife*, 4–8.

[162] See p. 29, n. 88. Vaguer appeals: so Dover, *Greek Popular Morality*, 245.

At least at first sight, however, that belief is undermined by the expressions of doubt which are a standard feature of what Athenians say about the afterlife in every context except that of ritual. A snappy title for a study of Greek afterlife beliefs would indeed be *If*; for expressions of the form 'if there is any awareness among the dead of events here'[163] or 'if there is any reward in Hades for the pious' are so common that they evidently embody not the doubts of individual speakers but a cliché of the culture. Neither of these expressions of doubt in fact entails doubt about the very existence of an afterlife; for even if there were no 'awareness among the dead of events here', the possibility would remain that the dead had a continuing, but detached, existence; and similarly a Hades might exist that failed to distinguish good from bad. And various permutations would be possible, since the traditional Hades has two functions, quite separate though each important in its own way: it is a place where the good are rewarded and the bad punished (probably by this date all the good and all the bad, not just the Homeric select few), and it is a place from which the dead observe the conduct of their living descendants. But the point of the 'if' expressions does not seem to be to open a negotiation with existing belief in order to explore options such as these. Though the doubt is expressed in relation to the particular aspect of the inherited conglomerate of afterlife beliefs that is immediately relevant, the real uncertainty surely concerns that conglomerate as a whole.

Yet that proposition immediately demands glossing, because it implies a much more corrosive scepticism than was actually at work. Given the epistemological basis of Greek religion, it was impossible even for a pious Greek not to feel 'uncertainty' about the traditional picture of the afterlife. As Demosthenes rather ponderously explains, no one has actually seen the heroes of old enjoying the delights of the islands of the blessed, but 'we entertain the opinion, by a kind of divination, that those whom we, the living, have treated as worthy of honours here on earth receive those same honours in the afterlife also.' Hyperides too speaks of the continuing perception of the dead as merely a matter of human 'supposition' or 'assumption'. For lack of better evidence about the realities of the underworld, painters' depictions and descriptions by poets are sometimes appealed to. In the absence of revelation, a proof of the continuing existence of the soul would have needed to be based on supposed empirical data. Xenophon's Cyrus, on his deathbed, attempts an empirical argument which has several strands (hauntings by the unjustly killed; grave cult; the experience of the soul in dreams), but concedes that his listeners may continue to believe that the soul dies with the body.[164]

---

[163] εἴ τις ἄρα ἔστιν αἴσθησις τοῖς ἐκεῖ περὶ τῶν ἐνθάδε γινομένων *vel sim.*: Lyc. *Leocr.* 136, cf. Eur. *HF* 490–1; *Or.* 1231–2 (both the Euripidean passages are prayers); Isocr. *Evag.* 2; Plat. 61; *Aigin.* 42; Hyperid. 6.43; 'if the dead could hear': Dem. 19.66; 20.87; 27.69 (cf. Isocr. *Bus.* 6); cf. Soph. *El.* 355–6 (εἴ τις ἔστ᾽ ἐκεῖ χάρις), Eur. *Heraclid.* 592 (εἴ τι δὴ κατὰ χθονός: this is unusually broad in its doubt). 'If there is any reward': *CEG* 559.2; 571.6; 603.5.

[164] Dem. 60.34, tr. Dover, *Greek Popular Morality*, 266; Hyperid. 6.43, ὥσπερ ὑπολάμβανομεν; Xen. *Cyr.* 8.7.17–22. Poets and painters: [Dem.] 25.52; Arist. *Pol.* 1334a 30–1; cf. Aeschin. 1.

Survival, therefore, could not be proved. But, despite Descartes' demonstration that one cannot strictly prove the existence of an external reality independent of the perceiving subject, most people have felt able to give reality the benefit of the doubt, and it might similarly be that the 'If' of the Greeks in relation to the afterlife was a merely formal disclaimer. Seldom is an 'if there is awareness among the dead of events here' followed by a 'but if there is not'; the conditional clause opens the possibility of continuing perception, and the speaker then draws the consequences favourable to his own position which follow from it. Even the slightly different formula used three times by Demosthenes, 'if the dead could perceive what is happening here', does not rule such perception out, while presenting it as difficult and uncertain. At the climax of the speech against murderous Eratosthenes, Lysias urges the jurors to avenge Eratosthenes' victims and declares 'I believe that they are listening to you and will be conscious of you casting your votes'; Orestes in tragedy can even be assured that 'your [dead] father, I know, hears [your prayers]' (where the uncertainty is acknowledged merely by an 'I know' which would be redundant in a simple statement of agreed fact). Twice an actual prayer to a dead person in tragedy is accompanied by a variant of the 'if the dead have perception' formula.[165] That occurrence suggests the possibility that the formulaic 'if', far from subverting the fiction of communication between the worlds created by grave cult, was itself part of the ritual.

Yet it would in turn be extreme to reduce Athenian reservations about the afterlife to an epistemological gesture. Hyperides' *Funeral Oration* contains an exception to the principle stated above that an 'if there is awareness among the dead' is seldom accompanied by an 'but if there is not'. Approaching the climax of his speech, the orator says 'If death is equivalent to not having been born, then [those who have died for Athens] are freed from disease and pain and the other accidents of human life.' He goes on, it is true, to the alternative that 'there is perception in Hades, and care from the divine, as we suppose', but it remains telling that on the most formal and solemn oratorical occasion in the Athenian year the chosen speaker could raise the possibility that, as characters in tragedy sometimes assert, whether with bitterness or relief, 'death is (the dead are) nothing'.[166] He could not by contrast possibly have suggested, even as the less favoured of two options, that perhaps the gods did not exist. Aeschines once asserts that funeral cult is performed for the sake of 'law and the divine', not for the dead man, who cannot perceive it; the particular circumstances of the case lead him to make this assertion, but

---

190 (tragedy). The unjustly killed/untimely dead constitute a special case (Johnston, *Restless Dead*, 127–60), and beliefs in this area cannot be generalized.

[165] Demosthenes' formula: see n. 163; Lys. 12.100; Eur. *El.* 684 (a similar 'I know' in Soph. *El.* 400); prayer to a dead person: n. 163 above. As in Lys. 12.100, the topos of 'what the dead will/would think/experience' has a closural function also in Dem. 27.69 and Hyperid. 6.43.

[166] Eur. *Tro.* 633; *IA* 1251; *Alc.* 381; *Hel.* 1421; fr. 532; cf. Eur. *Heraclid.* 593. The common tragic thought that death ends the pains of this life (Dover, *Greek Popular Morality*, 267; Eur. *Heraclid.* 595–6, with the note of J. Wilkins) is not necessarily so extreme. Hyperides: 6.43.

manipulation to suit a context is only possible with beliefs that are themselves flexible.[167] One fourth-century funerary epitaph declares that 'I enjoyed much sweet sport with those of my own age; I was born from earth, and have become earth again'. This sounds like a way of saying that 'death is nothing', but the sentiment is very isolated among Greek epitaphs if so.[168] Explicit denial of an afterlife is therefore a muted but not altogether silenced note within Athenian public discourse. As for less formal contexts, the fear that the soul dissolves and ceases to exist at the moment of death is treated in Plato's *Phaedo* as commonplace. There are also very many occasions in several genres where a speaker might have envisaged underworld rewards or compensations for the good, and punishments for the bad, but failed to do so.[169] Such silences can only be partially explained by generic constraints such as that which required tragedy to concentrate on life in this world.

Well over two hundred Attic verse epitaphs survive from the sixth to the fourth century.[170] The great majority simply describe the virtues of the deceased and lament their parting. Some speak in conventional language of the dead having gone to 'the chamber of Persephone' or having fallen victim to Fate or a *daimon* or the like. One famous public text (of 432) and a private imitation consign the bodies of the dead to the ground and their souls to the *aither*: this return of the soul to the *aither* was apparently a happy destiny that permitted the continuance of consciousness, not a blowing away on the wind.[171] A handful from the fourth century declare that the dead person is now enjoying the reward for piety or justice in Persephone's realm, if there are such rewards. Only three, as it seems, unreservedly predict a happy destiny for the soul (other than absorption into the *aither*), and it may not be coincidence that the dead person is not a native Athenian in the two identifiable cases: the soul of a young Theban has gone to the chamber of the pious, whereas an 'equally taxed foreigner' (*isoteles*) of unknown origin is now 'honoured among the chthonian gods'. (The origin of a woman whose

---

[167] 1.14: noted by Dover, *Greek Popular Morality*, 243, as 'exceptional' and ascribed to 'the flexibility of religious belief in the service of rhetoric' (a comparable case might be Ant. 5.95, where revenge is said to be of no use to a dead man). In Eur. *Hel.* 959–968 Menelaus states that an appeal to a dead man, useless in itself, may prove useful in shaming a living relative of the dead man; and he is right (1009–16: but the living relative sees the dead man as retaining perception).

[168] CEG 482; cf. R. Lattimore, *Themes in Greek and Latin Epitaphs* (Urbana, Ill.1962), 77. A similar formula is treated in a more complicated way in GVI 1126 (Eretria).

[169] Rudhardt, *Pensée religieuse*, 117; Dover, *Greek Popular Morality*, 266–7. Dissolution of soul: Pl. *Phaed.* 70a, 77b. Note too the counterfactual conditional in Philemon fr. 118 'if the dead had [not "have"] perception, as some say . . .'.

[170] See Sourvinou-Inwood, *Death*, 147–207: the contrast there well discussed between archaic epitaphs, with their predominant concern for 'memory survival', and those of the 4th c. does not concern me here.

[171] CEG 10.6 (IG I³ 1179) and 535; cf. Epicharmus fr. 213 and ps. Epicharmus fr. 254 (245 and 265 Kaibel) (both consolatory); Eur. *Suppl.* 531–4; *Hel.* 1014–16 (consciousness); fr. 971; Alexis fr. 163; and, for the underlying idea of 'recycling', Eur. fr. 839; for later developments see Bremmer, *Afterlife*, 137, n. 62. Ar. *Pax* 832–3, where the dead become stars, is more isolated, though introduced with an 'as they say': see the note of S. D. Olson ad loc.

'soul is on Olympus' is lost.)[172] But even the more qualified statement that so-and-so is being rewarded for piety, if such rewards exist, represents a change from the Homeric picture of the afterlife, where the ordinary dead are an ineffectual mass and rewards and punishment are reserved for exceptional individuals. Punishment too was now available to everyman, as we see for instance from the remark of old Cephalus in Plato that, as we near death, we come to fear the stories about underworld punishments that we laughed at when young.[173] On this model each one of us after death treads a path which at a certain point divides, and leads either to a place of bliss or of affliction. One of the influences which led to this democratization of the underworld is likely to have been the Eleusinian promise. But at no other level—and this is the notable conclusion to which the long digression has been leading—does that promise influence the things said about the afterlife in non-Eleusinian contexts. Allusions to the cheerful message received in the *telesterion* are all but unknown is epitaphs, whether from Attica or elsewhere.[174]

That panhellenic silence of tombstones is indeed so eloquent that one might be inclined to attribute it to a convention of reserve, an onward extension of the mystic secrecy. Many of those who lay beneath monuments so unexpressive in this regard will certainly have been initiates.[175] But it was not a secret that Eleusis offered the initiate 'fair hopes' for the afterlife; yet statements about the underworld continue to be qualified by an 'if' which is never either countered by a reference to those 'fair hopes' or phrased in terms of them ('if, as the *Mysteries* teach, the dead have perception even after death'). The argument presented earlier for the epistemological necessity of that 'if' contained in fact a loophole: for the *Mysteries* derive from things shown and taught by Demeter herself, and thus constitute the one great exception to the general truth that Greek religion was not based on revelation. Yet the loophole was not exploited, and the transition from 'fair hopes' to firm belief was not made. Eleusinian initiates were not cranks, or rare enthusiasts: the cult was a foundation of Attica's panhellenic prestige, and most Athenians

---

[172] Rewards: *CEG* 559.2, 571.6, 603.5. Unreserved promise: *CEG* 545.2, 595.5. Olympus: *CEG* 558. Dionysius of Kollytos in 593 is assured that his soul is immortal but is promised no special abode. 'Funerary banquet' reliefs may represent a variation on the theme of 'dead person(s) in a familial setting' (so Dentzer, *Banquet Couché*, 539–41, cf. 353–55, on his catalogue nn. R 207–19), rather than an assimilation of the ordinary dead to the heroes for which the iconographic type was first developed; the type is anyway very rare amid the huge numbers of surviving Attic gravestones.

[173] Pl. *Resp.* 330d–e; other references to afterlife punishments Aesch. *Supp.* 228–31; Dem. 24.104, 25.52–3; com. adesp. fr. 707 (a joke). On the squeezing out (never complete) of the Homeric middle ground for the ordinary dead see Dover, *Greek Popular Morality*, 265–6.

[174] O. Kern, *Die griechischen Mysterien der klassischen Zeit* (Berlin 1927), 12; Dover, *Greek Popular Morality*, 265. But note a new epitaph from northern Greece (n. 160 above) which describes the dead person as an initiate at Samothrace and Eleusis and urges Hades to lead him to the place of the pious; see too a new Posidippus epigram as interpreted by the editors of the epitaph, *Chiron* 33 (2003), 343.

[175] See Sourvinou-Inwood, *Death*, 173–4.

were probably initiated. But, from the language used about the afterlife in other contexts, we would never know that such a cult existed.

The other source of eschatological reassurance available to Athenians is archaeologically no less invisible. A handful of texts prove that Orphic poems about the afterlife were promoted at Athens by wandering seers and 'Orphic-initiators'.[176] At his most rigorous, Orpheus required vegetarianism of his initiates as one of the prices of salvation. But in actual religious practice those harsh demands were perhaps softened; the interchange mentioned earlier between 'Eleusinian' and 'Orphic' may have been two-way. However that may be, no example of the famous Gold Leaves buried with initiates in many parts of the Greek world has been discovered in Attica; so many Attic graves have been investigated that the discovery of a Gold Leaf would by now be a considerable surprise. The majority view is that the Gold Leaves were sold to initiates by Orphic-initiators; a minority view associates them with weakly attested Bacchic Mysteries.[177] On either view (since *ex hypothesi* the Bacchic Mysteries existed in Athens if they existed anywhere), the absence of Gold Leaves from Attic tombs is an anomaly and a puzzle.

Much more was hoped in Attica than was recorded on tombs, or in them. But, as we have seen, it is not only on tombstones that a tentative attitude to the afterlife prevails. We see here very clearly the difference which divides a religion that offers hopes from one which imposes firm beliefs.

---

[176] See p. 120, n. 18.
[177] Majority view: see e.g. F. Graf in *Masks of Dionysus*, 239–58. Minority view: Schlesier, 'Dionysos in der Unterwelt'; C. Calame, *Der Neue Pauly*, s.v. *Orphik, Orphische Dichtung*, 66–9.

16

Festivals, Rituals, Myths: Reprise

This chapter looks back unsystematically over the eight that precede it. Some points are drawn out, some added. Those chapters were about festivals, but there has been much talk in them of ritual and rituals. Festival has a clear Greek equivalent, *heorte*, problematic, as we saw earlier, only in its precise field of application. 'Ritual' is a term of analysis which emerged in the late nineteenth century and lacks, it seems, a close equivalent in any natural language.[1] But it is the concept of ritual, not of festival, that has been theme of a rich anthropological debate, to which distinguished contributions have been recently made.[2] Ritual and festival are at some points so hard to disentangle that this debate should certainly be touched on here. But a central dilemma in the analysis of ritual has been that of giving it an effective definition, and, though the difficulty is compounded once so-called secular rituals are taken into account, it quickly emerges even within the confines of religious activity. Not all Greek rituals are festivals, obviously; an oath sworn, a vow contracted, a sacrifice performed by an individual is not a festival. But are festivals rituals, and in what sense?

The question is not as scholastic as it may seem. One of the mechanisms of ritualization, it has been attractively suggested, relates to naming. Rituals are not perceived by the person who performs them as sequences of action which he or she puts together at will; the sequence of action is given, predetermined, and a characteristic way of emphasizing this 'facticity' of the ritual is to give it a distinctive name (or set of names: the parts can be subdivided).[3] But in Greek practice special names for what we might be disposed to identify as distinctive ritual sequences are not common. A scrap of exegetical writing prescribes the actions by which a 'pot is set up for Zeus Ktesios', but does not give those actions a name.[4] It is, as we have seen repeatedly, at the level of the festival that special naming flourishes, with names for whole festivals and for days and ritual sequences within them. And evidently, for every participant, a festival is precisely a thing 'accepted' from tradition (as, almost by definition,

---

[1] See J. N. Bremmer, ' "Religion", "Ritual" and the Opposition "Sacred vs. Profane" ', in F. Graf (ed.), *Ansichten griechischer Rituale* (Stuttgart and Leipzig 1998), 9–32, which builds on T. Asad, *Genealogies of Religion* (Baltimore and London 1988).

[2] See p. 158, n. 10.   [3] See Humphrey/Laidlaw, *Archetypal Actions*, 120–1.

[4] Autokleides *FGrH* 353 F 1.

is ritual),[5] not a thing created. In that sense a festival can be seen *in toto* as a ritual. But different elements of a festival will display in very uneven measure the rule-boundedness, formality and differentiation from everyday activity that we tend to associate with ritual. Ritual obscenity and ritual abuse are 'ritual' only in the sense that an expectation exists that at certain points abuse and obscenities may or should be uttered without causing offence;[6] there were not to our knowledge any fixed formulae. (The same example suggests, incidentally, that, of the characteristics of ritual just named, differentiation from everyday norms may be more basic than formality.) Even the language of prayer and invocation normally differed from that of ordinary speech in its addressee alone. And the line between ritual and secular dining is one that can scarcely be drawn.

A proposal to deal with this difficulty and with others is to substitute for the concept of ritual that of ritualisation.[7] We will no longer need to decide whether this or that activity is, in all its parts, a ritual; odd outcrops of ritualized activity within everyday life will not cause us to stumble, nor of everyday life within a 'ritual'. A festival will count as a ritualized framework containing a number of unequally ritualized parts. Nor will we need to seek the shared essence of all rituals. But it will remain necessary to describe or define ritualization, and such a description is likely to have a more formal cast than descriptions of rituals have tended to have: 'how does ritualization work?' will replace 'what do rituals do?' Such a theoretical shift will not come without a cost. Many vivid and illuminating observations about the social or psychological functions of particular rituals will lose their claim to be answering the question (now deemed a non-question) 'what does ritual do?' But perhaps proposed answers to that question have never been more than illustrations of some of the things that ritual can do, disguised as general accounts.[8] The notion, for instance, that ritual and social bonding are intimately associated is almost a truism. But the entailment works in one direction only: if it is hard to conceive of group formation that lacks some basis in ritual, there are many undeniable rituals, not just the obsessive rituals of the neurotic, that have no obvious connection with group dynamics. Monks and magicians alike conduct rituals in private.

Whether one favours the language of ritual or of ritualization, the difficulty is in fact, in relation to festivals, the same. Festivals are, whereas rituals are not, necessarily a collective activity; what happens at festivals, therefore, cannot be 'the ritual process' *tout court*. Unless a rigorous justification can be offered for setting aside non-group rituals as secondary, no generalization about either ritual or ritualization that appeals by way of definition to a social

---

[5] See e.g. Rappaport, *Ritual and Religion*, 119–24.
[6] Cf. Humphrey/Laidlaw, *Archetypal Actions*, 121–2.
[7] So, in different ways Bell, *Ritual Theory*, and Humphrey/Laidlaw, *Archetypal Actions*.
[8] See Humphrey/Laidlaw, *Archetypal Actions*, 70–1.

dimension can be valid. Yet the extraordinary social power of 'rituals' (the word is inescapable, for all its faults) is perhaps their most remarkable characteristic. To this I now turn. The theme is no longer 'theory of ritual', at least not in the sense of 'towards a unified theory of ritual', but at best 'some of the things that ritual can do'.

A central issue is the way in which the festivals defined and prescribed the social roles of those who participated in them. The most important mechanism here is a very simple one. Whether rituals can properly be seen as communicative or even as expressive is controversial.[9] But one does not need to invoke any content that may have been communicated during the festival itself in order to see the sense in which the *Thesmophoria* defined the citizen wives of Athens. Simple rules of inclusion and exclusion constituted a most unmistakable and indisputable declaration. Such rules are seldom known in detail, but the following pair of crucial propositions is likely to be sound:[10] (1) at a large number of festivals sacrificial meat was distributed to all male citizens and to them alone; (2) participation in public women's festivals was in theory confined to the wives and daughters of Athenian citizens. Neither proposition is intended to deny non-citizens some ceremonial role in Athenian festivals, under licence as it were, and it is hard to believe that, if a metic chose to hold a banquet at the *Choes*, say, in his own house, anyone would have cared to prevent him. But there remained a very strong sense in which citizenship and the right of full festival participation were synonymous. The two conduits to citizenship were themselves festival-celebrating bodies. Boys were admitted to phratries at a public festival, the *Apatouria*, which existed primarily for this purpose. And, though admission to the deme was not a ritual procedure, the deme was both an organizing principle through which citizens participated in the festivals of the city, and had a busy ritual life of its own.

If the festival cycle as a whole confirmed the citizenry in their position of privilege, particular festivals, as we have seen, had special significance for particular subgroups. Interpretative issues become more complex here, and even the tentative analyses offered above are subject to the warnings issued by recent ritual theorists against the arbitrary arrogance of the decoding observer.[11] A woman celebrating the *Thesmophoria* could not fail to know that she was a woman entitled to celebrate the *Thesmophoria*, but what it meant, in terms of a woman's ideal role, to do that was no doubt a more open

---

[9] See Humphrey/Laidlaw, *Archetypal Actions*, 73–81, with 85, n. 14.

[10] Proposition (2) is the less strongly based, being for lack of other evidence a mere extrapolation from the *Thesmophoria* (and even here such exclusiveness has been disputed, though wrongly in my view). In relation to the *Haloa* some inconclusive evidence goes the other way (p. 283). But the point survives, if in weakened form, as long as the central women's festival, the *Thesmophoria*, was exclusive in this way.

[11] The issue is central to G. Lewis, *Day of Shining Red: An Essay on Understanding Ritual* (Cambridge 1980); see too e.g. Humphrey/Laidlaw, *Archetypal Actions*, 180.

question, and for some women perhaps simply not an interesting one. What the little bears at Brauron may have made of their experiences is a curious enquiry, and the real issues here may rather concern the imaginings of parents about the growing up of their daughters. But with older children— the ephebes who competed in races before critical audiences, 'basket-bearers', chorus-members, and others—exposure at the festivals to the public gaze must indeed have been a challenge to live up to a role.

The capacity of festivals to make particular social arrangements seem inevitable becomes particularly intriguing when we come to more explicitly political relationships. The comparative literature bursts with case-studies of ritual used in the service of power, while also containing some of rituals used against it. The imperial twist given to the *Panathenaea* in the fifth century can count in its way as a textbook example of the former. We discussed too, in relation to the *Panathenaea*, the ceremonial prominence permitted to the wealthy *Hippeis*, and a few further instances can be assembled of ritual positions reserved for the wealthy or the well-born; the *gene* too retained their traditional cultic roles.[12] But what deserves to be emphasized in a comparative perspective is surely the extent to which Athenian festivals were not a regime for the imposition or maintenance of social hierarchies. Though we do find a kind of 'hierarchization' at the *Panathenaea*, in the sense that certain individuals get extra cuts of meat, the recipients are not selected on the basis of wealth or birth but of civic function.[13] The social order ritually orchestrated and celebrated throughout the festival year is that of the city administered by a democratically elected boule; members of the boule, magistrates, and 'performers of rites' (*hieropoioi*) selected from the boule are omnipresent. At the level of representations, it is true, it is hard to trace much influence of the democracy on Athenian religion. At best one can quote the worship of the tyrannicides Harmodius and Aristogeiton and the elevation of Theseus to become a symbol of democratic values (the cult of Democracy itself is not clearly attested before the 330s), perhaps too the prominence given to the craftsmen's god Hephaestus; Zeus, however, remained a king, and Olympus was no heavenly projection of a democratic polis.[14] But every citizen was entitled to eat as much sacrificial meat at the festivals of the city as any other, and even to participate actively in the ritual as a magistrate or *hieropoios*. At this level Athenian religion was very profoundly democratized. The claim that the Athenians celebrate 'twice as many festivals' as other Greeks comes from that same observer, the 'Old Oligarch', who documents what he regards as the extremes of Athenian democracy, that dire society

---

[12] See p. 220, and *Athenian Religion*, Ch. 5.   [13] See p. 267.

[14] See H. S. Versnel, 'Religion and Democracy', in W. Eder (ed.), *Die athenische Demokratie im 4. Jahrhundert v. Chr.* (Stuttgart 1995), 367–87; for the other aspect see M. H. Jameson, 'Religion in the Athenian Democracy', in I. Morris and K. Raaflaub (eds.), *Democracy 2500? Questions and Challenges* (Dubuque, Ia. 1998), 171–95, and *Athenian Religion*, 122–9.

where slaves fail to give way to free men in the streets.[15] The Athenians are famous for the success with which they stayed all but free of civil strife over long periods. It is an intriguing if unverifiable thought that their unique abundance of shared festivals, at many levels, may have helped to keep the Athenians in some measure in harmony with one another. The worst exception to the Athenians' record of civic peace was the rule of the 'Thirty tyrants' in 404–403, a regime eventually overthrown by a counter-movement originating in the Piraeus. Very strikingly, the 'men from the Piraeus' marched to Athena on the acropolis in what must have been felt as a respectful variant on the Panathenaic procession.[16] The restoration of the democracy was celebrated with an evocation of its most compelling ritual.

Yet to present the whole festival programme as nothing but a disguised template for the social and political system would be very reductive. Doubtless every festival conveys some message about social ordering and roles. But the same might be said of every social activity. Unitary theories of how festivals work have a certain intuitive plausibility in that festivals of the most diverse types in some ways resemble one another. But within the shared framework very different concerns are addressed. The central day of *Anthesteria* was a 'white day for slaves', but the *Anthesteria* was much more than a device for temporary inclusion of slaves within the social group. The *Dipolieia* honours Zeus of the city, but the problem that it dramatizes is that of the legitimacy of ox-slaying. The *Mysteries* are organized by the city, yet have as their central concern a possibility, open to all Greeks, of access to a better lot in the afterlife. At every festival, even the most political, a special shaping was also added by a whole range of further factors, chief among them the season and the god. After all the chapters that have preceded, the point does not, I hope, need to be elaborated further.[17]

The festivals discussed in the preceding chapters have, in the main, been festivals of the city. One exception was the *Adonia*, wholly unofficial yet occupying a kind of recognized place in the festival calendar. But much ritual activity of Athenian citizens took place neither in the context of public festivals nor yet of the groupings of kinsfolk and friends discussed in Chapter 2. There were initiations for Sabazius or the Corybantes or those conducted by Orpheus-initiators; there were Dionysiac *thiasoi*, and privately conducted rites for Pan or Aphrodite or Hecate; there were semi-permanent cult associations of diverse types, whether honouring heroes or Asclepius or Mother or others besides. Most of this activity took place on the edge of our field of vision:

---

[15] [Xen.] *Ath. Pol.* 3.8.

[16] See B. Strauss, *AJAH* 10 (1985), 67–83 (on Xen. *Hell.* 2.4.39 and Lys. 13.80–1). Note too the strong appeal to civic harmony in the name of shared rituals (μετεσχήκαμεν δὲ ὑμῖν καὶ ἱερῶν τῶν σεμνοτάτων καὶ θυσιῶν καὶ ἑορτῶν τῶν καλλίστων) put by Xenophon in the mouth of the Herald of the *Mysteries* a little earlier in the same sequence of events (Xen. *Hell.* 2.4.20).

[17] Cf. D. Gellner's argument for pluralism, 'Religion, politics and ritual. Remarks on Geertz and Bloch', *Social Anthropology* 7 (1999), 135–54.

we are aware that it occurred—though much undoubtedly eludes us entirely—but can seldom offer a description of much precision or specificity.[18] The question must be whether the opacity of this world radically distorts our understanding of Athenian religion, or merely leaves the picture hazy at the edges. The question has a quantitative and a qualitative aspect. On the one hand, we would like to know how much such activity there was, how many Athenians belonged to permanent private associations or occasionally joined the revels of ad hoc *thiasoi*, what proportion, so to speak, of the total volume of Athenian religious traffic went through these channels. On the other hand, it would be still more important to know whether the religious experience offered by the elective cults was felt to be qualitatively different from that otherwise available. Could the worship of Mother in a private society in the Piraeus stir depths of feeling untouched by Athena on the acropolis?

Answers to both questions can only be impressionistic. In regard to the first, perhaps we should once again take Aristophanes and Theophrastus as guides. Both are among our most important sources for elective cults; yet, in both, allusions to the festivals of the city and its subgroups are much more frequent than to the private societies. There is no obvious reason to detect ideology in this emphasis; a simpler view is that the established cults and festivals of the city were indeed a main focus of interest, that 'official' and 'popular' religion coincided. As for the second question, we have seen that the 'priestesses' who assembled *thiasoi* could be exposed to prosecution, while Aristophanes in a play fantasized about the expulsion of 'non-native' gods from the city.[19] Prima facie then there was something outside the norm about some elective cults. But the objection to the priestesses seems to have been not religious innovation but the socially subversive behaviour that flourished in their entourage. Some of the *thiasoi* did not offer 'new gods' but old gods such as Dionysus in a new context. There were ecstatic elements in the cult of Sabazius and Mother and the Corybantes, but so too were there in the civic cult of Dionysus; the Mother of the private associations was not clearly distinguished from the Mother who was honoured in public cult at Agrai and who watched over the documents of the city in the Metroon.[20] The matter is ultimately irresoluble,[21] but it is a tenable position that what the elective cults offered was à la carte access to a familiar range of religious experiences, rather than something fundamentally different.

Aitiological myths have been mentioned here and there in the preceding chapters, and the relation between myth and festival needs now to be addressed directly. Several urgent but largely unanswerable questions can

---

[18] For what can be said see *Athenian Religion*, 109–11, 158–63, 188–98, 214–17, 333–42; pp. 13, 166 and 325 in this volume; Mikalson, *Hellenistic Athens*, 144–55; I. N. Arnaoutoglou, *Thusias heneka kai sunousias. Private religious associations in Hellenistic Athens* (Athens 2003).

[19] See p. 133; *Athenian Religion* 158, n. 20.

[20] See p. 407.   [21] Cf. *Athenian Religion*, 198.

merely be registered here: the question of who knew particular myths, who knew of the association between particular myths and particular festivals, and how such knowledge might have been disseminated. Actual prose narration of myths is attested at only one Athenian festival, the *Oschophoria*.[22] One possibility was that a relevant myth could be chorally presented, but this was largely precluded at Athens by the special development that choruses there underwent. Myths were indeed very regularly performed and recreated there with rare magnificence, but this occurred in the main at the specialized choral and dramatic festivals; it was not a process diffused throughout the festival cycle. Yet it is arguable that even this arrangement preserved what was most essential about the relation between myth and ritual. The essential in that relationship has often been sought in a one-to-one connection between a particular myth and a particular ritual. But the matter can be viewed in a more general way that still has meaning. We can invoke here an elegant solution to the old problem raised by Aristotle's assertion that only a few spectators at the theatre actually knew the myths. Only a few may have known the detail of the myths, it has been countered; but everybody knew that there had been a time of myths, that 'generation of heroes' to which Herodotus alludes and which is the Greek version of Eliade's 'illud tempus'.[23] An awareness that there had been such a time, and of its huge significance, was kept vividly alive by all the dithyrambs and epic recitations and tragedies and even comedies presented to the public each year.[24] The festival cycle was rooted in a belief in that special time. Almost all festivals were held to have their origin then or to commemorate occurrences during it. The details of that origin or of the occurrence commemorated mattered less than the belief that the festival did indeed derive its power and legitimacy from the special time.

There is reason to believe that a whole succession of Attic festivals acquired new myths of origin during the fifth or fourth centuries; for the myth of Theseus, which was connected by the fourth century with some six festivals,[25] seems in the sixth to have been too obscure to have served as such an aitiological panacea. We mostly know of these Thesean aitiologies from the citations of Atthidographers by Plutarch in his life of Theseus; the source is a learned one, and it is possible that some of this rewriting of tradition occurred in the study and did not spread far beyond it. Earlier aitiologies for the festivals in question have all but vanished. The tie between a festival and a particular

---

[22] Plut. *Thes.* 23.4.

[23] Veyne, *Mythes*, 56; Arist. *Poet.* 9, 1451b 25–6; Hdt. 3.122.2. For ἡρωικοὶ χρόνοι cf. Ar. *Pol.* 1285b 4, 21. On Eliade's '*illud tempus*' see e.g. G. S. Kirk, *The Nature of Greek Myths* (Harmondsworth 1974), 63–6; it illuminates a central function of Greek myths, however inadequate it may be as a general theory.

[24] Cf. p. 140.

[25] *Kybernesia, Oskhophoria, Pyanopsia, Synoikia,* perhaps *Boedromia* and at a local level *Hekalesia*; he was also sometimes founder of the *Panathenaea*: cf. Table 1 below, and Calame, *Thésée, passim.*

myth of origin was often loose; poets and other men of words were free to suggest improvements and new connections. What they could not do was to cut the umbilical cord linking the festival to the 'generation of heroes'.

In the discussions of particular festival in earlier chapters, myths had very uneven prominence. Gaps in our documentation will be partly responsible.[26] But the argument so far suggests that the significance of associated myths for particular festivals was in fact very uneven. The foundational importance of the myth of Demeter's advent for the *Eleusinian Mysteries* is not the typical case. The rites of the second day of the *Anthesteria* commemorated hospitality offered to Orestes by Demophon, those of the third day a meal taken by survivors of Deucalion's flood, and yet further myths may also have been adduced. So there was no single myth which, as it were, provided a plot for the whole festival. The myths used to explain festival usages were usually details picked out from larger mythological sequences or added to them (so for instance Orestes' entertainment by Demophon). Myths freshly cut from whole cloth to explain a rite do exist—Sopater and the first ox-killing commemorated by the *Dipolieia* is an instance—but are the exception. This bricolage or redeployment of fragments from a different context served well the function of attaching the festival to the best-known incidents of *illud tempus*. But the gain in name recognition entailed a loss in close correspondence between myth and rite. There were also myths that illuminated aspects of a god's cult in Attica with a strong light but did not relate very closely to a particular festival. The various disasters that accompanied Dionysus' arrival in Attica illustrate fundamental Athenian perceptions of the nature of the god. Myths tell of a drunkenness confused with poisoning, of murder, of male sexual frenzy expressed in a permanent state of erection.[27] But what they characterize is Dionysiac cult as a whole rather than a particular one of his festivals.

None the less, a mythical explanation was attached to most festivals. But there are exceptions which bring the simple formula 'without myth, no festival' into doubt. Particular manifestations of divine favour in historical time—the epiphany of Pan before Marathon or the arrival of Asclepius in Athens in 421—could be commemorated by a festival, though in the second case it is noticeable that an explanatory myth set in mythical time also eventually emerged.[28] The complex ritual of an obscure festival on Salamis

[26] It is odd for instance that no myth explains the *thargelos* part of the *Thargelia* ritual.

[27] Icarius was taught winemaking by Dionysus himself; he gave wine to shepherds but they drank it neat and, drunkenly supposing themselves to have been poisoned, killed him in revenge (e.g. Apollod. *Bibl.* 3.14.7). Some versions add that to punish the shepherds Dionysus came to them as a lovely youth but vanished when they were most aroused; to escape their ensuing state of permanent erection they first made clay phalli (Σ Lucian 211.14–212.8 Rabe, cf. ibid. 280.4–12; rejection of Pegasus similarly leads to a priapism eventually allayed by instituting phallic cult in Σ Ar. *Ach.* 243a).

[28] Philostr. *VA* 4.18: the festival *Epidauria* intrudes within the sequence of the *Mysteries* because Asclepius arrived late for the *Mysteries* and was initiated on that day. On Asclepius' coming to Athens in 421 see *Athenian Religion*, 175–85. On Pan see ibid., 163–4; the great sacrifice to Artemis Agrotera commemorating the victory at Marathon (p. 461) is a comparable case.

came to be understood as imitation of an incident during the struggle for the island in the time of Solon; here too an event of high significance in the historical period has the power to ground a festival.[29] This capacity of festivals to commemorate national achievements—whether they were founded in order to do so, or partially reinterpreted in this sense over time—was indeed fundamental to their continuing appeal.[30] But there are other festivals that seem to have been instituted in the historical period (*Olympieia, Hephaisteia, Diisoteria*) which do not obviously derive from such 'epiphanies' (displays of mythical power in historical time, as one might see them). Perhaps it was sufficient in such cases that the power of the god in question was illustrated in numerous myths; an ad hoc justification for the particular festival was not required. Yet one may feel that the distinctive character of, say, the festival of Zeus Meilichios, the *Diasia* – an ancient Ionian festival this one—would have merited an explanation distinct from Zeus' general mythology. Whether it received one we do not know; none is recorded.

An issue related to that of myth is what one might pretentiously call 'the time of the festivals'. In writings of an Eliadian persuasion, the notion sometimes surfaces that festivals transport participants back to *illud tempus*, a primal time before the world achieved its final form. However that may be, it is not in doubt that festivals often play tricks with time, treating the past as if it were present or recurrent, and retrojecting the present into the past. 'Christ is risen', declare the Orthodox at Easter; hymn-singers of northern Europe describe the birth of Christ in that 'bleak midwinter' which surrounds them at the time of singing, much milder though conditions in Bethlehem are likely to have been. There is also a kind of timelessness about festivals which can allow them, simultaneously and seamlessly, to commemorate both myths and (as we have just seen) actual historical events perceived as being of transcendent importance.[31] The problem in studying the 'time of the festivals' is that the matter is almost impervious to enquiry. The claim is not (we may take it) that participants in festivals 'really believe' that they have been transported back to the time before the flood, or whenever it might be; these are not doctrines or dogmas that a sober prose account would record, but, at most, fantasies and emotions of the actual experience. Behind the sober statement in a heortological source that such and such a festival action 'imitates' such and such a mythical event there may or may not lie a ritual occasion at which some participants felt themselves briefly to shed something of their contemporary selves. One could study the different ways in which sources speak of such a relation to the past: sometimes the rite is said to

---

[29] Plut. *Sol.* 9; cf. p. 484.

[30] See App. 1 s.v. *Aianteia*, Artemis Agrotera, Democracy, [*Eleutheria*], *Mounichia*, Sphragitic Nymphs; cf. *Athenian Religion*, 187; 273–4.

[31] See *Athenian Religion*, 187, 273–4.

imitate the past event, sometimes to commemorate it, sometimes the action is simply said to have been repeated 'ever since', as if the logic needed no explanation.[32] But such an enquiry would not give access to the emotions of participants while imitating or commemorating or repeating the supposed original event. Only very occasionally does a source collapse the distance between present and past completely, and speak of participants in the ritual as if they were actual actors in the mythical events: Lactantius' statement that the initiates at Eleusis 'hunt for Kore' is an instance, and perhaps the only one. Here too the *Mysteries* are likely to represent the extreme case. But, if we postulate a spectrum, it will still be hard to know where upon it a particular festival is to be put.[33]

It is very important to bring such imponderables into the open. What mattered about festivals was the experience of the participants, however limited and problematic our knowledge of it may be. A further imponderable concerns the intensity of festival experience. This is a special form of a larger question concerning the intensity of Greek religious experience as a whole. The question has perhaps never been posed in that abstract form, though implicit answers to it can be tracked down in the literature. For some, Dionysiac experience is intense, all other forms of cult much less so. Intensity can be sought in sacrifice, envisaged as a *mysterium tremendum*, or in the synaesthetic excitement of choral dancing. Or perhaps, like the better type of eighteenth-century Englishman, the Greeks were 'religious without enthusiasm'. What is clear is that whatever intensity there was in Greek religious experience was a product of ritual, and of festivals above all. Some 'hot spots' have been emphasized above: the marriage of Dionysus to an Athenian woman during the *Anthesteria*, the 'extraordinary experience' of the *Mysteries* as a whole. Rituals of cleansing (the *Thargelia*, with its sadistic expulsion of scapegoats; the *Plynteria*, with its dramatization of impurity while Athena's statue was veiled) had a certain grim power; so too did the penitential *Diasia*. But at some festivals nothing more is attested than ceremony and fun and food. Our sources may often be defective; the hot spots of women's festivals would tend to be hidden from us, and (to repeat a point) it is only by chance that we hear of the simulated human sacrifice that occurred at the *Tauropolia*. But about the *Panathenaea* we know, perhaps, enough to be confident that it was always dignified but never intense, never emotionally strong. Here too

---

[32] On imitation (μίμημα) and commemoration (ὑπόμνημα) see *Liverpool Classical Monthly*, 14 (1989), 154–5; *Athenian Religion*, 273–4 and note already Eur. *Ion* 1429; for a simple 'ever since' or similar e.g. Eur. *IT* 958–60, Plut. *Thes*. 18.2, 22.4, 24.4. Alternatively the initiative could be presented as coming from a god or hero who founded the rite (*Eleusinian Mysteries*; Triptolemus and the *Proerosia* (p. 331, n. 20); also e.g. Eur. *IT* 1458–61; *Hipp*. 1423–30). The logic underlying 'ever since' would doubtless normally, if spelt out, have been that of 'imitation' (cf. Eur *Ion* 20–6 with 1427–9).

[33] Cases to think about would include the *Kronia* and, in contrasting ways, the second and third days of the *Anthesteria* (see pp. 202, 293 and 295–6). Lactantius: see p. 355.

we are likely to be dealing with quite a broad spectrum of possible experiences.

Pericles in Thucydides' Funeral Oration speaks of 'year-round competitions and sacrifices' that provide a 'relief from labour'; other sources too present Athens as a city of festivals and spectacles on a scale unparalleled in the rest of Greece.[34] 'Festivals and spectacles': theoreticians sometimes distinguish ritual from drama in the sense that drama has an audience whereas ritual has only participants.[35] Such a distinction cannot be pressed in relation to Greece,[36] but it is hard to deny that an Athenian's role at many festivals of the city had become largely that of spectator and consumer of meat. Athens, we must remember, was an 'archaic city', not a village community. Centralized festivals which 25–30,000 citizens were entitled to attend could scarcely avoid pushing the participants in the direction of spectatorship.[37] The proliferation of elective cults discussed above is another distinctively urban phenomenon. Yet, as we have seen, not all festivals even of the city were like that, since some took place primarily in individual houses and gave a role to families. And every Athenian remained involved in a good number of rites of smaller bodies such as deme and phratry which must have had a much more face-to-face feel to them.[38] The *Thesmophoria* was so organized that women too probably did not feel themselves submerged in an anonymous mass. Citizens were constantly involved (the experiences of metics and foreigners must have been very different) in a complex range of ritual activities at many different levels of civic organization. This co-presence of (so to speak) the village with the city is perhaps the central characteristic of the ever varied festival life of the archaic city.

---

[34] Thuc. 2.38.1; [Xen.] *Ath. Pol.* 2.9; Theopompus *FGrH* 115 F 213 (final sentence); Pl. *Alc.* ii. 148e; F. Pfister, *Die Reisebilder des Herakleides* (Vienna 1951), § 1.

[35] See Rappaport, *Ritual and Religion*, 39–43.

[36] See the brilliant critique by Kavoulaki, 'Ritual Performance', 154, and above, pp. 163 and 182, on the perception of processions and *pannychides* (undeniable ritual forms) as spectacles.

[37] Archaic city: see p. 3. Levy, *Mesocosm*, 61, associates 'the expansion and differentiation of dramatic, attention grabbing ... religious forms' (cf. Attic developments in the 6th c., *Athenian Religion*, ch. 6) with the archaic city; he ascribes actual theatre of Greek style to the 'rationalism' which increasingly distinguished the Greek from the 'archaic' city.

[38] On the denial of this claim by Edward Cohen see p. 3, n. 8.

TABLE I. Aitiological myths of Attic festivals

Festival	Aitiological myth	Reference
Anthesteria:		
Pithoigia	Arrival of Dionysus in Attica?	See p. 292
Choes	Orestes entertained by Demophon	See p. 293
Chytroi	Aftermath of Deucalion's flood	See p. 296
? Aiora	Death by hanging of 'Erigone'	See p. 301
? Marriage of Dionysus	(Theseus and Ariadne—probably irrelevant)	See p. 305
Apatouria	The trick of Melanthos against Xanthos	Hellanicus *FGrH* 4 F 125 = 323a F 23; cf. p. 461
Arrephoria	(Daughters of Cecrops?)	See p. 221
Boedromia	(*a*) aid given by Ion in the war against Eumolpus ? (*b*) a counter-attack during Theseus' battle with the Amazons	(*a*) Philoch. 328 F 13 (*b*) Jacoby, comm. on Philoch. loc. cit, p. 281
Brauronia	(*a*) Sacrifice of Iphigeneia (*b*) killing of a bear Iphigeneia is also to be a priestess in the cult	See p. 238 Eur. *IT* 1462–3
Chalkeia	(Hephaestus' relationship to Erichthonius?)	
City Dionysia	Bringing of an image of Dionysus by Pegasus of Eleutherae	*Athenian Religion*, 94
Delia/annual *theoria* to Delos	Theseus' voyage to Delos	See p. 81
Delphinion, procession to	Commemorated a supplication by the seven maidens prior to Theseus' expedition against the Minotaur	Plut. *Thes.* 18.2

Dipolieia	Slaying of ox by Sopater/ Diomos	See p. 187
Eleusinia	Founded to celebrate Demeter's gift of corn to mankind	See p. 202
Epidauria	Arrival of Asclepius at Athens during the *Mysteries*	Philostr. *VA* 4.18
Greater Mysteries	Demeter's coming to Eleusis	See pp. 341–2
Hekalesia	Commemoration of Hekale, who showed hospitality to Theseus	Plut. *Thes.* 14.2
Hephaisteia	(Hephaestus' relationship to Erichthonius?)	
Hieros Gamos	Zeus' marriage to Hera	See p. 76
Kallynteria	Because Aglauros as priestess was first to 'adorn the gods'.	Phot. κ 124 s.v.*Καλλυντήρια*
Kronia	'The age of Kronos'	See p. 202
Kybernesia	Honours members of Theseus' crew	Philochorus *FGrH* 328 F 111
Lesser Mysteries	Initiation of Heracles	See p. 345
Metageitnia	A move (in mythical time?) from Melite to Diomeia	Plut. *De exil.* 6, 601b
Mounichia	Killing of a bear; trick of Embaros	See p. 238
Oschophoria	Disguise of two companions of Theseus	See p. 213
Panathenaea	(*a*) Commemorates death of giant Aster (*b*) established by Erichthonius or (*c*) by Theseus	See pp. 254–6
Plynteria	Commemoration of the first washing of the sacred vestments, left unwashed for a year after the death of Aglauros	Hesych. s.v. *Πλυντήρια*; Phot. κ 124 s.v.*Καλλυντήρια*; *Anecd. Bekk.* 1.270.1–5.

Continues

TABLE I. *Continued*

Festival	Aitiological myth	Reference
Procession for Semnai	Aftermath of trial of Orestes	Aesch. *Eum.* 1021–47
Procharisteria	'*Anodos* of the goddess'	See p. 196
Proerosia	Established by Triptolemus, later revived/extended at the time of a great famine	See pp. 330–1
Prometheia	Theft of fire by Prometheus?	
Pyanopsia	(a) a meal eaten by Theseus' companions on return; the *eiresione* recalls their suppliant branch (b) the 'abundance of foods' visible when the Athenians brought a great famine to an end (c) how the Athenians fed the children of Heracles.	(a) and (c) Plut. *Thes.* 22.4–7; (b) p. 205
Pythaïs	Apollo's journey to Delphi from Delos	See pp. 86–7
Rural Dionysia	The phallic procession commemorates the priapism that afflicted shepherds at the time of the introduction of Dionysus' cult	See p. 376, n. 27
Synoikia	Synoecism of Theseus	Thuc. 2.15.2; Plut. *Thes.* 24.3–4 (*Metoikia*)
Tauropolia	Founded to house the image of Taurian Artemis brought to Attica by Iphigeneia and Orestes; the ritual commemorates the human sacrifices of that cult	Eur. *IT* 1449–61
Thargelia	The pharmakos ritual was instituted to remove the pollution caused by the killing of Androgeos	Helladius ap. Phot. *Bibl.* 279 p. 534 a 2–12. See p. 482

Thesmophoria	(a) the 'chambering' rite commemorates the loss of Eubouleus' pigs at the time of the rape of Kore	See p. 273
	(b) the festival was instituted by Celeus after Demeter's coming to Eleusis, the incident of the 'child in the fire', and the mission of Triptolemus	*Serv. Dan.* in Virg. *Georg.* 1.19, etc.*
	(c) an unidentified myth in Callim. fr. 63 explains the exclusion of virgins	

Note: Festivals of some prominence for which no *aitia* are known include *Diasia, Diisoteria, Hephaisteia, Lenaea, Olympieia, Pompaia, Skira, Stenia.*

* See H. J. Rose, *Hygini Fabulae* (Leiden 1933), 184.

III

17

Gods at Work I: Protecting the City

Greek polytheism is indescribable. The major gods have so many special forms; there are so many lesser gods, and heroes; they can all combine in such a multitude of ways. After the heroic efforts of the early writers of *Theogonies*, no Greek ever attempted to offer a thorough account of the pantheon, or anything like it;[1] Greeks called on 'the gods and heroes who occupied' their territories to lend aid in times of crisis, but never tried to list who they might be. It was not, far from it, that the traditional gods attracted no intellectual speculation. Attempts to reveal the hidden essence of particular gods or to identify this god with that were not rare. But neither the ordinary politicians who kept the cults going nor speculative thinkers were concerned to quantify the pantheon, to list all the gods, or to explain the relations between them. Gods overflowed like clothes from an over-filled drawer which no one felt obliged to tidy. That lack of felt need is itself an important datum. But it does not aid the task of the investigator. An account runs the risk of becoming that meaningless parade of many cults which Durkheim feared.[2]

Yet the gods cannot simply be ignored. If one attempts today to describe the indescribable, the best starting-point is the application of structuralist ideas to the study of Greek polytheism that occurred in the 1960s and 1970s.[3] What was most significant about the new approach was perhaps the recognition that the analysis of a pantheon is a problematic exercise. The structuralists offered for the first time (can this really be true?—but so at least it seems today[4]) a systematic position which one could either accept or react against. The central and defining proposition is that Greek gods need to be studied not

---

[1] We come closest perhaps in Hellenistic listing of cult titles and analysis of 'different gods bearing the same name': G. Wentzel, Ἐπικλήσεις Θεῶν sive De deorum cognominibus per grammaticorum graecorum scripta dispersis (diss. Göttingen 1889); W. Michaelis, De origine indicis deorum cognominum (diss. Berlin 1898).

[2] E. Durkheim, *The Elementary Forms of the Religious Life*, tr. J. C. Swain (London 1915), 5.

[3] First by J. P. Vernant alone, then, with some change of emphasis, in association with M. Detienne. Four landmarks: Vernant, 'Hestia-Hermès', in *Mythe et pensée*, I, 124–70 (1963); id., 'La société des dieux', in his *Mythe et société*, 103–20 (Paris 1966); Detienne, *Jardins* (1972); Detienne/Vernant, *Mètis* (1974).

[4] Before structuralism, there were perhaps two main implicit models for the analysis of a god's powers, both subdivisions of the overarching model of 'historical development'. One, which we will meet again, was (so to speak) 'the great earth-mother' and the erosion of her powers; this told of gods of all-but-universal competence being gradually cut down to size. The other, by contrast,

one by one but with reference to one another, as members of a pantheon. The powers of one god are defined and limited by those of another, and one cannot usefully contemplate the powers of Artemis, say, in isolation, any more than one can isolate the powers of the bishop in chess: Artemis is what she is by contrast with other gods, just as is the bishop by contrast with knights and pawns.

Needless to say, just as Saussurian structuralist linguistics can be seen as a formalization of the 'best practice' of earlier studies,[5] so too there had always been scholars who were aware that the powers of particular gods were constrained by those of others. How could there not have been, given that the structuralist position is only a reformulation of the Greeks' own stories of how functions, *timai*, were divided out in the early times among the various gods? Indeed, one might assemble *obiter dicta* of earlier scholarship and construct from them an alternative, 'free-market' model, whereby gods seek always to extend their powers but are usually inhibited by the prestige of established rivals.[6] Yet *obiter dicta*, not a theory, are what they were; and there always were also (and still are) accounts which cheerfully credit individual gods with almost unrestricted powers. Perhaps there *are* examples of gods who exercise functions not assigned to them in the familiar panhellenic distribution of *timai*. But structuralism teaches us not to acknowledge such cases without a fight; and, where they cannot be denied, we also need a theory to account for them. It is recognized, for instance, that the distribution of functions in local pantheons may differ significantly from panhellenic norms.[7] But even in such cases there is usually a distribution, only not the familiar one. There might also be circumstances in which the principle of distribution, which is also a principle of economy, breaks down. We would need then to define what they are.

A natural correlate to the first proposition is that, where different gods appear to be exercising the same function, they are not necessarily doing so in reality. If we cease to lump together as 'marriage goddesses', for instance, all those powers invoked by a girl during her transition from maid to wife, we can recognize them rather as a team, each contributing her own speciality.[8] Even where gods share an epithet it does not mean that they share a function:

---

told of gods gaining in functions by a process of 'one thing leads to another': if a god can do *x* for me, asks the worshipper, why can he not also do the closely related *y*? This second approach stresses the role of worshippers in creating gods (Farnell, *Cults*, v, 29; Nilsson, *Geschichte*, 386 (cf. 250)).

[5] See A. Morpurgo Davies, *La linguistica dell' ottocento* (Bologna 1996), 374, n. 51, 391.

[6] For such language see e.g. Nilsson, *Geschichte*, 440 (Athena Hygieia as a characteristic instance of great god expansionism), 451 (Poseidon's expansion obstructed by river gods; similarly 401 on Zeus and agriculture), 538 ('erfolgreiche Konkurrenz' of healing heroes against Apollo).

[7] C. Sourvinou-Inwood, *JHS* 98 (1978), 101–21 = ead., *'Reading' Greek Culture* (Oxford 1991), 147–88.

[8] So L. Bruit Zaidman/ P. Schmitt Pantel, *Religion in the Ancient Greek City*, tr. P. Cartledge (Cambridge 1992), 186–8.

Hermes is Agoraios because the agora is a place of trade, Zeus because it is also a place of political speech.[9] All this is too manifestly true to require further emphasis. Doubts and difficulties arise only at the margins. One intriguing case relating to Athens is that of Poseidon Hippios and Athena Hippia, who were worshipped together at Colonus; there was also a sole cult of Athena Hippia at Acharnae (and one of Poseidon Hippodromios perhaps at Phaleron[10]). On the basis of extra-Attic evidence, it can be argued, elegantly and persuasively, that the two gods relate to horses in different ways: Poseidon symbolizes the raw power of the mighty beast, Athena the technological skill needed to master that power through bridle and reins.[11] But, according to Sophocles in a glorious ode, it was Poseidon who at Colonus first tamed the horse with reins. This need not mean that the distinction between Poseidon Hippios and Athena Hippia is a delusion, but it does seem to indicate that in certain contexts it could cease to matter. What, after all, is a god of Horses? Surely more than anything a god of horsemen: it is the existence of riders, and probably riders organized as cavalry, that creates a demand for such powers. Details of the dealings between the horsemen and their gods unfortunately escape us entirely. But it is surely plausible that they felt able to approach both Poseidon and Athena about all their horse-related concerns. The distinction between the lord of the horse and the mistress of the rein would therefore be blunted in actual cult practice.[12]

The difficulties of this particular case, however, do not affect the main point. Central areas of human life elicit the involvement of many different gods, but each comes at them from his or her own angle. Conversely, each major god is active in many different spheres, and very often in a way that straddles all the divisions that we might like to set up between public and private, male and female, natural and social worlds.[13] Aphrodite is involved with (for instance) sexuality, marriage, seafaring and political life, and this multiplicity of diverse interests is the norm for a great god. Gods differ from mortals, therefore, not merely in power but also in this multi-dimensionality; they are not superhuman humans but bundles of powers quite inconceivable in human terms. Yet myth and art alike represent them as more like humans, with personalities, than are the gods of almost any other polytheistic system; their radical otherness is unmistakable when pointed out, yet constantly

---

[9] Farnell, *Cults*, i, 58.

[10] *LSS* 19.89–90, probably to be associated with the hippodrome at Echelidai near Phaleron. The occasion of the sacrifice by the *Salaminioi* is uncertain: could the *Kybernesia* (*Athenian Religion*, 314–15) have included a horse-race? Kolonos: Paus. 1.30.4; Soph. *OC* 55 and 669–715; *IG* I³ 383.59 and 405; p. 57, n. 29. Acharnae: Paus. 1.31.6, with *IG* II² 1206–7.

[11] Detienne/Vernant, *Mètis*, 176–200 (187–213 in the Engl. tr.); they discuss the ode of Sophocles, *OC* 668–719, at 198, n. 92 (212, n. 92).

[12] For display of decrees honouring cavalry commanders 'beside the Posidonion' (in Colonus?) see *SEG* XXI 525.43.

[13] J. P. Vernant, *Mythe et société* (Paris 1966), 105 (94 in the Engl. tr.).

disguised.[14] Humans seek to do business with them, as with other mortals, through the idiom of gift-giving and reciprocity.

Each major god, we have said, is active in many different spheres, and the question arises of what if anything unifies these disparate activities. The original structuralist answer was that each god was marked not by a distinctive sphere of activity (for, as we have noted, 'marriage', for instance, was common to many), but by a distinctive mode of action or of intervention or a distinctive *locus standi*: Zeus manifests sovereignty in all that he does, Athena *metis*, and so on.[15] This was, in a sense, a very conservative position, because it gave back to the gods an essence and an essential unity that had often been denied to them:[16] Athena might have ceased to be that goddess of war and weaving and reason of whom we learnt at school, but she re-emerged, more splendid, as a manifestation of a particular form of intelligence and of that alone ... This approach has been shown to be so powerfully effective in many areas that one is tempted to hail it as a panacea. It works for most of Artemis, for most of Athena, for all perhaps of Aphrodite (who applies to storms and political affairs the same conciliatory charm that unites lovers). But stubborn difficulties remain. Callimachus, at the start of the *Hymn to Artemis*, describes the goddess as a little girl sitting on her father's knee and asking him for a series of attributes and spheres of activity when she grows up: may I have many names, may I be a virgin and a huntress, may I roam mountains and never enter cities except when I come to the aid of women in labour. This is a familiar image of the wild and timid goddess. But her father responds that he will give more than she asks for, including thirty cities which will honour her alone (great hyperbole this, surely), and a place in many others. It is hard not to feel, with some paranoia, that the great ironist Callimachus[17] is here ridiculing our attempts to discover the logic of polytheism, so devastatingly difficult are the extra powers accorded by Zeus to accommodate in any general theory.[18] Or consider the military role of Athena, which has caused her often to be seen as a kind of bipolar goddess, part technological, part warlike. The most promising approach here is to contrast Athena, rational violence, with Ares, mere blind bloodlust (the *vis temperata* and *vis consilii*

---

[14] On the 'power or personality' debate about Greek gods see Bremmer, *Greek Religion*, 22–3, with references. Seen from Bhaktapur in Nepal, Greek gods have far more personality than the members of many pantheons: Levy, *Mesocosm*, 282.

[15] Detienne/Vernant, *Mètis*, 167, n. 2 (183, n. 2 in the Engl. tr.) ascribe this insight to G. Dumézil, *La Religion romaine archaïque* (Paris 1966), 179, 229.

[16] Cf. C. J. Herington, *JHS* 89 (1969), 168–70.

[17] P. Veyne, *L'Élégie érotique romaine* (Paris 1983), 32.

[18] For an attempt see Vernant, *Mortals and Immortals*, 204–5: Artemis expresses both 'the other', and also the capacity of culture to integrate it. On the particular case of Artemis Metaxu and Phylake at Eretria see D. Knoepfler in M. H. Hansen (ed.), *The Polis as an Urban Centre and as a Political Community* (Copenhagen 1997), 376–7. See too Cole, *Ritual Space*, 182–4.

expers of Horace).[19] Yet Athena is regularly associated with 'battle and war' without any contrast with Ares being drawn or implied; nor is that greater restraint which she brings to the business of warfare exactly a matter of *metis*. She is, it is true, a war-god of a different stamp from Ares, and the principle of separate functions is thus more or less preserved. But her military role can scarcely be derived from the simple exercise of *metis*.

Hermes is another good case to ponder. Most of his activities can be related to a core which cannot be captured in a single phrase (unless it be 'Hermes'!) in any language, but can be roughly paraphrased as transition/communication/exchange. Indeed Apollo in the *Homeric Hymn to Hermes* describes his sphere of activity, in a strikingly modern-sounding phrase found here only, as 'the activities of exchange' (ἐπαμοίβιμα ἔργα). But Hermes has also a strong association with pasture lands, and in particular with the successful and productive mating of the stock, which seems distinct from this core.[20] And, by the fourth century, the first context in which any young Athenian will have encountered Hermes was as patron, along with Heracles, of the *palaistra* and the gymnasium. His link with these places probably derives from an early attested role (itself not easy to explain)[21] as ἐναγώνιος, a patron of competitions. But, even if the link derives from that role, it goes beyond it. Hermes is not present in the gymnasium only on days of competition; he is always there, he occupies and fills it. Innumerable dedications from the whole Greek world in the hellenistic period attest the fact. Hermes did not expand at the expense of another god; rather, he moved into an empty space created by the growth of the institution of the gymnasium. And his modest place in the Olympian hierarchy made him an appropriate patron for the young users of those places. None the less, the emergence of Hermes of the gymnasium looks like

[19] See the works cited by S. Deacy, 'Athena and Ares', in H. van Wees (ed.), *War and Violence in Ancient Greece* (London 2000), 285–98, at 285: she begins with an unexpected structuralist, John Ruskin. Detienne/Vernant, *Mètis*, 167–75 (177–86 in the Engl. tr.) emphasize rather the association of Athena with bronze and thus with technology. But (1) the aegis of Athena is a natural product and (2) the argument fails in terms of their own contrastive principles, given that Ares too is 'brazen'.

[20] Exchange: *Hym. Hom. Herm.* 516. Mating: ibid. 491–4; Hes. *Theog.* 444. Vernant's answer is in terms of a contrast between a household's stored wealth in charge of Hestia and its mobile and potentially growing wealth in charge of Hermes (*Mythe et pensée*, i, 158; 152 in the Engl. tr.). But the binary opposition here is based on the rather questionable introduction of 'wealth' as *tertium comparationis*, while omitting other gods associated with forms of wealth (Zeus Ktesios, Plouton/Ploutos). Hermes' patronage of thieves and deceit is another interesting point of division between approaches. Structuralists parcel it up with communication/exchange, as if the patron of these functions necessarily patronized also the tricky exercise of them. But the matter is not so simple: as a patron of heralds, for instance, Hermes stands for straight dealing only. Nilsson (*Geschichte*, 507) and others argue that a god of herdsmen naturally became also a god of cattle-theft, an approved practice if exercised against outsiders.

[21] Competition is a form of interaction or exchange: Vernant, *Mythe et pensée*, i, 127 (129 in the Engl. tr.); competition demands cunning, a sense of the right moment: L. Kahn, *Hermès passe* (Paris 1978), 15. Farnell, *Cults*, v, 29–30, is baffled. N. Marinatos in *Initiation*, 130–52, puts a case, using the evidence of Kato Symi in Crete, for Hermes as a god intrinsically connected with the young through initiation, a form of transition.

a case of the extension of a god's sphere of competence not on the basis of the internal logic of a central core; the principle at work is more that of 'one thing leads to another'.[22] Where such extensions occur, they are sometimes local and transitory. Hermes, again, provides an example: at Athens he became somewhat associated with cavalry commanders, apparently because the cavalry's place of muster chanced to abut the region of the agora known as 'the Herms'.[23] This local development had no influence outside Attica, and such phenomena could easily be accommodated within the structuralist model by the addition of a footnote. The expansion of Hermes into the gymnasium, by contrast, happens throughout the Greek world, and in permanence.

In the early structuralist classics, the attempt was made to tease out the gods' distinctive modes of activity by systematic comparison: *A* would be contrasted with *B* not only at points of open intersection between them, such as that between Poseidon Hippios and Athena Hippia, but throughout the whole gamut of their activities. The difficulty with this procedure is that *A* ought to be compared not just with *B* but with every other power in the pantheon. The pairings and oppositions found in cult vary like the configurations of a kaleidoscope,[24] and nothing suggests that a Greek god's nature is defined by a binary special relationship with a particular partner. Binary comparison and the quest for single, distinctive modes of activity led, some now feel, to too stiff and fixed a picture of a pantheon that was recreated and reordered day by day, if within certain constraints, through the decisions made by individual worshippers.[25]

---

[22] The question of what is to count as 'development structured by a central logic' and what as 'one thing leads to another' or 'snowball' growth is itself very difficult. A close reading of any account of a god's functions, whether written by a structuralist or non-structuralist, reveals diverse slips and slides from one function to another. See for instance n. oo below on Zeus' association with wealth.

[23] Decrees honouring phylarchs/hipparchs were displayed 'by the Herms' (*SEG* XXI 357.9, 435.11, 525.44), and Mnesimachus fr. 4.3–4 speaks of the Herms as a place where phylarchs go, presumably because the *hipparcheion* (*IG* II² 895.6 = *SEG* XXI 436) was there; monuments celebrating victory in the *anthippasia* were displayed in the region (*IG* II² 3130, and T. L. Shear Jr., *Hesperia* 42, 1973, 179); note too (with C. Habicht, *AM* 76, 1961, 136–8) Xen. *Eq. mag.* 3. 2 and Ath. 167f. Cavalry commanders accordingly dedicate to Hermes (*SEG* XXXVI 269; XLVII 197) and have their honours proclaimed at the *agon* of the *Hermaia* (*IG* II² 895.5 = *SEG* XXI 436), perhaps to be envisaged as a largely equestrian competition held near the Herms (so Habicht, op. cit., 140: Demetrius of Phaleron the younger won a chariot victory at unspecified *Hermaia*, *IG* II² 2971.13), distinct from the *Hermaia* of gymnasia.

[24] Cf. J. D. Reed, *AntCl* 14 (1995), 326.

[25] See P. Borgeaud (who acknowledges input from M. Detienne), 'Manières grecques de nommer les dieux', *Colloqium Helveticum* 23 (1996) 19–36, esp. 19–23 and the citation of V. Bouillier and G. Toffin (eds.), *Classer les dieux? Des pantheons en Asie du sud* (Paris 1993); M. Detienne, 'Expérimenter dans le champ des polythéismes', *Kernos* 1997 (English version in *Arion*, spring/summer 1999, 127–49). Borgeaud writes, 23, 'C'est dans la relation concrète de l'interlocuteur à la puissance que s'opère le classement du pantheon'. The worshipper strikes back (cf. n. 4)!

No structuralist has yet questioned the prominence given in such analyses, under the influence of Levi-Strauss, to myth. Yet the unconscious assumptions of the individual worshipper were obviously not shaped, in the typical case, by knowledge of the whole corpus of Greek mythology. The competition between myth and cult for the title of 'best source' for the study of Greek religion is an old and, one would like to think, superannuated one. Myths reveal who and what the gods worshipped in the rituals are (a fundamental truth obscured by the 'myth and ritual' debate), and in that sense myth and cult should complement and not oppose one another. But myths do not do that alone, and it remains true that an account of the Greek gods based primarily on myths is likely to differ greatly from one based primarily on cults. The marriage of Zeus and Hera is represented in a succession of myths as a troubled one; yet in cult it remains the model of the institution of marriage.[26] A less drastic but still interesting case concerns that contrast between Poseidon and Athena which was mentioned earlier. In the myth of the Argonauts as told by Apollonius, they are both involved with seafaring, but in different ways: Poseidon with the sea itself, Athena with the art of the helmsman. This is a replication of the difference that separates Poseidon from Athena of Horses. But in cult, though a great variety of gods are variously associated with seafaring, Athena is not, or scarcely so. (But let us note an Athenian 'Steering' festival (*Kybernesia*) which has no securely attested honorand: Athena could make a claim ...). Of this it might be said that myth reveals a full panoply of Athena's potentialities,[27] of which only some become actualized in cult.

There are also, which is more serious, actualities of cult which fail to give rise to myths. In the last twenty-five years of the twentieth century, many of the most acute students of ancient religion offered accounts of Apollo. A stroll among these very varied portraits is most instructive, but the most fundamental point of difference lies in the emphasis given to the god's role in the rearing up of boys to manhood. Some accounts ignore what for others lies at the heart of Apollo's civic importance. This is a cultic function not prominent in the myths of Apollo but attested, with unusual clarity, in two early texts.[28] A final relevant difference between myths and cults: myths present, in the main, the clearly defined figures of major Olympians in interaction with one

---

[26] But Christiane Sourvinou-Inwood points out to me that it is not coincidence that it is precisely in relation to the 'archetypal' marriage that myth explores marital troubles. J. Redfield, *Arethusa* 15 (1982), 182, writes: 'the figure of Hera predicted to the Greek bride that her marriage would be a struggle resolved at best in uneasy compromise'.

[27] Or, as Marcel Detienne often calls them, 'virtualités'. On Athena and the sea see Detienne/ Vernant, *Mètis*, 201–41 (215–58 in the Engl. tr.). *Kybernesia*: *Athenian Religion*, 314–15, and p. 410 below; note too p. 410, n. 93 below on Athena and the steersman Phrontis.

[28] Hom. *Od.* 19.86; Hes. *Theog.* 347. Portraits of Apollo: see W. Burkert, 'Apellai und Apollon', *RhM* 118 (1975), 1–21; Versnel, 'Apollo and Mars', in his *Transition and Reversal*, 290–334, and the works of Graf, Jameson, Dumezil and Detienne cited below. Broadly Burkert, Jameson, Graf and Versnel engage in various ways with Apollo as a god of ephebes or (Jameson) post-ephebes; Dumezil and Detienne follow quite different paths.

another; cults swarm with lesser figures, not just heroes, though there are these in huge abundance, but also functional gods such as Kourotrophos and Pankrates and Nymphe. The gods of myth are familiar, plastic figures, though they may lose some of their sharpness of outline in cult. But myths did not speak of figures such as Pankrates, and the various stabs at identification made by worshippers suggest that they struggled to decide who he might be.

Structuralism sometimes speaks of polytheism as a system with a logic. But system and logic are both elastic terms. A local pantheon is not a product of system-building or the attempt to impose a logic in the same way as is, say, the *Theogony* of Hesiod. Consider, for instance, the chopping up of experience into segments put under divine patronage. Alone among land-animals the horse gives rise to a divine epithet, Hippios; yet this epithet is born not by one god, but by two. Grain crops are the concern of Demeter and vines of Dionysus, but who exactly should one pray to for one's figs[29] and fruit and pulses? The traveller by land prays to Hermes, but the traveller by sea must make his choice between a plethora of helpers: Poseidon, Aphrodite, Zeus Soter, the Dioscuri, the Great Gods ... Explanations for this inconsistent distribution of divine protection are usually not at all difficult to find. There are Poseidon and Athena of Horses but no Dionysus of Donkeys nor Hera of Cows (despite their affinities with those animals) because horsemen count for more in Greek society than riders of donkeys or drivers of cows. Poseidon Hippios makes sense, then; but it is not the sense of abstract thought or systematic taxonomy or map-making. If a Greek pantheon is a map of experience, we must understand by 'map' a working sketch on the back of an envelope.[30]

The pantheon here studied is that not of Greece but of Athens. The restriction imposes a discipline, and confers a rigour, which surely ought to be the ideal. If one is studying the gods in their interrelationships with one another, one must distinguish the interrelationships that exist in Athens from those of Sparta; and one must aim at comprehensiveness, to prevent hard cases from simply being left on one side. A comprehensive study of the gods of Greece is an impossible ideal: within a particular city one can at least come closer to it. Propositions that appear plausible in a panhellenic perspective become problematic once one attempts to work them through in relation to all the details of an actual pantheon. Certainly, there is a danger here of misplaced positivism: our evidence does not present a total picture of the functions which the various gods will have exercised at Athens, far from it. But the local view remains a powerful stimulus to thought even if what it

---

[29] In Attica, the answer seems to be that Demeter has a mediated relation with the fig, via the hero Phytalos: see Paus. 1.37.2, and for the importance of the place 'sacred fig' in the Eleusinian procession p. 347, n. 85.

[30] Our explanations of polytheism, like our explanations of history, are all post eventum. No one could successfully predict the shape of a pantheon. Cf. Burkert, *Greek Religion*, 217–18.

reveals may in a given case be a gap in the evidence rather than a real local anomaly.

It is time to bring these preliminaries to a close. Many more problems have been raised than have been resolved. But one principle for the organization of material perhaps imposes itself. Greek gods, we have seen, very regularly act in teams; and the attempt to distinguish their separate contributions or competences in such cases is of great theoretical importance. It will be best, then, to study the gods not one by one but in groups: the groups (best of all) in which they actually appear in sacred calendars and the like; the groups also which we can assemble of gods particularly concerned with particular departments of human life. The methodological ideal in the study of polytheism, which would be to consider every aspect of every god in relation to every other god, is completely unrealizable; the procedure suggested here can claim to be the best practical protection against studying the individual gods in isolation. It has the disadvantage that, whereas the categories of 'Apollo' and 'Artemis' are givens, it is the observer who must create the categories of warfare and politics and the like used to organize a topic-based treatment. I acknowledge the artificiality, and proceed. The order of presentation too is somewhat arbitrary. In *Eumenides*, Athena draws a distinction between, roughly, protection of the citizens in warfare, which is her own function, and care for their growth and flourishing, which she assigns to the Eumenides (903–15). An approximation to that structure will underly the division between this chapter and the next. But analytically it is not designed to bear weight.

The approach to gods through functions may seem to square ill with the earlier insistence, in relation to festivals, that the search for simple purposes and functions is misguided and reductive. But there is a real difference between the two cases: one approaches a healing deity when one is ill, whereas the regular festivals are never thought to bring immediate benefits either to individuals or to the community in that way. Festivals are there to be experienced, but gods can help with specific needs.

GODS OF THE ACROPOLIS, CITY-PROTECTORS

I start with protection of the city, in order to cede to Athena that first place which she demands, in a city where appeals were often made in the name of 'Athena and the (other) gods'.[31] She towers over all the other gods in the city's pantheon: the sacred treasures were divided between those of Athena and of 'the Other Gods', and in the Peloponnesian war period Athena seems to

---

[31] Ar. *Eccl.* 476; Alexis fr. 247.14; Lycurg. *Leoc.* 1; Din. 1.64.

have been about five times as rich as all the other gods put together[32]. She is
the paradigm case of what one might call the 'local special god' within Greek
polytheism. No Greek epithet catches the sense of 'special god' and the status
is far from being a formalized one, but it is not in doubt that some[33] cities were
felt to have a special relationship with single divine protectors. Polynices in
Euripides' *Phoenissae* addresses a prayer to 'Mistress Hera', and explains 'for I
am yours, since I have married the daughter of Adrastus, and live in Argos'.
The chorus in *Rhesus* generalize the point, speculating about the identity of a
mysterious intruder from the Greek camp. Who was he, they wonder, from
what part of the Greek world? 'What highest god does he invoke?' ($\pi o \hat{\iota} o \nu$
$\dot{\epsilon} \pi \epsilon \dot{\upsilon} \chi \epsilon \tau \alpha \iota \ \tau \grave{o} \nu \ \ddot{\upsilon} \pi \alpha \tau o \nu \ \theta \epsilon \hat{\omega} \nu$).[34] Very many are the texts that illustrate Solon's
image of Athena stretching out her hands over Athens to protect it. Athens is
the 'city of Pallas', and the Athenians are 'Pallas' citizens'. Athena 'has Attica
as her portion', she 'holds' or 'lives in' or 'rules' the city of which 'she is called
key-holder'. For Athenians she is 'mistress of this land' and 'our local goddess'
($\dot{\epsilon} \pi \iota \chi \dot{\omega} \rho \iota o \varsigma \ \dot{\eta} \mu \epsilon \tau \acute{\epsilon} \rho \alpha \ \theta \epsilon \acute{o} \varsigma$).[35] 'Yours is the ground, yours the city, you are its
mother and queen and guardian', the chorus of men of Marathon in Euripi-
des' *Heraclidae* insist to her; the chorus of Athenian women in *Ion*, sightseeing
at Delphi, catch sight of a sculpture of Athena and hail her gleefully as 'my
goddess', with a sudden intimacy that refutes all attempts to contrast 'civic'
with 'private' in Greek religious experience.[36]

The case of a special goddess as honoured as Athena raises crucial questions for any theoretical study of Greek polytheism. In a pantheon of divided
functions, how can a single goddess grow so great? Different gods have
different functions or *timai*; different gods love different cities best: these
truisms coexist in Greek texts without any attempt being made to show
how the one relates to the other. Scholars sometimes assemble evidence for
Athena's supposed power over the fertility both of the fields and the womb, as
though inviting us to fall down in reverence before a primeval all-powerful

---

[32] 'In the years 433–426 the Athenians borrowed over 4,001 T. from Athena Polias and over
766 T. from the Other Gods': R. Meiggs and D. Lewis, *A Selection of Greek Historical Inscriptions to
the End of the Fifth Century B.C.* (Oxford 1969), 217. Note too e.g. Dem. 24.120: 10% of booty
goes to Athena, 2% to the Other Gods.

[33] But not all: see U. Brackertz, *Zum Problem der Schutzgottheiten griechischer Städte* (diss. Berlin
1976), 238–9; S. G. Cole, 'Civic Cult and Civic Identity', in M. H. Hansen (ed.), *Sources for the
Ancient City-State* (Copenhagen 1995), 292–325, with the comments of W. Burkert, in Hansen
and K. Raaflaub (eds.), *Studies in the Ancient Greek Polis* (Stuttgart 1995), 201–10.

[34] *Phoen.* 1365; *Rhes.* 703. With the first case cf. Men. *Sic.* 144, where Theron, hoping that an
exposed child will turn out to be Athenian, urges Athena to 'make him yours'.

[35] One example in each case: Aesch. *Pers.* 347; *Eum.* 1045; Lycurg. *Leoc.* 26; Ar. *Thesm.* 1140;
ibid. 318–19; *Eq.* 763; *Thesm.* 1142; Aesch. *Eum.* 288; Ar. *Nub.* 601. There are many further
instances: see C. J. Herington, *Athena Parthenos and Athena Polias* (Manchester 1955), 55–8;
Brackertz, op. cit. 22–6 with notes. Solon's image: fr. 4.1–4 West.

[36] Eur. *Heraclid.* 770–2; *Ion* 211 (cf. 453–4).

Mother.[37] This is to push the model of gods' love for particular cities to an extreme, whereby at the limit each city would need in its pantheon only one great goddess (who would, however, differ from city to city). Yet, despite the pre-eminence of Athena, Athens has many more attested gods and goddesses than any other Greek state. Athena has manifestly not suppressed or supplanted rivals in any simple way; nor have we reason to postulate a process whereby those rivals encroached upon Athena and eroded her powers. Special goddess and ordinary gods each go about their business. How this can be is a question that must underlie much of this chapter. For the moment let us note merely that, at Athens,[38] Athena's special position develops out from her ancient function as mistress of the acropolis, protectress of the city, Polias. It is also, of course, powerfully underwritten by the homonymy between goddess and city.

With Athena Polias on the rock was Zeus Polieus. His great festival the *Dipolieia* did not, in the part known to us (the *Bouphonia*), bear on the safety of the city, though it certainly dramatized collective concerns with sacrifice and perhaps with agriculture. But it was as her father's daughter that Athena was so powerful to protect her citizens,[39] and the pairing of Zeus Polieus and Athena Polias brought out the genealogical connection. (In other cities Hera functioned similarly as a protectress, as her husband's wife.) The third major deity of the acropolis was Poseidon Erechtheus, who is not explicitly credited with protective functions and whose double name expresses an ambivalent relationship with the city: he has coalesced with the primeval Athenian and nursling of Athena, Erechtheus, but in order to coalesce with Erechtheus he had, according to myth, first to kill him. All the same, the linkage of Zeus Polieus, Athena Polias and Poseidon was sufficiently characteristic for the Erchians to reproduce it on their own acropolis.[40]

WARFARE

When Athena's power to save cities is appealed to in hymns, it is associated with her ferocity in war.[41] To warfare therefore I turn. As witnesses to their

---

[37] For references and criticism see Nilsson, *Geschichte*, 443; S. Deacy and A. Villing in *Athena in the Classical World*, 10, n. 37. Even the scrupulous Rudhardt, *Pensée religieuse*, 98–9, is affected by this old idea, which still surfaces here and there.

[38] No necessary connection exists, however, between the role of 'special god' and a particular function picked out by an epithet: Athena is Polias in many places (Sparta, for instance) where she is not a special goddess, whereas Hera at Argos, another goddess who symbolizes national identity, bears no functional epithet but is just 'Argive Hera'.

[39] Aesch. *Eum.* 996–1002; cf. J. Neils, 'Athena, Alter Ego of Zeus', in *Athena in the Classical World*, 219–32. For the precinct of Zeus Polieus see Hurwit, *Acropolis* 190–2. *Bouphonia*: see pp. 187–91.

[40] See p. 68, n. 69, and for Poseidon on the acropolis Parker, 'Myths,' 199–200.

[41] *Hymn. Hom.* 11.1–4 and 28.3 (παρθένον αἰδοίην ἐρυσίπτολιν ἀλκήεσσαν). The latter passage also juxtaposes her city-saving function with her virginity; I do not know that the familiar

oath, which was largely concerned with military matters, the ephebes of each
year invoked (after Agraulos and Hestia) Enyo, Enyalios, Ares and Athena
Areia. Our surviving copy of the oath was set up by the priest of Ares and
Athena Areia at Acharnae, and was found there along with a decree of the
deme Acharnae relating to the altars of those two gods. Acharnae was
unusual in hosting a deme festival of Ares, the *Areia*, even though the god
apparently lacked an actual temple.[42] When one has mentioned this unelaborate deme cult, a precinct of Ares of uncertain character (but hosting a
statue by Alkamenes) in the Agora, a precinct of Enyalios on Salamis and an
annual sacrifice (context unknown) by the polemarch to the same god, one
has almost exhausted the evidence for worship of mono-functional gods of
war in Attica.[43] Bloodstained Ares, the pariah among immortals,[44] could not
be honoured with a full festival of the city. Responsibility for aiding the
Athenians under arms was instead distributed, as in most Greek states,
among a variety of other gods. First comes Athena Areia, closely followed
by Athena Nike, who brought Victory primarily, and perhaps exclusively, in
war. As a character on the Athenian side explains in Euripides' *Heraclidae*,
'our allies are no weaker than those of the Argives. Hera, the wife of Zeus,
protects them, and Athena us; and this contributes to success, to have
superior gods. For Pallas will not endure to be defeated (νικωμένη γὰρ
Παλλὰς οὐκ ἀνέξεται)'.[45] The passage is a model illustration of the idea of

modern image of the raped city ('the 1689 Siege of Derry, the Maiden City that was besieged but
never penetrated': R. Moore and A. Sanders, *Anthropology Today* 18.6, Dec. 2002, 11) has ancient
analogues, the imagery relating to headdresses found in Homer (*Il.* 16. 97–100, with R. Janko's
note) being much milder.

[42] Oath: RO 88 (Tod, *GHI*, ii, 204); decree: *SEG* XXI 519 (Lawton, *Document Reliefs*, nos. 177
and 143; cf. too no. 125). For Augustan evidence for Ares at Acharnae see *IG* II² 2953. On the
lack of a temple see the following note. During the Peloponnesian war Acharnian bellicosity
became notorious (Thuc. 2. 20–1; Ar. *Ach.* 204–36): was it then that they took up the cult of
Ares?

[43] The temple of Ares seen by Pausanias (1.8.4) in the agora is generally identified with the
5th-c. temple, of unknown origin, that was relocated in the agora perhaps in the Augustan period
(Thompson/Wycherley, *Agora*, 162–5). That temple has now been identified, by M. Korres, as
fitting the foundations of a classical temple (presumably that of Athena Pallenis) recently found at
Gerakas/Pallene (*Horos* 10–12, 1992–8, 83–104): cf. H. R. Goette, ibid. 105–18 or in *Kult und
Kultbauten*, 116–31; Goette, *Attica*, 236); it had not therefore (cf. *Athenian Religion*, 154, n. 7)
migrated from the precinct of Ares at Acharnae. There had presumably been a sanctuary of Ares
of some kind in the agora before the arrival of the temple: the temple seen by Pausanias contained
two statues of Aphrodite, an Ares by Alcamenes, an Enyo by the sons of Praxiteles, and an
Athena by an unknown Parian sculptor, Locrus. The offerings to Ares made by the priestess of
Aglauros (p. 434, n. 64) were perhaps brought to the agora shrine. Salamis: Plut. *Sol.* 9.7,
supposedly founded by Solon (not discussed in Taylor, *Salamis*). Polemarch: Arist. *Ath. Pol.* 58.1 ὁ
δὲ πολέμαρχος θύει μὲν θυσίας τήν τε τῇ (τῇ τε Wilamowitz/Kaibel) Ἀρτέμιδι τῇ ἀγροτέρᾳ καὶ τῷ
Ἐνυαλίῳ, διατίθησι δ' ἀγῶνα κτλ. I take the sacrifice to Enyalios probably to be distinct from the
well-known one to Artemis (on the issue see Rhodes's references ad loc.).

[44] Hom. *Il.* 5.31, 890; Soph. *OT* 215.

[45] Eur. *Heraclid.* 347–52. On Athena Nike see *Athenian Religion*, 90 with n. 94 [+]. Informally
she often reverts to plain 'Nike': Ar. *Lys.* 317, where the reference to the acropolis cult is
unmistakable, and even in the epitaph of her first priestess, *IG* I³ 1330 (*CEG* 93).

special gods watching over different communities. It also presents the success of Athenian arms as what philosophers would call an analytical truth, entailed by the very meaning of Athena Victory. Athena's first victory was that over the giant Enceladus,[46] and since the sixth century she had been consecrated on the acropolis bastion under the title of Athena Nike. We hear by chance of a statue of Athena Nike dedicated there to commemorate a cluster of successes during the Archidamian war, and there must have been many such offerings. Indeed the many monuments of the acropolis are a symphony in which victory is the dominant theme. In 304 the Athenians still resolved to sacrifice to Athena Nike (and to others; but she comes first) 'for the safety of those on campaign'.[47]

Ares (or Enyalios) and Athena are, as it were, divine equivalents to human warriors; they and they alone are regularly depicted in armour, and the *Panathenaea* is the only Athenian festival to our knowledge at which celebrants wore arms. But other powers, even if not military professionals in the same way, were involved in the outcome of battles, each after their own fashion. The number potentially so concerned even with a single battle was rather large; we can compare a well-known inscription in which the Selinuntians list nine gods or heroes or groups of them 'because of whom we conquer', and then add 'and because of the other gods too'. Before leading out an Athenian army on campaign, the generals were expected by public opinion to secure 'fair omens'. Details are very uncertain, but one group of powers is known to whom pre-battle offerings ($\pi\rho\delta\tau o\mu a$ $\pi o\lambda\epsilon\mu\acute{\iota}o\upsilon$ $\delta o\rho\acute{o}\varsigma$), whether identical or not with the divinatory sacrifices, were made (sometimes? always?).[48] They are the Hyakinthides Parthenoi, who according to myth had saved the city by themselves serving, on a variously identified occasion, as the pre-battle offerings demanded by the gods as price of victory. Other Attic heroines, as we shall see, had died for the city, or were patrons of young proto-warriors, or both; but, as actual recipients of pre-battle offerings, the Hyakinthides are the most striking embodiment (Athena aside) of the paradoxical symbolic role of females in military affairs.

---

[46] Eur. *Ion* 1528–9.

[47] Archidamian war: *IG* II² 403 (for a comparable case see Paus. 4.36.6); campaign of 304: *Agora* XVI 114.14–16. But it is not clear that all the Gold Victories of the acropolis commemorated specific successes. Symphony: see the vivid pages of Hurwit, *Acropolis*, 230–1; on the sculptural decoration of the precinct of Athena Nike see most recently E. Harrison in *Architectural Sculpture*, 109–25 (frieze); E. Simon, ibid. 127–43 (and M. Jameson in *Ritual, Finance, Politics*, 307–24). Offerings are vowed, oddly, 'to Athena and to Victory' in the spurious Themistocles decree, ML 23.39. Heraclitus of Athmonon dedicated to her a record of Antigonus' valorous deeds in defence of Greece against the barbarians, *IG* II² 677.4.

[48] See Eur. *Erechtheus* fr. 65 Austin (370 Kannicht) 83–9, with Kearns, *Heroes*, 59–63; 201–2. The 'pre-battle offerings' are not literally that but 'cuts prior to the enemy spear', i.e. (?) first cuts against that spear. On securing good omens cf. p. 103. In the spurious 'Themistocles decree' the Athenians resolve to offer an $\dot{a}\rho\epsilon\sigma\tau\acute{\eta}\rho\iota o\nu$ to Zeus Pankrates, Athena, Nike and Poseidon Asphaleios before embarking (ML 23.38–40). Selinuntians: ML 38.

Less paradoxical is the role of Zeus. All decisive turns in human affairs depend on Zeus, including the turn in battle: battle trophies were normally dedicated to Zeus 'Of the Turn' (Tropaios), and he was still honoured as such on Salamis by the ephebes in the late Hellenistic period, in commemoration of the battle of 480. Zeus might direct the tide of battle in the cause of the political ideal of freedom; thanks were then owed to Zeus Eleutherios, as after the battle of Plataea and on many subsequent occasions.[49]

Between Artemis too and battle there was a connection which was not contingent but structural. Each year a procession took 600 goats to the sanctuary of Artemis Agrotera at Agrai, where they were sacrificed by none other than the polemarch; the offering derived, in aitiology and very likely in reality, from a vow made before the battle of Marathon, which itself is likely to have been based on a custom of making a pre-battle 'slaughter-sacrifice' (*sphagion*) to Artemis Agrotera. What is more, the shrine of (Artemis) Eukleia was said to have been founded from the spoils of Marathon, and that of Artemis Aristoboule to have commemorated the good counsel given by the goddess to Themistocles in 480; the festival of Artemis Mounichia came to be seen as commemorating the bright moonshine that preceded the battle of Salamis, and similar timely 'light in darkness' was given by Artemis Phosphoros to the democratic forces returning from Phyle during the civil war of 403.[50] The Homeric Artemis abandons the battlefield in humiliation, and the goddess evidently does not owe her military role to her own prowess as a warrior. She has a place, it has been suggested, because battle is the point of intersection between civilization and savagery, and it is precisely this border-zone between nature and culture that she regularly, if in very different ways, patrols.

The explanation fits neatly the preliminary 'slaughter-sacrifice' perhaps brought to Artemis Agrotera, the one that signifies, among other things, 'let the killing commence'. (Yet it would have been hard to predict a priori that a sacrifice with this function would have to be offered to Artemis rather than to Enyalios or Ares.) To explain Artemis' saving role it has been suggested further that she intervenes in situations of a special type, not ordinary battles

[49] Salamis: *IG* II² 1028.27, etc. (Pélékidis, *Éphébie*, 248); for the trophy cf. Timotheus, *Persae*, 210 Wilamowitz, 196 Page (*PMG* no. 791); *IG* II² 1035.33; Paus. 1.36. 1; Taylor, *Salamis*, 106. The trophy honoured Zeus (the normal recipient, ML 93.11, despite the doubts of Pritchett, *War*, ii, 272, n. 78), even though the battle was fought at sea. There was a trophy at Marathon (E. Vanderpool, *Hesperia* 35, 1966, 93–106), but no reliable trace of a cult of Zeus Tropaios there (S. D. Lambert plausibly proposes [Ἀπο]τροπαίοι for the received [Διί] τροπαίοι in *IG* I³ 255 A 11: *ZPE* 130, 2000, 71–2). Zeus Eleutherios: Thuc. 2.71.2, cf. *Athenian Religion*, 157, n. 17 and 239, n. 76.
[50] Artemis Agrotera: Xen. *Anab.* 3.2.12; Arist. *Ath. Pol.* 58.1. The normal recipient of *sphagia* in Athens is never specified; in Sparta it was Artemis Agrotera (Xen. *Hell.* 4.2.20). See M. Jameson, 'Sacrifice before Battle', in V. D. Hanson (ed.), *Hoplites* (London 1991), 197–227, at 210–11. Eukleia: Paus. 1.14.5. Aristoboule: Plut. *Them.* 22.2. Mounichia: Plut. *Glor. Ath.* 7.349f. *Lys.* 15.1 See further, respectively, *Athenian Religion*, 154, n. 6; 156, n.11; 155, n. 8; 155, n.10. Phyle: Clem. Al. *Strom.* 1.24.163. 1–2 (p. 102. 3–8 St.) (not mentioned in Xen. *Hell.* 2.4.2–7).

but those that form part of a 'war of total destruction', one that threatens the annihilation of an independent state. Such an annihilation would mean the destruction of temples, agora, a laying waste of civilized forms; Artemis is patrolling the borders again, therefore.[51] But a complication is that in legends of this type (the clearest instances of which are non-Attic) the goddess's intervention always occurs at night and always relates in some way to light or to vision: what defines the type is not exclusively the postulated situation of total war (hard to define, and not obviously applicable in every case) but also a distinctive mode of action on the part of the goddess.[52] What remains clear is that Artemis' role is not to serve as a symbol of ordinary hoplite valour, to stiffen the sinews of one side in an encounter taking place in a plain by day. She seems rather to occupy what Thucydides strangely calls 'the blank space of war', the area inaccessible to ordinary preparation and training.[53]

Pan too occupies that blank space. 'Panic' is named from Pan, and the honours paid to the god after the battle of Marathon may reflect a panic attack sent against the Persians. But nothing of the kind is recorded; we can merely note the possibility, and pass on. Artemis' nocturnal interventions are a form of epiphany, and with the possibility of epiphany or other invisible ad hoc assistance the range of potential divine helpers is extended almost beyond limit.[54] Any god or hero worshipped near a battlefield might offer aid, spontaneous or solicited; Delphi was available to offer advice on what powers to solicit. In the Persian war period, assistance is said to have come in 490 from Heracles, Theseus, Marathon and even rustic Echetlos, in 480 from Boreas, Ajax and the Aiacids, and in 479 from a rich cluster of gods and heroes of the Plataea region including the 'Sphragitic Nymphs'.[55] Thucydides has no time for such irregulars, but the possibility of intervention by local heroes is still envisaged in several passages in tragedy during the Pelopon-

---

[51] On all this see Vernant, *Mortals and Immortals*, 244–57, developing the ideas of P. Ellinger finally expressed in *La Légende nationale Phocidienne. Artémis, les situations extrêmes et les récits de guerre d' anéantissement* (Paris 1993). The idea of 'war of destruction' is clearly expressed by Xen. *Anab.* 3.2.11 in this context. Homeric Artemis: *Il.* 21.489–96.

[52] See Graf, *Nordionische Kulte*, 231. The situation when Artemis intervenes is always critical, but actual destruction of a polis is not at issue in the aid given to the democrats from Phyle, nor probably in the conflicts between Philip and Byzantium (Steph. Byz. s.v. Βόσπορος; Hesych. Mil. *FGrH* 390 F 1.27) or the Sicyonians and Hyperasians (Paus. 7.26.2–3).

[53] Thuc. 3.30.4: but note Hornblower's arguments ad loc. for the reading καινόν of codd. plurimi (for κενόν of CM).

[54] See S. Hornblower, 'Epic and Epiphanies', in D. Boedeker and D. Sider (eds.), *The New Simonides* (Oxford 2001), 135–47; ibid. 143–5 on Pan.

[55] 490: see p. 448, n. 117 below. Whether anyone had heard of Echetlos before the battle is uncertain. 480: Hdt. 7.189, 8.64. 479: Delphi told the Athenians under Aristides to pray to Zeus, Hera Kithaironia, Pan, the Sphragitic Nymphs, to sacrifice to seven Plataean heroes (whose names are given), and to fight in their own land in the plain of Eleusinian Demeter and Kore: Plut. *Aristid.* 11.3. Thank-offerings were regularly sent thereafter to the Sphragitic Nymphs: Plut. ibid. 19.5–6 and *Quaest.conv.* 1.10.3, 628e–f. The oracle is topographically too bifocal (this is not the famous Delphic ambiguity) to be historical as given, but may contain genuine elements: for various views see A. R. Burn, *Persia and the Greeks*, ed. 2 (London 1984), 515–16; C. Hignett, *Xerxes' Invasion of Greece* (Oxford 1963), 418–21; Schachter, *Cults*, II, 55–6.

nesian war;[56] and a thank-offering to Theseus made in 429 will be mentioned shortly. No more need be said about such occasional allies. If each military enterprise was typically preceded by a vow to a group of gods,[57] a new set of divine helpers will have been recruited for each campaign, though doubtless containing on each occasion a good number of familiar names.

One might have expected Heracles, so popular in Attica, to have a recurrent military role, but the thing has slipped through our documentation if so.[58] There is also a question about Apollo. The Athenians always continued to send spoils of war to Delphi, even though they cannot be shown to have consulted the god about any campaign which they undertook after 479.[59] But the dispatch of spoils, a matter of display, was linked only loosely if at all with the expression of thanks for specific assistance: after his victories in the Corinthian Gulf in 429, Phormio hung up spoils to Apollo at Delphi but performed a sacrifice on the spot to Poseidon and Theseus, his immediate helpers.[60] Spoils at Delphi and occasionally in Athens[61] aside, Apollo is not immediately associated with Athens' military activities. Yet the *temenos* of Apollo Lykeios a little way east of the city was the main training ground for the cavalry and hoplites of Athens, and a decree which imposes an annual levy on cavalry, hoplites (a secure supplement) and archers for the maintenance of a precinct of Apollo has been convincingly connected with this cult. Apollo Lykeios should for an Athenian have been associated, above all, with service in the cavalry or infantry; conversely, the god most intimately associated with such military service must have been that Apollo. 'You too, Wolfish Lord, prove wolfish to the enemy army' would therefore seem a natural appeal for the Athenian state to have made to the god on behalf of the hoplites who exercised in his precinct. Yet it is from a play of Aeschylus set in Thebes, not from a state document, that the quotation comes.[62] The only battle for help in which Apollo (no epithet) is thanked is, strangely, one fought

[56] See p. 448, n. 118 below. Does Soph. *OC* 621–3 refer to an actual intervention by Oedipus (see Kearns, *Heroes*, 51 with n. 33)?

[57] Before Arginusae a vow was supposedly made to Zeus Soter, Apollo and the Semnai (Diod. Sic. 13.102.2).

[58] The dedication in the Herakleion at Thebes made by Thrasyboulos and the other democrats of 403 (Paus. 9.11.6) speaks primarily of something different: gratitude for Theban support.

[59] See p. 109 above.

[60] Paus. 10.11.6; Poseidon also received a ship on the spot, Thuc. 2.84.4. On recipients of spoils see Pritchett, *War*, iii, 240–95; R. Lonis, *Guerre et religion en Grèce à l'époque classique* (Paris 1979), 157–78.

[61] *IG* II² 2789 (*Syll.*³ 166), a dedication by the Athenians and their allies (of the Second Athenian Confederacy) 'from the enemy', apparently set up in the Pythion. Lykomedes' motive for dedicating Salamis spoils to Apollo Daphnephoros of Phlya in 480 (Plut. *Them.* 15.3) was doubtless a hereditary association with that shrine, controlled by the *Lykomidai* (ibid. 1.4).

[62] Aesch. *Sept.* 145–6; cf. the prayer to him to protect the νεολαία (young men under arms, Aesch. *Pers.* 669) in Aesch. *Suppl.* 687. On all this see M. Jameson, 'Apollo Lykeios in Athens', *Archaiognosia* 1 (1980), 213–35. Training ground: e.g. Ar. *Pax* 353–6. Decree: *IG* I³ 138. Arginusae: Diod. Sic. 13.102.2.

at sea, Arginusae. Training warriors is, it seems, a distinct function from lending aid in war.

In the hellenistic period the concept of 'the gods who share in the campaign' or 'all the gods in the expedition' emerges.[63] It probably reflects a new sense of the army as a discrete entity with its own gods, whereas earlier the 'city-holding' gods had also protected its troops. From the third century decrees passed by military units become a commonplace in Attica;[64] these reveal a monotonous, but portable, commitment to 'Zeus Soter and Athena Soteira' for protection by both sea and land.

Sharp distinctions were not necessarily drawn between aid given on sea and on land: a trophy was set up for Zeus Tropaios after the naval victory of Salamis. But, as we have seen, Phormio thanked Poseidon and Theseus for aid in his naval campaigns of 429; and the dedication of a bronze spear-butt to the Dioscuri 'from the Lesbians' probably reflects a prayer for safe passage to the island in 427.[65]

POLITICAL LIFE, AND TRADE

The political gods of Greece or the political functions of Greek gods prove difficult to circumscribe and define. In speaking of cities other than Athens, we tend to identify gods as 'civic' or 'political' on the basis of several loose criteria: gods who bear the epithet 'of the agora', or have important shrines in an agora; gods in whose shrines public documents are displayed; gods who are invoked as protectors of laws. Sometimes the categories of 'city-protecting' and political are in effect conflated. But (to name only two difficulties) many things happened in most Greek agoras that were not politics in the narrow sense, while in Athens itself (though not in its demes) the agora was not in fact the place of political assembly. More fundamentally, political gods are hard to identify in Greece, it has been suggested, because they do not exist in the same comparatively straightforward sense as gods of healing or of warfare.[66] 'From Zeus come kings', perhaps, but in the world of the cities no such simple relation exists between political authority and the divine. The Olympian world and the human political world are cut from different templates; the points of contact are glancing and occasional. It is these glancing contacts that we must now investigate.

---

[63] Θεοὶ οἱ συστρατευόμενοι|θεοὶ πάντες οἱ κατὰ στρατείαν: Polyb. 7.9.2–3 (oaths of Philip V and Hannibal); contrast Aesch. *Sept.* 271–8.

[64] See *Athenian Religion*, 240, n. 81.

[65] So Hornblower, *Commentary*, I, 441, on *Hesperia* 47 (1978) 192–5 (*SEG* XXVIII 24). Zeus Tropaios and Salamis: n. 49 above.

[66] See Detienne/Sissa, *Vie quotidienne*, 228–30, with their reference to L. Gernet in Gernet and L. Boulanger, *Le Génie grec dans la religion* (Paris 1932) (which they call 'livre rare, le meilleur dans pareille domaine'), 171.

Here too we should no doubt 'start from Hestia', in this case the 'common hearth' located in the symbolic centre of the government of the city, the Prytaneum. Hestia herself was the unmoving emblem of permanence and legitimacy. Along with her was honoured, at least from the late fifth century, Apollo the exegete, in recognition of the city's reliance on the counsel of Delphi in all matters of cult. Regular entertainment (theoxeny) was also offered there to the Anakes or Dioscuri, those demi-gods always willing to accept mortal hospitality and thus available to the city too as points of immediate contact with the divine sphere.[67]

Away from the Prytaneum, the path to political activity led, one might say, past several altars: those of Zeus Herkeios and Apollo Patroos, about which questions were asked at the scrutiny of potential magistrates; and more particularly those of Zeus Phratrios and Athena Phratria, the two powers at the centre of the life of every phratry. Phratries were political bodies in the sense that they controlled access to citizenship, and it was surely as the base units from which the city was made up that they had the two poliadic deities of Athens as their patrons. In that sense poliadic gods were also political gods. There were also altars of Zeus Boulaios and Athena Boulaia, 'to whom members of the council pray on entry', in the council-chamber itself, exact equivalents to Zeus and Athena of Phratries. Hestia of the Council too had an altar, a very sacred place, scene of one of the most dramatic moments in Athenian history, the unavailing supplication of Theramenes in 403.[68] (Hera Boulaia, by contrast, is known from a single dedication, made, intriguingly, 'on the instructions of the god'.[69])

But the gods to whom sacrifices were made 'before the assemblies' by the serving *prytaneis*, as we learn from 'prytany inscriptions' stretching over several centuries, were not these but 'Apollo Prostaterios and Artemis Boulaia', to whom from early in the second century 'Artemis Phosphoros' is added.[70] The choice is a little surprising. There are, it is true, one or two

---

[67] See *IG* I³ 131, with Jameson's commentary; Chionides fr. 7 ap. Ath. 137e; *Athenian Religion*, 27, n. 59 [+].

[68] Ant. 6.45 (the passage quoted); Xen. *Hell.* 2.3.52–5; for the joint priest of Zeus Boulaios and Athena Boulaia see *IG* II² 3543–44, 5054. See further Rhodes, *Boule*, 34–5. On the phratry gods and Apollo Patroos see *Athenian Religion*, 106; on Zeus Herkeios p. 16 above.

[69] *IG* II² 4675. This short text is full of puzzles (see references in Kirchner's commentary). It derives from the precinct of a male deity, whose priest was serving for the fifth time, who apparently sent advice through dreams (προστάξαντος τοῦ θεοῦ, a phrase often used of Asclepius at Athens). In this case an individual was advised to make a dedication to Hera under an otherwise unattested epithet, but one suggesting civic and not personal concerns. The only Athenian parallel I have found for 'in the second priesthood of *x*' *vel sim.* is *IG* II² 4991: the whole formula type 'in the second *x* of *x*' is first attested to my knowledge *c*.125 BC, and may suggest that the corpus 3rd-c. date for *IG* II² 4675 is too early.

[70] See *Agora* XV, pp. 4–5. The formula first appears in the early 3rd c., soon after it became standard to pass decrees in recognition of all groups of *prytaneis*, but there is no reason to doubt that the practice of such pre-assembly sacrifices goes back much further. In addition to the regular sacrifices performed before every assembly, *prytaneis* might also be required to sacrifice at public festivals which chanced to fall in their period of office (*Agora* XV, ibid.); the sacrifice at

other traces of Apollo filling a political role in the archaic state. The temple of Apollo Delphinios served as one of the five murder courts, and we happen to know of a meeting of the assembly held in the precinct of Apollo Lykeios around the beginning of the fifth century.[71] But whereas the Apollos Delphinios and Lykeios apparently had a connection, from which political functions might derive, with particular age-classes, Apollo Prostaterios was a very general protector, a figure who stood in front of an individual or group or place to shield it from harm.[72] Artemis Boulaia was primarily 'Artemis of the Council' rather than 'Artemis of Good Counsel', though Themistocles' 'Artemis of Best Counsel' appears to play on the ambiguity of the epithet. She too was perhaps conceived as a protectress, like the 'Light-bringer' who came to be regularly associated with her. The oddity that Artemis should discharge a civic role at all was noted earlier.[73] So neither of the two gods who received sacrifice before meetings of the assembly sounds very political. What was sought was not political wisdom but a kind of safety or reassurance outside politics.

At the start of each meeting of the assembly, a herald prayed to a succession of gods for the beneficial outcome of the meeting, and uttered curses against various categories of public offender. Our best source for these prayers and curses is the burlesque version in Aristophanes' *Thesmophoriazousai*, where comically appropriate gods and goddesses have been substituted for those of reality;[74] no list of those actually invoked survives. Among them was perhaps Zeus Agoraios, a god mentioned both in tragedy and comedy as a patron of political persuasion, yet lacking a clear context in cult practice.[75]

---

the *Galaxia* mentioned in the first allusion to sacrifices by the prytaneis (Theophr. *Char.* 21.11: cf. Agora XV no. 180.10) is apparently a case in point. Dem. *Proem.* 54 purports to be a report to the assembly of the successful outcome of preliminary sacrifices to Zeus Soter, Athena, Nike, Peitho, Mother of the Gods and Apollo. If a genuine 4th-c. document (it is accepted as such by the latest editor, R. Clavaud, *Démosthène, Prologues*, Paris 1974, 8–9, 166–8), it was spoken by a practising politician who chanced to be serving among the *prytaneis*, and the choice of offerings is likely, being singular, to have been determined by a particular military crisis. But the epigraphic evidence can scarcely be said to confirm its authenticity, *pace* A. Rupprecht, *Philologus* 82 (1927), 399.

[71] *IG* I³ 105.34: on the date see M. Ostwald, *From Popular Sovereignty to the Sovereignty of Law* (Berkeley 1986), 31–40 [+].

[72] See Detienne, *Apollon*, 123–33, 232–4. Detienne suspects a connection between Apollo's political role and the delineation of places of assembly through rites of purificatory encirclement. The long series of dedications by magistrates to 'Apollo under the Long Rocks', on the slopes of the acropolis (Wycherley, *Testimonia*, 179), seems to begin only in the 1st c. AD.

[73] p. 390. 'Of Best Counsel': p. 400 above.

[74] Ar. *Thesm.* 295–311; 331–4 (the distortion in the latter goes beyond the addition of 'goddesses' to 'gods': there was no general class of 'Pythian' or 'Delian' gods). Cf. p. 100.

[75] See Wycherley, *Testimonia*, 122–24 (but *Syll.*³ 526 has no bearing on Athens). The main texts are Aesch. *Eum.* 973; Ar. *Eq.* 410, 500; Eur. *Heraclid.* 70 (his altar, as a place of supplication); *IG* I³ 42.5 (oath witness). Hesych. α 710 speaks of an altar at Athens (and Ar. *Eq.* 410 implies sacrifices): for a monumental 4th-c. altar found opposite the Metroon and conjecturally identified as his see Thompson/Wycherley, *Agora*, 160–2 (with the suggestion that it was originally located on the Pnyx).

Occasionally the assembly would vow to bring a procession and sacrifice to a
list of deities if a particular policy on which it had just resolved turned out
well. By a quirk of recording, just two such vows are known to us, both from
the year 362/1: one accompanied an alliance with four Peloponnesian
powers and was made to Olympian Zeus, Athena Polias, Demeter and Kore,
the Twelve Gods and the Semnai Theai; the other concerned the dispatch of a
cleruchy to Potidaea, and was for the Twelve Gods, the Semnai Theai and
Heracles.[76] The Semnai Theai are probably there in both cases to threaten the
Athenians with punishment should they break their vow. It is perhaps
because the cult at Eleusis embodies the panhellenic dimension of Athenian
religion that Demeter and Kore are honoured in connection with an alliance.
As for Heracles, it may have been hoped that 'Heracles Hegemon' would give
good guidance to the cleruchs.[77] These groups of gods illustrate the kinds of
selection that could be made from the pantheon to suit particular public
enterprises. But they do not reveal the gods presiding over the political
process.

Thus far we have assigned principal roles to Zeus and Athena, sucked into
the life of phratries and boule by their functions as poliadic deities, preparatory or protective roles to Apollo Prostaterios and Artemis Boulaia/Phos-
phoros, and minor parts to some other gods. Several further powers must
now be brought in. It was not only in the context of vows that the Semnai
Theai from their cave below the Areopagus kept the Athenians to their
principles. They watched over the results of murder trials; and Aeschylus in
an extraordinary set of passages identifies fear of the Semnai with that
reverent respect for legality, based on fear of punishment, that is the foundation of life in a community.[78] How much of this is singular Aeschylean vision,
how much common Athenian perception, is not easy to determine. But the
part played in the cult by figures of the stamp of Demosthenes and Lycurgus is
surely suggestive. The goddesses worshipped at Rhamnus, Nemesis and
Themis, probably had similar functions, though concrete evidence about
this famous and puzzling cult is extraordinarily elusive. The oddity is not so
much the large investment from which it benefited in the third quarter of the
fifth century, in the form of a fine temple and giant cult statue by either
Phidias or Agoracritus; a connection was already made in antiquity with the
Nemesis inflicted on the hybristic Persian invaders.[79] What lies beyond even
rational conjecture is why the inhabitants of the region, and they alone,

[76] *IG* II² 112.6–12 and 114. 6–12.

[77] For Heracles Hegemon see Xen. *Anab.* 4.8.25, 6.2.15, 6.5.24.

[78] Aesch. *Eum.* 517–565, 696–706; on the cult see *Athenian Religion*, 298–9. Murder trials:
cf. Paus. 1.28.6. On the relation of Erinyes/Eumenides/Semnai see Johnston, *Restless Dead*,
267–73 [+]. At issue is not just that problem, but also the way in which Aeschylus makes the
Semnai responsible for the whole fabric of social order in Athens.

[79] Paus. 1.33.2, and sources cited by Herter, *RE* s.v. *Nemesis*, 2349; on the temple cf. *Athenian
Religion*, 154 and on its dating most recently Petrakos, *Rhamnous*, 223 (shortly after 450). Also
relevant is the establishment of the fort in the same period (Petrakos, 26).

should already have held such a goddess in high honour in (as it seems) the sixth century.[80] The suggestion that she is by origin 'a divinity of nature connected with the vegetative world'[81] is an attempt to meet the difficulty, but finds no support either in the goddess's name or that of her associate: 'righteous indignation' and 'divinely ordained order' can scarcely be dissociated from the moral world, though offences against them would also no doubt affect the natural order. Unlike most personifications, Nemesis had a colourful myth which associated her twice over with feelings of moral outrage: she responded with outrage (so the *Cypria*, our first source) to Zeus' amorous designs against her; when he had had his way all the same, she became mother of the scandalous Helen, at whom she is shown pointing an accusing finger on a remarkable amphoriskos in Berlin.[82] Many of the things said by Aeschylus' *Semnai* about crime and punishment she could surely have said too.

The documents of Athens were in charge of the Mother of the Gods. The wild goddess from the Phrygian mountains as whom the Mother sometimes appeared is a surprising choice for the role; but the imprecision of the name or non-name 'Mother' allowed her in some contexts to be that wild outsider, in others a more demure and ancestral figure.[83] Still less predictable, according to common understandings of the goddess's nature, is the political role of Aphrodite. The real questions about Aphrodite Pandemos, 'Of All the People',[84] were long obscured by the playful sophistry of Plato and his pretence that the epithet identified a vulgar, in contrast to a spiritual, form of love. The issue is rather whether 'Of All the People' indicates merely that this is a cult not confined to a restricted group, or whether Aphrodite is also

---

[80] On the 6th-c. (and even earlier) evidence from the site see Petrakos, *Rhamnous*, 192–7.

[81] Farnell, *Cults*, ii, 493; cf. Herter, *RE* s.v. *Nemesis* (the best treatment), 2438 [+]. Herter, 2348–50, is sceptical of attempts (H. A. Shapiro, *Personifications in Greek Art*, Zurich 1993, 173–7 [+]; Petrakos, *Rhamnous*, 188–9) to interpret the iconography of her cult statue in this sense, though she is undoubtedly portrayed as a tranquil figure (see Petrakos, fig. 162).

[82] *Cypria* fr. 7 Davies ap. Ath. 334b–d (cf. fr. 8); Berlin West 30036, ARV 1173, 1 (Heimarmene Painter), Shapiro, op. cit., figs. 151–4. [Eratosth.] *Catast.* 25 locates the myth (on which see Herter, op. cit. 2342–6) in Rhamnus. The same myth also usually made her mother of the Dioscuri (who are present on her statue base), but exploitation of that theme in the cult is not demonstrable. The report of Sud. ρ 33 and Phot. s.v. ʿΡαμνουσία Νέμεσις that she 'reigned' in Rhamnus and that her cult was established by Erechtheus her son is dismissed as a 'rationalistische Erzählung' by Herter, 2346; but her relation to Erechtheus may be implied by Callim. *Hecale* fr. 1 Hollis (cf. A. S. Hollis, *ZPE* 93, 1992, 3). The most interesting offering that she receives is a 6th-c. bronze wheel (*IG* I³ 1018 quater; *IRhamnous* 76), an object often associated with her in late antiquity (for the various interpretations then offered—movement, transience, punishment—see Herter, 2375). Themis was a subordinate figure without her own priestess (see *IRhamnous* 120–2 with Petrakos' commentary), though she could receive independent dedications (e.g. ibid. 120); the old view that the smaller temple was hers has no foundation (Petrakos, *Rhamnous*, 190).

[83] See *Athenian Religion*, 188–9, and now the subtle account by Borgeaud, *Mère des Dieux*, 31–55, of 'une déesse conjoignant les notions d'alterité et d'ancestralité'.

[84] See Pirenne-Delforge, *L'Aphrodite grecque*, 26–40; *Athenian Religion*, 48–9, 234; and, on the new evidence from Cos, H. F. J. Horstmanshoff and others (eds.), *Kykeon. Studies in Honour of H.S. Versnel* (Leiden 2002), 143–60.

seen as a power who by her gentle charms creates friendship and concord among the citizens (and perhaps other inhabitants of Attica too). How emphatically was this perceived as a cult of civic unity? An important question here ought to be that of why it was precisely Aphrodite, rather than any other Olympian, who received an 'open' cult under the title 'Of All the People'. A tempting answer is that she was chosen, in a striking illustration of the power of Greek gods to span the division between private and public, because of her capacity to bring citizens together no less than lovers. Peitho, 'Persuasion', too, to whom a public sacrifice was made each year, probably within the precinct of Aphrodite Pandemos, was both political rhetoric and erotic allure. In the hellenistic period Aphrodite acquired an explicitly political role as 'Aphrodite Leader of the People'; in the fortress at Rhamnus she was simply 'Aphrodite Leader', perhaps with a twist towards the idea of military leadership. But for her worshippers she remained surely also the goddess of sexual dalliance.[85]

Before we leave the agora, let us note the other main activity associated with it. The most conspicuous divine presence in the physical agora was certainly Hermes. In addition to the bronze statue of Hermes Agoraios there was also, close by, the whole sector known as 'the Herms' from the abundance of Herms set up in it.[86] There were Herms everywhere in Athens, and those of the agora had diverse functions not necessarily closely connected with Hermes; all the same, the region of 'the Herms' was strongly evocative of the god. Hermes Agoraios was patron of the 'activities of exchange' that took place in the agora. The Erchians made a sacrifice to Hermes 'in the agora' at Erchia and prescribed, engagingly, that 'the herald' was to preside and to receive equal shares with the demarch: we are reminded that the agora was the main place of activity of those not insignificant functionaries, the public heralds.[87] No god other than Hermes is connected with trade; Apollo 'Of Profit' ($\kappa\epsilon\rho\delta\hat{\omega}os$) is, bizarrely, a power confined to Thessaly, and it was the cult of maritime gods, not special gods of trade, that shipowners at Athens found themselves required willy-nilly to subsidize.[88]

---

[85] Aphrodite Hegemone: *IG* II² 2798; *IRhamnus* 32.12, 33; 35.8; Petrakos, *Rhamnous*, 131–34; *Athenian Religion*, 272, n. 72 (ibid. 234, n. 59 for Peitho). Theseus received Delphic instructions to 'make Aphrodite his guide' (Plut. *Thes*. 18.3): the *aition* contains an erotic element (Ariadne).

[86] See Wycherley, *Testimonia*, 102–8, with the new evidence mentioned by Thompson/Wycherley, *Agora*, 94, nn. 62 and 63, and the possible reference to sacrifices in the tiny scrap *IG* II² 819. Hermes Agoraios is linked with deceit and perjury in Ar. *Eq*. 296–8. We would like to know why the 4th-c. politician Callistratus dedicated an altar to this god ([Plut.] *XOrat*. 844b). In Erythrae, the priesthood of Hermes Agoraios was sold, remarkably, for a much larger sum than any other: see Graf, *Nordionische Kulte*, 270. Ar. *Ach*. 816 has a Hermes Empolaios.

[87] See S. Lewis, *News and Society in the Greek Polis* (London 1996), 52–6. Erchia: *LSCG* 18 E 47–58. 'Activities of exchange': see p. 391.

[88] *Athenian Religion*, 125, n. 15. $\kappa\epsilon\rho\delta\hat{\omega}os$: I have found little discussion of this remarkable epithet more recent than that of O. Gruppe, *Griechische Mythologie und Religionsgeschichte* (Munich 1906), 1233, n. 6; Wilamowitz, *Glaube*, I, 322, treats it simply as an aspect of the covergence of functions between Apollo and Hermes.

METIS, CRAFTS

Athena has been involved in all the areas (barring this last) that we have surveyed so far, and we can stay with her a little longer. As Ergane she is patroness of the works of women, and receives quite numerous dedications in that function, which is hers alone unless perhaps she shares it with the Graces.[89] In supervision of fire-based crafts, metal-working above all, she is teamed with Hephaestus and with Prometheus, and their functions dovetail neatly: Prometheus is the mythical bringer of fire, Hephaestus is the worker with fire (while also himself being fire), and Athena contributes technological subtlety, *metis*. All three are honoured with torch-races (though so too eventually are Pan and Bendis, gods unconnected with fire and craft). This trio represents one of the most remarkable configurations of the Attic pantheon. Hephaestus and Prometheus were no doubt familiar as mythological characters in most Greek states, but it was only in Athens to our knowledge that either received honours on any substantial scale. Technology therefore was given a unique degree of cultic emphasis in Athens.[90] A correlate of this emphasis is the myth which made Hephaestus father of Erichthonius and thus the Athenians en masse 'children of Hephaestus'. No other Greek state appears to claim such an ascendence. A counter-note can be heard here, which awaits interpretation, to the more familiar and more dominant themes of Athenian self-representation.[91]

THE SEA, AND EARTHQUAKES

From the domains of Athena (and others) I turn now to those of Poseidon (and others); the move is an obvious one because of the contiguities between their territories. The role of both gods as patrons of horses and horsemen has already been discussed. They were also juxtaposed at Cape Sunium at the

[89] See Graf, *Nordionische Kulte*, 212, n. 31. B. Wagner-Hasel, 'The Graces and Colour Weaving', in L. Llewellyn-Jones (ed.), *Women's Dress in the Ancient Greek World* (London 2002), 17–32, adduces *Il.* 5.338; Bacchyl. 5.9 to illustrate the connection made in her title. The idea is attractive, if not supported by specific dedications (cf. below).

[90] Was it ignored altogether in other states, or did Athena take up the slack? I have no answer. Prometheus: the rest of Greece produces only a disputed claim to host his tomb (Argos v. Opus, Paus. 2.19.8) and a statue at Panopeus which some claim represented him (ibid. 10.4.4; cf. W. Kraus in *RE* s.v. *Prometheus*, 656–7). For his Athenian cult see Appendix 1 s.v. *Promethia*; Σ Soph. *OC* 56, which cites Apollodorus *FGrH* 244 F 147, Lysimachides *FGrH* 366 F 4; *RE* s.v. *Prometheus*, 654–6. Hephaestus is in effect worshipped only in Athens and on Lemnos: Nilsson, *Griechische Feste*, 428–9; L. Malten, *R.E.* s.v. *Hephaistos*, 362–3 (on temples cf. 324). For the Athenian association of Hephaistos and Athena see App. 1 s.v. *Chalkeia* and especially Pl. *Critias* 109c (cf. 112b).

[91] Cf. Parker, 'Myths' 194, n. 34. It was recognized throughout Greece that Athenian potters and painters produced the best ceramic fineware (R. T. Neer, *Style and Politics in Athenian Vase-Painting*, Cambridge 2002, 212–15). But of the crafts under Hephaestus' patronage metalworking is doubtless more important.

eastern tip of Attica, where Poseidon had his most famous Attic temple[92] and Athena too a smaller but still important one. A Poseidon so located was manifestly the god of the sea; he seems to have borne the title Soter. Possibly Athena was there in that contrasting role mentioned earlier, as a patroness of the application of technological thought to seafaring: it is quite likely that Menelaus' steersman Phrontis received a hero-cult just in the vicinity of her temple. But the idea may rather have been to echo, at the very limit of the goddess's territory, the pairing of Athena and Poseidon found at its centre on the acropolis. Athena had no other connections with seafarers, except that she could be invoked as Saviour, along with Zeus, by any persons in distress. (There were some nautical themes at the *Panathenaea*, but they derive from the character of the festival as an occasion of comprehensive civic display rather than from the nature of Athena.)[93]

As for Poseidon, the evidence that relates to him as god of the sea is fragmentary and frustrating, but just enough survives to illustrate a variety of possibilities: he had a priesthood, probably in the Piraeus region, as 'Of the Sea' (Pelagios); two fishermen at Eleusis brought him a dedication to commemorate a catch; Phormion made a sacrifice to him and to his son Theseus to celebrate a naval victory during the Archidamian war.[94] The 'Steering' festival (*Kybernesia*) may have honoured him, but the only attested addressees are two seamanly heroes, Theseus' pilot Nausithoos and his lookout Phaiax; another nautical hero is 'Save-ship' (Sosineos) of Thorikos, about whom we know nothing beyond his name.[95] Poseidon was a god of the old-fashioned, ambiguous type who had power to quell storms because he also had power to raise them. Other deities whom sailors might invoke were helpers only. Aphrodite Euploia from her large temple in the Piraeus caused the sea to

---

[92] Ar. *Eq.* 560; *Av.* 868; Eur. *Cycl.* 293–4. On the Sunium sanctuaries see Travlos, *Bildlexikon*, 404–29; Goette, *Sounion*, 18–43 and *Attica*, 203–9. The modern consensus (defended in Goette, *Sounion*) that the main temple belonged to Poseidon, and not, as Pausanias apparently thought (1.1.1: but W. K. Pritchett, *Pausanias Periegetes*, ii, Amsterdam 1999, 39–45, 161, suspects a lacuna in the text), to Athena, is based on the findspot of *IG* II² 1270.

[93] Phrontis: see Detienne/Vernant, *Mètis*, 233–5 (overlooked in *Athenian Religion*, 35); the 8th-c. plaque perhaps showing Phrontis is figured in Camp, *Athens*, 306, fig. 267. Poseidon Soter: *IG* II² 1300.9, by supplement (but viewed from the city he was 'Poseidon at Sunium', *IG* I³ 369. 62). Robertson, 'Palladium Shrines', 438–75, argues for a link between Athena and promontories. Athena Soteira: *Athenian Religion*, 240, n. 81. On seafaring deities in Attica see M. R. Recio, *Cultos Marítimos y Religiosidad de Navegantes en el Mundo Griego Antiquo* (BAR international series, 897, Oxford 2000), 141–50, who however too quickly assigns maritime interests to gods on the basis of a coastal location of their shrine. *Panathenaea*: p. 262.

[94] *IG* II² 410.18 (the two following priesthoods there mentioned are of the Piraeus); *IG* I³ 994 (but in *IG* I³ 828 a dedication is made to Athena from a catch 'given by Poseidon'); n. 60 above. Lambs thrown into the sea, presumably for Poseidon, were called κάθετοι (Harpocr. κ 7).

[95] *Kybernesia*: Plut. *Thes.* 17.6–7; cf. *Athenian Religion*, 315. Robertson, 'Palladium Shrines', 445–7, unpersuasively makes it a part of the *Oschophoria*. Sosineos: *SEG* XXXIII 147.50. On sailing heroes see Kearns, *Heroes*, 36–43, with mention also of Paralos, patron hero of the state galley of that name and now attested as having a priest at Aixone (Steinhauer, Ἱερὸς νόμος Αἰξωνέων); note too N. Robertson, *ZPE* 127 (1999), 179–81, on the ἥρως ἐπιτέγιος worshipped with the Anakes (*IG* II² 5071, ? cf. *IG* I³ 383. 346–7).

smile like herself, for those she favoured; the Dioscuri/Anakes made their saving interventions, maritime equivalents to 'Artemis Bringer of Light', amid the worst violence of the storm. Some Athenians too were doubtless initiates of the Great Gods of Samothrace, another set of protectors at sea.[96] We can merely note that the aid of all these powers (and eventually of others too) was available to those setting out from the Piraeus. We cannot track the rises and falls in popularity of the various competing saviours.

As a protector against earthquakes, by contrast, Poseidon 'Of Safety' (Asphaleios), 'Earth-holder' (Gaieochos) and 'Foundation-holder' (Theme-liouchos) had no competitors.[97] Little needs to be said about the function, therefore, important though it is. It would be interesting to know how the propitiation of a god so full of dangerous potential was organized. There is no trace of a specific annual festival. But it would have been very rash to wait until the first tremors were felt. Perhaps we should imagine regular sacrifice, not on the scale of a festival, by a restricted group.

HEALTH, HEALING, AVERSION OF EVIL

The chapter can conclude with protectors against other threats: gods of health, healers, and finally averters of evil. Most of the divine healing of Attica was done by heroes—Amynos, the variously identified 'Doctor Hero', Asclepius (with his flurry of assistants: Hygieia, Iaso, and the rest), and Amphiaraus.[98] How if at all their respective healing methods differed is not clear, but by the rules of polytheism there was no need for them to do so; two

---

[96] Aphrodite Euploia: Paus. 1.1.3; on Aphrodite's mode of intervention at sea Pirenne-Delforge, *L'Aphrodite grecque*, 434–7. Samothrace: Ar. *Pax* 277–8, cf. Alexis fr. 183.4–6, com. adesp. 1063.15–16, and presumably Theophr. *Char.* 25.2. Anakes: that they, like the Dioscuri with whom they were identified, had maritime interests is proven beyond doubt by the tax levied on shipowners to support their cult, *IG* I³ 133 (cf. N. Robertson, *ZPE* 127, 1999, 180); for Attic allusions to saving interventions by the Dioscuri at sea see Eur. *El.* 990–3, 1347–56, *Hel.* 1495–511; *Or.* 1635–67; Pl. *Euthd.* 293a (and in general e.g. *Hym. Hom.* 33); cf. n. 65 above. This is the function of the Dioscuri stressed in literature (note too ἐμπόλω or ἐμπόρω Διοσκόρω, Ar. fr. 316); what else may have been sought from the Anakes is unclear, though we know that they were also recipients of theoxeny (Chionides fr. 7 ap. Ath. 137e) and could have 'parasites' (Ath. 6. 235b). For the sources on the Anakeion see Wycherley, *Testimonia*, 61–5. Note too *Athenian Religion*, 339, n. 33, on *IG* II² 1291. The Dioscuri appear as such in Phegaia, *IG* II² 1932. 15.

[97] Asphaleios: Ar. *Ach.* 682 with Σ vet. 682a, where the odd explanation is offered ἵνα ἀσφαλῶς πλέωσιν (the 'Themistocles decree', ML 23.40, prescribes an offering to him, unexpectedly, in a military context); Gaieochos: *IG* II² 5058, with 3538 (a further title given to Poseidon Erechtheus of the acropolis); Themeliouchos: a priesthood held in 20/19 BC by a member of the genos *Kerykes* (Clinton, *Sacred Officials*, 51, line 17). Poseidon is a god poor in festivals, not in Attica alone (Nilsson, *Griechische Feste*, 66): for the Attic evidence see Appendix 1 s.v. *Posidea*.

[98] See *Athenian Religion*, 176, and now A. Verbanck-Piérard, 'Les héros guérisseurs: des dieux comme les autres!', in V. Pirenne-Delforge and E. Suárez de la Torre, *Héros et héroïnes dans les mythes et les cultes grecs* (Liège 2000), 281–332. On Asclepius as hero see now J. W. Riethmüller in R. Hägg (ed.), *Ancient Greek Hero Cult* (Stockholm 1999), 123–43; for interesting new votives to Amphiaraus see *BCH* 124 (2000), 782.

gods should not have identical functions, for gods can work anywhere, but heroes are tied to particular localities and many are needed to do the same thing in different places. Such at any rate was the initial framework of assumptions which the cults of Asclepius and (to a lesser extent) Amphiaraus were partly to outgrow. Some goddesses (Aphrodite at Daphni, and in Athens; Artemis Kalliste and Ariste) must also have acted as healers if the presence of 'anatomical votives' in a sanctuary in itself proves that they have such a role. But the goddesses receive only breasts and (almost always female) genitalia, and it has been plausibly suggested either that they specialized in 'women's diseases', or that vulvas refer to childbirth and breasts to lactation; in that case the relevant function was not 'healing' but 'aid in and after pregnancy'.[99] In the Roman period Zeus Hypsistos (or more often just Theos Hypsistos) receives anatomical votives. The healing cult of Zeus/Theos Hypsistos is unquestionably a novelty which assigned to Zeus a function that he never exercised in the classical period. The mysterious 'Good Goddess' (Agathe Theos) of the Piraeus, however, is shown with a leg which she must have healed c.300 BC, and a relief which shows Heracles with body parts must date from roughly the same period. So in the hellenistic period a small god (Agathe Theos) and a big hero (Heracles) could intrude on the healing heroes' monopoly.[100]

Further gods, too, had an association of some kind with health. Apollo Paion is one of the 'Other Gods', though we do not know where he had his shrine; and the Athenians dedicated an altar to him and to Athena on Delos in the late fifth century, possibly at the time of the great plague. Any business he may have had as a healer of individuals he seems to have lost by the time the bulk of the epigraphic evidence begins; some think that Apollo's role had been always, above all, to turn his bow against the onset of those collective

---

[99] For such views, which go back to P. Baur, *Eileithyia* (Chicago 1902), see B. Forsén, *Griechische Gliederweihungen* (Helsinki 1996), 133–4, who agrees. For the evidence see ibid. 29–83, which builds on van Straten, 'Gifts', 105–22.

[100] On Theos Hypsistos as healer see S. Mitchell in P. Athanassiadi and M. Frede, *Pagan Monotheism in Late Antiquity* (Oxford 1999), 106: in Athens the votives start in the 2nd c. AD. Agathe Theos: *IG* II² 4589, van Straten, 'Gifts', 120 10.2. Heracles with body parts: Athens, Acr. Mus. 7232 (van Straten, 'Gifts', 106 1.1 with fig. 50; Vikelas, *Pankrates-Heiligtum*, pl. 37.1: 4th or early 3rd c., according to a personal communication from Professor O. Palagia); for Roman period anatomical votives perhaps dedicated to Heracles see Vikela, *Pankrates-Heiligtum*, 55–6, pls. 33.2–3 (Forsén, op. cit. 59–60; that Heracles rather than the 'elder god' was the recipient of these votives is not, however, certain: cf. p. 423, n. 26 below). Dedications to Heracles found on the s. slope of the acropolis are sometimes taken to prove that he had a place in the Asclepieum, sometimes to attest a separate cult (though perhaps again of healing character): *IG* II² 4571, 4611, 4613 (on this cf. p. 438, n. 82 below), 4986: see e.g. Woodford, 'Herakles in Attika', 219–20 [+]; van Straten, *Hierà kalá*, 87. The provenance 'in Asclepieo' given by Kirchner for *IG* II² 4986–9 is a plausible guess of Koehler's disguised as a fact: the stones were found prior to the excavation of the Asclepieum. The provenance of Athens, Acr. Mus. 7232 (above) is merely 'acropolis museum storeroom', i.e. unknown. A. Frickenhaus, *AM* 36 (1911), 139, n. 1, thought all this material had come from elsewhere. There is certainly little profit in associating it with the unlocated shrine of Heracles Menytes known from literary sources (*Vit. Soph.* 12; Cic. *Div.* 1.54), since the epithet Menytes does not suggest a healing cult.

plagues which he could also send.[101] However that may be, Apollo was father of Asclepius, and there was no sharp conceptual distinction between the two functions. A more shocking figure to find active in this area is Athena; yet she was certainly honoured on the acropolis as Athena Hygieia by the fifth century.[102] The principle of division of functions between gods seems here to be blatantly violated. Or can health be prised a little apart from healing? Possibly it was Athena Hygieia's function to keep her people healthy rather than to cure them when ill. Any public sacrifice to any god in Athens was accompanied by a prayer for the 'health and safety' (ὑγίεια καὶ σωτηρία) of the people of Athens; and Aristophanes in a striking comic image speaks of Athena pouring 'Wealth-health' (πλουθυγίεια) over the city from a ladle. This would be an aspect of Athena's protective poliadic function, of the way in which, in Solon's image, she 'held her hand over' the city. In favour of this approach one might cite a Delphic response of the fourth century by which, in a context unfortunately unknown, Apollo urged the Athenians to 'pray and sacrifice for health to Zeus Hypatos, Heracles, Apollo Prostaterios'. These are helpers and protectors, not specialized healers. On the other side works the story that Athena Hygieia once appeared to Pericles in a dream and pre-scribed the treatment for a workman who was lying close to death after a fall during the building of the Propylaia.[103] Here the goddess operates exactly as if she were Asclepius. But there is no other sign that she did so.

If 'preservation of the citizens' health' bleeds into the general protecting function of the city's special goddess, defence against plague similarly blurs with the broader function of 'aversion of evil': it was believed, though wrongly, that both Apollo and Heracles received statues as Alexikakoi in recognition of help given during the great plague of 430.[104] The 'Averters of

---

[101] Apollo Paion: *IG* I³ 383.163–4; *IG* I³ 1468 *bis* (*CEG* 742); cf. Paus. 1.34.3 (Oropos). Apollo never primarily a healer of individuals: Detienne, *Apollon*, 227–9 (but the graffiti dedications to Apollo Ietros from Olbia, L. Dubois, *Inscriptions grecques dialectales d' Olbia du Pont*, Geneva 1996, nos. 54–9, make the case hard to sustain for that region); for the other view (that Apollo was Asclepius' precursor) see Nilsson, *GGR*, 538–44. In Attica, it looks as if most business went to healing heroes such as Amynos even before the coming of Asclepius. But Apollo was still envisaged as ἰατρόμαντις, Aesch. *Eum.* 62.

[102] See *IG* I³ 506, and *Athenian Religion*, 175, n. 78 (add *LSCG* 33 (RO 81) B 9). Note too Athena Paionia, Paus. 1.2.5 (a statue, in the precinct of Dionysus Melpomenos); ibid. 1.34.3 (sharing an altar segment at Oropos with Aphrodite, Panakeia, Iaso and Hygieia). So a 'healing Athena' exists; but she is not credited with much independent power.

[103] Wealth-health: Ar. *Eq.* 1091. Response: Dem. 21.52 (cf. too *IG* II² 783, where the priest of Zeus Soter makes offerings to Zeus Soter, Athena Soteira, Asclepius and Hygieia), adduced in this context by Kearns, *Heroes*, 14–15. Story: Plut. *Per.* 13.12–13 (and sources quoted by P. Stadter in his commentary ad loc.); cf. N. Robertson, *ZPE* 127 (1999), 177–9.

[104] Paus. 1.3.4; Σ Ar. *Ran.* 501a. Chronologically this appears impossible: see the works cited in *Athenian Religion* 186, n. 121. For the exclamation Ἄπολλον ἀποτρόπαιε see Ar. *Eq.* 1307, *Vesp.* 161, *Av.* 61, *Plut.* 359, 854; ἀλεξίκακε similarly used Ar. *Nub.* 1372. Note too Eur. *HF* 470, the ἀλεξητήριον ξύλον of Heracles (and the allusion in Ar. *Vesp.* 1043); ibid. *HF* 821 (appeal to Paian to be ἀπότροπος of evil); Soph. *El.* 637, prayer of Clytemnestra to Phoibos Prostaterios. Zeus is ἀλεξητήριος in Aesch. *Sept.* 8 and Soph. *OC* 143; θεοὶ ἀποτρόπαιοι are an anonymous group in Aesch. *Pers.* 203, Eur. *Phoen.* 586, Xen. *Symp.* 4.33; cf. Pl. *Leg.* 854b. The uneaten 'dinners of

Evil' are often mentioned in literary texts, and it is frustrating that little that is concrete can be said about this important function, which was not so much a specialized and isolated compartment within the competences of Apollo and Heracles as a permanent aspect of their nature, occasionally brought to the surface by application of a specific epithet; they always, that is to say, were guardians against ill whether invoked under that title or not. The protection offered by Apollo was generally imagined spatially: the god stood in front of one (Prostaterios) with his bow. But we do not know of physical realizations of this symbolism apart from the images of Aguieus outside house doors (which lacked the bow).[105] One of the two sacrifices to Apollo Apotropaios (indistinguishable from Alexikakos) in Erchia was made 'towards Paiania', as if to avert evil approaching from that quarter. The only other precise cultic context which we know is that Apollo Alexikakos received sacrifice at the *Thargelia*.[106]

The cult of Hecate was a different form of 'aversion of evil', if at a domestic more than a civic level. The triple-faced goddess certainly has a markedly double aspect. On the one side she is a familiar and surely not a forbidding domestic presence, with her shrine outside the front door; a woman in Aristophanes speaks of holding a 'party' (παιγνία) in her honour. In some of her functions she is indistinguishable from Artemis, with whom she sometimes coalesces as Artemis Hekate. On the other side she is the patroness of magicians, a goddess who revels in pollution and can attack or be conjured against a house; 'meals' are sent to her at the crossroads, to keep her away. To make her worshippers' psychology comprehensible, we must surely suppose that her two aspects are the sides of a single coin. Hecate is honoured at the door of the house to discourage her from stepping inside, and that form of

---

Hecate' (below, n. 107) could be envisaged as being shared by the ἀποτρόπαιοι (Plut. *Quaest. conv.* 7.6.3, 708e), but it is wrong to envisage them (J. W. Hewitt, *HSCP* 19, 1908, 109–12; Nock, *Essays*, 600–1, is more cautious) as 'chthonians': there are named Olympians among them, and there is no sign that sacrifices to Apollo Apotropaios were not eaten (n. 106). Heracles is designated Alexikakos on one votive relief from the Piraeus (*SEG* XXVIII 232; *LIMC* s.v. *Herakles*, no. 1378; Tagalidou, *Weihreliefs*, pl. 12 no. 32), where he appears beside a 'columnar shrine' probably in company with Hermes. Travlos, *Pictorial Dictionary*, 274–7, and Tagalidou, *Weihreliefs*, 22–7, revive Frickenhaus' old identification of the supposed site of the temple of Heracles Alexikakos in Melite, but see Wycherley, *Stones*, 187, 195, n. 46. The possibly Attic calendar from Miletupolis (p. 484) includes separate but consecutive offerings to Heracles and Alexikakos.

[105] On 'in front of the door gods', the more local version of 'aversion of evil', see p. 20. The dedications to Apollo in these functions are undated/Roman period: *IG* II² 4719 (Aguieus, a dedication by the πυλωροί: propylaea region); 4727 (Prostaterios, from near the acropolis); 4850, Aguieus Alexikakos (found 'beside the Acharnian gate', which may be significant); 4995, Aguieus Prostaterios and four other titles; 5009, Apotropaios (?), Piraeus. On Apollo Prostaterios see Detienne, *Apollon*, 124–5.

[106] Erchia: *LSCG* 18 α 32–3; γ 31–5. Thargelia: *LSS* 14.49, 54. Sacrifice to Apotropaios also in the Marathon Calendar (*ZPE* 130, 2000, 45–7), col. 1, 26 and probably in *IG* I³ 255 (n. 49 above).

intimacy which is cultivated with her is a way of making the threat that she poses psychologically manageable.[107]

[107] On Hekate before the door see pp. 18–20 above; on Artemis Hekate p. 431, n. 53 below; on Hekate and pollution Parker, *Miasma*, 30, 222–4; for a discussion of her double aspect, Johnston, *Restless Dead*, ch. 6. The role of Artemis or Hekate as Propylaios (Artemis/Hekate Epipurgidios on the Athenian acropolis, Paus. 2.30.2; cf. *IG* II² 5050 and Clinton, *Sacred Officials*, 51, line 10; Artemis Propylaia at Eleusis, Paus. 1.38.6) is an extension of the domestic door-keeping function. Party: Ar. *Lys.* 700.

18

Gods at Work II: The Growth of Plants and Men

Black Earth, according to Solon, was 'greatest mother of the Olympian gods'.[1] She was the source of agricultural wealth, and the nurse of children. We will investigate these two functions in turn. Earth herself was a figure more of thought and of myth, a very important one, than of cult, but she had some place at that level too. Thucydides, for instance, mentions her among the deities whose ancient shrines were situated south of the acropolis, and deme calendars have provided important new evidence. In Marathon she has two cult places and receives three offerings (all in late winter–early spring), a pregnant cow (an expensive offering this), a sheep, and an 'all black goat'. In Erchia she is one of the honorands, along with the Nymphs, Achelous, Alochos and Hermes, in a mini-festival held on the deme's 'Hill' late in Boedromion.[2] Whereas the other powers receive a plain 'sheep', she is given a 'pregnant sheep, not to be carried away'. The presence of Alochos, 'wife', in Erchia may indicate that the emphasis there is on earth's role as a nurse of children. But even so she receives, as once in Marathon, a pregnant victim; the 'all black goat' at Marathon too is clearly an offering specifically appropriate to Black Earth. Within the language of Greek ritual, that 'lexicon with few glosses',[3] the use of pregnant victims is perhaps the signifier that can be interpreted with most confidence. Such economically wasteful offerings go to distinctive recipients, earth and Demeter and powers such as them. Here the much-abused and over-extended concept of 'fertility' is for once in place.

I turn to other agriculturalists. Demeter, Kore and Plouton/Ploutos have had their due in the Eleusinian chapter, and Dionysus' relation to the vine needs merely to be noted. Zeus' involvement with agriculture is not very marked, but he does receive pre-ploughing offerings in some demes; and the

---

[1] Fr. 36.4–5 West.

[2] Thuc. 2.15.4 (later called Ge Olympia, Paus. 1.18.7; Plut. *Thes.* 27.6); note too the precinct of Ge Kourotrophos near the entrance to the acropolis, Paus. 1.22.3; late priesthood of Ge Themis, *IG* II² 5130. *Hieron* of Zeus Meilichios, Ge and Athena at Alopeke: *IG* I³ 1084. Marathon: *ZPE* 130 (2000), 45–7 col. 2.9, 13, 17–18; Erchia: *LSCG* 18 α 14–16, β 21–25, γ 26–30, δ 24–27, ε 16–21. 'This is a group concerned with fertility and birth': Kearns, *Heroes*, 23, n. 71. Ge in the Mysteries at Phlya: Paus. 1.31.4. Ge probably received an offering at the *Eleusinia*, *IG* I³ 5.3.

[3] M. H. Jameson, *BCH* 89 (1965), 165. On pregnant offerings see R. M. Simms, *Hesperia* 67 (1998), 96–7.

ploughing ox is the central character at the *Dipolieia*, even if the importance of agriculture to that festival is unclear. Zeus controls the weather, in Attica (where the evidence for this function is abundant) as elsewhere.[4] Perhaps his agricultural role is mainly derivative from this. Poseidon has a complicated relation with Demeter in many parts of the Greek world, and has a presence at Eleusis. One of his common panhellenic titles, attested also in Attica, is 'Phytalmios', which derives from the root φυ- indicating growth. (The -αλμ is now commonly seen as part of a suffix, not as a second signifying element in a compound.) To Plutarch it was self-evident that Poseidon Phytalmios was a god of farmers; sweet waters no less than bitter come from Poseidon, and springs such as Hippokrene are very often associated with Poseidon's animal the horse, in a coalescence of one divine function with another which is very characteristic of Greek religious imagination. But one of Poseidon's best-attested activities in Attica is the siring of children (Theseus, Eumolpus, Hippothoon, Halirrhothios), some of whom (Eumolpus, Hippothoon) had a particular association with Eleusis. And the title borne by Poseidon at Eleusis is precisely 'father'. Perhaps, it has been suggested, the title Phytalmios too once related to paternity and not the growth of plants; one may also wonder whether there is a metaphorical relation between the two things. However that may be, the Attic context in which Poseidon was honoured as Phytalmios eludes us; we cannot pin down any association he may have had with agriculture.[5]

The Sun and the Seasons were honoured with a procession;[6] their relevance to agriculture needs no demonstration. But that procession perhaps formed part of a festival of Apollo, the *Thargelia*, and Apollo's role in this area is more problematic. If we see the *Thargelia* as a festival of general purification, which also looked forward, in part prophylactically, to the coming harvest, we can keep Apollo himself at a distance from direct involvement in helping plants to grow.[7] But a second Apolline festival too appears more closely associated with agriculture than can readily be reconciled with the god's familiar set of concerns. At the *Pyanopsia* children parade with ripened agricultural products, while bean stews are eaten in the home. Children fit Apollo's general persona more readily than do nuts and ripe berries and bean stew, but the agricultural emphasis of the festival is too marked to be explained away as a metaphor for something else. A brief nostalgia might even seize the interpreter at this point for the discredited old understanding of

---

[4] Pre-ploughing offerings: Hagnous (?) *IG* II² 1183 (RO 63) 33; perhaps Thorikos, p. 196, n. 14. Zeus Georgos receives an offering in Maimakterion in a private calendar of the Roman period, *LSCG* 52.12. Dipolieia: pp. 187–91. Weather: *Athenian Religion*, 29–33.

[5] Poseidon and springs: e.g. Aesch. *Sept.* 308–10; Nilsson, *Geschichte*, 450; and paternity, F. Schachermeyr, *Poseidon und die entstehung des griechischen Götterglaubens* (Munich 1950), 37; Graf, *Nordionische Kulte* 207–8, who reinterprets Phytalmios in this sense. Phytalmios: *IG* II² 5051; Plut. *Conv. sept. sap.* 15, 158d. Poseidon Pater at Eleusis: Paus. 1.38.6.

[6] See p. 203.

[7] Cf. Parker, *Miasma*, 25–6; on this festival and *Pyanopsia* also pp. 203–6 above.

Apollo as a sun-god. But it is wiser merely to acknowledge a problem which fuller information might resolve. There is a difficulty also in respect of Athena. A long tradition of scholarship allows the goddess to have a finger in every pie, agriculture included. Most of the evidence assembled can, it is true, be dismissed without great difficulty. It is probably only a lexicographer's misunderstanding of a phrase of Lycurgus that has caused a sacrifice of 'Preliminary Thanks' (*Procharisteria*) brought 'when the crops were beginning to grow' to be associated with Athena, instead of its more likely recipient Demeter. And if Athena protects olive-trees, that is doubtless because they, like her, are a national symbol; if the function is more political than agricultural, it is not surprising that a Zeus of Olive Trees also guards them. Again, though Athena Nike's statue held a pomegranate in its right hand, it held a helmet in its left; the idea must be that victory in war allows that agricultural flourishing of which the pomegranate is a symbol, not that Athena is directly a source of fertility. A phrase that has seldom been much attended to in a sacred law is much more serious. It runs, scandalously, 'For Athena Skiras a pregnant sheep'. What has Athena, most virginal virgin of Attica as she has been called, to do with a pregnant sheep?[8] We noted earlier the unambiguous meaning of such an offering. The context provides no explanation. But we cannot readjust the whole allocation of agricultural functions in Attica on the basis of this anomalous minor offering in the calendar of a subgroup. Earth, Demeter, Kore, Plouton, Zeus, Poseidon, Sun, Seasons, and in some sense Apollo remain the accredited agricultural team.

The Semnai/Eumenides do not, to our knowledge, help plants to grow. But if angry they could prevent them from doing so; if favourable, therefore, they are a protection against storms and blights and murrains. When enraged they are the vehicles and embodiments of pollution, one symptom of which is agricultural desolation. When pollution is absent, then all things flourish. They represent the moral dimension to fertility, the sense in which a people's flourishing depends on observance of certain rules of conduct.[9]

WEALTH-GIVING GODS

The hill men of Attica knew how to cap verses like the shepherds of Theocritus, but pastoralism was of minor importance in Attica, and this is not the

---

[8] *Procharisteria*: see p. 196. Olives: see *Athenian Religion*, 144, n. 88 [+]; Zeus Morios: Soph. *OC* 704–6. Athena Nike: Harpocr. *v* 17 s.v. Νίκη ʾΑθηνâ, citing Heliodorus the Periegete *FGrH* 373 F 2. Athena holds a pomegranate also on a white ground lekythos by the Bowdoin painter (Brit. Mus. D 22; D.C. Kurtz, *Athenian White Lekythoi*, Oxford 1975, pl. 63.2). Pregnant sheep: *LSS* 19.92. Most virginal: Sissa/Detienne, *Vie quotidienne*, 235. But in truth a better formulation (its origin escapes me) is that Artemis is an embodiment of virginity, whereas Athena is beyond sexuality altogether.

[9] See the whole conclusion of Aesch. *Eum.* (from 778); Parker, *Miasma*, 107, 279–80. Pollution and fertility are the two sides of a coin.

region in which to study pastoral cults; there is, for instance, no trace of Apollo Nomios.[10] Nor can much be said about the devotions of those other wanderers over the mountains and other rough places of Attica, the hunters; Artemis Agrotera was much their most important goddess, and Xenophon also recommends prayer to Apollo.[11] From agriculture I move instead, since agricultural abundance was conceived as the primary form of wealth,[12] to the subject of 'wealth-giving' gods. Abundance had a symbol, the cornucopia, which was characteristically seen in the hands of the two Eleusinian gods of agricultural wealth, Ploutos and Plouton, but not in theirs alone.

At this point it is appropriate to digress in order to introduce a small and minor sanctuary unmentioned in literary sources. It was situated a little way east of the walls of Athens beyond the Ilissus, which bordered it on one side, and had the form of an open-air court approximately delimited by outcroppings of bedrock; the natural steppings in these on one side could have been used as seats. Near the middle of the court was a natural cleft which may have been interpreted as a point of access to the underworld; beside it two rough low walls perhaps indicated, but did not in fact enclose, an inner sanctum.

A humbler emplacement for gods could scarcely be found; but for us it is rendered remarkable by the extraordinarily rich assemblage of stone votive reliefs from the period *c*.350 to *c*.250 which have been recovered from it.[13] A majority of them depict, in the usual way, processions of worshippers approaching a deity, to whom they are often leading an animal victim; what is less common is that in several cases a woman or servant kneels directly in front of the god. Iconographically two deities appear, each in a score or so of examples. One is an older, bearded god who wears a cloak which leaves his chest bare; he is almost always seated, and typically holds a large cornucopia (less often a sceptre) in his left arm, a libation vessel in his right

---

[10] But for a 6th-c. herm dedicated to Hermes as]καὶ βοτὸν ἐπίσκοπον see *IRhamnous* 74. For Apollo Proopsios and other possibly relevant evidence see *Athenian Religion*, 32, n. 13. For Pan and herds see Aesch. *Eum*. 943; Hermes Nomios, Pan and Nymphs are invoked together in Ar. *Thesm*. 977–8. Capping: Ar. *Vesp*. 1223. Dedication of a goatherd to the Nymphs: *IG* I³ 974. W. Peek, *AM* 67 (1942), no. 104 (*IG* II² 4833) mentions 'shepherds' but is not necessarily a dedication by such; if it is, the recipient is lost. The shepherds' graffiti discovered by M. Langdon (see *SEG* XLIX 2) may however when published transform the picture.

[11] Xen. *Cyneg*. 6.13; Artemis is just 'the goddess' in 5.14, 13.18. Arrian in a different age adds Pan, the Nymphs, Hermes and all the mountain gods to these two (*Cyn*. 35.3), and some of these very likely received offerings from Attic huntsmen. On this one point the rich iconographic evidence yields little: A. Schnapp, *Le Chasseur et la cité* (Paris 1997), 324.

[12] 'They say that a field is the horn of Amaltheia': Phocylides fr. 7 Diehl.

[13] Published with splendid photographs in Vikela, *Pankrates-Heiligtum* [+], which is now basic on all aspects of the cult; see in brief Travlos, *Pictorial Dictionary*, 278–80. Inscriptions, known only from preliminary reports, reveal both citizen *orgeones* and non-citizen *thiasotai* based at the shrine (*SEG* XLI 247; *Athenian Religion*, 346–7). No find is held to predate 350 except a 5th-c. inscription (Vikela, 58): the kind of 'clear out' of votives often necessary in small shrines may explain the dearth of early material (Vikela, 58, postulates a sudden emergence of Pankrates *c*.350).

Fig. 28. Dedication to the bearded 'elder god' from the sanctuary of Pankrates (? late fourth century). Inscribed [- - -] ἐνη τῶι Παλαίμονι ἀνέθηκε.

hand. At least once he is accompanied by a goddess with sceptre and libation vessel, and once the two appear in the characteristic iconography of a 'banqueting hero' relief. The other figure is unmistakably a Heracles: he is young (whether bearded or beardless), naked, and adorned with a lion skin; usually he stands, and sometimes he holds cornucopia or club.[14] Heracles appears once as a large head (*protome*) resting on the ground, and once both as such a *protome* and as a full-size figure. Once Heracles is shown with a

---

[14] See the summary in Vikela, *Pankrates-Heiligtum*, 4–9. Kneeling: Vikela, 166, citing F. T. van Straten, *BABesch* 49 (1974), 159–89. 'Banquesting hero': A 22 (pl. 17) in Vikela's catalogue. *Protomai*: B 10 (pl. 22.2), with the older god (cf. Vikela's discussion, 145); B 13 (pl. 24.1); B 18 (pl. 26.1).

protome which appears to depict the older, bearded god, in a combination which confirms that the shrine had two distinct honorands (see Fig. 3). The elder god is named as Pankrates, Plouton, Palaimon and Theos, once in each case; the young figure is four times Pankrates, once Heracles Pankrates. A further fragmentary dedication to Palaimon could have related to either god.[15]

No surviving dedication names the elder god 'Zeus', but he was surely sometimes so understood. Pankrates is independently attested as a cult epithet at Athens of Zeus and of no other god;[16] in one relief from the sanctuary an eagle perches beneath the god's throne; and the elder god is iconographically identical with representations of Zeus Meilichios and Zeus Philios, holding cornucopia (or sceptre) and phiale, found elsewhere in Attica[17].

The argument can now revert to wealth-bringing gods, and their symbol the cornucopia. By the end of the fourth century the cornucopia is certainly borne by Agathe Tyche, by Agathe Theos, and by Agathos Daimon in addition to the gods already mentioned (Zeus Meilichios and Philios, and the two gods of the sanctuary by the Ilissus). Dionysus has it occasionally, and rather more often it is held by a member of his circle or otherwise associated with him.[18] Ploutos and Plouton bear the cornucopia as a direct expression of their nature. As for the various Zeuses, we know much less than we would wish of the benefits that they were felt to bestow on the families and other groups based on kinship in which their cult is so prominent, but wealth is seen as being in the gift of Zeus Meilichios in a well-known passage of Xenophon's *Anabasis*,[19] and the cornucopia should reflect that side of his personality; so too, we can perhaps infer, with the cornucopia held by Zeus

[15] On the Isthmian hero-cult of Palaimon see E. R. Gebhard and M. W. Dickie in R. Hägg (ed.), *Ancient Greek Hero Cult* (Stockholm 1999), 159–65, emphasizing Pindar frs. 5–6 Snell/Maehler. The relations of Heracles and Palaimon are obscure. According to Pherecydes *FGrH* 3 F 76, Heracles wrestled (παλαίω) with Antaios and then sired a son called Palaimon by Antaios' wife Iphinoe (a variant on this in Apollod. *Bibl.* 2.7.8 ad fin); for Plaut. *Rud.* 160–1 they are *socii*, and in Lycoph. *Alex.* 663 Palaimon is a title of H. (cf. Hesych. s.v Πάλαιμων), which alludes according to the Σ to H.'s wrestling with Zeus or Antaios or Achelous. In the dedication from Coroneia *IG* VII 2874 ['Ηρακλ]εῖ Παλαίμονι καὶ τῇ [πόλ]ει Μελάντιχος Ἀρί[σ]τωνος τὸν ναὸν ... ἀνέθηκε Melantichos would almost certainly have written Ἡρακλεῖ καὶ Παλαίμονι if he meant two distinct figures: the normal Greek for 'Tom, Dick and Harry' is 'Tom and Dick and Harry', or occasionally for brevity, in dedications of a different style from this one, 'Tom, Dick, Harry'. But for Attica the presence in the sanctuary of Pankrates of a defixio which binds a legal adversary πρὸς τὸν Πάλαιμον and invokes Palaimon's aid in securing revenge is of central importance (D. R. Jordan, *GRBS* 41, 2000, 10, no. 14): it shows Palaimon to have been functionally equated with, say, Plouton, but distinct from Heracles (for all defixiones are addressed to underworld gods: see p. 126).
[16] In the 'Themistocles decree', ML 23.38–9 (probably a 4th-c. composition) and by Hesych. s.v. Παγκρατής· Ζεύς. Ἀθηναῖοι. As a cult epithet it seems only otherwise to be given to Nike (*IGBulg.* 1. 300; cf. Vikela, *Pankrates-Heiligtum*, 66–70).
[17] See Vikela, *Pankrates-Heiligtum*, 73–5 [+] (but Zeus Naios has no place here); the essential already in Cook, *Zeus*, ii, 1104–21, 1162, 1173–8. Eagle: Vikela no A 14, pl. 12.
[18] See K. Bemmann, *Füllhörner in klassischer und hellenistischer Zeit* (Frankfurt 1994), 11–81; on Agathe Tyche see now I. Leventi in *Macedonians in Athens*, 128–39.
[19] 7.8.1–6. Zeus Meilichios and kinship groups: see p. 42.

Philios and (Zeus?) Pankrates. Agathe Tyche, Agathos Daimon and Agathe Theos could all, doubtless, confer wealth, but in the case of Agathe Theos a different element is also present: we know her from a single votive, and, though she has a cornucopia, a leg dangling in the left of the field shows the primary concern of the dedicators to have been healing. Perhaps she could bestow both wealth and health; alternatively the symbol had lost in specific force and become a vague expression of the propitious. When associated with Dionysus it perhaps evoked no more than the immediate pleasures of the symposium.[20]

The most complicated and interesting case is that of Heracles. No myth is needed in order to explain the association of Plouton with the cornucopia, which is simply an expression of part of his nature. Heracles by contrast had to acquire his, whether it was the horn he broke off from the brow of the bull-river Achelous or 'the horn of Amaltheia' given him by Achelous in exchange for the other.[21] What is probably a different myth associating Heracles with a cornucopia is murkily revealed by a dozen or so depictions showing Heracles in various forms of interaction with a mature (and sometimes definitely old) cornucopia-holding god.[22] In the most extreme case, seen thrice, Heracles carries the other on his back, once it seems over water, and various other permutations are found: the two look at one another, Heracles holds the cornucopia while the other looks on, both have their hands on it as if it were being passed from one to the other. It is obviously conceivable that the myth, whatever it is, underlies the co-tenancy of the Pankrates shrine by Heracles and an elder god, both associated with the cornucopia.[23] There are mysteries here which cannot for the moment be resolved. What is clear is that, however Heracles acquired the cornucopia, for cultic purposes he also retained it; he holds it in Attic votive reliefs, not just those deriving from the Pankrates shrine.[24] What he was conceived to do with it is less obvious. Heracles surely

[20] Cf. Pherecydes, *FGrH* 3 F 42: the horn of Amalthea could provide in abundance whatever food and drink one might pray for.

[21] See Pindar fr. 249a Snell/Maehler, and T. Gantz, *Early Greek Myth* (Baltimore 1993), i. 41–2.

[22] See J. Boardman in *LIMC* V.1. s.v. *Herakles*, nos. 3488–97 [+]; Vikela, *Pankrates-Heiligtum*, 117–23; Bemmann, op. cit. 28–36.

[23] F. van Straten, *BABesch* 49 (1974), 170–72, writing before the full publication of the votive material but aware that the 'bearded god' could be called Palaimon, suggested that this identification was applicable to the old man in all related scenes; Vollkommer, *Herakles*, 43–5 and Boardman in *LIMC* V.I. 179 take up this idea. But we now know that 'Palaimon' was just one name among several possible for the old man; Palaimon was variously associated with Heracles (n. 15), but nothing else in his known mythology helps to explain this particular interaction over the cornucopia. Gantz, op. cit. i, 456, draws attention to the late notice (Lactantius Plac. on Stat. *Theb.* 4. 106) that Heracles took Achelous' horn with him to Hades, and wonders whether it was Heracles who gave Plouton his horn. For some other views see Tagalidou, *Herakles*, 132–5 (but the supposed 'Heracles carrying Dionysus' has no textual basis).

[24] Athens NM 7232 (van Straten, 'Gifts', 106 with pl. 50; Vikela, *Pankrates-Heiligtum*, pl. 37.1; Tagalidou, *Herakles*, pl. 3); Petrakos, *Rhamnous*, 279, fig. 189 (cf. Tagalidou, *Herakles*, 137–9 and pl. 17); for a problematic Theban instance (Thebes Mus. Inv. 48, *IG* VII 2461) see Tagalidou, 129–39.

Fig. 29. Heracles carrying old man with cornucopia, 380–360 BC.

stands for the vitality of the body, not of the earth, even if there was an Attic convention of 'sacrificing' apples to him in lieu of bulls. (An iconographical type, found in the Pankrates shrine, which shows Heracles holding apples probably derives hence.[25]) In the hands of Heracles the cornucopia appears to have lost its specific meaning. One relief which shows him with it was addressed to him as a healer.[26]

Another source of wealth was the dead; at least, a standard prayer formula addressed to them was the request to 'send up good things'.[27] On a cup by the Tarquinia painter in the British Museum the figure otherwise known as Pandora, 'All Gifts', is labelled 'Anesidora', 'Sender up of Gifts'; Pandora herself is sometimes shown emerging from the earth. The place if any of Anesidora/Pandora in cult is uncertain.[28] But both with the dead and with

[25] See Vikela, *Pankrates-Heiligtum*, 160 on her B 13–15, pl. 24. 1–3 (note too pl. 39 and Athens NM 3952, *LIMC* s.v. *Herakles*, no. 330/1388, Tagalidou, *Weihreliefs*, fig. 13, no. 23). Sacrifice: Apollod. *FGrH* 244 F 115 and texts cited ad loc. by Jacoby. The practice is associated by the sources both with the Herakleion at Melite and also, perhaps wrongly (Schachter, *Cults*, II, 21), with Boeotia: it is discussed by S. Georgoudi in C. Jourdain-Annequin and others, *Le Bestiaire d' Héraclès* (*Kernos* suppl. 7, Liège 1998), 301–17.

[26] Athens NM 7232 (see n. 24 above). The 'body part' votives from the Pankrates shrine (p. 412, n. 100 above) cannot be specifically associated with a particular representation of either god; and they are dated to the Roman period.

[27] See Ar. fr. 504.14 with K/A's note.

[28] On all this see most recently J. Boardman in Καλλίστευμα (*Festschrift* for O. Tzachou-Alexandri, Athens 2001), 233–44. He also discusses, 240–1, the controversial vases (Bérard,

Anesidora we are skirting close, it must be clear, to the traditional scholarly
concept of 'chthonians', powers associated alike with death or the underworld and with growth: earth teems, and sends up, and receives back, as
Aeschylus says.[29] Plouton and the dead are model examples of such double-
sided powers, while Zeus Meilichios and Zeus Philios are often represented in
the form of a snake, a creature regularly associated with the earth and with
heroes; Zeus Meilichios seems seldom to have received ordinary 'Olympian'
sacrifice, and both Zeus Epiteleios Philios and (Zeus?) Pankrates could be
represented in the 'banqueting' schema characteristic not of gods but of
heroes.[30] Pankrates could even be given the name of an underworld power,
Plouton or Palaimon or plain 'God'. Athena and Apollo and Artemis (for
instance) are never treated in these ways.

Yet it is not clear that anything is gained by classifying these three forms of
Zeus as chthonians. Moderns speak (or spoke, until a recent revolt against the
concept)[31] of 'chthonians' or 'gods with a chthonian aspect' much more
frequently than the ancients did; a way of looking that the ancients occasionally found useful was transformed into a permanent classification. Moderns
seem also to have brought a much wider range of gods under the rubric. Was
Zeus Meilichios a chthonian? No source says so. And if he has a 'chthonian
aspect', is it right to lump this partial chthonian together with pure chthonians
and with other gods who have a larger, or smaller, or just different, chthonian
aspect? 'Chthonian', it might be said, is a useful translation into scholarly
language of what the ancients conveyed by endowing Zeus Meilichios with a
cornucopia, or alternatively by figuring him as a snake, and by sacrificing to
him in non-standard ways. It underlines what we surely ought to see as a
paradox, the interchangeability in Zeus' hands of sceptre and cornucopia,
symbol of sovereignty and pledge of abundance. Many religious systems keep
these things at opposite ends of the symbolic spectrum.[32] The last point is a
powerful one, and identifies an important issue within the theoretical analysis

---

Anodoi, passim; p. 325, n. 123) showing a goddess emerging from the earth, usually amid satyrs
bearing hammers (?); on these see too E. Simon in H. U. Cain and others (eds.), *Festschrift für
Nikolaus Himmelmann* (Mainz 1989) 197–203. The rescue of the goddess Peace from a cave in Ar.
Pax uses comparable language of 'bringing up, coming up' (307, 372, 417, 445).

[29] Aesch. *Cho.* 127–8. See in general A. Henrichs, 'Namenlosigkeit und Euphemismus: zur
Ambivalenz der chthonischen Mächte im attischen Drama', in H. Hofmann (ed.), *Fragmenta
Dramatica* (Göttingen 1991), 161–201.

[30] Zeus Meilichios and Philios: Cook, *Zeus*, II, 1108–110; 1174–6. Irregular sacrifice to Zeus
Meilichios: Thuc. 1.126.6; Xen. *Anab.* 7.8.4; *LSCG* 18 a 40–3. 'Banqueting hero': above n. 14 and
Ny Carlsberg Glyptotek 1558 (*IG* II² 4627).

[31] See R. Schlesier, *Der Neue Pauly*, s.v. *Chthonischer Götter* [+].

[32] I am thinking of the Dumezilian three Indo-european functions. Scholars commonly take
the middle term between 'sovereignty' and 'wealth' to be 'the household': what the king is to his
people, the paterfamilias is to the house; and the paterfamilias naturally has charge of the
household's stored wealth (so e.g. Vernant, *Mythe et société*, 108–9; 97 in the Engl. tr.). That
may well be a correct description of an associative logic deployed by the Greeks, though Zeus
Meilichios, for instance, does not quite fit. But such chains of association are scarcely inevitable.

of the pantheon. But did all chthonians have such traits? If not, it will be more precise to identify the traits of the individual god than to apply the broad label. The concept is analytically blunt; it does not sharpen description, but blurs it.

Yet there are real questions about the ancients' understanding of such powers, and the expectations that they had of them. The 'greatest festival of Zeus' at Athens was, according to Thucydides, the *Diasia* celebrated in honour of Zeus Meilichios; and evidence for private devotion to the god is also very abundant. The *Diasia* was conducted, in an often quoted phrase of a scholion to Lucian, 'with a certain grimness'. The god is associated in several ways with purification.[33] The exact character of that 'grimness' puzzles the imagination. Zeus Meilichios was not a punisher of transgressors, like the Semnai. Nor was he a simple god of the underworld, like Plouton. But perhaps some of their characteristics rubbed off on him. Then there is the question of the benefits that he could bestow. He was a wealth-giver, but was he that alone? There may have been a more general and uneasy sense that every group needed to propitiate him in order to prosper in any way. E. R. Dodds's famous account of the ill-defined guilts and anxieties that beset the archaic Greek soul is a strange distortion of the attitude of those high-spirited pessimists. But it may catch something of the mood in which they confronted Zeus Meilichios.[34] Just the same questions arise with Pankrates. The urgency of the supplications addressed to him on the votive reliefs, where some worshippers are even on their knees, is not in doubt. But in no single case do we know what they are asking for. Zeus Philios has, on the surface, a much more cheerful aspect, and has even been mistaken for a god who emerges from the symposium.[35] He embodies rather the ties that bind small social groups, but also, we must presume, their sense of the need for a beneficent patron if they are to prosper.

As Zeus Herkeios and Zeus Ktesios lack an attested iconography in Attica,[36] we cannot tell whether either or both might have carried a cornucopia. But Ktesios bears his relation to property and thus to wealth in his name. Lines between these various forms of Zeus are very difficult for us to draw. If Zeus Ktesios was concerned both with safe husbanding of the household's property and with extending it,[37] one may wonder what more there was for Zeus Meilichios to contribute. Perhaps Zeus Ktesios was an emblem of prudent management, while Zeus Meilichios controlled more incalculable factors. Perhaps it was a matter of the different groups within which the two gods were honoured. And perhaps the difference was no more clear to Athenians than to us.

---

[33] *Σ* Lucian p. 107.15 Rabe; on the festival cf. p. 466. On Zeus Meilichios Jameson *et al.*, *Selinous*, 81–102, is now basic (for purification see 95).

[34] Dodds, *The Greeks and the Irrational* (Berkeley 1951), ch. 2. High-spirited pessimist: R. Jenkyns, of Homer (*JRS* 75, 1985, 76).

[35] So Nilsson, *Geschichte*, 808–9; cf. *Athenian Religion*, 241–2 [+].

[36] See p. 16.   [37] See p. 15 above.

The relation of Hermes to wealth, however, was certainly of a different type. He seems in fact to have been associated with it in two distinct ways. Archaic poetry speaks of him as the god responsible for multiplication of livestock and so for wealth in herds. But he is also (to say nothing of the profits of trade) the god of luck and of the lucky strike, including it seems the lucky strike in mining.[38]

CHILD-NURTURING

Earth, I noted earlier, rears both crops, source of wealth, and children. Having followed one path leading from that crossroads, we can now turn back and take the other. Erichthonius, we are told, established the custom that those sacrificing to any god should first make an offering to Kourotrophos; and deme calendars have shown that such preliminary sacrifices to Kourotrophos, though not invariable, were indeed extremely common.[39] Earth and Kourotrophos are separate figures in all cultic texts of the pre-Roman period, when the composite Ge Kourotrophos emerges, and Kourotrophos is thus a model example of a functional 'Sondergott' as defined by Usener.[40] But earth was already a 'rich nurse of children' ($\lambda\iota\pi\alpha\rho\dot{\eta}$ $\kappa o\upsilon\rho\acute{o}\tau\rho o\varphi o\varsigma$) for Solon and 'bore the whole labour of training ($\pi\alpha\iota\delta\epsilon\acute{\iota}\alpha$)' in Aeschylus,[41] and it was supposedly from gratitude to his own mother/nurse Earth that Erichthonius established the custom of the preliminary sacrifice to Kourotrophos. Evidently any worshipper bringing such an offering was always free, and even likely, to envisage Earth as the recipient.

No god other than Ge is formally Kourotrophos in Attica until a late theatre seat attests a priestess of Demeter Kourotrophos Achaia.[42] But very many are the gods who are associated in various ways either with Kourotrophos herself or with the child-nurturing function. As has just been noted, many but not all major sacrifices were preceded by a minor one to Kourotrophos: it may be that, when one was, the recipients were functionally related to Kourotrophos in some way. Table 2 table lists the gods with whom Kourotrophos is linked in

---

[38] Livestock: Hom. *Il.* 14.490–1; *Hymn. Hom. Herm.* 491–5 (for the link with wealth ibid. 171, 529). Mines: Aesch. *Eum.* 946. Whether his popularity in the mining region of Attica (Goette, *Sounion*, 106–7) is a consequence of this is not clear

[39] Suda κ 2193. Deme calendars: see below. The evidence of the calendars decisively defends the text against Mommsen's change of τοὺς θύοντάς τινι θεῷ to θύοντας τῇ θεῷ (*Feste*, 116, n. 4). For the sources see Hadzisteliou Price, *Kourotrophos*, 101–23; Kourotrophos is distinguished from Ge by Nilsson, *Geschichte*, 457; but Hadzisteliou Price, op. cit. 111–12, argues that identification was always implied (her argument from the interpolated text of Ar. *Thesm.* 295–300, however, is bad).

[40] H. Usener, *Götternamen*[3] (Stuttgart 1948; 1st edn. 1896), 73–272.

[41] Solon fr. 43; Aesch. *Sept.* 17–19; cf. the play made with the topic in funeral orations (*Athenian Religion*, 138 and 252).

[42] *IG* II[2] 5153.

TABLE 2. Gods linked with Kourotrophos

ERCHIA				
1. Artemis				
2. Artemis Hekate				
3. Apollo Delphinios	? Apollo Lykeios			
4. Hera	Zeus Teleios	Poseidon		
5. Aglauros	Athena Polias	Zeus Polieus	Poseidon	?
THORIKOS				
6. Demeter	Zeus Herkeios			
7. Athena				
8. Leto	Artemis	Apollo		
MARATHON				
9. ?				
10. Earth	Zeus Hypatos	Ioleos		
11. Hyttenios				
12. Athena Hellotis				
13. Hera	?			
SALAMINIOI				
14. Ioleos	Alcmene	Maia	Heracles	Three heroes and, in alternate years, Ion

Note: In the Marathon calendar Kourotrophos also receives two independent offerings.

offerings in four sacrificial calendars.[43] Each numbered line indicates Kourotrophos' co-recipient or recipients on a particular occasion; so at Erchia, for instance, she received offerings on five occasions, at the fourth of which the group of honorands was Kourotrophos, Hera, Zeus Teleios, Poseidon.

In most of these cases one can detect a specific propriety in the involvement of Kourotrophos. Gods such as Apollo, Artemis, Leto, and Hera have obvious connections with the world of childrearing and family life. Zeus Polieus and Poseidon do not (offering 5), but Athena Polias and Aglauros intervene as middle terms between them and Kourotrophos. Probably then the associations are significant in all cases;[44] they illustrate, if so, the threads that lead out from Kourotrophos to most other deities in the pantheon.

[43] Erchia: *LSCG* 18; Thorikos: *SEG* XXXIII 147; Marathon: *ZPE* 130 (2000), 45–7; *Salaminioi*: *LSS* 19. 84–5.

[44] We know too little of (e.g.) Athena Hellotis and Hyttenios to build an argument in either direction. But note the suggestion of Kearns, *Heroes*, 35, that the whole offering 14 is 'kourotrophic'.

The tendency of the Greeks to appeal to a plurality of gods, to recruit a team, appears in this area of life perhaps more clearly than in any other. Often we can see, according to the structuralist principle, how different gods approach the common ground down different paths. But worshippers perhaps did not always preserve the initial distinctions with rigour. Birth and childcare are distinct functions, and Eileithyia is a specialist in the former. But it was a custom for parents or grandparents to dedicate to Eileithyia statues of children up to the age of about 6.[45] It looks as if Eileithyia is also being thanked for rearing the child through the most dangerous years (at the least, the parents have prudently withheld their investment until that point). The votives at Brauron seem to tell the same story: Artemis is a birth goddess and a protector of 'future maidens' (girls from the age of about 6), but the museum also contains statues of crawling boys. Perhaps Artemis' care for little girls and boys was an extension of her care (of which Aeschylus speaks[46]) for the young creatures of the wild. She would be a protectress then, in contrast to the more normal type of *kourotrophos* whose symbolic role was actually to feed the child. But one may wonder how many parents who had dedicated a statue at Brauron would also have found it necessary to make a separate offering to Kourotrophos. The functions are likely to have blended.

A different complication is that the endpoint of kourotrophy was not sharply defined. The main concern doubtless was with the early years, but there was no point prior to adulthood at which children formally passed out of the care of their *kourotrophoi*.[47] Alongside the *kourotrophoi* the figure of Apollo (if he is indeed, as is generally supposed, a patron of young men) comes gradually into view.

---

[45] See the statues Athens NM 693–6 with e.g. S. Karousou, *ArchEph* 1957, 77–80; Pingiatoglou, *Eileithyia*, 61–5; these illuminate the dedications (given in rough chronological order— they range from ? 4th c. BC to 2nd c. AD) *SEG* XXXV 141; *IG* II² 4669, 4682; *SEG* XVIII 88; *IG* II² 3895; *SEG* XXIV 226; *IG* II² 4048; *AM* 57 (1942), 56, no. 94; *IG* II² 3965, 4066. The similarities between these dedications prove decisively that Eukoline in *IG* II² 4682 is a little girl (so W. Peek, *AM* 57 1942, 57, n. 1) not (so e.g. A. E. Raubitschek, *Hesperia* 35, 1966, 242) a goddess. In Isae. 5.39 a mother protests against ill-treatment by her son by supplication at a shrine of Eileithyia.

[46] Aesch. *Ag.* 140–3; cf. Xen. *Cyneg.* 5.14. But Diod. Sic. 5.73.4–5 assigns help in birth to Eileithyia, the 'discovery' of childcare and of suitable sustenance for children to Artemis, 'who is called Kourotrophos' for that reason; like a good structuralist, he is trying to give different gods different functions. The Spartan festival of *Tithenidia*, in honour of Artemis Korythalia, bore a connection with nursing in its name. For nursing mother votives from Brauron see Hadzisteliou Price, *Kourotrophos*, 121, n. 106, and *Mesogaia*, 123. Σ vet. Ar. *Vesp.* 804b claims that it was as a *kourotrophos* that Hecate had shrines outside housedoors in Athens: one of her many convergences with Artemis if so.

[47] Pl. *Leg.* 784d prescribes that disorderly husbands are to be excluded from weddings and from ἐπιτελειώσεις of children, disorderly wives from various privileges including attendance at weddings and γενέθλια. LSJ and all translators known to me (but not O. Walter, *ArchEph* 1937, 108) identify ἐπιτελειώσεις and γενέθλια, which is linguistically very implausible. The ἐπιτελειώσεις surely refer to phratry-induction rituals of some kind, here seen, remarkably, as signifying a 'completion' of the child. That would suggest a ritual of adolescence rather than of childhood. (Walter compares the gloss of Hesych. ε 5315 ἐπιτελείωσις· αὔξησις; but the word ought to indicate 'achievement of maturity' rather than the process of growing.)

Fig. 30. Xenokrateia presents her son to Cephisus and other gods: early fourth century Attic marble votive relief.

A minor shrine unknown to literary sources, again, brings many of these points into sharp focus. It was situated at Echelidai, on or near the Cephisus, about half way between Piraeus and Phaleron. The shrine itself has not been uncovered; what we have are two fine marble reliefs (one a double relief) and an inscribed stele, all of about 400 BC, found together in that region. The double relief was dedicated by Cephisodotus (note the name) 'to Hermes and the Nymphs in order that …': what follows is indecipherable, but the next word was probably a part of ἀέξω/αὔξω, to grow or cause to grow. (Rings specially made for children are known which bear the inscription 'grow!' or 'growth'.[48]) On one side is shown the local hero Echelos bearing off his bride Iasile in a four-horse chariot; on the other six deities, among whom the Nymphs and Cephisus can be confidently identified. The other relief was dedicated by a mother Xenokrateia 'to Cephisus and his altar-sharing gods' and describes itself obscurely as 'this gift of [in gratitude for? for the sake of?] teaching (διδασκαλία)'. At the front stand a woman, surely Xenokrateia, and her very small son, who is reaching out to a figure who must be Cephisus. No clearer expression is found anywhere in Greek art or literature of the idea of putting a child under divine protection than this little group. Around and behind them are shown, rather larger, a crowd of gods. It is frustrating that among these only Pythian Apollo and Achelous can be certainly identified. But we can still note the remarkable fact that ten gods attend the formal presentation of the little boy to the river-god. The stele bears a list (in the dative case) of what are either 'Cephisus and his altar-sharing gods' or a closely related group. They are: Hestia, Cephisus, Apollo Pythios, Leto, Artemis Lochia, Eileithyia, Achelous, Kallirhoe, Geraistan Nymphs of Birth, Rhapso.[49]

Rivers and springs, this sanctuary reminds us, are almost as important *kourotrophoi* as is earth. Cephisus, main god of the shrine, has first place after Hestia, goddess of good beginnings; and later appear both the greatest of rivers, Achelous, and Kallirhoe, the spring from which the bridal bath was supposed to be drawn. Earth provides nourishment, rivers provide fructifying moisture. 'The ancients used to cut their first locks for rivers, as a token of the

---

[48] See O. Walter, *ArchEph* 1937, 108, n. 3: αὖξε or αὔξησις.

[49] The inscriptions are *IG* I³ 986 (*CEG* II 743), 987 (*CEG* II 744), *IG* II² 4547–8. From the large bibliography (see the editions named) the outstanding item is O. Walter, *ArchEph* 1937, 97–119; on the reliefs (*LIMC* s.v. *Kephisos* [1], nos. 1 and 2) see most recently G. Güntner, *Göttervereine und Götterversammlungen auf attischen Weihreliefs* (Würzburg 1994), 21–3, 78–80. Guarducci's arguments against seeing the figure with Xenokrateia and her son as Cephisus are not strong (*Φόρος. Tribute to B.D. Meritt*, New York 1974, 61–2). The idea that Xenokrateia founded the whole sanctuary rests in my view on an impossible translation of the start of *IG* I³ 987: *IG* I³ is right against Hansen. *IG* I³ 986 accepts Wilhelm's supplement Ἑρμῆι καὶ Νύμφαισιν Ἀ<λ>εξὸ [τήνδ' ἀνέθηκεν] which appears, implausibly, to make different individuals responsible for the two faces of the double relief. Walter's Ἑρμῆι καὶ Νύμφαισιν ἵνα ἀέξοιεν φ[ίλον υἱόν] is palmary in sense and Greek (cf. Hom. *Od.* 13.360) but is rejected as incompatible with the traces by Hansen (though not by *IG* I³); Hansen accepts Guarducci's ἵνα ἀέξοιεν Φαλερ[ές], which is very implausible sense. For the 'presentation' of the young Plato to patronal gods see n. 51 below.

fact that the growth of everything comes from water', explained ancient commentators faced with texts that mentioned such hair offerings. They were surely right, and Orestes in Aeschylus explicitly describes the lock he will bring to the river Inachus as a 'nurture offering' ($\theta\rho\epsilon\pi\tau\eta\rho\iota o\nu$).[50] (Here again, we can note, the period of 'nurture' is stretched right up into adolescence.) But moisture was doubtless needed to quicken the seed as well as to sustain it during growth, and names such as the Cephisodotus, 'given by Cephisus', of one of our inscriptions attest a practice of praying to rivers in order to conceive. Once again, 'kourotrophy' proves hard to circumscribe, if the powers responsible for it have also been responsible for conception. Earth and Demeter straddle the two stages in just the same way, since they provide sustenance for the growing child and are also the prototype for the swelling womb. Spring nymphs, daughters of rivers, are described in Aeschylus as 'life-giving', which covers both functions.[51]

The other gods who shared the altar at Echelidai also have clear relevance. The triad of Leto, Apollo and Artemis has an iconic significance in Greek religion: Leto's achievement in bearing twins, and such twins, was the supreme instance known to man of 'fair birth'. Artemis is also given a more precise role by addition of the epithet Lochia, 'of birth'. In this role, which is often hers in Attica,[52] she is functionally identical with Eileithyia[53] (with whom in fact she coalesces in many parts of the Greek world, as Artemis Eileithyia); but the two goddesses can coexist in the same region, and even in this one shrine. Apollo perhaps also points forward to the growth of boys into youths. The Geraistan Nymphs of Birth are a rarity, and may reflect an individual's selection from the vast panorama of possibilities presented by mythology. Nymphs, it is true, are among the most familiar nursing figures both in myth and in cult, perhaps again because of their association with water.[54] But these precise nymphs are otherwise known only from a late reference to 'Geraistian Nymphs' who brought up the baby Zeus in Gortyn.[55]

---

[50] Σ Pind. *Pyth.* 4. 145 (cf. Σ B Hom. *Il.* 23.142); Aesch. *Cho.* 6; 'Simonides' XXXII (b) in Page, *FGE*. Paus. 1.37.3 mentions a dedication to Cephisus showing a youth 'cutting his locks'. Cf. (also on the whole question of 'potamonymy') Parker in S. Hornblower and E. Matthews (eds.), *Greek Personal Names* (Oxford 2000), 59–60. Appropriately, a phratry also had a shrine of Cephisus: *Agora* XIX H9.

[51] Fr. 168.17. According to legend, the young Plato was taken by his parents to Hymettus in order to be presented to Pan, the Nymphs and Apollo Nomios (Olympiodorus, *Vit. Plat.* 1). If the story (which culminates with bees smearing honey on the boy's lips) has been shaped by actual practices, it reveals a different association between childrearing and the world of nature, in this case a link with the gods of the world beyond the ploughed fields.

[52] See Ch. 11 on Brauron. Leto: e.g. *Hymn. Hom. Apoll.* 14–18, or the votive relief from Brauron, *Mesogaia*, 116–17.

[53] In Aesch. *Supp.* 676–7 it is Artemis Hekate who has this function.

[54] See Eur. *El.* 626; M. L. West's note on Hes. *Theog.* 347. They also aid conception, and receive offerings from pregnant women: H. Herter, *RE* s.v. *Nymphen*, 1549; Nilsson, *Geschichte*, 248–9.

[55] *Etym. Magn.* 227.39–41 s.v. Γεραιστιάδες; id. 227.44–6 s.v. Γεραίστιον also associates the place of that name in Arcadia with the swaddling of Zeus. As for the adjective γενέθλιος, in Pl. *Leg.* 729c the γενέθλιοι θεοί confer children (in 879d they appear to prevent offences against parents).

As for Rhapso, 'stitcher', she is not known at all. Perhaps she stitched the unformed child in some way. Marriage, conception, birth, and nurture (perhaps even up into the teens) all seem to be attended to somewhere within the group—without Kourotrophos herself being present at all.

Other goddesses may have had relations of a less direct kind with the world of childcare. Rich Athenian mothers put gold snake bracelets on their children's wrists in commemoration of the real snakes who guarded Erichthonius, the archetypal Athenian child whom Athena 'reared' and the daughters of Cecrops were supposed to tend. So Athena could perhaps be seen as a kind of honorary *kourotrophos* to the whole people, though it is not clear to what extent this conception was activated in cult: the best that can be quoted is one votive relief of the late fourth century which shows a tiny boy presented to the goddess by his father.[56] Demeter was multiply qualified: she was mother of Kore and nurse of Demophon; and Fair Birth was worshipped at one of her greatest festivals.[57] But perhaps the perpetual cycle of Demeter festivals in which Athenian women were involved was enough, and women turned elsewhere if they wished specialized aid when faced with motherhood.

Even sensual Aphrodite could not dissociate herself wholly from the drabber cares of women, as we see from the intriguing case of Genetyllis or (the plural is rather commoner than the singular) the Genetyllides. These were 'daimones from the circle of Aphrodite', worshipped in her sanctuary at Cape Kolias. Women gathered there in what as far as we can tell were privately organized groups (that is to say, no formal structures are attested, though there was a priestess of Aphrodite Kolias). Aristophanes mentions Genetyllis or the Genetyllides several times, and they are invariably seen as a symbol of female sensuality; they find themselves linked with gluttony, deep kisses, effeminate and erotic music. But Genetyllis is simply a diminutive formation from γενετή, birth, and we are told that the Genetyllides received dog sacrifices like other goddesses of birth.[58] What really happens at group rituals is never reducible to their formally declared purpose, as we saw in relation to festivals, and the cult of the Genetyllides can count as a model illustration of that truth (so much it seems safe to infer from the Aristophanic portrayal). Women brought together to contemplate the grim prospect of childbirth take hearty

[56] Commemoration: Eur. *Ion.* 20–6, 1427–9; 'rearing' by Athena; Hom. *Il.* 2.547–9; votive relief: Athens Acr. Mus. 3030 (Walter, *Aeropolismuseum*, no. 46, B. Holtzmann, *L'Aeropole d'Athènes*, Paris 2003, 179).

[57] On Demophon and Fair Birth see p. 340 and p. 275. Note too what was said above about Earth and Demeter as concerned both with conception and nurture. Cf. Kron, 'Frauenfeste', 629 (non-Attic evidence). IG II² 4025, a dedication to Demeter and Kore of a statue of a girl by her mother (4th c.), may be relevant.

[58] Ar. *Lys.* 2, *Nub.* 52, *Thesm.* 130, fr. 325; cf. Paus. 1.1.5 with the Σ ad loc. (this last compares Genetyllis to Hecate and speaks of dog-sacrifice), Suda γ 141, which mentions uncertainties (cf. Jessen in *RE* s.v. *Genetyllis*, 1150) whether she/they were associates of Aphrodite or Artemis (*similia* in the Σ on the cited passages of Aristophanes). For the etymology see P. Chantraine, *Dictionnaire étymologique de la langue grecque* (Paris 1968–80), s.v. γίγνομαι, 223.

pleasure instead in one another's company. Aphrodite, for all her importance in the life of women, is not usually associated directly with childbirth. Nor is she here, but through the mediation of Genetyllis; and Aphrodite's own contribution, we may suppose, is the gaiety. Here, then, she intrudes on a sphere alien to her while retaining her own distinctive identity. In other cases we merely see her exercising functions that others too could have fulfilled, without the Aphrodisian trademark being visible. A spring on Hymettus which brought pregnancy and easy labour was sacred to her,[59] and, if we accept that votive breasts may relate not to disease but to lactation,[60] the feeding mother was a chief client at all her sanctuaries. On the other hand, a votive pinax from the archaic acropolis which shows Aphrodite holding two children does not simply assimilate her to a young mother like any other, a responsible *kourotrophos*: for the two children here are identified by inscription as Desire and Love.[61]

What, amid all these maternal concerns, of Mother? According to a rationalizing account found in Diodorus, a human Cybele was an expert in curing the diseases of young children and animals by purifications and charms (ἐπῳδαί), and in the course of treatment often had occasion to take them in her arms. By this account, votives showing Mother holding a child represent her not as a mother herself, but as a healer of the young. In fact, in the small votive Mothers from Attica, the object she holds on her lap is usually not a child but a lion. But perhaps this standardized image of the goddess could thank her for any kind of aid. The little marble images of Cybele to be seen in all the museums of Attica (and there are usually many more in the storerooms) pose a puzzle by their very frequency. Do grateful memories of the ecstatic dance explain them all? Perhaps they reflect rather a pediatric role.[62]

As was noted earlier, no sharp line divides the divine protectors of very tiny children from those who guide older ones. But let us now shift the emphasis to the latter function. The disastrous attempt at nursing by the daughters of Cecrops in myth related to a very small child. But those two of the three daughters who have an independent role in cult, once indeed sharing a priestess with Kourotrophos, are associated with rather larger

---

[59] Suda κ 2672, citing Cratinus fr. 110; Hesych. κ 4521, citing Ar. fr. 283; cf. E. K. Borthwick, *AJP* 84 (1963), 225–43; W. Bühler, *Zenobii Athoi Proverbia*, iv (Göttingen 1982), 283–90. Aigeus established the Athenian cult of Aphrodite Ourania because of childlessness, according to Paus. 1.14.7 (cf. Artemid. 2.37 p. 171. 20–1 Pack).

[60] See p. 412.

[61] Athens NM acropolis 2526; on this, and on the similar kantharos fr. ib. 603, see H. A. Shapiro, *Art and Cult under the Tyrants in Athens* (Mainz 1989), 120–1.

[62] So Borgeaud, *Mère des dieux*, 53: 'c'est sans aucun doute la protection des petits enfants qui fut, dans la région quasi silencieuse des pratiques individuelles, (sa) fonction majeure'; cf. L. E. Roller, *In Search of God the Mother* (Berkeley 1999), 159, 210. Diodorus: 3.58.2–3. Votives: M. J. Vermaseren, *Corpus Cultus Cybelae Attidisque*, ii. *Graecia atque Insulae* (Leiden 1990), 1–120; for an Attic instance with a child see Hadzisteliou Price, *Kourotrophos*, 64–5 with fig. 50. Note the dedication to Agdistis and Attis ὑπὲρ τέκνων n. 83 below. On the cult cf. *Athenian Religion*, 188–94.

ones. Pandrosus was patroness of the 7-year-old *arrephoroi*, and perhaps of any girl of that age.[63] More paradoxically, Aglauros was the chief divine patroness of the ephebes: it was in her sanctuary that they swore their famous oath (to which she was first witness, prior even to Hestia), and her priestess was required to make sacrifice, at certain mysterious 'entry rites', to a long list of gods closely comparable to those to whom the ephebes made their oath.[64] A new myth was even invented which allowed her, true role model for the ephebes, to sacrifice herself for her country.[65] To contemplate the cults of the acropolis is to stare into the unfathomable recesses of history. What has a foolish girl such as Aglauros to do with the rising generation of young men? Or, if she is by nature a fostering power (her sisters' names, though not her own, speak of nourishing dew),[66] how has myth made her into a foolish girl? Let us duck the unanswerable questions, and note instead that she is the first divine witness to the ephebic oath, while Heracles is the last. Perhaps she is best seen as a feminine influence, in counterpoise to the aggressively masculine ideal set before the ephebes by Heracles. Like Pandrosos, Aglauros is an oath goddess for women only. She mattered to women because she was their divine surrogate in rearing their sons. She and Pandrosos were also, as it were, representatives of Athena in this area. Athena's association with an 'Ephebes' rite' at the *Oschophoria* is something of an anomaly. But the possibility was raised in Chapter 10 that her intermediaries Aglauros and Pandrosos were also involved.[67]

[63] On Pandrosos and the *arrephoroi* see p. 219; on the joint priesthood p. 216. That Herse is much less rooted in cult than her sisters is widely agreed (see e.g. Jacoby, n. 3 to comm. on Philoch. *FGrH* 328 F 105; Brulé, *Fille d'Athènes*, 38–9).

[64] See the new text of the 240s published by G. S. Dontas, *Hesperia* 52 (1983), 48–63 = *SEG* XXXIII 115; cf. XXXVI 169. The priestess sacrificed εἰσιτητήρια, also called εἰσαγώγεια, to Aglauros, Ares, Helios, the Hours, Apollo and the other customary gods; the ephebes swore (RO 88) to 'Agraulos' (= Aglauros), Hestia, Enyo, Enyalios, Ares and Athena Areia, Zeus, Thallo, Auxo and Hegemone, Heracles, boundaries of the fatherland, corn, barley, vines, olive-trees, figs. Aglauros is common to both lists, Ares in the new inscription is a simplification of the military group Enyo, Enyalios and Athena Areia, while Sun, Hours and Apollo correspond as sources of growth to Thallo, Auxo and Hegemone: Thallo was in fact an Hour at Athens, while Auxo and Hegemone belonged to the closely related group of Graces (Paus. 9.35.2). One might suppose (despite the objections of P. Gauthier, *Bull. Épig.* 1996, 582–3, no. 175) that the εἰσιτητήρια/εἰσαγώγεια in question were those of the ephebes (εἰσαγώγεια in particular would suit their induction better than the priestess's own entry to office): the priest of Demos and the Graces associated with these in 2nd-c. texts did not exist at the date of the Dontas decree, and it would be very reasonable to speculate that the priestess of Aglauros preceded him in that function. That hypothesis is much weakened, however, by *IG* II² 948, dated by S. V. Tracy to *c.*190 (*Attic Letter-Cutters*, 84), a fragment of a decree which was evidently closely comparable to the Dontas decree (N. Robertson, *AJP* 105, 1984, 392, n. 47): *ex hypothesi* the priestess should have surrendered these functions by that date to the priest of Demos and the Charites (a post created in the 220s).

[65] Philochorus *FGrH* 328 F 105. On Aglauros see R. Merkelbach, 'Aglauros: die Religion der Epheben', *ZPE* 9 (1972), 277–83; Sissa/Detienne, *Vie quotidienne*, 245–9; Kearns, *Heroes*, 23–7, 57–63.

[66] Steph. Byz. s.v. Ἀγραυλή speaks of them as 'named from the things that make the crops grow' (ἀπὸ τῶν αὐξόντων τοὺς καρπούς).

[67] See p. 216. Oaths: p. 270.

The ephebes swore also by Thallo, Auxo and Hegemone. According to Pausanias,[68] Graces and Seasons (Horai) originally came in twos in Attica: Auxo and Hegemone were Graces, Karpo and Thallo were Seasons, but the Athenians eventually adopted the new panhellenic fashion and installed a triad of Graces in front of the entrance to the acropolis. Details remain slippery (Pausanias fails to name the Athenian triad for us), but Pausanias' report is enough to make plain the kind of thing that the ephebes' group of Thallo, Auxo and Hegemone were. And yet the Graces and, to a lesser extent, the Seasons, evade all our attempts to categorize them. We call them powers of growth, the Graces more linked with humans, the Seasons with plants,[69] because several bear speaking names which so present them—Auxo links with growth, Thallo with flourishing, Karpo with fruiting. Ephebes honour powers of vegetable as well as of human growth partly because it is their duty to protect the produce of the land, and partly because they are themselves a portion of that produce. But the name Charites itself (for which Graces is in this respect a good equivalent) forbids our reducing or confining them to this sphere of mere production. The Charites are associated with 'Splendour' (Aglaia) and 'Merriment' (Euphrosyne) and 'Festivity' (Thalia—linked etymologically with θάλλω) even when they are not so named (as they sometimes are[70]). They are also associated with charming behaviour and the repaying of favours and sexual pleasure and much else that is gracious. The central point in what is arguably the first character sketch in western literature, Xenophon's obituary of the Spartan Clearchus, is that this talented military man lacked the charm conferred by the Graces.[71] They embody a superbly comprehensive and celebratory vision of human flourishing, a reproach to the puritanisms of all ages. One would be glad to get a clearer view of the contexts in which these great powers were honoured. Some important votive reliefs survive from their sanctuary on the Nike bastion of the acropolis; the reliefs display a distinctive iconography, but give no clue as to the occasions on which they were offered.[72] The association with the young is the cultic role of the Graces which we know best.

---

[68] 9.35.2. For Robert's challenge to Pausanias and the subsequent debate see Habicht, *Studien*, 85–93.

[69] H. Usener, *Götternamen*, ed. 3 (Frankfurt 1948: text unchanged from the 1st ed., 1895), 143. On the Seasons cf. pp. 203–4. For the association of Graces, Seasons and Nymphs see Xen. *Symp.* 7.5.

[70] e.g. in Hes. *Theog.* 909.   [71] *Anab.* 2.6.12.

[72] See O. Palagia in *Opes Atticae. Miscellanea ... R. Bogaert et H. van Looy oblata* (The Hague 1990), 347–56. On the basis of the new specimen which she publishes, Palagia makes the important suggestion that the Graces are regularly shown as half-figures to suggest a form of *anodos*. On the Graces see B. MacLachlan, *The Age of Grace* (Princeton 1993), esp. ch. 3, and V. Pirenne-Delforge, *Kernos* 9 (1996), 195–214, who gives the Attic poetic references on p. 198. For their possible association with weaving see p. 409, n. 89. They are honoured in association with the *Eleusinia* (*IG* I³ 5; cf. the Nicomachus calendar *BSA* 97, 2002, 364, fr. 3.81, with the caution on p. 329) and *Thesmophoria* (Ar. *Thesm.* 300); perhaps in an uncertain context in *IG* I³ 234.14. A singular Charis is joined with two Pans in *IG* I³ 976.

Of the relation of Artemis to girls, more than enough has been said in Chapter 11. That of Apollo to boys poses a puzzle. As was noted earlier (p. 393), Apollo's capacity to 'make youths grow' (κουρίζειν), aided by the Nymphs, is one of the best-attested facets of his panhellenic cultic persona. Theophrastus' 'Man Proud of Trifles' takes his son to Delphi to cut a (first?) lock of hair.[73] One would assign to Apollo the hair-offering associated with phratry entry, were it established that every phratry had a cult of Apollo.[74] In Attica there are signs that it was particularly under the epithet Delphinios (one shared, significantly, by Artemis) that Apollo presided over youths' growth to manhood. Two separate instances of oaths sworn before arbitrators about a boy's legitimacy are known from the orators, and both were taken in the temple of Apollo Delphinios. This is rather unlikely to be coincidence. Mythologically, it was outside this temple that the young Theseus was mocked for his girlish appearance—and responded by throwing a bull over its top; there too Aegeus was tricked into attempting to poison his still unrecognized son, whose identity then emerged. This then was the place where youths revealed who they were, and what. A supplication by maidens to the temple is also attested, and it has been plausibly suggested that Apollo Delphinios was the god of the *Pyanopsia*, at which boys had leading parts. Delphinios was honoured in the demes as well as in Athens itself.[75] So far, so good. The oddity is that the ephebes, who honour all the gods (so to speak), do not in fact honour Apollo Delphinios. Ought not he, rather than Aglauros, to be their patron? Perhaps one might argue that Apollo makes youths grow all the way from infancy up to manhood, whereas the ephebate is a mere brief stage within that process; they need not approach him specially, because he has long been their protector.

[73] Theophr. *Char.* 21.3. Such had once been the custom for οἱ μεταβαίνοντες ἐκ παίδων, according to Plut. *Thes.* 5.1; for another instance see Theopompus *FGrH* 115 F 248 ap. Ath. 605a. For Apollo as recipient of hair-offerings see Euphorion I in Gow/Page *HE* (*Anth. Pal.* 6. 279), with the editors' parallels. On such haircuts see E. B. Harrison in R. Hägg and others (eds.), *Early Greek Cult Practice* (Stockholm 1988), 247–54; D. D. Leitao in *Initiation*, 109–29.

[74] See *Athenian Religion*, 64, n. 31; hair-offering: p. 458 below.

[75] Oaths: [Dem.] 40.11 (39.3–4); Isae. 12.9. Men from different tribes (Aigeis and Akamantis) were involved. We know that for arbitration tribes were paired and that arbitrations for each pair occurred in fixed places, and thus the theoretical possibility exists that Aigeis and Akamantis were a pair and their arbitration seat, for all cases, was Apollo's temple. But it is much easier to suppose that in both cases the parties adjourned for the oath to the court of the appropriate deity (J. H. Lipsius, *Das Attische Recht und Rechtsverfahren*, 228, n. 33). Artemis Delphinia: Poll. 8.119. Myths: Paus. 1.19.1; Plut. *Thes.* 12.4–6. Supplication: Plut. *Thes.* 18.2. Pyanopsia: Calame, *Thésée*, 319–22. Demes: *LSCG* 18 a 23–30; *SEG* XXXIII.147.6. On all this see F. Graf, *MH* 36 (1979), 2–22. Delphinios receives a hair-offering and is asked explicitly κοῦρον ἀέξοις in Rhianus VIII Gow/Page *HE* (*Anth. Pal.* 6.278). From the 2nd c. BC an association between the ephebes and the gymnasium of the Lyceum is also visible (Graf, *Nordionische Kulte*, 224, n. 61) and may well go back further; S. F. Schröder, *AM* 101 (1986), 167–84, stresses the 'pre-ephebic' depiction of the god which can be reconstructed for the 4th-c. statue in the Lyceum (Lucian, *Anacharsis*, 7) and sees the influence of Lycurgus; cf. O. Palagia, *LIMC* s.v. *Apollo*, no. 39. But Lykeios too is absent from the ephebic oath.

A similar difficulty arose with Apollo Lykeios;[76] there too good evidence pointed to an association between the god and the adult citizenry under arms, and yet credit for military successes was not accorded him. A large question hovers here. To put it crudely, what is Apollo for? Prophecy was very important, of course; then there was protection, individual and collective, against disease. But even functions as crucial as these do not fully explain why the deme of Erchia, say, sacrificed to the god under six different titles. Apollo has considerable prominence in the world of men's private associations in Attica.[77] Apollo as a god who grows boys into men, under whose aegis grown men train for war, a patron of male sociability and men's societies: once we acknowledge this Apollo, our question as to what the god is for becomes much easier to answer.

Heracles is straightforward by contrast, that demi-god so intimately associated with youth that he even had her as his wife. According to a lexicographer, 'at Athens those who were about to become ephebes, before they cut off the lock of hair, brought a measure of wine as an offering to Heracles, and after they had poured a libation gave it to their companions to drink; this libation is called *oinisteria*.'[78] There is a distinctive tall lebes which is sometimes shown with Heracles and on one document relating to his cult is even used, on its own, to evoke him. If this vessel that could symbolize Heracles was, as has been suggested, the one used for the *oinisteria*, the ceremony must have had a central place in the Athenian perception of Heracles.[79] A relief which shows an elderly man presenting a naked adolescent to the god must relate to the same circle of ideas.[80] It was admission to the phratry that was achieved by a ritual haircutting, and this (not the later entry to the corps of ephebes) was doubtless the occasion of the *oinisteria*; but Heracles stayed with the young men when they did become ephebes, presiding over many of the gymnasia in which they exercised, and serving as one of the divine witnesses to their oath. Heracles was also, to an even greater extent than Apollo, a god who was honoured by restricted groups of adult males dining together; and his was one of the cults (Apollo's was another) in which the archaic

[76] See p. 402.

[77] See *Athenian Religion*, 336, on *Hebdomaistai* and *Eikadeis*.

[78] Hesych. o 325; for other references see the testimonia to Eupolis fr. 146. Ath. 494f treats *oinisteria*, probably wrongly, as the name of a particular drinking-vessel.

[79] See F. T. van Straten, *BABesch* 54 (1979), 189–91, who builds on O. Walter, *AM* 62 (1937), 41–51. One document: the new decrees from Eleusis relating to the cult of Heracles, *SEG* XXIX 131; for the crucial detail see van Straten, fig. 1. The newly attested Ἡράκλεια σπονδεῖα of two demes (*SEG* XXXIX 148) also connect Heracles with libations.

[80] Athens NM 2723, *LIMC* s.v. *Herakles*, no. 760, Tagalidou, *Weihreliefs*, pl. 12 no. 21; here Fig. 31. Various other dedications to Heracles may have a similar occasion, but (*pace* O. Walter, *AM* 62, 1937, 49) lack the spotlight on a single adolescent which is decisive: 'the iconography of the votive reliefs to Heracles is not exceptional' (J. Boardman in *LIMC* s.v. *Herakles*, p. 805). For Heracles' relation to maturity rituals in general see e.g. Paus. 3.14.6; Diod. Sic. 4.24.4–6; C. Jourdain-Annequin, 'Héraclès Parastatès', in *Lire les polytheismes 1: Les grandes figures religieuses* (Besancon/Paris 1986), 283–331, M. Osanna, *Santuari e culti dell'Acaia antica* (Naples 1996), 48–51.

Fig. 31. Presentation of youth to Heracles, fifth-fourth century.

institution of formally nominated dinner-companions or 'parasites' was found.[81] In both cases it seems that the god of the ephebes carries on as the god of the grown man.

At the end of the fourth century, one Lysistrate made a dedication to Heracles 'for her children': the two visible on the very damaged relief are clearly pre-adolescent.[82] As the regular recipient of dedications 'for' a dedicant's children is Asclepius (or Hygieia), it is usually assumed that Heracles is here assuming the role of a healing god. (Other occasional recipients are

---

[81] Ath. 6.234d–235d; cf. *Athenian Religion*, 331. Heracles and banquets: *Athenian Religion*, 333–4; A. Verbanck-Piérard, 'Herakles at Feast in Attic Art: A Mythical or Cultic Iconography?', in R. Hägg (ed.), *The Iconography of Greek Cult in the Archaic and Classical Periods* (Athens/Liège 1992), 85–106. O. Walter, *AM* 62 (1937), 41–51, linked the type of roofless columnar shrine that is constantly associated with Heracles (*LIMC* nos. 1368–1380) with rites of theoxeny for him (so too van Straten, *Hierà kalá*, 88–89); but Heracles is seldom actually shown dining in the columnar shrine.

[82] *IG* II² 4613; Kearns, *Heroes*, pl. 1B (the best photo); *LIMC* s.v. *Herakles*, no. 1387; Tagalidou, *Weihreliefs*, pl. 8, no. 15; van Straten, *Hierà kalá*, 87; Löhr, *Familienweihungen*, no. 168 and p. 204. On Heracles and healing see p. 412 above.

Agdistis and Attis, Artemis Diktynna, Artemis (of Mounichia).[83]) But even when addressed to an accredited healer, dedications for a plurality of children are perhaps a form of prophylaxis rather than a response to a specific disease. It is impossible to say whether Lysistrate turned to Heracles as doctor, as 'averter of ill' or just as a good grower-up of children.

With Heracles we have perhaps slipped from 'kourotrophy', even its upper reaches, to something different. Heracles is a gauge of masculinity for the young future warriors. The god of gender ambiguity, by contrast, is Dionysus. At the *Oschophoria* Dionysus too comes into contact with ephebes. His formal point of entry is via the vintage, which the festival celebrated. But there was no necessity to select the celebrants of a vintage festival from a particular age group, nor to require the two leaders of the procession to dress as girls. Dionysus' other contacts with the young are glancing,[84] and probably relate to their future place within the community of drinking men. But at the *Oschophoria* the womanish god is patron of a rite which dramatizes, we assume, the need of the ephebes to set all unmasculine qualities behind them.

CONCEPTION, CHILDBIRTH, MARRIAGE

We have been looking at 'kourotrophy', not primarily at the experiences of the mothers of these children; but the one thing has repeatedly brought in the other. One reason indeed why functions become somewhat blurred in this area is likely to be that mothers experienced pregnancy-childbirth-childrearing as a single, transforming experience. As goddesses who aid conception we have noted Aphrodite (explicitly so attested), and, by strong implication, Demeter (with her companion Kalligeneia) and the watery powers, rivers and nymphs; two more groups to whom one could pray for children during the preliminaries to marriage will be mentioned below. Aristotle in his dry way recommends that pregnant women should take a walk each day in order to honour the gods concerned with birth—the exercise will be good for them.[85] Was he thinking of Aphrodite's scandalous companion Genetyllis, whom we met earlier? Perhaps rather of Eileithyia and Artemis, the two other birth helpers attested in Attica.[86] But the options open to an individual

---

[83] *IG* II² 4671; 4688; *SEG* XXVI 267 (where I would supplement [ὑπὲρ τῶν παιδ]ίων), dedicated by women in each case. Asclepius: *IG* II² 4400 and often.

[84] For the crowning of children at *Choes* see p. 298; offerings to Dionysus Melanaigis at the *Apatouria* are very uncertain (p. 460). The relation of Dionysus to transitions is, by contrast, a central theme of Isler-Kerenyi, *Dionysos* (see the index s.v. *iniziazione*); this seems to me exaggerated. On *Oschophoria* see pp. 216–17.

[85] *Pol.* 1335b 12–16: πρὸς θεῶν ἀποθεραπείαν τῶν εἰληχότων τὴν περὶ τῆς γενέσεως τιμήν.

[86] Both are present, for instance, in the shrine at Echelidai, p. 430 above. Hera is not attested as a birth-helper in Attica; in addition to Genetyllis, there was another relevant cult of Aphrodite at the foot of Hymettus (n. 59 above). The Nymphs too could be honoured πρὸ μέλλοντος τόκου (Eur. *El.* 626): advance childcare arrangements? or extra birth-helpers? (for the second possibility see Herter, *RE* s.v. *Nymphai*, 1550, who cites *IG* XII.5.1017.11 (*GVI* 1815), μεδεωδίσι Νύμφαις).

woman disposed to take Aristotle's advice would be constrained by availability of shrines, and she might be forced to improvise.

The gods associated with marriage have not so far been mentioned, and need a few extra words. Our knowledge of them unfortunately is heavily dependent on unreliable lexicographical sources. According to Pollux (whose perspective is normally Attic) the pre-marriage sacrifices (*proteleia*) for girls were made to Hera Teleia, Artemis and the Moirai. A different encyclopaedist records that the sacrifices made within his phratry by a young man on the occasion of his marriage honoured Hera, Aphrodite and the Graces of Marriage.[87] The second item is surprising in the form given. The offering within the phratry was not a celebration of marriage and its joys, but a way of registering an event which was liable to lead in due course to the introduction of new young members to that body. One might have expected Zeus and Athena of Phratries to be the recipients. The trio of Hera, Aphrodite and the Graces of Marriage could, on the other hand, very well have been offered *proteleia*. The Suda defines *Proteleia* as a day (*sic*) on which 'her parents took the maiden who was getting married to the acropolis to the goddess and performed sacrifices'. 'The goddess' here in normal usage would certainly indicate Athena, but Artemis too had a precinct on the acropolis (the Brauronion), and one virgin goddess may have been confused with the other at some point in transmission.[88] Late sources also speak of the priestess of Athena calling at the houses of newly-weds with the aegis and a collecting box; this report too has been impugned, on the grounds that in the classical period the priestess of Athena cannot have comported herself like a 'begging priestess' (a term of abuse). A single black figure krater, however, shows what looks like Athena, but must rather be her priestess, waving farewell to a nuptial cortège.[89] If Athena was indeed involved, she must have represented the civic aspect of the proceedings, the importance of marriage for the city.

Alongside these rickety sources can now be set firm evidence from the early fourth century, an object which calls itself 'offering box for Aphrodite Ourania' and solicits '*proteleia* for marriage: one drachma'.[90] In this case the

---

[87] Pollux 3.38; *Etym. Magn.* 220.54-7. Plutarch names the gods involved in marriage as Zeus Teleios, Hera Teleia, Aphrodite, Peitho, Artemis (*Quaest. Rom.* 2, 264b). On the tricky question of timing and location of such sacrifices see Vérilhac/Vial, Le *Mariage grec*, 291.

[88] So Deubner, *Attische Feste*, 16, and Burkert, *Le orse*, 25 (for Burkert's view see further p. 233, n. 70) on Sud. π 2865 s.v. Προτέλεια (but the 'kanephorie der athenischen Bräute zu ehren der Artemis Brauronia' which Deubner extracts from Σ Theocr. 2.66 is a phantasm). We do not normally think of the Brauronion as a place of actual cult activity, but see G. Despinis in *Kult und Kultbauten*, 209–17, and for possible votives E. Vikela, *AM* 112 (1997), 183–4.

[89] Late sources: for the fullest version (in Cod. Gr. 676 of the Bibliothèque Nationale) and inferior variants see Nilsson, *Op. Sel.* iii, 173, n. 27, who argues that this is primarily a (late) begging custom only loosely associated with marriage. It runs ἡ γοῦν ἱέρεια τὴν ἱερὰν αἰγίδα Ἀθήνησι φέρουσα ἀγείρει ἀπὸ τῆς ἀκροπόλεως ἀρξαμένη πρὸς τὰ ἱερὰ καὶ πρὸς τοὺς νεογάμους. Krater: Paris, Louvre Cp 11269, *CVA*, France 12, pl. 166: *City of Images*, 98, fig. 136.

[90] *SEG* XLI 182; for possible visual evidence of a bride's offering to Aphrodite see Oakley/Sinos, *Wedding*, 14, with figs. 3–6.

possibility was apparently being offered of commuting a sacrifice into a cash payment. Two further sets of recipients of pre-marriage offerings are known, though without the term *proteleia* being used explicitly: the Atthidographer Phanodemus says that before marriage the Athenians pray and sacrifice to the Tritopatores for the birth of children, while in Aeschylus Athena promises the Semnai 'offerings for children, and the fulfilment of marriage'.[91] As for Demeter, the symbolism of the corn-eating life as the life of comfort was evoked at several points during the ceremony.[92] But actual offerings to the goddess are not attested.

We have then at least seven potential recipients (individuals or groups) of marriage sacrifices—Hera Teleia, Artemis, the Moirai, Aphrodite (Ourania), the Graces of Marriage, the Tritopatores and the Semnai (doubtful are Athena and Demeter). Perhaps individuals made their own choice of three or four, who will normally have included Hera Teleia (who probably brought Zeus Teleios with her). The great goddess Hera, hitherto wholly absent from our survey, at this point finally regains her rights. Attic Hera is a model illustration of the elasticity of polytheism, and of the limits of that elasticity. All those functions belonging to a poliadic deity which Hera exercises in Samos or Argos are swallowed up in Attica by Athena. None of the other optional extensions of Hera's powers seems here to have been made, either; she does not appear as a *kourotrophos*, or as a birth-helper. She is reduced to her smallest possible extent. But that relation to marriage which lies at the very centre of her panhellenic personality she retains, unchallenged, in Attica too, both in cult and in literature.[93] Her one festival, the *Hieros Gamos*, is a celebration of marriage, and a very popular one.

Hera embodies the institution of marriage. Aphrodite is its sensual realization. Artemis is propitiated by those about to abandon her virgin realm. It was certainly of high importance to tend Artemis at this point, even if a special explanation can be found for certain passages of tragedy that seem to associate her particularly closely with *proteleia*.[94] *Proteleia* aside, the familiar practice of the girl's premarital hair offering is attested for Attica, if with maddening vagueness, and analogy indicates that the recipient will have been a virgin, either Artemis or a heroine.[95] Athena was honoured, if

[91] FGrH 325 F 6; Aesch. *Eum.* 835 θύη πρὸ παίδων καὶ γαμηλίου τέλους. A. H. Sommerstein argues in his edition (Cambridge 1989) ad loc. 'if πρό is to bear the same meaning with both nouns, that meaning must be 'before' ... πρὸ παίδων will then mean 'before childbirth'. That sense for πρὸ παίδων is very unpersuasive; I take πρό as equivalent to a vague ὑπέρ, and understand a reference to premarital sacrifices accompanied by a prayer for the birth of children, like those to the Tritopatores mentioned by Phanodemus.

[92] See pp. 282–3.

[93] See I. Clark, 'The gamos of Hera: myth and ritual', in *The Sacred and the Feminine*, 13–26. On *Hieros Gamos* see p. 76.

[94] Aesch. *Ag.* 227 (demanded by the mythological situation); Eur. *IA* 718–19 (Artemis is here the local goddess). Cf. pp. 242–3; and Oakley/Sinos, *Wedding*, 14, with figs. 6–8.

[95] Pollux continues, immediately after the sentence about *proteleia* quoted in the text (cf. n. 87), 'And at this time girls made hair-offerings to the goddesses'. Analogy: see Vérilhac/Vial,

honoured she was, in recognition of the civic importance of every marriage, source of future citizens; but we have seen that the bride's family may possibly have taken her to the acropolis to honour Artemis instead. The Moirai appear because it is they who bring together the partners to a marriage; one's marriage choice is part of one's destiny (more perhaps in the sense of the fixed contours of one's life than of anything predetermined). At the moment of childbirth too they are present.[96] The Graces of Marriage need, let us hope, no exegesis. The role of the Semnai must represent an application to individual lives of what they represent within the state, that is to say the dependence of fertility on avoidance of pollution, and thus of certain forms of wrongdoing. The Tritopatores probably stand for something different, the ideal of family continuity. One gives to one's son one's father's or one's wife's father's name, and one prays to one's ancestors for descendants. The sources do not indicate in the main which of the two uniting families were likely to bring which set of offerings, though it is obvious that those to Artemis came from the bride's side. Those to the Tritopatores seem to belong rather to the groom. Grooms performed a torch-race in honour of Pan, it has been argued from a confused citation of Philochorus in a scholiast, as a farewell to the wild sexuality embodied in that god.[97] The idea is most intriguing, and finds some support in the frequent presence of wedding *loutrophoroi* as offerings in caves of Pan and the Nymphs. But that is probably not what Philochorus was saying; the confusions of the scholiast are more readily explained in other ways. Nor do we hear of wedding sacrifices to Dionysus, model of conjugality though he was in some ways.[98]

Yet another power must now be named, one called simply Nymphe, woman ripe for marriage, bride. Her shrine on the south slope of the acropolis has yielded a spectacular but largely unpublished array of marriage-related votive material, probably the richest such assemblage from anywhere in the Greek world.[99] The full corpus will doubtless eventually become the central

Mariage grec, 287–8. (Artemis) Eukleia, a goddess well known in Attica, was a recipient of pre-marriage offerings in neighbouring Boeotia: Plut. *Aristid.* 20.8.

[96] e.g. Eur. *IT* 205–7, and often: Pingiatoglou, *Eileithyia*, 95–7. Little that is concrete is known about the Attic cult of the Moirai. The *Praxiergidai* sacrifice to them and Zeus Moiragetes in *IG* I³ 7.12, and they probably have a place in the Piraeus Asclepieum, *IG* II² 4971 (*LSCG* 22: the text mentioned in *ArchDelt* 1973 [1977], *Chron.* 48 may be similar). They receive a small independent offering in Marathon (*ZPE* 130, 2000, 45–7, col. 2. 28: Thargelion), and have a late-attested priestess in the city (*SEG* XII 95.46 = *IG* II² 1092 B 27; *IG* II² 5137). Graces of Marriage: Eur. *Hipp.* 1148, συζύγιαι Χάριτες, should allude to them (E. W. Bushala, *TAPA* 109, 1969, 23–9; *aliter* W. S. Barrett ad loc.).

[97] Borgeaud, *Pan*, 226–31, on Σ Patm. on Dem. 57.43.

[98] Isler-Kerenyi, *Dionysos*, 58, 87 and often (index s.v. *nozze*) makes an oblique case for him as 'divinità nuziale nel contesto del simposio'. But Plutarch fr. 157.2 Sandbach, on the symbolic hostility between Dionysos and Hera at Athens, should not be forgotten. Sissa/Detienne, *Vie quotidienne*, 254, note the exclusion of Dionysus, 'qui semble pourtant rôder dans les environs'. On the conjugality of Dionysus see p. 323, n. 114.

[99] See Travlos, *Pictorial Dictionary*, 361–4; *Athenian Religion*, 299. I have not been able to see C. Papadopoulou-Kanellopoulou, *Iero tis Numphis. Melanomorfès loutrophoroi* (Athens 1997).

resource for all study of the iconography of weddings. What it perhaps will not reveal is why, in addition to the bevy of gods variously concerned with marriage whom we have already surveyed, the Athenians also felt the need for a specialist concerned, it seems, with nothing else; nor precisely how her functions related to those of the others.

ATHENA AND 'THE OTHER GODS'

Well over a hundred gods and heroes (if we allow the Zeuses Meilichios and Phatrios, say, to count as two gods) have had functions pinned to them in these two chapters, and not every conceivable function has been covered. We can reopen at this point the question broached earlier of the relation of the special goddess Athena to all these other powers. One or two cases have been noted where Athena exercises functions that do not obviously derive from her panhellenic persona: she is Athena Hygieia, she has some involvement, if through her intermediaries Aglauros and Pandrosos, with the rearing and training of young citizens, possibly also with weddings.[100] It is very questionable whether she receives *Procharisteria* sacrifices for the shooting corn; but the scandalous and inexplicable offering of a pregnant sheep to Athena Skiras cannot be denied.[101] But this is almost all on a very small scale. It is misleading to credit the Athena of Athens with an interest (say) in healing, child rearing, and agriculture, if one does not go on to list the other deities whom the Athenians continued to regard as the real specialists in those areas. Athena Hygieia, even if she was concerned with healing as opposed to 'preservation of health' at all, was no kind of rival to Asclepius; as for her putative agricultural role, Attica was not a region in which the cult of Demeter languished. Athena was so great that she spilled over a little into the spheres of others, but the balance of the polytheistic pantheon was not disturbed. Such modest 'imperialism' was not the source of her pre-eminence, but a consequence of it. In what then was that pre-eminence grounded and expressed? It seems to have had two bases. On the one hand, every aspect of Athena's panhellenic personality is developed to the full. She has, for instance, important cults as Athena Nike and Athena Hephaistia.[102] Both functions derive naturally from her Homeric character, but it was not necessary that either should be picked out and given special emphasis in this way, by a temple and priesthood in the one case, by a great statue and festival in the other. On the other hand, the goddess assumes honours, functions and revenues that had been left unassigned in the panhellenic division and were open to any special god to claim. Competitions in music and athletics could be attached to the festival of almost any god in the archaic period; and so Athena

---

[100] See pp. 413, 434 and 440.   [101] See p. 418.
[102] See *Athenian Religion*, 90, and App. 1 below s.v. *Chalkeia*.

became patroness of the great cultural and sporting event of the Athenian year, the *Panathenaea*. A festival commemorating political unification might have fallen to any of the gods concerned with political life; but at Athens it was natural that the *Synoikia* should be assigned precisely to Athena.

Apart from festivals, there were other important forms of private and public cult that had no necessary association with one god of the panhellenic pantheon rather than another. A clear case is the vow of 'first fruits' (ἀπαρχή) or a 'tithe', the pledge to pay to a god a tenth of, as it might be, the income from a particular field during the forthcoming year.[103] Athena receives vastly more tithes than any other god at Athens. A number of the dedicators are craftsmen and so may be supposed particularly devoted to Athena Ergane (even where they fail to mention that specific title), but in the majority of cases the reason for choosing Athena seems simply to be that she is 'our goddess'. In Cyrene, Apollo's city, it is Apollo who receives a preponderance of the tithes. This fluctuation in tithe-receiving gods from city to city is possible because the good to which the tithe relates is often good luck very generally conceived. One Athenian dedicator declares:

> Maiden on the acropolis, Telesinos son of Ketis dedicated
> This statue. May you delight in it, and grant to him to dedicate another.

In order to dedicate another, Telesinos will need to stay alive and prosperous; and similar dedications ask the goddess explicitly to 'keep safe' the dedicator, his family and property.[104] One pays a tithe in gratitude that things are going well, in hope that they will continue to do so.

Publicly too gifts were constantly made to Athena, and, if she owes her disproportionate share of battle spoil to her status as a goddess of war, her panhellenic personality does not explain why at Athens she benefits so much more than other gods from fines, confiscated property and tribute from the empire. As the individual paid his tithe in hope and gratitude, so the state showered money on the goddess, to acknowledge her protection and persuade her to continue it. Both privately and publicly what was sought was something very general, well-being. Well-being depends on the gods as a whole rather than on any individual god; but the special god serves as an accessible local representative of that distant body. What in strict theology only 'the gods' can grant, an Athenian seeks from Athena. And on the public level the special god serves as a symbol of national identity. Athena *is* Athens; the coins bear her image and symbols; her treasury is in a sense the state reserve; the subjects of the Athenian empire subsidize 'Athena who rules Athens',[105] and the

---

[103] See Lazzarini, 'Formule', 87–93; Burkert, *Mystery Cults*, 12–15 (votive religion); R. Parker, article 'Dedication (general)', in *Thesaurus Cultus et Rituum Antiquorum* I (Los Angeles 2005), 269–81, at p. 275, and now the fine study of C. M. Keesling, *The Votive Statues of the Athenian Acropolis* (Cambridge 2003).

[104] IG I³ 728 (CEG 227); 872 (CEG 275); probably 745 (CEG 228).

[105] See *Athenian Religion*, 144.

Athenians themselves know no more obvious way to spend the profits of empire than in glorifying the goddess. In embodying the Athenians' pride in themselves, Athena was evidently not intruding on the territory of any other god.

What of 'the Other Gods'? Much more detail has, I fear, been here presented than any reader can readily assimilate. But that is the way with polytheism. It is difficult to read a sacrificial calendar or a few pages of Pausanias without bewilderment. The situation where a single god discharges a clearly isolable function (as for instance Poseidon protects against earthquakes) is not the typical one. Functions blur into one another, as we have seen repeatedly in looking at conception and birth and childrearing. And several gods, sometimes half a dozen or more, typically have some association with a particular function. The key structuralist postulate that, in such cases, each god brings to the same problem a different expertise is often convincing, and always the best working hypothesis. Yet we have encountered several problems and hard cases. The standard and not unreasonable response to such difficulties, and indeed to the chaotic aspect of polytheism as a whole, is that the implicit logic will have been intuitively understood by the Greek themselves, with their rich stores of cultural knowledge. But post-structuralism has questioned the postulate of homogeneous societies in which every single mind is rutted deep by a large number of fixed collective representations.[106] A campaign, an alliance, a colonizing expedition impends, and the assembly resolves to make a vow to a team of gods: will there be instant consensus as to the appropriate powers to approach? How does an anxious young woman faced with a first pregnancy determine which helper to turn to? She has visited sanctuaries of both Artemis and Aphrodite, and has seen identical votives probably relating to the anxieties of such a time in both.[107] It will be obvious that for certain tasks certain gods cannot possibly be chosen, and to that extent the situation is not one of extreme post-structuralist flux. But it is perhaps not quite one of structuralist clarities and certitudes either.

ANNEXE: HEROES AND HEROINES

Some of the heroes and heroines of Attica have appeared here and there in what precedes.[108] As a group they have been admirably studied by others,

---

[106] Cf. p. 392, n. 25 above.   [107] See p. 412, n. 99.

[108] See Kearns, *Heroes*, now supplemented by Larson, *Heroine Cults*. Addenda to Kearns: F. Willemsen, *AM* 85 (1970), 105–7, no. 9 (*SEG* XXXVII 143), Kerameikos, c. 280, Σίμυλος ἥρωι ἐπηκόωι ὑπὲρ Λακράτου εὐχήν; P. G. Themelis, *Horos* 10–12 (1992–8), 77–82 (*SEG* XLVI 260, cf. XLIX 224), Kamariza, base of an offering table inscribed |Τ|ελέστης Εὐδώτηι εὐξαμέν|ος| (mid 4th c.), cf. Eudosia, *IG* II² 4591; S. Lambert, *Rationes Centesimarum* (Amsterdam 1997), 70, F 14. 9, property ῞Ηρω ᾽Αλκιμάχου; apparently too Athens NM 1522, Svoronos pl. 130 [not in *IG* II²] (cf. *IG* VII 3089; van Straten, *Hierà kalá*, 96), a hero Praxiteles in the Asclepieum; perhaps IRhamnous, 109, if Hegeleos there is a hero. The regulation in the new fragment of a sacred law from Aixone (G. Steinhauer, ῾Ιερὸς νόμος Αἰξωνέων᾽, 159, lines 36–7) for sacrifices made by *pentekostyes* (unattested in Attica) ἐν τοῖς ἡρώοις πο introduces a new concept of clustered ἡρῷα.

and an extended treatment would be out of place here. But the question poses itself of how the functions of heroes and heroines differed from those of gods, of what they had to offer the people of Attica that was distinctive to themselves.[109] To that issue I briefly turn.

To start with a truism: no god was an Athenian, whereas many heroes and heroines had so been. They were therefore necessarily the main vehicles for myths of national identity, for the imagination of an Athenian past. Narrative rather than cult was the crucial medium for this function, and Theseus could in principle have served as an embodiment of Athenian ideals without a single animal ever being slain in his honour. But cultic honours reinforced the effect, and the central figures of Athenian mythology (Cecrops and his daughters, Erichthonius/Erechtheus, Theseus and his sons, Ion) were all so honoured; so too was Codrus, that exemplar of patriotism, though there are grounds for supposing that he only acquired cult at quite a late date.[110] There developed in Attica an elaborate mythology of patriotic sacrifice/self-sacrifice in which the victims were mostly young women,[111] and cult groups such as the Hyakinthides became sucked into it, in a way revealing of the tendency to ground potent myths in actual cult. Dying for Athens was evidently a thing no god or goddess could do. (The storied past did not need to be a narrowly improving one—myth cycles such as those of Prokne and Cephalus, who was also a hero of cult, are counter-cases—but the tendency was in that direction.)

The role of heroes as focuses for group identity derives from this broader role of creating an Athenian history. There are complications here: the ideal type may be represented by the ten Clisthenic tribes, each with its eponymous hero, but groups such as demes or *gene* are far from always recognizing a single hero with whom they have a special relationship.[112] Still, the general point that heroes often have this function is beyond dispute, and in the ideal type it is reinforced by cult: the Thorikians are united not just by the idea of their archegete Thorikos, but by coming together to eat a bovine in his honour.

Some non-Athenians too were recognized as heroes in Attica, and here too cult could support, and be supported by, a myth which motivated the for-

---

[109] G. Ekroth, *The Sacrificial Rituals of Greek Hero-Cults* (*Kernos* supplement 12, Liège 2002), in a very important study builds on Nock (*Essays*, 578–9) and argues that a typical heroic sacrifice was ritually indistinguishable from a typical divine sacrifice; similarly in brief, with reference to Attica, A. Verbanck-Piérard in V. Pirenne-Delforge (ed.), *Les Panthéons des cites* (Liège 1998), 109–28. Even if that is true, it does not follow that the two classes were functionally indistinguishable.

[110] See Kearns, *Heroes*, 107, on *IG* I³ 84; the idea goes back to Wilamowitz, *Kl. Schr.* V.I, 259.

[111] See Kearns, *Heroes*, 55–63, and on the paradoxical saving power of the very weak her 'Saving the city', in O. Murray and S. Price (eds.), *The Greek City* (Oxford 1990), 325–44; also Kron, 'Patriotic Heroes', 74–83. Little is known of what was evidently the important cult of the Hyakinthides; the pre-battle sacrifices mentioned in Eur. *Erechth.* fr. 65 Austin (370 Kannicht) 83–89 brought them into the military sphere.

[112] See Kearns, *Heroes*, 68, with 78–9; 93, with 101–2. On deme archegetes see p. 71, n. 83.

eigners' presence in Attica in ways flattering to Athenian self-esteem. A paradigm case is that of the Heraclidae, who are strangely prominent in the cults of east Attica; there must certainly have been interaction between these cults and the myth of the reception of the Heraclidae, which no patriotic orator ever failed to use in illustration of the Athenians' hospitality to the oppressed.[113]

A hero without a name, however, could scarcely be much of a focus for group identity or self-esteem. Yet, alongside the sheer abundance of heroes, the frequency among them of anonymous heroes is perhaps the most important modification brought by the inscriptions to what we learn from literary sources. (A rival claimant might be the frequency with which heroes are followed by an associated heroine or heroines.) The Marathonians sacrifice to 'Hero at (?) Drasileia', 'hero beside the Hellotion' and probably one other such; the Salaminians to the 'hero at the salt-flats', the 'hero at Antisara' and (probably) 'the hero on the bastion'; the Erchians to 'the heroines at Schoinos' and 'the heroines at Pylon'; the heroes 'above the plain' and 'gate-keeper' at Thorikos (Hyperpedios, Pylochos) may indicate similar figures.[114] What differentiates heroes such as these from gods is not Athenian identity but their relation to place, or at least the nature of that relation. It cannot be proved that the cult of 'the hero beside the Hellotion', say, was evoked by an ancient tomb or other notable feature there, but it must count as probable; however that may be, most heroes and heroines are, of their nature, pinned to a place and one place only in a way that most deities, of their nature, cannot be.[115] Indeed, the collectivities of 'heroines' who are sometimes associated with individual heroes can be compared with groups such as Nymphs; one can conceive that 'Thorikos and the heroines of Thorikos', say, served to populate the deme's landscape in much the same way as (unattested) Thorikian Nymphs might have done.[116] At all events, the network of heroic tombs in an ordinary deme meant that there was always supernatural power close to hand. The important military function of heroes derives in part from this local rootedness. Battles happen in a place, and one needs the aid of the powers distinctively associated with that place. A famous painting in the Stoa Poikile depicted the various heroes who aided the Athenians at Marathon, including the obscure local Echetlos, 'ploughshare-man'; a cup in Oxford may show a

---

[113] See *Athenian Religion*, 138, n. 65 (where the case of the Seven against Thebes is also mentioned).

[114] Marathon: *ZPE* 130 (2000), 45–7, col. 2. 3, 24, 25; Salaminians: *LSS* 19.85–6 (cf. S. Lambert, *ZPE* 119, 1997, 92; but 'the hero at Pyrgilios/on' is also possible); Erchia: *LSCG* 18 *a* 19–20, ε 3–5; Thorikos: *SEG* XXXIII 147. 48–50. Slightly different are 'hero at/associated with sandal' and 'hero at the stern' (Kearns, *Heroes*, 152, 196), since something functional is or may be believed about them.

[115] See Kearns, *Heroes*, 3–4 (with some necessary qualifications), 54; qualifications also in her 'Between God and Man', in *Sanctuaire Grec*, 5–107, at 65–8.

[116] For the Nymph/Heroine parallelism see the texts cited by Nock, *Essays*, 596, and the reservations of Larson, *Heroine Cults*, 31–3.

pair of heroes arising from their tomb to bring help at just that battle (which it postdates by only a few years).[117]

The other source of the military effectiveness of heroes is that they were once men, and as men were typically fighters; and they have preserved their prowess and their loyalties after death. We are dealing here with a 'role continuity' (unavailable to gods) displayed also, for instance, by Asclepius, a doctor both before and after death. If heroes retain loyalties, the possibility arises of suborning an enemy's heroes post mortem by paying them cult, or even of benefiting from a change of allegiance that had already occurred during their lifetime: the Oedipus of *Oedipus at Colonus*, rejected by Thebes but befriended by Athens, will side with Athens in a battle one day to be fought between the two states at the site of his tomb (the element of simple proximity appears again here); and the several variations on this theme in tragedy surely imply a foundation in actual belief.[118]

The roles mentioned so far have been those available to what one might call 'free-standing' heroes. But very often a hero was linked through myth, or within the sequence of a festival, or within the shape of a sanctuary, or in a combination of these ways, with a god. The heroes and heroines associated with the first reception of a god in Attica provide a particularly clear example in which the hero literally mediates between god and man: Ikarios and the daughters of Semachus received Dionysus; Keleos, Eumolpus, Triptolemus and others were involved with the establishment of Demeter's *Mysteries*,[119] and some of us still cling to the image of Sophocles earning heroic status by playing host to Asclepius.[120] Heroes may found rites, or may embody aspects of them: Hesychos, 'Silent One', receives preliminary sacrifice during the silent rites held in honour of the Semnai, we are told. Sometimes such sacral heroes serve to bring slightly unfamiliar areas within the ambit of a god: Phytalos bridges the gap between Demeter and the cultivation of the fig, and Athena's little team of heroines, the daughters of Cecrops, associate her not only with weaving, a familiar concern, but also with the crucial growing years of young male citizens. Occasionally a hero can embody a function too specialized to form a part of a god's recognized persona. There are many gods of the sea, for instance, but the skill of the helmsman is best expressed through heroic prototypes.[121] The distinction between the specialization conveyed

---

[117] Painting: Paus. 1.15.3 (cf. 1.32.4–5), with Kearns, *Heroes*, 45. Cup: Ash. Mus. 1911.615 and New York frags., Metr. Mus. Art 1973.175.2: see e.g. Kron, 'Patriotic Heroes', 65–8 |+|.

[118] See Kearns, *Heroes*, 46–53 on Aesch. *Eum.* 767–74; Eur. *Heraclid.* 1026–44; Soph. *OC* 616–23, 1331–2, 1518–34 (all these cases are of foreign heroes friendly to a host state); Plut. *Sol.* 9.1; Hdt. 5.89; Eur. *Erechth.* fr. 65 Austin (370 Kannicht) 87–9 (suborning).

[119] See Kearns, *Heroes*, e.g. 25, 70 and ead. 'Between God and Man' (n. 115 above), 77–93.

[120] The story (*Athenian Religion*, 184–85), doubted afresh by A. Connolly. *JHS* 118 (1998), 1–21, has acquired a picturesque new detail in the statement of Hurwit, *Acropolis*, 219, that the poet fed the god-as-snake with eggs.

[121] See p. 410, n. 93 on Phrontis and p. 410, n. 95 on the festival *Kybernesia*. The heroes of the *Kybernesia* were probably subordinated to Poseidon (or perhaps Athena; less probably they were

through a divine epithet and that embodied in a hero need not be very great, and there were those who thought, probably wrongly, that Aglauros and Pandrosos were mere epithets of Athena; in Attica Iphigeneia is a heroine worshipped in the precinct of Artemis Brauronia, in Hermione a title of the goddess.[122] But a heroine differs from an epithet in that she may have a myth which makes her a prototype of her human worshippers. Iphigeneia was tithed to Artemis by Agamemnon just as the little bears were tithed by their fathers.[123]

We have noted the possibility of a hero offering highly specialized expertise. But such is not the typical case. The area where heroes largely supplant gods is that of healing, but we do not find one hero specializing in wounds, one in fevers, and so on. The healing heroes too are general practitioners, and their advantage seems to lie in 'role continuity' with their human past.[124] The worshipper imagines an ideal healer who is like a human doctor, only more effective, and quondam mortals, especially if they have been healers themselves while alive, slip more readily into this role than do gods. Perhaps there was rather more specialization among the general run of heroes than we can now discern. But they probably owed their popularity above all to their proximity to man, their accessibility: a proximity which was grounded in their nature as ex-humans, but which found physical expression in the fact that their shrines were often literally just round the corner.[125] One could turn to them for almost anything, then; the point was that they were near at hand. That heroes were very popular with individuals is shown by the familiar 'banqueting hero' type of votive relief, as common in Attica as elsewhere. Unfortunately such dedications often fail even to name the recipient, still less to explain the motives for which they have been made. The most striking single exhibit is the fourth-century dedication from the agora made by Dionysius the cobbler and his sons, in honour of the hero Kallistephanos and *his* sons, in consequence of a dream vision.[126] The scene depicted is a rare and lively individualized composition: to the left a busy scene in a cobbler's shop, to the right two slightly larger figures (heads unfortunately missing),

---

free-standing); Phrontis was associated with Athena if he was worshipped in Attica at all. Hesychos: Polemon ap. *Σ* Soph. *OC* 489; see *Athenian Religion*, 298, and for comparable cases Kearns, *Heroes*, 70. Phytalos: Paus. 1.37.2. Daughters of Cecrops: see pp. 219, 432, 434.

[122] See p. 240. Aglauros: Harpocr. *a* 11. Pandrosos: *Σ* R*Γ* Ar. *Lys.* 439a.

[123] Cf. p. 241. Iphigeneia can in fact be seen as having three roles in the Brauronian cult: as honorand; as first priestess; as first victim (E. Kearns, 'The nature of heroines', in *The Sacred and the Feminine*, 96–110, at 104).

[124] Kearns, *Heroes*, 21. On what follows see ibid. 11. A model non-Attic example of specialized heroes is that of the Spartan kitchen heroes Matton and Keraon, 'Kneader' and 'Mixer' (Demetrius of Scepsis ap. Ath. 173f, cf. Polemon ap. Ath. 39c).

[125] See J. S. Rusten's important short study, 'Γείτων ἥρως', *HSCP* 87 (1983), 289–97.

[126] Still known only from the photo (of the relief only) and the English translation of the text in Camp, *Agora*, 147 (Löhr, *Familienweihungen*, no. 81); one phrase of Greek is quoted in Kearns, *Heroes*, 11. For 'heroes and sons of heroes' see Ar. *Av.* 881–2. Banqueting heroes: see references in *Athenian Religion*, 140, n. 71.

Fig. 32. Votive relief dedicated by Dionysius and his sons to the hero Kallistephanos and his sons.

seated face to face, beside a bench or table on which two sandals are visible. If the figures on the right are heroes, then we have a splendid counter-case to the claim made above about the rarity of specialized heroes: Kallistephanos and sons are cobblers like Dionysius and sons (the emphasis on the 'and sons' parallelism, sons of heroes being rare, may support this view). But the figures on the right may simply be further members of Dionysius' workshop. At all events, all that Dionysius requests in return for the gift is 'wealth and health', a very general formula which could probably have been addressed to almost any hero.

It would be odd to end without mentioning a 'mission statement' addressed to us by the heroes themselves, if only in a play by Aristophanes. The eponymous chorus of *Heroes* proclaim, probably to the audience in the *parodos*:

And so, men, be on your guard, and respect the heroes; for we are the stewards of good and ill: we watch for the unjust and thieves and robbers, and give them diseases [a list of especially uncomfortable diseases follows].

Doubtless this is not quite serious, not quite not serious. The possibility that illness might be sent by the gods as a punishment for transgression was one always familiar to the Greeks, though it was never more than one available diagnosis.[127] The heroes are not unique, then, in their capacity to send punitive disease. But it is probably, again, their close involvement with human life which allows the comic poet to ascribe to them such drastic and immediate responsibility in this area.

[127] See Parker, *Miasma*, 235–56. The passage cited is Ar. fr. 322. The ascription of this papyrus (both to author and to play) is conjectural, but surely correct.

Epilogue

In the Christian centuries religion has, we know, been a major motivation for political action, a factor that can seldom be ignored for very long in the writing of narrative history. Studies of Greek religion and of Greek history, by contrast, have traditionally gone their own, largely independent ways. Studies of Greek social and moral values are a more recent genre, but now that they exist they too follow a third path of their own which only occasionally intersects with the other two. But here again one would not think of investigating social and moral values in a Muslim or Christian country without constant reference to the teachings of those religions. How is one to react to this disparity between the way in which religion is treated by students of ancient and of modern history?

Specialists in Greek religion may be inclined, in proselytizing mode, to seek an explanation in the inadequacies of traditional approaches to Greek history. Superficial similarities between the Greeks and ourselves have created the illusion, they might urge, that their political behaviour like ours can be analysed in secular and rational terms; the omnipresent myths, rituals and expressions of respect for the gods are either ignored or treated as a form of wrapping which does not affect the content of the thing wrapped, whereas in reality they are the underpinning, the emotional and cognitive foundation, of the whole of communal life. Myth and religion are pervasive, inescapable, all-shaping; even where imperceptible to a casual view they are active below the surface: witness for instance the triakonter which still in the fourth century took a chorus of 'unwed young' to Delos, unmasked in Chapter 4 as supposedly the very boat in which Theseus conveyed his own twice seven 'unwed young' to the island.

Yet the very embeddedness of religion within Athenian society would have allowed a Protagoras to construct a pair of Competing Arguments on the topic. Religion is very important, because it impinges on everything. Religion is very unimportant, because it is so much a part of the life of the city that it has no independent position, no ground from which to assert distinct imperatives of its own. The blurring of functions between magistrate and priest symbolizes both the power and powerlessness of religion within the city. Of the tribute brought to Athens by the citizens of the empire, one-sixtieth was paid over to Athena: so piety demanded. But Athena's treasury could also be called on to make loans in support of Athenian war efforts; since the gods willed the good of the city, they could not be envisaged as objecting to such a use of their funds in a time of crisis. Religion was so close to the Athenians that it was easy to live with, like a comfortable old coat.

Religion provoked no revolutions in Greece, started no wars, inspired no new movements in thought and feeling. These negative claims are not merely consequences of the preference of ancient historians for secular explanations of events. Religion in Greece was not, in chemical language, a volatile substance. It was stable partly, to continue the metaphor, because it did not react explosively to other polytheistic systems, but could blend or coexist with them. There were no wars of religion in the ancient polytheistic world because there was nothing for such a war to be about. But it was a stabilizing and conservative factor above all because its organizational structures tracked so closely those of Greek society as a whole. The gods of deme and phratry and city were never in a position to lead a revolt against city and phratry and deme. To take a part in the civil wars that tore cities apart in the fifth and fourth centuries, gods of a much more free-standing type would have been needed. Elective cults existed which might in theory have offered more room for manoeuvre. But every individual's primary and shaping experience of religion was within exactly the structures through which he or she first experienced the existing social order. One's identity as a worshipper of the gods was also one's identity as a citizen. The ancient city, it has been elegantly argued, is characterised by a unique blend of Durkheimian (or Fustel de Coulangean) 'embedded religion' in its structures with Weberian rationalism in its political procedures.[1] But what kept religion from exercising a strong independent force was perhaps not primarily a countervailing rationalism. The point was rather that any argument which was seen to work against the interests of the city could not be accepted as a genuine religious argument at all. Between a sober and rational judgement of what was good for the city and the will of the gods there could not, in the long term, be any conflict.

But what of the relation between religion and 'Greek popular morality' or 'Athenian social values'? Much has been written and written well in recent years about the Greek man as an embodiment of a Mediterranean code of honour;[2] notably different positions have been adopted, yet the issue of religious constraints upon behaviour has played increasingly little part in the debate. Perhaps it is true that the strain of Greek feeling that values manliness is simply distinct from the one that enjoins piety; the two central values coexist but do not interact. Cynicism, the movement that set more

---

[1] O. Murray, 'Cities of Reason', in Murray and S. Price (eds.), *The Greek City from Homer to Alexander* (Oxford 1990), 1–25.

[2] I cite *exempli gratia* D. Cohen, *Law, Violence and Community in Classical Athens* (Cambridge 1995) and G. Herman, 'Ancient Athens and the Values of Mediterranean Society', *Mediterranean Historical Review* 11 (1996), 5–36.

value than any other on 'manly virtue', can appear indifferent or hostile to
the claims of religion.[3] On this view the most that religion does is to impose
certain brakes upon the extremes of manly self-assertion: one must not violate
sanctuary or break oaths,[4] nor (the myth of Tydeus suggests) should hostility
to an enemy be taken to the point of eating his brains when dead. Within the
arena so delimited, man shows his excellence by courage, resourcefulness and
furious resolve, and need not reck of the gods.

Yet there were important ways apart from the gods' anger against oath-
breakers in which piety was intertwined with social values.[5] The closest
Greek equivalents to the untranslatable 'religion' introduce 'the gods' in
some form (whether through a phrase such as 'cultivate/believe in the
gods' or the simple 'the things of the gods', τὰ τῶν θεῶν[6]). This book has
accordingly spoken much of the 'things of the gods'. But piety—let it be
stressed in conclusion—stretched into areas that do not concern the gods
directly. Piety is exercised, according to Plato's Eryximachus, in relation to
'parents living and dead and the gods'; Lycurgus too speaks of 'piety towards
parents and the dead'. It is the *nomos* to grant 'god-like honours' to one's
parents, according to a fragment of Menander; Plato in his hyperbolic late
manner speaks of an aged parent as a kind of living shrine. Greek literature
has no exemplary *pius Aeneas*, but the same value is unquestionably present.
Athenians excel all mankind, according to Lycurgus, in piety towards the
gods, scrupulous respect towards parents, eager commitment towards the
fatherland.[7] Patriotism and piety were indistinguishable because of the obligation to protect the sacred places of Attica.

Respect for the gods, respect for the fatherland, respect for ancestral tombs,
respect for parents: the deep conservatism inherent in Greek religion could
not be more clearly revealed. For some, the fascination in the study of ancient
religions lies in their wildness, their exoticism, their terrors; they are a rough
archaic hinterland to escape to from the disenchanted modern world. It was
not like that for those who lived with these gods every day of their lives. This

---

[3] See *Athenian Religion*, 279, n. 102.

[4] Mediterranean anthropologists often speak of values, such as truthfulness, which are recognized
by their informants as valid in an ideal world but only partially applicable in the actual one (where the
one absolute value is loyalty to the interests of one's group). It may be that Greeks saw fidelity to oaths
in the same way. But as an ideal, at least, oaths were certainly recognized as a constraint.

[5] Many more, in fact, than I mention here: see Dover, *Greek Popular Morality*, 250–4, on
'extensions of piety'.

[6] 'This very common phrase (singular or plural ...) represents anything willed, protected by
or associated with the gods': C. Collard in the note ad loc. in his commentary (Groningen 1975)
on Eur. *Supp.* 301–2. For prose instances see e.g. Xen. *Anab.* 3.2.9, *Cyrop.* 3.3.20, 6.2.40;
Theophr. *Char.* 25.2; the parody in Ar. *Pax* 868 τὰ τῆς πυγῆς καλὰ (for τὰ τοῦ θεοῦ καλὰ, as in
Phrynichus fr. 9) has been missed by commentators.

[7] Pl. *Symp.* 188c; Lycurg. *Leoc.* 94; Men. fr. 823 (600 Koerte); Pl. *Leg.* 931a; Lycurg. *Leoc.* 15;
cf. Mikalson, *Athenian Popular Religion*, 97–100.

work has sought to make Athenian religion not, I hope, more dull, but more liveable, more real.

$$\kappa\acute{o}\gamma\xi, \pi\acute{a}\xi^8$$

---

[8] The ambiguity of Hesych. κ 3184 κόγξ, ὁμ(οίως) πάξ. ἐπιφώνημα τετελεσμένοις has sometimes earnt this phrase a place in accounts of the *Eleusinian Mysteries*, as 'an acclamation over the initiated'. But, as has been known since Lobeck, one should rather translate 'exclamation over a completed task' (cf. Wilamowitz, *Glaube*, ii, 474).

Appendix 1: Attic Festivals: A Check List

This appendix is chiefly intended to provide information on festivals little treated in the main text of the book; but for completeness even those discussed *in extenso* elsewhere are briefly noted here. Festivals such as the *Ptolemaea* and *Diogeneia* that were certainly not in existence before 300 BC are excluded (the little-known *Charmosuna*, probably a festival of Isis, is excluded for the same reason). The main quarry for material, here as elsewhere, has been Deubner, *Attische Feste*. Certain 'festivals' exposed by Deubner as non-Attic or as not festivals at all (*Askolia, Daphnephoria, Paionia*) are also omitted. Some festivals not so exposed by Deubner, but open to doubt on similar grounds, appear here enclosed in squre brackets.

As was argued in Chapter 8, the line between a large sacrifice and a festival is not at all sharp: many 'sacrifices' known from deme calendars may have constituted festivals for those who participated. But it would serve no purpose to list all such instances here. Deme rites are normally included only where a distinctive name, such as *Amarysia*, is attested (but it should be stressed that such attestation is largely dependent on chance).

Adonia   Mourning for Adonis. Celebrated in private houses (and on their roofs), in (?) late spring. See pp. 283–8.

Agathe Tyche, sacrifice to   Sacrifices to her appear regularly in the Lycurgan skin-sale records, though with modest yields (*IG* II² 1496 A 76–7, 107–8, ?148–9); they fall between the *Lenaea* of Gamelion and the *Asklepieia* of Elaphebolion. On the cult see *Athenian Religion*, 231–2.

Aianteia   A festival held for Ajax on Salamis, possibly established or revived in gratitude for the hero's assistance at the battle of Salamis (Hdt. 8.64, 121) but known to us exclusively from the involvement of ephebes in the hellenistic period (first attestation *SEG* XXIX 116.17–22 of 214/13): attested elements are a 'long race' between Athenian and Salaminian ephebes, a ship race, a torch-race, a procession and a sacrifice to Ajax (*IG* II² 1011.16–18, 53–5: briefer references in many ephebic decrees). In the second century BC it was an occasion for the proclamation of honours accorded to a Salaminian gymnasiarch (*IG* II² 1227.32). A lectisternium for the hero (Σ Pind. *Nem.* 2.19 κλίνη μετὰ πανοπλίας, 'adorned', κοσμεῖν, by the Athenians: no precise place mentioned) may be distinct. Date unknown.

Aiora   A swinging festival or rite connected aitiologically with the death of Erigone, daughter of Icarius. Whether it was a part of the *Anthesteria* or an independent festival is controversial. See p. 301.

Amarysia   Pausanias reports (1.31.4–5) that Artemis Amarysia is worshipped not only in Amarynthos in Euboea (on the important Euboean cult see D. Knoepfler, *CRAI* 1988, 382–421; E. Sapouna-Sakellaraki, *Kernos* 5, 1992, 235–63; P. Brulé, *Kernos* 6, 1993, 57–65), but also in the deme Athmonon in Attica: the Athenian festival, he says, is just as splendid as the Euboean. *IG* II² 1203.17, a decree of, presumably, Athmonon found at Marusi, provides for honours to be proclaimed Ἀμαρυσίων τῷ ἀγῶνι. *IG* I² 865 (not in *IG* I³) is a pair of archaizing (second century AD?) '*horoi* of the *temenos* of Artemis Amarysia' found at Marusi. For discussion of the site of the sanctuary see I. A. Pikoulas, *Horos* 10–12 (1992–8), 205–14 (*SEG* XLVI 225). Pausanias' reference (loc. cit.) to 'the Athenians' holding the festival does not prove that the *Amarysia* were celebrated in the city as well as in Athmonon, since 'Athenians' there contrasts with 'Euboeans' (nor do Hesych. α 3649, Phot. α 1134 Ἀμαρύσια· ἑορτὴ Ἀθήνῃσι); but a shrine of 'Artemis Amarysia from Athmonon' in the city (Kydathenaeon) is attested early (*IG* I³ 426.66–9), and the festival at Athmonon is likely to have attracted a broad clientele and may have been state-funded. Date and ritual content unknown.

Ammon, sacrifice to   A sacrifice yielding a very modest sum (just under 45 dr.) in skin-sales was made to Ammon in 333 (*IG* II² 1496. 96), probably in the month Hekatombaion (it is listed between entries for the sacrifice to Peace and the *Panathenaea*, both in that month). On the cult of Ammon in Athens see p. 111, n. 76.

Amphiaraia   A penteteric athletic competition in honour of Amphiaraus at Oropos, first celebrated in 329/8 BC. The *penteteris* was an expansion of an existing competitive festival attested by victory dedications. Date unknown. See *Athenian Religion*, 149, n. 109, and 246, n. 100 (the case for associating *SEG* XXXII 86 with the festival may be strengthened by a new reading of Stephen Lambert κα]πηλίοις (pers. comm.; cf. *IOropos* 290.18) in line 33).

Anak(e)ia   An athletic festival, in honour of the Anakes (Dioscuri), known from two bronze prize-vessels (*Athenian Religion*, 97, n. 124), a fragment of an archaic regulation which mentions or implies sacrifice, a procession, a competition, and 'parasites' (Ath. 235b), and a single literary reference to a horse-race (Lysias fr. 75.3 Thalheim, xvii 2.3 Gernet/Bizos); presumably held at or in association with the Anakion (Wycherley, *Testimonia*, 61–5) in the centre of Athens. Paus. Att. α 111 speaks of the sacrifice having the form of a triple offering, τριττύα, and also honouring Helen. Date: unknown,[1] but I shall argue elsewhere the case for reading ἐξ Ἀνακίω]ν in *IG* II² 1496 A 120, which would give a date late in Skirophorion in the fourth (and second?) year of an Olympiad. It is indeterminable whether the payment made 'for the *Anakia*' by the deme Plotheia (*IG* I³ 258. 6) was for the central festival or a local homonym. Cf. s.v. *Great Gods, procession for*, and on the cult of the Anakes p. 411 above.

Antheia   A sacrifice/festival to Demeter attested in the demes Paiania and Thorikos, probably to be linked with the flowering of the corn. Held in Thorikos in Mounichion (the date in Paiania is unknown). See p. 195.

---

[1] On *IG* I³ 477. 8, which is almost certainly irrelevant, see p. 464, n. 24 below.

Anthesteria A three-day festival in honour of Dionysus, held on Anthesterion 11–13. The modalities are uncertain: perhaps celebrated both in Athens and in the demes. Thucydides simply calls it 'the older *Dionysia*' (2.15.4). See Ch. 13.

Apatouria The main festival of the phratries (Xen. *Hell.* 1.7.8). It occurred in Pyanepsion (Theophr. *Char.* 3.5, Harpocr. α 173, Hesych. κ 3843), probably in the second half of the month; the exact days are unknown.[2] The phratry of the Deceleans celebrated the *Apatouria* at its own altar in Decelea (*IG* II² 1237 (RO 5) 67); and though no other evidence bears directly on the matter, the presumption must be that other phratries used their own altars at different places in Attica. A central celebration in parallel to that of the individual phratries is not attested; one at Panakton associated with a garrison depends on a supplement in *IG* II² 1299.28–32 (whence also *IG* II² 1285.22).[3] According to two lexicographers both boys and girls were introduced to phratries (Suda α 2940; Pollux 8.107, in a confused notice), but the evidence of the orators suggests that girls were normally not so introduced, though an ἐπίκληρος might be (Is. 3.73).[4] An ἐπίκληρος was presumably present on the occasion of her introduction, but perhaps on no other. Such cases aside, the *Apatouria* may have been celebrated exclusively by men and boys.[5]

Three day names *Dorpia*, *Anarrhysis*, *Koureotis*, are widely attested, usually in that order;[6] a fourth day *Epibda*, 'Hangover', is added by Hesych. α 5842 (cf. ε 4622). The main activity was the induction of new members to the phratry, which was achieved by sacrifice (accompanied by an oath sworn by the sponsor),[7] supposedly by a hair cutting,[8] and by a wine libation (*oinisteria*) to Heracles (Eupolis fr. 146, and texts cited ad loc.). Suda α 2940 gives as the sequence of events: assembly of the *phratores* and banquet on the evening of *Dorpia*; sacrifice to Zeus Phratrios and Athena Phratria on *Anarrhysis*; induction of new *phratores* on *Koureotis*. But this neat scheme is partly influenced by interpretation of the day names (*Anarrhysis* from the 'drawing back' of the victim's neck for sacrifice, *Koureotis* from the haircut that supposedly accompanied induction) and may be too simple; the division between day two, the day of sacrifices, and day three, when new *phratores* were introduced, is too sharp given that it was by sacrificial ritual that new members were admitted to the phratry. At an early stage, probably on *Dorpia*, came the banquet of the 'pre-tasters' (*Protenthai*: Ath. 171c–e). At this or at some later feast it was the duty of the 'wine-watchers' (*Oinoptai*) to ensure equal shares for all (Eupolis fr. 219, and texts there cited).[9] Other attested activities— children's competitions in 'rhapsody' (Pl. *Tim.* 21b–c), processions honouring Hephaestus (see below, on Istros fr. 2 (a))—cannot be placed within the sequence.

---

[2] See A. Mommsen, *Heortologie* (Leipzig 1864), 302–5; *Feste*, 326–7; Lambert, *Phratries*, 157, n. 80.

[3] What a celebration of the *Apatouria* in the context of a garrison rather than an individual phratry might be is hard to understand.

[4] See Lambert, *Phratries*, 178–81 [+].

[5] Women have access to 'the meat from the *Apatouria*' (Ar. *Thesm.* 558), but it may have been brought or sent home.

[6] Suda α 2940, etc; Simplic. in Arist. *Phys.* 4.11, 708.17 Diels; but Σ Plat. *Tim.* 21b inverts the first two (in *Etym. Magn.* 533.41–53 there may be a lacuna).

[7] *Athenian Religion*, 105.

[8] Suda κ 2179; Hesych. κ 3843.

[9] The probability must be that individual phratries elected their own *Protenthai* and *Oinoptai*, but we have no details (Lambert, *Phratries*, 154–5).

Three types of sacrifice are attested. Γαμηλία is probably an offering brought by a male *phrator* on the occasion of marriage (Isae. 3.76; 8.18; Dem. 57.43; one view of Didymos ap. Harpocr. γ 2).[10] The lexicographical sources attest two further names for offerings, κουρεῖον and μεῖον, and though they sometimes (*Etym. Magn.* 533.35–40; Σ vet. Ar. *Ran.* 798c), identify the two, and never contrast them,[11] the inscription *IG* II² 1237 (RO 5) unmistakably shows them to be distinct: different priestly dues are owed for each (lines 1–8), less for the μεῖον than for the κουρεῖον (which in that phratry, at least, was evidently the more important occasion administratively). The κουρεῖον is associated with children of 3 or 4 in Σ Plat. *Tim* 21b; more commonly it is linked with ἡλικία (Poll.8.107) or the adolescent ἀποκείρεσθαι (Suda κ 2179, perhaps Hesych. κ 3843). The μεῖον too when given a location in time is linked with adolescents (Suda μ 828; Poll. 3.52–3, with Ath. 494f, Hesych o 325), though perhaps only in consequence of its confusion with the κουρεῖον. Given that two sacrifices of induction, and also two ages, are attested, there has been a temptation to postulate a two-stage process, and to assign the μεῖον to age 0–3 and the κουρεῖον to about 16.[12] Though this solution has no direct support in any source, it sits well with broad anthropological considerations and with the probably correct etymological association between κουρεῖον and ἀποκείρεσθαι;[13] and a close Delphic parallel is available. But, for literary sources, introduction to the phratry is a single process, which seems commonly to occur quite soon after birth;[14] in the only case in an extant speech where the relevant offering is named it is a κουρεῖον, but in that case the child was certainly not new-born and may have been an adolescent (Isae. 6.21–2).[15] It is puzzling that no orator alludes to a two-stage process if it existed, given the central importance in inheritance cases of proofs of legitimacy; and Isaeus 6.21–2 proves that in certain cases, at least, κουρεῖον sufficed without μεῖον. The difficulty could be met by the hypothesis that uncontested completion of either sacrifice was sufficient to enrol the child in the phratry: the orators would have had no reason to mention the performance of the other (if it occurred) if it provided no further evidence of the child's acceptance by the *phratores* as legitimate. At least in the Decelean phratry, however, it looks as if the crucial offering

[10] Only Pollux 8.107 associates it with the marriage of a daughter; the second view of Didymus ap. Harpocr. γ 2, that the wife on whose behalf the γαμηλία was brought became thereby a member of the phratry, finds no support in other evidence. Schmitt Pantel, *Cité au banquet*, 88, comments 'tout se joue en dehors de la femme'.

[11] Other references: Harpocrat. μ 16, Poll. 3.53, 8.107, Phot. κ 1028, Suda μ 828.

[12] See the references in Lambert, *Phratries*, 162, n. 113. K. Latte, *RE* s.v. *Phratrie*, 752 = *Kleine Schriften*, 429, compares the two-stage παιδῆια/ἀπελλαῖα of the *Labyadai* of Delphi. Only weak support can be derived from the possibility (still accepted in the etymological dictionaries of Frisk and Chantraine) that, as the ancients supposed, μεῖον the offering is identical etymologically with the comparative μεῖον meaning 'lesser', despite their different genitive formations; since *ex hypothesi* the word for the offering had developed a different declension (heteroclisis), it must have come to be perceived as semantically distinct.

[13] K. Latte, *RE* s.v. *Phratrie*, 752 = *Kleine Schriften*, 429 drew attention to the use of κουρεῖον apparently for a 'sheep-shearing' offering in *Inscr.Prien.* 362 (*LSA* 39) 13; see too J. Labarbe, *Bulletin de l'Académie royale de Belgique: Classe des Lettres* 39 (1953), 358–94, at 366–8.

[14] Andoc. *Myst.* 125–6; Isae. 8.19; Dem. 43.11–14, 57.54; Apollod. *Neaer.* 55–60 (attempted introduction); *P. Oxy.* 31.2538. fr. 1 col. 2.23–28; delayed introduction irregular: Lys. 30.2, Ar. *Ran.* 418. Cf. Lambert, *Phratries*, 162–3, nn. 115–16; 165, nn. 128–9.

[15] J. Labarbe's attempt, op. cit., to argue that the induction occurred in this case at the age of 16 has been effectively criticized, by Lambert, *Phratries*, 165, n. 128, and Golden, *Children*, 27. All that is certain is that the child introduced was the elder of two, i.e. not new-born.

for purposes of registration was the κουρεῖον, whether or not the μεῖον had been brought. Much here remains uncertain. See Lambert, *Phratries*, 161–78.[16]

As honorands of the festival Zeus Phratrios is named thrice only (*IG* II² 1237 (RO 5) *passim*, by implication; *LSS* 19 (RO 37) 91; Suda α 2940), Athena Phratria only once (Suda α 2940). (There are also occasional references to Zeus Apatourios/Apatenor, *Etym. Magn.* 119.15–16, Conon *FGrH* 26 F 1 (39).) But, as the only gods of whom all the phratries had altars (*Athenian Religion*, 106), the role of Zeus and Athena must have been central. The same consideration in reverse brings into doubt the claim of other gods to have been universally honoured at the festival. Also mentioned are Hephaestus (Istros *FGrH* 334 F 2 (a) ap Harpocr. λ 3), Artemis (Hesych. κ 3843), Heracles (Eupolis fr. 146, with sources there cited: see p. 437), and Dionysus Melanaigis (Suda α 2940; Σ vet. Ar. *Pax* 893a; *Etym. Magn.* 119.15–16; *Anecd. Bekk.* 1.417. 32; Conon *FGrH* 26 F 1 (39)) Could they have been honoured even though they lacked altars at most phratry centres? One could suppose that Hephaestus and Dionysus were sufficiently made present in fire and wine respectively. Hair cut for Artemis at the phratry centre could perhaps be delivered to one of her shrines after the festival. But there are grounds, of unequal strength, for doubting the sources that associate each of Hephaestus (see below), Artemis[17] and Dionysus with the festival: in particular, it is Dionysus Melanaigis, not Dionysus *tout court*, of whom sources speak in relation to the *Apatouria*, and the god can scarcely have been honoured under that specific title by every phratry. Melanaigis sounds like an epithet that should belong to a particular cult in a particular place, and it may be that he is a god not of the *Apatouria* but of north west Attica, who has entered the tradition via the aitiological legend for the festival, which is set in that region (*Athenian Religion*, 94, n. 116).

A corrupt fragment of Istros (*FGrH* 334 F 2(a) ap. Harpocration, λ 3) raises several complications:

Λαμπάς· Λυσίας ἐν τῷ κατ' Εὐφήμου. τρεῖς ἄγουσιν Ἀθηναῖοι ἑορτὰς λαμπάδος. Παναθηναίοις καὶ Ἡφαιστίοις καὶ Προμηθείοις, ὡς Πολέμων φησὶν ἐν τῷ περὶ τῶν ἐν τοῖς προπυλαίοις πινάκων. Ἴστρος δ' ἐν α΄ τῶν Ἀτθίδων < > εἰπὼν ὡς ἐν τῇ τῶν Ἀπατουρίων ἑορτῇ Ἀθηναίων οἱ καλλίστας στολὰς ἐνδεδυκότες, λαβόντες ἡμμένας λαμπάδας ἀπὸ τῆς ἑστίας, ὑμνοῦσι τὸν Ἥφαιστον θύοντες, ὑπόμνημα τοῦ κατανοήσαντας (de Valois: κατανοήσαντος codd.) <αὐτοὺς> τὴν χρείαν τοῦ πυρὸς διδάξαι τοὺς ἄλλους.

3 < > Jacoby; εἶπεν Blanchard. 4. Ἀθηναίων οἱ <καλλίστοι> Sauppe; οἱ <ἱερεῖς> vel <ἔφηβοι> Meier; οἱ <φρατέρες> Dindorf. 5 θέοντες de Valois.

De Valois' conjecture in 5 is an easy one, since initially Harpocration is here discussing torch-races. But Mommsen, *Feste*, 339, Wilamowitz, Aischylos, *Interpretationen* (Berlin 1914), 142–3, n. 3, and Jacoby ad loc. agree in rejecting the conjecture and seeing here not a torch-race but a torch procession, accompanied by hymns and conducted in smart clothes (not athletes' dress). That disposes of a form of ritual action (the tribal torch-race) which would be out of place at a phratry festival, at the expense of postulating a form of ritual action otherwise unknown, and one which it would still

---

[16] Jeanmaire, *Couroi*, 380, suggests that a κουρεῖον ritual originally associated with adolescence had moved down to early childhood by the classical period.

[17] 'wohl eine Verwechslung mit dem Haaropfer der Bräute', Deubner, *Attische Feste*, 234, on Hesych. κ 3843.

be easier to envisage at a centralized festival[18] than at the *Apatouria*. They may none the less be in the right, and Jacoby stresses that the absence of other evidence for a role of Hephaestus at the *Apatouria* proves little. But it is not inconceivable that ἐν τῇ τῶν Ἀπατουρίων ἑορτῇ is a product of error.[19]

A myth which explains the name of the festival through a 'deceit' (*apate*) perpetrated by Melanthos against the Boeotian king Xanthos first appears in Hellanicus *FGrH* 323a F 23 ap. Σ Plat. *Symp.* 208d, if Jacoby was right[20] to ascribe the whole content of the scholion to Hellanicus. Otherwise the first attestation is Ephoros 70 *FGrH* F 22. It is through a variant of this myth that Dionysus Melanaigis is associated with the festival (see above).

Aphrodisia   The deme Plotheia made contributions to an unidentifiable festival of this name (*IG* I³ 258. 5). See too s.v. *Aphrodite Pandemos, procession for* and *Eros, festival of*.

Aphrodite Pandemos, procession for   A procession in honour of Aphrodite Pandemos is known only from a decree of *c.* 283/2, in which the *astynomoi* are required to 'prepare a dove for purification of the shrine, wipe (περιαλείψαι) the altars, pitch the [doors] and wash the statues; and also prepare purple of weight two drachmas ...' (παρασκευάζειν εἰς κάθαρσι[ν] τοῦ ἱεροῦ περιστερὰν καὶ περιαλεῖ[ψα]ι τοὺς βωμοὺς καὶ πιττῶσαι τὰς [θύρας][21] καὶ λοῦσαι τὰ ἔδη· παρα[σκευάσαι δὲ κα]ὶ πορφύραν ὁλκὴν ⊢⊢: *IG* II² 659 (*LSCG* 39) 23–7). The destination of the procession was presumably the sanctuary of Aphrodite Pandemos on the south slopes of the acropolis (L. Beschi, *ASAtene* 29–30, 1967–8, 517–28). Date unknown.

Apollonia   A festival of the Epakrians, who were apparently a group of demes (Plotheia and others) of north east Attica (*Athenian Religion*, 330). Only the name is known.

Areia   A mid-fourth-century decree of the deme Acharnai provides for the building of altars for Ares and Athena Areia πρὸ τῆς θυσίας [τῶν Ἀ]ρείων (*SEG* XXI 519.16–17). This was presumably a regular festival of the deme.

Arrephoria   *Etym. Magn.* 149.14 ἀρρηφόροι καὶ Ἀρρηφόρια· ἑορτὴ ἐπιτελουμένη τῇ Ἀθηνᾷ ἐν Σκιροφοριῶνι μηνί. See pp. 221–2. This obscure ritual honouring Athena and Pandrosus was primarily and probably exclusively associated with the acropolis; but for the possibility that an Erchian version was held on Skirophorion 3 see p. 68, n. 69.

Artemis Agrotera, procession and sacrifice to   The polemarch (Arist. *Ath. Pol.* 58.1) sacrificed annually 500 goats to Artemis Agrotera (and also to Enyalios?—see

---

[18] J. Töpffer, *Attische Genealogie* (Berlin 1889), 107–8, supposed 'the hearth' to be that of the Prytaneion, at which the phratries assembled for a communal δορπία; but there is no other evidence that they did this. Wilamowitz thought more plausibly of individual phratry houses.

[19] This view has perhaps not hitherto been advanced; Jacoby was wrong to ascribe it to Wilamowitz.

[20] Against the scholars whom he cites in n. 1 to his commentary ad loc. The tradition that Melanthos came from abroad to acquire the Attic kingship is already in Herodotus (5.65.3).

[21] For the supplement see P. Roussel, *REA* 36 (1934), 177–9.

p. 398, n. 43), supposedly in fulfilment of a vow made before the battle of Marathon (Xen. *Anab.* 3.2.12: cf. Ar. *Eq.* 660–62, *Lys.* 1248–65; *Athenian Religion*, 153–4). An associated procession, in which in the hellenistic period the ephebes participated in arms (*IG* II² 1028.8, and often), was still performed in Plutarch's day (*De malignitate Herodoti* 26, 862a); the same passage of Plutarch confirms that the sacrifice took place at Artemis Agrotera's sanctuary at Agrai, and by a probable conjecture gives Boedromion 6 as the date: τὴν πρὸς Ἄγρας πομπήν, ἣν πέμπουσιν ἔτι καὶ νῦν τῇ ἕκτῃ (Valckenaer, for mss. Ἑκάτῃ: cf. Plut. *De glor. Ath.* 7, 349e) χαριστήρια τῆς νίκης ἑορτάζοντες. (Ael. *VH* 2.25 gives Thargelion 6 and 300 goats.) In the passages of Plutarch cited the festival is treated as a celebration of the victory at Marathon. Pfuhl plausibly suggested that in the classical period hoplites and perhaps cavalry participated as such in the procession (*De pompis*, 34–5).

Asklepieia Two distinct festivals of this name appear in the Lycurgan skin-sale records (*IG* II² 1496 A), one celebrated between the *Lenaea* and the *City Dionysia* (78–9, 109, 150), one after the *Eleusinia* and the sacrifice to Democracy and before the *Thesea* (133, 142). A regular formula in decrees honouring priests of Asclepius is that the priest ἐβουθύ[τησεν τοῖς τε Ἀσκληπιείοις] καὶ Ἐπιδαυρίοις καὶ Ἡρώιοις παρασ[τήσας θύματα ὡς κάλλιστα] [κ]αὶ τὰς τούτων παννυχίδας συν[ετέλεσεν (so *SEG* XVIII 26.11–12; cf. ibid. 21.8–9, 27.6–7: the supplement Ἀσκληπιείοις is secure, though not actually appearing on the stone in any case). *Epidauria* was a name for a festival of Asclepius, including a procession, celebrated on Boedromion 17 or 18 (see p. 348, n. 88), and can readily be identified with the second of the two *Asklepieia* of the skin-sale records; a *kanephoros* for the *Epidauria* already appears in *IG* II² 3457 ('IV/III c. B.C.'; cf. an *arrephoros* for the *Epidauria* in *SEG* XVIII 26.19), and the festival bore this alternative name right from its inception if it is correctly supplemented in the calendar of Nicomachus, *BSA* 97 (2002), 366, fr. 4.15. The first *Asklepieia* of the records will be identical with the 'sacrifice to Asclepius' attested by Aeschin. 3.67 for Elaphebolion 8 (also, ibid., the day of the *Proagon* to the City Dionysia). The two *Asklepieia* were, therefore, six months apart. It was probably at the two *Asklepieia* that the public doctors made their regular 'twice yearly' sacrifices to the god (*IG* II² 772.9–13). About the details we know nothing in either case beyond the sacrifices attested by the skin records, the *pannychides* mentioned in the decree quoted above, and the procession at the *Epidauria*.

Asklepieia in the Piraeus *IG* II² 47 = *LSS* 11 (of c. 370–350) treats of the affairs of the sanctuary of Asclepius in the Piraeus (*Athenian Religion*, 181–2). It goes on to regulate meat distribution at a publicly financed festival: portions from the 'leader ox' (ἡγεμὼν βοῦς) are to go to the prytaneis, the nine archons, the *hieropoioi* and (probably) 'the escorters', and the rest of the meat to … (the inscription breaks here). The festival must surely be one, otherwise unattested and of unknown date, celebrated at the Asclepieum in the Piraeus.

Athenaea The *Athenaea* which according to Pausanias (8.2.1) were transformed by Theseus into *Panathenaea* are a merely theoretical postulate. Real *Athenaea* are attested in the mid-second century BC by two lists of fifteen individuals who 'served as hieropoioi for the *Athenaea*'; a further list of names inscribed by a different hand on one of these stones may be a list of prizewinners.[22] According to Suda χ 34 (see *Chalkeia*, below) *Athenaea* was an alternative name for *Chalkeia*. But the *Athenaea* of the Hellenistic inscriptions were on an elaborate scale hard to reconcile with the 'craftsmen's festival' as which some sources describe the *Chalkeia* (Suda χ 35). And it is very unlikely that the same festival would have been referred to indifferently as both *Chalkeia* and *Athenaea* in public inscriptions of the same period. The hellenistic *Athenaea* are probably a distinct festival, of unknown antecedents.[23]

Athena Pallenis, festival of A regional festival (date unknown) of central Attica for which archons and 'parasites' were recruited, some at least from specified demes. See *Athenian Religion*, 330–1.

Attideia 'Both the *Attideia*' were celebrated by a private society of citizen worshippers of Mother in the Piraeus (*IG* II² 1315. 10, of 211/10: on the society see *Athenian Religion*, 192–3).

Balletys An Eleusinian rite in honour of Demophon, possibly an independent festival of unknown date but more probably a component of an unidentified festival: see p. 329.

Bendidea The *Bendidea* were celebrated in the Piraeus on Thargelion 19 or 20 (ὅτι γὰρ τὰ ἐν Πειραιεῖ Βενδίδεια τῇ ἐνάτῃ ἐπὶ δέκα τοῦ Θαργηλιῶνος ὁμολογοῦσιν οἱ περὶ ἑορτῶν γράψαντες Procl. on Pl. *Tim.* 9b, p. 26.13 Diehl, cf. Σ Pl. *Resp.* 327a; Ἀριστοκλῆς ὁ Ῥόδιος ἱστορεῖ τὰ μὲν ἐν Πειραιεῖ Βενδίδεια τῇ εἰκάδι τοῦ Θαργηλιῶνος ἐπιτελεῖσθαι, ἔπεσθαι δὲ τὰς περὶ τὴν Ἀθηνᾶν ἑορτάς Procl. on Pl. *Tim.* 27a, p. 85.28 Diehl). Attested elements are sacrifice on a large scale (*IG* II² 1496.86, 117), two processions, one of Thracians and one of Athenians, a horse-race on torchback, and a *pannychis* (all this from Pl. *Resp.* 327a–328a). The procession of the Thracians is later attested as starting 'from the prytaneum hearth' in the city, from where it proceeded to the Bendideion in the Piraeus (*IG* II² 1283.4–13). See further *Athenian Religion*, 170–3.

Boedromia The month name Boedromion (Trümpy, *Monatsnamen*, 291) and Apollo's title Boedromios are found outside Attica (Paus. 9.17.2; Callim. *Hymn* 2. 69; for Attica see *Etym. Magn.* 202.49–50), and two separate aitia are known for the Attic rite (p. 380). But all we hear of it in historic times is a scornful allusion in Demosthenes to orators who pander to the people by a promise to 'send the *Boedromia*' (3.31, whence Harp. β 14). It occurred in Boedromion (*Etym. Magn.* 202.49–50), perhaps on Apollo's sacred day, the 7th (Pfuhl, *De Pompis*, 35–6), and may have had a military character (Pfuhl, ibid.).

Brauronia A *penteteris* (probably including a *pannychis*) celebrated at Brauron in honour of Artemis Brauronia. A public *theoria* went to Brauron, very probably starting from the Brauronion on the acropolis. Date unknown See pp. 230–1.

---

[22] *IG* II² 1937; C. Habicht, *AM* 97 (1982), 171–84 = *Athen in Hellenistischer Zeit* (Munich 1994), 52–66 (*SEG* XXXII 216).
[23] So too Mansfield. *Robe of Athena*, 303, n. 8. On the *Athenaea* revived under Commodus see Follet, *Athènes*, 320.

Chalkeia A festival honouring Athena as a goddess of crafts in association with Hephaestus, probably centred on the Hephaisteion and supposedly in historical times celebrated mainly by craftsmen. The warp for the *peplos* presented to Athena at the *Greater Panathenaea* was set in the loom on the day of the festival (but presumably only every fourth year).

Performance of sacrifices at the *Chalkeia* by the prytaneis is mentioned in several decrees in their honour: *Agora* XV 70. 7 ('290–275'); *Agora* XV 78.16 (of 273/2), where the sacrifice follows the *Stenia* and is made to Athena Archegetis; by an uncertain supplement *Agora* XV 253. 9 (118/7), where a *pannychis* is mentioned; note too in fragmentary contexts *IG* II² 930.3 (early second century?); *IG* II² 990.2 (mid-second century?); ? *SEG* XLVIII 241. I would suppose that a sacrifice to Athena, made in the fourth prytany of a year in the last decade of the fifth century by the workers on the Erechtheum (*IG* I³ 477. 8), was brought Χα]λκείοις ('Αν]ακείοις vulgo).[24]

The main testimonia are:

1. Harpocration, χ 2 *Χαλκεῖα·* Ὑπερείδης ἐν τῷ κατὰ Δημέου ξενίας (fr. 90 Jessen). τὰ Χαλκεῖα ἑορτὴ παρ' Ἀθηναίοις <τῇ Ἀθηνᾷ addidit Meursius> ἀγομένη Πυανεψιῶνος ἕνῃ καὶ νέᾳ, χειρώναξι κοινή, μάλιστα δὲ χαλκεῦσιν, ὥς φησιν Ἀπολλώνιος ὁ Ἀχαρνεύς (*FGrH* 356 F 18). Φανόδημος δὲ οὐκ Ἀθηνᾷ φησιν ἄγεσθαι τὴν ἑορτὴν ἀλλ' Ἡφαίστῳ (*FGrH* 365 F 3). γέγραπται δὲ καὶ Μενάνδρῳ δρᾶμα Χαλκεῖα (cf. frs. 400–2).

2. Pollux 7.105 Χαλκεῖα ἑορτὴ ἐν τῇ Ἀττικῇ Ἡφαίστου ἱερά.

3. Hesych. s. v. Χαλκεῖα· ὑπομνήματα τῆς τῶν τεχνῶν εὑρέσεως.

4. Suda χ 34 Χαλκεῖα· ἑορτὴ Ἀθήνησιν, ἅ τινες Ἀθήναια καλοῦσιν, οἱ δὲ Πάνδημον διὰ τὸ ὑπὸ πάντων ἄγεσθαι.

5. Suda χ 35, *Etym. Magn.* 805. 43–7 (similia [- Πυανεψιῶνος] Eustath. ad Hom. *Il.* 2.552; and, combined with material from Harpocration, *Et. Gen.* p. 306 Miller). Χαλκεῖα· ἑορτὴ ἀρχαία καὶ δημώδης (δημοτελής Eust.) πάλαι, ὕστερον δὲ ὑπὸ μόνων ἤγετο τῶν τεχνιτῶν, ὅτι ὁ Ἥφαιστος ἐν τῇ Ἀττικῇ χαλκὸν εἰργάσατο. ἔστι δὲ ἕνῃ καὶ νέα τοῦ Πυανεψιῶνος· ἐν ᾖ καὶ ἱέρειαι μετὰ τῶν ἀρρηφόρων τὸν πέπλον διάζονται. Identified as deriving from Pausanias Atticista (χ 2) by Erbse.

Addressee: *Agora* XV 78.16 gives Athena Archegetis, and items (1) and (4) imply Athena; (2) and by implication (5) give Hephaistos. An excerpted Phanodemos (in (1)) ascribed it 'not to Athena but to Hephaistos', but his point may rather have been 'not only Athena, but also Hephaistos'.[25] A joint cult would explain the discrepancy of the sources, and is almost inevitably to be linked with the joint cult of Hephaistos and Athena Hephaistia in the Hephaisteion (Wycherley, *Testimonia*, 98–102)—one in which Phanodemos was interested, as his successful proposal to dedicate a statue there in 343/2 shows (*IG* II² 223 = *Syll.*³ 227). 'Athena Archegetis' is not necessarily incompatible, since Archegetis was a general honorific title not attached to a specific cult. Athena Ergane (introduced by supplement in *Agora* XV 253.9), by contrast, had a

---

[24] For that one would expect the form 'Αν]ακίοις. The timing is right for the *Chalkeia*, implausible for an athletic festival such as the *Anakia*. Stephen Lambert has kindly inspected the stone, and reports that it breaks halfway down the letters read as AK: the traces hitherto interpreted as a crossbar of A could arise from accidental damage.

[25] So Jacoby ad loc., and Mansfield, *Robe of Athena*, 328, n. 71.

cult place distinct from that of Hephaistos, on the acropolis. A work to be associated with Athena Ergane, the weaving of the *peplos*, none the less commenced on the day of the festival (5, *ad fin.*) But the only indication that she received direct worship on the day under that name is the doubtful one of Soph. fr. 844 (see below).

Alternative name? (4) offers two alternatives, of which the second ('Pandemos') has generally been ascribed to muddle;[26] on the first (*Athenaea*) see s.v. *Athenaea* above. The relevance of the following fragment of Sophocles (fr. 844) is uncertain:

> (a) βᾶτ' εἰς ὁδὸν δὴ πᾶς ὁ χειρῶναξ λεώς,
> οἳ τὴν Διὸς γοργῶπιν Ἐργάνην στατοῖς
> λίκνοισι προστρέπεσθε (b) <καὶ> παρ' ἄκμονι
> τυπάδι βαρείᾳ
> <καὶ> Gataker; <χοῖ> Jebb.

(a), which is quoted anonymously by Plut. *De Fortuna* 4, 99a (and also by Clem. Al. *Protr.* 10.97.3), was combined by Gataker with (b), extracted from Plut. *Praecepta gerendae reipublicae*, 5, 802b τὴν γὰρ Ἐργάνην οὗτοι μόνον θεραπεύουσιν, ὥς φησι Σοφοκλῆς, οἱ 'παρ' ἄκμονι τυπάδι βαρείᾳ' καὶ πληγαῖς ὑπακούουσαν ὕλην ἄψυχον δημιουργοῦντες. The two do not necessarily cohere directly, even if they derive from the same context. λίκνα in cult are usually envisaged as containers for agricultural produce (so Hesych. λ 521, quoting our fragment) and associated with Demeter and Dionysus, but Bérard has made the attractive suggestion that they could be offered to Athena Ergane in themselves, as products of the basketmaker's craft; he adduces a fragment of the Pan painter found, perhaps significantly, on the acropolis, showing a bearded male carrying an empty λίκνον perhaps as part of a procession.[27] The force of στατοῖς is obscure (Bérard suggests 'held still, immobile', not shaken as was normal for a winnowing basket).[28] Without knowing the setting of Sophocles' play to have been Athens or properly understanding the ritual details (does προστρέπεσθε necessarily entail a procession?), we cannot associate the fragment very confidently with a specific Athenian cult.

Date: Pyanepsion 30 (see (1) and (5) above).

Chloïa A sacrifice/festival to Demeter attested in the demes Thorikos, Paiania and Eleusis, and probably to be associated with the revival of the green corn shoots (χλόη) after winter. In Thorikos (where alone the date is identifiable) it falls in Elaphebolion. See p. 195, n. 10.

Delia A penteteric festival on Delos revived by the Athenians in 426. Neither the date of the *Delia* nor of the annual *theoriai* sent by the Athenians to the island is certainly known. See pp. 80–2.

Delphinion, procession to A supplicatory procession on Mounichion 6 by certain maidens to the Delphinion, linked aitiologically with the saga of Theseus (Plut. *Thes.*

---

[26] So e.g. Deubner, *Attische Feste*, 36, n. 5; Mansfield, *Robe of Athena*, 303, n. 8.

[27] C. Bérard, 'Le Liknon d'Athéna', *AntK* 19 (1976), 101–14, discussing ARV² 553.31 (= his plate 26.1).

[28] Bérard, op. cit., 110–12, surveys other views. It would help to know what a ψυκτὴρ στατός (LSJ s.v. στατός) was.

18.2); from the choice of Artemis' 6th (Diog. Laert. 2.44) rather than Apollo's 7th, Pfuhl inferred that Artemis Delphinia was the main honorand (*De pompis*, 79). Cf. p. 208.

Democracy, sacrifice to   A sacrifice (yielding 414 1/2 dr. in skin-sales) was made to Democracy in 332, and again (sum lost) in the following year (*IG* II² 1496.131–2, 140–1). The sacrifice of the skin-sales records falls between the *Eleusinia* and the *Asklepieia* (*Epidauria*), i.e. in Metageinion or before Boedromion 17. Given its position in the calendar, this sacrifice could be the same as a 'thanksgiving for freedom' on Boedromion 12 which is said by Plutarch (*De glor. Ath.* 7, 349f) to commemorate the return of the democrats from Phyle in 403. For this identification see *Athenian Religion*, 228–9 (and ibid. 229, n. 43, for a 'procession to Democracy' possibly on Salamis).

Diasia   'A very great festival of Zeus Meilichios, outside the city, at which en masse they sacrifice in large numbers not animal victims (ἱερεῖα) but <pure> local offerings' (Thuc. 1.126.6);[29] a deme calendar has shown that 'outside the city' means at Agrai (*LSCG* 18 α 37–42). Despite Thucydides' implication that vegetarian offerings were the norm, some animal victims were provided by participating demes (ibid. and *SEG* XXXIII 147.35), and some participants certainly ate meat with their kin (Ar. *Nub.* 408–9); the festival was also an opportunity to buy a toy for a child (Ar. *Nub.* 864). Whether wives normally attended is not known (cf. p. 167). A scholion on Lucian describes the *Diasia* as being celebrated 'with a certain grimness' (p. 107.15 and 110.27 Rabe; cf. Hesych. Δ 1312), though in Plutarch it is an occasion for good humour like any other festival (*De tranq. anim.* 20, 477d; cf. Lucian, *Timon* 7). A competition mentioned is a Lucianic work at which orators competed with encomia of mythological heroes for a prize of corn ears is likely to be a late innovation if it existed at all (*Charidemus* 1–3); elsewhere in Lucian Zeus complains that the festival is no longer celebrated (*Icaromenippus* 24). The heortologist Apollonius of Acharnae, probably writing in the late second century c. BC, is unexpectedly reported as 'distinguishing the *Diasia* from the festival of Meilichios' (*FGrH* 365 F 5, ap. Σ vet. Ar. *Nub.* 408c)—a paradoxical view which has not been explained (see Jacoby ad loc.). See *Athenian Religion*, 78, n. 41, and pp. 74, 162 and 425 above. Date: Anthesterion 23 (Σ vet. Ar. *Nub.* 408c).

Diisoteria   The name *Diisoteria* first appears in 139 (*IG* II² 971.42; cf. 1006. 29–30 and 78, where the ephebes race into the harbour at Mounichia at the festival, ibid. 1008.21, and 3483), but a procession to the shrine of Zeus Soter in the Piraeus, and subsequent large sacrifices, are already attested in the fourth century (Arist. *Ath. Pol.* 56.5, *IG* II² 380.20–1, 30–1; ibid. 1496. 88–9, 118–19). Two decrees of the 270s (*IG* II² 676; *Agora* XVI 186) honour *epimeletai* for their supervision of the sacrifice and (not in *IG* II² 676) procession for Zeus Soter and Athena Soteira and also for their

---

[29] πανδημεὶ θύουσι πολλά (C. F. Hermann: πολλοὶ mss) οὐχ ἱερεῖα, ἀλλὰ < ἀγνὰ add. Hemsterthuis e Polluce 1.26 > θύματα ἐπιχώρια. πολλοὶ of the mss. is defended against Hermann's generally accepted conjecture by M. H. Jameson, *BCH* 89 (1965), 154 ff., who points out the contradiction between the emended text and the evidence of the deme calendars. But πολλοὶ is very hard after πανδημεὶ. The addition of ἀγνὰ (possible, but as Jameson shows not obligatory) focuses but does not change the sense.

preparation of the couch and table (ἐπεμελήθησαν ... [τῆς στρώσεως τ]ῆς κλίνης καὶ [τῆς ἐπικοσμήσεως τῆ]ς τραπέ[ζης]); these additional elements presumably belong to the same festival. A comparable decree of the second century speaks only of sacrifices, but Asclepius and Hygieia are now added to the recipients (*IG* II² 783). The third-century decrees were found in the Athenian agora, and possibly attest a separate celebration in Athens itself at a time when Athens was politically divided from the Piraeus (*Athenian Religion*, 240, n. 79). Alternatively it has been suggested that the procession may have gone to the Piraeus from Athens (so tentatively Mommsen, *Feste*, 528, taken up by A. P. Matthaiou, *Horos* 10–12, 1992–8, 42–4 and G. J. Oliver in D. Jordan and J. Traill (eds.), *Lettered Attica* (Publ. of Canadian Arch. Inst. at Athens no. 3, 2003), 104–8).

Date: The evidence of the Lycurgan skin-sale records (*IG* II² 1496. 88–89, 118–19), if these observe strict chronological order, puts the sacrifice after the *Bendidea* (Thargelion 19 or 20) but early enough to leave time for two later sacrifices before the end of Skirophorion. *IG* II² 676 and *Agora* XVI 186, honouring the *epimeletai* of the festival, were passed respectively on Skirophorion 20 and 11, and, though honours were often long delayed, they could scarcely be carried over from one year to another: it will follow then, since Skirophorion was the last month of the year, that the sacrifice preceded Skirophorion 11. On the other hand, Lys. 26.6 shows that in the year 383/2 a sacrifice to Zeus Soter which was performed on Skirophorion 30 was sufficiently important for all public business to be suspended on this day. Such a suspension did not occur later in the century (Mikalson, *Calendar*, 181), and I shall argue elsewhere that the great sacrifice to Zeus Soter, originally located on Skirophorion 30, was moved between 383/2 and *c*.350 to a date earlier in the month.[30]

Dionysia, τὰ ἀστικά **or** ἐν ἄστει **or** τὰ μεγάλα (for these terms see Pickard-Cambridge, *Dramatic Festivals*², 56, nn. 1–2). A festival which dramatized the advent of Dionysus in the city on the occasion of the 'choruses' in his honour (see pp. 317–18). The great procession on Elaphebolion 10 was preceded (surely at no long distance) by the 'bringing in of Dionysus', and followed by several days of competitions (Pickard-Cambridge, *Dramatic Festivals*², 63–7).

Dionysia, τὰ κατ' ἀγρούς A festival of the demes typically held in Posideon (Theophr. *Char.* 3.5). In numerous demes it became a context for dramatic and choral performances, probably varying somewhat in date from deme to deme (Pl. *Resp.* 475d). The other attested element is a phallic procession. See p. 316 and Jones, *Rural Athens*, 124–58; Jones reattaches to the festival two elements dissociated from it by earlier scholarship, the game of jumping on greasy wineskins (Eubulus fr. 7) and a cock fight (Haghios Eleutherios calendar frieze, Deubner, *Attische Feste*, 251, with pl. 37 no. 13). Jones assumes that dramatic performances were a mandatory element in the festival, which will thus have been confined to demes equipped with a theatre, but Ar. *Ach.* 201–2, 241–79 may suggest otherwise.

[30] *Aliter Athenian Religion*, 240, n. 78. I judge the entry sacrifices offered by the priest of Zeus Soter (*IG* II² 689+ Acr. Mus. 14906 (A. P. Matthaiou, *Horos* 10–12, 1992–8, 31–2: *SEG* XLVI 134) line 20, *IG* II² 690.3) to be distinct; but for the other view see Matthaiou, loc. cit., 37–41.

Dionysia, τὰ ἐν Πειραιεῖ   The Piraeus *Dionysia* may have originated as the Piraeus form of the *Rural Dionysia*,[31] and continued to be seen as a festival of the deme (*IG* II² 1214. 20–25), but also came to serve as an extra dramatic and perhaps (*Athenian Religion*, 246, n. 100) choral festival of the city. *Pompe* and sacrifices on a large scale are attested in the fourth century (Dem. 21.10; *IG* II² 380. 21; ibid. 1496.70 and 144), and by the second century BC a ritual *eisagoge* of the god like that at the *City Dionysia* appears (Pickard-Cambridge, *Dramatic Festivals*², 44, n. 2). See Pickard-Cambridge, 45–7; R. Garland, *The Piraeus* (London 1987), 124–6; Jones, *Rural Athens*, 134–5.

Dipolieia   On the *Dipolieia* held on the acropolis on Skirophorion 14 in honour of Zeus Polieus see pp. 187–91.

Elaphebolia   The only testimonia are *Anecd. Bekk.* 1.249.7–9 Ἐλαφηβολιών· μὴν Ἀθήνησι πέμπτος. ἐκλήθη δὲ ἀπὸ τῶν ἐλάφων, αἵτινες τῷ μηνὶ τουτῷ ἐθύοντο τῇ Ἐλαφηβόλῳ Ἀρτέμιδι and Ath. 646e ἔλαφος· πλακοῦς ὁ τοῖς Ἐλαφηβολίοις ἀναπλασσόμενος διὰ σταιτὸς καὶ μέλιτος καὶ σησάμου. An Attic cult of Artemis as Elaphebolos is not otherwise attested. A modest public sacrifice (though scarcely of deer) cannot be ruled out, but the preparation of 'deer' cakes (in private houses?) attested by Athenaeus is all that we can be sure of. A month name Elaphebolion is known also from Iasos (Trümpy, *Monatsnamen*, 115); on the *Elaphebolia* of Hyampolis see Ellinger, *Légende nationale Phocidienne*, 243–6.

Eleusinia   A non-annual athletic competition in honour of Demeter and Kore, held at Eleusis. Receipts from it appear in the Lycurgan skin-sale records (*IG* II² 1496 A 130, 138) between those for the *Panathenaea* (end of Hekatombaion) and for the sacrifice to Democracy (Boedromion 12 or thereabouts); it must have fallen in Metageitnion or early in Boedromion.
   The periodicity of the festival is problematic. A set of fourth-century Eleusinian accounts records, over a four-year period, one payment 'for the *penteteris* of the *Eleusinia*' (doubtless the 'great *Eleusinia*' mentioned elsewhere) and one and no more 'for the *trieteris* of the *Eleusinia*' (*IG* II² 1672.258–62). That might seem conclusive evidence that the *Eleusinia* were celebrated twice and twice only over a period of four years, paradoxical though the idea of a *trieteris* held every fourth year may seem.[32] But the years in which *Eleusinia* are known to have been celebrated cannot, on accepted datings of certain crucial floating archonships, be made to fit into a pattern of alternate years.[33] 'Plain' annual *Eleusinia* have therefore been postulated, to give three different

[31] Such dating evidence as there is points to a date in Posideon, or is compatible with it: Pickard-Cambridge, *Dramatic Festivals*², 45, n. 7.
[32] For this approach see van der Loeff, *De ludis eleusiniis*, 100–36, who argued for *penteteris* in year 1 of the Olympiad, *trieteris* in year three.
[33] *IG* II² 1496. 126–30 (332/1, year one of an Olympiad) and II² 1304. 17–27 + 847. 23–5 (215/14, year two of the Olympiad) clash irreconcilably. (The date of the former is certain, of the latter all but universally accepted; it is, however, rejected by Follet, *Athènes*, 329, in order to preserve van der Loeff's scheme.) A popular compromise which puts *trieterides* in years one and three and the *penteteris* in year two (Boesch, *BPW* 1917, 157, accepted e.g. by Deubner, *Attische Feste*, 91, Kirchner on *IG* II² 1496 131, Healey, *Eleusinian Sacrifices*, 28–47) meets that difficulty

types of *Eleusinia*: Great (*penteteris*), Lesser (*trieteris*), Plain or annual.[34] Parallels for this 'Three Bears' structure may, however, prove elusive. Perhaps a promised revision of the archon dates for the period *c*.240 to 200 will put all back in order; or perhaps a reform took place in the third century whereby the 'lesser *Eleusinia*' became annual.[35]

[**Eleutheria** In his list of Athenian achievements commemorated in the festival calendar Plutarch mentions, with a date, three commemorative festivals of the month Boedromion, and continues 'On the third of the month they won the battle of Plataea' (*De glor. Ath.* 7, 349 f.; same date for the battle in *Camill*. 19.5). This is more likely to be a loose allusion to the panhellenic festival of *Eleutheria* held at Plataea on Boedromion 4 (Plut. *Aristid*. 19.8) than (so Mikalson, *Calendar*, 48) unique evidence for a separate Athenian rite. Cf. Pritchett, *Greek State at War*, iii, 182–3 and below s.v. *Sphragitic Nymphs, sacrifice to*.]

Enyalios, sacrifice to Brought by the polemarch (Arist. *Ath. Pol.* 58.1), whether as an independent offering or as part of the sacrifice to Artemis Agrotera (q.v.) on Boedromion 6 is unclear (cf. p. 398, n. 43).

Epidauria See s.v. *Asklepieia*.

Epikleidia Known only from Hesych. ε 4858 Ἐπικλείδια· ἑορτὴ Δήμητρος Ἀθήνησι. There is no reason to link the festival with the *Epikleidai* (on this group see *Athenian Religion*, 320), as recommended by A. von Premerstein, *AM* 35 (1910), 107f. (who also cites some different, earlier views).

Epitaphia A musical, athletic and equestrian competition organized by the polemarch in honour of those who had died in battle (Arist. *Ath. Pol.* 58.1; *Athenian Religion*, 132, n. 36). In theory the commemorative festival presumably followed on from the public funeral held in the Ceramicus for the dead of a particular year, though how the relation worked in practice is unclear (there will not have been a public funeral every year, and when there was the date may have varied). The *Epitaphia* reappear in the

---

and gives *trieteris* an easier sense, but appears incompatible with the indication of *IG* II[2] 1672 about the frequency of the *trieteris*. And on current dating of disputed archons celebrations in all four years of the Olympiad are attested.

[34] So R.M. Simms, *GRBS* 16 (1975), 269–70, who accepts Boesch's scheme of a 'plain' celebration in year four (his argument from II[2] 1672. 255–7 for annual celebration is fallacious: Smarzyck, *Religionspolitik*, 186, n. 87); K. Clinton, *AJP* 100 (1979), 9–12 (*penteris* year two, *trieteris* year four, plain celebration in one and three). But the postulate of 'plain' *Eleusinia* appears to issue in self-contradiction. They must have lacked competitions (since prize-money for plain celebrations does not appear in *IG* II[2] 1672): yet (on Simms's scheme) ephebes travelled to Eleusis to attend them (II[2] 1028), and (on Clinton's) they yielded substantial sums for skin sales (II[2] 1496) and might even require an agonothete (II[2] 2336. 207). Parallels: cf. T. Klee, *Zur Geschichte der gymnischen Agone an griechischen Festen* (Leipzig 1918), 69–70.

[35] Revision: J. D. Morgan, *AJA* 100 (1996), 395; cf. K. Clinton in *OCD*[3] s.v. *Eleusinia*. Reform: on this view we must also suppose that the *penteteris* changed year within the Olympiad (a proposal already made by Rhodes on *Ath. Pol.* 54.7). Proclamation of honours at a non-annual festival is not a wholly easy notion, despite van der Loeff, *De ludis eleusiniis*, 104–6 (*IG* VII 2411 is weak basis for an argument). And *IG* II[2] 847. 23–5 does not disprove the existence of annual *Eleusinia* at that date, given that the *Eleusinia* in question in that text are definitely 'greater'.

late hellenistic period when there is no longer any trace of a public funeral: races, torch-races and parades by the ephebes are the attested elements then (*IG* II² 1006.22–3, 1011.9; briefer references appear in many ephebic decrees). There is evidence that in the hellenistic period the festival was understood as commemoration of the Persian wars and particularly of the battle of Marathon: in an unpublished decree of 176/5 the ephebes are said to have 'visited Marathon and crowned the *polyandreion* and performed a funeral contest, according to what is customarily done [in front of] the city *polyandreion* ([πρὸ τοῦ] πρὸς τῶι ἄστει πολυανδρείου)'; this latter was apparently a cenotaph in Athens itself, from which one of the torch-races of the *Epitaphia* started (*IG* II² 1006.22), commemorating the dead of Marathon (see A. P. Matthaiou in P. Derow and R. Parker, eds., *Herodotus and his World*, Oxford 2003, 197, citing Ag. Inv. 7529). The ephebes of 123/2 similarly crowned the *polyandreion* at Marathon and made funerary offerings (ἐνήγισαν) to 'those who died in war for freedom' there, *IG* II² 1006.69.

The notice of Hesych. ε 4499 ἐπ' Εὐρυγύῃ ἀγών· Μελησαγόρας (*FGrH* 330 F 2) τὸν Ἀνδρόγεων Εὐρυγύην εἰρῆσθαί φησι τὸν Μίνωος, ἐφ' ᾧ τὸν ἀγῶνα τίθεσθαι ἐπιτάφιον Ἀθήνησιν ἐν τῷ Κεραμεικῷ is isolated and anomalous; the author may have intended to 'give a respectable pre-history' (Jacoby, comm. on *FGrH* 330 F 2, p. 606) to the late-established festival.

Epizephyra A festival known only from an entry in the calendar of the deme Skambonidai, *IG* I³ 244 C 19–21 Ἐπιζε[φύρο]ισι ἐμ Πυθίοι.

Eros, festival of A rock cut inscription from the vicinity of the precinct of Aphrodite on the north slope of the acropolis (Travlos, *Pictorial Dictionary*, 228–31) runs τὸι Ἔροτι hε ἑορτὴ [τ]ετράδι hισταμέν[ο] Μονιχιο͂[ν]ος μεν[ός] (*IG* I³ 1382). Nothing more is known of the festival.

Erosouria/Herosouria A festival of Athena known only from an entry in the calendar of the deme Erchia for Gamelion 9: Ἡροσουρίοις, ἐμ πόλει Ἐρχιᾶσι, ἀμνή, Γ⊢⊢ (*LSCG* 18 B 28–31). For a faint possibility that the festival name should rather be *Prosouria* see S. D. Lambert, *ZPE* 130 (2000), 5, n. 31.

Galaxia *Anecd. Bekk.* 1.229.25–7 (fuller than Hesych. γ 80): Γαλάξια· ἑορτὴ Ἀθήνῃσι μητρὶ θεῶν ἀγομένη, ἐν ᾗ ἕψουσι τὴν γαλαξίαν. ἔστι δὲ πόλτος κρίθινος ἐκ γάλακτος. On γαλαξία see p. 185. The festival is uninformatively mentioned also in Theophr. *Char.* 21.11 (by Wilamowitz's palmary conjecture) and in an ephebic decree (*IG* II² 1011.13: the ephebes sacrifice and make a dedication; dedications to Mother without mention of the festival occur ibid. 1006. 23–4 and often). Deubner inferred from the Delian month name Galaxion = Attic Elaphebolion that the Attic festival fell in that month (*Attische Feste*, 216): the inference is not inescapable (see *RE* s.v. *Galaxios*, *Galaxion*).

Genesia A festival honouring dead parents, held on Boedromion 5. The relation between the rite of Boedromion 5 and possible private *Genesia* performed by families is unclear; if a public rite distinct from private commemorations occurred on Boedromion 5, we do not know where it was held. See pp. 27–8.

Great Gods, procession for Known only from late hellenistic decrees in honour of the ephebes (*IG* II² 1006.29, 1008.18), and very probably a hellenistic introduction (but N. Robertson assigns it to the *Anakeia*, *ZPE* 127, 1999, 180); it was associated with a ship race in the Piraeus. Date unknown.

Haloa A festival (probably with *pannychis*) held at Eleusis, and probably there only, on Posideon 26 (Photius *a* 1080) and perhaps the following day, in honour of Demeter, Kore, Dionysus and apparently Poseidon: see pp. 167, 199–201, 279, 283, 329.

'Hekaleia' (the name is not attested). A sacrifice brought to Zeus Hekalos/Hekaleios and Hekale/Hekaline by 'the demes around Hekale [the place]' (Plut. *Thes.* 14.2; *Athenian Religion*, 111; for the form Zeus Hekaleios see Steph. Byz. s.v. Ἑκάλη and Hesych. ε 1231).

[**Hekatombaia** *Etym. Magn.* 321.6–8: Ἑκατομβαιὼν δὲ ὠνόμασται διὰ τὰς τοῦ Ἀπόλλωνος θυσίας· θύουσι γὰρ αὐτῷ Ἑκατομβαίῳ (*similia Anecd. Bekk.* 1.247.1–2); Hesych. ε 1270 Ἑκατόμβαιος· ὁ Ἀπόλλων παρὰ τοῖς Ἀθηναίοις. But no trace survives of an actual festival so named.]

Hephaisteia A festival of uncertain date in honour of Hephaestus and Athena, the organization or reorganization or a particular celebration of which is regulated in a fragmentary decree of 421/0 (*IG* I³ 82: see most recently H. B. Mattingly, *CQ* 47, 1997, 353–4); it is surely relevant that work on the 'statues for the Hephaesteum' began in just this year (see *IG* I³ 472). The *penteteris* mentioned in the decree (6, 33) is probably the *Panathenaea*, since the *Hephaisteia* does not appear among the list of *penteterides*, which presents itself as complete, of Arist. *Ath. Pol.* 54.7 (the new *penteteris* added in 329/8 there mentioned is probably not (*Athenian Religion*, 246, n. 100) the *Hephaisteia*; but if it were, the case for assuming a penteteric *Hephaisteia* in the fifth century would become still weaker). The references in the decree to other festivals (*Promethia*, 37, and *Panathenaea* if that is the reference of *penteteris*) might suggest that the *Hephaisteia* at this date was a new festival calqued on existing models; and in fact each of *Hephaisteia*, *Promethia*, and *Panathenaea* hosted a torch-race (see below; that at the *Hephaisteia* is mentioned in the decree, 34) beginning from the Academy. On the other hand, for Herodotus (8.98.2) the link among 'the Greeks' of Hephaestus with torch-races is primary, not a secondary product of bricolage. Probably then we should see in the decree (with Deubner, *Attische Feste*, 213) a reorganization, not a wholly new introduction; perhaps indeed it does no more than prescribe a single celebration on an exceptional scale (so Sokolowski, commentary to *LSCG* 13; Rosivach, *Public Sacrifice*, 154). In the legible portions the decree regulates the appointment of ten *hieropoioi* from the dikasts and ten from the boule (19–25); assigns three cattle to the metics, who are to receive the meat raw (25–6); provides for good order during the *pompe* (26–30); and apparently contains the first epigraphic allusion to the ritual of 'bull-lifting' (31–2; cf. van Straten, *Hierà kalá*, 109–113),[36] to be conducted by 200

---

[36] Van Straten, *Hierà kalá*, 111–12, draws attention, in connection with the *Hephaisteia*, to a r.f. kylix (Florence 81600) of *c.* 500 which shows bull-lifting by ephebes on the outside and Hephaestus in the tondo.

chosen Athenians. Given this emphasis on animal sacrifice it is surprising to find no trace of the *Hephaisteia* in the skin-sale records of the 330s (*IG* II² 1496a), if the regulations laid down in the decree were indeed intended to be permanent. Sacrifices to Poseidon and Apollo are also mentioned (36).

The torch-race between teams of ephebes from each tribe was funded as a liturgy by gymnasiarchs (cf. *IG* II² 3201; *SEG* XXV 177.29). [Xen.] *Ath. Pol.* 3.4 speaks of disputes between *khoregoi* at *Dionysia, Thargelia, Panathenaea, Promethia* and *Hephaisteia*. Either 'khoregoi' here is shorthand for 'khoregoi and gymnasiarchs', or we must postulate liturgically funded choral performances too (*IG* II² 1138. 9–11 is similarly ambiguous), a postulate that finds some support in the reference to μοσική (admittedly in a broken context) in the decree (16). On the problem see Wilson, *Khoregia*, 35.

The main source for the torch-race is Harpocration λ 3: λαμπάς· Λυσίας ἐν τῷ κατ᾽ Εὐφήμου. τρεῖς ἄγουσιν Ἀθηναῖοι ἑορτὰς λαμπάδος, Παναθηναίοις καὶ Ἡφαιστίοις καὶ Προμηθείοις, ὡς Πολέμων φησὶν ἐν τῷ περὶ τῶν ἐν τοῖς προπυλαίοις πινάκων. The three torch-races reappear in various scholia (vet. Ar. *Ran.* 129c and 1087a; in *Σ* Patm. Dem. 57.43 a race for Pan replaces the Panathenaea); the addition that they were all held 'in the Ceramicus' (*Σ* vet. Ar. *Ran.* 131b, c) derives from Ar. *Ran.* 129 and has no authority, though it is probably correct that they all passed through there, as the Panathenaic race certainly did (Ar. *Ran.* 1089–98). The Panathenaic race started from the altar of Eros in the Academy (Plut. *Sol.* 1.7; Herm. in *Phdr.* 231e), that at the *Promethia* from the altar of Prometheus also in the Academy (Paus. 1.30.2), that at the *Hephaisteia* doubtless from the same place, the cults of Prometheus and Hephaestus there being very closely associated (*Σ* Soph. *OC* 56). The Panathenaic race ended apparently at the great altar of the goddess on the acropolis (Herm. in *Phdr.* 231e), that at the *Hephaisteia* presumably at the Hephaisteion (and there too that for Prometheus?)

Herakleia at Diomeia Ἡράκλεια τᾶν Διομείοις are mentioned by Ar. *Ran.* 651; cf. Harpocration ε 50 Ἐν Διομείοις Ἡράκλειον· Ὑπερείδης κατὰ Κόνωνος. τῆς ἐν Διομείοις ἀγομένης ἑορτῆς τῷ Ἡρακλεῖ μνημονεύουσι καὶ οἱ κωμικοί. *IG* II² 1245 and 1247, decrees of the association (of uncertain character)[37] of *Mesogeioi*, regulate an otherwise unidentified ἑορτή (with θυσία and πομπή) of Heracles in which a priest of Diomos is involved. This may be the Ἡράκλεια τᾶν Διομείοις (*Athenian Religion*, 306); if not, nothing is known of that festival. Cf. the following entry. The location of the deme Diomeia is unknown, though it should abut the urban deme Melite if we change εἰς Διωμίδα (unknown) to εἰς Διόμεια in Plut. *De exil.* 6, 601b;[38] the findspot of two decrees of the *Mesogeioi* (a little west of the National Archaeological Museum: *AJA* 65, 1965, 110) may provide a clue if they are associated with the festival.

A date may be given by an incident of 346. Dem. 19.86 (cf. 125) tells how an abnormal decision was taken to 'bring women and children in from the fields and celebrate the *Herakleia* within the walls' for fear of Philip. The decision was made on Skirophorion 27 (Dem. 19. 60 with 125; cf. D. M. MacDowell's notes on Dem. 19.86). It follows that an extra-urban *Herakleia* was celebrated a little after that, presumably in the following month, Hekatombaion. Mommsen argued that only a festival normally

[37] Jones, *Associations*, 238, rejects Schlaifer's arguments for treating them as a *genos*.
[38] I do not know the origin of this old correction (Mommsen, *Feste*, 160 n. 2), strangely ignored in the Teubner.

held far from the city would have needed to be brought inside for safety, thus the penteteric *Herakleia* of Marathon (Mommsen, *Feste*, 161). But raiding parties could come right up to the walls, and Demosthenes' expression would in fact fit well a festival normally held a little way ἐκτὸς τείχους, such as the *Herakleia* in Diomeia.

In the Haghios Eleutherios calendar frieze (Deubner, *Attische Feste*, 226, with fig. 40, no. 37; the central figure in Simon, *Festivals*, pl. 2.3) a figure of Heracles appears in Metageitnion and presumably attests an important festival of Heracles held in that month. Unless we suppose that the Athenians in 346 chose on Skirophorion 27 to relocate a festival held in the next month but one, there were two *Herakleia* in successive months, that of Dem. 19.86 in Hekatombaion and that of the calendar frieze in Metageitnion.

[**Herakleia at Kynosarges**   The *Herakleia at Diomeia* have traditionally, but it seems wrongly (*Athenian Religion*, 306), been supposed to take place in the gymnasium of Heracles at Kynosarges. Monthly offerings with the involvement of παράσιτοι are attested at Kynosarges (Polemon ap. Ath. 234e), but no actual festival.]

Herakleia at Marathon   An athletic festival at which clients of Pindar from outside Attica competed (*Ol.* 9.89 with Σ; 13.110; *Pyth.* 8.79); *ARV*² 1044.9, a pelike of the Epimedes Painter which shows a citharode amid Nikai and is inscribed 'Victory at the *Panathenaea*, Victory at Nemea, at Marathon, at Isthmus', attests a citharodic contest too. *IG* I³ 1015 *bis*, found at Marathon near the findspot of *IG* I³ 2/3, on the interpretation of S. N. Koumanoudes commemorates an athletic victory in this festival.[39] An inscription from the first half of the fifth century gives some organizational details (*IG* I³ 3). In all probability these are the penteteric *Herakleia* mentioned by Arist. *Ath. Pol.* 54.7. Their date is unknown, unless the incident of 346 (see above, under *Herakleia in Diomeia*) concerned them.

***Herakleia* in demes**   On the *Herakleia* at Porthmos, a festival of the *genos Salaminioi* but apparently not confined to them alone, see *Athenian Religion*, 313–14 (cf. Goette, *Sounion*, 66–8 with figs. 144–6); on the Herakleia σπονδ<ε>ῖα καὶ θερινά of the two demes Kydantidai and Ionidai, ibid. 332; on the rites at the τετράκωμον Ἡράκλειον near Phaleron see *Athenian Religion*, 328–9; on the 'festival of Heracles at Akris' of the deme Eleusis see *SEG* XXVIII 103.32. There were doubtless many other such. On 'parasites of Heracles' in 'all the demes' (doubtless an exaggeration) see Diodorus comicus fr. 2. 23–30.[40]

Hermaia   Hermaia were celebrated (quite frequently?) by the young users of gymnasia (see p. 251), but a separate, largely equestrian, *Hermaia* for adults is perhaps attested by *IG* II² 895.5 and 2971.13 (see p. 392, n. 23). Date unknown.

Hermes Hegemonios, sacrifice to   A sacrifice in late Mounichion/early Thargelion known only from two entries in the Lycurgan skin-sale records, *IG* II² A 1496. 84–5, 115–16. See *Athenian Religion*, 238, n. 72.

---

[39] See A. P. Matthaiou in P. Derow and R. Parker (eds.), *Herodotus and his World* (Oxford 2003), 190–4. On this view the festival could be called the *Empylia Herakleia*.

[40] On the Attic Heracles see most recently C. Jourdain-Annequin, *Ktema* 23 (1998), 355–64.

Heroa *SEG* XVIII 26.11–12 honours a priest of Asclepius who ἐβουθύ[τησεν τοῖς τε Ἀσκληπιείοις] καὶ ᾿Επιδαυρίοις καὶ ῾Ηρώιοις παρασ[τήσας θύματα ὡς κάλλιστα] [κ]αὶ τὰς τούτων παννυχίδας συν[ετέλεσεν; ibid. 27.6–7 is very similar. Since Asclepius was himself, it seems, treated as a hero in the Asclepieum (*Athenian Religion*, 183, n. 109; p. 411, n. 98 above), this was presumably a third rite in his honour. J. W. Riethmüller (in R. Hägg (ed.), *Ancient Greek Hero Cult*, Stockholm 1999, 123–43) argues for a 'chthonic' sacrifice at what he identifies as a *bothros* in the Asclepieum; A. Verbanck-Piérard (in V. Pirenne-Delforge and E. Suárez de la Torre, *Héros et héroines dans les mythes et les cultes grecs*, Liège 2000, 281–332, esp. 329–32) contests the identification and denies the importance of chthonic sacrifice in Asclepian cult. *AM* 85 (1970), 109 is a dedication to Hermes made by a victor (perhaps in a torch-race) at the *Heroa*; the festival comprised games, therefore. Like *SEG* XVIII 26 and 27, this text is of the second century BC.

Hieros Gamos A festival celebrating the marriage of Zeus and Hera, probably observed in private houses throughout Attica (but also the occasion of sacrifices by demes). *Hieros Gamos*, not the *Theogamia* given by Σ Hes. *Op.* 783–4 Pertusi, is the classically attested name. *Date*: Gamelion 27. See p. 76.

Hydrophoria Either an unknown minor festival, or more probably a rite within a festival, perhaps on day three of *Anthesteria* (p. 296).

Iobaccheia The γέραραι who prepared the archon basileus' wife for her marriage to Dionysus, probably during the *Anthesteria* (p. 304), were required to swear that they would celebrate 'in accord with tradition' two otherwise almost unknown festivals of Dionysus, the *Iobaccheia* and *Theoinia* (q.v.) (Apollod. *Neaer.* 59.78). The '*Lenaea*' vases sometimes speculatively associated with the *Anthesteria* (p. 306) might, no less speculatively, be associated with one of these festivals.

Kalamaia A festival of Demeter celebrated at Eleusis (*IG* II² 949.9) and in the Piraeus (*IG* II² 1177.9), perhaps in Hekatombaion (to which the month Kalamaion corresponds in the calendars of Miletus and perhaps Perinthos: Trümpy, *Monatsnamen*, 89, 93). See p. 195.

Kallynteria Phot. κ 124 s.v. Καλλυντήρια καὶ Πλυντήρια· ἑορτῶν ὀνόματα· γίνονται μὲν αὗται Θαργηλιῶνος μηνός, ἐνατῇ μὲν ἐπὶ δέκα Καλλυντήρια, δευτέρᾳ δὲ φθίνοντος τὰ Πλυντήρια (*Etym. Magn.* 487.13 adds nothing). Photius explains the name from the fact that Agraulos as priestess was the first to 'adorn the gods' (τοὺς θεοὺς κοσμῆσαι), and 'adorning is a form of making brilliant' (καὶ γὰρ τὸ κοσμεῖν καὶ λαμπρύνειν ἐστιν). The general and surely correct assumption is that *Kallynteria*, like *Plynteria*, honoured Athena. It is also widely believed (after Deubner, *Attische Feste*, 20) that the festival was devoted to cleaning the 'old temple' containing the image of Athena Polias, in preparation for the *Plynteria* which focused on the image itself. Mansfield, *Robe of Athena*, 370–1, takes up Photius' *aition* and sees it as an 'Adorning-festival' concerned with the *kosmos* of the statue; a main officiant will have been the assistant to the priestess of Athena known as κοσμώ (Harp. τ 22 s.v. τραπεζοφόρος). But one might expect such a rite to have followed, not preceded, the *Plynteria* at which the *kosmos* was removed (Plut. Alc. 34.1); and καλλύνω and associated words typically refer to cleaning rather than decoration. The matter is uncertain.

Photius' date for *Kallynteria* is at the moment generally rejected (that for *Plynteria* is also disputed) on the grounds that (1) the *Bendidea* may have fallen on Thargelion 19 (but Thargelion 20 is also a possibility), and could not have been so located if there was an existing festival on that day; (2) Aristokles of Rhodes (as cited s.v. *Bendidea*) states that 'the festivals of Athena' (but is this a true plural?) succeed the *Bendidea*. These considerations have some force but are not quite conclusive. If unmoored from Thargelion 19 the festival is left to float in the last third of the month (Mikalson, *Calendar*, 163–4); the only ground for setting *Kallynteria* before *Plynteria* (so Deubner, *Attische Feste*, 18; Mansfield, *Robe of Athena*, 384, n. 16) is Photius' belief that this was the sequence.

Klematis The *kosmetes* of the ephebes in or near 39/8 BC is praised for having sacrificed with them τῇ τε Κληματίδι καὶ τῇ πομπῇ τοῦ Ἐλαφηβολιῶ[νος] (*IG* II² 1043. 31).[41] Commentators compare Plut. *De cupiditate divitiarum* 8. 527d, where a κληματίς or vine-branch is listed as a typical component of ἡ πάτριος τῶν Διονυσίων ἑορτή in its simple ancient form, and postulate a minor Dionysiac festival at which a vine-branch played some role (Deubner, *Attische Feste*, 147).

Kronia A festival of Kronos at which slaves were allowed unusual freedoms. The main context was the individual household, but the Prytaneis could also have some role (*Agora* XV 81.6). *Date*: Hekatombaion 12 (Dem. 24.26). See p. 162 and p. 202.

Kybernesia According to Philochorus (*FGrH* 328 F 111 ap. Plut. *Thes.* 17.6), a festival honouring Theseus' pilot Nausithoos and look-out Phaiax at their hero-shrines in Phaleron. A sacrifice offered to Poseidon Hippodromios, Phaiax, Teucer and Nauseiros by the *genos Salaminioi* in Boedromion (on the 8th?) may relate to the festival, in which case we acquire a date for it and an association with Poseidon: see *Athenian Religion*, 314–15, and p. 389, n. 10, p. 393 and p. 410 above.

Lenaea A festival of Dionysus celebrated at the Lenaion over several days in Gamelion, with Gamelion 12 perhaps the main day (Mikalson, *Calendar*, 109–10). Securely attested elements are a procession, mass sacrifice, and a competition in tragedy and comedy. See p. 317.

Metageitnia Known from Plut. *De Exilio* 6, 601b, Ἀθηναίων οἱ μεταστάντες ἐκ Μελίτης εἰς Διόμεια (mss. Διωμίδα: see n. 38 above) ... καὶ μῆνα Μεταγειτνιῶνα καὶ θυσίαν ἐπώνυμον ἄγουσι τοῦ μετοικισμοῦ τὰ Μεταγείτνια; Lysimachides (*FGrH* 366 F 1) ap. Harp. μ 24 mentions a sacrifice to Apollo Metageitnios in the month Metageitnion. Metageitnion is a common month name, and Plutarch is obviously recounting a secondary aitiology. It may follow that Diomeia hosted not just a Herakleion (p. 472 above) but also a significant sanctuary of Apollo.

Mounichia A festival honouring Artemis Mounichia at her shrine in Phaleron on Mounichion 16. The attested rite is a procession at which distinctive cakes decorated

---

[41] This 'procession of Elaphebolion' must be that at the *City Dionysia* (so Pélékidis, *L'Éphébie*, 246).

with torches were carried, but the festival was probably also an important moment in the lives of the young girls who served as 'bears' in the shrine of Artemis Mounichia, perhaps marking the end of their service. The festival came to be seen as commemorating the aid given by Artemis Mounichia during the battle of Salamis, and the ephebes became heavily involved. See p. 231, n. 59, 238. Pfuhl suggests that, if the association with Salamis arose in the classical period, hoplites and cavalry may have been added to the procession already then (Pfuhl, *De pompis*, 81).

Mysteries, Lesser   A festival honouring 'Mother at Agrai' held in Anthesterion (on the 20th?) and treated as a preliminary to the *Greater Mysteries* of Eleusis: see pp. 344–6.

Mysteries, Greater   A festival of initiation in honour of Demeter and Kore at Eleusis. Initiates from all Greece underwent preliminary rites in Athens beginning on Boedromion 15, and travelled to Eleusis on Boedromion 19 or 20; the final day of the Mysteries seems to have been Boedromion 23. See Chapter 15. Boedromion 16 hosted also an οἰνοχόημα commemorating Chabrias' victory off Naxos in 376 (*Athenian Religion*, 238, n. 74).

Nemesia   An athletic festival in honour of Nemesis of Rhamnus, probably first attested by *IG* II² 3105 + *SEG* XXXI 162 of the Lycurgan period (cf. *Athenian Religion* 254, n. 126); *IRhamnous* 7. 8–9 of the mid-third century BC speaks of '*Greater Nemesia*', and gives Hekatombaion 19 as the date of their 'athletic competition'. Plain *Nemesia* appear in a later third-century text, *IRhamnous* 17. 28. An unpublished text mentioned in *Ergon* 1998, 16, attests a *pannychis*.
    Dem. 41.11 speaks of a woman who spent a mna of silver εἰς τὰ Νεμέσεια τῷ πατρί, and lexicographers record Νεμέσεια as a festival of the dead (Σ Dem. 41.11, Harpocr. ν 11, *Anecd. Bekk.* 1. 282.32–3) and explain that ἡ Νέμεσις ἐπὶ τῶν νεκρῶν τέτακται (Σ Dem., *Anecd. Bekk.*). It seems impossible to associate such private *Nemeseia* with the rite at Rhamnus. A man unjustly slain could have a Nemesis (Soph. *El.* 792), but no other distinctive association between the goddess and the dead is known. I have suggested (*Athenian Religion*, 246, n. 101) that εἰς Νεμέσεια in Dem. 41.11 may be no more than an early corruption for εἰς Γενέσια. The comment of Harpocration (ν 11) on Νεμέσεια in Dem. 41.11 is interestingly tentative: 'perhaps it was a festival of Nemesis (μήποτε ἑορτή τις ἦν Νεμέσεως) at which they performed the customary rites for the dead'.

[**Niketeria**   Proclus *In Ti.* 53d, p. 173.9 Diehl, claims that 'Athena's victory is still celebrated among the Athenians, and they hold a festival as for the defeat of Poseidon by Athena' (ἔτι τοίνυν τῆς Ἀθηνᾶς τὰ νικητήρια παρὰ Ἀθηναίοις ἀνύμνηται, καὶ ἑορτὴν ποιοῦνται ταύτην ὡς τοῦ Ποσειδῶνος ὑπὸ τῆς Ἀθηνᾶς νενικημένου). But Plutarch reports that the Athenians always omit from the calendar the day on which the conflict supposedly occurred, Boedromion 2 (Plut. *De frat. amor.* 18, 489b, cf. *Quaest. Conv.* 9.6, 741b: Mikalson, *Calendar*, 47, misinterprets Plutarch's 'omit', ἐξαιροῦσιν). These claims are contradictory, and Mommsen's suggestion (*Feste*, 171–2) that the festival fell on the day following the suppressed day (which might be why the hypothetical

Athenian celebration of the victory of Plataea[42] was also set on Boedromion 3) does not explain how an event so ill-omened as to require the suppression of its anniversary was also occasion for a celebratory festival. Proclus has perhaps misunderstood Plutarch's anti-festival as a festival.]

Olympieia   An agonistic festival in honour of Zeus Olympios, presumably associated with his temple south-east of the acropolis. Skins sold from animals sacrificed at the *Olympieia* realized 671 dr. in 334/3 and 500 + dr. in 332/3 (*IG* II^2 1496 A 82–3, 113–4; a *hieropoios* at the festival is honoured in *IG* II^2 1257 B 6). A cavalry procession in honour of Zeus attested for Mounichion 19 (Plut. *Phoc.* 37.1, cf. Mikalson, *Calendar*, 145) probably belonged to the festival;[43] the date is compatible with that implied by the skin-sale records. The attested element is a tribal competion in ἀνθιππασία (*IG* II^2 3079.5; *Agora* XVI 203.2, both of the mid-third century; *Hesperia* 43, 1974, 312, no. 1, of the fourth-third century). On the revived Hadrianic *Olympieia* see Follet, *Athènes*, 345–8.

Oschophoria   A festival of Athena and Dionysus associated with the temple of Athena Skiras at Phaleron. The role of grape-clusters in the rite points to a date in autumn. If the figure of a grape-treading man holding a vine branch with grape clusters on the Haghios Eleutherios frieze (Deubner, *Attische Feste*, pl. 35, no. 3, with p. 250) alludes to the festival it may locate it specifically in Pyanopsion. Cf. pp. 211–17, and on the date *Athenian Religion*, 316, n. 85.

Pan, torch-race for   For Herodotus' account (6.105) of how the Athenians in 490 resolved to 'propitiate Pan with annual sacrifices and a torch-race' see *Athenian Religion*, 163–4 (note especially 164, n. 37, on a vase in Cape Town perhaps reflecting the torch-race). Herodotus does not explain the reason for choosing a torch-race: does it reflect the great run during which Philippides appeared to Pan? Other sources (Σ Patm. Dem. 57.43; *Anecd. Bekk.* 1.228.11–14; Phot. λ 66) add nothing, except an unreliable association in Σ Patm. Dem. 57.43 between the race and 'those about to marry' (cf. p. 442, n. 97). No trace exists of the liturgical structure (tribal gymnasiarchs) that supported the other torch-races (see above s.v. *Hephaisteia*). Nor is the course known.

Panathenaea   A festival of Athena comprising a sacrificial procession to the acropolis, athletic and musical competitions, and a *pannychis*; it was celebrated with especial splendour every four years as the *Great Panathenaea*. The main day was Hekatombaion 28 (p. 256). See Chapter 12.

Pandia   A little-known festival, probably of Zeus, held straight after the *City Dionysia* in Elaphebolion. The primary evidence consists merely of (*a*) a payment made by the deme Plotheia ἐς Πάνδια (*IG* I^3 258. 9); (*b*) a law cited in Dem. 21.8, whereby on the day after the *Pandia* an assembly is to be held in the theatre of Dionysus to discuss *inter alia* complaints concerning the *City Dionysia*; (*c*) an honorary resolution passed by the tribe Pandionis ἐν τῇ ἀγορᾷ τῇ μετὰ Πάνδια (*IG* II^2 1140). Phot. Πάνδια· ἑορτή τις

---

[42]   See above s.v. *Eleutheria*.
[43]   So already an unnamed predecessor of Mommsen, *Feste*, 466.

Ἀθήνησι μετὰ τὰ Διονύσια ἀγομένη ... ἄγεται δὲ αὕτη τῷ Διί clearly derives from (*b*); whether the association with Zeus (also in Poll. 1.37) is more than a probably correct etymological guess is unclear. *Etym. Magn.* 651.21–4 (abbreviated in *Anecd. Bekk.* 1. 292.10–11) offers alternative associations with Pandeia the moon, with Pandion, eponym of the tribe Pandionis, and with Zeus, and adds an etymology ἀπὸ τοῦ πάντα δινεύειν τῷ Διί. (*c*) suggests that the festival had already in the classical period become associated by popular etymology with Pandion (himself originally named from the festival, according to Wilamowitz, *Kl. Schr.* V. 2, 118). If (*a*) refers to the central celebration, it provides support for seeing here a 'festival of Zeus for all' (so Wilamowitz, *Glaube*, i, 222: cf. *Panathenaea*), which faded in importance in the historical period.

Peace, sacrifice to   Such a sacrifice was established, according to the best sources, in commemoration of the Peace that followed Timotheus' victory over the Spartans near Corcyra in 375; substantial receipts from it appear at the start (i.e. in Hekatombaion) of the skin-sale records for 333 and 332 (see *Athenian Religion*, 230, nn. 45 and 46). According to Σ vet. Ar. *Pax* 1019–20 it fell on the same day as the *Synoikia*, i.e. Hekatombaion 16. See too the note on a calendar from Miletupolis, p. 484 below. For the possibility, deriving from *Hesperia* 7 (1938), 294–6, no. 20, that a trieteric athletic, equestrian and musical *agon* was (briefly?) added in the Lycurgan period see J. D. Sosin, *MusHelv* 61 (2004), 1–8.

Plynteria   A festival apparently celebrated in Athens on the 25th (Plut. *Alc.* 34. 1) of Thargelion,[44] at which members of the *genos Praxiergidai* removed the adornments of Athena Polias' ancient image in the 'Old Temple' on the acropolis, veiled it, and performed secret rites (Xen. *Hell.* 1.4.12; Plut. *Alc.* 34.1–2). The day on which the goddess was thus covered was a ἡμέρα ἀποφράς (Xen. and Plut., locc. citt.) , and some (at least) temples were closed (Pollux 8.141). A procession attested for the festival (p. 178, n. 2 and p. 179, n. 5 above) is probably to be identified (*Athenian Religion*, 307, n. 63; for the other view see Mansfield, *Robe of Athena*, 424–33) with one at which the ephebes 'escorted Pallas to the sea (at Phaleron) and back ... with the *genos*-members' (sc. the *Praxiergidai*). The image was probably immersed in the sea; the name *Plynteria* suggests that certain of the goddess's robes may have been washed too, though the relation between this ritual and the presentation of a new *peplos* at the *Greater Panathenaea* is unclear. Maidens known as λουτρίδες or πλυντρίδες (Ar. Fr. 849) performed the cleansing. The rite was aitiologically connected (p. 381 above) with the Cecropid Aglauros. For the possibility of an allusion to the *Plynteria* on the south metopes of the Parthenon see Hurwit, *Acropolis*, 173–4, commenting on A. Mantis in *Architectural Sculpture*, 67–81. For a speculative reconstruction of the festival see Mansfield, *Robe of Athena*, 371–8.

---

[44] Phot. κ 124 (cf. s.v. *Kallynteria* above) gives Thargelion 29, but Deubner pointed out (*Attische Feste*, 18) that the assembly meetings attested for that day (Mikalson, *Calendar*, 160) prove it not to have been a ἡμέρα ἀποφράς. Offerings to Athena, including a 'robe', listed in the Nicomachus calendar (*BSA* 97, 2002, 364, fr. 3, col. I, 5–15) for (almost certainly) Thargelion are likely to be relevant: Mansfield's proposal to place them on the 24th rather than, as is generally accepted, the 29th (Mansfield, *Robe*, 392, n. 41), and to see them as preparatory, has its attractions.

The Thorikos calendar lists a sacrifice to Athena 'at the *Plynteria*' in the following month, Skirophorion (see p. 76). This is apparently a separate celebration in the deme. A calendar of uncertain origin (*IG* I³ 246 C 26) also attests a sacrifice to Athena at the *Plynteria*, but in this case in Thargelion.

Pompaia   Known only from Eust. in *Od.* 22.481, 1935.5, καὶ οἱ τὸ διοπομπεῖν δὲ ἑρμηνεύοντές φασιν ὅτι δῖον ἐκάλουν κώδιον ἱερείου τυθέντος Διὶ μειλιχίῳ ἐν τοῖς καθαρμοῖς φθίνοντος Μαιμακτηριῶνος μηνὸς ὅτε ἤγοντο τὰ Πομπαῖα. καὶ καθαρμῶν ἐκβολαὶ εἰς τὰς τριόδους ἐγίνοντο. εἶχον δὲ μετὰ χεῖρας πομπόν. ὅπερ ἦν, φασί, κηρύκιον, σέβας Ἑρμοῦ. καὶ ἐκ τοῦ τοιούτου πομποῦ καὶ τοῦ ῥηθέντος δίου τὸ διοπομπεῖν.

Posidea   The only festival of this name appears in a calendar (*IG* I³ 255.10) of uncertain character probably from the Marathonian region (S. D. Lambert, *ZPE* 130, 2000, 71–5); the *Posidea* there mentioned may be local. For traces of a festival at Sunium see p. 59, n. 36. The musical competition in the Piraeus attested by [Plut.] *X Orat.* 842a is probably a product of textual corruption (*Athenian Religion*, 246, n. 100). See too s.v. *Haloa, Kybernesia* and *Protrugaia*.

Proarktouria   See s.v. *Proerosia*.

Procharisteria   (variant form *Proschaireteria*). A sacrifice performed by the magistrates on the acropolis in spring to celebrate the return of Persephone; the recipient was probably Demeter, though our lexicographical sources link the sacrifice with Athena. See p. 197, n. 16.

Proerosia   A 'pre-ploughing' sacrifice/festival performed in several demes and with especial pomp in Eleusis. The honorand is commonly Demeter, but in Myrrhinus it is Zeus. The Eleusinian *Proerosia* was 'proclaimed' on Pyanopsion 5 (*LSCG* 7. 1–7) for celebration doubtless on the 6th; in Thorikos the rite fell in Boedromion. See p. 196, n. 14, and pp. 330–2. According to Hesych. s.v. Προηρόσια the festival was also called Προαρκτούρια (a corruption probably conceals as source the name of Kleidemos: *FGrH* 323 F 23), whence the uncertain supplement Προαρκτ]ουρ/ίοι[σι in the very fragmentary calendar *IG* I³ 232. 20–1. On the importance of the heliacal rising of Arktouros for the farmer see Hes. *Op.* 610; a sacrifice 'before' this rising (8 September in Greece) might seem to belong in Metageitnion (August–September), and it is not certain that *Proarktouria* and *Proerosia* were identical, though they were doubtless similar.

Promethia   A festival of uncertain date, first attested in *IG* I³ 82.32(?) and 35. It hosted a tribal torch-race (for references to the liturgy of training the tribal team see Lys. 21.3, Isae. 7.36), and possibly choral competitions: see above s.v. *Hephaisteia*.

Prosouria   See s.v. *Erosouria*.

Protrygaia   Hesych. s.v. Προτρύγαια· ἑορτὴ Διονύσου καὶ Ποσειδῶνος may relate to Attica; nothing more is known of the festival, though the linking of Dionysus and Poseidon recalls the *Haloa*.

Pyanopsia   A festival of Apollo, celebrated on Pyanopsion 7 (Harpocr. π 120; Plut. *Thes.* 22.4; cf. *LSCG* 7. 8–19). The best-attested public rite is that a 'boy with both parents alive' deposited an olive branch hung with produce (*eiresione*) at a temple of Apollo, perhaps that of Apollo Delphinios in Athens (p. 436, n. 75). But there was much carrying around of *eiresionai* by other troops of boys, and the offering/consumption of a bean-stew was a further central element; we should probably envisage this as a diffused rite celebrated throughout Attica, though priests from Eleusis seem to have attended a central celebration (including a *pannychis*) in Athens (*LSCG* 7. 9–19, as interpreted by G. Roux, *AntCl* 35, 1966, 562–73). See p. 185 and pp. 204–6.

Semnai, procession to cave of   An important civic procession, of date unknown, led by the *genos Hesychidai*: see *Athenian Religion*, 298–9.

Skira/Skirophoria   Only the date is uncontroversial, Skirophorion 12 (Σ Ar. *Ekkl.* 18). Early references suggest a women's festival of Demeter and Kore celebrated at various locales; later, but important, sources introduce an association with the cults of Athena and Poseidon on the acropolis, and a procession to a specific cult site west of Athens. See pp. 173–7 above. The date Skirophorion 12 was made 'more holy' (ἱερωτέρα) by the battle of Mantinea (of 362), according to Plut. *De glor. Ath.* 7, 350a; some element of commemoration was apparently added.

Sphragitic Nymphs, sacrifice to   An annual sacrifice brought by the tribe Aiantis to local nymphs in commemoration of the battle of Plataea (*Athenian Religion*, 104, n. 6). The date is unattested, but it may have occurred on the traditional date of the battle, Boedromion 3 or 4 (see above s.v. *Eleutheria*). Cf. p. 401, n. 55.

Stenia   Presented by the chorus in Ar. *Thesm.* 834–5, with the *Skira*, as one of the festivals which 'we', i.e. women, celebrate. The main source is Photius s.v. Στήνια· ἑορτὴ Ἀθήνησιν ἐν ᾗ ἐδόκει ἡ ἄνοδος γενέσθαι τῆς Δήμητρος· ἐλοιδοροῦντο δ᾽ ἐν αὐτῇ νυκτὸς αἱ γυναῖκες ἀλλήλαις· οὕτως Εὔβουλος (fr. 146 K/A, 148 Hunter); the women's mockery appears also in Hesych. s.v. Στήνια, while ibid. s.v. στηνιῶσαι· βλασφημῆσαι, λοιδορῆσαι attests a verb derived from the custom (whether regular slang, or a comic nonce word, is unclear). Σ Ar. *Thesm.* 834 dates the *Stenia* 'two days before the *Thesmophoria*, on Pyanopsion 9'. 'The coming up of Demeter' in Photius' notice is probably a slip for 'the coming up of Kore' (Demeter had no *Anodos*), but the timing remains inexplicable, since Pyanopsion is an autumn month and Kore's return is usually set in spring (Richardson, *Hymn to Demeter*, 284–5; Burkert, *Homo Necans*, 260–1). *Agora* XV. 78.6–8 unexpectedly praises the male prytaneis of 273/2 who ἔθ]υσαν δὲ καὶ τὰ Στήνια παρ᾽ α[ὐ]τῶν τεῖ Δήμητρι καὶ τεῖ Κόρει ὑπὲρ τ[ῆς βουλῆ]ς καὶ τοῦ δήμου.

Synoikia   A public festival in honour of Athena, supposedly commemorating the synoecism of Attica by Theseus (Ξυνοίκια ἐξ ἐκείνου Ἀθηναῖοι ἔτι καὶ νῦν τῇ θεῷ ἑορτὴν δημοτελῆ ποιοῦσιν, Thuc. 2.15.2). Plutarch speaks of Theseus after the synoecism 'sacrificing the *Metoikia* on the 16th of Hekatombaion, which they still sacrifice today' (ἔθυσε δὲ καὶ Μετοίκια τῇ ἕκτῃ ἐπὶ δέκα τοῦ Ἑκατομβαιῶνος, ἣν ἔτι νῦν θύουσι, *Thes.* 24.4); the date coincides with that given for *Synoikia* in Σ vet. Ar. *Pax* 1019–20, whence it follows that *Synoikia* and '*Metoikia*' are identical. '*Metoikia*' is probably a slip by Plutarch, who may have been remembering the *Metageitnia*.[45] No ritual action other than sacrifice is attested. Entries listed for Hekatombaion 15 and 16 in the biennial section of the calendar of Nicomachus, to be made by the trittys *Leukotainiai* of the pre-Clisthenic tribe Gleontis, almost certainly relate to the *Synoikia* (*Athenian Religion*, 112–13), but do not prove that the festival itself was biennial (cf. S. D. Lambert, *BSA* 97, 2002, 376–7). The offering of the *Leukotainiai* on the 16th was made to Zeus Phratrios and Athena Phratria, presumably at their shrine in the Agora (Thompson/Wycherley, *Agora*, 139–40). But the deme Skambonidai offered a full-grown victim on the acropolis (*IG* I³ 244 C 16–17 Χσυννοι[κίοις] ἐ[μ] πόλει τέ[λεον]). which was probably the central location of the festival.

Tauropolia A festival of Artemis Tauropolos held at her temple in Halai Araphenides, which supposedly hosted the image of the goddess brought from Tauri (Eur. *IT* 1450–7). Attested elements are the mock sacrifice of a young man, a *pannychis*, and probably a competition in pyrrhic dancing. There was considerable local involvement,[46] but participants from elsewhere in Attica are attested. See pp. 59 and 241–2. Date unknown.

Thargelia A festival of Apollo Pythios (but cf. p. 203, n. 50), closely associated with the Pythion in the south of the city. Attested elements are the expulsion of scapegoats; the preparation, presentation (and eating?) of *thargeloi*, a vegetarian foodstuff; a procession, in which an elaborate array of natural products was probably carried; a major competition in cyclic choruses.

Plut. *Quaest. Conv.* 8.1.2, 717d gives the 7th as the day, and ibid. 8.1.1, 717b confirms Thargelion as the month, of the *Thargelia*. Diog. Laert. 2.44 speaks of the Athenians 'purifying the city' on the previous day, Thargelion 6. It has long been customary (since Meursius, according to Mommsen, *Feste*, 479) to suppose a two-day festival, and at least since Mommsen (*Feste*, 479) it has been normal to assign the expulsion of the scapegoats to the 6th, the procession and the choral competitions (mentioned together by Dem. 21.10) to the 7th. Nothing contradicts, but nothing specifically supports, this reconstruction. A sacrifice to Demeter Chloe is also attested for Thargelion 6 by Σ Soph. *OC* 1600 (cf. p. 196, n. 15).

The main sources on the character of θάργηλοι are: Hesych. θ 104 s.v. Θαργήλια· Ἀπόλλωνος ἑορτή. καὶ ὅλος ὁ μὴν ἱερὸς τοῦ θεοῦ. ἐν δὲ τοῖς Θαργηλίοις τὰς ἀπαρχὰς τῶν φαινομένων ποιοῦνται καὶ περικομίζουσι. ταῦτα δὲ θαργήλιά φασι. καὶ μὴν Θαργηλιών. καὶ τὴν βυετηρίαν ἐκάλουν θάργηλον … καὶ ὁ θάργηλος χύτρα ἐστὶν ἀνάπλεως σπερμάτων; ibid. θ 106 s.v. θάργηλος· χύτρα ἱεροῦ ἐψήματος; Phot. θ 22 (Sud. θ 49) Θαργήλια· ἑορτή Ἀρτέμιδος καὶ Ἀπόλλωνος … θάργηλος ὁ τῶν σπερμάτων μεστὸς χύτρος ἱεροῦ ἐψήματος. ἥψουν δὲ ἐν αὐτῇ ἀπαρχὰς τῷ θεῷ τῶν πεφηνότων καρπῶν. ἵσταντο δὲ ἐν αὐτῇ καὶ χοροὶ καὶ ἀγών; Etym. Magn. 443.19 Θαργήλια· ἑορτὴ Ἀθήνησιν· ὀνομάζεται ἀπὸ τῶν θαργηλίων. θαργήλια δέ εἰσι πάντες οἱ ἀπὸ γῆς καρποί. ἄγεται δὲ μηνὶ Θαργηλιῶνι Ἀρτέμιδος καὶ

---

[45] The festival *Metageitnia* had a separate *aition* (see the entry above). But a tradition existed which explained the month name Metageitnion from Theseus' transfer of the population of Attica to Athens, which supposedly occurred in that month (Σ Thuc. 2.15.3; Photius μ 309 Μεταγειτνιών· μὴν Ἀθήνησι δεύτερος· ὠνομάσθαι δέ φασιν ἀπὸ τῆς μεταβάσεως τῆς εἰς τὸ ἄστυ, ταύτης τῶι μηνὶ τούτωι γενομένης ὑπὸ τοῦ Θησέως).

[46] Made explicit by Deubner's ingenious but uncertain correction (*Attische Feste*, 209) of a corrupt gloss of Hesych. Ταυροπόλια· Ἁλεῖς (ἁ εἰς mss.) ἑορτὴν ἄγουσιν Ἀρτέμιδι.

Ἀπόλλωνος (*similia* up to καρποί *Anecd. Bekk.* 1.263.23–5); Ath. 114a (types of cake are being discussed) παρεῖδε δὲ τοῦτον ὁ Βλεψίας, ὥσπερ καὶ τὸν θάργηλον, ὅν τινες καλοῦσι θαλύσιον. Κράτης δ᾽ ἐν β᾽ Ἀττικῆς διαλέκτου (*FGrH* 362 F 6) θάργηλον καλεῖσθαι τὸν ἐκ τῆς συγκομιδῆς πρῶτον γινόμενον ἄρτον.

On the rituals of (*ex hypothesi*) day two see pp. 185 and 203–4. The main sources for the scapegoat rite are:

1. Harp. φ 5:

> Φαρμακός· Λυσίας ἐν τῷ Κατ᾽ Ἀνδοκίδου ἀσεβείας (6.53), εἰ γνήσιος. δύο ἄνδρας Ἀθήνησιν ἐξῆγον καθάρσια ἐσομένους τῆς πόλεως ἐν τοῖς Θαργηλίοις, ἕνα μὲν ὑπὲρ τῶν ἀνδρῶν, ἕνα δὲ ὑπὲρ τῶν γυναικῶν. ὅτι δὲ ὄνομα κύριόν ἐστιν ὁ Φαρμακός, ἱερὰς δὲ φιάλας τοῦ Ἀπόλλωνος κλέψας ἁλοὺς ὑπὸ τῶν περὶ τὸν Ἀχιλλέα κατελεύσθη, καὶ τὰ τοῖς Θαργηλίοις ἀγόμενα τούτων ἀπομιμήματά ἐστιν, Ἴστρος ἐν α´ τῶν Ἀπόλλωνος ἐπιφανειῶν (*FGrH* 334 F 50) εἴρηκεν.

Pharmakos. Lysias in the prosecution of Andocides *For Impiety*, if it is genuine. At Athens they led out two men to be purifications of the city at the *Thargelia*, one on behalf of the men, one on behalf of the women. Istros in Book I of *Epiphanies of Apollo* says that Pharmakos is a proper name, that he was caught stealing the sacred cups of Apollo and stoned by the companions of Achilles, and that the rites performed at the *Thargelia* are imitations of these events.

2. Helladius ap. Phot. *Bibl.* 279 p. 534a 2–12:

> ὅτι ἔθος ἦν ἐν Ἀθήναις φαρμακοὺς ἄγειν δύο, τὸν μὲν ὑπὲρ ἀνδρῶν, τὸν δὲ ὑπὲρ γυναικῶν πρὸς τὸν καθαρμὸν ἀγομένους. καὶ ὁ μὲν τῶν ἀνδρῶν μελαίνας ἰσχάδας περὶ τὸν τράχηλον εἶχε, λευκὰς δ᾽ ἅτερος· συβάκχοι δέ, φησίν, ὠνομάζοντο. τὸ δὲ καθάρσιον τοῦτο λοιμικῶν νόσων ἀποτροπιασμός ἦν, λαβὸν τὴν ἀρχὴν ἀπὸ Ἀνδρόγεω τοῦ Κρητός, οὗ τεθνηκότος ἐν ταῖς Ἀθήναις παρανόμως τὴν λοιμικὴν ἐνόσησαν οἱ Ἀθηναῖοι νόσον, καὶ ἐκράτει τὸ ἔθος ἀεὶ καθαίρειν τὴν πόλιν τοῖς φαρμακοῖς.

It was customary at Athens to lead two scapegoats, of whom one was led for a purification on behalf of men, the other on behalf of women. The one for the men wore black dried figs around his neck, the one for the women white ones. They were called, he says, Sybacchoi. This purification was a means of averting plagues, and took its origin from the Cretan Androgeos: when he was killed in Athens lawlessly, the Athenians were afflicted by plague, and the custom prevailed thenceforth always to purify the city with scapegoats.

(1) appears to combine an account of the Attic rite with an *aition* derived from Istros for a comparable, non-Attic rite, since 'the locality, the persons, the singular number φαρμακός, the stoning show that Istros does not describe the Attic rite' (Jacoby on Istros *FGrH* 334 F 50). Of (2) Jacoby comments that 'it is not certain that this (the story of Androgeos) was the only *aition* given in the Atthides, still less that it is early' (on Istros *FGrH* 334 F 50, n. 8).

Various practices are ascribed to Athens in late scholia (on Ar. *Eq.* 1136; *Ran.* 733; *Plut.* 454; Aesch. *Sept.* 680), but the scholia in question derive from John Tzetzes (see the note of W. J. W. Koster on Σ rec. Ar. *Ran.* 733a), who demonstrably conflated evidence from different regions of the Greek world and even introduced elements from

Appendix 1

quite different rites. We cannot then know how the Athenians recruited their scape-goats (at Abdera the victim was 'hired', ὠνητός, Dieg. II. 29–40 on Callim. fr. 90). Note in particular that Ar. Eq. 1136 concerns the 'feeding up' of public slaves (ὥσπερ δημοσίους τρέφεις), not of scapegoats (see D. D. Hughes, Human Sacrifice in Ancient Greece, London 1991, 150), credible though it is that scapegoats were fed at public expense for a short (cf. Dieg. II. 29–40 on Callim. fr. 90, Abdera) or long (Petronius ap. Serv. in Aen. 3.57, Marseilles) period.

For Attic understandings of the scapegoat two key texts are Ar. Ran. 732–3, where it is said that nowadays the Athenians choose as political leaders persons of the vilest origins, 'whom in the past the city wouldn't readily have used even as scapegoats so carelessly' (οἷσιν ἡ πόλις πρὸ τοῦ/οὐδὲ φαρμακοῖσιν εἰκῇ ῥᾳδίως ἐχρήσατ᾽ ἄν) and [Lys.] 6. 53, 'you should think that by punishing and getting rid of Andocides you are purifying the city and performing an expulsion of evil and sending out a scapegoat and getting rid of a spirit of crime' (νῦν οὖν χρὴ νομίζειν τιμωρουμένους καὶ ἀπαλλαττομένους Ἀνδοκίδου τὴν πόλιν καθαίρειν καὶ ἀποδιοπομπεῖσθαι καὶ φαρμακὸν ἀποπέμπειν καὶ ἀλιτηρίου ἀπαλλάττεσθαι). The Lysias passage provides the strongest specific evidence that the Attic scapegoat was expelled, as we now know to have happened in Abdera (Dieg. II. 29–40 on Callim. fr. 90), not killed. Spectacular practices such as scapegoat-ing can survive in popular memory for long after they cease to be performed in reality, and neither of the texts just quoted proves that the ritual was contemporary. But, had it ended in (say) the sixth century, it would be hard even to guess at a possible source for the precise details known to the sources of Harpocration and Helladius.

Many details attested for similar rituals elsewhere in the Greek world are very likely to have applied also to Attica: see in general J. N. Bremmer, 'Scapegoat Rituals in Ancient Greece', HSCP 87 (1983), 299–320 (= Oxford Readings, 271–93), and Hughes, op. cit., 139–65.

[See the addendum on p. 485.]

Theogamia See Hieros Gamos.

Theoinia See s.v. Iobaccheia. Harpocr. θ 7 identifies the festival, wrongly, with the Rural Dionysia and attests a role for unidentified γεννῆται, i.e. probably (Athenian Religion, 299) members of the Theoinidai.

Theseia The sparse classical references to this festival reveal only that gruel was eaten (Ar. Plut. 627–8) and that sacrifices were made on a large scale (IG II² 1496.134, 143). Plutarch dates 'the greatest sacrifice to Theseus', i.e. probably our festival, to Pyanopsion 8 (Thes. 36.4; Mikalson, Calendar, 70); he also mentions a sacrifice to the Amazons performed before the Theseia 'in olden times' (ἡ γινομένη πάλαι θυσία ταῖς Ἀμαζόσι πρὸ τῶν Θησείων, Thes. 27.7) and the burnt-offering of a ram still in his day made to Theseus' teacher Konnidas on the day before the festival (Thes. 4). The festival emerges into the light of day in the mid-second century, when inscriptions, especially very extensive victor lists (IG II² 956ff.), attest for the 'Great Theseia' not just a procession and sacrifice but also an elaborate programme of torch-races and athletic and equestrian competitions for individuals, tribes, and military units (both Athenian and mercenary). Much of all this is likely to be a new creation of that very prosperous epoch in Athenian history (G. R. Bugh, ZPE 83, 1990, 20–37; Habicht, Athens from

Alexander, 240–2; Mikalson, *Hellenistic Athens*, 252–3; N. M. Kennell, *Phoenix* 53, 1999, 249–62).

Thesmophoria   Three-day women's festival of Demeter and Kore, apparently held at various locales in Attica. The dates normally given are Pyanopsion 11–13 (Σ Ar. *Thesm.* 80 with Phot. θ 134, Alciphron 2.37.1-2, and Mikalson, *Calendar*, 71–2), though learned ancient commentators on Aristophanes also uncovered a celebration at Halimus on the 10th (Σ Ar. *Thesm.* 80; cf. p. 75, n. 103). See Ch. 13.

Unknown god, festival of on Salamis   Plutarch in the life of Solon describes a particular version of the capture of Salamis by Solon, and goes on (9.6): 'This version seems to be supported by the rites performed (τὰ δρώμενα). An Attic ship used to sail up[47] initially in silence, then as (an opposing group?) approached with shouts and battle-cries one armed man leapt out and ran with a cry to cape Skiradion <lacuna> approaching from land. Nearby is the shrine of Enyalios which Solon founded.' This is the only source. A very implausible attempt by E. Peterson (*Jahrbuch* 32, 1917, 137–54) to detect a depiction on a red-figure kylix by the Telephos painter (Boston 95.28 & fragments elsewhere; Deubner, *Attische Feste*, pl. 24) did not commend itself to Beazley, *ARV²* 2, 816–17; but U. Kron has some sympathy, 'Patriotic Heroes', 69–71. The rite has been ascribed to festivals of Athena Skiras, Ajax and Enyalios (for references see Deubner, *Attische Feste*, 218–19; brief mention in Pritchett, *War*, iii, 207).

Zosteria   A deme festival of Halai Aixonides (but perhaps admitting some broader participation) known only from *SEG* XLII 112.5, ἡ θυσία τῶν Ζωστηρίων: cf. p. 59, n. 35.

Note on a calendar from Miletupolis

A substantial fragment of a sacrificial calendar of the fourth century has recently been published from Miletupolis in the region of Cyzicus (E. Schwertheim, *Die Inschriften von Kyzikos und Umgebung*, ii, *Miletupolis*, Bonn 1983, no. 1). The surviving portion begins in an unidentified month and proceeds to Skirophorion, a month name name hitherto known from Athens alone and certainly not found in the calendars of Cyzicus or its mother-city Miletus. On Skirophorion 14, day of the Attic *Dipolieia*, appears a sacrifice to Zeus Polieus. The first editor (E. Schwertheim, op. cit., pp. 107–12) took these strikingly Attic elements as an indication that Miletupolis had been founded or refounded under Attic influence *c*.410 BC. C. Habicht has countered (*Epigraphica Anatolica* 31, 1999, 26–9) that the text is too Attic to attest mere influence: it must be part of an Attic sacred calendar, perhaps of a deme, brought to the region of Miletupolis in circumstances unknown. He adduces the sacrifice to [Εἰρ]ήνηι, line 12, as a further sign of Attic origin. Yet the text does not fit wholly comfortably in

---

[47] So the mss: Madvig substituted a present tense here and later.
[48] But this date apparently changed to a date before Skirophorion 11 by at least *c*.350.

an Attic context. The designations for days within the month in general follow Attic practice, but τετρακαιδεκάτηι in 7 is a unicum (for τέτραδι ἐπὶ δέκα). An offering to Apollo Karneios (11) would, as has been noted, require a special explanation in an Athenian calendar; and the presumptive sacrifice to Peace falls on Skirophorion 17, whereas the attested Attic date is Hekatombaion 16 (see Peace, sacrifice to, above). The choice finally of a bull as offering no less than three times in a fourteen-line text is wholly unexampled in Attica (though also, it must be conceded, elsewhere).

Addendum to p. 483

The personnel involved in an expanded version of the 'sacrifices and processions at Kepoi at the festival of *Thargelia*' are listed in a decree of 129/8 (LSS 14): the priest of Apollo Pythios, the exegetes, the 'other priests', the nine archons, the 'hierophant, the daduch and those who have accompanied them', the *agonothetai*, the *choregoi* and the *hieropoioi* are all to pray (?) and process (33–7), while the priest of Apollo Pythios is to conduct the sacrifices at Kepoi to Apollo Alexikakos and Patroos and Pythios (52–5); various other officials, and 'the priestesses', are mentioned in unclear contexts (24–7, 32–3). The decree breathes the same late Hellenistic enthusiasm for Apollo Pythios that is expressed in the *Pythaïdes* (pp. 83–4 above; A. Wilhelm, *SBWien* 1947, no 224.4, 49–53 = *Akademieschriften zur griechischen Inschriftenkunde* 3, Leipzig 1974, 297–301; Mikalson, *Hellenistic Athens*, 272–4), and is an equally unreliable guide to classical practice.

TABLE 3: Dated Festivals

	Hekatombaion	Metageitnion	Boedromion	Pyanepsion	Maimakterion	Posideon
1						
2						
3			Sphragitic Nymphs?			
4						
5			*Genesia*			
6			Artemis Agrotera	*Proerosia* at Eleusis		
7			*Boedromia?*	*Pyanopsia*		
8			*Kybernesia?*	*Theseia?*		
9				*Stenia*		
10				*Thesmophoria* at Halimus		
11				*Anodos*[1]		
12	*Kronia*		Thanksgiving for Freedom[3]	*Nesteia*[2]		
13				*Kalligeneia*[4]		
14			Eleusinian sacra brought to Athens			
15			*Prorrhesis*			
16	*Synoikia/* Sacrifice to Peace		ἅλαδε μύσται[5]			
17			*Epidauria* (or 18th)[6]			
18						
19	*Greater Nemesia*		Iacchus procession (or 20th)			
20			Initiates at Eleusis ?			
21			Initiates at Eleusis			
22			Initiates at Eleusis			
23			*Plemochoai?*: end of Mysteries			
24						
25						
26						*Haloa*
27	Panathenaic games[7]					*Haloa?*
28	Panathenaic procession					
29						
30				*Chalkeia*		
Unknown	Sacrifice to Ammon *Herakleia? Kalamaia*	*Herakleia? Metageitnia Eleusinia?*[8]	*Proerosia* (Thorikos)	*Apatouria* (3 days) *Oschophoria?*[9]	*Pompaia*	*Rural Dionysia*

[1] First day of *Thesmophoria*.
[2] Second day of *Thesmophoria*.
[3] Commemorating return from Phyle:? = sacrifice to Democracy.
[4] Third day of *Thesmophoria*.
[5] Also wine-pouring commemorating victory of Chabrias.
[6] Potential initiates stay at home.
[7] And preceding days?
[8] Or in following month.
[9] Or in previous month.

	Gamelion	Anthesterion	Elaphebolion	Mounichion	Thargelion	Skirophorion
1						
2						
3						
4				Festival of Eros		
5						
6				Procession to Delphinion	*Thargelia*	
7					*Thargelia*	
8			*Asklepieia* Proagon to *City Dionysia*			
9	*Erosouria*		Bringing in of Dionysus?			
10			*City Dionysia* procession			
11		*Pithoigia*[10]	*City Dionysia* ↓			
12	*Lenaea* ↓	*Choes*[11]			*Skira/Skirophoria*	
13		*Chytroi*[12]				
14					*Dipolieia*	
15						
16				*Mounichia*		
17						
18						
19				*Olympieia?*	*Bendidea* (or 20th) *Kallynteria?*	
20		*Lesser Mysteries?*				
21						
22						
23		*Diasia*				
24						
25					*Plynteria*	
26						
27	*Hieros Gamos*					
28						
29						
30						Sacrifice to Zeus Soter/*Diisoteria*[13]
Unknown		Sacrifice to Agathe Tyche (or a month on either side)	*Pandia*[14] *Chloïa Galaxia?* *Elaphebolia?*	*Antheia Adonia?*		*Anakia? Arrephoria*

[10] First day of *Anthesteria*.
[11] Second day of *Anthesteria*.
[12] Third day of *Anthesteria*.
[13] But this date apparently changed to a date before Skirophorion 11 by at latest c. 350.
[14] Follows immediately end of *City Dionysia*.

Appendix 2: Alciphron as Heortologist

In studies of Attic festivals, passages from Alciphron's *Epistles* are occasionally cited. The letters seem to have been written late in the second century AD or thereabouts, but are set in the milieu of fourth-century Athens made familiar and romantic by the ever popular Menander.[1] The presumption, not unreasonable in itself, seems to be that Alciphron preserves authentic material which he has found in works of Menander now lost to us.[2] And some festivals are indeed treated in an unexceptionable way. In 2.37.2[3] the three days of the *Thesmophoria* are correctly listed: this will doubtless come from a handbook, not from Menander. The *Dionysia*, most obvious of festivals, are several times mentioned in rather general terms (1.9.3, 2.37.1, 3.35.2, 4.14.1), the *Panathenaea*, strangely enough, not at all. In 4.14.8 courtesans and their lovers feast together at a private celebration of the *Adonia*; in 4.16.3 Lamia and Demetrius Poliorketes celebrate *Aphrodisia* together. *Lenaea* appear once as an occasion for drama (4.18.10), once as a festival of Attic women (1.4.2). The 'yearly *Choes*' are a characteristic and valued feature of Attic life in 4.18.10. Gifts are sent to a hanger-on at the *Kronia* in 3.21.[4]

Other festivals, however, acquire strange attributes in Alciphron's depiction. He twice mentions the *Oschophoria*. In 1.11.1 a fisherman's daughter has fallen in love with 'a city ephebe, the *oschophoros*' whom she first saw when her mother sent her to the city at the *Oschophoria*. In 1.4.2 a fisherman reproaches his wife for abandoning the shore and rushing to the city to celebrate *Oschophoria* and *Lenaea* along with rich Athenian women. One detail here is authentic, that of the ephebic *oschophoros*. But far from being a lure to draw honest fisherfolk to the city, the *Oschophoria* almost certainly brought Athenians down to the shore at Phaleron, where the main part of the festival took place. And it is very unlikely that it was a women's festival of the type at which any woman who wished could take part. The only active female participants of whom we know, the *deipnophoroi*, were carefully selected.[5] Others could perhaps watch, but that is scarcely what is envisaged in Alciphron.

The *Apatouria* appears twice, and its third day *Koureotis* is once treated as if it were an independent festival. In 1.9.3 a fisherman hopes that the rich individuals to whom he sells his fish will send him some consideration (παραμύθια) at the time of the *Dionysia* or *Apatouria*. In 2.37.1 it appears in a list of 'city delights', of which a farmer's

---

[1] See E. L. Bowie in P. E. Easterling and B. M. W. Knox, *The Cambridge History of Classical Literature, i. Greek Literature* (Cambridge 1985), 679–80.

[2] On Menander as a source for the epistolographers, see the works cited by A. S. Gratwick, *CQ* 29 (1979), 309, n. 3.

[3] I cite by the numeration of M. A. Scheper's Teubner (Leipzig, 1905), which is also that of the Loeb of A. R. Benner and F. H. Fobes.

[4] I do not know Attic evidence for the practice of sending presents to dependents at festivals which is assumed here and in 1.9.3.

[5] On all this see pp. 211–17.

wife is depriving herself by staying in the country. In 3.10.1 we hear of a dinner-party to which a parasite was invited while 'the city was celebrating the festival *Koureotis*'. None of these allusions shows the slightest awareness of the special character of the *Apatouria*, a festival of the phratries which they celebrated not at a central site in Athens but at their individual centres throughout Attica. Whether a farmer's wife could have participated in the festivities of the phratry to which her own husband belonged, doubtless in the country, is uncertain. But to go up to the city at *Apatouria* time in search of spectacle would certainly have been a wasted journey.

The most striking feature of Alciphron's heortology is the prominence of the *Haloa*, which appears three times. In 2.37.1 it is one of the 'city delights' (along with *Apatouria*, *Dionysia* and *Thesmophoria*) . In 4.18.4 the courtesan Glycera is staying in the city 'because of the *Haloa* of the goddess'. And in 4.6.3 we hear that 'it was the *Haloa*, and naturally enough we (courtesans) all attended the all-night rite'. Here the question of Alciphron's authority becomes crucial, because it is on him that the conception of the *Haloa* as a kind of festival of convenience principally depends. We know indeed from Apollodorus' speech against Neaera that the hierophant Archias once performed a sacrifice for a courtesan at the festival.[6] But she might have had reason to be present at the sanctuary at a time when men gathered even if she was not entitled to participate fully in the rites. It is surely conceivable that the ultimate source for the association between courtesans and the *Haloa* found in Alciphron is none other than this passage of Apollodorus. The other items of information about the festival that he presents are of variable credibility. No other source speaks of a *pannychis*, and Alciphron might simply have transferred one hither from one of the other festivals at which Menander mentions them. But there are strong independent grounds, in the purchases of firewood recorded in the Eleusinian accounts, to believe that some such event took place.[7] This then may be a rare authentic detail, like the ephebic *oschophoros*. On the other hand his belief that the *Haloa*—it is otherwise attested only as an Eleusinian festival—[8] took place in Athens looks like simple error, and his reference to 'the *Haloa* of the goddess' may suggest that he supposed the honorand to be Athena.

---

[6] Apollod. *Neaer.* 116–17; cf. p. 283.
[7] See p. 200.
[8] See p. 329, n. 10.

Subject Index

Greek words are positioned alphabetically as if transliterated into English (aspirates are ignored). Please look for Greek names beginning with kappa under both C and K.

Mother (*Cont.*)
  temple in Agora 55
  see also *Galaxia*, *Mysteries* (Lesser)
Mounichia (festival) 209, 228, 231 n.
  59, 233, 242
  aition for *arkteia* 238–9
  in Thorikos calendar 75 n. 104, 76
Mounichion (month), festivals of 208–9
mountain shrines 69, 70 n. 77
Mouseia, in schools 251–2
mud, carried in procession? 204
mud, underworld 361
μυεῖν 345
murdered, pursue their killers 145
Musaeus 114, 121, 361–3
Muses 252
myrtle 97 n. 28
mystagogues 345 n. 78
Mysteries, Greater (of Eleusis) **342–363**
  aftermath 360–1
  ἅλαδε μύσται 347
  and agricultural year 207
  associated vases and coins 334
  birth of child ? 357
  books about 334 n. 35
  divine marriage? 356–7
  duration 350 n.100
  eschatological promise 354
  expressive media used 353
  fee for initiation 342 n. 65
  as festival of Athenian polis 343
  grades of initiation 344
  ἱερεία δεῦρο 347
  Homeric Hymn to Demeter and 341 n.
  61, 359
  individual preparatory offerings 342
  last celebration 327
  morality and 361–2
  mythical initiates 341 n. 58, 342 n.
  62
  mystai and *epoptai* 344, 350
  myth and 342, 359–60
  numbers of initiates 343, 348 n. 91
  open to all Greek-speaking adults 327,
  342
  pannychis at 166
  Plemochoai 350

  pre-initiation 345
  procession(s) to Eleusis 348
  proclamation in agora 347
  repeat initiation? 348 n. 91, 361
  revelations 354–360
  sacred objects brought to Athens 346
  sacrifices at 351
  search for Kore? 355
  secrecy 345
  slaves initiated 169–70, 342 n. 65
  teaching at/before 352
  see also *anaktoron*, Orpheus, *telesterion*,
  torches
Mysteries, Lesser (of Agrai) 56, **344–6**
  administered by Eleusinian
    epistatai 345 n. 77
  date of 344 n. 72
  Dionysus at 341
  formal requirement for *Greater*? 344
  founded for Heracles 345
  Zeus Meilichios and 344 n. 76
  see also Mother, at Agrai
myths
  and deme cults 71–2, 78
  as evidence for divine functions 393
  glorifying Athens 86
  told at *Oschophoria* 213
  underly cult 140
  see also aitiological myths, Delphinion,
    Dionysus, Eleusis (cult of Demeter
    and Kore), heroes and heroines,
    Mysteries (Greater), *phalloi*, self-
    sacrifice

nakedness, of girls 244
name
  changed at adoption 33 n. 103
  preservation of 29 n.88, 32 n. 102
  see also family name
Nausithoos 410
Neanias 71, 208, 209
necromancy 121 n. 21
Nekysia, of Bithynia 28 n. 85
Nemeseia, rites for parents? 31 n. 94,
  476
Nemesia (Rhamnus) 72, 476
Nemesis at Rhamnus

Select Index of Sources and Monuments

Literary Texts

33 B 14	261 n. 31, 268 n.70
33 B 25–7	74 n. 97, 260
33 B 31–4	257
36	*see IG II² 1177*
39	*see IG II² 659*
96.11–26	200
178	*see IG I³ 256*

LSS

3	*see IG I³ 6*
11	*see IG II² 47*
14.8–9	80 n. 6
14.49, 54	414
19	215
19.84–5	427 n. 44
19.89–90	389 n. 10
19.93	418
20.17–23	168
124	*see IG II² 1184*

ML

20.7, 16	9 n. 3, 13 n. 21
23.38–40	399 nn. 47, 48
23.39	399 n. 47
23.40	411 n. 97
38	399
52	*see IG I³ 40*
65	*see IG I³ 61*
78	*see IG I³ 93*
73	*see IG I³ 78*

NGCT

24	132

RO

46	*see SEG XLII 112*
58	*see IG II² 204*
63	*see IG II² 1183*
81	*see LSCG 33*
88	398
91	*see IG II² 337*

SEG

XVIII 26.11–12	462, 474
XXI 519	106
XXI 519.16–17	72, 461
XXI 525.43	389 n. 12
XXI 1064	298
XXII 117	67
XXIV 151	65 n. 55
XXIV 151.21	334
XXVI 267	439 n. 83
XXVIII 24	403
XXVIII 232	413 n. 104
XXIX 131	437 n. 79
XXXII 216	462 n. 22
XXXIII 115	203, 434
XXXIII 147.5–6	340 n. 55
XXXIII.147.6	436 n. 75
XXXIII 147.19	59 n. 36
XXXIII 147.22; left side by 41; right side by 44	17 n. 40
XXXIII 147.26–7	208
XXXIII 147.35	466
XXXIV 103	59 n. 37
XXXV 113	332–3
XXXVIII 232	413 n. 104
XXXIX 148	64 n. 50, 72 n. 91
XLI 182	440
XLII 112	59 n. 35
XLII 112.5	72, 482
XLIII 26 A 3–4	70
XLIX 141–3	69 n. 74

SGD

14	130
48	130

Steinhauer
'Ἱερὸς νόμος Αἰξωνέων'

64 n. 53, 66 n. 63, 71 n. 83, 335 n. 43, 445 n. 108

Lightning Source UK Ltd.
Milton Keynes UK
06 January 2010

148215UK00005B/7/P